*An Encyclopedia of
Shade Perennials*

An Encyclopedia of
Shade Perennials

W. George Schmid

Timber Press
Portland • Cambridge

All photographs are by the author unless otherwise noted.

Published in 2002 by
Timber Press, Inc.
The Haseltine Building
133 S.W. Second Avenue, Suite 450
Portland, Oregon 97204, U.S.A.

Timber Press
2 Station Road
Swavesey
Cambridge CB4 5QJ, U.K.

ISBN 0-88192-549-7

Printed in Hong Kong

Library of Congress Cataloging-in-Publication Data

Schmid, Wolfram George.
An encyclopedia of shade perennials / W. George Schmid.
p. cm.
ISBN 0-88192-549-7
1. Perennials—Encyclopedias. 2. Shade-tolerant plants—Encyclopedias. I. Title.

SB434 .S297 2002
635.9'32'03—dc21

2002020456

I dedicate this book to the greatest treasure in my life, my family:

*Hildegarde, my wife, friend, and supporter for over half a century,
and my children, Michael, Henry, Hildegarde, Wilhelmina, and Siegfried,
who with their mates have given us ten grandchildren whose eyes not only see
but also appreciate nature's riches. Their combined love and encouragement
made this book possible.*

Contents

Foreword by Allan M. Armitage 9

Acknowledgments 10

Part 1. The Shady Garden 11

    1. A Personal Outlook 13

    2. Fated Shade 17

    3. Practical Thoughts 27

    4. Plants Assigned 45

Part 2. Perennials for the Shady Garden A–Z 55

Plant Sources 339

U.S. Department of Agriculture Hardiness Zone Map 342

Index of Plant Names 343

Color photographs follow page 176

Foreword

As I read George Schmid's book, I am reminded that all gardeners are kindred in spirit and that—regardless of their roots or knowledge—the gardening they do and the gardens they create are always personal. As I follow George from the shady glens of Bavaria to his shady garden in Georgia, I am struck by his love of and passion for his avocation, this thing called gardening. And as I imagine a small boy stealing through a picket fence to be liberated by the shady forest beyond, I am mesmerized by his appreciation of the virtues of shade in the garden.

Shade is to gardening as Oreos are to cookies: having too many can give you a stomachache but having none is cruel and unusual punishment. George takes us through his personal thoughts on shade gardening, letting us know why shade gardening makes so much sense and what plants await the gardener. And plants are important to George, who has little use for the "biological desert" of turfgrass.

This man knows his plants. In each genus, he offers the "master" gardener no-nonsense botanical information concerning height, flower, fruit, and family; he also provides the newcomer with his thoughts on soil conditions, watering, and, more importantly, the reason one would put a certain plant in the garden in the first place. His favorites become obvious, and his knowledge of the great variety within a genus is enviable and ours to share.

I have a great deal of shade in my own garden, and I too wanted "a cooling refuge during the summer months." So as can be imagined, I plunged into this book and surfaced not only with a better appreciation of my shaded garden but with a broadened understanding of the diversity of perennials that can flourish in such conditions—not to mention a warm-all-over feeling.

I enjoy my shaded garden, yet there is always more to learn and to try, and so I visit George often to indulge our mutual shady tastes. He is a gentleman and a scholar, and I come away refreshed by having been with a man who revels in sharing his garden, his plants, and his knowledge. You will be similarly refreshed, and similarly educated.

Allan M. Armitage
Athens, Georgia

Acknowledgments

Information for this tome came from many sources, but I want to thank a few standout contributors for their help: Tony Avent, whose Juniper Level Botanic Garden was an inspiration; Darrell R. Probst, who gave generously of his specialized knowledge of epimediums; and Barry Yinger, a font of information on the genus *Asarum*.

As appreciative of the virtues of shade in the garden as I am, Allan Armitage agreed to write the foreword for this book, and I want to thank him for his sensitive words. Sigi Schmid, my youngest son, has accompanied me on many rewarding hikes through the Appalachians; his support, companionship, and keen eyes have helped me discover the many small wonders along the way. Sharing the paths of discovery with one of my own sons was and still is one of the highlights of being a father.

It is impossible for me to grow all the plants included in this encyclopedia on my half-acre garden, and in some instances I have had to rely on photographs taken by others. My thanks again to Allan Armitage, Tony Avent (Plant Delights Nursery), Hans Hansen (Shady Oaks Nursery), Lynne Harrison, Don Jacobs (Eco Gardens), and Sigi Schmid.

My thanks to Martin White, designer, and last but not least, I want to thank Franni Bertolino Farrell, my editor. Her attention to detail and intuitive grasp of what I wanted to say transformed my stiff, technical text into nicely flowing, eloquent writing, which makes for enjoyable reading.

Part 1

The Shady Garden

My grandmother, my mother, yours truly at age two, my father—and the picket fence in my grandfather's garden, Ottobrunn, Bavaria, late summer potato harvest, 1932.

CHAPTER 1

A Personal Outlook

Shade Remembered

One of my earliest childhood recollections is of shade. During my kindergarten days, frequent visits to my grandfather's home in the Bavarian hamlet of Ottobrunn allowed me to explore his wonderful garden. I remember clearly the many paths to run along, the vegetables, and colorful flowers everywhere. He even had a raspberry patch, which was strictly off-limits for me during the berry season. I did manage to sneak out a few hard-won berries now and then. Hard-won, because I always got tangled up in the spiny canes. All this was fascinating, but my secret wish was to go beyond the back fence to the dark, shady woods. The picket fence had a gate, which was always locked. I tried climbing, but the obstacle was too tall. Determined, I used sticks to pry loose a couple of the pickets. It took a while to get this done, always in secret and a little at a time, but one summer day I finished the job. The way to the mysterious woods was open.

I remembered the forbidding stories of bears and other wild animals Grandfather told, so at first I was satisfied to slip through to the other side and just sit there, waiting fearfully for the beasts to emerge from the woods' edge, just a few feet from the fence. After a few such visits I got up enough courage to leave the bright, hot sun at the fence and enter the dark woods. The tops of the young spruce trees formed a contiguous canopy that sunlight could not penetrate, creating a dry, gloomy world of shade. The trees had lost their lower branches, and the ground beneath was covered with a thick mat of fallen needles. I crawled on all fours to penetrate the thicket. There, a few feet into the woods, I found my favorite hiding place. Its cool, mysterious darkness enveloped me. It was at the same time soothing and scary. Once my eyes got used to the low light, the menacing wild beasts were forgotten, and the thick bed of soft, dry needles became my building material. Following Grandfather's example, I created a fantasy garden of my own, laying out imaginary garden paths, fences, and houses. My toy soldiers were the visitors, and I paraded them around my dream world. I will never forget the feeling of elation: I had conquered my fears and entered the dark world of eternal shade. With the boundless imagination of a child's mind, I built my first garden in that shady corner of the woods. Shade became my friend, and so it remains, as I live and garden in the South.

Design by Nature

I am telling my childhood story because gardening in the shade is not only possible in a child's imagination. It is gardening designed by nature. As I remember, nothing green grew on the forest floor of my secret garden. I seem to recollect a few mushrooms, but there was no moss and definitely no green plants. But this forest was not nature's work: it was man-made and badly so. The trees were planted too close. Nature rarely if ever commits such an abomination. In the natural world, shade is as ordained as the sunlight that produces it. Some plants are fated to reach high into the sky, capturing a disproportionate share of the sun's rays; others, evolved to live under these giants, flourish in the shade. In natural gardens a balance exists, providing myriad levels of light and shade, and various plant life prospers under these varying conditions. In natural forests some plants exist even in the darkest corners of the forest floor.

With growth, change becomes inevitable. Nature's garden is forever changing, and with it changes the shade. The sun-grabbing giants die and fall, making more light for others to rise. Plants below the canopy continue to evolve and persist under more or less shady circumstances. In this scheme, shade is not a nemesis. Over eons it has been embraced by many plant species. Shade in the natural plant world is simply a factor of evolution, a by-product of the existence of sunlight. Design by nature is worth emulating in one's own garden, and inevitably, some shade will be part of this design.

The Woodlands

Aside from playing in the dirt at home, one of my most cherished pursuits is visiting the shady, natural gardens of the southern Appalachians. Several times each spring, summer, and fall, I visit different remote spots there to hike and photograph the natural wonders of the area. To call such places gardens may be irrational, because a garden in the strict sense of the word has always meant an enclosed space set aside for the cultivation of plants; Teutonic tribes called such a place a garth, and that thought is echoed by modern gardeners when they refer to their garden as a yard. Notwithstanding, in many of these natural areas I see a garden, its nooks and crannies filled with wildflowers, ferns, and mosses, punctuated here and there by lichen-covered rocks. The inspiration of such a natural garden is boundless. My visits are particularly uplifting in the summer. While my plants at Hosta Hill—as I call my half-acre shady garden—are languishing in the summer heat of the South, a visit to the cool, shady valleys of the Smoky Mountains and beyond restores my gardening ambitions, and I am ready to dream, plan, and work to get things ready for the next season. Photographs taken in these natural gardens go a long way in providing new ideas and the stimulus to incorporate them into my garden design. Just as nature's shady gardens are forever changing, my own garden is in a constant state of flux. Not all my friends change or add to their gardens as frequently as I do, yet most are not content to leave things as they are and make some changes some of the time. Besides, nature constantly meddles with man-made gardens and sees to it that at least some part of the garden requires attention.

The first thing I realized during these visits was the futility of traditional garden design. In the mountains, I see the wild, shady garden grow more beautiful each year, while many of our home landscapes become more ragged. Perpetual-care lawns are rooted in sweeping, formal layouts in vogue a century and more ago; these small replicas of earlier gardens, often in the front and rear of the house, are rounded out by the addition of a flowering tree (usually a Bradford pear or other undesirable cultivar), a few foundation shrubs, and small beds of annuals and perennials. To maintain such a synthetic garden requires a lot of work: heavy applications of fertilizer, insecticides, herbicides, and fungicides; regular mowing and watering; and in some areas reseeding, redressing, and re-everything. Incredibly, this type of landscape is installed in new subdivisions to this very day; in some areas, building codes actually mandate lawn installation. This is hard to understand, given that natural resources like water are increasingly scarce and the environment is under attack from all sides. To make our own odious contribution to this fiasco is no longer acceptable. Years ago, I decided that spending weekends mowing the lawn, replanting annuals, or performing other repetitive garden tasks was wastefulness and slavery, not gardening. I used the pine straw provided free by my trees, which increasingly shaded out the warm weather grasses that came with the house, to suffocate what was left of my skimpy lawn. Shade-tolerant shrubs and perennials replaced it, and soon a wonderful, shady front garden provided a cooling refuge during the summer months.

Lawns, on the other hand, are biological deserts. Their wide-open character discourages birds and other wildlife. There are no nesting spots, no places to burrow (except for moles, perhaps), and absolutely no place to hide. The only critters living in or under lawns are grubs, army worms, and other nonbeneficial bugs. So we apply poisons to be rid of them, thus releasing more toxins into our already afflicted environment and leaving nothing but a green but genuine wasteland called a lawn. Not even the insect pests are alive, and birds and other visiting wildlife eating their toxic remains get poisoned as well. This is not gardening either!

The natural gardens remaining in wild areas the world over point to a better way. Year after year, my Appalachian visits prove to me that natural gardens should be the pattern followed. As a wild garden matures, its treasure of plants matures also. Nature has its own way of balancing the system, maintaining intrinsic native harmony. In man-made gardens, even those closely following the natural model, maintaining such harmony is much more difficult. Gardeners tend to add a personal touch, mix native and exotic plants, and combine natural and synthesized designs. Stability and balance are much more difficult to maintain under these circumstances, so gardeners are forever reminded by their surroundings that their input is required. Nevertheless, gardens made following designs by nature will be less demanding than those conceived along classic lines. Nature's composition is a blending of soft colors and textures. Its supple contours look relaxed; there are no straight lines that have to be maintained. Even weeds, the nemesis of classic gardens, have a hard time getting a foothold. While no garden is maintenance-free, following nature's example reduces a gardener's workload and provides more time for relaxation and enjoyment.

The Personal Touch

Visiting other people's gardens is another highlight of every season. I have never seen two gardens exactly alike, and I find it impossible to duplicate even small parts of another garden. The layout and permanent features could be copied, but the living occupants, trees, shrubs, and flowering plants have a mind, size, and shape all their own. But above all, it is the personal touch of individual gardeners that makes each garden unique. The reason for gardening's popularity is the almost unlimited freedom it gives to gardeners to express themselves. Gardening is like art, and our landscapes our canvas. This art is limited only by financial resources, the environment, and climate. If money is no object, even climate can be overcome by erecting and maintaining a conservatory.

Garden visits provide an infinite display of what to do—or not to do—when making your own garden. A few years ago I was invited to a garden that was whimsical in the extreme, with multi-colored ornaments intermixed with a riot of annuals and perennials. Nature's soothing green was nowhere to be seen. It looked like a Jackson Pollock canvas. It was not *my* type of garden. Nevertheless, I respected what I saw, because it was *her* type of garden. It matched the owner's bubbly, colorful personality perfectly. What I thought of it mattered not. In gardens as in art, everyone is free to like or dislike what they see, just as gardeners everywhere are free to make gardens that have their own personal touch and so appeal to their own taste.

I have learned from my own early efforts that the personal touch of beginning gardeners can be guileless and even crude. I have only to look at photographs taken in my garden in Nashville, Tennessee, in 1957, and it becomes obvious to me how my tastes have changed: trying to mimic the gardens of Versailles on a sunny quarter-acre backlot is no longer my own personal touch.

My Garden's Embrace

It has been many years since I shaped my first simple garden with the dreams and imagination of a small child. Hosta Hill, now more than three decades old, shows what can be accomplished when a child's fantasy becomes reality. Friends and visitors alike admire the maturity of my garden and wonder who did all the considerable work evidenced by its hardscaping and plantings. When I tell them I placed every brick and stone, shaped the ground to plotted design, dug every hole to plant in, and placed every tree—except for the native pines—and all the shrubs and perennials, I see skepticism in their eyes. They know I spent most of my time making a living, away from the garden, so how did I have time to do all this? The answer is simple: I love my family and gardening. It was the love of my family that sustained me, and it was the embrace of my garden that provided the respite required to emerge refreshed for another battle with the madding crowds away from home. Gardening was therapy for me; it filled my mind with the pleasure of nature and growing things. The rigors of building and planting kept my otherwise deskbound body strong. Gardening allowed me to reach a balance between the necessity of making a living and the fundamental human desire to keep both mind and body healthy and happy. I honestly do not know what would have become of me without the embrace of my garden.

Aside from supporting a sane mind and a sound body, gardening has endowed me with many traits, not the least of which is patience. All the gardeners I know are patient people. In following the rhythms of nature, year after year, they develop a knowing patience that influences their daily interactions with the rest of the world. Gardening also brings many little successes, which in turn kindle happiness and personal satisfaction. I have derived a lot of enjoyment from planning and designing my own Shangri-la. Gardening has taught me how to lay bricks and stone, how to smell soil, how to build and maintain water features, how to cope with disastrous but nevertheless natural events like ice storms and high winds. It has imparted an understanding of how nature works. It has inspired me to protect our precious environment. Best of all, through gardening, I have made many friends, all of whom share their love of gardens and their lives with me.

CHAPTER 2

Fated Shade

Of Nature and Shade

Where there is light, there must be shadow. Everything on earth with three dimensions is fated to shade. Mountains cast a shadow that darkens the valley below. As long as the sun shines, anything that moves—man, animal, or machine—is trailed by its own shadow. Lamplight or even a flickering candle generates shade. And having been out hunting slugs and other nasty critters in the middle of the night, I can vouch that the full moon's eerie shadows abound in the garden. Gardeners must realize that for living plants, shade is as inevitable as life-giving sunlight. Survival of the fittest applies not only to the animal kingdom but to plants as well. In dense, primeval forests, the crowns of the tallest trees receive most of the sunlight. Descending into the forest's lower levels, the nourishing sunrays become sparser; here plants have evolved to propagate themselves at reduced levels of light. On the forest floor, wildflowers have adapted to rise and procreate in late-winter sun, before their giant neighbors leaf out. Even in the shade cast by these succeeding light-reducing layers, non-flowering plants like mosses and fungi have found a way to exist. All kinds of plants flourish in varying degrees of shade.

As always, nature has important lessons for gardeners. The first and most important one is to copy as much as possible the natural conditions under which garden plants have developed. Most plants grown in gardens are hybrids and cultivars of long standing, yet they have their ancestors' genetic imprint, and it is this built-in memory that makes them fail or succeed in the cultivated environment of the garden. Many wildflowers, for example, require sun in late winter and early spring and fairly deep shade after they have bloomed. Some even go dormant after the leaf canopy closes, using stored-up energy to ripen seeds and provide for another season's bloom. It is useless to cultivate such plants in full sun; they will wither and die. On the other hand, growing these wonderful natives in full shade year-round accomplishes the same depressing result. With no life-giving sun for them in spring, no vitality is stored for survival and increase. Nature is adaptable, however, and the amounts of light and shade provided in the wild need not be faithfully duplicated in gardens. Many plants, even delicate wildflowers, thrive in conditions somewhat above or below these means.

In days gone by, shade was considered bad. Majestic shade trees and tall shrubs were ruthlessly eliminated, sacrificed to the idea that gardens, parks, and lawns must be open to the sun. But to consider shade a detriment to gardening is incorrect. Shade in the garden reduces the burden on our environment and saves valuable natural resources. Many informed gardeners now make the most of shade. Perhaps years of gardening and many harsh lessons have taught me to instinctively categorize shade and then make the right choices for planting. Yet shade must be defined somehow for gardeners whose learning curve on shady gardens has not yet reached a satisfactory apex.

Shade Defined

Defining shade is more an art than a science: it is impossible to establish a permanent value for a given spot in the garden. Light levels vary, from morning to sunset, for sunny and cloudy days, and with the passing of the seasons. Theoretically, full shade is where direct rays of sunlight never reach. It is not, however, the total absence of light. Full shade requires a source of light to produce it, and in the case of gardens, it is the sunlight that causes it. Plants grow in full shade by utilizing reflected sunlight. I wanted to establish, to my mind at least, what full shade really means; I finally resolved that full shade must be on the north side of my house, where I had planted a bed of hostas. Direct sunlight never reaches into that corner, yet the hostas thrive, because the open corner receives plenty of reflected light. Many gardens have a similar north-facing corner created by a permanent structure.

Full shade is modified by where it is produced. Because the summer sun is higher in the sky at Hosta Hill (in Tucker, Georgia, 34 degrees North latitude), the full shade cast by the north wall of my house is shorter than that in my mother's garden north of Detroit, Michigan (42.5 degrees North latitude): Mother's house casts a longer field of full shade. Also, my north corner receives more reflected light because the wall is open to the sky and unencumbered by trees and tall shrubs; my mother's house, on the other hand, has a wide roof extension and trees planted along the wall, so the amount of reflected light is much reduced. Nothing much grows in Mother's shady north corner; even reflected light is blocked. It is almost like that absolute shade I remember near my ancestral home.

Defining shade that is anything less than full is more difficult. Most shade in nature is produced by trees and shrubs, yet even low-growing plants can provide shade. In wet meadows in central Japan, tall grasses shade the leaf mounds of wild species hostas, yet flowers on even taller scapes extend above the grasses, inviting pollination by insects. Any living plant, short or tall, will produce some shade, but trees are the prime natural shade givers. Here, in the morning, with the sun low in the sky, almost full sun reaches under the loblolly pines, brightening the garden. Later in the day the sun's rays are filtered through the long-needled, open tree branches and dapples the plants underneath with ever-changing patterns of light and shade. Further back in the garden, a Canadian hemlock casts a much denser shade; a little patch of English ivy is the only thing that grows beneath it, limbed up though it is. Along the eastern fenceline, a willow oak planted by a squirrel three decades ago allows almost full sun to reach under its leafless branches in midwinter, while in summer the large, multibranched tree crown casts cooling, dense shade. The hemlock's branches are horizontal yet somewhat pendent, and close to the ground, giving shade that is much deeper underneath; the willow oak permits more sun exposure from the sides. Thus, three different trees—loblolly pine, hemlock, and willow oak—give various shade patterns throughout the year, changing with each season. Even the same tree species grown under different cultural situations can cast different intensities of shade. Most of my trees are pines, so Hosta Hill shade is dappled most of the time.

Keeping records of where, when, and to what extent shade exists during different seasons is essential to defining shade in the garden and a critical task for beginning gardeners. The main purpose of this exercise is to identify the shady areas (and coincidentally, the areas where more sun than shade prevails). Look at the trees, shrubs, and other shade-givers in your garden. Visit the garden during winter to determine where shade exists once deciduous trees and shrubs have lost their leaves, and again in spring and early summer, as the tree canopy regenerates itself. Once conditions are known, the gardener can concentrate fully on plant selection and layout. Many perennials thought suitable for sunny areas only can in fact be grown where they receive a half-day's sun. I grow daylilies on the southeast side of the house, where they receive sun from morning until about one o'clock in the afternoon, and they bloom faithfully every year. Other sun-loving garden perennials can be grown successfully with a few hours of morning sun; full sun does not seem to be required for flowering. And remember that the shade perennial that endures relatively long periods of exposure to direct sun in northern latitudes will wither and die if exposed to high, hot noon or afternoon sun in southern gardens.

In gardening, homework always pays. Homework for gardeners is primarily studying the garden literature, visiting other gardens, and, above all, talking to other gardeners. Doing homework before digging greatly increases the chance of success. Nonetheless, over the years I have found out that learning the hard way is sometimes the only way and an inescapable part of gardening. There are just too many variables. The cultural requirements of many established cultivars are well known and information about them is readily found, but it is often difficult to determine how best to place plants that have recently entered commerce. Nurseries have developed methods of propagating these plants under controlled conditions, but once they are planted out in the open, gardeners—and the plants—are usually on their own. The only way to cultivate these plants is by trial and error, which frequently means learning about their needs the hard way. Many of my gardening friends invite this process; they are compelled to push the envelope and plant things where they are not supposed to grow. The fun is trying things no one else has attempted and finding new ways of being successful—or failing miserably, as the case may be.

Happily, most so-called shade plants are content with some sun exposure, and it is often surprisingly easy to cultivate sun-loving perennials in part-shade. On the other hand, no flowering garden plant requires constant full shade, and even shade-tolerant ferns and mosses are able to thrive with considerable sun exposure. Nearly all the herbaceous perennials considered in this work show a wide tolerance in the amount of shade they require, and most need some sun for reliable flowering. Hence, just about any mixture of sun and shade becomes acceptable: each plant will flourish within a substantial range of sun/shade and geographic location and altitude. Given too much sun a plant actually burns; given too much shade it may stop flowering or fade away altogether. Drought and heat tolerance are also a concern, as is cold hardiness. When there is too much moisture the plant may rot, while a severe lack of moisture makes the plant wither and die. Some shade-tolerant plants demand dry shade; others need moist shade. Plants grown in the open in the South become houseplants in the North.

I try to avoid the term "shade garden" because the word "shade," standing alone, simply implies the relative absence of light and nothing more. But beyond that basic meaning, dozens of adjectives—most subject to considerable and sometimes contentious interpretation—have been used to define a specific type of shade. Following are two ways to characterize shade in the garden. I recommend readers study both. The first characterizes shade by using popular terms and simple definitions; the second gives a more detailed analysis of shade conditions.

The easy way out

Here are what I consider popular definitions of shade, sometimes in conjunction with the degree of sun exposure, rated from zero to 100, with zero denoting total absence of direct exposure to sun, 50 indicating half direct sun and half shade (with full sun occurring usually mornings and afternoons, and shade prevailing while the sun is high in the sky), and 100 representing full-sun conditions from sunrise until sunset.

1. Total and perpetual shade exists where the direct rays of the sun never reach and where there is an absence of reflected light. Sun exposure and reflected light are practically zero. Few plants, if any, grow under these conditions.

2. Full shade (FS) occurs under wide- and low-branching deciduous tall shrubs and trees or evergreen trees with tight branching structure and dense foliage that cast deep shadows during most daylight hours in the main growing season in spring and summer. Under deciduous trees, sun exposure can be near 100 during winter. Some plants grow and thrive under these conditions, particularly the many wildflowers that rise in late winter or very early spring, before deciduous trees leaf out, and then go dormant late in spring or early summer, when the woodland leaf canopy provides nearly full shade. Out in the open, the areas beneath solitary trees or small groups of closely spaced trees receive considerable sunlight in the early morning hours or late in the afternoon. Although some sun exposure may occur at sunrise and sunset for short periods of time, full shade conditions prevail for most daylight hours. Effective average sun exposure is less than 10 (perhaps one or two hours of direct sun exist at low angles). In gardens, where closely spaced groups of trees and shrubs are common, full shade may be prevalent even at sunrise and before sunset. Although considered full shade, these conditions may nevertheless provide high light at low sun angles, so many shade-tolerant plants can be cultivated in full shade, provided high light levels exist at least part of the time.

3. Medium shade (MS), also called filtered shade or dappled shade, exists under high-branching deciduous trees that have an open structure and foliage that is not heavy, and under groups of high-branching evergreens with a similarly open structure. Sun exposure is between 30 and 50, with direct sun exposure occurring for two or three hours after sunrise and before sunset for trees in the open. For the remainder of the day, exposure to direct sunrays is intermittent and filtered. Obviously, morning sun is much more beneficial for shade garden plants than hot afternoon sun.

4. Woodland shade (WS) is as complex as the forests themselves, something between medium and light shade. It is impossible to assign it a numerical degree of sun exposure. In densely forested areas, it might approach full shade for part of the day; in lightly wooded areas, medium shade

may prevail most of the time. Forested areas of various types are found all over the temperate regions of the world. Large deciduous forests exist in some areas, while in others evergreen tree species, mostly conifers, abound. In many locations conifers are in decline, and mixed woods flourish. Many forests are natural or may even be old growth, where the spacing of trees is determined by the inherent rise and fall of dominating tree species and other vagaries of nature; others are managed or even man-made. Dense woods close in on us and even intimidate, while open woods invite and enchant. The reason for this is simple: dense forests are dark and dank, with sunlight reaching the ground at clearings only. Open woodland is lighter and brighter; shade is dappled, and sunlight dances across the forest floor, supporting considerable undergrowth and a multitude of thriving, shade-tolerant herbaceous plants. Our garden "woodlands" are frequently open, with the trees of neighbors contributing to the shading. Unfortunately, poor selection of tree species can turn such urban woodlands into dark, unproductive places. Offending trees may have to be limbed up (their lower branches removed) or even cut down. If the trees are "good" shade trees, we try at all costs to maintain the trees we planted or inherited. Most city gardeners realize that only woodland conditions can turn their gardens into the urban refuge they long for. For the purpose of building a garden with shade-tolerant perennials, woodland shade is ideal.

5. Light shade (LS), also called open shade or traveling shade, exists where shade occurs for only part of the day, with full sun exposure, possibly exceeding two-thirds of daylight hours, for the remainder of the day. The shade may be filtered through singular, small trees or may be a dense shadow cast by a man-made structure or a tree with a concentrated leaf mass. Sun exposure under these conditions exceeds 60. Areas that receive some midday shade will see considerable direct sun during morning and afternoon. Even during times of shading, the open exposure allows considerable reflected light to reach the shaded area, and bright light conditions exist. Many plants considered sun-loving can be planted in light shade; care must be taken when siting shade perennials, however, because exposure to direct sun in midafternoon can lead to leaf burning, particularly in southern regions.

Three ways to solve the puzzle

My method, based on my own experience, begins with three simple questions. Where are the shady areas in the garden? When does this shade exist, during a given season or during the course of each day? And, is the shade a full shade, or is it modified to some degree? The answers, or three attributes necessary to qualify and quantify shade conditions and limits in the garden, are shade location, shade timing, and shade intensity.

Most important is shade location. Areas where summer shade exists may offer no shade whatsoever in early spring before the trees leaf out. As the sun becomes stronger in spring, the first cloudless late March sky wreaks havoc with the tender growth of many shade-tolerant plants that have already emerged in southern regions. Further north, the same plants are still safely dormant or even snow-covered, so the early, burning sun has no detrimental effect. Latitude, which influences climate, must therefore be considered, meaning that the first simple question has a two-part answer: the location of the garden on the map, and the location of shady areas in the garden.

Latitude (location north or south of the equator) determines the length and consequently the coverage of shadows as well as the intensity of the sunlight, but it does not exactly demarcate climate. Climate not only depends on the sun's rays received at any given latitude, but by a garden's altitude (above sea level), the proximity of oceans, the atmosphere, and other factors. For simplification, climatologists have organized the earth's climate into zones. Most gardens on earth are located in the north and south temperate zones, which can be considered the seasonal belts of the Earth. Practically all the plants discussed in this work have their origin with or are species growing in the north or south temperate zones. Within these zones several different climates exist. The shade-giving plant species growing in one climatic region—oceanic, continental, mountain, coastal, desert—are often very different from those occurring in another. Ultimately—shade houses, pergolas, and other man-made structures aside—the relative nature of shade in gardens is determined by the species of trees and tall shrubs that cast the shade.

The timing of shade in the garden also bears investigation, for many perennials selected for the shady garden require shade during the hot noon to afternoon hours. Plants that can tolerate less shade or even some sun in the early to mid-morning hours need protection from the much more intense sun later in the day. Further away from the equator, more sun can be tolerated by the same plant, because the intensity of the sun diminishes. Thus, shade timing must coincide with the requirements of a given perennial. Shade timing has two main components: seasonal timing and diurnal timing.

Seasonal timing is simply the recognition of changes in shade patterns caused by seasonal changes in the shade-giving tree and shrub canopy. Deciduous trees lose their leaves in fall, while the foliage of evergreen trees remains with the tree until the next season's leaves replace it. In spring, anything growing under deciduous trees will be in almost full sun. The bare branches will cast some shadow, but for gardening objectives, such shade is insignificant. Evergreens represent another parameter in shade timing. One group, broadleaf evergreens, is important to all gardeners; it includes hollies, rhododendrons, and other usually small trees and shrubs that hold onto last season's leaves throughout the winter before dropping them in spring, coincidental with a new flush of leaves. As a result, they give considerable year-round shade. With this group, the shade timing exercise is obviously identical to that of a fully leafed-out deciduous tree in summer. Conifers are another group of evergreens. These trees and shrubs have very high garden importance and winter-persistent foliage that typically takes the form of needles. As a consequence, they give some shade throughout the seasons and usually show some increase in shade during late spring and summer, when a flush of new needles replaces last year's. Yet another group of evergreens, tropical evergreens, are of marginal importance to temperate zone gardeners and are not considered here.

Diurnal timing is easily established by observation: it is simply the existence of shade during a given time of day. The sun's rays are strongest when the sun is high in the sky. During that time, shadows are shortest and shade coverage is at its minimum. Most perennials suitable for the shady garden will prefer morning sun and noon to late afternoon shade. Siting them accordingly increases the chances for success in a shady garden. Here the hot afternoon sun is most damaging. I do plant in such areas, but the plant selection is limited to those that tolerate full sun.

Shade intensity is the third quality to be determined. This is paramount to determining what tree species occur in the garden, but even novice gardeners can gauge the various shade intensities by observation alone. Obviously, few plants thrive in conditions of full and uninterrupted shade; but most garden areas with some tree and shrub cover receive varying intensities of shade and are therefore capable of supporting many shade perennials. In the main, Hosta Hill receives almost continuous overhead shade beneath a contiguous canopy of towering longleaf and loblolly pines. Understory dogwoods and Japanese maples cast a more intense shade, just right for many eastern wildflower species. A 40-year-old evergreen *Magnolia grandiflora* on the western border casts year-round shade so dense, nothing will grow underneath it; its branches touch the ground all around it, forming suckers that further deepen the shade.

When too much shade is the problem, the remedies are simple (and much faster than "growing" shade). The most obvious and frequent solution is to cut down trees or tall shrubs. Trees that have become dangerous because of disease, lightning strike, or storm damage must be removed; healthy trees should be removed only if their presence threatens the garden environment, which does happen. A good friend of mine had a large black walnut tree shading the entire rear garden. He loved the tree but did not like the patch of bare ground beneath it, so one spring he planted shade-tolerant perennials and small shrubs underneath the giant. Soon he found everything smashed by falling walnuts or stunted by the chemicals the tree produced. He tolerated this magnificent yet lethal tree for a few years more, but finally he cut it down. With proceeds from the sale of the wood, he purchased and planted three fast-growing pin oaks, and the restored garden now thrives in their more benevolent shade.

Limbing up or pruning is another way to control or maintain shade intensity. Even if not required at first, such measures are often necessitated by growing and expanding shade trees and shrubs. Most tall shrubs need periodic pruning for best performance anyway, so this pruning can be performed with ultimate shade requisites in mind.

Bones of the Shady Garden

In nature as well as in gardens, shade is never a constant: it depends on a fluctuating framework of trees and shrubs—the bones of the garden. This framework changes steadily, and with it changes the location, timing, and intensity of the shade provided by it. As trees and shrubs grow larger in time, their shade becomes more influential. Eventually they die and must be removed. Sometimes storms topple them, and their shade is suddenly gone. With the passing of time, all gardens change.

It takes time to build the bones of a garden. Gardeners who have an established skeleton of trees and shrubs are lucky indeed; owners of new homes with a treeless landscape should educate themselves very carefully about tree and shrub species suitable for making a shady garden. In 1957 we moved into our first home, in Nashville, Tennessee. Our newly seeded front lawn came furnished with the obligatory sugar maple. I planted a bed of iris and daylilies around it, and they did well for a while. Within a few short seasons, however, the tree had shaded out the flower bed and part of the lawn, and the shady area around the tree was nothing but a sea of hungry tree roots. I finally covered the sore spot with a mulch of pine bark. Back then family obligations did not allow much time for horticulture, so the selection of a sugar maple did not appear a bad choice. It was. Upon returning to the place many years later, I found the maple gone, replaced by flowers in sunny borders with a small patch of a lawn. This example illustrates that the "man-made" shade created by planting an undesirable tree impaired the garden environment in front of my first home for decades. Not only was I affected by this poor choice, but subsequent owners had problems as well. Besides Japanese maples and dogwoods, good choices for understory trees include Carolina silverbell (*Halesia carolina*), fringe tree (*Chionanthus virginicus*), Japanese snowbell (*Styrax japonicus*), and saucer and star magnolias (*Magnolia ×soulangeana* and *M. stellata*).

Many gardeners struggle with the problem of having too much shade in their gardens. At Hosta Hill some of the increasingly detrimental shade can be controlled, but inevitably my sunny flower borders turn into shady beds and small trees planted years ago became giants. I and many other gardeners with the same dilemma have to change the selection of perennials and small shrubs to those tolerant of some shade. That many shade perennials require less maintenance is an added benefit to gardeners of advancing age.

Shade Without Trees

Gardening is fundamentally a waiting game. Gardeners wait for trees to mature, for perennials to attain blooming age, and for bulbs planted in fall to show up in spring. Unfortunately patience is not an inborn virtue for many of us, so the prospect of having to wait a decade or more to grow shade-giving trees appears unacceptable at first. In time even the most eager gardeners learn to be patient and might even consider planting a tree for their grandchildren.

For the very impatient, however, gardening in shady areas is possible by erecting structures to provide such shade, which gives the gardener freedom to select the shade's location, timing, and intensity. Easily the most artificial of these designs is the shade house, usually a simple edifice consisting of an open roof framework covered with shade cloth or a wooden trellis and supported on columns. The material is typically treated wood. Size is limited only by economics and available space. Large nurseries erect entire complexes of rudimentary shade houses for the purpose of plant propagation. In gardens these shade structures take on a more architectural tone and are embellished with trim work and other decorations. Pergolas fit this purpose as well but some patience is required, because the roof cover is commonly a living vine; sometimes shade cloth is utilized until the vine or other living cover has grown enough to fill in the roof openings. Pergolas are more open on the sides and therefore admit much more light than shade houses, which may have shade cloth cover on the east or west wall (or both). Densely overgrown pergolas, on the other hand, give 100% shading during high noon because the covering vines frequently exclude the sun's rays completely. Open greenhouses too use shade cloth to control the sun; for this purpose, woven polypropylene or UV-polyethylene shade fabric is commercially available in several degrees of shading, measured in percentage. These shade-giving structures can be made as attractive as money and talent allows, and they can contribute greatly to the design aesthetics of open gardens. As decorative, functional, and useful as they may be, they can never replace the living beauty of shade-giving trees and shrubs in a woodland garden.

A few treeless gardeners fated to sun may have neither the space nor the money to erect such shade-giving structures. While they may not have overhead shade, they can nevertheless take advantage of shade cast by small shrubs, their house, or solid fences. As long three-dimensional objects exist, shade will also be present. Even full shade can be found on the north side of a dwelling, for example, so a shady nook can be planted and maintained in gardens that have an abundance of sunshine elsewhere. Indeed, if no trees are present, a few surveys of the property carried out during morning, noon, and evening hours will reveal a shady niche here and there where at least some perennials for the shady garden can contribute to the overall attractiveness of the garden. Every gardener deserves at least one shady corner.

CHAPTER 3

Practical Thoughts

A few years ago, I gave a lecture to the Georgia Hosta Society. The topic was troubles in the garden, and the outcome was unexpected. A few seasoned gardeners were appreciative, but many novice members were turned off by "all that talk about slugs and bugs." A frequently heard question: if gardening in general—and growing hostas in particular—is that much trouble, who needs it?

One trait that separates man from the apes, I explained, is man's innate urge to create art, and nature is the stage upon which gardeners perform their temporal art. With this comes all the good and bad nature brings, be it life-giving sun and rain or damaging wind and hail. Pollinating bees are good, and many consider the beauty of butterflies very good, but behind the charm of butterflies, I reminded my audience, lurks the destructiveness of their larvae before they metamorphose into fluttering loveliness. Nature does not care about gardens. It goes on finding its own balance, as it must, and in so doing interferes with the artful ways of the gardener. Succesful gardeners work with rather than against natural progression, I concluded. Rather than "Garden and never mind the bugs," the message should be "Garden and *know* the bugs!"

The best gardeners are practical gardeners. They know their bugs and are attuned to the physical environment of the garden. They understand soils, the weather, and all the other things important to versed gardening. Practical thoughts may not fit into the romanticized image of fine gardening, but behind those wonderful vistas of garden art is the application of a gardener's basic and practical know-how.

The Garden's Floor

The wild woodland floor is made up of the by-products of tree growth and life in the woods. Millions of particles rain down constantly: leaves, needles, pieces of bark, small and large branches torn loose by storms; all manner of fruit, seed cones, and other seed-bearing encasings; windblown dust and dirt, rain, snow, and ice; animal hair, feathers, and droppings, and even the bones of long-dead creatures. Even trees die and fall, and their decaying trunks become part of the forest floor. Over time, nature shuffles and reshuffles the mixture. Fungi, lichens, bacteria, and other tiny creatures break it down to its basic components. Burrowing animals see to it that a liberal sprinkling of earth's mineral matter is added to the mix. Eventually, layer upon layer of this rich, organic debris makes up the soil of the forest floor. This soil is not static and changes constantly. New debris is added, particles of old are absorbed by roots, and so the seasons' successional process never ends.

For gardeners, the soil produced by nature's workings is to die for. Rarely, if ever, is such "gardener's gold" available. I had it once but lost it, and it is worth telling the story . . . The half-acre of Hosta Hill sits on the crest of a hillock. In days long gone, an old farmhouse sat on the site, and I still discover pieces of china and small farm implements when I dig in the garden. The loblolly pines are second growth; their random placement shows they are volunteers on former farmland. Judging by the growth rings of some of the trees removed for construction, farming in the area must have stopped around 1910. Loblolly pines are notorious for shedding their large needles in bushel-basket quantities, and when we started the house, 60 years' accumulation had built a carpet of gardener's gold. I remember sinking my hands into this soft, dark, spongy soil, dreaming of carpeting the back-half with wildflowers. Indeed, some wildflowers were already there: wild ginger, cranefly orchid, and Solomon's seal, mixed in with Christmas and lady ferns. Sadly, my dream was not realized. One day, visiting the site to inspect ongoing construction, I found to my horror that all that woods soil had been pushed aside and carried off—wildflowers, ferns, shrubs, and all. Only the trees were left standing. The contractor wanted to put in a lawn. It was too late for protestations, so I shed a few silent tears. At least I still had my trees. But to make my garden, I had to build new soil atop a solid layer of exposed, brick-hard Georgia red clay.

Most gardeners these days have a similar problem. In many developments, the landscape, whether woodland or old farmland, is so thoroughly disturbed, gardeners must "create" their own soil. Plant rescues are an excellent way to save wildflowers from destruction where development is planned, and many local native plant societies, including the Georgia Native Plant Society, arrange such rescues. As a participant, I see the before and after of such development. A few small wildflowers, ferns, and some smaller shrubs can be rescued, but everything else falls to the bulldozers. House construction on this bare ground is more economical, and it is easier to install the "new landscape," an ornamental tree, perhaps, a lawn, of course, and foundation planting. It is sad indeed. It will take years to grow new shade providers and to build soil. A few contractors are beginning to realize how devastating such methods are, and they try to save a few trees, at least.

Organic matter

To take available soil and improve it to attain good physical structure and openness (a condition sometimes referred to as good tilth) is time-consuming, labor-intensive, and often expensive. The addition of organic matter to clay or sandy soils—indeed, to any natural soil composed chiefly of mineral particles—is essential. Organic matter can actually be bought in raw form, which, for practical reasons, usually takes the form of packaged products. Fine-graded ground bark, coarse sphagnum peat, or ground natural waste products, like peanut hulls or corn cobs—all are available at nurseries. Ground tree clippings and sawdust can be obtained cheaply by the truckload and are sometimes free for the taking; these require the addition of slow-release, high-nitrogen fertilizers to feed the decomposition process. Gardeners can collect pine needles, leaves, or other natural waste; once composted, they make fine soil amendments. When raw organic materials are digested in compost piles by soil organisms, they become humus.

Technically, humus is an amorphous, colloidal, black or brown substance that has the ability to retain water. This makes it an excellent amendment to natural garden soils, particularly rapid-draining, sandy soils. It also helps the formation of soil crumbs in clayey soils, improving aeration and drainage. Humus comes in two forms: mor humus, formed in acid conditions, and mull humus, formed in neutral or alkaline environments. The addition of humus is one of the best ways to improve garden soil because its chemicals are directly available to plants. Gardeners often take the brown, decayed matter on their compost piles for pure humus, but it is actually a mixture of raw and decomposed organic matter: colloidal humus, moder (an intermediate form of humus), and reduced, raw organic matter in different stages of decomposition. Raw vegetable garbage, grass clippings, and plant waste materials should be composted before being used in the garden. Diseased plant waste and materials should never be placed on the compost pile but conveyed away from the garden.

Knowing the soil

Knowing the soil is essential to making a garden, and it is important for gardeners to find out which of the multitude of different natural soils they have. Many county extension offices of the United States Department of Agriculture (USDA) provide a soil analysis service either free or for a nominal charge. At Hosta Hill the natural soil is a dense, red clay, suitable for making bricks and, in fact, widely used for this purpose. For gardening it is simply appalling.

The five major soil types, categorized by the ratio of coarse to fine particles, are sandy, silty, loamy, chalky, and clayey. Gravelly sands, fine sands, silt loams, sandy clays, heavy clays (like those at Hosta Hill), and other intermediate types occur. Loams (mixtures of mineral particles with an optimum combination of coarse and fine particles) are best for gardening. Herbaceous shade perennials require a loose, well-drained soil, high in organic matter.

Soils can be acid, alkaline, or neutral, which level is indicated by the pH number. Neutral is represented by pH 7. Readings above 7 indicate increasingly alkaline conditions (with 14 being absolute alkalinity). Readings below 7 indicate increasingly acid conditions (few plants can exist below pH 4). Soil tests will determine, among other things, what pH number the soil has, and inexpensive pH meters are available at nurseries, so gardeners can do their own testing. Pine and oak forests impart acidity to the surrounding soil; woodlands growing on limestone rock or in chalky soils have soil that is more alkaline. A wide variety of pH levels are tolerated by most herbaceous perennials suitable for shady gardens. Most perennials listed in this book have great adaptability, preferring slightly acid soils, a condition found in most garden soils, so adjustment of pH is normally not required.

Chlorosis, in which the leaves turn slowly yellow but the veins stay dark green, is a condition caused variously by overfertilizing, poorly drained soils, chemical soil imbalance, or a virus. Spray the leaves with iron sulphate (1 oz. per 2 gallons/4 g per liter): if the leaves temporarily turn green after this treatment, the pH balance of the soil requires adjustment, usually toward the acid side, to make the iron in the soil more available. Adding chelated iron may be necessary.

Water: too little or too much

Many plants with large leaves have high transpiration rates, which means they lose uncommonly high amounts of water through the leaves. Such plants require considerable available amounts of water in the soil to replace the transpired water. With rare exceptions, wild populations of large-leaved plants grow in relatively moist soils or near water, and these conditions are fortified by high humidity and rainfall in many natural woodlands. Garden soils for such plants should have a high water-holding capacity. This can be accomplished by the addition of organic matter like peat moss, ground organic waste products, or thoroughly composted material containing humus. During the spring growing season, soil moisture must be maintained at field capacity: the amount of water that can be held by capillary action in the soil after excess, gravitational water has percolated to the water table. As moisture is withdrawn from the soil by absorption through roots or evaporation, the moisture amount becomes less than field capacity. Soil moisture deficit is the difference between the actual amount of moisture in the soil and its field capacity; this deficit can be held to a minimum by regular watering and the addition of clean mulches to reduce surface evaporation. Maintaining moisture in the soil is one of the most important obligations a gardener has. In the shady garden, insufficient moisture is invariably detrimental to lush growth and plant survival.

There can also be too much water in the soil. The slow-draining clay soil at Hosta Hill is an example. Initially, I tried to fool nature and grow perennials in barely improved clay. The results were dismal. A few hostas hung on to a skimpy existence and did not begin to flourish until I took pity on the plants, dug them up, and amended the soil with an abundance of pine bark and peat moss. The hostas took off and grew to their full glory; some remain happily in the same location after three decades.

A breath of air

Soils must be able to breathe. Good garden soils have a high percentage of pore space (the empty space in soils usually occupied by air and water)—the best have around 50% solid matter and 50% pore space. In the very fine, natural clay soils of Georgia, the volume of the individual pore spaces becomes very small but surface tension increases, so the soil can hold large amounts of water. Thus, heavy clay soils have poor percolation (the rate at which water can move through the soil). These soils are usually sticky and wet and retain large quantities of water but, once they dry out, are difficult to bring back up to field capacity because of poor percolation. Percolation in these soils can be improved by the addition of liberal amounts of coarse, organic matter. Sand can sometimes be beneficial, but here another story bears telling...

Many years ago I read somewhere that sand was a fine amendment for clay soils, making the soil percolate and breath better. Dutifully, I purchased several bags of coarse builders' sand and mixed it with my Georgia clay in proportions long forgotten. I planted a few perennials in that mix and eagerly awaited their bursting forth next spring. To me, few things are more exciting than the emergence of new plant shoots in spring. But nothing happened with the new perennials, and finally I decided to dig and find the cause of their disappearance. The sand-clay mixture, through chemical interaction, had turned into something akin to concrete. Not even a spade could break the clod. After this, I never mixed sand with Georgia red clay again.

Minerals in the soil

Agricultural topsoil is composed of 90% mineral and 10% organic matter. Old, undisturbed woodland soil, by contrast, can be as much as 50% organic matter. A high volume of organic matter is preferred in soil for the shady natural garden. Although organic content is important, a percentage of mineral content should be maintained for balance. At Hosta Hill various planting areas are installed above the underlying clay surface. These raised beds are filled with soil composed of 10% screened clay, 20% composted humus or cow manure, 20% peat moss, and 50% ground pine bark. This mix holds a lot of water during dry summers but also drains well during excessively wet periods.

To fertilize or not

Many cultivated garden plants are relatively heavy feeders. Wildflowers are not, however, and fertilizing at Hosta Hill is thus kept to a minimum. Nutrients can be added in many ways. Because they are absorbed at a fairly high rate, particularly by fast-growing perennials, the danger of overfertilizing is always present. So I use only one type of fertilizer, which contains nitrogen, phosphorus, potassium, and many required trace elements, such as magnesium, iron, and calcium. This fertilizer, Osmocote Plus®, comes in the form of osmotic pellets and feeds through osmosis for extended periods. It comes in two formulas; I use the 18–6–12 formula, with eight- to nine-months' time release. A 50-pound (23 kg) bag, applied sparingly in early spring, feeds my entire garden. In most areas application should be made in early spring, but in more southern latitudes, where the ground rarely freezes and with some root growth continuing through winter, fertilizer can be applied in late winter. Other slow-release, urea-based fertilizers will do, but many are water soluble and their nutrients are washed away by heavy spring rains. I do not recommend raw chemical fertilizers, such as ammonium nitrate or superphosphate, due to the danger of burning; wildflowers and other natives are particularly sensitive to such injury. I do not employ foliar feeding; it deposits a residue that spoils the attractive surface of many large-leaved perennials.

Making garden soil

To be happy, gardeners need some measure of success. The first step to such success is good soil, but few gardeners are lucky enough to have good garden soil ready for planting. I have already detailed my mixture for raised beds, but it is by no means the only one I use. Specific soil requirements, when known, are given for individual plants described in Part 2. Some require constantly moist or even wet soils; others require soils with rapid drainage. Gardeners can accommodate their plants by creating soils and conditions that mimic the natural habitat. Wet soils can be duplicated by building artificial swamps, and rapid drainage is easily achieved by creating elevated rock gardens with porous soils and sublayers.

Making soil does not mean replacing existing topsoil. To simplify, it means adding organic matter to the surface layer of soil, the layer in which cultivation occurs. How much must be added depends on the make-up of this existing soil and its depth. Some topsoil layers are only 1–2 in. (2.5–5 cm) deep, while others may be over 12 in. (30 cm) thick. It also depends on the topsoil type, so it is important to get the soil analyzed. The basic tenet is to add enough organic matter to make slow-draining clay soils like my brick yard soil percolate faster and rapid-draining sandy soils hold more water. Make most of this organic matter a relatively coarse material, like rough-ground tree bark. These are available prepackaged from local plant nurseries. Bark, peanut hulls, or corn cobs in ground form can also be purchased by the truckload. Such materials open clay soils and permit them to breathe and freely drain any excess water.

For soils that drain too fast, I recommend water-holding organic matter, such as humus from the compost pile or peat moss. A little peat moss goes a long way; the problem with it is its rapid deterioration in the soil. In years past I added as much as 30% (by volume) peat moss to some beds. In a few short years, the surface of the beds had literally sunk as much as several inches because the peat moss simply disappeared. I now use peat moss sparingly, usually in wildflower beds.

Where good, loamy topsoil already exists naturally, only small amounts of organic amendments are required. Some experimentation may be necessary to find the best formula. Just as a garden cannot be made in one day, development of its soil base takes some time to accomplish. When large quantities of amendments are required, economics may also play a decisive role. When it comes to a decision of buying either soil amendments or plants, the amendments should come first, because if the plants are not given correct soil conditions, they may die anyway.

At Hosta Hill it took many years to arrive at suitable soil conditions. After seeing plants excel at first and then decline, I realized that the fertility and tilth of my soil is not a permanent condition. The bed where a lot of peat moss had disappeared gave the first clue. There was nothing wrong with the plants. I watered, fertilized, and did all the things gardeners are supposed to do, but to no avail. Trying to reestablish the former elevation, I removed the plants and started digging. The soil appeared to be of good tilth, too good perhaps, because nearby dogwood trees had greedily invaded the bed over the years, forming a thick mat of roots. No wonder the plants had declined. I replenished the soil, and, back at their old level, the plants showed renewed vigor the following spring.

Maintaining garden soil

The story of tree root invasion just related illustrates the necessity of soil maintenance. It is not enough to improve the soil. From time to time it will be essential to inspect the soil, to have it retested perhaps, or to make the soil over again. This is even more essential in planting areas that can be invaded by the roots of trees and shrubs. Some popular garden trees (dogwoods and maples, for example) and shrubs (stewartias come to mind) have greedy, dense, far-reaching root systems that can choke nearby planting beds.

There can be other problems. Some amendments may be absorbed and disappear; it is not enough to just top the area or bed with more amendment because this will bury the tops of plants with layers of new material, which can lead to rotting or suffocation. Many perennials are fussy about how deep they are planted, so it will be necessary to dig the plants, amend the soil, screen it to remove tree roots, and then replant. In thriving gardens, plants may start to crowd each other out, so periodic digging is a must anyway. The soil of shady gardens under pines and oaks can become more acid in time, and it is prudent to test the acidity now and then. Judicious applications of pelletized lime can correct conditions of too much acidity. Some plants are very sensitive to lime; use caution whenever using lime in shady woodland gardens. In short, successful gardening is not possible without some maintenance, and maintaining the soil is imperative.

Trouble from Above

In most shady gardens as in the wild, trees are the shade givers; but in gardens, shade trees are a roof bringing trouble—namely, damage to the underlying plants. Physical damage is common: trees bombard the garden below with large cones, nuts, and other seedpods or heavy fruit. Avoid planting large-leaved perennials under many of the pine trees, magnolias, and other trees that produce large seedpods or fruit. Falling pinecones can cause considerable leaf damage, and even pine needles driven by wind or falling from a height can pierce the leaves of hostas and other large-leaved perennials. Another type of damage is caused by tree droppings, such as the resinous droplets that descend from many pines or the sticky nectar exuded by some flowering trees. These secretions are impossible to remove and usually turn black in short order by way of fungal action, discoloring the leaves and flowers. Impact damage by falling branches is an obvious hazard under trees, principally those with brittle wood. Not so obvious are falling, spent flower petals (or bracts in some cases), which attach themselves to rain-moistened leaves and, because of the sugars in their chemical composition, become literally glued to the leaves of perennials. In North America the dogwood is one such flowering tree. If left on the leaves, fungal action eventually decays the covered leaf tissue. Smaller particles can accumulate in the pockets of rugose or cup-shaped leaves. Neither rain nor wind will dislodge them, and they eventually become attached, adversely affecting the appearance of a leaf or the entire plant.

Only careful siting and selection of suitable shade tree species under which to plant can reduce or eliminate these problems. In gardens where existing shade trees bring trouble, plant a shield of leafy, understory trees, such as redbud (*Cercis canadensis*) or flowering dogwood, so that the fall of some objects tumbling down from greater heights can be blocked or broken to some extent. I use this method at Hosta Hill. But remember: while the flowering dogwood will shield leafy plants like hostas, partially at least, from falling objects, it may itself present a hazard. Indeed, the shady garden is not without conflicts and troubles! It used to disturb me greatly when the perfect leaf of a hosta got smashed and torn by a spiny pinecone falling from great height. Over time I got over it, and now I just tuck the damaged leaf under the others or remove it. It is not worth worrying over such minor troubles in Paradise.

Trouble Underneath

Nature has another surprise waiting, hidden from view. Shade trees stretch their feeder roots over large areas. They feed on the splendidly friable, fertile soil provided in the planting areas and beds on the shady garden floor with a rapacity that can eventually damage the plants grown there. It may take several years for the harm to show up, but there will be a general decline in plant vigor, a cessation of bloom, and an eventual wasting of the plants. Check for invading tree roots at regular dividing time. If root invasion has occurred, remove the roots, screen the soil, and replant everything, while you are at the routine lifting and dividing. If the offending trees are mature, remove a portion of their feeder roots; normally this is not harmful to the trees. I have installed landscape fabrics, designed to prevent root invasion, in the bottom of planting areas and beds before backfilling and planting. They definitely hinder root invasion and lengthen the time a plant can grow unimpeded. Eventually, though, the tree roots find a way into the planting beds. These fabrics are available in most large garden centers.

In most shady gardens, trees are the primary shade givers, so the problem with tree roots is unavoidable. For new gardens it can be reduced by carefully selecting shade trees with nonaggressive root systems. Maples, dogwoods, magnolias, and many other tree species have aggressive root systems; dwarf Japanese maples are tolerable, but large native and exotic maple trees can be very destructive.

A not-so-new school of thought has reemerged of late. Gardeners emulate their native landscape and let plants fend for themselves. After all, that is what happens in nature. But replicating nature's delicate balance is difficult. In the garden, too many factors can upset the balance, not least of which are the gardeners themselves. At Hosta Hill, I find that other garden necessities can be efficiently accomplished during periodic checks for root invasion: plants can be divided for increase, the presence of harmful insect grubs detected, soil amendments added, weeds removed—it is even possible to redesign the entire area. Usually several years pass before root removal is required, so I find this radical procedure not unwelcome. Gardens are never finished, so never mind a little trouble underneath: it is part of it all.

Gardeners' Enemies

A horde of bugs, slugs, and other assorted pests can plague gardeners, some invisible, like bacteria, fungi, and viruses. Over the years, I have become philosophical about these enemies. Because they attack and damage precious garden plants, they command the thoughtful gardener's full attention, and as a consequence, many beneficial creatures in the garden are forgotten—insect pollinators, soil bacteria, earthworms and mycorrhizas, symbiotic soil fungi, and other helpers.

Focusing on the bugs and slugs, gardeners forget that other problems can be the cause of trouble. I have learned—sometimes the hard way—that sickly looking plants may not be diseased after all. Injury to plants may be brought about by a late freeze, sun scald, fertilizer burn, waterlogged or parched soil, herbicide or other chemical injury. Before fixing blame on bugs, seen or unseen, I try to determine if the cause of sickness is associated with the environment—perhaps I have unintentionally stepped on an emerging plant or done something else wrong. Only after eliminating these causes, referred to as physiogenic factors, do I go after pathogenic causes. Pathogens are living organisms that cause diseases in garden plants. Most are very small, so powerful microscopes are required to detect them. All we gardeners can do is to become proficient in recognizing the symptoms brought about by these invisible hordes.

Viruses

Viruses are ultramicroscopic, nucleoprotein molecules that, once inside a living being, behave like living organisms. Some, like the one that mottles forms of *Farfugium japonicum* (leopard plant), are beneficial. Others, however, are deadly when they interact with people, animals, or plants. While gardeners may care little about what viruses actually are, they become very worried when they get the flu or, worse yet, when symptoms show up in the garden. These include chlorosis (yellowing of the leaves), mottling or mosaicism (white or yellowish spots), blotching (whitened areas larger than spots), wilting and collapse of plant tissue, leaf curl, mosaic and ring spots, general reduction in vigor, and stunting. Viruses partially or completely shut down the plant's vascular system and consequently photosynthesis. Worse, a virus can be spread by any action that transfers cell sap from one plant to another; cutting or sucking insects accomplish this, as do gardeners who use the same garden tools first on infected and then on healthy plants. Viruses can also spread through asexual propagation methods, like dividing, and often through seed.

Mosaicism is almost always a viral infection, but leaf yellowing can have several causes, for example the normal yellowing that occurs at the onset of dormancy. Many leaves turn yellow during very hot, dry weather, a normal signal of heat stress due to lack of water; leaves thus affected remain firm for quite some time and dry up slowly, just as they do at winter's onset. More often than not, a visit to the county USDA extension office or a university's plant pathology department can help identify viral diseases. Plant breeders have developed garden varieties, both edible and ornamental, that have inbred resistance to viruses; gardeners should select such cultivars whenever possible.

As no effective treatment against viral infections is known, the best strategy for most gardeners will be the one I use at Hosta Hill: any plant suspected of being infected by a virus is ruthlessly eliminated. I dig up the plant and consign the remains, soil and all, to the waste heap; infected plant waste should never be conveyed to the compost pile. The spade used in the procedure is afterward thoroughly cleaned with heavily chlorinated water. It is better to lose even expensive or rare plants, thereby avoiding the spread of infection in a tightly planted garden.

Bacteria and fungi

Bacteria and fungi are the most prevalent pathogens. They usually enter plant tissue that is cut, torn, or abraded, and once inside the plant tissue multiply rapidly. They can cause decay, contribute to secondary infections, and may result in the plant's demise. When the sad results show up in the garden, it is often too late to do anything about the predicament; many bacterial and fungal diseases start in late fall, after the leaf drop of herbaceous perennials, and the destructive action continues below ground until spring. By the time the plants are expected to produce their spring flush of leaves, the underground portion of the plant may have turned to mush. Crown rot, a frequently observed problem in herbaceous perennials, belongs in this category. At Hosta Hill, even with good fall sanitation, crown rot occurs once in a while. In years past, I spent a lot of time worrying about hosta rhizomes rotting in the ground, but I am more practical now. Losing a plant now and then is inevitable in gardens, and most certainly such losses should not result in unreasonable grief, even if it is an old, cherished keepsake from Grandmother's garden.

Practical thoughts must also include a respect for the environment. It is absolutely unconscionable and impractical to try to save commonly available garden plants by dousing them with fungicides and insecticides. This is not to say that in rare cases the application of systemic insecticides or fungicides can be employed under rigidly controlled conditions, but in my experience such measures would be justified only when an "irreplaceable" plant becomes diseased. Plants that can be readily bought in plant nurseries should simply be replaced when a malady strikes. A gardener's first priority should be to stem further infection of neighboring, healthy plants, and that is best accomplished by removing and discarding all diseased plant material. This is no time to be sentimental.

Early detection of symptoms is essential. Once a crown is affected, the decay process is irreversible; there is no magic bullet for curing diseases affecting the root portion of a plant. In early spring, when herbaceous perennials do not resprout at all or the young leaves turn yellow just after sprouting, trouble exists just below the surface. Good gardeners spend a lot of time in their personal landscape visiting the plantings and checking everything. Thus they can detect problems before they become disasters.

If a garden is generally healthy, afflictions are rarely seen; healthy, robust, and well-cared-for plantings are in the main disease-resistant. And luckily, virtually all plants sold by nurseries are disease-free, and packaged soil and soil amendments are safe. Nonetheless, I practice exclusion for all plants and any other materials brought in from outside. I have a quarantine area in the rear of Hosta Hill where I keep "newly imported" plants in pots for about six months, to determine their general health. Obviously, the problem of excluding pathogens becomes much more complicated when dealing with wind-borne diseases or those brought in by insects or other carriers. Gardens are wide open to such carriers; it is impossible to erect barriers to exclude them.

Be alert. If you live in an area where prolonged snow cover exists, visit your plants often to detect storm and snow damage to trees and shrubs. Corrective measures, such as pruning, may prevent the development of disease in the aboveground plant tissues. In areas where the ground remains open, inspect the herbaceous perennials that are resting for the winter. Falling dead branches can pierce the ground and damage the underground portions of plants, allowing pathogens to enter. Gardeners should know where their plants are located, so as to avoid stepping on fragile rhizomes and emerging plant shoots. Above all, use all your senses: look, touch, and smell.

Bacterial and fungal diseases are easily spotted during the growing season, and gardeners should become familiar with their symptoms. Examples of these maladies are leaf spot, anthracnose, crown gall, slime flux, wilting, mildews, rusts, smut, cankers, black spot, and some blights. Leaf yellowing is often attributed to a virus but can also be caused by bacteria or fungi. A visit to a county USDA extension office is particularly valuable; some pathogens are concentrated in certain regions of the country, and these offices are aware of such infections.

Improper growing conditions—too much shade or sun, too much or too little water, too much or inadequate feeding—result in unhealthy plants, which are much less able to resist all manner of plant pathogens. Avoid siting plants in low spots that get flooded every spring; improve soil if it is mostly clay; do not apply heavy, rotting, organic mulches in the fall—instead, use light, clean mulches, like pine needles, bark, salt hay, or similar products. Take steps to reduce physical damage to the plants caused by slugs, insects, and other animals, which can result in secondary infections. Plant pathogens, particularly bacteria and fungi are everywhere, so backfilling with clean planting soil will eliminate them as well as insect larvae and other subterranean pests.

Nematodes

Nematodes are unsegmented worms; most are very small, 0.5–5.0 mm in length, although some grow much larger. Nematodes specializing on agricultural crops cause an estimated $1 billion in damage yearly to world agriculture. Common horticultural afflictions are rootknot eelworms or root gall nematodes; these cystforming nematodes invade the root structures and lay eggs in cysts formed from root tissue. These cysts or galls, visible when roots are exposed, release poisons or enzymes that alter cell content, leading to stunted growth or loss of vigor. The cysts, full of eggs, then detach themselves, awaiting another cycle and staying viable for many years. Other species form permanent galls that remain as part of the roots, and the nematodes do not leave the host plant until it dies or the roots are severed. No truly effective control exists for living plants, but the ground can be fumigated before planting, a process best left to professionals. Some granular nematicides are available and can be tried, but the environmental consequences must be considered. Good cultural practices can overcome some of the damage.

Foliar nematodes invade the aboveground portions of plants, particularly the leaves, disfiguring them. Hostas, chrysanthemums, some ferns, and other cultivated garden plants are favorite targets. These eelworms invade the rising shoots on the rootstock very early in the spring, hatching from overwintering eggs, and grow in cell pockets of the elongating plant tissue, usually winding up in the leaf structure. There they consume the inner cell layers and lay a new crop of eggs inside the leaves. The damage does not show up until early in summer. Total eradication is possible only with extremely dangerous chemicals and is not advised. Again, gardeners must be practical and learn to live with these pests. The best way to keep populations down is to remove any disfigured leaves as soon as they show up, thus preventing the eggs from escaping into the ground when the leaves disintegrate in fall.

Bugs and other critters

Of late, conscientious gardeners have replaced chemical insecticides with beneficial predatory insects, which take over the role of biological insect control in gardens. With that understanding, and even with another grateful nod to the extremely beneficial pollinating insects, it must be said that a huge number of "bad" insect species in the north and south temperate zones still, in some way, make life miserable for gardeners. Insects have only two goals in life: to eat as much as possible and to procreate as much as possible (and furthermore, to do both as quickly as possible). The way caterpillars can devour the leaves of a favorite garden plant easily qualifies them as ultimate eating machines, and the impulse to be utterly rid of such pests is understandable to most gardeners, who may remember a wonderful rose chewed to bits by Japanese beetles or that perfect hosta leaf cut to ribbons by army worms. But many gardeners have made a conscious decision to stop constant use of toxic chemicals to control pests in the garden. For this reason I shall dispense with giving advice on how, when, where, and in what amounts to use chemical protection. Even occasional and prudent use of selected, biodegradable insecticides and fungicides should be considered a last resort. Biological controls and exclusion are the best ways to protect against bugs.

Various predators, parasites, and even beneficial diseases can be introduced into the garden to combat specific garden pests. Ladybugs control aphids, mealybugs, and other soft-scale insects; predatory mites fight thrips and spider mites; predatory wasps are used against whiteflies. Beneficial nematodes are very effective against any pest that lives just below the ground or crawls upon it, like the grubs and adults of weevils, borers, Japanese beetles, wireworms, army worms, root maggots, and a host of others. Green lacewings predate on aphids, scales, and whitefly; tiny parasitic wasps combat insects both as larvae and adults. The product Bt (strains of the bacteria *Bacillus thuringiensis*, available in powder form) paralyzes those ravenous caterpillars; another strain of Bt is marketed for control of mosquito larvae, which should appeal to gardeners who are bothered by the adult version of this blood-sucking menace during their insect-hunting jaunts in the garden. Most important, encouraging songbirds to visit the garden is a very effective control of all insect pests. Several mail-order houses specialize in providing such environmentally friendly solutions for bug control.

Exclusive methods may be as simple as setting a trap to catch Japanese beetles or hanging up flypaper, one of the oldest exclusionary devices known. Many more are available at garden centers or comprehensive hardware stores: animal and insect traps; sticky plant collars or tapes to intercept insects climbing tree trunks; tacky baits that use either color or synthesized sexual attractants to snare specific insects. Light can also be used as a nonspecific attractant; some light traps kill the offenders in an electric grid. And bugs can be caught in the beam of a flashlight and hand-picked at night; coordinate such activities with neighbors beforehand, to prevent their thinking something more sinister is taking place. Observant gardeners even hand-pick moth egg cases or Japanese beetles, albeit after damage has been done.

Slugs and snails

Slugs and snails, classified as mollusks, have horny, rasplike teeth (radulas, or radulae) that can cut through even the most substantive perennial leaf or sprout. Adults cause extensive damage, occasionally eating an entire shoot at the ground line in spring; some plants will resprout, but the surviving initial leaves remain extensively damaged. Slugs and snails are hermaphrodites: they can produce offspring without benefit of a sexual union, but they do also mate. The egg clusters are produced in batches, from a few to many, laid in moist places under abandoned flower pots, woodpiles, and vegetation, and in other hiding places, including soil fissures and hollows. Depending on the species involved, hundreds to thousands of eggs are produced during a life cycle, each with a high survival rate. Many become sexually mature very early on, so the generation gap is brief, creating a continuing problem for the gardener throughout the growing season. The fight against mollusks is constant.

During lazy summer days, resigned gardeners often put up with mollusks, figuring that the first freeze is not too far away. Unfortunately, the many eggs laid in summer hatch new broods that hibernate during winter and literally overrun the garden during the spring warm-up (or, in the warmer sections of the temperate regions, the late-winter warm-up), shortly before early perennial sprouts appear. This is when the application of a molluskicide is most effective. A thorough cleanup, as early as possible in spring (or even begun in late fall), is another absolute must; leaves, sticks, pinecones, and other debris must be removed from beds, paths, and planting areas. Inspect the garden for possible hiding places and eliminate them. Anything that is lying on the ground can be a hiding place for mollusks during the daytime when ultraviolet rays endanger their existence, forcing them to seek cover. On cloudy days, they can be seen climbing atop leaves. Feeding takes place at night. Hand-picking of slugs during the night is an effective exclusionary method, albeit a bothersome one.

I have found a highly effective product that contains a selective, mollusk-specific attractant; a small, beadlike amount suffices, so the environmental impact is minuscule. Drawn out of their hiding places by the attractant, the mollusks consume the product, which also contains a synergist, resulting in fast dehydration and death. Unlike poisoned bran products, this gray slug killer does not attract birds and other wildlife. Plastic slug houses are also available; the toxic bait, fortified with chemical attractants, is enclosed, preventing birds from being poisoned. A dish sunk into the ground and filled with beer is a famous exclusion device for slugs; slugs absolutely love that beverage and promptly drown themselves in it. Other lures include inverted grapefruit skins, lettuce, and other preferred foods around which slugs congregate during the night for feeding; gather them at their table in the early morning, before sunrise, and dispose of them.

Nonpoisonous controls include spreading diatomaceous earth, wood ashes, soot, sharp cinders, broken cedar shingle fibers (shingle tow), and other, similar material around the plants. I have tried some of these but unsuccessfully. Finely ground pine bark seems to have some effect; it coats the gastropods' feet with bark fines, which apparently cannot be overcome by increased secretion of slime, so repels them, but this is only marginally useful because the bark fines must be loose and dry, a difficult state to achieve during rainy springs. Biological controls include birds, skunks, shrews, and turtles. At Hosta Hill a family of chipmunks (*Tamias striatus*) consumes a considerable number of snails, judging by the piles of broken shells at their burrow's entrance, and they probably eat slugs, too, without leaving a trace. Unfortunately, they dig extensive tunnels and can themselves be a real nuisance.

Weevils

The snout beetles or weevils are a large group of 50,000 insect species. Many specialize on specific plants and have become a significant pest for azaleas, rhododendrons, and other ornamentals. Visual damage, caused by the adult beetles feeding at night, consists of irregular notches eaten out of leaf margins. Even more destructive are the cream-colored, orange-headed beetle larvae, which feed on the roots. The beneficial nematode *Heterorhabditis heliothidis* is an effective biological control; once eaten, it causes death in weevils by releasing blood-poisoning bacteria and also by penetrating the skin of the insect and feeding on its blood cells. This selective, specialized nematode is harmless to plants and humans and should be the control of choice.

Butterfly and moth larvae

The order encompassing butterflies and moths includes 112,000 species, many endemic to the temperate zones. The adults are mostly very attractive and admired as beautiful insects. Nevertheless, during their larval stage (the second stage of metamorphosis), many species cause great damage to food crops and ornamentals. Some are migratory in the adult stage, infesting certain areas overnight. Even the larvae of some species are migratory; army worms, striped caterpillars, and other moth larvae of the Noctuidae occasionally move in huge numbers. Fortunately, many butterfly and moth larvae have specialized feeding habits; the well-known migratory monarch, for instance, feeds only on milkweed and bypasses garden ornamentals. The larvae of some night-feeding moths, however, have a voracious appetite for anything green, and their damage can be devastating to cultivated garden plants.

Both chemical and biological controls are available. Only chemical methods work fast enough to control overnight infestation; they are the only choice in difficult, but usually localized situations. Even so, many gardeners now opt to forgo such measures, given their toxicity and potential ill effects on the environment. Relatively slow-acting biological controls include predatory wasps and insect-eating birds and mammals. Repeated applications of Bt (*Bacillus thuringiensis*), which is eaten by the caterpillars and kills them, have proven effective. Timing is of the essence with this biological control, and slight damage caused by newly hatched larvae may have to be tolerated. Examine emerging plants for signs of early damage during the spring warm-up; apply Bt if necessary and repeat applications throughout the spring and summer growing season.

The search for organic, biological, and botanical products that are environmentally safe continues with urgency as toxic pesticides are withdrawn from the market. The neem tree is the source of a spray reputed to be effective against caterpillars and other insect pests. Beneficial nematodes have proven highly effective and long-lasting at Hosta Hill, but their application must be timed in concert with the appearance of caterpillars. Botanicals like rotenone are useful, but I have never used them because they are toxic to birds and other wildlife. Organics include dormant oil sprays, biodegradable soap solutions, and the application of home-brewed pesticides containing garlic, pepper, vinegar, deodorant soaps, and other household organics.

Mammals

Deer and rabbits are among the worst offenders when it comes to wildlife feeding on garden plants. Feeding principally occurs in spring, when the growth is young and tender; damage consists of everything from partially eaten sprouts to the erasing of entire, emerging leaf bundles. Rabbits are easily fenced out, but deer are another matter: many species can and will jump a standard chain-link fence 4 ft. (1.2 m) in height to get to a food supply. To reliably exclude deer, animal control experts recommend fences with a minimum height of 8 ft. (2.5 m) topped with barbed and electric wire, but many gardeners have neither the funds nor the inclination to convert their property into a cage. Other available methods, usually involving a repellent, are unfortunately are not very long-lasting. Some gardeners concoct foul-smelling preparations, use human hair collected at barbershops or urine of questionable origin to "mark" their territory, but such measures are often to no avail.

Nor are the root structures of plants immune from animal attack. Voles use abandoned chipmunk tunnels to get to the roots and rhizomes of garden plants, with occasionally lethal consequences. There is no better defense against destructive voles than a hungry cat. Unfortunately, most domestic cats are fed so well, they have no intention of chasing down mice or voles. My grandfather had a half dozen barn cats; all they got from him was a dish of milk each morning—all their solid food came from the barns and fields. I still remember my grandfather's stinging rebuke when, as a little boy, I innocently fed one of the cats with leftovers from the table. As with most good cures, the hungry domestic cat has a serious side effect: a preference for songbirds over quadruped rodents. Most gardeners entice the lovely birds (which themselves are so effective against insects) with birdbaths, feeding stations, and berried shrubs, so cats usually find a satisfying hunting ground for birds in our gardens.

Squirrels damage individual perennial clumps by digging holes to bury acorns and other nuts in the fall and retrieving them in spring; smaller plants can be completely dug up and thrown aside during this search for buried food. Terrestrial squirrels, such as the striped ground-squirrel or chipmunk, eat insects and slugs, but unfortunately, their extensive burrows can damage root systems in beds and plantings. Other burrowing rodents, principally gophers and moles, ravage plantings by their extensive tunneling. While gophers actually eat subterranean root systems, so injuring the plants, moles are attracted by grubs, and their extensive tunneling in search of them causes physical damage to plantings. Getting rid of grubs is the best way to combat moles.

Exclusionary methods, such as fencing or chaining, are not very effective against such tunneling, climbing, leaping mammals. More often, active controls, principally poisoning or lethal trapping, are employed. Gardeners should investigate local laws and search their conscience before deciding to use such drastic measures. Many responsible gardeners capture wild animals in non-injurious traps and release the wild animal in natural areas.

Biological controls (as, for example, cats against voles or trained dogs against rabbits) can backfire, when the "beneficial" animals engage in fast pursuit through a garden, inflicting severe, physical damage on plantings. The same thing happens when children, sometimes innocently, other times not so, play or cavort in the flower beds. To me, developing in young children a love for nature and plants kindles respect for anything living and growing. We have ten grandchildren, and not one of them has ever cavorted in my beds.

Stretching the Limits

You would think the workings of the natural world just arrayed would present gardeners with enough problems to conquer. But gardeners merrily create some of their own by knowingly stretching the limits of plants. One such stretch was my mother's desire to grow tropical plants without benefit of a greenhouse in Detroit, Michigan. Another is my desire to dabble in Bavarian alpines in my hot and humid Dixie climate. Extensive plant collecting and improved propagation methods make it possible to obtain plants from faroff habitats. The lure of growing difficult plants out of their native habitat or to adorn gardens with bewitching exotics is just too strong to be ignored. Many gardeners are spurred on by alluring magazine articles and local "experts," who proudly showcase wondrous rarities during spring garden tours. Others, trying to satisfy a craving for being the first on the block to cultivate an uncommon Chinese import, become entangled in the web of plant collecting. Suddenly the very human goal—gardening as art, recreation, and refuge—becomes unbridled desire to acquire and display as many curiosities as possible. As long as this desire does not develop into a garden-destroying obsession, the cultivation of difficult plants in even more difficult habitats is a good way to learn.

Plants are very good at letting gardeners know whether they are satisfied or unhappy. Given the right cultural conditions, they reward with lush foliage and bloom; if unhappy, they simply perish, mostly sooner than later. Finding out what makes plants thrive under less than ideal circumstances is always a welcome challenge to gardeners, because most of us understand that the path to becoming a successful gardener is composed of many small steps of achievement. For many, the road never ends, and, while they happily repose in the Shangri-la of their own making, their mind wanders to greater challenges ahead. Truly, never is there a dull moment—there is always something to look forward to. Perhaps that is why so many good gardeners grow very old so cheerfully.

Eventually, gardeners will strike a balance between their own skills and the demands of the plants whose limits they are trying to stretch. They understand what is possible and what cannot be attained. Above all, they realize that fooling Mother Nature has a high price in both time and money. When these costs become too high, gardeners may give up some of these "stretching" projects, content in knowing that they have traveled that road and learned a lot on the way. If lucky, some of the exotics may still grace their garden, pleasing them and garnering the praise of visitors.

Contained in the Shade

Container gardening has been practiced for millennia: potting plants was one of the most practical things ancient Egyptians ever came up with. Mobility is the root of this practicality. Potted plants can be moved around easily; even very large, heavy containers are made transportable with the aid of casters or rollers. With this method, plants can be sited just about any place in the garden, shifted from sun to shade, and brought inside during stormy or freezing weather. Container gardening allows complete freedom in the choice of plants. Almost any plant can be grown just about anywhere in a pot, provided the gardener knows what the plant's cultural needs are. With its exact soil conditions, feeding, and watering requirements met, any plant listed in this book can be grown outside its listed hardiness zone.

Potting is a superb way to give importance to exceptional plants; even when placed among ground plantings, a potted plant stands out among other garden plants. Another very obvious benefit is the ability to store dormant plants over the winter. Many tender and subtropical perennials go dormant when cold weather arrives and can subsequently be moved to frost-free locations like a heated garage or basement. Safely stored in a dry, warm haven, the plant's root system is protected from freezing and the rotting caused by wet soil conditions.

Garden design and plant layout can be finetuned by using potted plants in experimental locations. Many gardeners do not have the ability to visualize a change to a garden scene or what a plant might look like at maturity. I suggest they keep their perennial plants, and even small shrubs, in plastic pots of adequate size. These can then be placed in prepared holes in the garden, pot and all, and backfilled as required. A particular design can be observed for a season or two, and modification, if necessary, will be easy. If a plant looks out of place, simply lift it out of the ground—again, pot and all—and move it to a more appropriate location. Potted perennials are not hurt by these moves. When the final position is found, the plastic container is removed and the plant claims its permanent spot in the earth. Some will call this a shotgun approach, but it works.

Some skilled gardeners use potted plants similarly but with a twist. They place the pots on top of the ground, mound up topsoil or bark around them, and dress the berm with decorative mulch. Simple and effective, this method is used principally to eliminate competition from trees with greedy root systems near the surface. A good friend of mine uses this method for another reason. He lives in an area where late hard freezes are as common as very early warm days, which pattern causes many perennials to emerge too early, only to be cut down. To protect his plants from this calamity, he grows them in pots. They are stored in an unheated garage in winter; in spring, after all danger of frost has passed, the emerging, potted plants are moved outside and installed within a berm, in a new layout each spring. This, of course, creates more work for him, but he claims the peace of mind is worth the effort.

Gardeners who are looking for reduction of garden maintenance are hereby put on notice: gardening in pots is more arduous than in-ground cultivation. Regular watering of container subjects is vital; the potted soil concentrates the roots and dries out faster. Trickle irrigation to each pot is ideal. Also, some perennials grow rapidly, and a few are sensitive to potting and dislike being confined in such way. I have kept some perennials, including hostas, in pots for up to eight years without ill effect, but inevitably, potted plants must be set free and their usually crowded, rootbound underpinnings released. This creates additional work, but dividing for increase can be accomplished at the same time, making the effort worthwhile.

For me, one of the most practical aspects of pot culture is the ability it gives me to experiment. Keeping an untried plant in a pot, in the fore, reminds me to keep watching over it and to learn all about it. It may take some time to determine its likes and dislikes, but eventually the plant will find its way into the garden and happily add its beauty and character to all the others gathered there.

Plants Assigned

Shade-loving or Shade-tolerant?

Many plants are described as shade-loving. This is utter nonsense. All gardenworthy plants require some level of light to photosynthesize and create chlorophyll. They do this by absorbing light energy, which is used to produce carbohydrates and all other materials essential for growth. The chlorophyll pigments absorb red and blue-violet light and reflect green light (hence, plants look green). Some nonblooming specialty plants, like mosses, can persist under very low light conditions. Flowering plants are another matter. Hostas, for instance, are often called shade-loving plants, when in fact their progenitor species in the natural habitat grow in open meadows and forest clearings and receive a lot of sunshine. In gardens, hostas may be more efficient than other plants in converting light energy into chlorophyll, but to consider them shade-loving is stretching the truth.

All flowering plants slow down their growth rate and stop blooming when light levels become too low. One might argue that it does not matter if a garden plant sustains its life cycle by pollination and the generation of seeds—after all, gardeners usually lift, divide, replace, and in general look after the welfare of their plants. But when there is too much shade, the plant's growth rate goes to zero and flowering stops. The result is a plant that barely exists. To call this condition "shade-loving" is preposterous.

In my opinion, "shade-tolerant" better characterizes plants that can be grown in shade. Some plants are more shade-tolerant than others. Many regarded as suitable only for the sunny border can be successfully grown and will flower in some degree of shade. Many can be grown in full shade, and in certain cases, shade is necessary for their survival. Many nonflowering garden plants, ferns for example, prefer considerable shade, but most flowering plants require a measured amount of sunlight. The perfect sun exposure for plants mimics the conditions found in their natural habitat. Our native wildflowers, which are often described as shade plants, receive some sun during their spring flowering and pollination period and increasing amounts of shade as the trees leaf out. A study of wild plant populations of the same species shows that sun exposure can vary considerably from one population to another. Remember this leeway when trying to mimic nature's purported ideal exposure.

Every garden has unique conditions of light and shade. In many gardens, north or south, the only way to gauge the shade tolerance of a plant is to place it in a site considered suitable and then "listen" to it. If it turns yellow, it may not have enough water; sometimes it is not too much shade but a very dry location that keeps a plant from thriving. If it stops growing and flowering and just "sits there," it may have too much shade—give it more light, either by moving it or by limbing up the offending tree. Neither solution is definitely permanent. The new location may turn out to be too sunny, and the limbed-up tree will continue to grow larger. Sooner or later, it becomes necessary find yet another solution.

Fortunately, most garden plants have a wide latitude of shade tolerance. I grow daylilies and iris, both considered plants for full sun, with just a few hours of unimpeded morning-till-noon sunlight, and they bloom for me nicely. I also successfully grow shade-tolerant hostas in sunny areas of Hosta Hill by providing extra water during droughts. The best way to decide where a given shade-tolerant cultivar should be sited is to be informed about a plant's cultural requirements. Reading about it helps a lot, but the best teacher is to actually experience the plant by planting it in the garden. They will tell us when their shade tolerance has been exceeded—if we are listening. Successful gardeners spend a lot of time listening . . .

The Worth of Plants

The number of garden plants available to gardeners is staggering. Some were collected in the wild only recently, and their respective garden value has yet to be determined. Many others have been in cultivation the world over for centuries, and their importance is well established. In either case, the gardenworthiness of a given plant has to be judged by the individual gardener for his or her particular location and microclimate. Each square foot of the garden has a different microclimate that can influence the worth of plants: humidity and other climatic conditions, annual rainfall, sun exposure, snow cover, soil conditions and fertility, orientation, land contour, available moisture—all are contributing factors. Most important is the amount of attention the gardener pays to the plant's requirements. The worth of a plant depends not only on its hardiness, longevity, and aesthetic contributions to the garden (form, texture, color, and accent) in a particular microclimate but also on its ability to be fruitful and multiply.

Hardiness

A plant's hardiness must be among the first considerations in determining the relative gardenworthiness of a plant. A tropical palm that would make a fine garden addition in southern Florida will not be worth much planted out in northern Minnesota. Yet one can enjoy a tropical palm at the Canadian border if it is potted and placed on a sheltered patio during the warm summer time. The enjoyment will be brief, and the poor palm will have to spend the long cold season in a greenhouse, in the living room, or worse, the basement. To some gardeners, challenging plants are worth the effort, but most of us who like to play in the dirt grow plants in a microclimate that suits them.

Whether a plant is hardy enough to be worthy of inclusion in a given landscape depends primarily on the geographic location of the garden and the plant's own genetic makeup. The term "hardy" in a general sense means that a plant lives and survives local cold, heat, and other factors. All wild plants are considered hardy in their own natural habitat; they have evolved and adjusted to a life cycle dictated by local climatic and environmental conditions. Evergreen perennials like hellebores are able to maintain a minimum cell water content in their top growth, so survive freezing conditions with their top growth intact; herbaceous perennials like hostas have nonhardy top growth, which is unable to maintain cell water content during freezing conditions. The natural response of these plants is to shed their top growth and survive such conditions by storing food in underground organs such as rhizomes, tubers, corms, or bulbs. In their native habitat, this dormancy normally occurs in winter.

Another process, heat dormancy, is a reaction to extremely dry, hot conditions. The first symptom of this process is yellowing of the leaves, indicating shutdown of the vascular system. The plant loses some or all of its leafy top growth, depending on the severity of the weather. Occasionally, leaves resprout when normal conditions return. In deciduous plants, yellowing of leaves is normal at the onset of winter dormancy, but at times of active growth, it invariably signals a condition of stress or disease. Heat dormancy rarely occurs in the native habitat, but it is frequent in cultivated plants, particularly in warmer regions. Because it occurs during a period of active root growth, heat dormancy is extremely damaging; the plant will be smaller and less vigorous the following season. At Hosta Hill some exposed hostas have gone heat-dormant during extremely hot, dry summers; fortunately, plants have the ability to recover between such events, unless they repeat themselves in successive years, as around Atlanta ("Hotlanta" to locals) in 1998 and 1999.

Hardiness is also the ability of plants to readjust to a new habitat. Even if temperatures are about normal (for the plant), rainfall may be more or less, and soil conditions may be different. Hostas, for example, are temperate-region plants that are considered hardy even in extreme winter conditions. But, as retiring gardeners transplanting their hostas to Florida have found out, hostas do not like the Florida climate and soil, and so decline and wither away.

Freezing, on the other hand, is regular and cyclic in temperate zones, so one of the main regulating factors of garden hardiness is cold hardiness, the ability of a plant to withstand a given average minimum temperature. The USDA has prepared a map that is divided into zones based on the average minimum annual temperatures (in degrees Fahrenheit and Celsius) recorded throughout North America from 1974 to 1986 (similar maps showing the European cold hardiness zones are published in *The European Garden Flora*). Most gardeners can expect some periods when the temperatures fall below the average shown on the map, and some adventurous gardeners like to experiment with plants considered tender in their area. Such "stretching" requires preparation; tender plants must be protected with coverings and mulches when the eventual below-average low-temperatures hit. The courageous experimenters should also be prepared to lose plants if temperatures reach record lows for long periods and coverings or mulches fail to protect. The effect of cold temperatures is to some degree affected by microclimate. Snow cover, for example, can ameliorate the effect of extremely low temperatures.

Gardeners must try to learn what plants need for cold survival, but even diligent researches occasionally disclose only incomplete results. It is a known fact: the USDA hardiness zones as printed in most books, including this one, are approximate guides only. Their small scale makes it is impossible to include all the geographic details that modify the general outlines of the map. Many county USDA extension offices have larger, more detailed maps available for local areas.

Beginning gardeners especially should pay close attention to all hardiness zone information available for their region. Determining the entire range of conditions for your garden is essential for success. Keep temperature records in winter and spring: late-spring freezes can be more damaging to emerging plants than midwinter cold. Use an outdoor thermometer; it is not enough to call the local weather station, whose records reflect conditions at their particular location only.

Longevity

The longevity of a given perennial must be considered when selecting plants for gardenworthiness. Herbaceous perennials lose their green stems and leaves in fall and reappear in spring with renewed vigor and often in increased size. The very best garden plants do this reliably, year after year. But some plants are simply not suited for the open garden, and, as attractive and seductive as they may be, they simply will not survive there. This is true not only true for exotic plants gathered in faraway places but for some of the wildflowers blanketing woodlands just a few miles from our gardens. These wonderful natives flower generation after generation in their native habitat, but they barely idle on when removed to gardens and disappear after a few years. Herbaceous perennials assigned to the shady garden are best picked from a list of tried and proven plants whose longevity in the garden is well established. Obviously, longevity alone does not imply gardenworthiness. Much to my chagrin, many of the perennial weeds in my garden have unbelievable longevity (not to speak of the many annual weeds), and with them longevity becomes a nuisance.

Plant longevity is chiefly dependent on the provision of good soil, watering, fertilizing, and tender loving care. Even when basic maintenance is provided diligently, however, some normally long-lived perennials are nonetheless short-lived. Even the hosta, the Methuselah of flowering plants, can have problems. On aged clumps, the center part of the rhizome may die out and root rot sets in; in most cases, parts of the surviving, now ring-shaped rhizome keep on growing, and little can be noticed after the plant leafs out and covers the center hollow. Many other long-lived perennials, daylilies and iris, for example, have a root system that becomes crowded with age. When the crowding becomes severe, flowering diminishes or stops entirely, and the roots must be lifted, divided, and replanted. In heavy soils, heuchera cultivars have a habit of "growing out of the ground." The exposed roots dry out, and the plant deteriorates. Lifting and replanting is the only remedy. So longevity is to some degree affected by periodic root maintenance.

Form and texture

That form and texture are mentioned here, before color, might appear peculiar to many gardeners. After all, the key elements in the garden are flowering plants. Unfortunately, the flowering glory of many perennials is transitory, and for the shady garden, the selection of flowering perennials for year-round bloom is not what it is for the sunny border. Additionally, the flowers of shade perennials are frequently smaller and less conspicuous. Thus, the importance of flowers in the shady garden is transcended to a considerable degree by the many diverse forms and unusual textures found in the leaves of shady garden plants. Some of the best plants for shade, in fact, are the nonflowering ferns. Combining the lacy fronds of ferns with the bold, highly textured leaves of hostas and the elegant, leafy stalks of Solomon's seal makes a shady garden corner rich in forms and textures. There will be short periods of flowering, of course, from the hostas and Solomon's seals, but the visual content of such plantings is sufficient to make flowering a secondary consideration. And, as with most perennials suited for the shady garden, the display of green forms and textures, having lasted the entire season, ends with a glorious display of fall colors. It is not essential to create rich tapestries of color in the shady garden; to me, they somehow do not support my goal of tranquillity. Admittedly, in my garden I enjoy the riotous spring display of color provided by native wildflowers, azaleas, dogwoods, and redbuds. But by late spring the blossoms are gone, and now comes the extended period of time when I look for the cooling envelope of a shady green garden, with its multiplicity of fascinating plant forms and textures.

Another significant reason for recommending form and texture over color is the reduction of labor. I realize some gardeners get a lot of pleasure spending their weekends or more staking and deadheading flowers. To them, activity is the main goal of gardening, and they welcome the exercise occasioned by maintenance. I enjoy garden work to a point but much prefer to relax in a cool corner in midsummer, relishing the fruits of my labors.

Most important, opting for the form-and-texture garden reduces the initial investment required for a new garden and can decrease the costs associated with established gardens. For one thing, less plants are needed for the shady form-and-texture garden. Sunny borders require a multiplicity of flowering plants designed to give multilevel, year-round bloom; the result is an expensive, high concentration of individual plants in a relatively small area. In the woodland, on the other hand, plants look more correct and spontaneous in small colonies. Complete coverage of the ground is not necessary; it is all right to expose some of the garden floor. In this way, individual plants and plant groupings become more visible and hence more important. While the flowering plants of a sunny border must subordinate themselves to the overall color display and design, plants and plant groups in the shady garden can exert their individuality of both form and texture. This is important to the natural gardener, who seeks out native plants to duplicate the surrounding, indigenous landscape, as well as the collector, who wants to showcase his treasures individually and in a setting akin to the natural habitat.

Color and accent

Color is a device. It is as essential to gardens as it is to the artist's canvas. There are, of course, two sources of color in the garden, one provided by flowers and the other by leaves. Flowers give relatively short-lived color, while leaves provide year-round color. Luckily, green is no longer the only color in a garden of leaves. Modern horticulture has developed trees, shrubs, and perennials that produce leaves in excellent colors, from silvery white, yellow, and chartreuse to blue-green, blue-gray, whitish gray, purple, brownish, and even black. Some tree groups, like dogwoods and Japanese maples, offer exciting new solid leaf colors, and there are even specimens with three colors on the same tree—tri-colored beech, for example.

Everybody seems to know what color is but very few gardeners can explain it. Scientifically, color is reflected light of different wavelengths. What makes the subject so difficult is the distinction between the physical basis of this reflected light (wavelength in angstroms) and the different sensations produced by these light waves in humans. Most of us feel colors more than we see them; the color combinations we see in gardens can evoke either pleasure or disdain. These color feelings have a lot to do with personal likes and dislikes: some individuals are drawn toward warm colors, like yellow or red, while others prefer cool colors, like blue or even white (yes, white is a color). And even when we see colors, we see them differently because the impulses transmitting light waves from the optical nerve register in slightly dissimilar fashion on the human brain; indeed, some of us are color blind in more than just the clinical sense.

Because colors are reflected light, the quality of the natural light being reflected influences color. Brilliant, direct sunshine is not the same as light filtered through clouds. In the shady garden, light is transmitted through trees before it is reflected; the result is more muted, and a softening of colors takes place. Moreover, colors are almost never viewed in isolation but in combination with others, and so are visually (and mentally) modified. Complicating things further is the shifting nature of plant colors, which undergo changes from spring until after the first frost. Flower colors are ephemeral at best; they arise with the opening of the bud, perhaps deepen in full bloom, and fade with the dropping of the petals. Leaf colors are more permanent; they arise with bud break in spring and last through leaf drop in fall. Colors change from the soft green hue of the buds to the brilliant fall foliage display. Evergreens retain their color all season, but they too show different pigmentation in spring and fall.

Many gardeners, not interested in the intricacies of color theory, are satisfied with feeling their way through the world of color, perhaps discerning only good or bad and likes or dislikes. This approach works well in the natural, shady garden because it is feeling that creates a relaxing ambience. Creating a poem of color in sunny borders, by contrast, requires considerable skill. The handling of color combinations and placement of plants by size, bloom season, and habit requires a very delicate and professional touch. Too often sunny borders are simply overwhelming; occasionally, with colors out of balance, they can become distasteful.

Accents are highlights in the garden, and, admittedly, against the green backdrop, the human eye is drawn to bright colors first. Many flowering plants are suitable for shade, but they are ordinarily used as accents and embellishments in concert with the shapes and textures structuring the shady garden. Most gardeners now shun well-established models and develop their own idea of what a garden should look like. Shade is increasingly becoming a requisite in modern gardens, and shade precludes a dominant display of flower color. Leaf colors are more at home in the shady garden.

A word about variegation is in order here: novice gardeners sometimes mistake an atypical solid leaf color, such as yellow, to be variegation. This is not true. Solid leaf colors, however unusual, are not variegation. Variegated leaves show a combination of two or more colors, with patterns ranging from narrow to wide margins, bright centers on dark surrounds and the reverse, and multicolored streakings and splashings. Some herbaceous perennials, like hostas and heucheras, are so colorfully variegated, their leaf mounds—splashed yellow, cream, and white—look almost like flowers, particularly in the shady garden. Careful siting of such plants creates bright accents in the shady garden.

The astonishing range of leaf colors, along with their form and texture, are prime considerations when weighing the gardenworthiness of plants for shady gardens. The color of flowers, even the glorious pinks and yellows of lady slipper orchids, takes a secondary role.

A bounteous harvest

Many plants that flourish in the natural shady garden are grouped in communities of individual plants. Rarely, a singular plant is seen, but the norm is dominant groups of like plants, scattered among the trees and shrubs. These wonderful colonies of individual plants can get quite large—to see hundreds of large-flowered white trilliums carpet a forested mountain slope is a magnificent sight indeed. One advantage of herbaceous perennials for the shady garden is their ability to form such colonies: rapid increase is the final element of gardenworthiness. Some perennials do this much faster than others, so their value is greater; by forming colonies, they hasten the creation of the natural shady garden's unique look. Of course, the gardener can help even such eager colonizers by planting several specimens in a group to begin with.

Not one of the many excellent garden books and photo essays on the subject of the natural look teaches as much as a day's visit to the mountains. Their text and illustrations combine to give a fair idea of what natural gardens look like, but there is one important aspect they fail to provide: the natural garden must be felt body and soul. I did not become a true gardener until I experienced these feelings and carried them back home, inspired to create my garden in the image of nature. Plants that give a bounteous harvest are key to this image. They also make friends, so many of them are prominently featured in Part 2.

Success guaranteed

Many plants are easy to grow, but not all are suited for shady places. Further, many of those that can be planted in the shade are not easy to maintain: they simply do not have the general hardiness and longevity required for plants to be considered gardenworthy in the shady garden. Gardening success is almost guaranteed once these difficult and transitory shade plants are banished from shady gardens. Notice the word "almost." Sometimes a gardener manages to kill off even hostas or hellebores, among the most durable of all shade-tolerant plants, but that takes considerable and determined effort. Plants that are easy to grow and keep are the backbone of a shady garden. The plant species and cultivars listed in Part 2 are selected with this in mind, and each in its own way will contribute to a successful shady garden.

The Glory Season

Spring is the glory season for many natural gardens. The blooming of many wildflowers coincides with the rays of the warming spring sun reaching the forest floor before the canopy of leaves closes in. From late March through May, spring beauty (*Claytonia* spp.), twinleaf (*Jeffersonia* spp.), liverleaf (*Hepatica* spp.), bloodroot (*Sanguinaria* spp.), violet (*Viola* spp.), trout lily (*Erythronium* spp.), mayapple (*Podophyllum* spp.), foamflower (*Tiarella* spp.), campion (*Silene* spp.), lady slipper (*Cypripedium* spp.), and many other wildflowers join the carpet of trilliums in the mountain forest's glory season. In the shady garden at home, the same dazzling display can be accomplished. At Hosta Hill, charming natives, many of them rescued from the bulldozers, now provide their own resplendent spring display. They join the native dogwoods and indigenous and exotic azaleas to give my garden its own wonderful glory season.

Hosta Hill, however, is different from the floral display in the mountains. There the show is temporary and by the onset of summer, with the canopy fully leafed out, a quiet, green silence settles in. Here and in many other shady gardens, the color display continues. As the wildflowers fade, variegated hostas, heucheras, dwarf Japanese maples, and other colorful foliage plants take over and extend the glory season. It continues through the summer heat, providing colorful groupings and accents until the first frost turns everything into a riot of reds, yellows, oranges, and purples. Finally, the first hard freeze cuts down the display. Trees and shrubs lose their colorful leaves, and the herbaceous perennials slump to the ground, ready for the winter's rest. Yet, in the many shady southern gardens that lack snow cover, a few hardy evergreen perennials hang on and continue to please the eye. Hellebores decide they can compete and open their flowers, Italian arums unfold their colorful leaves, and wild gingers finally have enough elbow room to be noticed. It is not really a glory season, but anything blooming is welcome as winter approaches. In the North, snow finally covers all. To gardeners, it too is a glory season of sorts, and many call it their winter wonderland.

In the shady garden it is possible to have a long glory season provided the plants assigned to the garden have uncommon, long-lasting leaf color or variegation. A majority of the plants recommended in Part 2 contribute both flower and leaf color for the entire season. Their attributes combined with the wonderful shapes and textures available makes the modern shady garden a visual pleasure and a soothing refuge.

About the Encyclopedia

The plant descriptions presented in Part 2 are in alphabetical order, according to genus. In some cases, closely related genera with similar cultural requirements (*Asarum* and *Saruma*, for example) are combined; the same reasoning drove my decision to lump together a few genera of bamboo suitable for shady gardens. Plants whose names appear in **boldface** are pictured in the color photograph section, which is also arranged alphabetically.

The science of plant taxonomy is in a constant state of flux, and taxonomic diagreements are not easily solved. The problem as to whether or not *Achlys triphylla* var. *japonica* is actually a distinct species, *Achlys japonica*, cannot be solved in this work. Many placements are based on minuscule botanical details in the flower structure that matter not to gardeners. My decisions concerning the generic and specific names used as main entries are based solely on simplifying things for gardeners, so, for example, I have kept all wild gingers under *Asarum*. Plants that are new to horticulture enter commerce with tentative scientific names that may have to be changed later, and even some established plants are incorrectly labeled in commerce. Most gardeners understand this and adjust when the true names become known. In general, the latest taxonomic revisions are applied, but in some cases I have maintained the old, established Linnaean order. All possible synonyms are included as cross references in the Index of Plant Names.

Descriptions begin with general comments relating to the genus as a whole, including my own experience with certain of its members; its general habitat and cultural range with emphasis on performance and hardiness in hot and cool regions; its naming and placement in higher orders; its historical use in medicine and folklore; its soil requirements and other cultural recommendations; its propagative characteristics; and any concerns regarding pests and diseases. Descriptions of recommended species and cultivars follow the general comments, again alphabetically presented. Most species descriptions begin with a range of shade gradients (see Chapter 2 for details), abbreviated as follows:

FS = full shade
MS = medium shade
WS = woodland shade
LS = light shade

All descriptive terms are rendered in plain English—for instance, "heart-shaped" instead of "cordate." In time, even casual gardeners primarily interested in cultivars may want to learn some of the more frequently used descriptive latinate terms. For a comprehensive reference, consult William Thomas Stearn's *Botanical Latin* (fourth edition published in 1992 by Timber Press, Portland, Oregon).

Many of the odder common names are of regional occurrence only and not in general use. Transliteration of names conforms to international standards and is in accord with Hepburn for Japanese, Pinyin for Chinese, and McCune-Reischauer for Korean. Although it is against the rules of the International Code of Nomenclature for Cultivated Plants, foreign cultivar names are often translated into English or even renamed by the nursery industry. Perhaps my listing these translated names and renamings as synonyms—for example, *Anemone* ×*hybrida* 'Géante des Blanches' ('White Giant', 'White Queen'), one a translation, one a renaming—will prevent duplication of orders by unsuspecting gardeners.

The only standard for inclusion was availability in commerce. Obviously, some plants are found in garden centers the world over, while others may be had only from specialty nurseries in certain countries. Often I have included rare North American wildflowers—but always with the admonition that none of these should ever be removed from the wild; rather, they should be sought out from nurseries specializing in propagating these rare treasures. See Plant Sources for a list of nurseries.

Part 2

Perennials for the Shady Garden A–Z

Acanthus

Bear's breeches are the Mediterranean plants whose leaves inspired the classic decoration on Corinthian columns. They are magnificent plants with gorgeous, incised, tropical-looking leaves and pinkish white flowers, each propped up by spiny, nefarious-looking, leaflike bracts. Most species require full sun and a stony, well-draining soil; in my experience, all dislike long, hot summers. In winter, the soil at Hosta Hill is cold and wet—another condition they abhor. But the spring display is astounding. A plant I suspect is a hybrid (*Acanthus mollis* × *A. spinosus*) has flourished here for years, thriving in partial shade with about three hours of morning sun. After the spikes go to seed, I cut most of them, leaving only the lower part of one to produce a few seeds. If I let all spikes go to seed, the plant dies off and loses its magnificent leaves by midsummer. In the cool days of autumn, the plant regenerates and produces many new leaves, which overwinter. I cover them during the coldest days with dry pine straw supported by aluminum screens, to prevent matting. I also have *Acanthus* 'Summer Beauty', which I bought for its intriguing name.

Bear's breeches like some sun but grow in partial shade, preferring sunny morning hours. They are in general suitable for cultivation in zone 7 and warmer. I observed a population of *Acanthus spinosus* in northeastern Italy, which has a climate slightly colder than zone 7, but further north into the foothills of the southern Alps it does not exist. In colder regions, bear's breeches are a subject for potting and thrive on a sunny, protected patio. They may require overwintering in a cool greenhouse and the withholding of some water, but their soil should not dry out. Their grandeur, however, is well worth the extra effort. *Acanthus* is from the Greek *acanthe* (= thorn). The genus is classified in the acanthus family, Acanthaceae.

Propagate by taking root cuttings in very early spring. Plant cuttings in a well-draining potting soil and keep them moist and warm. Fresh seed can be germinated under the same conditions.

Large slugs and snails attack the young growth and even mature leaves. In summer, army worms, striped caterpillars, and other moth larvae feed on the leaves, but the damage is hard to see on the incised leaves.

Species and cultivars listed are evergreen in zone 7 but may become deciduous in zone 6, requiring maximum protection during extreme winters.

Acanthus hungaricus, Hungarian bear's breeches. Southeastern Europe, Balkans, Romania, Greece.

Morning sun, LS to WS; flowers pink to mauve, tubular, lower lip 3-lobed, with 4 spiny, reddish purple, oval, pointed bracts (calyces), crowded on flowerstalks 2–4 ft. (0.6–1.2 m) tall; May–July; plant clump-forming, to 36 in. (90 cm) wide and high; leaves 24–36 in. (60–90 cm) long, glossy dark green, cut into deep lobes with winged midrib, more toothed than spiny in the margins. This species lacks the monster appearance of other bear's breeches. It is rarely seen in gardens, probably because it is not as showy as other species and cultivars. Hardy to zone 7, heat- and drought-tolerant. Other species from the Mediterranean region include *Acanthus dioscoridis*, *A. hirsutus*, *A. montanus* (mountain thistle), and *A. syriacus*, all of which are too tender to be grown in zone 8 and colder. Rarely available, they might make good pot subjects, but none is as showy as *A. hungaricus*.

Acanthus mollis, bear's breeches, common bear's breeches. Southwestern Europe, northeastern Africa.

Morning sun, LS to WS; flowers white, sometimes shaded to pink, tubular, lower lip 3-lobed, with 4 spiny, mauve bracts (calyces), crowded on flowerstalks 3–7 ft. (0.9–2 m) tall, often 2–5 racemes per plant are produced; May–July; plant clump-forming, to 4 ft. (1.2 m) wide and high; leaves large, to 36 in. (90 cm) long and 18 in. (45 cm) wide, very glossy dark green, arching on the stem, cut and dissected into lobes, with soft spines in the margins. Plant in a sheltered spot to keep the huge, sail-like leaves from being tattered by spring storms, high winds, and hail. The overwintering leaves of this large plant break under the weight of our occasional winter ice storms, but they are replaced by new leaves in early spring. Hardy to zone 7a, 6 with protection.

'Holland's Lemon', leaves like the typical species but greenish yellow.

Latifolius Group, selected cultivars with larger, more shallowly lobed, glossy dark green leaves to 4 ft. (1.2 m) long.

'Niger', leaves very dark green, glossy.

'Oak Leaf', leaves shaped like a red oak leaf, dark green, shiny.

Acanthus spinosus, spiny bear's breeches. Southeastern Europe and eastern Mediterranean region, northeastern Italy, Balkans, to western Turkey.

Morning sun, LS to WS; flowers white, sometimes shaded to pink, with 4 spiny, purple bracts (calyces) on a tall raceme to 40 in. (1 m), often 2–6 racemes per plant are produced; May–July; plant clump-forming, to 4 ft. (1.2 m) wide and 36 in. (90 cm) high; leaves large, to 12 in. (30 cm) long and 10 in. (25 cm) wide, glossy dark green, arching on the stem, deeply cut and dissected to the midrib, with soft spines in the margins. Hardy to zone 6. This is a great accent plant when surrounded by hostas and ferns; during flowering it is spectacular. Probably the best species for gardens.

Spinosissimus Group, selected hybrids (*Acanthus mollis* × *A. spinosus*); leaves extremely narrow, deeply incised and heavily bristled; they are mean-looking but have more bark than bite because the spines are soft and not penetrating. **'Spinosissimus'** is typical.

'Summer Beauty' is an outstanding representative of the Spinosissimus Group. Morning sun, LS; flowers white, with spiny, purple bracts (calyces) on tall racemes to 6 ft. (1.8 m), often 2–5 racemes per plant are produced; May–July; plant clump-forming, to 5 ft. (1.5 m) wide and 40 in. (1 m) high; leaves large, to 12 in. (30 cm) long and 10 in. (25 cm) wide, glossy dark green, arching on the stem, deeply cut and dissected to the midrib, with soft spines in the margins. Garden origin.

Achlys

It is unfortunate that some of the western North American wildflowers are so rarely cultivated. Admittedly, the wonderful, deep woodland soil found in the moist forest communities of the western mountain ranges is a difficult habitat to match, but happily, dedicated shade gardeners are not deterred and sometimes succeed in cultivating these beauties out of their natural range. *Achlys triphylla* is one of these western denizens. When I first saw it in flower it reminded me of the eastern *Amianthium muscaetoxicum* (fly poison). Its leaves are something else, having three large, jagged-toothed lobes. The leaves overlap in mature colonies, solidly covering

the ground. Widely creeping rhizomes assure the spread of this plant, particularly when it is happy with its microclimate. I observed a blooming colony of these plants in British Columbia—truly a spectacular sight. Accustomed as they are to cool moisture, I have not been able to duplicate this natural display at Hosta Hill, though plants should do better in cooler locations, provided soil moisture levels can be kept high. American Indians called this wildflower deerfoot; colonists noticed the sweet fragrance of drying leaves and named it vanilla leaf or sweetleaf. Sweet-after-death describes the propensity of the leaves to retain their fragrance after drying.

To successfully cultivate this species, the cultural conditions of its natural habitat must be approximated as closely as possible. Like most North American wildflowers, vanilla leaf resents fertilizing. I never fertilize but add years-old compost to the soil. Hardy to zone 5, 4 with protection and in a very sheltered position. Heat resistance is limited. *Achlys* (= mist) is from the Greek, a reference either to the delicate, wispy flowers or the plant's preferred habitat in the western woods. The genus is classified in the barberry family, Berberidaceae.

Propagate by taking rhizome cuttings in very early spring. Fresh seed can be sown in the ground or in a seed tray.

Large slugs and snails can damage young leaf growth and even mature leaves. In summer, army worms and striped caterpillars feed on the leaves.

Achlys triphylla, deerfoot, sweet-after-death, sweetleaf, vanilla leaf. Western North America, British Columbia south to northern California, eastern Asia, northern Japan and Korea.

MS to FS; flowers tiny, numerous, clustered together on a narrow, slightly conical or cylindrical raceme, to 2 in. (5 cm) long, tepals absent, stamens white, 8–12 per flower, filamentous to petal-like, flowerstalks 12–20 in. (30–50 cm), leafless; May–July; plant herbaceous, clump-forming, rhizomatous; leaves green, to 6 in. (15 cm) across, divided into 3 lobelike leaflets, middle leaflet larger, all leaflets 5- to 7-lobed and/or toothed. The many airy white stamens give the inflorescence its wispy appearance; strangely, neither sepals nor petals contribute to this filmy display. Still scarce, but available. Excellent for a solid cover in deep, moist shade. *Achlys japonica* (Japanese deerfoot), sometimes ranked as a variety of *A. triphylla*, is slightly smaller in stature and has fewer stamens in the raceme. The leaves are more lobed than divided, and the leaflets 3-lobed. This species from northern Honshu and Hokkaido is rarely offered.

Aconitum

One early summer day, while hiking in the Bavarian mountains as a young boy, I picked some stems of *Eisenhut*, the German name for monkshood. I wanted to bring this flower home to give to a beautiful neighbor girl I secretly adored. It was probably *Aconitum napellus* subsp. *compactum* or *A. napellus* subsp. *tauricum*. I shall never forget my father's scolding, when he found out. That day, I learned a lot about preservation of wildflowers—and the poisonous nature of wolfsbane. After that, I had a healthy respect for the aconites growing in the Bavarian garden of my grandmother, and much later, in my mother's garden in southern Michigan.

Most aconites are listed as perennials (sometimes biennial or vining) for full sun to part shade, so their inclusion in a book of plants for the shady garden is somewhat arguable. Yet, their beauty will unfold in partial shade. They make colorful additions to open woodland gardens, or they can be planted in shady perennial beds. Aconites are native to the northern temperate regions of North America and Eurasia. They dislike the warm temperatures of the south temperate zones and are not suitable where summer night temperatures exceed 70°F (21°C) for extended periods. Experience has shown that the warm night (and day) conditions in zones 7 and 8 are simply not appropriate for successful cultivation. Species are reliably hardy in zones 3 to 6, unless otherwise indicated.

Aconitum is the Latin version of an ancient name used by Theophrastus for a poisonous herb. All parts of the plant are poisonous when ingested; its root extract was used to poison wolves, a scourge of European farmers (hence, wolfsbane). *Aconitum napellus*, the classic European monkshood, has served as a source of aconite, a heart sedative. The genus *Aconitum* is classified in the buttercup or crowfoot family, Ranunculaceae.

Nomenclature of aconites is confused. Many species are of garden origin, and many interspecific crosses of uncertain makeup exist. For example, hybrids between *Aconitum carmichaelii* and *A. carmichaelii* var. *wilsonii* are variously combined either as *A. ×arendsii* or listed under *A. carmichaelii*. *Aconitum napellus* is divided into subspecies, each of which has given rise to many cultivars. I have attempted to assign cultivars with proper appellation, but the best advice may be for gardeners to concentrate on cultivar names exclusively when searching for plants.

Most aconites suitable for the garden have similar morphology. With flowerstalks 3–4 ft. (0.9–1.2 m) high, they should be placed at the back of the border. Avoid siting plants in open and accessible plantings near walks, not only because of their poisonous nature, but because wind gusts will blow them down unless they are staked individually. Keep small children away from the plants; broken flower stems and torn leaves exude a poisonous sap that can be absorbed through cuts and scratches. Flowers show well above the leaves; they are usually borne in terminal clusters, commonly a raceme or panicle, to 24 in. (60 cm) long. They are predominantly blue or purple, but yellow, white, pink, and bicolored flowers are also available. The flowers are 1–2 in. (2.5–5 cm) long and have five sepals, the upper of which is enlarged and shaped like a hood or helmet (hence, monkshood), and five petals, the upper pair shaped like spurs and included in the hood, the lower triplet insignificant or absent. The leaves are divided fingerlike, lobed or cleft. In most cultivars the leaves clothe the lower half of the stem. The rootstock is thickened or tuberous.

Propagate by division in early autumn or late winter to early spring. Seed can be sown as soon as ripe.

Aconites demand soils that are high in organic content, loose, and free-draining. It is futile to plant them in heavy, waterlogged soils. Flooding and standing water is fatal. Under these conditions, fungal diseases develop in the crowns. Rust appears as gray and black encrustation on the shriveling growing tips and spreads quickly. Crown rot caused by *Sclerotium rolfsii* is also seen. Slugs and snails can be very damaging to the young growing tips, as can infestations of aphids.

Species and cultivars listed are perennial and nonvining; only diverging morphological traits are included in the plant descriptions.

Aconitum alboviolaceum. Mountains of South Korea.

Sun, LS; flowers creamy white to very pale yellow; July–August; plant to 32 in. (80 cm) tall and

12 in. (30 cm) wide; leaves large, dark green, divided into 5–7 lobes with added incisions similar to wild geraniums. This new collection is a great aconite for southern gardens; its cold hardiness is uncertain, however, and further north than zone 6 it may need some protection.

Aconitum anthora. Mountains of Europe to the Caucasus.

Sun, LS; flowers light yellow, occasionally blue to blue-violet; July–August; plant to 32 in. (80 cm) tall and 12 in. (30 cm) wide; leaves large, dark green, divided into 5–7 lobes with added incisions. Hardy in zones 5 and 6.

Aconitum bartlettii. Korea.

Sun, LS; flowers light to medium blue on branched racemes; July–August; plant to 4 ft. (1.2 m) tall and 12 in. (30 cm) wide; leaves dark green, finely divided into 5–7 lobes with diminutive divisions. This recent importation brings a ferny look to the open woodland garden. Hardy in zones 5 and 6.

Aconitum ×cammarum. Garden hybrid (*A. variegatum × A. napellus*).

Sun, LS; a collection of sterile hybrid cultivars of garden origin and often with uncertain attribution; June–August; plants from 32 in. (80 cm) to 4 ft. (1.2 m) tall; leaves large, mostly glossy sometimes dull, medium to dark green, divided into 3–7 lobes. Hardy in zones 3 to 6.

'Bicolor', blue and white flowers on branching panicle; 4 ft. (1.2 m) tall and 12 in. (30 cm) wide; subject to wilting, so transplant often.

'Blue Scepter', flowers blue and white; 28 in. (70 cm) tall and 12 in. (30 cm) wide; subject to wilting, so transplant often.

'Coeruleum' ('Caeruleum'), flowers dark blue on straight, branching panicle; 4 ft. (1.2 m) tall and 12 in. (30 cm) wide.

'Doppelgänger' (= body double), flowers dark blue on branching panicle; 4 ft. (1.2 m) tall and 14 in. (35 cm) wide.

'Francis Marc' ('Franz Marc', 'France Marc'), flowers large, dark blue on straight, branching panicle; 4 ft. (1.2 m) tall and 12 in. (30 cm) wide.

'Nachthimmel' ('Night Sky'), flowers very large, dark violet with bulging hood on loose panicle with nodding branches; 4 ft. (1.2 m) tall and 12 in. (30 cm) wide.

'Spark's Variety' ('Spark'), flowers large, dark blue on straight, branching panicle; 5 ft. (1.5 m) tall and 14 in. (35 cm) wide. Over a century old and once attributed to *Aconitum henryi*, a Chinese species.

Aconitum carmichaelii, azure monkshood. Eastern Russia to China.

Sun, LS; flowers blue to blue-violet on dense panicles; September–October; plant to 6 ft. (1.8 m) tall, but often less, to 40 in. (1 m) and 18 in. (45 cm) wide; leaves large, glossy dark green extending into the upper reaches of the stem, leathery substance, divided into 3–5 lobes. My mother grew this species on the south side of her home, protected from strong north winds; she never needed to staked the plants. Hardy in zones 3 to 6. **'Arendsii'** ('Arends') has deep blue flowers on branched panicles; 4 ft. (1.2 m) tall and 12 in. (30 cm) wide. 'Late Crop' has blue flowers.

Aconitum carmichaelii var. *wilsonii*. Central China.

Sun, LS; flowers blue to blue-violet on loose panicles, more elongated and open than the type; September–October; plant to 5 ft. (1.5 m) tall and 16 in. (40 cm) wide; leaves large, medium green, extending into the upper reaches of the stem, strongly divided into leaf bases, 3–5 lobes. Hardy in zones 3 to 6. 'Barker' ('Barker's Variety'; pure violet flowers) and 'Kelmscott' (light blue-violet flowers) are as tall as var. *wilsonii* but a little wider, to 18 in. (45 cm).

Aconitum lycoctonum, wolfsbane, wolf's bane, badger's bane, northern monkshood. Mostly northern Europe, central Europe in the Alps.

Sun, LS; a species long known in central Europe with wide distribution. Taxonomists have separated subsp. *vulparia* (Moldavian monkshood) to the east and var. *pyrenaicum* of the western Alps and Pyrenees, based on minor morphological differences. To simplify, all forms are combined here. Flowers are pale to creamy yellow or yellowish white, but forms with purple flowers are known; on straight, sometimes twining racemes or panicles, loosely arranged; June–August; plants from 32 in. (80 cm) to 5 ft. (1.5 m) tall; leaves dark green, rounded to kidney-shaped, deeply divided into 3–9 lobes, with additional 3–4 clefts. The epithet derives from its use to poison wolves (*lyco* = of wolves).

These European plants, all slightly different, make excellent subjects for the woodland garden, where they naturalize under the right conditions. The yellow flowers add bright color to shady areas. Interplant them with green and blue hostas, ferns, and wildflowers. Tolerates more shade than most aconites. Hardy in zones 5 and 6. Among the bushiest aconites available for the garden is the hybrid 'Ivorine', with flowers pale yellowish white on dense racemes; to 36 in. (90 cm) tall and 18 in. (45 cm) wide; the much-divided leaves form an attractive mound topped by ivory flowers.

Aconitum napellus, common monkshood, helmet flower, friar's cap, turk's cap, soldier's cap, bear's foot, garden monkshood, garden wolfsbane. Northern and central Europe, Alps.

Sun, LS; flowers deep blue, occasionally white or pinkish, usually on straight panicles, branched at the base; June–August; plants from 32 in. (80 cm) to 4 ft. (1.2 m) tall; leaves mostly glossy, sometimes dull, medium to dark green, divided into 3–7 lobes that are again deeply incised, appearing feathery, and reaching far up the stem, upper part of plants hairy or felty. Hardy in zones 5 and 6.

'Album' ('Albidum') has off-white flowers.

'Bergfürst' ('Mountain Prince'), flowers very dark blue on dense, branching panicle; 5 ft. (1.5 m) tall and 16 in. (40 cm) wide.

'Bressingham Spire', flowers uniform dark violet-blue on straight, branching panicle; 36 in. (90 cm) tall and 12 in. (30 cm) wide. Valuable cultivar with flowers held high above foliage, requires no staking.

'Carneum' ('Roseum', 'Rubellum'), flowers rose-pink. The color is brought out only in areas of cold nights; further south, color turns off-white.

'Gletschereis' ('Glacier Ice'), flowers white on branching panicle; to 4 ft. (1.2 m) tall and 14 in. (35 cm) wide; flowers are early and long-lasting; good cut flower.

'Nanum', flowers dark blue on branching panicle; smaller, to 32 in. (80 cm) tall; scarcely seen in cultivation, but available.

'Newry Blue', dark navy-blue flowers on branching panicle; to 5 ft. (1.5 m) tall and 14 in. (35 cm) wide; erect, similar to 'Bressingham Spire'. Often listed as a hybrid, but the originator places it with *Aconitum napellus*.

Acorus

Acorus is the classic name for a plant with aromatic roots. *Acorus calamus* (sweet flag) is a North American aquatic perennial that might be considered unsuitable for the woodland garden, but I have successfully grown selections of it and another species in the genus away from their normal, watery home and found them to be excellent for adding texture and color to the shady garden. *Acorus* belongs in the Acoraceae.

Acorus calamus 'Variegatus' (variegated sweet flag) is a marsh plant with larger, strap-shaped, green leaves attractively striped with creamy white. I planted a few of these years ago in the clefts of a man-made rock ledge, where they fend for themselves with no maintenance or watering. The clay soil between the rocks stays moist, and there they slowly increase, making a wonderful display.

Acorus gramineus 'Minimus Aureus' is a recent introduction to horticulture. It is a darling little plant that looks like a small, golden tuft of grass. I have several planted next to dwarf hostas, ferns, and astilbes, where they get considerable shade during the day. The expand slowly, making wonderful bright spots in shady corners. I water them only when their neighbors need it.

Both are hardy even under these alien growing conditions. My variegated sweet flag plantings get no winter protection. With a light cover of pine straw, the little golden bunches of *Acorus gramineus* 'Minimus Aureus' have withstood temperatures down to 15°F (−10°C); with some protection, this cultivar should be hardy in zone 6, possibly zone 5. Further north it is a good pot subject, overwintering inside. *Acorus calamus* 'Variegatus' is hardy to zone 4.

With few exceptions, grasses are limited to sunny areas. *Acorus* distinguishes itself by serving as a good grass substitute, adding a dimension to the texture of shady gardens.

Propagate by dividing the rhizome.

Root rot, leaf spot, and rust are reported, but I have not experienced them here. Application of a fungicide should hinder the spread of such diseases.

Acorus calamus, sweet flag, calamus, calamusroot, flagroot, myrtle flag, sweet calamus. Pandemic in the northern hemisphere.

Morning sun, LS to MS; flowers greenish yellow in a dense spadix, protruding from a spathe (leaf-like flowering stem); May–July; evergreen leaves sword-shaped, green with distinct midrib, to 4 ft. (1.2 m) in water, much shorter when growing in garden soil, to 14 in. (35 cm); plant rhizomatous, rootstock is aromatic. Hardy to zone 4. 'Variegatus' (variegated sweet flag) has leaves striped with creamy white to white.

Acorus gramineus, grassy sweet flag. China, Japan.

Morning sun, LS to MS; tiny flowers in a spadix to 3 in. (8 cm) long on a short spathe; leaves grass-like, no distinct midrib, 6–12 in. (15–30 cm) long, in dwarf forms 2–4 in. (5–10 cm) long; plant rhizomatous, arranged in a tuft, rootstock not aromatic.

'Albovariegatus' ('Argenteostriatus') has white-striped leaves, dwarf stature.

'Minimus Aureus' (dwarf golden sweet flag) has very short and narrow, bright yellow leaves, 2 in. (5 cm) and shorter in center, the outer leaves to 4 in. (10 cm) long. It is a highlight in corners of the garden that get filtered sunlight and some morning sun. Makes a wonderful underplanting for perennials with bluish or dark green leaves. Hardy to zone 5, but some protection may be required. It is evergreen at Hosta Hill, and the leaves come through mild winters in good shape. Severe winter weather can disfigure leaves.

'Oborozuki' has bright yellow leaves.

'Ogon' ('Wogon') has yellow leaves with creamy yellow variegation. Sometimes reverts to all yellow.

'Pusillus' is a compact clump of green leaves to 3 in. (8 cm). Not as dwarf as 'Minimus Aureus'.

'Variegatus' ('Aureovariegatus') has yellow leaves with creamy yellow variegation.

'Yodo-no-Yuki' ('Yodonoyuki') has green leaves variegated with whitish green.

Actaea

Of the several common names connected with this genus of woodland plants, my favorite is doll's eyes, given to *Actaea alba* for its beautiful white berries with a black spot at the tip, which recall a doll's eye. More frequent is baneberry, from the archaic English *bane* (= to kill, to hurt). Many old names gave some hint as to the plants' medical use or their effect on humans when ingested. In this case, all parts of the plant—and in particular the berries—are poisonous, hence the forewarning name. The white or red berries are very appealing to children, so much so that in bygone times they strung the berries (hence, necklaceweed). Cautious gardeners site these plants in areas inaccessible to small children, or they avoid planting them altogether. Aside from being baneful, the berries are a powerful purgative; American Indians used minute amounts of the berries for pain and menstrual and postpartum problems.

Actaea is native to shady woodlands in the temperate regions of North America and Eurasia. The genus *Actaea* gets its name from the classical Greek *aktea* (= elder), for the similarity of its leaves to those of *Sambucus* spp.; Linnaeus adopted this name for baneberries. *Actaea* is classified in the Ranunculaceae.

Despite their toxic properties, baneberries are attractive plants for the shady garden. Their pinnate, much-divided leaves holds their fresh, dark green color well into the early days of fall, even in the warm climate of Hosta Hill. In spring their small, white flowers form a ball-shaped, terminal raceme and are held over the leaf mound by strong stems. This display is followed by glossy white, red, or black berries. It is the berries that give added color to the autumn garden. Years ago, I discovered the white-berried form in the North Georgia mountains. In an otherwise bleak woods, the white-berried colony stood out like a beacon. Later I rescued some plants locally and bought a few others. I grow all the North American species and a few exotics as well—I would not be without them. Needless to say, I watch our youngest grandchildren when they are visiting while the berries are on the clumps.

Baneberries thrive in considerable shade and may be used in dark corners of shady gardens, where the white berries show up well. I grow the red berries where some sun filters into the garden, which brings out their wonderful red color. They do best in a light, well-draining woodland soil, rich in organic matter and preferably not too acid. I sweeten the soil by mixing in turkey grit, made from crushed seashells and sold in farm supply stores (poultry growers use it as a bedding material). The grit also aids soil drainage. Baneberries like cool soil, but they will succeed even in warmer regions if ample moisture is available. Hardy in zones 3 to 7. Intrepid gardeners may want to try them in deep shade and with abundant watering in the hotter areas of zone 8.

Propagate by dividing the rhizome in autumn after the leaves have dropped. Each division should have a growing tip. Employ a clean, sharp knife for cutting and apply a dusting of fungicide to keep the cuts free of fungi-caused smut or rust. Seed propagation is cumbersome and arduous, requiring a regimen of warm, freezing, and cold temperature periods. Even with successful germination, results are variable at best.

Occasionally, clumps develop leaf spot, leaf smut, or black rust, fungal diseases that can affect the entire plant unless fungicides are employed. Check plants often while young leaves are emerging in spring. Other insect pests do not seem to bother them, but I see occasional weevil damage.

Species and cultivars listed are clump-forming herbaceous perennials. All are suitable for zones 3 to 7; certain microclimates in zone 3 may be too challenging in severe winters.

Actaea alba, white baneberry, doll's eyes, necklaceweed, white cohosh, whitebeads. Eastern North America, eastern Canada south to New England and south to Georgia and west to Oklahoma, Missouri, and Minnesota.

LS to FS; flowers white, small, 4–10 fringed petals, grouped in a small, globose, terminal raceme, 2.5 in. (6 cm) long in mature plants, smaller when young, flowerstalks red, to 36 in. (90 cm) elongating to as much as 4 ft. (1.2 m) and thickening as the berries develop; April–July; leaf mound to 30 in. (75 cm) tall and wide with dark green, slightly hairy, triple compound and pinnate leaves, to 20 in. (50 cm) long, divided into 3–12 leaflets that are ovate at the base, toothed and pointed, some deeply cleft, to 2 in. (5 cm) long; fruit a glossy, oval, white berry carried on thick, red stalks. The red-fruited f. *pachycarpa* can be distinguished from *Actaea rubra* (red baneberry) by its thick pedicels, a contrast to the slender ones of *A. rubra*. *Actaea asiatica* (Japanese baneberry), endemic to China, Korea, and Japan, is smaller in size than *A. alba*; its flowering racemes are more spherical, and its black berries are held horizontally on elongating and thickening stalks that turn reddish brown. It may be an Asian derivative of *A. spicata*, which also has black berries. Its garden merit rests on the flowers

and the handsome, leafy clump alone, since the black berries are more inconspicuous than those of the white- or red-berried forms.

Actaea erythrocarpa, European red baneberry. Northern Europe east to the western Caucasus.

LS to FS; this dark red-fruited baneberry is very similar to *Actaea spicata* and formerly was considered a variety of it. The berries are a very dark red, almost maroon, like the fruit of the sweet chestnut (*Castanea sativa*) of Europe. Sometimes available, but its berries are not as outstanding as the white and bright red forms.

Actaea rubra, red baneberry, coralberry, snakeberry. Eastern North America, eastern Canada south to Pennsylvania and west to South Dakota and Nebraska.

LS to FS; flowers white, small, 4–10 petals, broad at the base and tapering at the tip, grouped in a small, globose, terminal raceme, 2.5 in. (6 cm) long; flowerstalks green, to 32 in. (80 cm); April–July; leaf mound to 24 in. (60 cm) tall and 30 in. (75 cm) wide with dark green, slightly hairy, triple compound and pinnate leaves, to 14 in. (35 cm) long, divided into 3–15 leaflets, ovate at the base, deeply toothed and pointed, some deeply cleft, to 2 in. (5 cm) long; fruit a glossy, round to oval, red berry carried on thin green stalks. Forma *neglecta* ('Neglecta'), a white-fruited baneberry native in western North America, from British Columbia to southern Oregon, is smaller than the type. Subspecies *arguta* has much smaller leaves and grows to 18 in. (45 cm) tall and wide; it has round, red berries. This species and its variants are considered the most poisonous of all baneberries, so site plants away from easily accessible areas.

Actaea spicata, black baneberry. Northern Europe east to northern Turkey.

LS to FS; flowers white, sometimes with a bluish hue, small, grouped in a small, egg-shaped, pointed, terminal raceme; flowerstalks green, to 24 in. (60 cm); June–July; leaf mound to 20 in. (50 cm) tall and 18 in. (45 cm) wide with dark green, triple compound and pinnate leaves, to 14 in. (35 cm) long, divided into 7–15 leaflets, ovate at the base, lance-shaped, toothed, to 2 in. (5 cm) long; fruit a black, egg-shaped berry carried on thin, green stalks. Its black berries are not as attractive as the white- and red-fruited baneberries. Variety *acuminata* is a regionally modified form ranging from southeastern Europe to northern India; it has elongated, acuminate leaf tips and is rarely seen.

Adiantum

Maidenhair ferns are among the most popular of all ferns. Although many species are tropical, a few inhabit the temperate zone; one is *Adiantum pedatum*, easily one of the most attractive and distinctive ferns for temperate gardens. It needs a fair amount of shade and can tolerate deep shade. I grow several clumps of this herbaceous, long-lived fern, which emerges every spring without fail. It expands slowly by means of a creeping rootstock, branching from time to time and forming a large group of upright stalks that bear the horseshoelike fronds. When it comes to ferns with grace and beauty, few can match this native American species. More delicate and refined is *A. capillus-veneris* (southern maidenhair), but it is not very hardy. Many southern nurseries sell this delightful fern but give no instructions as to its cultural requirements. My single clump has been growing and expanding for years here in zone 7a, at elevation 1185 ft. (361 m) above sea level. The stalks and fronds die down every autumn, but with some overwintering protection to keep the soil from freezing, this beauty springs forth every spring with renewed vigor. It gets plenty of water during the long, hot, dry summer. Those gardening further north should plant the graceful *A. venustum* instead; in its natural habitat, this fern occurs in protected areas, primarily in southeastern Georgia, but I have seen colonies of it on Lookout Mountain in northwestern Georgia and in White County, Georgia, where it grows in the spray of a small waterfall, protected by overhanging rock ledges. It is definitely worth trying even in colder areas, if protection can be provided or if it can be brought indoors during winter.

Maidenhair ferns are native to shady woodlands in the warmer regions of North America and Eurasia. The genus gets its name from the classical Greek *adiantos* (= not to wet), alluding to the water-shedding surface of the fronds of some species. *Adiantum* is classified in the Adiantaceae.

Maidenhair ferns thrive in considerable shade and may be used in dark corners of a shady garden.

They are also successfully cultivated in areas where some sun filters into the garden. They do not tolerate direct sun except during the early morning hours. They do best in a light, well-draining woodland soil, rich in organic matter and preferably alkaline. I sweeten the soil by mixing in poultry bedding material made from crushed seashells and sold in farm supply stores as turkey grit. The grit also opens up the soil mixture and aids drainage. Maidenhair ferns require abundant moisture. *Adiantum pedatum* withstands some drought and considerable heat if grown in shade and is very hardy; despite its delicate appearance, it is a tough fern for the garden.

Propagate by dividing the creeping rhizome in autumn after the fronds have dropped or in very early spring. Each division should be large; it is better to cut a plant in half rather than take small pieces, which are difficult to grow on. Propagation by spores is also relatively easy under the right conditions. The spores must be sown as soon as they are ripe on a coarse commercial mix with a pH of 7 to 8.5 maintained moist at 70°F (21°C). My brick borders are an excellent growing medium for spores, but I find the small ferns are difficult to dislodge from the cracks in the brick. Taking divisions is much faster.

Maidenhair ferns are sometimes attacked by scale insects. Root rot caused by fungi is also reported, but I have never seen it here, perhaps because my ferns are in raised beds. Foliar nematodes may infest maidenhair plantings and are difficult to eradicate. Usually not fatal, but they do disfigure the leaflets and reduce the vigor of the plants.

Species and cultivars listed form slowly expanding clumps and lose their top growth in areas where temperatures go a few degrees below freezing; in warmer areas, maidenhair ferns are evergreen.

Adiantum capillus-veneris, southern maidenhair, southern maidenhair fern, black maidenhair, duddergrass, Venushair fern, Venus maidenhair. Southern Europe, North America from Virginia south to Georgia and Alabama, west to Missouri, and along the West Coast in California.

LS to FS; fronds are produced on slender, unbranched stalks (stipes), emerging directly from the rhizome and scaly at the base, shiny black to dark brown, drooping or leaning; topped with light green fronds composed of thin leaflets (pinnules), wedge-shaped at the base and rounded, cleft, with several lobes at the apex, arrangement at base first 2- to 3-compound, then single and alternate toward the tip of the frond; frond and stipe 12–26 in. (30–65 cm) long, fronds to 16 in. (40 cm) long and 8 in. (20 cm) wide; spore cases (sori) covered by reflexed tip of the lobes, half-moon-shaped. This most charming native maidenhair fern can be grown in the ground or potted and brought outdoors during summer in colder areas. Its delicate appearance adds grace and beauty to the garden. It shudders in the slightest breeze, animating its spot. Site large clumps near walks or seating, where they can be appreciated. Hardy to zone 7. Available cultivars are more tolerant of cold and expand the usefulness of the species.

'Banksianum', vigorous grower, more upright stalks. Comes true from spores. Hardy to zone 6 with protection.

'Fimbriatum', the lobes are fingerlike and extended.

'Imbricatum', a dwarfed form with deeply cut lobes. Fronds hang down.

'Mairisii', the fronds are broadly triangular with pinnules elongated triangular; an older cold-resistant hybrid.

'Scintilla', twisted leaflets, deeply cut, almost skeletonized.

Adiantum pedatum, northern maidenhair, northern maidenhair fern, American maidenhair, American maidenhair fern, five-finger fern, horseshoe fern. North America from Quebec to Alaska, south to northern Georgia and California, eastern Asia from northern India to Japan.

LS to FS; fronds are produced on strong stalks (stipes), emerging directly from the rhizome and scaly at the base, shiny black to dark brown, erect; stipes more or less equally forked at the top, each fork bears 5–7 curving leaflets on the upper side, spreading out to form a flat, horseshoe-shaped frond with light green, in some forms bluish green, thin, mostly oblong leaflets (pinnules), with the out-facing side cleft and lobed; stipe and fronds to 30 in. (75 cm) long, fronds 16 in. (40 cm) long and 10 in. (25 cm) wide; spore cases (sori) covered by reflexed tip of the lobes, half-moon-shaped, on the upper margin of the pinnules. Every gardener in North America can grow this native maidenhair fern. It is unique among ferns with its horseshoe-like fronds, carried high on strong stalks. Its rootstock creeps widely and branches, enlarging the plant constantly. A sturdy, valuable garden plant, long-lived and suitable for areas of full shade, where mass plantings can brighten up otherwise dark areas. Excellent as a companion plant when overtopping smaller perennials. Hardy to zone 3. The only problem I have had with this fern is the early appearance of the bronze-colored young croziers. At this early stage the emerging croziers, with their tops beautifully rolled like the scroll of a violin, are extremely fragile and snap at the slightest stress. If you must remove mulch in spring from areas where the croziers appear, be very careful in the process. Ferns are also damaged by late frosts and freezes and require occasional protection. All this extra effort is rewarded by elegant stands of these splendid ferns. To me they are, as someone once said, the wings of my garden.

Subspecies *aleuticum* (Aleutian maidenhair fern, true northern maidenhair fern) is very similar but slightly smaller than the type. It is native to northwestern North America, including the Alaskan Peninsula and the Aleutian Island chain; some consider it a separate species, *Adiantum aleuticum*. When young, the new fronds are pinkish, and the pinnules are bluish green and more triangular. 'Compactum' and 'Nanum' are dwarf forms of the Aleutian maidenhair fern. Subspecies *subpumilum* (dwarf maidenhair fern) has small fronds to 4 in. (10 cm) with bluish green pinnules. This cute dwarf fern, which grows to 6 in. (15 cm) tall and 10 in. (25 cm) wide, should be placed up close to garner attention; it is offered as 'Minor' and 'Minus'. Subspecies *calderi*, which is occasionally available from specialists, forms a very tight, upright clump with small, glaucous bluish green pinnules.

'Asiaticum' has drooping fronds.

'Imbricatum' may simply be a select form of *Adiantum pedatum* subsp. *calderi* with a tight, upright clump with small, glaucous bluish green pinnules. Often confused with *A. capillus-veneris* 'Imbricatum'—which illustrates the folly of using identical cultivar names for different species within the same genus (and, incidentally, violates the rules of the International Code of Nomenclature for Cultivated Plants). Caution is advised when ordering under these names.

'Japonicum' (early red maidenhair fern) is closely related to *Adiantum pedatum* subsp. *aleuti-*

cum and has young pinkish to reddish bronze fronds that later turn darker green.

'Laceratum' has deeply cut leaflets.

'Miss Sharples' has yellowish fronds.

'Montanum' makes a very compact clump.

Adiantum venustum, Himalayan maidenhair fern, mountain maidenhair fern, Venus' hair fern. Himalayas, northern India and Nepal, western China.

LS to FS; fronds evergreen, produced on slender, unbranched stalks (stipes), emerging directly from the rhizome, shiny black to dark brown, drooping or leaning, when growing on vertical rock walls hanging down; topped with compound, triangular fronds, first reddish bronze, medium green later, composed of thin leaflets (pinnules), wedge-shaped at the base and rounded, cleft, with several lobes at the apex; the compound fronds are 3- to 4-pinnate; stem 12–32 in. (30–80 cm) long, fronds to 12 in. (30 cm) long and 8 in. (20 cm) wide; spore cases (sori) covered by reflexed tip of the lobes, half-moon-shaped. This mountain fern is much more hardy than *Adiantum capillus-veneris*, which it closely resembles. Some have characterized it as a little coarser, but for garden purposes, it easily replaces the much more tender southern maidenhair and allows gardeners in northern climates to add a delicate and charming fern to their landscape. Coming as it does from a sharply draining mountain environment, at elevations reaching 7900 ft. (2400 m), it must be cultivated in rapid-draining soil with the rootstock barely covered. The widely creeping rhizomes form a nice colony in time, to 6 in. (15 cm) high, with leaning, overlapping fronds. A great fern in the wild garden near rock features or in the low-growing border. Hardy in zones 5 to 8 and evergreen to 15°F (−10°C).

Aegopodium

Occasionally, even pernicious weeds—like bishop's weed—are selected by gardeners to solve landscape problems of one sort or another. There are locations in shady gardens where nothing else will grow (the back corner of many gardens, planted with evergreens, comes to mind), but I have seen bishop's weed thriving in many gardens, planted under great tree canopies where darkness reigns and tree root competition sucks the soil dry. Bishop's weed does not seem to mind and carries on year after year with little or no care. Its only fault is that it dies down every fall. Bishop's weed is a good but invasive herbaceous perennial, attractive and of easy culture, which forms a thick, low ground-cover of nicely variegated leaves that brighten dark corners of the garden. I would never plant it in the open border or even in good woodland soil: it is almost impossible to contain under such conditions. Its aggressively spreading rhizomes would soon take over, and the dense leaf cover would overwhelm all other low-growing plants. In areas where the soil is dry, sterile, or just plain bad, however, bishop's weed might be the solution to cover bare ground. Many gardeners use it in pots, where it can be contained, but because it also spreads by seed, the flowers should be cut back on potted plants kept near open borders. Not surprisingly, bishop's weed escaped from gardens has naturalized in some areas of North America. Bishop's weed requires some moisture in the soil and dies back during very hot, dry summers, becoming ragged and unsightly. In this case, mow the entire planting, after moisture returns, to rejuvenate it.

All species in the genus *Aegopodium* are herbs that spread aggressively. The genus is classified in the Umbelliferae.

Propagate by dividing the creeping rhizome in autumn or in spring. Seed propagation is also easy, but take care the seed does not spread to areas where the plant is not wanted.

Now and then, leaf blight browns the foliage. Usually, new shoots will replace the dead stems.

***Aegopodium podagraria* 'Variegatum'**, bishop's weed, goutweed, ashweed, herb Gerard, ground ash, ground elder. Northern and central Europe east to Siberia, western and northern Asia.

LS to FS; flowers very small, creamy white to white, carried 10–16 on loose, flat compound umbels to 3 in. (8 cm) across, stems to 14 in. (35 cm); June–August; leaf stems green, 12–24 in. (30–60 cm) long, leaning, with compound, ternate or 2-ternate leaves, lower leafstalks winged and clasping, leaflets toothed, dark green with a creamy white margin and occasional white splashes in the leaf; rootstock with aggressively spreading rhizomes; fruit seedlike, aromatic. The all-green typical species, native to shady woodlands in Eurasia, is sometimes seen in gardens, but only this variegated cultivar is worth growing. Whether used as a groundcover or in containers, steady vigilance is required to keep it from escaping. Hardy to zone 4.

Ajuga

The name bugleweed is applied both to *Ajuga*, a fine genus of garden plants and groundcovers, and to *Lycopus*, which has several North American species and is far less desirable (my apologies to those who grow Virginia bugleweed in their bog or wildflower gardens). *Ajuga reptans* (carpet bugle) is a popular creeping groundcover, and several other bugle species are used as specimen plants in the front of a border or along paths in the woodland garden. I have grown several forms of *A. reptans*, the species most frequently offered in nurseries, for years; it has the most diverse selection of cultivars, many of them with variegated leaves. My main bugle planting provides groundcover around a fountain, where it gets considerable morning sun. It is in shade after midmorning. One of the negative traits of bugle is its propensity to grow where it is not wanted and to die out where it is desired. *Ajuga reptans* likes to grow more on brick paths than it does in the good soil intended for it, so watch it along paths. Some gardeners like their bugle large, and their desire is now satisfied by the really big *A. reptans* 'Catlin's Giant'. One plant of this giant may be enough for many gardens. I keep a close watch on mine—I do not want this creeping bugle to get out of hand.

Other species in the genus *Ajuga* are better behaved. They lack the wandering stolons of *Ajuga reptans*, so can be used as specimen plants. I particularly like *A. pyramidalis* 'Metallica Crispa', with its gleaming cushion of purple curlicue leaves. A rare variegated form of *A. incisa* from Japan has been made available recently; the leaves of this 'Bikun' (= beautiful decoration) are deeply cleft and toothed and have a wide yellow margin.

Ajuga is native to shady woodlands in the temperate regions of Eurasia, including central and southern Europe, south to North Africa and east to the Caucasus and beyond. The genus gets its name from the classical Latin *ajugatus* (= not yoked), alluding to the five-toothed, disconnected calyx. *Ajuga* is classified in the Labiatae.

Bugle dislikes wet and waterlogged soils and thrives in considerable shade. *Ajuga reptans* becomes more docile in shady areas; morning sun is required for it to make a tight groundcover. In northern gardens it tolerates considerable, if not full, sun; in southern gardens the dark leaves may scorch in too much sun. Both the species and its cultivars may be used in full shade as long as they have a moist environment. They do best in a light, well-draining, moist woodland soil, rich in organic matter. Nutlets of *A. reptans* are dispersed by insects, usually wood ants, and the resulting small plants set up housekeeping in the middle of some of the garden paths at Hosta Hill, which have a base of pure, unimproved Georgia red clay, covered with a thin coating of pine bark. There they thrive on neglect and do not mind being stepped on occasionally. Their best use is for covering the ground, and they make colorful companions; the cultivars with variegated and purple leaves are particularly good when juxtaposed with plants of opposing colors. The clump-forming bugles grow out of the ground and may need occasional dividing to keep them nicely clumped and attractive. Their great colors make this effort worthwhile. Hardy to zone 3; their garden use can extend to zone 9 if they are planted in the shade and supplied with moisture during hot, dry summers.

Propagate by separating the individual rosettes that arise along the stolons or by dividing the clumps. This can be done almost all year if the resulting plants can be well cared for after transplanting. Otherwise, late summer is a good time to separate rosettes or take root cuttings.

Occasionally, under wet and warm conditions, clumps develop leaf spot or crown rot (southern blight) caused by *Sclerotium rolfsii* (white silk fungus, white mold fungus). Check plants often while young leaves are emerging in spring. Other insect pests do not seem to bother bugle.

Species and cultivars listed are clump-forming evergreen or semi-evergreen perennials; *Ajuga reptans* develops stolons. All are suitable for zones 3 to 7; certain microclimates in zone 3 may be challenging in severe winters.

Ajuga genevensis, blue bugle, blue bugleweed, Geneva bugle, upright bugle, upright bugleweed. Temperate Eurasia, including central Europe north to southern Sweden, and east to southwest Asia.

Some sun, LS to FS; flowers 3–18, bright blue, rarely white or pink, small corolla to 0.5 in. (1 cm) long, among bluish bracts, arranged in false whorls (verticilaster) on a terminal spike, 4–6 in. (10–15 cm) tall; April–June; plant evergreen, clump-forming, rhizomatous, without stolons, and with upright, hairy stems to 15 in. (38 cm), lower leaves with long leafstalks arranged in a rosette, to 5 in. (13 cm) long and 2 in. (5 cm) wide, light green, hairy, ovate to spoon-shaped, with lobes or toothed; fruit an egg-shaped nutlet. Differs from other species by its upright habit and its need for somewhat drier soil. It makes a good companion plant in front of the shady border yet is infrequently seen. Cultivars include 'Alba' (white flowers), 'Jumbo' (a large form), 'Pink Surprise' (pink flowers), 'Robustum' (another large form), and 'Rosea' (rose-pink flowers).

Ajuga lobata. Himalayas, Nepal.

LS to MS; flowers lavender-blue, arranged on short flowerstalks, 3 in. (8 cm) tall; May–June; plant evergreen; leaves small, rounded, green, emerging along training, stoloniferous stems, making a dense groundcover. A great addition to the shady garden where a bright green groundcover is desired. Uses are similar to *Ajuga reptans*.

Ajuga pyramidalis, pyramidal bugle, northern bugle. Northern and central Europe, Scandinavia, Iceland, and in the mountains further south, and east to the Caucasus.

Some sun, LS to FS; flowers 5–18, deep blue, rarely white or pink, small corolla to 0.8 in. (2 cm) long, among purple-margined bracts, arranged in dense, pyramidal whorls on flowerstalks 4–6 in. (10–15 cm) tall; April–June; plant evergreen, sometimes semi-evergreen depending on microclimate, clump-forming, rhizomatous, without stolons, and with upright, hairy stems to 12 in. (30 cm), lower leaves with long leafstalks arranged in a rosette, to 4 in. (10 cm) long and 2 in. (5 cm) wide, dark green, hairy, ovate to spoon-shaped, toothed; fruit an egg-shaped nutlet. Makes a good companion plant along woodland paths or in the shady border. **'Metallica Crispa'** ('Metallica'), which produces a shimmering purplish bronze cushion of crinkled leaves, is popular for its compact habit, to 8 in. (20 cm) high and 14 in. (35 cm) wide. An attention-getter when planted with masses of small yellow hostas like *Hosta sieboldii* 'Subcrocea' and light green ferns, but this cultivar has a sloppy growth pattern and gets out of shape easily. I keep

it in shape by frequent dividing. It is well worth the effort, which also produces more plants for the garden or to give away.

Ajuga reptans, carpet bugle, carpet bugleweed, common bugleweed. Northern and central Europe, south to North Africa and east to Asia Minor.

Some sun, LS to FS; flowers 4–8, corolla blue, rarely white or pink, small, among blue-tinged bracts, arranged in false whorls (verticilaster) on a terminal spike, 4–6 in. (10–15 cm) tall; April–June; plant evergreen, rhizomatous, developing above ground, leafy stolons, 4–12 in. (10–30 cm) long, rooting at the leaf nodes; central lower leaves with long leafstalks arranged in a rosette, to 2 in. (5 cm) long and 1 in. (2.5 cm) wide, dark green, hairy, ovate to spoon-shaped, smooth or scalloped margins; fruit an egg-shaped nutlet. This popular species is an excellent and colorful groundcover used by many gardeners. A rapid spreader, it can invade adjacent border areas or lawns, resulting in what Southerners call "buglelawn."

'Alba', flowers white.

'Arctic Fox', silvery gray leaves and a narrow, dark green margin. Reversions to green are reported.

'Atropurpurea', easily the most popular and widely available form. It has coppery leaves with a purple tinge and bright blue flowers on fairly tall spike.

'Botanical Wonder', bright blue flowers on tall spike, to 6 in. (15 cm).

'Bronze Beauty', brilliant, deep bronze, metallic leaves.

'Brownherz', coppery, very dark purple-brown leaves.

'Burgundy Glow', leaves with silvery green centers, suffused with pink and cream toward the margins. Pink bracts and light blue flowers.

'Catlin's Giant', the largest bugle available, runs as fast as the species. Leaves are very large, purple, and nicely fluted. It needs careful watching so as not to stray out of bounds.

'Cristata', leaves all twisted out of shape the entire mound is distorted. For those who like grotesque plants, this one will satisfy.

'Gaiety', flowers lilac, coppery purple leaves.

'Jungle Beauty', large, indigo-blue flowers, crinkled bronze-green leaves.

'Multicolor' ('Rainbow', 'Tricolor') bronze leaves mottled reddish pink and yellow, sometimes speckled with silvery gray, or gray speckled with green, margined leaves, and all-green leaves. Some leaves have pink hues. Every leaf on the plant is different and to give an accurate description is impossible. Flowers are dark blue.

'Pink Beauty', flowers deep pink, smaller than 'Rosea'.

'Pink Delight', flowers bright pink, leaves crinkled green.

'Pink Elf', flowers pink, smaller than 'Rosea'.

'Pink Spire', flowers pink on taller pink spikes, to 7 in. (18 cm).

'Rosea', flowers rose-pink.

'Silver Beauty', leaves green overlaid with silvery gray and margined in white.

'Silver Carpet', leaves overlaid with silvery gray.

'Tottenham', flowers with pinkish shading to lilac. May be a hybrid with *Ajuga genevensis*.

'Valfredda' ('Chocolate Chip'), flowers on short stems to 3 in. (8 cm), bright to dark blue, leaves small, brown-tinted. This new miniature bugle stands out among yellow-leaved small hostas.

'Variegata', leaves flecked with creamy white.

Amianthium

Amianthium muscaetoxicum (fly poison) is one of those obscure wildflowers hardly seen in gardens, yet it deserves better. I first saw this beauty along the Blue Ridge Parkway in Great Smoky Mountains Park, growing in a meadow near the tree line —a marvelous sight: cylindrical racemes of white flowers held aloft on 24 in. (60 cm) spikes. I took several photographs and left the sizeable colony for others to admire. It took me a while to find a responsible wildflower nursery that offered the plants, but now I have a small group that delights all with a showy display every May. I have them interplanted with fairy wands, native trilliums, wild gingers, and uvularias. When in bloom, this species never fails to elicit comments of wonderment from visitors admiring the progression of white buds, greenish white flowers, and green flowers, all on the same raceme. The spent flowering spike and raceme remain on the plant, making a modest but interesting early autumn display.

All parts of the plant are toxic, particularly the bulbous root. In agricultural meadows it has been wiped out to prevent livestock from being poisoned. It does carry on in mountainous areas of the Appalachians and in Atlantic coastal areas. Early settlers of the region used crushed bulbs with some honey to make their own flypaper or crushed roots in sugar water for fly bait (hence, fly poison). Pesky crows raiding vegetable gardens also met an untimely end by ingesting poisoned bait made with the plant. Wash your hands after handling the bulbous roots or other parts of the plant, and, as with baneberry, take care to keep small children and the attractive flowers separate. As with all native wildflowers, fly poison should be purchased only from environmentally certified sources; this plant is threatened in several areas, so wild populations must remain untouched by greedy shovels.

The specific name comes from the Latin *muscae* (= flies) and *toxicum* (= poison). The generic name is a combination of the Greek *amiantos* (= immaculate) and *anthos* (= flower). *Amianthium* is classified in the Melanthiaceae.

Fly poison thrives in open woods and meadows and is seen in sandy bogs along the coast. It requires damp, acid soil with a pH of 5. It tolerates considerable shade but prefers a more open site with light shade and some sun. Hardy to zone 4.

Propagate by taking bulblets. Seed propagation is difficult.

I have not seen any disease or insect damage.

Amianthium muscaetoxicum, fly poison, crow poison. Eastern North America, coastal plains from New York to Florida, in mountains from Pennsylvania to North Carolina, west to Missouri and Oklahoma.

Some sun, LS; flowers small, numerous, 3 petals, 3 sepals, white turning greenish with maturity, persisting on the spike as fruit matures, arranged in a dense, first conical then cylindrical raceme, 2–4 in. (5–10 cm) long on tall flowerstalks with small, leafy bracts, to 36 in. (90 cm), but usually less, 12–24 in. (30–60 cm); May–June; plant herbaceous, clump-forming, with bulbous root; basal leaves are straplike, green, smooth, to 14 in. (35 cm) long and 0.8 in. (2 cm) wide, blunt-tipped; 3-beaked capsule. Many gardeners find a place for poisonous plants like philodendrons and dieffenbachias in their homes; surely the risk of planting this beauty in the open garden is minor, and this elegant native should find a place in the wildflower garden.

Amorphophallus

Until recently, the genus *Amorphophallus* was a curiosity in botanical gardens and in a few intrepid gardeners' greenhouses. Exaggerated reports of a penetrating foul odor during bloom season contributed to its rarity in cultivation. There is some truth to the reports; but the exciting and unusual flowers of these aroids (as plants of the arum family, Araceae, are known) make it well worth opening your eyes wide while holding your nose shut for a spell around these trendy plants, and gardeners are now in a race to see who can grow the tallest, meanest-looking amorphophallus. *Amorphophallus titanum* (titan arum) garnered worldwide television news coverage when its bulbs (actually tubers or cormlike rhizomes), some weighing over 50 lbs. (23 kg), finally issued their monstrous, mesmerizing spathe and spadix, widely reported as being the largest flower in the plant kingdom. (Actually, the flowers of this plant are very tiny and crowded onto the spadix, familiar to many as the Jack—as in jack-in-the-pulpit, a related North American native; I guess many gardeners consider the combination of spathe and spadix a flower, and so to simplify things, I may sometimes call it that too.) At the Atlanta Botanical Garden, people waited patiently in long lines to get a look at the spectacle; the same scene was repeated in England and on the Continent—and the rest is history. A demand has developed for this and other species of *Amorphophallus*, and several are now available that have smaller but equally bizarre "flowers." They are not as huge and expensive as *A. titanum*, which can cost the aficionado as much as dinner for four in a fine New York restaurant, but then, not every gardener has the room to grow that giant.

Some time after flowering, these exotic Asian marvels send up a large, single leaf that has the generalized shape of an umbrella palm (*Hedyscepe canterburyana*) atop a thick stalk, which is brownish green mottled with white or greenish spots and brown and purple speckles, reminiscent of the patterned skin of many tropical serpents (hence, snake palm). Although the snake palms have been touted as the latest in gardening, they have been around for years. The first flowering of *Amorphophallus titanum* in North America took place in the conservatory of the New York Botanical Garden on 8 June 1937. Some gardeners have grown the smaller varieties as curiosities in greenhouses and potted on Florida or southern California patios.

Most available snake palm species come from Southeast Asia, and being of tropical origin, their tubers must not be exposed to freezing. I have grown *Amorphophallus rivieri* var. *konjac* for years, always setting the corms out after the last freeze and bringing them in during winter. Soon I found that some of the offsets left behind came up in spring even after harsh winters with temperatures down to 0°F (−18°C). I started to leave the large mother corms in the ground at a depth of 12 in. (30 cm), on top of a well-draining coarse bark and gravel layer and surrounded by good garden soil. They proved remarkably hardy. The rhizomatous corms develop an indentation on top, so I plant them tipped at about 45 degrees, to let the water drain out during winter rains. I brought a few rhizomes to my mother in Detroit, where they became curiosities for all the neighbors. She planted them after the ground warmed up and removed them in autumn before the ground froze and brought them inside to overwinter. Most snake palms may be safely left in the ground in zone 7; however, those who have spent a bunch of dollars for their snake palms may want to overwinter the tubers inside.

Snake palms are ideally suited to our temperate Western shady gardens. I plant them among large hostas and tall ferns in the woodland, where they overtop their neighbors. First they send up 5–6 ft. (1.5–1.8 m) flowerstalks; they follow this display, after some rest, with a towering single leaf that soon reveals why they are called snake palm. Let me caution against placing them in a windswept area. The large, sail-like leaf caught in a moderate wind gust can exert considerable force on the pulpy stem, breaking it occasionally; a sturdy stake usually solves the problem.

Amorphophallus is from the Greek *amorphos* (= deformed) and *phallos* (= penis), referring to the phallic shape of the spadix. Taxonomists classify some species under the genus *Hydrosme*, which I consider a synonym.

Propagate by taking offsets. The mother rhizome sends out rhizomatous "branches" that form another cormlike swelling at their termination point. I have not tried seeds; propagation by offsets is much faster.

Viral diseases (mosaic virus), bacterial rot, and leaf spot (anthracnose) are reported but unknown in my experience.

Amorphophallus bulbifer, Indian snake palm, bulb-bearing snake palm. Northeast India.

MS to FS; inflorescence to 18 in. (45 cm) tall; spathe widely expanded to 4 in. (10 cm) wide, hooded, rose-colored in the throat becoming pinkish tan inside the hood, outside pinkish with green markings; spadix pink, with sterile appendage to 4 in. (10 cm) long and 1 in. (2.5 cm) wide; leaf on thick petiole to 0.8 in. (2 cm) wide and 4 ft. (1.2 m) tall, petiole dark olive-green with silvery sea-green irregular spotting; leaf solitary, 3-parted, to 36 in. (90 cm) wide, with each leaflet 2-pinnate, light to dark green with prominent veins; bulblets, to 1 in. (2.5 cm) in diameter, form at the apex junction of the petiole and at major leaf divisions; seed black. It makes its own bulblets on top of the leaf, which can be removed and planted to make additional plants. This smaller snake palm has a slight but not pungent odor.

Amorphophallus paeoniifolius, punga pung, elephant yam, peony-leaved snake palm, Telingo potato. India, New Guinea.

MS to FS; inflorescence to 12 in. (30 cm) tall; spathe widely expanded, cup-shaped, with upper margin incurved, recurved and very undulate, wide, purple and spotted with rusty cinnamon in the throat; spadix impossible to describe but roughly cone-shaped, with many folds, distortions, and waves on its surface, cinnamon to honey-colored, leaf on thick petiole to 2 in. (5 cm) wide at the base, tapering toward top, to 8 ft. (2.5 m) tall, petiole medium to light green marbled with irregular silvery light green to gray-green markings, tiny protuberances that feel nubby to the touch occur along the entire length; leaf solitary, 3-parted, to 7 ft. (2 m) wide, with each leaflet pinnatifid, light to yellowish green with prominent veins. A very large snake palm with a huge tuber; this Telingo potato is an important food starch from northeast India to Vietnam and the Philippines. The flower structure is the weirdest I have ever seen on any plant—so outlandish only a photo can do it justice. The smell is noticeable but all are willing to stand it just to see the macabre flower, a conversation piece for the garden if there ever was one.

Amorphophallus rivieri, devil's tongue, leopard palm, konjac, konjac snake palm, snake palm, umbrella arum. Indonesia, Malay Archipelago, Sumatra.

MS to FS; inflorescence to 6 ft. (1.8 m) tall; spathe funnel-shaped to 5 in. (13 cm) wide, with expanded collarlike limb, wavy at top, blackish red to dark purple; spadix purple, tapering toward the top, to 36 in. (90 cm) long and 2 in. (5 cm) wide, supported by white-spotted flowerstalk to 18 in. (45 cm) long; leaf on thick petiole to 2 in. (5 cm) wide and 5 ft. (1.5 m) tall, tapering, dark olive-green to very dark greenish brown speckled progressively with silvery sea-green irregular spots toward the top, some stems of mature plants have few spots and are dark to the leaf, tiny protuberances that feel nubby to the touch occur at the base; leaf solitary, 3-parted, to 36 in. (90 cm) wide, with each leaflet 2- to 3-pinnate, light to dark green with prominent veins; seed black; mature tubers are to 12 in. (30 cm) wide and form stolons bearing small tubers. Variety *konjac*, the most frequently offered snake palm, is somewhat larger but otherwise indistinguishable from the type, which is seldom seen. Given fertile soil and plenty of water, it will grow very large. Leaving this one in the ground gives succeeding offsets a chance to form a large colony, which will need plenty of space; I give away an increasing number of small tubers. If there is room for only one snake palm, this is it—the hardiest and most prolific of them all. Its huge, colorful flower structure, one of the tallest among snake palms, will be the "thing" everyone wants to see and smell in spring. The foul odor lasts but a short time and draws flies from miles away.

Amorphophallus titanum, corpse flower, titan arum. Malay Archipelago, Sumatra.

MS to FS; peduncle spotted purplish brown, to 40 in. (1 m); inflorescence to 9 ft. (2.7 m) tall; spathe openly vase-shaped, to 4 ft. (1.2 m) across and 5 ft. (1.5 m) tall, with recurved collarlike limb irregularly margined, with ribbed walls of reddish purple changing to creamy pink below; spadix prodigiously protruding and up to 7 ft. (2 m) tall, dirty, dull yellow, furrowed, tapering toward the blunt top; leaf on thick petiole to 6 in. (15 cm) wide and 18 ft. (5.5 m) tall, tapering, dark olive-green to very dark greenish brown speckled progressively with silvery sea-green irregular spots toward the top, some stems of mature plants have few spots and are dark to the leaf, protuberances that feel nubby to the touch occur at the base; leaf solitary, 3-parted, to 15 ft. (5 m) wide, with each leaflet pinnatifid and deeply lobed, medium to dark green with prominent veins; mature tubers are to 20 in. (50 cm) in diameter and form stolonlike offsets. A snake palm of truly titanic proportions and even television fame. So large it is seldom seen in small gardens, but temperate zone botanic gardens feature them in their conservatories for all to see and smell. The inflorescence has a foul odor (hence, corpse flower). Some daring and wealthy gardeners have bought immature tubers and are growing them on.

Anemone

Windflowers are a mixed blessing in the wildflower and woodland garden. I have tried *Anemone sylvestris* and other spring-flowering species and cultivars, but they were gone by July, dormant even before the heat of the summer arrived, leaving holes in my garden. The same can be said for another group of windflowers that are usually mat-forming, creeping perennials, like *A. blanda*, which require full sun and a dry soil in dormancy—a condition that is difficult to provide when they are planted with woodlanders that require moist soil year-round. I have had some success with anemones that flower in late summer and autumn, but their growth is rampant: some gardeners call them downright invasive. This spreading habit is subdued when the plants are grown in more shade, but windflowers respond to reduced sun exposure with diminished flowering. Another flaw: some exotic anemones have a penchant for giving up the ghost after a couple of seasons and quietly disappear from the garden scene. The native North American wood anemones, however, are well suited to the shady woodland garden. Just exactly which species and cultivars will work in a given garden is up to the individual gardener, and some experimentation may be the best way to select specific plants. The main consideration is to match the anemone's native growing conditions to the cultural conditions attainable in gardens. This may be difficult with some species but is certainly worth trying, given their beautiful flowers.

Anemones are found all over the temperate zones, both in the northern and southern hemispheres. Their habitat is enormously diverse, ranging from shady woodlands to sun-baked alpine screes. This accounts for the many failures in gardens where an unsuitable habitat is provided. The best windflowers for the shady garden are easily the wood anemones, common in woodlands in the temperate regions of North America. They range from eastern Canada to the moist woodlands of the Carolinas and Georgia. Unfortunately, they are somewhat fussy in the lower parts of the southeastern states, where long periods of summer heat and drought dry out the soil.

Nomenclature of the garden cultivars is confused. The many garden clones and hybrids are variously assigned to *Anemone hupehensis*, its variety *japonica*, or the hybrid group *A.* ×*hybrida*. Since most are sold under the genus name alone (for instance, *Anemone* 'Prinz Heinrich'), the specific attribution becomes less important. The genus *Anemone* derives its name from the classical Greek *anemos* (= wind). *Anemone* is classified in the Ranunculaceae.

Despite their sometimes invasive and occasionally demanding properties, anemones have been grown in gardens for many years. Their flowers are in the shape of a shallow dish with a concentric tuft of bright yellow stamens, much like a daisy. The number of tepals varies considerably, depending on the species, and some flowers are double, in shades of white, creamy yellow, yellow, pink, red, violet, purple, and blue. Specific windflowers like the wood anemones are short-stemmed and make good groundcover, particularly those that spread; most of the fall-blooming varieties bloom on taller stems. Anemones do best in a light, well-draining woodland soil, rich in organic matter, but I know of plantings that thrive in ordinary garden soil. They like cool soil, but they will succeed even in warmer regions if ample moisture is available; most wood anemones require moist soils year-round. Sometimes, they are slow to establish from small plants, but by the third year they bloom abundantly and spread vigorously. The spreading woodland and meadow species are best planted where they will not overrun other delicate wildflowers or woodlanders. The anemones native to North America and northern Europe are hardy to zone 4; those from Mediterranean regions are somewhat tender.

Propagate by taking root cuttings of autumn-flowering anemones in spring. For summer-dormant species, divide the tubers after they go dormant, usually in summer. Divide rhizomatous species in early spring. Seed can be sown as soon as ripe. Utilize a cold frame and liberate the seed from the woolly casing before sowing.

Anemones are prone to develop leaf galls, leaf spot, or leaf smut. Powdery mildew is very common, particularly in humid climates. Late-blooming anemones are subject to foliar and root nematodes. Slugs and snails, moth and butterfly larvae (caterpillars), and various beetles and their grubs all favor the plants.

Species and cultivars listed should receive at least four hours of sunlight, as present in open woods, for reliable and abundant flowering. All are suitable for zones 4 to 7, unless otherwise noted; anemones in difficult microclimates in zones 4 and 5 may require winter protection.

Anemone hupehensis, Chinese anemone. Western and central China.

LS to WS; flowers 5–15 in loose cymes, 5–6 rounded tepals, to 2.5 in. (6 cm) across, white or pink with the outer being red or deep pink; flowerstalks 20–36 in. (50–90 cm), slightly hairy; August–October; plant with suckering, fibrous rootstock; leaves basal, dark green, slightly hairy, lobed and deeply toothed, divided into 3–5 leaflets, 5–8 in. (18–20 cm) long. This species is the basis for many autumn-flowering anemones. Variety *japonica* (Japanese anemone) is taller, to 4 ft. (1.2 m), and has 20–25 narrow, light pink tepals so tightly arranged as to appear double or semi-double; known in Japanese gardens since the 17th century, it was introduced into cultivation by Robert Fortune in 1844. Cultivars of this species and variety that bloom September–October may in fact be cultivars of *Anemone ×hybrida*.

'Bodnant Burgundy', flowers deep pinkish purple to 3 in. (8 cm); plant to 40 in. (1 m).

'Bowles' Pink' ('E. A. Bowles'), flowers pink to 3 in. (8 cm).

'Bressingham Glow', flowers uniform pink, semi-double, to 3 in. (8 cm) with a bright, shiny appearance produced by silky threads on the outer surface; plant to 36 in. (90 cm).

'Elegans', flowers pale rose-pink; plant to 28 in. (70 cm).

'Hadspen Abundance', flowers bicolored, pink and purple; plant similar to the species but more vigorous and floriferous.

'Praecox', plant to 32 in. (80 cm) with purple-pink flowers.

'Prinz Heinrich' ('Prince Henry'), flowers reddish purple, semi-double; plant to 32 in. (80 cm), spreads rapidly.

'Rubra', flowers red; plant to 32 in. (80 cm).

'September Charm' ('September Glow'), flowers silvery pink, darker outside, drooping.

'Splendens', flowers purplish pink; plant to 32 in. (80 cm), robust.

'Superba', flowers pink to 3 in. (8 cm); plant to 36 in. (90 cm). A selected clone of the species with good vigor and larger stature.

Anemone ×hybrida, Japanese anemone of gardens. Hybrid (*A. hupehensis* var. *japonica* × *A. vitifolia*).

LS to WS; flowers 12–20 in loose umbels or cymes, 6–15 tepals, to 3.5 in. (9 cm) across, semi-double light pink, seldom white, single, semi-double, and double flowers occur; flowerstalks stout, erect, 4–5 ft. (1.2–1.5 m); August–October; plant with suckering, sometimes invasive, fibrous rootstock; leaves basal, medium green, slightly hairy beneath, 3-lobed and deeply toothed, divided into 3–5 leaflets, 4–8 in. (10–20 cm) long. This hybrid group is the mainstay of autumn-flowering anemones and includes some of the most popular garden varieties. Since it flowers a week or so later than *Anemone hupehensis*, combining these hybrids with that species lengthens a windflower bloom display. Most flowers are a light pink, but white sports have appeared; both colors contrast beautifully with the round tuft of bright yellow stamens in center. The flowerstalks are very tall but strong; notwithstanding, stake them in unprotected areas before they are bowed by autumn winds. Some *A. ×hybrida* cultivars are very old, and I am not alone in preferring the tried-and-proven ones listed: **'Honorine Jobert'**, a white sport first described in 1858, remains the most popular single-flowered garden anemone. Its broad, pure white tepals overlap and show a little pink on the underside; the stems are 4 ft. (1.2 m) tall, and the plant is a vigorous, lively spreader.

'Alba', plant to 36 in. (90 cm) with single white flowers to 3 in. (8 cm).

'Alice', plant to 32 in. (80 cm) with semi-double pink flowers to 2.5 in. (6 cm).

'Elegantissima', plant to 5 ft. (1.5 m) with pink flowers, semi-double.

'Géante des Blanches' ('White Giant', 'White Queen'), flowers semi-double, to 3 in. (8 cm), broad, clean white, overlapping tepals, greenish shading on the underside; plant to 36 in. (90 cm), spreads rapidly.

'Königin Charlotte' ('Queen Charlotte', 'Reine Charlotte'), flowers large, semi-double pink, to 4 in. (10 cm), with broad, overlapping outer tepals; plant huge, to 5 ft. (1.5 m).

'Kriemhilde', flowers semi-double, pale purple-pink, darker outside.

'Luise Uhink', flowers large, to 5 in. (13 cm), almost semi-double, white; plant to 4 ft. (1.2 m).

'Margarette' ('Lady Gilmoure'), flowers almost double, pink, to 4 in. (10 cm), with pink shading to dark pink toward the outside; plant to 4 ft. (1.2 m).

'Max Vogel', flowers numerous, 20–32, single pale pink, to 4–5 in. (10–13 cm), with the outer tepals darker pink; plant to 4 ft. (1.2 m).

'Pamina', double, rosy red flowers, to 4 in. (10 cm); plant to 36 in. (90 cm).

'Profusion', flowers rosy pink, to 4 in. (10 cm).

'Rosenschale' ('Pink Shell'), flowers large, dark pink, to 4 in. (10 cm), with broad, overlapping outer tepals; plant to 32 in. (80 cm).

'Whirlwind', flowers semi-double, pure white, to 4 in. (10 cm), greenish shading on the tepals in center; plant to 4 ft. (1.2 m), very hardy.

Anemone tomentosa. Northern and central China.

LS to WS; flowers 9–15 in loose cymes, 5–6 tepals, to 3 in. (8 cm) across, light pink, single; flowerstalks stout, erect, 4–5 ft. (1.2–1.5 m); August–September; plant clump-forming, with fibrous rootstock that spreads by underground runners; leaves on the stem and basal, medium green, covered with fine, woolly white hairs below, 3-lobed, cleft and toothed, 2–5 in. (5–13 cm) long; fruit a woolly capsule. This species gets its name from the whitish (tomentose), woolly covering of the leaves. It is clump-forming but can become invasive if not watched. The woolly fruit stays on the stems all winter long and adds interest. 'Robustissima' is hardier than the species (to zone 3); 'Superba' is smaller in all respects. The species and its cultivars, especially 'Robustissima', are frequently mixed up, so caution is advised; in fact, many sources ship

Anemone tomentosa and *A. vitifolia* and their cultivars interchangeably.

Anemone vitifolia, grape leaf anemone, clumping anemone. Afghanistan to Nepal and western China and Burma.

LS to WS; flowers 3–7 in loose cymes, 6–8 tepals, to 2.5 in. (6 cm) across, white, single; flowerstalks stout, erect, to 36 in. (90 cm); August–September; plant clump-forming, with fibrous rootstock; leaves on the stem and basal, medium green, 5-lobed, 4–8 in. (10–20 cm) long; fruit woolly. One of the earliest autumn-flowering anemones, it can be combined with other species to give several weeks of bloom in the fall. The lobed leaves of this species (the epithet means "vine-leafed") are unlike those of other anemones in appearance, thus bringing diversity, and they stay fresh, lasting from spring until autumn, an important trait for shady gardens. The woolly fruit stays on the stems during winter and adds interest. Unlike other anemones, this species forms a slowly expanding clump and is better behaved in the border than the runners; it nevertheless spreads by stolons, which root a distance away from the mother plant and form new clumps. Remove these in spring, and either plant them elsewhere or give them away to friends.

Anemonella

Delicate native woodland plants are often overlooked by shade gardeners. Their dainty and fragile beauty is frequently overpowered by bold hostas, large ferns, and carpeting plants with dense habits. So I place my rue anemones where they can be appreciated. *Anemonella thalictroides* (rue anemone) is found in moist, fertile, open woodlands in eastern North America. It is perfect planted by itself in a shady corner under a pine tree with moist and acidic soil. There, away from more boisterous neighbors, its charm can be seen. Plant small ferns or a patch of moss next to it, whose bluish green leaves will contrast with their soft green.

Taxonomists have had a field day with this plant. As the generic name indicates, the only species in the genus was formerly included with the anemones as *Anemone thalictroides* (= the anemone that looks like a thalictrum), as its leaves resemble those of *Thalictrum dioicum*. Latest placements favor inclusion in the genus *Thalictrum*, but many gardeners still grow it under the older name *Anemonella*, a fitting diminutive of anemone. *Anemonella* is classified in the Ranunculaceae.

Despite its fragile charm, rue anemone is long-lived given the right conditions. Find a permanent place for this beauty: it resents being moved or otherwise disturbed. The soil must not soggy, or the tubers will rot. Choose a site that is sheltered from strong winds. The only fault of this little plant is its relatively early dormancy, which occurs after the seeds have ripened; nevertheless, the early-spring flowers and attractive leaves provide a lovely display well into early summer. Rue anemone is a bit slow to establish itself, but after a few seasons it forms a nice colony if larger adjoining plants are prevented from obliterating it. Watering is necessary in hot, dry summers. Hardy to zone 4.

Similar are *Isopyrum biternata* and *I. thalictroides*, false rue anemones, common in central and eastern North America and Europe, respectively. Differentiated only by minor botanical details and their smaller size, these species serve equal purposes in gardens. *Isopyrum biternata* is hardy to zone 3, *I. thalictroides* to zone 5.

Propagate rue anemones and false rue anemones by removing some outer tubers from the periphery of larger plants, without disturbing the mother plant. Do this in early autumn, after the plant goes dormant, or in very early spring. When happy, rue anemone will seed itself, or seed can be sown in a cold frame as soon as ripe.

Leaf smut, rust, and powdery mildew are common in humid climates. Slugs and snails can decimate plantings in early spring, so frequent checks are advised.

Anemonella thalictroides, rue anemone, windflower. Eastern North America, southwest Maine west to Minnesota, south to Georgia, Alabama, northwest Florida and Mississippi and west to Arkansas and Oklahoma.

LS to MS; flowers 2–4 in loose umbels, usually 9 tepals, cup-shaped to 0.8 in. (2 cm) across, single, white, or white shaded with very light pink; flowerstalks thin, fragile, erect, 3–10 in. (8–25 cm); March–May; plant with slowly expanding tuberous rootstock; leaves basal, bluish green, 2- to 3-ternate, divided into 5–9 oval leaflets, 4–6 in. (10–15 cm) long; fruit one-seeded, ribbed. A lovely native no garden should be without.

'Alba Plena', flowers white fully double.

'Cameo', flowers pink double.

'Green Hurricane', flowers small, lime-green, button type.

'Oscar Schoaf' ('Flore Pleno', 'Schoaf's Double', 'Schoaf's Pink'), flowers rosy pink double.

'Rosea', flowers rosy pink.

'Rosea Plena', flowers long-lasting, rosy pink double.

'Rubra', flowers rosy red.

'Semidouble White', flowers semi-double white.

Anemonopsis

Occasionally, unusual plants are received from Asia and I just have to try them. *Anemonopsis macrophylla* (false anemone) is one such plant. It has been around since Siebold, the dauntless German doctor, brought it and many other species back from Japan in the 1830s. Forewarned that plants disappeared in hot, dry summers in short order, I planted one in full shade, in very deep woods soil. Few hot breezes could reach this nook, which was wind-protected by a board fence at back and mature azaleas to the left and right. I provided water unfailingly, even misting the plant at times. It thrived in the cool nights and warm days of early spring, and when the hot days and nights of August arrived, the plant continued in good condition. I was looking forward to seeing its flowers—and then took a fortnight's vacation to escape the unbearable Georgia heat, high up in the North Carolina mountains. The plant dried out and gave up.

In more northern areas, however, gardeners should have no problems. The false anemone is a valuable shade garden plant where summers are cool and the environment replicates to some degree its native habitat in Japan. False anemone is a great companion to hostas, ferns, astilbes, and native wildflowers in the moist woodland border. Although its leaves look more like those of the baneberry, the generic name indicates a resemblance to anemone (Greek, *opsis* = resembling). The flowers do resemble those of the anemone, but they nod, and only the back of the tepals shows. *Anemonopsis* is classified in the Ranunculaceae. It is sometimes confused with *Amenopsis*, a tender California native.

The rhizomatous rootstock spreads slowly, forming a nice colony in time. Watering and misting is necessary in hot, dry summers. False anemones suffer severely in dry, hot winds, so a sheltering position in full shade should be selected in southern gardens. In the South, this is not a plant for weekend gardeners. Hardy to zone 4.

Propagate by carefully dividing the fleshy dormant rhizome. Seed is unreliable.

Slugs and snails left my plants alone, even with abundant moisture present. No other pests or diseases are reported.

Anemonopsis macrophylla, false anemone. Japan, central Honshu, Japanese Alps.

MS to FS; flowers 2–5 in open racemes, usually 7–13 tepals, the sepals larger and waxy, nodding cup-shaped to 1.5 in. (4 cm) across, pink to pale violet; flowerstalks upright, blackish purple, 24–32 in. (60–80 cm); August–September; plant clump-forming with slowly expanding rhizomatous rootstock; leaves 2- or 3-lobed on very long petioles, substantially toothed and incised, shiny dark green, leaflets, 3–6 in. (8–15 cm) long. An excellent plant for the shady northern garden. Difficult further south unless cool, moist conditions can be maintained during hot summers.

Aplectrum

Hardy woodland orchids native to North America are not much seen in gardens. Many are small, unassuming plants and are often overlooked in the wild. This is fortunate because most are rare and thus protect themselves by being inconspicuous. My first acquaintance with *Aplectrum hyemale* was during a late autumn walk on a North Georgia mountain trail, where it is fairly common. Fallen leaves covered the ground and I almost overlooked it, but a second glance revealed a splendid colony of strange green leaves with a hint of silvery white striping. One leaf twisted to show the shiny purple back. I had to have one, and in time I found one at a wildflower nursery. This orchid is locally called resurrection orchid because it "has things all turned around," as mountain people express it: its leaves appear in autumn, remain on the plant over the winter, and die down the following midspring. After a short period, the plant resurrects itself and the flower spikes appear. I like this unusual orchid, with its peculiar life cycle. The content of its paired corms was used by American Indians as a dressing

for wounds and on abscesses. It was also taken for respiratory problems.

The genus *Aplectrum* (= without horns) is classified in the orchid family, Orchidaceae. The epithet (*hyemalis* = pertaining to winter) indicates its fascinating persistence during that season.

This is an attractive curiosity for southern gardens. It is useful in the wildflower garden in deep, moist soil with a pH of 5.5 to 7. Hardy to zone 4. It is a less interesting plant in areas of long-lasting snow cover, where the unusual leaves cannot be seen.

Propagate by carefully dividing the tuberous corm.

In my garden, nothing seems to bother this native orchid. In more southern areas, slugs are a scourge during winter warm-ups.

Aplectrum hyemale, puttyroot, Adam and Eve orchid, resurrection orchid. Southeastern Canada and northern New England, south into the Ohio River Valley and the central Appalachians, northern Georgia, Alabama, and Arkansas, west to the Rockies and Cascades.

LS to FS; flowers tiny, greenish purple or white and yellow tinged with purple, insignificant, 6–24, in a loose spiral on an erect spike 18–24 in. (45–60 cm) high; June–August; leaf solitary, basal, elliptic, from connected underground corms in autumn, dark gray-green above, shiny purple on the underside, pleated, thinly silvery-white striped, to 7 in. (18 cm) long and 3 in. (8 cm) wide, disappearing before flowering. An orchid with winter interest for discriminating gardeners. As with many North American species, it has a Japanese counterpart in *Aplectrum unguiculatum*, which is rarely offered.

Aquilegia

Hybrid columbines are a mainstay of sunny borders, but they require a fair amount of full sun to provide the stimulating flower display promised on the seed packets. Unfortunately, many of the hybrid groups are short-lived, and this inherent problem is aggravated by a little too much shade. I tried some McKana Hybrids in woodland shade, and they did give a nice display for a couple of seasons, after which they rapidly declined. Still, I wanted some columbines in my garden. One day, while on a hiking trip in the Little River Valley of the Smoky Mountains, I stumbled upon a colony of wild columbines growing in full shade near a moss-covered rock formation. Hundreds of fabulous, bright scarlet, long-spurred flowers with yellow skirts could not be missed—an unforgettable sight. Happily, I was able to purchase a few pots in a wildflower nursery off the Blue Ridge Parkway. This wonderful native, *Aquilegia canadensis*, which now thrives in the moist shade of my garden, is so vigorous, some gardeners consider it an annoyance when seedlings show up in unexpected places. In so seeding, the clumps renew themselves, and there is no die-back as seen in many hybrid columbines.

The native habitat of columbines is remarkably diverse, ranging from shady woodlands to sun-baked alpine meadows. Easily the best columbines for the shady garden are the various species native to woodlands. Hardy to zone 3.

The common name appears to be rooted in the Latin *columbinus* (= like a dove), although I cannot see anything dovelike in the flowers. The genus name derives from the Latin *aquila* (= eagle), alluding to the resemblance of the five flower spurs to an eagle's talons. *Aquilegia* is classified in the Ranunculaceae.

Columbines have been popular garden plants for many years. Their foliage is attractive and long-lasting. The colorful flowers attract hummingbirds, which are simply mesmerizing in the garden. Hummingbirds have long tongues so can easily reach the nectaries; bees, on the other hand, cut holes into the sides of the nectaries to get to the sweet fluid. Some species, like the Canadian columbine, have flowers that nod, supported by thin stems; others have up-facing flowers. Color combinations (sepals and petals) seen in species include blue and white, blue and blue, yellow and red, yellow and yellow, and white and white. Species columbines do best in a light, moist, but well-draining woodland soil, rich in organic matter; many species columbines are deep-rooted so do well during the long, hot, dry summers of the South.

Propagate by dividing the dormant rhizome. Seed germinates easily, and in most cases new plants flower within two seasons. Established clumps self-seed abundantly; seedlings can be removed where they are not wanted and planted where they are. To harvest seed, wait until the seeds turn black and sow as soon as ripe; move young plants in autumn, digging to a depth sufficient to liberate all roots. Expect hybrids in gardens where several species and cultivars are present; because they are frequently open-pollinated, most columbines rarely come true in such gardens.

Leaf miners, those pesky bugs that construct twisting roadways on otherwise attractive foliage, mysteriously appear whenever a columbine is planted, disfiguring the leaves. Combat this affliction by cutting off all affected leaves and sending them to the dump; this removes some of the active insects, and new, unaffected leaves soon develop. Systemic insecticides are useful, but they should be used as a last resort and sparingly. Fortuitously, the Canadian columbine does not seem to be as affected by this blight. Columbines are also subject to rust, fungal leaf spot, and powdery mildew. Crown rot (southern blight) caused by white silk fungus (white mold fungus) is sometimes problematic. Butterfly and moth larvae (caterpillars) and various beetles, particularly weevils, and their grubs also do damage. A general-application insecticide may be the only way to solve these problems. Slugs, present in just about every moist woodland garden, have not been problematic at Hosta Hill.

Species and cultivars listed are suitable for zones 4 to 8, unless otherwise noted. Short-lived hybrid columbines requiring full sun or very light shade are excluded in general; those that are included should be considered for tentative use; microclimate will be decisive in these cases.

Aquilegia canadensis, Canada columbine, Canadian columbine, wild columbine, rock bells. Eastern North America, Ontario and Quebec, New England west to Wisconsin and Minnesota, south to Georgia, Florida, and Tennessee.

LS to MS; flowers many, nodding, somewhat bell-shaped, on terminal, leafy racemes, 1–2 in. (2.5–5 cm) long, 5 slightly diverging but forward-pointing bright red sepals, 5 petals with yellow blades tapering backward into straight or slightly outward-curved bright red spurs to 0.5 in. (1 cm) long, yellow stamens bundled and projecting; flowerstalks 20–30 in. (50–75 cm); April–July; plant clump-forming with deep-seated rootstock; leaves basal, 2-ternate, light green, 4–6 in. (10–15 cm) long, leaflets 9–25 per leaf, each lobed and deeply divided into 3 segments; fruit many-seeded, dehiscent. One of the best columbines for the shady garden. Here its brilliant scarlet flowers with yellow accents go on five to six weeks; when this species is combined with August-flowering hostas and autumn-flowering anemones, some color can be had in the shady garden during most of the summer. For best effect and to follow natural patterns, combine several plants to form a colony. This species was used by American Indians as a narcotic and aphrodisiac and to treat headaches, fevers, and gastrointestinal complaints. Seems to grow larger in the warmer areas of its habitat; it can be grown in warmer areas extending to zone 8. Cultivars include 'Corbett' (yellow flowers) and 'Nana', a smaller version of the type to 12 in. (30 cm).

Aquilegia coerulea, Rocky Mountain columbine. Western North America, Rocky Mountain area from Montana to northern Arizona and New Mexico.

LS to WS; flowers many, upright on terminal, leafy racemes, 5 flaring blue to bluish purple sepals to 2.5 in. (6 cm) across and 5 white petals with long, straight or outward-curved spurs to 2 in. (5 cm) long with knobs at the ends; flowerstalks 20–30 in. (50–75 cm); May–July; plant clump-forming with deep-seated rootstock; leaves basal, 2-ternate, medium gray-green, leaflets lobed and deeply divided, to 1.5 in. (4 cm) long; fruit many-seeded, dehiscent. Not as robust as some species (but long-lasting compared to the hybrid groups), which fault is easily corrected by rejuvenating the planting with raised seedlings. An excellent species for woodland shade and the basis for many long-spurred hybrids. Combine several plants to form a colony.

'Albiflora', flowers yellowish white.

'Candidissima', flowers large, pure white.

'Citrina', flowers lemon-yellow.

'Crimson Star', flowers bicolored, red and white or creamy white; hybrid origin.

'Cuprea', flowers red with metallic, coppery glow.

'Haylodgensis', flowers bright blue; hybrid origin.

'Helenae', flowers bright blue; hybrid origin.

'Himmelblau' ('Heavenly Blue'), flowers deep blue with white petioles, long spurs; probably hybrid origin.

'Koralle' ('Coral'), flowers salmon-pink, coral; hybrid origin.

'Maxistar', large flowers, bright yellow, very long spurs, pointed outward; hybrid origin.

'Olympia', flowers red and yellow; hybrid origin.

'Rotstern' ('Red Star'), flowers red and white; hybrid origin.

Aquilegia vulgaris, common columbine, European columbine, European crowfoot, garden columbine, granny's bonnet, true columbine. Pandemic in Europe.

Sun, LS; flowers blue or violet, 5–18, nodding, on leafy stems from branched racemes, 0.8 in. (2 cm) long, 5 forward-pointing sepals, 5 petals with blades tapering backward into short, strongly hooked, incurved spurs terminating with rounded knobs; flowerstalks to 36 in. (90 cm); June–August; plant clump-forming; leaves basal, 2-ternate, medium bluish green, glaucous beneath, divided into lobed leaflets. Suitable in the shady garden if some sun is available. The subject of widespread breeding with other wild species in Europe, the type is rarely available. Variety *stellata* has spurless flowers with widely spreading tepals and comes in white, blue, and pink. The bizarre double and almost triple flowers have an outline almost like pompon-shaped semi-cactus dahlias; prudence is advised before introducing such a jarring element into the restful green garden. Several cultivars with variegated leaves have been combined as *Aquilegia* Vervaeneana Group; flower colors in this group range from purple, violet, and blue to pink, yellow, and white, and leaves are margined, mottled, or streaked with whitish yellow or yellow. Consult the latest nursery catalogs for details and availability.

'Adelaide Addison', flowers blue, blue edge on double, white center.

'Alba', white flowers, much like (and sometimes sold as) 'Nivea'.

'Alba Plena', flowers double white.

'Atrorosa', flowers rose-red.

'Caryophylloides', flowers red tinged white.

'Clematiflora Alba', flowers spurless, white; erect habit.

'Double Red', flowers double, dark red; smaller stature.

'Erecta', flowers white; erect habit.

'Flore Pleno' ('Pleno'), flowers double of various colors.

'Gisela Powell', flowers yellow-orange.

'Nivea' ('Munstead White'), flowers pure white contrasting with gray-green foliage. Nothing approaches it for brightening up a lightly shaded corner.

'Nora Barlow', flowers double (pom-pom), pink and whitish green.

'Olympia', flowers blue and white. Often confused with *Aquilegia coerulea* 'Olympia'.

'Red Star', flowers red with white. Often confused *Aquilegia coerulea* 'Rotstern'.

'Tom Fairhurst', flowers pink and red.

Arachniodes

If one fern I have comes close to being as ornate as the Japanese painted fern (*Athyrium nipponicum* 'Pictum'), it is *Arachniodes simplicior* (variegated shield fern). Its glossy, bright green fronds carry a pronounced yellowish band on each side of the midrib. In many ways, this fern is more showy—it literally shines in a garden. Not usually considered hardy in zone 9 and colder, but I have found both *A. simplicior* and *A. standishii* to be hardy here in zone 7a and evergreen in a protected area, although during particularly cold winters, the top growth becomes deciduous; with some protection, they could be grown in the ground a little further north. The attractiveness of *A. simplicior* particularly is worth a try. In the very cold northern regions, it makes an excellent container plant; in such situations, its handsome, variegated fronds can be closely examined in an elevated position.

The ferns in the genus *Arachniodes* are endemic to the temperate and tropical regions of eastern Asia. The generic name (*arachniodes* = like a spider) suggests the spidery habit of a clump. The genus is placed in the shield fern family, Dryopteridaceae.

Propagate by dividing the creeping rhizome in autumn or in very early spring. Propagation by spores is also successful; spores should be sown as soon as they are ripe on a coarse commercial mix with a pH of 7 to 8.5 maintained moist at 70°F (21°C).

Slugs seem to like my variegated shield ferns; other maladies and insects do not seem to bother them.

Arachniodes simplicior, variegated shield fern. Japan, China.

LS to FS; fronds to 4 ft. (1.2 m), produced in rosettes on slender stalks emerging directly from the rhizome, scaly at the base, stalk green, leaning; leaves 2- to 3-compound, lustrous dark green with a yellowish band along the midrib on both sides of the stalk, to 16 in. (40 cm) long and 10 in. (25 cm) wide, broadly ovate, tapering at the tip; leaflets (pinnae) wedge-shaped, narrow, pointed top; subleaflets deeply cut and toothed, mostly blunt-pointed; veins prominent. It grows to 28 in. (70 cm). Sometimes incorrectly sold as a selection ('Variegata') of *Arachniodes aristata*. *Arachniodes standishii* (upside-down fern) is similar but slightly smaller, to 20 in. (50 cm) and without variegation; its veins protrude conspicuously on the upper face of the leaflets, whereas in other species they can be seen on the underside only (hence the common name). Clones from northern Honshu and Hokkaido seem to be more hardy than those originating further south. Both species form slowly expanding clumps and should be placed in a shaded position, where no direct sun reaches during the heat of the day. Early morning sun is tolerated. They do best in a light, well-draining, acid woodland soil, rich in organic matter, and do well in the hot, humid southern regions of North America. Provide supplemental water during periods of drought.

Aralia

Large, leafy perennials are crucial to the success of the shady garden. This is abundantly epitomized by hostas, whose leaves play a major role in adding texture and color. Hostas, though, stay close to the ground—some taller, leafy presence is needed. Large perennials like those of the genus *Aralia* (spikenard) add such highlights and vertical emphasis. The genus includes shrubs and trees, including the very popular *Aralia elata* (variegated Japanese angelica tree), but the stately herbaceous perennial spikenards are practically unknown and rarely seen, perhaps because they are considered weedy by some. Indeed, *A. racemosa*, the native American spikenard, forms considerable colonies in the right conditions. Other spikenards are better behaved. *Aralia cordata* (Japanese spikenard), brought into Western cultivation by Siebold in the 1830s, is increasingly appreciated for its large, striking leaves and tall roundish umbels of white flowers. Several other species are available, all preferring moist shade, although they will tolerate considerable sun if grown in moist soil along stream banks or ponds. I made my first acquaintance with aralias during a summer trip through the Smoky Mountains. There I found *A. spinosa*, a shrubby aralia whose fitting common name, devil's walking stick, was inspired by its monstrous spiny trunk, prickly stalks, and bristly leaves. At least 15 ft. (5 m) tall, it was topped by huge umbels of greenish flowers, and the display was simply breathtaking. Although too large for my small garden, I made a mental note of it. Much later, I found the more restrained *A. cordata* in a friend's garden, and I was hooked.

Spikenards are native to North America and Asia. The species listed are benign—mostly lacking spikes and bristles altogether—so undeserving of the name spikenard. Most are hardy to zone 4. Their habitat is diverse, ranging from shady woodlands and thickets to open ravines and stream banks. Michel Sarrazin, physician at the Court of Quebec, sent various northern species of this group from North America to Europe in the early 1700s; the generic name stems from the French-Canadian *aralie*. *Aralia* is classified in the ginseng or aralia family, Araliaceae.

The Japanese spikenard's attractive large foliage adds a tropical flavor to the shady garden. The Japanese eat the young, blanched shoots of this plant; I use it as a bold accent plant, overtopping glades of hostas and ferns, its prominently veined leaves adding texture to the garden. It looks much like an oversized astilbe, providing striking vertical accent, particularly when in bloom in late summer. Flowers are followed by many purplish black berries. A sheltered location is recommended for this tall plant, whose large leaves catch the wind like sails; in very windy locations the flowerstalk may have to be staked. The soil must stay moist if this aralia is to be kept happy.

Propagate by dividing the dormant rhizome.

Aralias are prone to develop fungal leaf spot, which may require application of a fungicide. Aphids and other sucking insects can be controlled biologically or with a mild general-application insecticide. Stem-boring insects sometimes attack the plants; vigilance is required to detect this problem early.

Species listed are suitable for zones 4 to 8, unless otherwise noted.

Aralia californica, elk clover, California spikenard. Western North America, British Columbia to northern California.

Some sun, LS to WS; flowers many, arranged in roundish umbels on upright, branched racemes, white, inflorescence to 30 in. (75 cm) long; flowerstalks to 9 ft. (2.7 m), less in cultivation to 5 ft. (1.5 m); September; plant with rhizomatous rootstock, spreading; leaves 2-, sometimes 3-pinnate, 36 in. (90 cm) long, with 5–15 ovate leaflets, medium green, bristly, irregularly double-toothed, to 10 in. (25 cm) long; fruit many, black berries. A fine tall accent for the background of larger woodland gardens.

Aralia cordata, Japanese spikenard, *udo* (Jap.). Japan.

Some sun, LS to WS; flowers many, on upright, branched racemes, greenish white, inflorescence to 10 in. (25 cm) tall; flowerstalks 5–7 ft. (1.5–2 m), dark green to black; September; plant with rhizomatous rootstock, spreading; leaves 2- to 3-pinnate, 12 in. (30 cm) long, with 3–9 leaflets, medium green attractively marked lighter green along the veins, irregularly toothed, with acute tip, to 6 in. (15 cm) long; fruit many, purplish black berries. A stately accent in the garden. Its leaves are robust, and the plant is long-lasting. In fertile, moist soil this species forms colonies by means of creeping rhizomes; check each spring to curtail its spread. Hardy to zone 5, 4 with protection. *Aralia continentalis* from Korea is similar; its leaves are more finely textured, and the flower panicles are white, rounded, and pendulous. *Aralia cachemirica* from the Himalayas has long been grown in England but is seldom seen in North America; it can reach 10 ft. (3 m) and may be too large for many smaller gardens. Coming from sunny, exposed, mountainous positions, it may be marginal in very shady gardens. Hardy to zone 6.

Aralia nudicaulis, wild sarsaparilla. North America, British Columbia to Newfoundland, south to Georgia and west to Colorado.

Some sun, LS to WS; flowers many, in usually 3 ball-shaped umbels to 2 in. (5 cm) wide, on separate, upright, branched stem, white, to 12 in. (30 cm); May–June; plant with carrot-shaped taproot, spreading; leaves on separate, single stalk, to 20 in. (50 cm), rising above flowers, umbrellalike, 3-branched, each with 3–5 leaflets, ovate, light green, veins impressed, finely toothed, to 6 in. (15 cm) long; fruit many, black berries. This native species is much smaller than the other species listed, providing a nice spring accent in the wildflower garden. It spreads actively, so occasional attention is required to contain the colony. Similar to *Panax quinquefolius*, which is distinguished by its single umbel of flowers and red fruit. Wild sarsaparilla was used as a substitute for authentic sarsaparilla flavoring.

Aralia racemosa, American spikenard, spikenard, life-of-man, petty morel. North America, eastern Canada south to North Carolina and west to Arizona and Utah.

Some sun, LS to WS; flowers many, arranged in umbels on upright, branched racemes, white, inflorescence to 15 in. (38 cm) long; flowerstalks to 8 ft. (2.5 m), in cultivation to 5 ft. (1.5 m) or less; September; plant with rhizomatous rootstock, spreading; leaves 2-, sometimes 3-pinnate, 30 in. (75 cm) long, with 3–7 ovate leaflets, medium green, not bristly, irregularly toothed and serrated, to 8 in. (20 cm) long; fruit many, brownish purple berries. Similar to *Aralia californica* but not quite as large and a little more refined, making it more acceptable in smaller gardens. American Indians used it medicinally.

Arisaema

In 1969 our family moved to Tucker, Georgia, to build the home we live in today. Although the area had not been farmed since the 1930s, it was still known as Atlanta's "farm country," a hill-and-dale spot covered in second-growth loblolly pine forest punctuated by ancient oak trees, with some farm terraces still discernible coursing through the woods. As the area began to be built up—and long before we had a Georgia Native Plant Society—I raced bulldozers all over developing neighborhoods to rescue ferns and wildflowers. On one of these rescue missions, I discovered a colony of jack-in-the-pulpit that stood out among the undergrowth. I still have some of these particularly vigorous plants, whose leaves are taller, almost 4 ft. (1.2 m), than most jacks I have added since. "Jack" is the preacher—the clublike spadix standing in the "pulpit" formed by the encircling spathe, with a sheltering, pointed hood above it. The hood frequently covers the spadix and has to be lifted slightly to reveal it. The North American native jack-in-the-pulpit (*Arisaema triphyllum*) is so well

known and widespread in shady wildflower corners that many gardeners just call it jack.

With flower structures unlike most garden flowers, arisaemas have become an obsession; and with the recent importation of hardy exotic arisaemas from the Far East, not just collectors but many regular gardeners pride themselves on their latest acquisitions. Although the collective common name cobra lily (an allusion to the similarity of the flower to the raised head of a cobra) is most proper for arisaemas that come from the Himalayas, it is applied to other Asian arisaemas.

Many relish the diversity of arisaemas, and their size allows several to be included in a shady woodland garden. Happily, their growth in general is more up than out, so they can be mixed with lower-growing underplantings. And arisaemas provide an attractive display from spring until autumn. They are better garden plants than snake palms because they do not rest for a month or more between flowering and sending up a leafstalk; with snake palms, nothing shows above ground during this respite. Arisaema leaves emerge first, followed by the flower, and remain on the plant long after fruiting, when the withering spathe reveals an attractive seed cluster of tightly packed, colorful berries.

Botanists have known about *Arisaema triphyllum* since the mid-1700s. It was familiar to American Indians, who either cooked the tubers for a lengthy period and then used them as a source of starch (hence, Indian turnip) or sliced and dried the corms and ground them into flour. Early settlers dried the tubers, ground them, and used them as a pepper substitute. The corms contain calcium oxalate, which causes an intense burning sensation in the mouth if the corms are eaten raw; this same chemical was the basis for an insecticide. Wildlife loves the fleshy red fruit; I have observed chipmunks making off with them before I can harvest. Not as showy is another, lesser-known jack endemic to North America, *A. dracontium* (green dragon), which was also used as a source of starch and as a medicine for female problems. It has a light green leaf and flower, but the most notable feature is its whiplike spadix, which extends like a long mouse tail beyond the pointed spathe. My children always looked for a mouse caught in the spathe.

Both native North American arisaemas are now joined by an ever-increasing number of species from Nepal, northern India, western China, Taiwan, Thailand, Korea, and Japan. Some 150 species are now known, and plant hunters continue to scour Asian habitats to find additional species suitable for cultivation, which are then propagated from seed. Some newer species are still rare and therefore expensive, but most gardeners can afford to add one or two to their gardens. It may be just as well to grow and preserve a few of the Himalayan arisaemas in the West, in fact, because they may not be altogether safe in their habitat. Indian author Udai Pradhan writes about *Arisaema speciosum* being used as pig fodder. He recalls seeing whole populations being ripped out of the ground with the vegetative parts fed to the pigs and the tubers left behind. Fortunately, the farmers of Nepal and Sikkim have found it much more lucrative to sell the corms for horticultural use, and plant collectors oblige them.

Arisaemas are native to many different habitats. The North American arisaemas are hardy to zone 4 with protection; the Asian arisaemas vary in cold hardiness from zone 4 to zone 8. They require abundant water during their active growth cycle, but most must have a dry winter rest period. Tubers left in the ground demand fairly deep planting, to 4 in. (10 cm) for the larger tubers, less for the really small ones. The roots emerge from the top of the tuber, so the soil surrounding the tuber over the top and to the sides must be fertile, loose, and moisture-retentive. On the other hand, near perfect drainage is a must below the tuber to prevent rot. The tubers resent wet and cold soil in winter and so are difficult to grow outside where the ground stays soggy. During the winter rest period, they prefer a nearly dry soil but resent drying out completely. Where all this would be difficult to accomplish, tubers should be lifted and stored in barely moist peat in a cool garage or basement, where temperatures stay above freezing. Early-rising species can be kept inside until all danger of frost has passed. Examine tubers for soft spots before planting them out in spring, and remove any offsets (small corms emanating either directly from the mother tuber or on short, rhizomatous extensions) from the large tubers (they sap strength from the large tuber and may reduce top growth). Small tubers may be used to expand the planting or given away to friends. A similar recommendation holds true for the seed clusters, which are enormous in some species (*Arisaema taiwanense*, for example). The production of these fruiting bodies depletes the tubers energy reserves and diminishes future top growth, so the fading flowering structure should be removed. During their inevitable decline, the inflorescence of arisaemas is anything but ornate: their early removal not only helps conserve energy in the tuber but also improves the appearance of the plant.

I keep some of my better arisaemas in good commercial potting soil in large plastic pots, with plenty of room for the roots to grow. The pots have a gravel layer below the tuber to guarantee drainage. In spring, I plunge these pots into previously prepared holes, where they stay during the growing season. In autumn or whenever the plant goes dormant, I remove the pots and store them inside in cool but frost-free areas. The following spring they are returned to their former locations (I save their spots by inserting empty pots of the same size after removing the potted tubers in autumn). This method is best for all gardens where winters are wet and cold; by overwintering, even some half-tender species can animate northern gardens.

Arisaemas, like snake palms, never fail to become topics of conversation. They are ideally suited for the shady garden, rising above large and small hostas and woodland ferns, wildflowers, or groundcover, their distinctive, colorful flowers, striking leaves, and beautifully marked petioles accenting the panorama. Their neighbors must be chosen with care: some arisaemas are small, while others grow to 6 ft. (1.8 m). Do not place the tall ones in windy areas; the large leaves act like sails, and high winds can break the pulpy stems. Allow enough room between tubers for leaf expansion above; some leaf overlap is acceptable, but too much overlap hides the attractive flowers.

Arisaema is from the Greek *aron* (= arum) and *aima* (= blood-red), referring to the red markings of some leaves and the petioles. The genus belongs in the Araceae.

Propagate by taking offsets in autumn. Seed can be sown in autumn in a cold frame.

Viral diseases (dasheen mosaic virus) are reported. Large slugs and snails attack the fresh, young shoots in spring. Weevils are known to take bites out of the leaves, but at Hosta Hill—with weevils ever present, causing damage to azaleas—none have developed an appetite for arisaemas.

Species and cultivars listed tolerate considerable sun, preferably morning sun in more southern regions. Fruit for all is a cluster of red, brown, or blackish berries that remain on the plant until winter. Tubers should be overwintered indoors in northern areas wherever the soil freezes. Identification of arisaemas in commerce is sometimes problematic, as is the variability within a given species. It is not unusual to see green and purple flowers on different plants of the same species. Size also varies greatly in cultivation, so adjustments may be necessary.

Arisaema amurense, Amur cobra lily. Northern China and Korea, Amur river region, northern Japan.

LS to FS; inflorescence on short peduncle below or even with leaf; spathe to 5 in. (13 cm) long with light green tube, with flaring hood, purple to deep violet with 5 whitish green stripes, the central one wider; spadix with cylindrical appendage, green, slightly longer than tube; May–July; petiole 8–12 in. (20–30 cm) tall, purple to chiefly purple-mottled, sheathed below, with pseudostem to 4 in. (10 cm) long; leaf solitary, sometimes 2, with 5 radiating green leaflets, oblong lance-shaped, prominently veined, 4–5 in. (10–13 cm) long. A variable, hardy arisaema. Variety *robustum* is no more robust than the type, though its name suggests otherwise; var. *denticulatum* is differentiated from the species by toothed leaves. All are colorful arisaemas that fit well in a deeply shaded corner with other diminutive companion plants, such as small hostas, ferns, and astilbes. Hardy in zones 6 to 8.

Arisaema angustatum. Korea.

LS to FS; inflorescence to 18 in. (45 cm) tall; spathe to 6 in. (15 cm) long, hooded, green with narrow white stripes, light green, striped pinkish white outside, lighter inside; May–July; petiole to 40 in. (1 m), occasionally taller in the wild, compound leaf solitary, green with some grayish marbling in the leaflets. **Variety *peninsulae*** is very similar, distinguished only by the height of the inflorescence, which rises above the leaves on 4 ft. (1.2 m) flowerstalks. The bright red fruit held up high is eye-catching. A recent introduction, *Arisaema angustatum* var. *peninsulae* f. *variegata*, is similar to the species but has beautiful, pronounced irregular silver markings running along the midrib of the leaflets. Hardy to zone 5.

Arisaema candidissimum, white cobra lily. Western China.

LS to FS; peduncle below leaf, 3–4 in. (8–10 cm) long; spathe to 5 in. (13 cm) long, hooded, light green to pinkish white-striped outside, hood is a greenish pink with elongated tip, white-margined and -striped inside; spadix darker green toward top, with tapering appendage; June–July; petiole to 18 in. (45 cm) tall, light green with brownish, basal bract; leaf solitary, with 3 shiny green leaflets, broadly ovate, to 8 in. (20 cm) long. In some clones of this superb arisaema, the flower emerges before the leaves; in others the leaves unfold before the flower rises, which difference may be due to environmental conditions. I have grown this exquisite Chinese jack for several years, and from the initial two tubers a colony of more than a dozen plants has developed; their leaves unfold first, followed closely by the slightly fragrant flowers—you must get really close and have a good nose to detect it. The pinkish white flowers glow in the shade and cannot be missed. This lovely flowering jack deserves a special place in the garden, where it can be inspected at close range. The epithet is the Latin *candidissimum* (= the whitest), pointing to the very white spathe and hood. Hardy to zone 6, but it can be grown further north by potting the tubers and overwintering them inside. *Arisaema franchetianum*, also from western China, has almost identical leaves; differentiating these species is difficult when plants are not in flower. The flower of *A. franchetianum* is quite different, sitting on a long peduncle to 10 in. (25 cm), which is sheathed by purplish mottled bracts (cataphylls); the spathe tube is purple to brownish purple, striped white, hooded, with an elongated, pendulous tip. The spadix is club-shaped and contained in the spathe tube. Another jack with white flowers is *A. saxatile*; its inflorescence is smaller and more narrow than *A. candidissimum*.

Arisaema concinnum, elegant cobra lily. Himalayas, northern India, western China, Nepal, Bhutan.

LS to FS; peduncle 10 in. (25 cm), shorter than or sometimes even with the petiole, mostly green, rarely mottled with purple; spathe to 6 in. (15 cm) long, hooded, light green, rarely purple, with 5 wide white stripes, hood with elongated, down-pointing tip to 4 in. (10 cm) long; spadix darker green toward top, slightly longer than tube; May–June; petiole to 24 in. (60 cm) tall, same color as peduncle; leaf solitary, with 7–13 radiating, green to yellowish green leaflets, narrowly lance-shaped, with irregular piecrust margins, sharp-tipped, 6–12 in. (15–30 cm) long. Some clones of this superb rhizomatous arisaema have green spathes, others have purple spathes. In the wild, both forms are seen growing side by side. The epithet comes from the Latin *concinnus* (= elegant), and a refined plant it is, with striking narrow leaves hovering umbrellalike above the flower. Hardy in zones 6 to 9.

Arisaema consanguineum, consanguineous cobra lily. Himalayas, southern Tibet, northern India, western China, Nepal, Bhutan, Taiwan.

LS to FS; 10 in. (25 cm) peduncle, mostly green, rarely mottled with pink and brown, sheathed at the ground; spathe to 5 in. (13 cm) long, hooded, uniform light green or white-striped purple, flaring hood with elongated, drooping, threadlike tail to 6 in. (15 cm) long; spadix darker green or brownish toward top, slightly longer than tube; May–June; petiole to 40 in. (1 m), taller in cultivation, to 5 ft. (1.5 m), same color as peduncle, purple to chiefly purple-mottled, sheathed below, with pseudostem to 24 in. (60 cm) long; May–June; leaf solitary, with 11–22, usually 15, leaflets, to 14 in. (35 cm) long and very narrow, 0.5 in. (1 cm) or less, radiating, green to yellowish green leaflets, smooth margin, wavy, very narrowly lance-shaped, with tips lengthened into threadlike, drooping extensions, to 3 in. (8 cm) long; fruit cluster of red berries. This species is superficially similar to *Arisaema erubescens* and *A. concinnum*; the epithet (*consanguineum* = of the same blood) probably alludes to such a relationship. The most visible differences are the very long, threadlike extensions of the spadix hood and the equally long, thin leaf tips, both hanging down. In the wild, two clones of this arisaema are found, some with green and others with white-striped, purple spathes; some nurseries offer the purple flower, the more desirable jack, as 'Red Form' and the green one as 'Himalayan Form'. Variable plants from seedlings are also available. Hardy in zones 7 to 9.

Arisaema costatum, ribbed cobra lily. Eastern and central Nepal.

LS to FS; peduncle below leaf, 6–10 in. (15–25 cm) long; spathe tube to 5 in. (13 cm) long, cylindrical, slightly flattened into the hood at the top, dark reddish purple with clear white stripes outside, with elongated tip, striped inside and out, ribbed along stripes; spadix darker green toward top, with tapering, threadlike appendage often to 20 in. (50 cm) long; June–early July; petiole to 16 in. (40 cm) tall, light green tinged purple or brownish red, 2–3 basal bracts; leaf solitary, with 3 green leaflets, broadly ovate, the middle leaflet much larger, to 14 in. (35 cm) long, the leaves have distinct, closely spaced, parallel ribbed veins on the underside, hence the Latin epithet (*costatum* = elevated, ribbed). This arisaema has a graceful flower with the lines in the spathe tube flowing uninterrupted into the hood. Hardy to zone 7 with protection but best overwintered.

Arisaema dracontium, green dragon, dragon arum, Indian turnip. Eastern North America, Ontario, southern Quebec, and New Brunswick south through Appalachians to Georgia and along the coastal plain to Florida, west to eastern Texas, Michigan, and Wisconsin.

LS to FS; peduncle 10–20 in. (25–50 cm) long; spathe tube 4–8 in. (10–20 cm) long, tubular but open on the spadix side, light to medium green, flaring hood upright or bending, somewhat darker, small; spadix whitish at base, darker green tinged, with tapering upright, sometimes bending, appendage projecting to 10 in. (25 cm) above hood, in the upper part thinning, threadlike, slightly bending at the tip or straight; May–June; petiole to 36 in. (90 cm) tall, dull light green tinged, sometimes mottled with, brown, 2–3 basal bracts; leaf solitary, compound, with 5–15 dull green leaflets, ovate, acuminate, central ones larger to 8 in. (20 cm) long; fruit cluster of red berries. The spathe and long spadix is a fanciful portrayal of a dragon's tongue, hence the Latin epithet (*dracontium* = dragonlike). This native North American jack is not as showy as the exotic cobra lilies, but it is a graceful addition to the shady woodland, where it attracts attention by rising above smaller companions. A small colony of plants is better than a single specimen. Hardy in zones 4 to 9. Widely available from wildflower nurseries and of easy culture in the garden.

Arisaema elephas. Western China.

LS to FS; peduncle to 5 in. (13 cm); spathe a very dark purple-black with white lines, hooded; spadix thick, blackish purple extending beyond the spathe tube, to 12 in. (30 cm) long; June–July; petiole to 30 in. (75 cm) tall; leaf solitary, with 3 bold green leaflets, broadly ovate and pointed; fruit cluster of bright red berries. Scarcely available, it will eventually make an unusual addition to the Western shady garden.

Arisaema erubescens, blushing cobra lily. Himalayas, northern India, Darjeeling, Nepal, Bhutan.

LS to FS; peduncle, rose-colored and streaked red, shorter than petiole; spathe to 2 in. (5 cm) long, widening at the top, brownish purple sometimes red or purple, with 3–5 white stripes extending into hood, covered with a pinkish white bloom, hood flaring wide with reflexed lips and long, down-pointing tip to 3 in. (8 cm) long; spadix darker green or brownish, slightly longer than the spathe tube with a blunt, rounded tip; May–June; petiole to 20 in. (50 cm) tall, rose with brown mottling; leaf solitary, with 7–15 radiating leaflets, 5–10 in. (13–25 cm) long, shiny dark green above, smooth and glaucescent below, narrowly lance-shaped, broadest above the middle, with sharp, tapering tip. This rhizomatous, spreading Himalayan jack has striking shiny, undulate leaves and a flower with a whitish bloom (indumentum) that imparts a blush-pink appearance, to which the Latin epithet (*erubescens* = blushing, reddening) refers. A showy jack—makes a great solitary accent. Sometimes considered synonymous with or a variety of *Arisaema consanguineum*. Reported hardy to zone 4—questionable considering its native habitat. It is reliably hardy here in zone 7a; best to pot and overwinter it further north.

Arisaema exappendiculatum, appendixless cobra lily. Himalayas, Nepal.

LS to FS; peduncle to 9 in. (23 cm), spathe tube without hood but tapering from a roundish base to an elongated, erect tip, mostly purple-striped green, rarely purple, to 3 in. (8 cm) long, in-rolled margins, fully enclosing the cylindrical spathe tube; spadix small, to 1 in. (2.5 cm) long, fully enclosed; May–July; petiole to 20 in. (50 cm) tall, greenish to grayish purple; pseudostem short, leaf solitary, with 9–13 radiating leaflets, lance-shaped, broadest above the middle, 4–9 in. (10–23 cm) long, to 4 in. (10 cm) wide, green, median leaflets shorter. Differs from most Himalayan jacks by having an erect spathe, which looks like the tip of a

lance, without the usual hood-shaped limb. It is vigorously rhizomatous and spreads briskly in good garden soil. Its species name alludes to the missing spadix appendage. Scarcely tested in Western gardens but may be as hardy as other species from the area, to zone 6 or 7, with precautions or potted and overwintered. Where hardy, its spreading habit may be boon to gardeners.

Arisaema fargesii. Western China.

LS to FS; spathe a very dark purple-black with white lines, hooded; spadix with very long, thread-like, tapering appendage to 24 in. (60 cm) long; June–July; petiole to 30 in. (75 cm) tall; leaf solitary, with 3 shiny, light green leaflets, broadly ovate, to 15 in. (38 cm) long. A relatively new jack with bold leaves of heavy substance, similar to those of *Arisaema ringens*. Yet untested but nevertheless promises to be an exciting addition to many gardens.

Arisaema flavum, yellow-flowered cobra lily, owlface cobra lily. Himalayas from Afghanistan east to western China.

LS to FS; spathe tube almost globelike to 0.8 in. (2 cm) long and of lesser width, pale yellow to yellowish green, in the upper part brownish purple with purple stripes; junction of spathe tube and hood very constricted, hood yellowish green, purple inside at lower end, tip reflexed, pointing down; spadix small, contained in spathe tube; June–early July; pseudostem to 16 in. (40 cm), streaked brown, petiole to 18 in. (45 cm) tall; leaves 2, rarely 1, with 5–11 radiating, green leaflets with conspicuous veins, oblong lance-shaped, to 5 in. (13 cm) long. The small yellow flower gave this jack its name (*flavum* = yellow); it is a midget compared to others jacks, and if there is such a thing as a cute jack, this is the one. The leaves are not small, but this arisaema requires a place up front to assure the cute inflorescence is not overlooked. Hardy here in zone 7a but best overwintered further north. The tuber is small, so mark its location carefully. Being from a subalpine region, it requires perfect drainage under the tuber. In a locality to its liking, it will seed itself around.

Arisaema griffithii, Griffith's cobra lily. Himalayas, northern India, Darjeeling, Nepal, Bhutan.

LS to FS; peduncle short; spathe very large and decorative, tube to 3 in. (8 cm) long, purple with white stripes, ribbed, hood very wide at the top, to 8 in. (20 cm), winged, folded over and downward, centrally convex above the tube and with a tapering tip to 4 in. (10 cm), deep violet-purple with closely spaced lines of pale yellow to white on the facing surface, with large lateral lobes forming ovate flaps, deep violet with yellowish or greenish veins all over; spadix clublike, purple, to 5 in. (13 cm) long, with tapering, threadlike appendage often held in the hood, but mostly reaching the ground, very long, tortuous, to 40 in. (1 m); March–May; petiole to 30 in. (75 cm) tall, purple or brownish red speckled with light green, 2–3 large basal bracts; leaves 2, with 3 leaflets, puckered, green with yellowish, red, or purplish wavy margins, 8–10 primary veins impressed above and elevated below, broadly ovate, sometimes rhombic in outline, the middle leaflet much larger, to 18 in. (45 cm) long. This somewhat tender arisaema has not only the largest flower but the most bizarre inflorescence in the genus—the entire plant looks menacing, but it is, nevertheless, fascinating and attractive. Most likely the common name of the genus, cobra lily, is traceable to this Himalayan jack: the winged hood of the flower suggests the raised head of a cobra. Variety *pradhanii* is said to be larger; var. *verrucosum* differs from the type by having a smaller spathe hood that is ovate above the spathe tube, not convoluted, and warts on the very dark, almost black petiole and peduncle, hence the varietal name, from the Latin *verruca* (= wart). *Arisaema griffithii* resents our cold, wet soil and comes up early in spring; I found it best to pot the tuber and overwinter it inside, allowing for it to be brought inside during late freezes, after it emerges. Hardy to zone 8. *Arisaema utile* is very similar but smaller, to 20 in. (50 cm) high, with a much shorter peduncle, a shorter hood tip extension, and a much longer spadix appendage, to 8 in. (20 cm) long.

Arisaema heterophyllum. Korea.

LS to FS; spathe to 5 in. (13 cm) long, hooded, uniform light green, white-striped, flaring hood with elongated, downward-drooping threadlike tail to 6 in. (15 cm) long; spadix darker green, slightly longer than tube; June–July; petiole to 40 in. (1 m) tall, dull green, with pseudostem to 24 in. (60 cm) long; May–June; leaf solitary, with leaflets to 10 in. (25 cm) long and very narrow, radiating from the petiole, dull light green, smooth margin, wavy, very narrowly lance-shaped, with tips lengthened into threadlike, drooping extensions; fruit cluster of red berries. The epithet *heterophyllum* (= different leaves) alludes to the leaves being different from other species in the area. *Arisaema consanguineum* is superficially similar and is sometimes supplied in lieu of *A. heterophyllum*; caution is advised before ordering.

Arisaema intermedium, Blume's cobra lily. Himalayas from Afghanistan east to western China.

LS to FS; spathe recurved, green, rarely purple-tinged, hood yellowish green, striped whitish, with a long, tapering tip to 3 in. (8 cm) long; spadix extending beyond spathe tube with very long, tapering, threadlike appendage, to 24 in. (60 cm), sometimes longer; May–June; petiole to 12 in. (30 cm) tall; leaves 2, with 3 green leaflets, broadly ovate, networked with many veins, piecrust margins, to 10 in. (25 cm) long. Attractive leaves, a fascinating flower, and a curious spadix tail that meanders down and across the ground make this an interesting jack. Hardy to zone 6 with protection; pot in areas of wet winters. Native to the higher elevations of the Himalayas, at above 8000 ft. (2800 m), it requires a cool spot in deep shade and dislikes hot summer temperatures. The same goes for var. *biflagellatum*, which is distinguished by a longer tail on the hood but is otherwise much like the type.

Arisaema iyoanum, Japanese cobra lily. Japan, Shikoku.

LS to FS; peduncle very short, spathe with hood blackish purple striped pinkish green, with a long, tapering tip; spadix club-shaped, green with dark brown, almost black spotting; May–June; petiole spotted dark brownish purple, to 24 in. (60 cm) tall; leaf solitary, compound, with 9–13 green leaflets, ovate lance-shaped, arranged like a horseshoe. Hardy to zone 7. Can be tried in colder areas with protection. It should be potted in areas of cold and wet or freezing winter soils. Also available is subsp. *nakaianum*, which has rolled edges on its clublike spadix.

Arisaema jaquemontii, Jaquemont's cobra lily. Himalayas, Afghanistan, southeastern Tibet, northern India, Darjeeling, Nepal, Bhutan.

LS to FS; flowers carried above leaves; spathe to 6 in. (15 cm) long, widening at the top, a very light whitish green, sometimes barely white-striped, hood flaring, extending over the spathe tube, tip of green, barely striped, hood elongated into a vertically ascending, green, rarely purple, tail-like tip to 5 in. (13 cm) long; spadix slender, darker green purplish toward top, slightly longer than the spathe tube, bending forward and down; June–July; petiole to 20 in. (50 cm) tall, but mostly less, shorter than the inflorescence, light green; leaf solitary, occasionally 2, with 3–9, usually 5, radiating leaflets, to 7 in. (18 cm) long, light green with prominent veins, lance-shaped, broadest above the middle, wavy in the margins, with sharp, tapering tip. One of the hardiest Himalayan species, outstanding for carrying its flowers above the leaves, where the unusual long, upright tail extending from the hood can be observed. I planted a small colony in a shady corner underplanted with white-flowering *Mazus reptans*. Hardy to zone 6, with pot culture required in colder regions. Where it can be left in the ground, it soon propagates by offsets.

Arisaema kiushianum, Kyushu cobra lily. Japan, Kyushu.

LS to FS; without pseudostem, peduncle to 6 in. (15 cm) arising from the ground next to petiole; spathe to 5 in. (13 cm) long, widening at the top, purple, hood broadly flaring, extending over the spathe tube with long up-slanting, pointed tip, dark purple with white T-shaped marking inside; spadix club-shaped, projecting, with threadlike extension rising up, then hanging down; July; petiole dark brownish green to 16 in. (40 cm) tall; leaf solitary, with 9–11 radiating leaflets, to 8 in. (20 cm) long, green, lance-shaped, broadest above the middle, with sharp, tapering tip. A showy species with prominent white markings inside the hood. Hardy to zone 6b. It emerges late and blooms in July, so late freezes are not a problem.

Arisaema limbatum. Japan, east-central Honshu.

LS to FS; spathe on 10 in. (25 cm) long peduncle emerging between the leaf petioles, spathe rising above leaves, to 5 in. (13 cm) long, hooded, uniform green with whitish green stripes outside, purplish green, white-striped inside hood, flaring hood that is blunt or pointed with broad, drooping ear-like lobes (auricles); spadix short, inside spathe tube, whitish green, darker green toward top, slightly longer than tube; April–May; petiole to 30

in. (75 cm), taller in cultivation, to 5 ft. (1.5 m), greenish purple, mottled darker purple, sheathed with pseudostem to 24 in. (60 cm) long; leaves 2, digitate, with 3–9 medium green leaflets, smooth margin, wavy, broadly egg-shaped, tapering to a sharp, extended tip. Occasionally, the leaves are marked with irregular, whitish gray markings along the midrib, with tips lengthened to a sharp point; some cultivated specimens lack the tail. This tall, attractive Japanese jack from Chiba Prefecture is an early riser. Here it is always too early and gets nipped by a late freeze. I keep it in a pot in a cool, dry place until mid-April, when it gets buried outside, pot and all. With warming weather, it comes up quickly and keeps pace with the other jacks, blooming here in late May. This lets me enjoy its commanding presence without freeze worries. In autumn the pot with the tuber gets put back into storage again.

Arisaema maximowiczii. Japan, Kyushu.

LS to FS; spathe to 5 in. (13 cm) long, widening at the top, whitish at the base, light green tube with white stripes, hood extending over the spathe tube, green, white-striped; spadix club-shaped with projecting, slender extension to 7 in. (18 cm) long, drooping; June–July; petiole to 16 in. (40 cm) tall, green, with basal bracts marked dark brown; leaf solitary, with 3–9 radiating leaflets, green, lance-shaped, broadest above the middle, with sharp, tapering tip. Hardy to zone 6b.

Arisaema minamitanii. Japan, Kyushu.

LS to FS; spathe green, widening at the top, hood extending over the spathe tube; spadix club-shaped; June; petiole to 16 in. (40 cm) tall, green, with basal bracts marked dark brown; leaf solitary, with 5 radiating leaflets, green, lance-shaped, broadest above the middle, with sharp, tapering tip. This species, recently discovered on Kyushu in Miyazaki Prefecture, is similar to *Arisaema robustum* and is reported to be a durable garden plant. Hardy to zone 6.

Arisaema negishii. Japan, Kyushu.

LS to FS; peduncle arising between the leaf petioles; spathe held above foliage, shiny green, striped reddish brown, widening at the top, hood extending over the spathe tube; spadix whip-shaped, exserted; May–July; petiole to 36 in. (90 cm) tall, green; leaves 2, compound, with 3–9 leaflets, green, ovate lance-shaped, with tapering tips, arranged like a horseshoe. This Japanese jack also occurs in extreme southern Honshu and many of the southern islands. Hardy in zones 6 to 9.

Arisaema nepenthoides, nepenthes-like cobra lily, yellow cobra plant. Himalayas, northern India, Nepal east to Sikkim, Bhutan, Darjeeling, northern Burma, western China.

LS to FS; peduncle long, with flower held at, beneath, or slightly above the leaves, mottled dull brownish purple; spathe tube to 7 in. (18 cm) long, greenish red or brown, spotted darker, with 3–5 wide lines on the back, hood whitish inside, yellowish outside, as wide as the spathe tube, slightly flaring, tapering tip incurved; spiraling, earlike appendages projecting 1 in. (2.5 cm) each side at the base of the hood, purple, green spotted brown with purple margins; spadix projected, clublike, white to pale yellow; May–June; pseudostem tall, yellow tinged pink on top, yellowish brown toward base, with large, spotted bracts; petiole to 18 in. (45 cm) tall, yellowish brown, with striated dark reddish brown lines; leaves 2, rarely 3, each with 5–7 palmate leaflets, glossy dark green above, glaucous beneath, narrowly lance-shaped, broadest above the middle, middle larger, to 20 in. (50 cm) long. The spathe tube of this Himalayan jack is colored like the pitchers of *Nepenthes refflesiana* (monkey cup), a tropical, climbing pitcher plant, hence the epithet *nepenthoides* (= like a nepenthes). Marvelous and showy in the garden. Hardy to zone 8, but I have had it potted in the ground during mild winters in zone 7a. Because this species resents cold, wet soil, I find it is better to bring the potted tubers inside, pot and all, to overwinter, then place them back in the accustomed spot the following spring. As the tubers grows, they may need repotting from time to time. This jack is occasionally available under one of its synonyms, particularly *Arisaema ochraceum*, signifying its pigmentation (*ochraceus* = ochre-yellow, yellowish brown). Its showy flower and unusual color display are well worth the extra effort. Variable in height.

Arisaema propinquum, Wallich's cobra lily. Himalayas, Kashmir, Nepal, Bhutan, southeast Tibet.

LS to FS; peduncle long, but shorter than petioles, mottled dull brownish purple; spathe to 6 in.

(15 cm) long, cylindrical, deep purple with white stripes with hood widened, flaring, dark reddish purple with white stripes, latticed white toward margin, with pointed, elongated tail, bending down; spadix darker green or purple, slender, with tapering, threadlike appendage to 2 in. (5 cm) long, extending from mouth and held subhorizontally, sometimes hanging down; May–June; petiole to 18 in. (45 cm) tall, green or green spotted purple or brownish red; leaves 2, each with 3 glossy green leaflets on short leafstalks, broadly ovate, the middle leaflet sometimes shorter, to 8 in. (20 cm) long, with closely spaced, reticulate veins on the underside. The epithet is from the Latin *propinquus* (= near, neighboring; in the sense of "related to"), indicating its affinity to *Arisaema costatum*, which has prominent parallel, as opposed to reticulate, veins. Plants hailing from the subalpine regions of Sikkim (available under the name *sikkimense*) are slightly different and are better planted in a rock garden. The common name honors the botanist Wallich, who first described the Nepalese arisaemas in 1824. This jack is suitable to more northern gardens, being hardier than *A. costatum*. Hardy to zone 5 with protection; in areas of wet and cold winter soils, it is best overwintered.

Arisaema ringens, ringent cobra lily, gaping mouth cobra lily. China, Taiwan, Korea, Japan, Shikoku.

LS to FS; peduncle short to 2 in. (5 cm); spathe tube to 3 in. (8 cm) long, purple with light green stripes, sometimes uniform pale green, hood wide, sharply incurved, sitting helmet-shaped atop the spathe tube, with deep purple, almost black, curled, earlike appendages each side; spadix enclosed, not visible, club-shaped, white to pale yellow; May–June; petiole to 18 in. (45 cm) tall, brownish with green markings at the base fading to solid green further up; leaves 2, with 3 leaflets, glossy medium green with prominent depressed veins above and elevated beneath, broadly ovate, 18–36 in. (45–90 cm) long, with brownish purple, threadlike but stiff leaf tip extensions to 2 in. (5 cm) long. The best of all exotic jacks when it comes to uncomplicated culture and long-lasting display value in the shady garden. Its leaves are among the largest I have seen and exceed many published descriptions; I have measured as much as 50 in. (1.3 m) across the leaflets of a leaf. The leaflets have great substance and come through hot, dry summers here with aplomb. Like the large-leaved hostas, they need plenty of water, but when left alone during a few days of absence, no harm was done by the heat and dryness. Here the leaves emerge a light green, ripening to a darker green, and they are never without their beautiful gloss; they stay on the plant until early November, providing a continuing accent from early spring until autumn. Aside from the superb leaves, the spring-blooming flower is something to behold: as the epithet indicates, it looks much like the gaping mouth of a sinister, dark monster. This is inferred by the Latin *ringens*, which usually characterizes a one-petaled flower with the upper limb (hood) pressed against the lower one (spathe tube). The construction is impossible to describe, and in this case a picture is worth more than a thousand words. One of the most impressive and showy arisaemas for the open garden, it has survived temperatures to 0°F (−18°C) here for short periods with protection to keep the soil from freezing. Hardy to zone 5, but it can be grown in pots anywhere if the corm is overwintered in a frost-free place. *Arisaema ringens* is variable—for example, the lips of the spathe, which are mostly purple, can also be green. Forma *glaucescens*, a form from the Ryukyu Islands with a glaucous, whitish coating covering the flower, is available but still rare. In Europe *A. ringens* of gardens is actually *A. robustum*, so be cautious when ordering from European sources. The easiest way to tell these species apart is by the number of leaflets: 3 for *A. ringens*, 5 for *A. robustum*.

Arisaema robustum, robust cobra lily. Eastern Russia, Sakhalin, Japan, Korea.

LS to FS; short peduncle; spathe green, rarely purple, with white stripes outside, white-striped dark purple inside, to 3 in. (8 cm) long, with ear-like coils at junction with tube, widening at the top, hood held obliquely upward or horizontal over the spathe tube, slightly incurved, with long extended tip; spadix club shaped, truncate, green; June–July; pseudostem to 14 in. (35 cm) with large basal bracts, with petiole to 10 in. (25 cm) tall, green; leaf 1, rarely 2, with 5 radiating leaflets, green, obovate with sharp, tapering tip. This large, and as the epithet indicates, robust arisaema makes an excellent landscape plant for the open garden, whether used as an accent in mass plantings of ferns and smaller hostas or to punctuate ground-

cover in the shady woodland. Many available plants of this variable jack are raised from seed, so expect minor differences. Hardy to zone 5; in areas of wet and cold winter soils, it is best overwintered.

Arisaema saxatile, rock-dwelling cobra lily. Japan.

LS to FS; spathe long, narrow tube, perfect white outside, long hood upright to slightly oblique; spadix cylindrical, green, tapering and extending beyond the spathe tip; June–July; petioles to 15 in. (38 cm) tall; leaves 2, with 3 leaflets, green, narrowly lance-shaped with sharp, tapering tip. This recent introduction is a distinctive, elegant jack for the garden. Hardy to zone 7. Its epithet is from the Latin *saxatilis* (= dwelling among rocks), alluding to its native habitat. The flowers are lovely, brightening up shady corners with their glowing white spathes.

Arisaema sazensoo. Japan.

LS to FS; spathe emerging on peduncle between the leaf petioles, to 5 in. (13 cm) long, widening at the top, purple outside, whitish inside, long hood extending over and beyond the spathe tube, purple, with 5 greenish white stripes; spadix cylindrical, truncate; June–July; petioles to 12 in. (30 cm) tall, green or greenish with dark brown markings, basal bracts; leaves 2, with 5 radiating leaflets, green, lance-shaped, broadest above the middle, with sharp, tapering tip. This Japanese jack is new to Western gardens and a good garden plant. Its epithet is from the Japanese *sazen* (= meditation), for the drooping hood, which looks much like a bowing Buddhist monk. A rare albino form is available; its spathe is a translucent light jade-green. This species and *Arisaema sikokianum* are mixed up in commerce, so verification before ordering is advised. Hardy to zone 6b.

Arisaema serratum, Japanese cobra lily. China, Korea, Japan, Kurile Islands.

LS to FS; peduncle long, but shorter than petioles, mottled dull brownish purple; spathe to 5 in. (13 cm) long, cylindrical, pale green with white stripes or purple spots, or dark purple; hood slightly widened, flaring, with pointed tip, pale green with purple spots or dark purple with whitish green stripes; spadix darker green, short, with blunt, round tip; May–June; pseudostem to 20 in. (50 cm) with petioles to 20 in. (50 cm) tall, green mottled with dark brownish purple; leaves 2, each with 7–9 green, radiating leaflets, wavy, narrowly lance-shaped, to 10 in. (25 cm) long; the leaflet margins can be smooth but are frequently toothed, hence the epithet, from the Latin *serratus* (= toothed). This species is variable in other details as well, including the color of the spathe and the height of the plant; a detailed description should be obtained before ordering. I have measured some plants at almost 5 ft. (1.5 m) tall; at Hosta Hill it has reached 4 ft. (1.2 m). In most clones, the flower exceeds the leaves in height. This tall addition to the shady garden looks fabulous popping out of plantings of woodland ferns or larger hostas, and it can replace Asiatic lilies in the more shady areas of the garden. Hardy to zone 5, possibly zone 4. **'Silver Pattern'**, with attractive silver markings, provides outstanding interest even when not in flower and is well worth the considerable additional cost. If only one example of this species can be planted, this is the one.

Arisaema sikokianum, Shikoku cobra lily. Japan, Shikoku.

LS to FS; peduncle long, to 12 in. (30 cm), but shorter than petioles, mottled dull brownish purple; spathe to 8 in. (20 cm) long, the base of the tube arising decurrent to the peduncle, with no abrupt transition, tube pinched at the center, flaring at the top, interior yellowish white to pure white, dull brownish purple at the base, exterior dark purple or deep reddish brown; hood pinched at the base then widening, erect, with up-pointed tip, margins slightly incurved, purple inside with 5–9 whitish green stripes, darker purple outside; spadix pure white, short, erect, slightly emerging above tube, cylindrical with enlarged, knoblike top; May–June; petioles to 20 in. (50 cm) tall, green mottled with dark brownish purple; leaves 2, unequal in height, the lower with 3 leaflets, the upper with 5, leaflets wavy, broadly ovate, dark green or dark green with whitish gray markings along the midrib, toothed, sometimes smooth-margined, with slightly depressed veins, to 6 in. (15 cm) long. This is the cobra lily everyone talks about, and with its unequal leaflet count and gaping flower (whose white mouth contains a jack like that of no other arisaema), it is also the easiest to identify. Some gardening duffers compare it to a smooth golf ball sitting on a fat tee. Flowering-size tubers exact a premium price, but its commanding presence when in flower makes this investment worth every penny. It has, as Barry Yinger puts it, a "wow" impact. Occasionally sold as *Arisaema sazensoo*. Although most clones in commerce are variegated, some nurseries have selected outstanding clones with silvery gray markings along the leaf midrib; these are available as *A. sikokianum* 'Variegata'. Hardy to zone 5. Potting is the best way to protect this valuable jack. Hybrids are rare in the wild, but some have been made in cultivation, most recently *A. sikokianum* × *A. takedae*, a vigorous cross that reaches 4 ft. (1.2 m) with leaflets attractively silver-marbled; the light yellowish green flowers are otherwise similar to those of *A. sikokianum*.

Arisaema speciosum, showy cobra lily, pig arisaema, *sungure-to* (Punjabi). Himalayas, Nepal east to western China.

LS to FS; peduncle short, rising from the ground; spathe to 8 in. (20 cm), very dark purple, striped white and ribbed, white inside with purple margins at the mouth; hood very long, purple inside and out, margins rolled up, long tip projecting over and far beyond the mouth, elongated, tapering tip bending down subhorizontally; spadix greenish yellow fading to purplish green toward top, bending forward, with very long, tapering, reddish purple, threadlike appendage, to 32 in. (80 cm), sometimes longer; early May–June; no pseudostem; petiole to 28 in. (70 cm) tall; leaf solitary, with 3 large, green leaflets, the middle one larger, broadly ovate, margins sometimes flushed red, to 18 in. (45 cm) long. Attractive leaves and a large flower with an outlandish spadix tail that extends far beyond the fascinating flower, meandering down and across the ground, make this an interesting jack. It comes up early, so protection from late freezes is in order. The epithet comes from the Latin *speciosus* (= showy). Hardy to zone 8, 7 with protection, but potting is suggested. Variety *mirabile* differs by having a spadix that is distended at the top and somewhat rugose. It is rarely available.

Arisaema taiwanense, Taiwanese cobra lily. Taiwan.
LS to FS; spathe to 8 in. (20 cm), emerging from the ground on very short stalk (peduncle), slightly widening at the top, blackish purple outside, very large hood extending over and beyond the spathe tube, dark purple; spadix cylindrical with a long

tapering tip coming to a blunt, bent-forward end; white; May–June; petioles to 4 ft. (1.2 m) tall, green or greenish with dark reddish brown or purple markings; leaf solitary, rarely 2, with 9–17 radiating leaflets, 12 in. (30 cm) long, green, ovate, with tapering tips that terminate in a threadlike, vertically drooping 2 in. (5 cm) tip extensions; fruit cluster very large, egg-shaped, first green then scarlet-red. Hardy in zone 6, but given its subtropical origin, I pot and overwinter it. There is no reason to take chances with this beautiful jack, described as being the python-skinned queen of the genus. Abundant fruiting under favorable conditions lowers the vitality of this Taiwanese jack, so removal of the fruit cluster at an early stage is advised. Seed may not come true if this species is grown in the vicinity of other Japanese jacks. Remove offsets from the corm to propagate true offspring.

Arisaema tashiroi. Japan.

LS to FS; spathe green with white interior, hood erect with up-pointing tip extending over the spathe tube; spadix green, cylindrical, truncate; May–June; petioles to 36 in. (90 cm) tall, green or greenish with dark brown to purple markings, basal bracts; leaves 2, with green leaflets, lance-shaped, broadest above the middle, with sharp, tapering tip. A recent introduction and reportedly a good garden plant. Hardy to zone 6b.

Arisaema ternatipartitum. Japan.

LS to FS; inflorescence emerging on long peduncle at leaf juncture, to 12 in. (30 cm); spathe to 3 in. (8 cm) long with green tube with flaring hood, with small, earlike extensions; spadix short, green; May–July; petiole 8 in. (20 cm) tall, mottled, with pseudostem to 2 in. (5 cm) long; leaves 2, each with 3 green leaflets, oblong lance-shaped, 4–6 in. (10–15 cm) long. Rhizomes are sent out from the small tuber, forming colonies. This petite arisaema is a cute addition to gardens. Its size limits use in the open garden; better to plant it in a raised bed or rock garden or near a path. Definitely worth a try. Hardy to zone 6b.

Arisaema thunbergii, Thunberg's cobra lily. Southern Japan.

LS to FS; peduncle to 8 in. (20 cm) long, shorter than petioles, mottled dull brownish purple; spathe tube cylindrical, greenish mottled heavily with dark brownish red or dark purple or whitish green with wide purple stripes; hood slightly widened, flaring and arching over the mouth of the tube, with pointed tip with a thin, tapering extension, dark purple with whitish green stripes outside, brown with pale greenish stripes inside; spadix green with threadlike appendage to 20 in. (50 cm), thickened and wrinkled at the base, with the outer portion hanging down; May–June; petioles to 24 in. (60 cm) tall, green spotted with dark brownish purple; leaf usually solitary with 9–17 wavy, dark green leaflets, compound, arranged horseshoelike, narrowly lance-shaped with elongated tip, to 10 in. (25 cm) long. At Hosta Hill this tall addition to the shady garden has reached 28 in. (70 cm). Goes dormant fairly early, so should be combined with companion plant able to fill in a bare spot, like larger woodland ferns or hostas. Remove the numerous offsets; if allowed to remain, they make colonies too dense for good cultivation. It is of easy culture and vigorous when planted out in the open woodland garden. This jack is named for early plant hunter Carl Peter Thunberg, who wrote a compendium of Japanese plants, *Flora Japonica*, in 1784. Hardy to zone 6b but might require potting in certain microclimates. Subspecies *urashima* has a spadix apppendage that is smooth at the base. The subspecies is also offered as *A. urashima*; plants I have seen under this name, however, have rougher and wider leaves, bloom later, and are hardy to zone 5, although these differences may be attributed to cultural conditions.

Arisaema tortuosum, tortuous cobra lily, tall cobra lily. Himalayas, northern India, Kashmir, Nepal, Sikkim, Bhutan, Darjeeling, northern Burma, southwestern China.

LS to FS; peduncle long, with flower occasionally held above leaves, but sometimes of equal height or shorter, mottled dull brownish purple; spathe to 8 in. (20 cm) long, usually green, rarely purple, with barely discernible light green lines; hood whitish inside, green outside, as wide as the spathe tube, slightly flaring, bending over and extending beyond tube; spadix extension tail-like, green to blackish purple, smooth, thick, projecting from the mouth of the tube first erect, then outward in a shallow, upright S-curve, tapering to a thin tip, to 10 in. (25 cm) long; May–June; pseudostem to 8 ft. (2.5 m), heavily mottled reddish brown or purple, occasionally green, with large, spotted bracts below; compound leaves 2, rarely 3, each with 5–17 leaflets, green, ovate to lance-shaped, broadest above the middle, to 12 in. (30 cm) long; fruit cluster bright scarlet. If *Arisaema taiwanense* is the queen of arisaemas when it comes to size, this Himalayan jack is definitely the king. Even small tubers give rise to 5 ft. (1.5 m) tall plants. This jack is variable in its colors, but the berry cluster's color is always a beacon to all. The spathe may not be the most colorful in the genus, but its tortuously bending spadix extension (to which the epithet refers) is usually held high above the leaves, becoming a serpentine focal point in the garden. Gardeners who have had trouble showing off a jack among taller plantings should definitely plant this one—there is no way anyone can miss this giant. I have it popping up between large blue and gray hostas and established clumps of reddish dark green autumn fern, where the color contrast brings out the best in this jack. Also offered under its synonym *A. helleborifolium*, which epithet indicates the similarity of its leaves with those of the hellebore. Hardy to zone 7a. Pot in colder areas; it comes up early, so protect from late freezes.

Arisaema triphyllum, jack-in-the-pulpit, Indian turnip, dragonroot. Eastern North America, southeastern Quebec and New Brunswick south through Appalachians to North Carolina, Georgia, and Florida, west to Louisiana and eastern Texas.

LS to FS; peduncle short; spathe 2–3 in. (5–8 cm) long, spathe tube tubular, light to medium green or reddish purple; hood flaring, margins recurved, bending forward and sometimes slightly down over the spathe tube, with the hood tip sharply pointed and extending far beyond the tube, pointing down or curving back up; spadix appendage green or purple, cylindrical with rounded top, exerted beyond tube; April–June; petiole 12–36 in. (30–90 cm) tall, dull light green or dark brownish purple with greenish linear markings; leaves 2, with 3, rarely 5 leaflets, dull medium green, sometimes dark green, conspicuously veined, ovate, with sharp tip, central ones slightly larger, 3–8 in. (8–20 cm) long; long-lasting fruit cluster of red berries. This native North American jack got its name from the usual arrangement of the leaflets (*triphyllum* = three leaves). Taxonomists have treated this variable jack variously, sometimes classifying its distinct forms as separate species. The main difference is color, though sizes vary considerably as well. **Variety *atrorubens*** ('Atrorubens'; purple jack, ruby jack) is the most desired form, with its fine reddish purple coloration; the leaves are sometimes grayish green underneath. Subspecies *stewardsonii* (Indian turnip), a northern form, grows in swamps and bogs of eastern Canada and south in the northern Appalachians; its spathe tube has prominent ridges. Frequent in wet soils along the Atlantic coastal plain and the Piedmont from New England to Georgia and Florida is a smaller form with light green leaves and a spathe that is sometimes blackish inside; both the spathe tube and hood are lightly, sometimes barely perceptibly, striped with a whitish green. This jack frequently has only a solitary leaf with 3 leaflets. A form with ridged white stripes is available as 'Zebrinus'. I am growing an unusual variation saved from the bulldozers; it easily reaches 4 ft. (1.2 m) and has very large leaves, to 14 in. (35 cm) long and 27 in. (69 cm) across. While the spathe hood of the smaller forms is usually closed, the hood of this large form is open, and the petioles, pseudostem, and leaf veins have a dark purple color. The purple jacks are most striking but any of these native North American jacks makes a great addition to the shady garden. They are of easy culture, going on year after year with minimum care. Seed can be saved and sown in the garden as soon as ripe, after removing the pulp. Hardy in zones 4 to 9.

Arisaema yamatense. Japan, southern and central Honshu.

LS to FS; peduncle short, rising from the petiole; spathe to 5 in. (13 cm), variable in color, but usually green outside, white inside, margins recurved at opening; hood green with short tip projecting over and beyond the mouth, yellowish white inside; spadix cylindrical, white with a green, slightly expanded blunt head; early May–June; petiole to 5 ft. (1.5 m), very light green mottled with brownish purple, sometimes almost white with the same pattern; leaf solitary, rarely 2, with 7–11 green leaflets, finger-leaved (pedate), with pointed tip, to 15 in. (38 cm) long; fruit cluster large, reddish orange. A variable species. Some specimens have an extremely attractive snake pattern of purple on white or green on purple; some have variegation along the midrib of the leaflets, but they are most often plain green. The spathe is plain green, but the inside of the hood is an attractive white. Hardy to zone 6. Variety *sugimotoi* is distinguished by having 2 leaves per stem but is otherwise similar; its more copious leaf mound makes it a better garden plant.

Arisaema yunnanense. China, Yunnan.

LS to FS; spathe and hood green, white-striped; spadix tapering, extending horizontally from spathe tube, light green to green; May–June; petiole to 18 in. (45 cm) tall; leaf usually solitary, with 3 green leaflets, the middle one larger, broadly ovate. This modest, mostly green jack is occasionally available.

Arisarum

Found in the Mediterranean region, southwestern Europe, and the Atlantic islands, the arisarums are very similar to the cobra lilies, *Arisaema*, only smaller. Of the three species in the genus, only one, the fairly tender *Arisarum proboscideum*, is suitable for gardening in deep shade.

The generic name is from *arisaron*, the classical Greek name for *Arisarum vulgare*, which needs sun. *Arisarum* belongs in the Araceae.

Propagate by dividing the tubers in autumn or very early spring. Seed can be sown in autumn or spring in a cold frame.

Diseases and attacks by insects are uncommon.

Arisarum proboscideum, mouse plant, mousetail plant. Italy, Spain.

LS to FS; peduncle short, to 6 in. (15 cm); spathe to 7 in. (18 cm) long with red to dark brown tube fading to pure white in the basal part; hood red to pinkish brown with the upper part forming a thin, whiplike tip to 6 in. (15 cm) long, reddish or brownish pink at base turning to pinkish white toward tip; spadix enclosed in tube; April–May; plant tuberous-rhizomatous; leaves simple, glossy green, arrow-shaped to 6 in. (15 cm) long on petioles to 10 in. (25 cm), emerging in crowded bundles. The tufts of shiny leaves are attractive and add diversity to shady gardens; they all but obliterate the small spathe, from which the long spadix extension emerges (hence its common names). The mouse plant comes from warm woodlands, where it grows in very moist, humus-rich soil or in shady marshes. It fits well in a deeply shaded corner with other small companion plants, such as small hostas, ferns, and the dwarf astilbes. Hardy to zone 7, 6 with protection. Withstands 15°F (−10°C) for short periods with protection. Where the ground freezes, pot and overwinter indoors. This plant is for patient collectors who are willing to brush the leaves aside to reveal the curiously pretty flowers partially hidden among them.

Arum

Arums are not considered true shade garden plants. But one species, *Arum italicum* (Italian arum), handily adds the leaf texture and color so important in shady gardens. It does not flower in more than the lightest shade, hence no colorful, glowing cluster of orange-red berries follow, but this might be just as well, because the fruit is very poisonous. Even if I have to do without the colorful berries, I would keep a few tubers of Italian arum just for the beautiful leaves. Plants are sited where they get a couple of hours of morning sun—and where the disappearance of their leaves in early summer matters not. New leaves emerge in late autumn; here they are usually larger and more striking than those of plants situated in full sun. They provide a wonderful display of interesting, curiously marbled leaves throughout autumn and winter, helping the hellebores bring some color to the garden during the off-season. The leaves have withstood freezing temperatures on many occasions; they droop a little, but spring right back when warmer days arrive. In areas colder than zone 6 and where snow would cover the leaves, they are definitely houseplants.

Found all around the Mediterranean region, *Arum italicum* is one of the hardiest garden arums available. It grows in moist, shady marshes of woodlands and is much more attractive than *A. maculatum* (Austrian arum), a central-European species widespread in Austria and Bavaria (I remember the leaves of Grandfather's *Aronstab*, but it is to the bicolored spathe of red and white that another of its common names, lords-and-ladies, refers). Arums should be planted in protected locations with light shade and some sun. Exceptional in areas with winter-wet soils, arums require watering in gardens where the soil dries out in winter. Although the soil must be moist during the active growing season, dry soil is required during dormancy in summer, so withhold watering after the leaves die down. The addition of slow-release fertilizer at the beginning of leaf emergence in autumn is beneficial.

The generic name is from *aron*, the classical Greek name used by Theophrastus for *Arum*. *Arum* belongs in the Araceae.

Propagate by dividing the tubers after flowering. Seed can be sown in autumn after all the pulp is removed with care, due to its toxic nature. Seed may require a long time to germinate, so division is faster and more productive for gardeners.

Diseases and attacks by insects are uncommon.

Arum italicum, Italian arum. Mediterranean region, Turkey, Syria, North Africa, Italy, also England and south-central Europe.

Morning sun, LS; spathe to 15 in. (38 cm) long, spathe tube pale green to greenish white, sometimes light purple, blade (hood) pale green to yellowish, unmarked or marked with purple, flower develops only in mostly sunny positions; June–July; plant tuberous; leaves simple, glossy, triangular, arrow-shaped to 16 in. (40 cm) long on longer petioles, medium to grayish green with silver, whitish to light grayish or yellowish green markings along the principal veins, occasionally with purplish dots and markings. This species is extremely variable so expect differences in color shading and markings. Some supbspecies, like subsp. *albispathum* and subsp. *neglectum*, are without showy leaf markings; they are not noteworthy in gardens, and they are, as the latter name might indicate, neglected by nature. The leaves of the selection 'Immaculatum' (sometimes assigned to *Arum maculatum*) are also an unmarked, plain green. Hybrids (*A. italicum* × *A. maculatum*) have, aside from the typical marbling of the species, some yellowish markings and purple spots. Grow this species and its cultivars for their beautiful leaves, which emerge in autumn, stand overwinter, and crumble at the time of flowering in late spring or early summer. Site in a protected corner and combine with hostas, pulmonarias, heucheras, or other bold-leaved plants that can fill in during the arums' summer dormancy. Excellent for winter color where there is little or no snow cover and the soil does not freeze solid.

'Chamaeleon', leaves broad, marbled yellowish green and greenish gray.

'Marmoratum' (var. *marmoratum*), leaves large, marbled in yellowish white.

'**Pictum**', leaves smaller and narrower, marbled silvery gray with creamy undertones.

'Tiny', leaves small, no more than 4 in. (10 cm) long, triangular, arrow-shaped, and beautifully marbled with yellowish white. For gardeners who appreciate dwarf plants.

'White Winter', leaves narrow, marbled with pure white; plant small.

Aruncus

Centuries ago, *Aruncus* was given the name goatsbeard because its flowers have a fancied resemblance to the white beard of a goat. The name goatsbeard also applies to spirea, which itself is used as a synonym for *Aruncus dioicus*; in fact, *Aruncus* is closely related to *Spiraea* and *Filipendula* and is frequently mislabled as one or the other.

Goatsbeard grows in moist, shady woodlands, often in mountainous areas, throughout the entire northern hemisphere, and our native as well as the Asian goatsbeards are supremely adapted to these conditions; I have seen spectacular blooming specimens in a ravine in the North Georgia mountains. Goatsbeards are very long-lived if the microclimate is to their liking. They require a fertile woodland soil with plenty of humus and a pH of 5 to 6. The one thing they do not like is a lack of moisture. Provide supplemental water during prolonged droughts and a spot in deep, moist shade to keep them happy, but such a location also reduces flowering, unfortunately. Sadly, the giant native goatsbeard, *Aruncus dioicus*, does not do well in the Georgia Piedmont, so I stopped growing it. There is some hope for southern goatsbeard lovers, however, in a new hybrid, *A. aethusifolius* × *A. dioicus*, which was developed at the Mount Cuba Center for the Study of Piedmont Flora; though not as tall as the native species, this *Aruncus* 'Southern White' has been successful in the hot, dry summers of zone 8a.

Goatsbeards are herbaceous, clump-forming perennials with short rhizomes as well as some fibrous roots. *Aruncus* is the classic name bestowed upon these plants by the Roman polymath Pliny. The genus belongs in the rose family, Rosaceae. Many species form large to very large, slowly spreading clumps and a dense, billowing shrublike form; smaller species are available for gardens that cannot accommodate large plants. Flowers are their crowning glory; individually, they are very small, but they are assembled in plumes of off-white clouds drifting high above the leaf mound, pyramidal panicles often exceeding 20 in. (50 cm) in length. Unfortunately, the spectacular display does not last very long, and the flowers brown rapidly. The sometimes fernlike, medium to dark green leaves die back in autumn, but the faded flower panicles remain upright and like astilbes provide winter interest. Large goatsbeards should be located at the periphery of the garden; fronted with plantings of hostas or other bold-leaved plants, they form a superb summertime screen. The dwarf species are great companion plants for miniature hostas and can be used as fern substitutes where spring flowering is desired.

Propagate cultivars by dividing the completely dormant rhizome in the first warm days of late winter. Carry the roots with a large ball of soil attached. Most species self-seed unless deadheaded. I dislike deadheading and let the plants seed as they will. There will always be something to give away to friends and neighbors. Seed propagation too is easy, but why do it if the plant takes over that chore?

Occasionally clumps at the soil level develop black rust on emerging leaves; in these cases only systemic fungicides seem to work. Attacks by some fly larvae and tarnished plant bugs are reported; insects do not otherwise seem to bother goatsbeards.

Species and cultivars listed are dioecious: a plant has either male or female reproductive organs and requires cross-fertilization from other individuals for successful seed production. In gardens, locally isolated female plants do not produce seed. All flower from late May to August, depending upon location.

Aruncus aethusifolius, dwarf goatsbeard, Korean goatsbeard. Korea, Cheju Island, Japan.

LS to MS; flowers tiny, white to light yellow, carried on erect, open, panicles to 6 in. (15 cm) long, above the leaves; plant compact, to 15 in. (38 cm) high and wide, with compound, 2- to 3-pinnate leaves, to 10 in. (25 cm) long, divided into small, ovate, green leaflets, deeply incised. A wonderful small addition to gardens that cannot accommodate the larger goatsbeards. Its leaves turn a bright yellow in autumn, brightening the garden together with the hostas that change color at that time. The

selection 'Hillside Gem' is similar but smaller, with a neat habit. Hardy to zone 5.

Aruncus astilboides, Japanese goatsbeard. Japan.

LS to MS; flowers tiny, white to light yellow, carried on erect, open, panicles to 8 in. (20 cm) long; plant delicate, to 4 ft. (1.2 m) high and wide, with compound, 2- to 3-pinnate leaves, divided into small, ovate, deeply serrated, green leaflets tinted with reddish brown, a little more than 1 in. (2.5 cm) long. Very similar to an astilbe (*astilboides* = like an astilbe), and a good goatsbeard for smaller gardens. Hardy to zone 6, 5 with protection.

Aruncus dioicus, goatsbeard, goat's beard, bride's feathers. Europe to eastern Siberia, North America from Pennsylvania south through the Appalachians to Georgia and west to Alabama, Arkansas, Missouri, and Illinois.

Some sun, LS to MS; flowers tiny white to creamy white in male plants, greenish white and more nodding in female plants, carried on large panicles with spikelike clusters of densely arranged flowers branching off a tall, central stalk reaching 7 ft. (2 m), but in gardens more often 4–6 ft. (1.2–1.8 m); plant bushy, 4–5 ft. (1.2–1.5 m) tall and 4 ft. (1.2 m) wide, large green alternate compound leaves, to 15 in. (38 cm) long, 2- to 3-pinnate leaflets to 5 in. (13 cm) long, smooth, medium green, with deeply toothed margins. A very large goatsbeard whose large shrublike proportions composed of ferny leaves cannot be missed, even as a background, for which garden use it is most suited. Needs plenty of space to develop to maturity. Long known: it has been used as an herbal bath for swollen feet, American Indians dressed bee stings with a poultice made from its roots, and the airy, white flowers were collected in the woods for wedding decorations (hence, bride's feathers). When mature it has a woody rootstock, making propagation by division difficult, but it self-seeds copiously when cross-fertilized and produces abundant seedlings. Hardy in zones 4 to 7; reported growing as far north as zone 2 but loathes hot, dry summers further south. I have grown **var. kamtschaticus** from the eastern Russian Kamchatka Peninsula for some years; it is about the same size as 'Kneiffii'. The flowers are white, similar to those of the type but not as showy: the inflorescence is only about half the size. The leaves are compound, with the leaflets medium to dark green, lobed and toothed. The leaf mound is to 24 in. (60 cm) tall. This small variety is suitable for any garden and does well in hot southern climates as long as the soil is kept moist. *Aruncus sinensis* (Chinese goatsbeard) has a tighter structure with more luxuriant leaf growth and leaves whose bronze undertone is imparted to the entire plant; easily distinguished from *A. dioicus* and more suited to warmer regions, to zone 6.

'Glasnevin', flowers in feathery plumes of creamy white; plant grows to 5 ft. (1.5 m).

'Kneiffii' is considerably smaller than the species, 3.5–4 ft. (1–1.2 m), with whitish flowers and a more ferny appearance in leaf. Possibly a selection of var. *kamtschaticus*.

'Southern White', a hybrid (*Aruncus aethusifolius* × *A. dioicus*) with multibranched, slender spikes of white flowers that resemble those of *A. aethusifolius* but are much more dense and numerous; plant vigorous and suited for hot-summer areas in zones 7 and 8; size is intermediate between the parents.

'Zweiweltenkind' ('Child of Two Worlds'), ivory-white flowers, a selection of *Aruncus sinensis*.

Aruncus parvulus, dwarf goatsbeard. Japan.

LS to MS; flowers tiny, white to light yellow, carried on erect, open, feathery panicles; plant compact, to 12 in. (30 cm) high, with compound, 2- to 3-pinnate leaves. As the epithet *parvulus* (= dwarf) indicates, this is another good goatsbeard for smaller gardens. Most often represented in commerce by its selection 'Dagalet' (which is frequently offered as *Astilbe* ×*crispa* 'Dagalet').

Asarum and *Saruma*

Wild gingers bring out the collector in gardeners. This has certainly been the case with me at least, as the following story relates . . . Over time, a few meandering creeks have carved deep valleys into the Georgia red clay, and some 20 years ago I explored just such a steep, rocky gorge near my home. Because it is unsuitable for building, the landscape remains pristine to this day; it is wild, dark, and eerie, even with unseen houses nearby. Old stands of trees persist, mostly towering, centuries-old oak trees, loblolly pines, and tulip poplars. There is always a shallow stream flowing, fed by underground springs and a small lake upstream. Old fallen trees

litter the area, and their decay feeds all manner of forest floor plants. Mosses and wildflowers abound. Near the stream, growing by a fallen giant, I detected a plant that day with splendid shiny leaves marbled with silvery veins. I admired this wild ginger for a while, took a few pictures, and continued on. But when my developed slides came back, showing the splendor of this particular wild ginger magnified many times, I just had to return, shovel in hand, to find it. Heavy spring rains had transformed the gentle stream into a raging torrent; the old, decaying log was gone, and the area was now thinly covered with red clay and debris. I searched for hours and returned very disappointed. The little beauty was nowhere to be seen.

A week later, I went back one more time—and a few tiny, unmistakable, silvery marbled leaves had pushed through the clay. The thick, long roots, anchored in deep native clay, had withstood the onslaught of the flood and saved the plant from being washed away. The plant has been growing at Hosta Hill ever since, happy in the same soil it came from, in the deep shade of pines and a hemlock. It is still my favorite native wild ginger, and I even gave it a name, 'Gosan Valley', one of the most beautiful forms of *Asarum shuttleworthii* I have seen. Finding this native wild ginger started my *Asarum* collecting fever, and I have most of the many new species and forms now available. I must admit, some are more spectacular than my 'Gosan Valley', but who can argue with a first wild ginger love?

Premier plants for the shady garden, wild gingers come from the shady woodlands of the temperate regions of North America, Europe, and eastern Asia. *Asarum* is the classic Greek and Roman name for these plants. Taxonomic splitters have had a good time with the genus, dividing it into a plethora of new genera, so gardeners be warned: any time now, you may find your favorite wild ginger under an alias like *Heterotropa*, *Hexastylis*, *Asarabacca*, *Japonasarum*, or *Asiasarum*. Well over 100 species are known, and dedicated and daring plant collectors like Dan Hinkley, Barry Yinger, and Bleddyn and Sue Wynn-Jones are adding to this number all the time. Most new species are found in Japan and China. *Asarum* belongs in the birthwort family, Aristolochiaceae. The related *Saruma henryi*, taller than most wild gingers, has been growing at Hosta Hill for some time. It too belongs in the Aristolochiaceae.

Whenever the roots of wild gingers are cut or their leaves broken, the strong, gingerlike aroma drifts over a considerable area, hence the common name. This is particularly noticeable when the plants are divided for increase. In the garden, wild gingers serve as groundcover and specimen plants in light to deep shade. Native gingers require considerable shade; some Japanese and Chinese species are happy with a bit of sun exposure. Except for the widely grown deciduous *Asarum canadense* (Canadian ginger) and its equally deciduous Japanese counterpart, *A. caulescens*, most are evergreen. Their leaves have great substance and are usually shiny; many are attractively marbled along the veins or all over the leaf surface. Leafstalks arise directly from the rootstock. The roots are thick and penetrate the soil deeply. Wild gingers do best in a light, well-draining woodland soil, rich in organic matter and preferably acid. Good drainage is essential. With their deep-rooting habit, both native and Asian wild gingers can withstand long periods of drought, but they will not tolerate continued dry soil.

At Hosta Hill wild gingers abound. A few have rounded leaves, with lobes that overlap frequently. All have attractive silvery veining or mottling reminiscent of cyclamens. Most Japanese and Chinese wild gingers have distinctly heart-shaped leaves, some with overlapping lobes. To me, the finest wild ginger is the variable Japanese *Asarum kumageanum*; planted near one of the walks, my golden-mottled specimen elicits inquiry from every visitor. Another wild ginger from Japan is *A. hirsutisepalum*, which has the largest leaves of any asarum I grow. A splendid wild ginger from China is the aptly named *A. splendens*, whose large leaves are a very dark green mottled with large silver blotches.

Notice that so far I have said nothing about the flowers of wild gingers. To me, leaves are the most important value point in plants for the shady garden, and this applies to *Asarum* as well. Most wild gingers are evergreen: their endowment to the garden lasts the entire year, provided there is no snow cover in winter. Most of my wild gingers are planted in the ground, but I have *Asarum hirsutisepalum* in a nice, elevated pot on the patio just to show off the gorgeous, beaker-shaped flowers covered with purple specks. Other wild gingers, like *A. speciosum*, have erect leaves on long leafstalks, so their flowers show advantageously even when planted in the ground. The flowers of our natives *A. arifolium*, *A. ruthii*, *A. shuttleworthii*, and *A. virginicum* are hidden in spring under a dense cover of leaves, which must be pushed aside to reveal the little brown jugs. In short, the flowers of some wild gingers are spectacular, even bizarre, but all are ephemeral. It is the leaves of *Asarum* that add so much to the shady garden.

Wild gingers from Japan—where the passion for unusual mutations of *Asarum* has become an obsession called *saishin*—are another story. Japanese collectors concentrate on unusual flower forms, including albino, and have selected as many as 150 different variants of *Asarum minamitanianum* alone. Of more interest to me is their selection of different leaf forms seen in this species, for example the yellow-leaved *A. minamitanianum* 'Koki'. Other leaf mutations include center variegations, called *hon fu* (= true variegation) in Japan, seen, for instance, in *A. savatieri* 'Otome aoi shirofukurin', which has a uniform, narrow white leaf margin (*shirofukurin* = white margin). The book *Toki no Hana*, translated from the Japanese by Asian plant guru Barry Yinger, gives a glimpse of these unique selections, which bring great sums of money in commerce.

Propagate by division. Employ a fungicide during this process to keep the cuts free of black rust. Seed propagation is possible, but ants seem to have better success with this method than I shall ever hope to attain.

Occasionally, black rust develops on emerging leaves at the soil level. This malady appears as gray and black encrustations on the shriveling growing tips and spreads quickly. Entire plants can be affected unless systemic fungicides are employed; I have not been able to find an effective yet environmentally friendly cure. Crown rot too is problematic as are slugs, which seem to prefer tender young leaves. Check plants often while leaves are emerging in spring. Other insect pests do not seem to bother my wild gingers.

Given the tremendous diversity of leaf and flower seen in both native and Asian species, I offer descriptions for some wild gingers with trepidation. In many species, the leaves can be either variegated or plain green, and the usually bright patterns of the emergent leaves in spring become more dull with the progressing seasons. Variability is normal in species populations and should be expected in purchased plants. Unless otherwise noted, all asarums are evergreen in zones 6 to 9 (in colder regions, even evergreen asarums become herbaceous and may lose their top growth) and hardy to zone 5 with protection.

Asarum arifolium, arrowhead ginger, heartleaf, heartleaf ginger, little brown jugs, pig flower, pig ginger, wild ginger. Eastern North America, Virginia, the Carolinas, Georgia, west to Louisiana.

MS to FS; flowers brown, shaped like little brown jugs, 3-lobed, darker inside, to 1 in. (2.5 cm) long, with spreading sepal lobes; April–May; plant clump-forming, 6 in. (15 cm) tall to 18 in. (45 cm) wide; leaves of many different shapes but mostly triangular, arrow-shaped with rounded lobes, to 5 in. (13 cm) long, dark green with varying lighter gray-green patterns. This species has a profusion of different leaf forms and variegation patterns; in some plants, large triangular leaves are distinctly mottled and veined, while smaller forms are almost heart-shaped with little mottling. I grow more than 20 forms, most rescued locally from construction sites. This is a good garden plant, deep-rooted and very drought-resistant. It does not like overly wet soils, where it is subject to fungal rot of the crown. Here in Georgia, it thrives in dense clay, which dries out completely during droughts; it may need some dry summer weather to flourish. The Appalachian native *Asarum ruthii*, also called little brown jugs, is very similar but has erect sepal lobes 0.1 in. (3 mm) long, while *A. arifolium* has spreading sepal lobes, 0.3 in. (8 mm) long; its leaves are similarly colored but more heart-shaped.

Asarum asaroides, *tairin aoi* (Jap.). Japan, Honshu, Kyushu.

MS to FS; flowers brownish with dark purple tint and whitish center, tub-shaped, 2 in. (5 cm) across; May; plant clump-forming, 6 in. (15 cm) tall to 14 in. (35 cm) wide; leaves to 6 in. (15 cm) long, heart-shaped, dark grayish green with cloudy silver markings. The epithet means "the asarumlike asarum." Albino forms and variants with tortoise-shell variegation in the leaves are available. *Asarum muramatsui* (*amagi kanaoi* in Japan), a species from central Honshu, has similar but smaller flowers and glossy, patterned foliage with deeply sunken veins. Both are good garden plants, hardy to zone 6. Very similar is *A. satsumense* (*satsuma aoi* in Japan), which differs from *A. asaroides* by having boldly ruf-

fled and tubercular flowers and grayish green, patterned leaves. Similar too is *A. unzen* (*unzen kanaoi* in Japan) from northern Kyushu's Shimabara Peninsula; it flowers April–May. The brownish flowers are like those of *A. asaroides* but smaller, very constricted at the top, and with sharply pointed lobes. The roughly triangular leaves are evergreen and patterned. Hardy to zone 6b.

Asarum asperum, *miyako aoi* (Jap.). Japan, central Honshu, western Kansai (Kinki), Shikoku, Kyushu.

MS to FS; flowers whitish outside with dark purple inside center, inflated, tub-shaped, very contracted at throat, with 3 rounded lobes, similar to native "fat" little brown jugs, 1.5 in. (4 cm) across; May; plant clump-forming, 6 in. (15 cm) tall to 9 in. (23 cm) wide; leaves to 3 in. (8 cm) long, heart-shaped, dark green with varying silver patterns. The albino forms have pale green, not white, flowers. Hardy to zone 6. A related evergreen species is *Asarum controversum* from Nagasaki, Japan, which also has patterned leaves and flowers that look like those of Dutchman's pipe, *Aristolochia macrophylla*. Hardy to zone 7.

Asarum blumei, *ranyo aoi* (Jap.). Japan, central Honshu, Shizuoka, Kanagawa.

MS to FS; flowers brownish with dark purple tint, tub-shaped, lobes widely spreading, rounded, networked or stippled white throat, small; May; plant clump-forming, 8 in. (20 cm) tall to 12 in. (30 cm) wide; leaves to 5 in. (13 cm) long, arrow-shaped, glossy dark grayish green with cloudy silver markings along the margins and leaf veins. Still scarce, this variable species promises to be a good garden plant.

Asarum campaniforme, kiwi asarum, kiwi ginger, *kiwi kanaoi* (Jap.). Southern China.

MS to FS; flowers elongated, tubular, to 2 in. (5 cm), whitish green outside, a conspicuous, blackish purple ribbon appears inside on the edges of the sepals; May; deciduous; plant clump-forming, 12 in. (30 cm) tall to 16 in. (40 cm) wide; leaves to 6 in. (15 cm) long, narrowly arrow-shaped, variable, either glossy green without markings or marked with variable, unpredictable designs. In a genus known for its bizarre flowers, this species stands out as one of the most peculiar: its flowers have a spoke pattern like a kiwi fruit cut crosswise and are carried flat on the ground—strange but weirdly attractive. Suitable to zone 7b and south. Further north it needs to be potted and moved inside during freezing periods. The unconventional flowers are well worth this effort.

Asarum canadense, Canadian ginger, wild ginger, Canadian snakeroot, ginger root, Indian ginger snakeroot. Eastern North America, Quebec to New Brunswick, south to South Carolina and Georgia, west to Missouri and Minnesota.

MS to FS; flowers reddish to greenish brown, tub-shaped, emerging between leafstalks, 1.5 in. (4 cm) wide with 3 rounded sepal lobes, no petals; April–May; deciduous, plant rhizomatous, widely creeping and forming large colonies in time, to 12 in. (30 cm) tall; leaves paired, to 6 in. (15 cm) long, kidney-shaped, hairy, rich green with no markings. An excellent, widely grown ginger that faithfully returns year after year with a luxurious, fast-growing, ground-covering carpet of large leaves. It stands up well to cold or heat and drought. Hardy to zone 3, 2 with some leaf cover. This wild ginger was used by American Indians and early settlers to season cooking and to treat colds, coughs, fevers, and stomach disorders; raw, it serves as a powerful emetic and antiseptic. Variety *acuminatum* from the Great Smoky Mountains has more pointed, sometimes tailed sepal lobes; var. *reflexum* is more like the type. The two are usually not separated in commerce.

Asarum caudatum, western wild ginger. Western North America, British Columbia, Washington, Oregon to Montana.

MS to FS; flowers reddish to greenish brown, tub-shaped, to 1 in. (2.5 cm) wide with 3 pointed, tailed lobes, tails to 2 in. (5 cm); May–July; plant rhizomatous, creeping and forming colonies, to 12 in. (30 cm) tall; leaves to 5 in. (13 cm) long, heart-shaped, rich green with no markings. This wild ginger from the deeply shaded redwood and pine forests of the Pacific Coast needs moist soil and considerable shade. It does well in some gardens out of its native range, but here it has failed miserably—while a few miles away, at a friend's garden, its growth is luxuriant, year after year. I suspect that soil moisture content and composition as well as day and night time temperature ranges have a lot to do with this. Worth a try—but may give southeast-

ern gardeners fits. 'Alba' (f. *alba* of gardens; *soshinka* in Japan), a rare albino form of the type, has white flowers. Nor do *Asarum lemmonii* (Lemmon's wild ginger), another western wild ginger from southern Oregon to northern California, and the closely related *A. wagneri* grow here; these two fussy species may not be of great garden value, but as native North American wild gingers, they should be represented in collections, if at all possible.

Asarum caudigerum. China, Taiwan.

MS to FS; flowers brownish green to brown, hairy, tubular, of minor importance; May; plant clump-forming, 10 in. (25 cm) tall to 12 in. (30 cm) wide; leaves to 4 in. (10 cm) long, arrow-shaped, on 5 in. (13 cm) petioles, dark grayish green to green. All parts of this wild ginger are covered with minute hairs, which add an exceptional, silky luster to the plant, something rarely seen in this genus. It reminds me a little of the luminous appearance of sunlit *Saruma henryi*, but the shine is more brilliant and conspicuous. Still rare, this asarum makes a fine addition to gardens. Variety *cardiophyllum* has fuzzy, green, heart-shaped leaves with yellowish brown flowers borne in the leaf axils in early spring. Cold hardiness is not yet determined; potting is advised in zone 7b and colder.

Asarum caulescens, Japanese wild ginger, *futaba aoi* or *kamo aoi* (Jap.). Japan, Honshu, Shikoku, Kyushu.

MS to FS; flowers usually reddish brown, bowl-shaped, emerging between the base of leafstalks on relatively long, hairy pedicel, flower small, to 1 in. (2.5 cm) wide, with 3 reflexed lobes covering tube; April–May; deciduous, plant rhizomatous, creeping and forming colonies, to 6 in. (15 cm) tall; leaves to 3 in. (8 cm) long, round to oval, deeply sunken veins, dark green with no markings. The Japanese equivalent of *Asarum canadense*, only smaller and with daintier flowers. A good groundcover for small areas. Some better forms with white to pinkish white flowers are in commerce. Another deciduous species from Japan with nearly black flowers and bright green leaves is *A. dimitiatum*, which is rare but available for a price. Hardy to zone 4.

Asarum celsum, *miyabi kanaoi* (Jap.). Japan, southern Kyushu, Kagoshima.

MS to FS; flowers purple-brown, pear-shaped, with ridged opening; March; plant small, clump-forming; leaves triangular with oval base, green with no markings. A very early-blooming, rare species. In zone 8 and colder, use in a pot on the shady patio or in the cold greenhouse.

Asarum costatum, Tosa wild ginger, *tosano aoi* (Jap.). Japan, southeastern Shikoku, Kochi.

MS to FS; flowers dark purple, some with white band around lobes, cylindrical, 6-angled, contracted at throat, with 3 pointed lobes, 1 in. (2.5 cm) across; April–May; plant clump-forming, 6 in. (15 cm) tall to 9 in. (23 cm) wide; leaves to 5 in. (13 cm) long, heart-shaped, dark green with varying silver patterns.

Asarum dissitum. Japan, Ryukyu.

MS to FS; flowers inflated, tubular, contracted at throat, large, pointed lobes; April–May; plant large, clump-forming, 8 in. (20 cm) tall to 15 in. (38 cm) wide; leaves to 8 in. (20 cm) long, glossy green with silvery blotches. Also from Ryukyu are *Asarum gelasinum* and *A. gusk* with velvety, succulent leaves and variable, usually furry flowers; *A. leucosepalum* with velvety, dark green, faintly patterned leaves and pure white flowers; and *A. monodoriflorum* with similar leaves. All are semi-tender subjects for shady patio pot culture, not hardy enough to be planted in the open ground in gardens in zone 8 and colder. I grow *A. monodoriflorum* in the ground during the summer in zone 7a and pot it in autumn before the cold season arrives; it makes a nice display in a sunny south window during our very short winters.

Asarum europaeum, European ginger, European asarabacca. Europe east to the Caucasus.

MS to FS; flowers brown, bell-shaped with short lobes, to 0.5 in. (1 cm) long, narrow; April–May; plant rhizomatous, prostrate, mat-forming, to 4 in. (10 cm) tall and 12 in. (30 cm) wide; leaves to 2 in. (5 cm) long, kidney-shaped, rich glossy green with little or no markings. Variety *caucasicum* has triangular, extended leaves. An excellent garden plant and one of the hardiest asarums, reportedly thriving in zone 4.

Asarum fudsinoi. Japan, Ryukyu.

MS to FS; flowers brown, tubular, contracted at throat, 3-lobed; May; plant clump-forming, 6 in. (15 cm) tall to 9 in. (23 cm) wide; leaves to 4 in. (10 cm) long, heart-shaped, soft uniform green, sometimes with silvery blotches. A semi-tender subject for shady patio pot culture in zone 8.

Asarum hartwegii, Sierra wild ginger, Hartweg's ginger. Western North America, Oregon to northern California.

MS to FS; flowers reddish to greenish brown, urn-shaped, to 0.5 in. (1 cm) wide with 3 pointed, tailed lobes, tails to 2.5 in. (6 cm); May–June; plant rhizomatous, shortly creeping and forming colonies, to 12 in. (30 cm) tall; leaves to 4 in. (10 cm) long, heart-shaped, rich green with pale, silvery veins. A nicely marked ginger with good drought tolerance but fussy when planted in a spot not to its liking.

Asarum hexalobum, *sanyo aoi* (Jap.). Japan, Honshu, western Chugoku, Shikoku, northern Kyushu.

MS to FS; flowers small, white, sometimes pink, inflated, pear-shaped; April–May; plant vigorous, clump-forming, 5 in. (13 cm) tall; leaves to 3 in. (8 cm) long, rounded, dark green speckled with silver-gray in varying patterns. Hardy to zone 6.

Asarum hirsutisepalum, *oni kanaoi* (Jap.). Japan, Kyushu, Kagoshima, Yakushima.

MS to FS; flowers whitish gray, inflated, tub-shaped, contracted at throat, with 3 pointed lobes, occasionally a purple-veined, white ring at throat, 2 in. (5 cm) across; April; plant clump-forming, 12 in. (30 cm) tall to 18 in. (45 cm) wide; leaves triangular heart-shaped, 7 in. (18 cm) long and 6 in. (15 cm) wide, deeply lobed, of thick substance, uniform shiny light green in spring, later dark green with the veins outlined in light green. The flowers are absolutely stunning, and although the leaves are not mottled, they are very large; a mature clump stands out in the garden or in a container. Great with ferns and wildflowers with lacy foliage. In Japan, sports with different leaf variegation patterns such as white, silvery gray, or yellow mottling are available; used exclusively in pot culture, they have become objects of great desire and command princely sums. 'Kinkonkan' (= golden crown) is a yellow-variegated cultivar.

Asarum infrapurpureum. Taiwan.

MS to FS; flowers dark or purplish red, tubular, contracted at throat, to 1 in. (2.5 cm) across; April–

May; plant spreading, 6 in. (15 cm) tall to 9 in. (23 cm) wide; leaves to 3 in. (8 cm) long, heart-shaped, wavy margins, purplish brown or purple leaves, spotted with white above, purple underneath. This species should be placed in an elevated bed or potted and displayed at eye level so that the contrast between the purple underside of the leaves with the white-dotted surface can be closely observed. Hardy to zone 7. Albino forms are available.

Asarum kiusianum, *tsukushi aoi* (Jap.). Japan, Kyushu.

MS to FS; flowers yellowish, uniformly spotted with bright purple inside lobes, inflated, tub-shaped, contracted at throat, with 3 rounded lobes; April–May; plant clump-forming, 6 in. (15 cm) tall to 12 in. (30 cm) wide; leaves to 3 in. (8 cm) long, heart-shaped, usually with silvery white veins. The flowers of this species are gorgeous and very showy. Variety *tubulosum* has pure white flowers, peculiar-looking yet very attractive. Forms with greenish white flowers are also available.

Asarum kumageanum, *kuwaiba kanaoi* (Jap.). Japan, Kyushu, Tanegashima, Yakushima.

MS to FS; flowers brownish purple, inflated, tub-shaped, contracted at throat, with 3 wavy, rippling lobes, purple-spotted, yellowish lobe margins and ring at throat, to 2 in. (5 cm) across; April; plant clump-forming, 10 in. (25 cm) tall to 16 in. (40 cm) wide; leaves to 6 in. (15 cm) long, triangular to heart-shaped, of thick substance, shiny, rich dark green base color with the leaf interior mottled with large patches of a yellowish green, almost golden mottling. Later in the season, the bright green turns to dark green, and the variegation becomes a very light green, with a grayish cast. Several forms offered have silver rather than golden markings. Variety *satakeanum* is very similar, differing only in minor flower characteristics.

Asarum macranthum. China, Taiwan.

MS to FS; flowers dark brownish to purple, small; April–May; plant rhizomatous, forming expanding clumps, 8 in. (20 cm) tall; leaves to 5 in. (13 cm) long, arrow-shaped, dark green with variable and uneven silvery and whitish gray splotches and a surface glowing with a refined luster. Both it and the virtually identical *Asarum maculatum*, also from China, are still rare in gardens.

Asarum magnificum. China.

MS to FS; flowers blackish purple outside, with a plaited white throat, urn-shaped, large, to 2 in. (5 cm) across; May; plant 10 in. (25 cm) tall to 18 in. (45 cm) wide; leaves to 6 in. (15 cm) long, triangular to heart-shaped, dark green with outstanding, cloudy silvery white to greenish white markings, similar to *Asarum splendens* but without its active rhizomatous behavior. Clones of this very attractive wild ginger are highly variable; expect differences in plants from commercial sources.

Asarum maximum, panda face ginger, *panda kanaoi* (Jap.). China.

MS to FS; flowers black with pure white 3-lobed interior; May; plant clump-forming, 10 in. (25 cm) tall to 14 in. (35 cm) wide; leaves to 6 in. (15 cm) across and 7 in. (18 cm) long, triangular, of thick substance, uniform shiny light green in spring, later dark green. Another variable wild ginger; the forms with silvery gray markings in the leaf center are most gardenworthy. The flowers are outstanding; with some imagination, they do look like the face of a panda. May be too tender for outside planting, except in protected areas of zone 7 or warmer. Further north it should be potted in an elevated position, where the striking flowers can be observed and the plant carried inside during the cold season.

Asarum megacalyx, *koshino kanaoi* (Jap.). Northern Japan.

MS to FS; flowers bell-shaped, almost black; September–November; plant spreading by runners, low-growing; leaves to 3 in. (8 cm) long, triangular, of thick substance, uniform shiny light green in spring, later dark green. Some forms have patterned leaves. This running wild ginger forms a splendid groundcover. *Asarum fauriei*, which has very small, usually plain green, rounded leaves and variable flowers, makes a dainty, small-leaved evergreen groundcover. One of the best cold-climate, spreading evergreen gingers is *A. ikegamii* (*yukiguni kanaoi* in Japan), with leathery, dark glossy green leaves. All are from northern Japan, in commerce, and hardy to zone 5.

Asarum minamitanianum, mouse tail ginger, *onaga kanaoi* (Jap.). Japan, Kyushu.

MS to FS; flowers variable, reddish pink to blackish purple, contracted at throat, with 3 long-tailed lobes, with tails to 5 in. (13 cm) long, lobes deep purple with whitish margin and white throat; April–May; plant clump-forming, 6 in. (15 cm) tall to 9 in. (23 cm) wide; leaves to 5 in. (13 cm) long, heart-shaped, dark green with varying silver patterns. A variable species with hundreds of different flower forms. Those with extremely long-tailed sepals and leaf variegations have been collected in the wild in Japan to the detriment of natural populations. Use in protected areas in zone 7 or put it in a pot. A definite conversation piece during mouse tail bloom time.

Asarum minor. Eastern North America, New England south to North Carolina.

MS to FS; flowers reddish to greenish brown, urn-shaped, to 1 in. (2.5 cm) wide with 3 pointed lobes; plant to 12 in. (30 cm) tall; leaves to 4 in. (10 cm) long, heart-shaped, rich green with pale, with silvery gray markings. A nicely marked wild ginger with good drought tolerance. 'Honeysong' is a large-leaved, distinctly marked selection.

Asarum naniflorum, small-flowered ginger. Eastern North America, Virginia south to the Carolinas.

MS to FS; flowers reddish brown, urn-shaped, to 0.5 in. (1 cm) with 3 pointed lobes to 0.2 in. (0.5 cm); plant to 8 in. (20 cm) tall; leaves to 2 in. (5 cm) long, rounded, heart-shaped, rich green with pale silvery gray markings. A species that will be of more interest to collectors than to gardeners, it is threatened and should never be collected in the wild. Plant this small wild ginger in an elevated spot in a shady rockery or along a path, where it can be spotted. 'Eco Decor' is a silver-marked clone introduced by my gardening neighbor Don Jacobs.

Asarum niponicum, Japanese wild ginger, *kanto kanaoi* (Jap.). Japan, central Honshu, Kansai, Chūbu, Kanto.

MS to FS; flowers brown, 3-lobed; July–August; plant clump-forming, 6 in. (15 cm) tall to 9 in. (23 cm) wide; leaves variable in size, averaging 3 in. (8 cm) long, oval to heart-shaped with extended lobes, dark green with varying silvery gray patterns. A good, hardy garden plant with highly variable leaves. Similarly varied in leaf variegation and size is *Asarum savatieri* (*otome kanaoi* in Japan), also from central Honshu; it blooms more than a month later than *A. niponicum*. In Japan many variegated

sports of these two species have been selected and are collected by aficionados; with luck, the more stable varieties will reach Western gardens. Both species are hardy to zone 5. Other evergreen species from central Honshu are *A. kooyanum*, with mostly medium green, unmarked leaves, and *A. rigescens* (*atsumi kanaoi* in Japan), with 3 in. (8 cm) long, glossy, leathery leaves with depressed veins and unusual patterning. Both are good garden plants, hardy to zone 6. Even more hardy (well into zone 5) is *A. tamaense* (round-leaved Japanese ginger, *tamano kanaoi* or *maruba kanaoi* in Japan) from Kanto in central Honshu; it is a clump-forming ginger with evergreen, shiny, leathery roundish leaves, either plain green or patterned but always with deeply sunken veins. The leafstalks are purple; the flowers, which appear March–April, are usually brownish and have pear-shaped tubes with very wavy lobes.

Asarum sakawanum, *sakawa saishin* (Jap.). Japan, Shikoku, Kochi.

MS to FS; flowers brownish purple, contracted at throat, with 3 wavy lobes, deep purple with whitish margin and white throat; April–May; plant clump-forming, 6 in. (15 cm) tall, 9 in. (23 cm) wide; leaves to 5 in. (13 cm) long, heart-shaped, glossy green with varying silver splashings and speckles. A good garden plant and companion for small hostas. Albino forms are available.

Asarum shuttleworthii, little brown jugs, mottled wild ginger, Shuttleworth's ginger, wild ginger. Eastern North America, Virginia, the Carolinas, northern Georgia, to Alabama.

MS to FS; flowers brown, 3-lobed, darker inside, to 1.5 in. (4 cm) long, narrow; April–May; plant slowly spreading by creeping rhizomes, 6 in. (15 cm) tall to 18 in. (45 cm) wide; leaves variable, to 3 in. (8 cm) long, round with rounded, sometimes overlapping lobes, rich green with striking silvery markings. All forms have a prostrate growth habit, forming mats of leaves that hide the "little brown jug" flowers in spring. Variety *harperi* from west-central Georgia has smaller, rounded leaves to 1 in. (2.5 cm). Hardy to zone 6. A similar native species with longer rhizomes, *A. lewisii*, is rarely available.

'Callaway' (seen in photo of *Pulmonaria longifolia* 'Bertram Anderson') was named by Fred Galle for its point of discovery, Callaway Gardens in

Georgia. Leaves to 2 in. (5 cm) with good mottling; vigorous; spreads slowly by creeping rhizomes, making a striking effect in time.

'Gosan Valley' is a selected clone of the type. Leaves to 2.5 in. (6 cm) long and 2 in. (5 cm) wide, with very pronounced mottling of silvery white on dark green.

Asarum sieboldii, *usuba saishin* (Jap.). North-central Japan, Korea.

MS to FS; flowers brownish purple with 3 wavy, flaring, pointed lobes; April–May; deciduous, plant rhizomatous, to 10 in. (25 cm) tall; leaves to 4 in. (10 cm) long, heart- to kidney-shaped, with wavy margins, and overlapping lobes, dull green with no markings. This species may represent an Asian relative of *Asarum canadense*, judging by the similarity of the flowers; not quite as large and vigorous as Canadian ginger, it serves the same purpose in gardens.

Asarum sinense, Chinese ginger. Southern China, Sichuan.

MS to FS; flowers ball-shaped, dark brown to brownish purple, with down-turned sepal lobes, covered with fine, whitish hairs, tubular, of minor importance; May; plant clump-forming, 10 in. (25 cm) tall to 12 in. (30 cm) wide; leaves to 4 in. (10 cm) long, heart- to elongated heart-shaped, on long petioles, variable, either solid light green or marked. Just like the flowers, the upper leaf surface and petioles have a dense cover of fine hairs, which imparts a greenish sheen. The high mountains of Sichuan province in China are the habitat of another Chinese species, *Asarum himalayicum* (Himalayan wild ginger), reportedly the only wild ginger native to the Himalayas, where it occurs above 9000 ft. (2700 m), growing in cold, moist, cloud-soaked woods. It may be a challenge to grow these Asian gingers in southeastern North America.

Asarum speciosum. Eastern North America, Appalachians in Virginia and the Carolinas.

MS to FS; flowers mushroom-shaped when unopened, opening wide, 3 lobes rounded and pointed, with white margin and purple inside, showing a creamy white sunburst pattern in the throat, to 1 in. (2.5 cm) long and wide; April–May; plant clump-forming, to 8 in. (20 cm) tall and wide; leaves to 6 in. (15 cm) long and 3 in. (8 cm) wide,

arrow-shaped with rounded lobes, light green in spring, dark green later and usually unmarked. All forms I have observed have an erect growing habit. Although the leaves are usually plain green, they are large, and the long-lasting display of gorgeous flowers is among the best of the native North American wild gingers, rivaling that of *Asarum campaniforme*. During spring bloom time, it is one of the most popular wild gingers at Hosta Hill. 'Buxom Beauty' is a distinctly marked and rounder-leaved selection.

Asarum splendens, Chinese wild ginger. China.

MS to FS; flowers dark purple, urn-shaped, large, to 2 in. (5 cm) across; May; plant vigorously rhizomatous, 10 in. (25 cm) tall to 18 in. (45 cm) wide initially but eventually spreading over a wide area; leaves to 6 in. (15 cm) long, triangular to heart-shaped, dark green with outstanding, cloudy silver markings. Not only a very attractive wild ginger but one of the easiest to grow and propagate, and by far the most vigorous garden asarum: I dug a plant to divide it, leaving many creeping rhizomatous rootlets in the ground; each produced a new plant very quickly. In another place, remnants of a dug-up clump traveled under mortared brick and came up in the middle of a walk composed of compacted Georgia red clay. The leaves withstand winters in zone 6b to −10°F (−23°C). Herbaceous in colder regions. Sometimes offered as *Asarum magnificum*.

Asarum stellatum, starry ginger. Japan, Shikoku.

MS to FS; flowers brownish purple, contracted at throat, with 3 tailed lobes, deep purple with whitish margin and white throat, tails to 1 in. (2.5 cm) long; April–May; plant clump-forming, 6 in. (15 cm) tall to 9 in. (23 cm) wide; leaves to 5 in. (13 cm) long, heart-shaped, glossy green with each half being mostly covered with a silvery cloud leaving a dark green center and margin. The leaf is dotted as if spangled with bright, silvery stars, hence the scientific and common names. A good garden plant.

Asarum subglobosum, *marumi kanaoi* (Jap.). Japan, central Kyushu.

MS to FS; yellowish brown to yellowish white, ball-shaped tube, contracted at throat, with 3 pointed lobes, deep purple with whitish margin and white or brown throat; March–May; plant clump-forming; leaves evergreen, to 5 in. (13 cm) long, rounded heart-shaped, grayish green with varying patterns. Another of the wild gingers subject to pot culture in Japan; many forms, including a white-flowered albino with jade-green flowers, are available. *Asarum trigynum* (*sanko kanaoi* in Japan), a very rare species from Kagoshima Prefecture, is similar but has only 3 pistils instead the usual 6. The jade-green flowers are more elongated and tubular, and the patterned green leaves are triangular. Both are good plants for gardens in zone 7a and south.

Asarum takaoi, small Japanese wild ginger, *hime takaoi* (Jap.). Japan, Honshu, southern Tohoku, Kanto, to Kansai, Shikoku.

MS to FS; flowers usually reddish brown, bowl-shaped, small, to 1 in. (2.5 cm) wide, with 3 straight lobes; April–May; plant rhizomatous, creeping and forming colonies, to 4 in. (10 cm) tall; leaves to 3 in. (8 cm) long, round to oval, dark veining over light gray-green mottling, sometimes with no markings. A widespread species in Japan, extending into the northern regions of Honshu, and among the hardiest species for the garden, hardy to zone 5. Spreads slowly and makes an excellent groundcover in time. Its extreme variability exceeds that of our native *Asarum arifolium*; the many forms in commerce offer random uniformity of leaf variegation at best. Two representatives of the *A. takaoi* complex selected by Japanese collectors for pot culture are the yellow-variegated 'Kinkazkan' (= Mount Kinka) and 'Setsu Getsu Ka' (= snow-moon flower), with light jade-green flowers and leaves variegated with gray and silvery white.

Asarum virginicum, Virginia heartleaf, little brown jugs, pig flower. Eastern North America, Pennsylvania, West Virginia, and Virginia south to northern Georgia.

MS to FS; flowers reddish to greenish brown, urn-shaped, to 1 in. (2.5 cm) wide with 3 pointed, spreading sepal lobes to 0.5 in. (1 cm) long, inside of flower networked with low ridges; plant to 12 in. (30 cm) tall; leaves to 4 in. (10 cm) long, heart-shaped, rich green with pale, with silvery gray markings. A nicely marked wild ginger with good drought tolerance. It is related to *Asarum minor*, which it closely resembles, but at Hosta Hill, I have found *A. virginicum* to be a better garden plant.

Asarum heterophyllum is distinguished by its much shorter flower lobes and a high-relief network of ridges inside the flowers.

Asarum yoshikawae, black dwarf Japanese wild ginger, *kurohime takaoi* (Jap.). Japan, Honshu, Chūbu.

MS to FS; related to *Asarum takaoi* and similar to it, but with larger leaves. Offered in an albino form with light jade-green flowers with a white center. Very rare and still expensive. Hardy to zone 6.

Saruma henryi, pyramidal Chinese ginger, upright Chinese ginger. Western China.

MS to FS; flowers bright yellow, small, to 0.8 in. (2 cm) wide, with 3 flat, rounded lobes; April–September; plant to 24 in. (60 cm) tall and 30 in. (75 cm) wide, stems branching; leaves mostly opposed on long, hairy leafstalks, sometimes singular, to 5 in. (13 cm) long and wide, distinctly and broadly heart-shaped with nicely rounded lobes, depressed veining over leaves, which are shiny, light green at first, turning a dull dark green; stems and leaves covered with tiny hairs, giving them a felty look. Scarce but available, this species is an excellent garden plant here in zone 7a and may be hardy to zone 5. Under the right conditions, it grows taller and much more rapidly than *Asarum* species. Flowering starts early (here, in April) and continues sporadically throughout spring and summer, although heat and drought put it to rest. This newcomer to cultivation makes an excellent accent plant in the shady garden, particularly when planted with all-green hostas, small ferns, and wild gingers. I have it underplanted with small yellow hostas, yellow club moss (*Selaginella kraussiana* 'Aurea'), and dwarf golden sweet flag (*Acorus gramineus* 'Minimus Aureus'), where its erect, dark green, heavily veined leaves make a fine pyramidal accent. With supplemental water, it has withstood droughts with aplomb, continuing to grow and flower all during the summer's heat.

Aspidistra

Aspidistra elatior (cast-iron plant) is sometimes the only houseplant still alive when the owners return from a lengthy vacation. Some say it thrives on neglect, which is how it earned its common name. Its tough constitution together with its beauty—exemplified by long-lasting, leathery leaves—attracted multitudes of indoor gardeners during the Victorian period. Flower arrangers found the leaves indispensable because they stayed fresh almost permanently after cutting. Barkeepers, looking for something better than plastic greenery, took up with the aspidistras and soon it acquired its other common name, barroom plant. It is a classic indoor plant, tolerant of dust, fumes, general neglect—and extremely low light levels. From time to time, a gardener brings a potted cast-iron plant outside, letting it spend the warm season on a shady patio. In 1959, I decided to plant a few clumps out in my Nashville garden, and more than 40 years later both they and their children continue to grace Hosta Hill with their elegance and beauty. Here in zone 7, they have survived intact every winter except one, when temperatures dipped to −10°F (−23°C); the top growth became tattered and unsightly, but the rhizomatous roots survived, sending up fresh leaves in spring. Infrequent local ice storms can bombard the leaves with melting ice particles, falling out of the pine trees; I just cut off the damaged leaves in early spring and let new growth take over.

Cast-iron plants are eminently adated to even the deepest shade, and though their cold hardiness limits them to zone 7 and warmer, they are useful in most northern shady gardens as well. My mother took a few of my extras back to Michigan and potted them in plastic nursery pots, which she plunged every spring into prepared holes lined with empty plastic liners. Before the big freeze started, she brought them back inside, where, slipped into decorative containers, they graced my parents' home all winter. Aspidistras frequently fail to flower in homes or gardens, but this is no problem because the flowers are insignificant and hidden within the foliage.

Aspidistras are endemic to the Himalayas, southern China, and Japan, in moist, shady woodlands. Several of the variegated forms found in China have been propagated and are now available. These can brighten the darkest corners of any garden, but they should not be fertilized because they may turn all green. Cast-iron plants are extremely long-lived and, I daresay, almost permanent. They are evergreen, clump-forming perennials with short rhizomes, usually near soil level. The genus name comes from the Greek *aspidion* (= small, round shield), an allusion to the shape of the stigma. It is classified in the lily-of-the-valley family, Convallariaceae.

Propagate by dividing the rhizome before new growth starts in late winter or spring.

Aspidistras are relatively disease-free; anthracnose and leaf spot are reported but have not been noticed here. Slugs and snails are the natural pollinators of aspidistras, but they seem to munch on juicier things, like hostas or lettuce. Mealy bugs, mites, and scale insects too are occasionally described as pests, but not in my experience. The only insect damage I have seen is the vine weevils' scalloping of the leaf margins.

Species and cultivars listed are hardy to zone 7; further north, best to pot and overwinter them.

Aspidistra caespitosa, jade ribbon plant. China.
  MS to FS; plant compact, clump-forming, to 24 in. (60 cm) high; leaves upright, elongated lance-shaped, jade-green, arising directly from the rhizome, to 25 in. (63 cm) long and 0.5 in. (1 cm) wide. The tight clumps of leaves, which have been compared to those of daylilies (*Hemerocallis* spp.), add texture to the shady garden. 'Jade Ribbons' is an available selection.

Aspidistra elatior, cast-iron plant, iron plant, barroom plant. China, Japan.
  MS to FS; plant clump-forming, to 4 ft. (1.2 m) high; leaves erect or slightly leaning, elongated elliptic, dark glossy green, arising directly from the rhizome, to 36 in. (90 cm) long and 3–5 in. (8–13 cm) wide, held on rigid, stout petioles to 14 in. (35 cm) long. This is the ubiquitous cast-iron plant of Victorian days. Its appealing leaves present themselves in tight, upright bundles; thick and stout—even high winds will not knock them down. Many variegated forms from China and Japan are available.
  'Akebono' (= dawn of day), to 30 in. (75 cm) high, with oblong-elliptic leaves, to 20 in. (50 cm) long and 4 in. (10 cm) wide, on stout petioles to 10 in. (25 cm) long. Leaves have a white stripe in the center. Remove the occasional all-green leaf.
  '**Asahi**' (= morning sun), to 25 in. (63 cm) high, with oblong-elliptic leaves, to 20 in. (50 cm) long and 4–5 in. (10–13 cm) wide, on stout petioles to 10 in. (25 cm) long. Leaves have progressive whitening and streaking toward the tip and are almost all white at the apex.

'Hoshi Zaro' (= starry sky), to 36 in. (90 cm) high, with oblong-elliptic leaves, to 30 in. (75 cm) long and 4–5 in. (10–13 cm) wide, on stout petioles to 10 in. (25 cm) long. Leaves are white-speckled all over, much like a starry sky.

'Milky Way' ('Minor'), to 20 in. (50 cm) high, with oblong-elliptic leaves, to 16 in. (40 cm) long and 3–4 in. (8–10 cm) wide, on stout petioles to 8 in. (20 cm) long. White-speckled leaves, similar to 'Hoshi Zaro' but smaller.

'Okame', to 30 in. (75 cm) high, with oblong-elliptic leaves, to 24 in. (60 cm) long and 4 in. (10 cm) wide, on stout petioles to 8 in. (20 cm) long. Leaves have white blotches throughout.

'Variegata', to 40 in. (1 m) high, with oblong-elliptic leaves, to 32 in. (80 cm) long and 4–5 in. (10–13 cm) wide, on stout petioles to 10 in. (25 cm) long. Leaves have irregular white stripes, narrow and wide, throughout. Remove the occasional all-green leaf.

'Variegata Ashei', to 38 in. (95 cm) high, with oblong-elliptic leaves. The leaf center is pale. Leaves are irregularly white-striped more or less equally throughout.

'Variegata Exotica', to 38 in. (95 cm) high, with oblong-elliptic leaves. The leaves have bold, irregular white stripes throughout.

Aspidistra linearifolia, narrow-leaved cast-iron plant. China.

MS to FS; plant clump-forming, to 30 in. (75 cm) high; leaves erect or slightly leaning, elongated straplike, dark shiny green, arising directly from the rhizome, to 28 in. (70 cm) long and 0.8 in. (2 cm) wide. A relatively new species from China. **'Leopard'** has green leaves richly speckled with yellow spots. Hardy to zone 8, 7 with protection.

Aspidistra lurida, small cast-iron plant. China.

MS to FS; plant clump-forming, to 8 in. (20 cm) high; leaves erect or slightly leaning, elongated elliptic, dark glossy green, arising directly from the rhizome, to 10 in. (25 cm) long. Hardy to zone 8. The variegated 'Irish Mist' grows to 18 in. (45 cm) high, with oblong-elliptic leaves, to 10 in. (25 cm) long and 2–3 in. (5–8 cm) wide, on stout petioles to 4 in. (10 cm) long; yellow speckles and markings appear all over its mature leaves. Hardy to zone 7; further north, a subject for potting only.

Aspidistra typica, cast-iron plant. China.

MS to FS; the following cultivars are of uncertain parentage but may turn out to be connected with *Aspidistra typica*.

'China Moon', plant compact, clump-forming, to 10 in. (25 cm) high, with small oblong-elliptic leaves, to 9 in. (23 cm) long and 3 in. (8 cm) wide, on thin, rigid petioles 6–7 in. (15–18 cm) long. Leaves are spotted with creamy yellow and brighten up a shady corner.

'China Star', plant clump-forming, to 20 in. (50 cm) high, with oblong-elliptic leaves, 8–10 in. (20–25 cm) long and 2 in. (5 cm) wide. Leaves are spattered with yellow specks.

'China Sun', plant clump-forming, to 24 in. (60 cm) high, with oblong-elliptic leaves, to 20 in. (50 cm) long and 2 in. (5 cm) wide. Leaves are specked with light yellow dots.

Asplenium

The most tropical-looking hardy ferns available for the shady garden are members of the genus *Asplenium*, the highly decorative and long-lived spleenworts. Some, like maidenhair spleenwort (*Asplenium trichomanes*) and brownstem spleenwort (*A. platyneuron*) are considered delicate, but I can vouch for their rugged nature. They spread spores, with resulting baby ferns, all over Hosta Hill; their favorite anchorage is cracks in bricks or between rocks, but they will also find a place on dense, acid Georgia red clay. Once established in a garden, *A. trichomanes* makes itself at home, showing off its petite, tidy rosettes here and there without the gardener's intervention. Leave it be or move it, it is attractive anywhere. Many spleenworts are of tropical origin and so not suitable outdoors in temperate zone gardens, although widely grown as houseplants and in greenhouses. The many hardy species, with their variety of leaf forms, textures, and colors, are the ones considered here: no shady garden should be without a few of these valuable assets.

The hardy spleenworts are native to shady woodlands and are cosmopolitan in the temperate regions of North America and Eurasia. The classification of certain fern groups is still debated; I follow those who include *Camptosorus*, *Ceterach*, *Phyllitis*, and several other genera with the spleenworts. The genus gets its name from the classical Greek *a* and *spleen* (= no or without [the] spleen), alluding to its medicinal properties. Some species are used as a treatment for parasitic worms, chest complaints, and digestive tract disorders, and as poultices for bruises and burns. *Asplenium* is classified in the spleenwort family, Aspleniaceae.

Spleenworts are successfully cultivated in medium shade and where some sun filters into the garden. Morning sun is ideal, but they do not appreciate direct sun from noon through late afternoon. They do best in a light, well-draining woodland soil, rich in organic matter. Some species prefer alkaline soil (I sweeten the soil by mixing in dolomitic limestone or turkey grit made from crushed seashells), others an acid soil, so species descriptions include soil preference. Spleenworts like abundant moisture, but all species listed tolerate dry conditions to some extent. Some are difficult to establish—*Asplenium ruta-muraria* (wall rue), for example; removing a small start of this tiny, delicate fern, which is sometimes seen growing luxuriantly on old walls, usually ends in its demise, so it is best admired in its natural habitat. Cosmopolitan species like *A. trichomanes* and *A. platyneuron* are best for gardens. With their great diversity of leaf shape and texture, the spleenworts make great companion plants for wildflowers, other ferns, and hostas and fit in well anywhere in the shady garden. They are particularly useful in isolated places along walks, where they add greenery between rocks and along watercourses. The American and European hardy spleenworts are hardy to zone 4, with some like *A. platyneuron* usable in zone 2. All species grown at Hosta Hill are of very easy culture, maintaining themselves with little or no care. They are ideal ferns for the shady garden.

Propagate spleenworts by raising them from fresh spores. Once established, they are very prolific and will naturalize in many places of the garden, whence the fledgling plants can be lifted and transplanted to suitable locations.

Occasionally spleenworts are attacked by scale insects and mealy bugs, but I have not seen such damage. Infestations of foliar nematodes are usually not fatal, but they do disfigure the leaflets and reduce the vigor of the plants.

Most species and cultivars listed form slowly expanding clumps and are evergreen, though the leaves may be disfigured by ice and heavy snow.

Asplenium ceterach, scale fern, rusty-back fern. Central and southern Europe east to the Caucasus, Mediterranean region, western Asia, India, Himalayas.

Some sun, LS to WS; evergreen, rhizomes short, upright; fronds produced in rosettes, short, lance-shaped, divided into alternate leaflets (pinnae) of oblong to rounded tips, deeply cleft between leaflets nearly to the midrib; fronds 5–8 in. (13–20 cm) long, with heavy substance, dark green above and covered with yellowish to silvery brown scales beneath; spore cases (sori) few, short. A tough fern for the rockery, dry places, and alkaline soils. Like *Polypodium polypodioides* (resurrection fern), it rolls up its fronds to conserve water during droughts. It does not like soggy or wet soils and is best in elevated situations that guarantee good drainage. Site where leaves will remain dry; continuous moisture on them brings decline. Difficult to establish where high humidity and rainfall keep the soil saturated. *Ceterach* is the Arabic name for this fern. Hardy in zones 5 to 8.

Asplenium platyneuron, brownstem spleenwort, ebony spleenwort, blackstem spleenwort. North America, Ontario to Quebec, south to Georgia, west to Texas and the Rocky Mountains.

Some sun, LS to WS; evergreen to semi-evergreen in colder areas, rhizomes short, upright; fronds produced in rosettes, fertile fronds to 20 in. (50 cm) tall, erect, tapering at top and bottom, dark green, fertile leaflets narrowly oblong, pointed tip, with prominent earlike lobe at base, toothed and serrated margins, alternately spaced; sterile fronds more numerous, to 10 in. (25 cm), not erect, bending down, often flat on the ground, light green, evergreen, leaflets more rounded, spaced closer, lobe present but not as manifest, margins less toothed; veins on all leaflets are forked; spore cases (sori) short, straight, running together. The epithet (*platyneuron* = with broad veins) stems from an old, inaccurate illustration. This is a small, rugged fern for dry places; it is abundant in the wild and prevalent in suburbia, where it pops up, weedlike, in the most unexpected places. It is always welcome in gardens, however, where its small size and charming looks are appreciated. It does not like soggy or wet soils and is best in elevated situations that guarantee good drainage. At Hosta Hill, it shows up in both alkaline and moderately acid soils, in mortar joints of brick curbing, next to rocks, or on rock ledges—almost anywhere in the garden. Occasionally grows in full sun. Hardy in zones 3 to 8; alkaline, neutral, and acid soils to pH 6. *Asplenium resiliens* (blackstem spleenwort) is similar, with more rounded and more opposite leaflets, but not quite as hardy, zones 6 to 9. Its stems are a true glossy black.

Asplenium rhizophyllum, walking fern, walking spleenwort. North America, Ontario to Quebec, south to northern Georgia, west to Oklahoma and Minnesota.

Some sun, LS to WS; evergreen, rhizomes short, upright, with glossy brown scales; fronds simple, produced as single leaves to 7 in. (18 cm) long, 1 in. (2.5 cm) wide at base, supported by a short stalk, brown and scaly at the base, smooth green above; leaves elongated triangular, heart-shaped at the base, arching, tapering to a long, thin point that touches the ground as leaves mature, evergreen, leathery, shiny green above and dull green below; veins free, networked; spore cases scattered over undersurface from base to tip. Site this small conversation-piece fern where it can be observed closely: in mature specimens the leaf arches over, and its tips touch the ground, at which point new ferns sprout, hence the epithet (*rhizophyllum* = root-leaved) and common names. Years ago, I saw these most unusual ferns flourishing on moss-covered limestone rocks in the Appalachian Valley of northeastern Georgia; the mother fern had formed colonies of smaller ferns all around. It is now scarce in the wild and should not be collected. Requires moist, alkaline soil; add dolomitic limestone to acid topsoils. Hardy in zones 5 to 8.

Asplenium scolopendrium, hart's tongue fern. Europe, western Asia, eastern North America, Ontario, New Brunswick, New York, Tennessee.

MS to FS; evergreen, rhizomes short, upright, creeping, hidden under the leaf bases; fronds simple, produced as single leaves to 15 in. (38 cm) long, 2 in. (5 cm) wide; supported by a short stalk, brown and scaly; leaves produced in crowns, elongated strap-shaped, with wavy edges, in European forms lobed, incised, arching, heart-shaped at base, tapering gradually to a point, either blunt, or often forked, leathery, glossy light green above and duller below; veins free, ending uniformly distant from edge; spore cases scattered over undersurface from base to tip. Veins free, networked; spore cases linear, elongated, mostly in pairs. At one time this extremely variable spleenwort was the rarest fern in North America, but new colonies of rescued and propagated individuals have been reintroduced to the wild. Requires ever-moist, alkaline to neutral soil; slightly acid soils are occasionally tolerated. Prefers high humidity; benefits from misting or overhead watering during droughts. Hardy in zones 5 to 8. The American form, var. *americanum*, is seldom offered.

Selected cultivars with similar features have been grouped as follows: Cristatum Group (crested tips); Marginatum Group (toothed and irregular margins, ridged leaves); Ramocristatum Group (fronds branched near the tip, each branch tip crested); and Ramomarginatum Group (fronds branched near the tip, each branch toothed or irregularly margined). Cultivars are widely available from wildflower nurseries.

'Angustifolium' (narrow-leaved hart's tongue fern), fronds to 18 in. (45 cm) long, only 1.5 in. (4 cm) wide.

'Capitatum' (tasseled hart's tongue fern), fronds to 14 in. (35 cm) long with crested tip.

'Crispum' (wavy-frond hart's tongue fern), fronds to 20 in. (50 cm) long, evenly undulate, deeply folded and ruffled margin. Often confused with 'Undulatum'.

'Crispum Bolton's Nobile', fronds to 25 in. (63 cm) long and 10 in. (25 cm) wide, ruffled margin.

'Crispum Golden Queen' (golden hart's tongue fern), greenish yellow fronds to 20 in. (50 cm) long, evenly undulate and ruffled margin.

'Crispum Moly', fronds to 30 in. (75 cm) long, quickly tapering to a sharp tip, ruffled margin.

'Cristatum' (cockscomb hart's tongue fern), fronds to 14 in. (35 cm) long with crest divided many times, each division with a spreading, crested tip. Sterile.

'Digitatum' ('Digitatum Cristatum'), fronds to 20 in. (50 cm) long, many-branched, each ending in a flat crest.

'Fimbriatum', fronds to 30 in. (75 cm) long, heavily fringed.

'Laceratum Kaye' ('Kaye's Lacerate', 'Kaye's Laceratum'; Kaye's hart's tongue fern), broad fronds to 14 in. (35 cm) long, deeply and unevenly divided, shredded, with crested tip.

'Marginatum' (hart's tongue fern), narrow fronds to 18 in. (45 cm) long, deeply lobed margins.

'Muricatum', fronds to 14 in. (35 cm) long, pleated and wrinkled surface.

'Ramocristatum', fronds to 14 in. (35 cm) long, branched, with branch terminals crested.

'Ramosum' (twin hart's tongue fern), fronds to 14 in. (35 cm) long, divided into 2 branches, forming two blades.

'Sagitatum' (arrowhead hart's tongue fern), lobes produced at the base, creating elongated, arrowhead-shaped fronds to 18 in. (45 cm) long.

'Sagitocrispum', fronds arrowhead-shaped like 'Sagitatum', to 18 in. (45 cm) long, frond terminals crispate.

'Sagitocristatum', fronds arrowhead-shaped like 'Sagitatum', to 18 in. (45 cm) long, frond terminals crested.

'Speciosum', fronds to 30 in. (75 cm) long, deeply folded and pleated.

'Undulatum' (undulate hart's tongue fern), fronds to 18 in. (45 cm) long, darker green than 'Crispum', with wavy, less undulate margins. Fertile.

Asplenium trichomanes, maidenhair spleenwort. Cosmopolitan in North America, Europe, and Asia.

LS to FS; evergreen to semi-evergreen in colder areas, rhizomes short, upright, with dark brown scales; fronds produced in rosettes, fertile fronds 4–7 in. (10–18 cm) tall, erect, tapering at top and bottom, dark green, fertile leaflets round to oval, lacking the earlike projections of *Asplenium platyneuron*, slightly toothed, opposite, tightly spaced in upper half, spaced apart toward the base; sterile fronds usually flat on the ground; veins on all leaflets are free and forked; spore cases (sori) few, short, running together. This dainty, pretty fern requires a special position in the garden to be fully appreciated; an elevated site in the rock garden or between limestone rocks near a path would be ideal. It grows in alkaline soil and does not like soggy or wet soils. The common name comes from the resemblance of the leaflets to those of the southern maidenhair fern, *Adiantum capillus-veneris*. Hardy in zones 5 to 8; alkaline soil. In gardens with acid soils, *Asplenium pinnatifidum* (lobed spleenwort), with lobed leaflets, and *A. montanum* (mountain spleenwort), with more triangular leaflets, can be substituted; they are somewhat larger and grow here in granitic, more acid soils. Cultivars with in-

cised fronds are combined in the *A. trichomanes* Incisum Group.

'Cristatum', fronds to 5 in. (13 cm) long, leaflets (pinnae/pinnules) with the capitate frond tip (leaflet) only crested.

'Greenfield', Incisum Group, fronds to 6 in. (15 cm) long, leaflets (pinnae/pinnules) triangular and deeply incised.

'Incisum', Incisum Group, fronds to 6 in. (15 cm) long, leaflets (pinnae/pinnules) triangular and deeply incised.

'Incisum Moulei' ('Moulei'), Incisum Group, fronds to 4 in. (10 cm) long, leaflets (pinnae/pinnules) linear and deeply incised.

'Ramocristatum', fronds to 6 in. (15 cm) long, leaflets (pinnae/pinnules) branched with frond tip (leaflet) on branches crested.

'Trogyense', Incisum Group, fronds to 4 in. (10 cm) long, leaflets (pinnae/pinnules) triangular and deeply incised; a selection of *Asplenium trichomanes* subsp. *pachyrachis*.

Aster

Asters are primarily plants for the sunny border. Gorgeous flowers are their glory, but in shade, they stop blooming. I do grow *Aster tataricus* (Tatarian aster) in the southeast corner of the garden, where it gets full sun from morning until noon. To increase bloom count, I cut it back in early summer to about half its ultimate height of 7 ft. (2 m). Its flowers are beautiful, like lavender-blue stars, as the classical generic name indicates (*aster* = star). Years ago, I found **A. divaricatus** (white wood aster), low-growing and still topped with white flowers, on an outing to North Georgia in late October. It grew near the path, where the woods opened up somewhat, but I figured it was in considerable shade during the day, so I collected seeds from a few heads gone over. In a few years, the wood aster had seeded itself all over Hosta Hill, obliterating more attractive, showy woodland plants. I did like the nice, dark green, elongated heart-shaped leaves, but I found the flowers ragged and unkempt—so no longer are there wood asters in my woods. Certainly *A. divaricatus* is a candidate for lightly shaded areas of the garden, but it must be deadheaded constantly to prevent its taking over. Other woodland asters also seed prolifically, requiring the gardener's endless attention during fruiting. A good one is *A. lateriflorus* (calico aster) with white or pale purple flowers, growing to 5 ft. (1.5 m). Another for light shade with some sun is *A. umbellatus* (flattop aster), which has ragged, white petals with yellow or pinkish centers carried umbrellalike atop the stems; but it is a giant at 8 ft. (2.5 m) and therefore hard to place in a garden of usually low-growing woodlanders. Both are of easy culture in moderately acid, moist soil. Other than the incredibly sturdy *A. tataricus*, I no longer grow asters here: they are subject to all sorts of fungal diseases; attract mites, aphids, slugs, and snails; and serve as a host for nematodes. With well over a thousand species in the garden, I can do without plants that become a burden rather than a joy.

Astilbe

Astilbes have been favorites since the importations of Thunberg and Siebold in the late 1700s to early 1800s; like hostas, they are indispensable—a "must have" for every shady garden. I have grown astilbes in my shady garden for several decades, and they become more appealing to me with each passing year. Astilbes are herbaceous, rhizomatous, long-lived perennials of the saxifrage family, Saxifragaceae, originating in moist woodlands of North America (two species) and Southeast Asia (all others). All are well adapted to shady, moist conditions. Many of the available hybrids form large, slowly spreading clumps resembling subshrubs, and in larger gardens, they can be massed with grand effect. Their crowning glory are the plumelike panicles wafting above the leaf mound. After the flowers fade and the leaves die back in autumn, the long-lasting panicles remain upright, turn brown, and provide attractive garden highlights throughout the winter; some people use them dried in flower arranging. Individually, the flowers are very small, but they drift above the leaves in large plumes of white, red, pink, and purple. Tall as they are, the flowering panicles require no staking, though after a hard rain they may droop a little. The medium to dark green leaves, which in some varieties show a bronze to reddish tinge, arise directly from the rhizome. They are compound, usually 2- or 3-ternate, with each leaf divided into three to five leaflets. Each leaflet is toothed and, depending on the hybrid's parentage, either ovate to lance- or heart-shaped.

Several interesting species recently imported from the Far East have been added to those of Chinese origin, which have been in commerce for some time. One of these I like very much is *Astilbe chinensis* var. *pumila*, a great, small companion plant for miniature hostas. I am also quite fond of one of our two native North American astilbes, *A. biternata*, as a large background plant for shady corners; its imposing plumes of white to yellowish white flowers and shrublike proportions cannot be missed. I remember seeing a blooming colony of *A. biternata* in the North Georgia mountains, and I shall never forget that sight. Hosta Hill now has a specimen of this wonderful native backing up Japanese anemones and toad lilies at the base of a loblolly pine.

By far the largest of the several groups of hybrids in commerce is *Astilbe* ×*arendsii*, named for German nurseryman Georg Arends. *Astilbe* ×*arendsii* now includes not only Arends' complex crosses (which he made between 1900 and the 1930s using *A. chinensis* var. *davidii*, *A. astilboides*, *A. japonica*, and *A. thunbergii*) but those contributed by hybridizers in France, the Netherlands, and other countries. The nomenclature of these hybrids is confused. Many previously considered *A.* ×*arendsii* have been reassigned to species with which they are ostensibly more closely associated—for example, *A.* ×*arendsii* 'Deutschland' is now *A. japonica* 'Deutschland'. Most gardeners will forgo the precision and simply refer to it as *Astilbe* 'Deutschland'; nevertheless, I have listed all cultivars under these latest species affiliation.

I feature *Astilbe* ×*arendsii* 'Cattleya' prominently around the patio in the rear garden of Hosta Hill. There it is combined with hellebores, hostas, ferns, Chinese mayapples, variegated Hakone grass, foamflowers, and epimediums to form a loose, natural-looking border that provides plant contrast and color all year. In late spring, its pink flowers continue the show started by 'Pink Pearl' azalea. Elsewhere the pure white spires of *A. japonica* 'Deutschland' and *A.* ×*arendsii* 'Diamant' brighten up the shady borders. The compound mass of toothed foliage provides an excellent contrast to the bold leaves of hostas and native mayapples. I prefer astilbes with white flowers because they stand out more in a shady garden, and of course the smaller ones fit into half-acre Hosta Hill much better. *Astilbe simplicifolia* 'William Buchanan' has deeply toothed, dark green leaves; it flowers fairly late, here in late June, and its creamy white plumes combine well with a group of small, white-margined *Hosta* 'Allan P. McConnell'.

Astilbes must have water; I have learned to pay attention to their emerging panicles, which begin to droop as soon as there is a lack of moisture at the roots. This unmistakable signal requires immediate action, after which the plants recover rapidly. (Successful gardeners pay attention to their plants. Not paying any attention when plants "talk" can result in losses and disappointment.) Wherever astilbes are placed at Hosta Hill, the native acid clay soil has been amended with liberal amounts of peat moss, pine bark, compost, and other water-retaining organic components. Because pine bark mulch and chips contribute to the drainage, I do not use sand. Watering is by buried soaker hoses, the kind made out of recycled automobile tires. This is the easiest way to keep astilbes and other perennials with thirsty roots and rhizomes happy and healthy. Although astilbes can be grown in full sun when situated in a boggy site, in shady corners their water requirements are considerably reduced; my established clumps come through periods of hot Southern drought without damage even when I am not there to water them.

Astilbes are reliably winter hardy. Most thrive in zones 4 to 8.

The genus name *Astilbe* (= without shine) refers to the flowers' lack of brilliance; the leaves of some species are quite shiny, however, a feature easily more conspicuous.

Propagate by dividing the completely dormant rhizome in late autumn, late winter, or in spring, after the ground thaws. I dig the rhizomes with a large ball of soil attached so as not to disturb the roots, and carry as much of the attached soil as possible along to the new location or the pot, as the case may be. Some species can be propagated by seed, but the seeds are short-lived, remaining viable for less than three weeks. To me, division is a lot easier.

Leaf spot and powdery mildew are reported but never—not in 50 years—seen here.

Astilbe ×*arendsii*. Garden hybrid.

A very few of this group of garden hybrids are limited to zone 5, and gardeners in zone 4 may have to use extra protection to push their limit. Be-

ware of ordering duplicate plants under both the original German cultivar name and its English translation.

'Amethyst', lilac to pink flowers, early; 36 in. (90 cm) tall and wide.

'Anita Pfeifer', salmon-pink flowers; 32 in. (80 cm) tall.

'Bergkristall' ('Mountain Crystal'), white flowers, midseason; 40 in. (1 m) tall.

'Brautschleier' ('Bridal Veil'), white, nodding flowers, early; 36 in. (90 cm) tall and wide.

'Bressingham Beauty', light pink flowers, midseason, bronze-tinted leaves; 36 in. (90 cm) tall and 24 in. (60 cm) wide.

'Cattleya', lilac flowers, late; 4 ft. (1.2 m) tall and 36 in. (90 cm) wide.

'Ceres', lilac flowers; 36 in. (90 cm) tall and wide.

'Diamant' ('Diamond'), white flowers, early; 30 in. (75 cm) tall and 24 in. (60 cm) wide.

'Else Schluck', carmine-red flowers, midseason; 36 in. (90 cm) tall.

'Fanal', dark crimson flowers, early; leaves dark; 32 in. (80 cm) tall and 18 in. (45 cm) wide.

'Feuer' ('Fire'), salmon to carmine-red flowers on narrow panicles, late; 32 in. (80 cm) tall and 24 in. (60 cm) wide.

'Gloria' ('Glory'), dark pink flowers, early; 32 in. (80 cm) tall and 24 in. (60 cm) wide.

'Glut' ('Glow'), dark red flowers, late; 36 in. (90 cm) tall and 24 in. (60 cm) wide.

'Granat' ('Garnet'), crimson-red flowers; 32 in. (80 cm) tall and 24 in. (60 cm) wide.

'Grete Pungel', light pink flowers, early; 40 in. (1 m) tall and 24 in. (60 cm) wide.

'Hyazinth' ('Hyacinth'), dark pink flowers, midseason; 36 in. (90 cm) tall and 18 in. (45 cm) wide.

'Irrlicht' ('Jack o' Lantern', 'Will-o'-the-Wisp'), white flowers, early to midseason; 18 in. (45 cm) tall.

'Lilli Goos', dark bronze-tinted leaves, midseason; 32 in. (80 cm) tall.

'Obergärtner Jürgens' ('Headgardener Jürgens'), carmine-red flowers, early; 36 in. (90 cm) tall.

'Rosa Perle' ('Pink Pearl'), reddish pink flowers, early; 30 in. (75 cm) tall.

'Rotlicht' ('Red Light'), bright red flowers, bronze-tinted leaves, midseason; 36 in. (90 cm) tall and 24 in. (60 cm) wide.

'Salland', carmine-red flowers, midseason; 6 ft. (1.8 m) tall.

'Spartan', deep red flowers, midseason; 24 in. (60 cm) tall.

'Spinell', salmon-red flowers; 36 in. (90 cm) tall.

'Venus', very light, shell-pink flowers; 36 in. (90 cm) tall.

'Weisse Gloria' ('White Glory'), white flowers, late; 36 in. (90 cm) tall and 18 in. (45 cm) wide.

Astilbe biternata, false goatsbeard. North America, Virginia, Kentucky, south to Georgia.

Sun, LS to MS; tiny white to light yellow flowers carried on tall, open, drooping panicles; plant to 4 ft. (1.2 m) tall and 36 in. (90 cm) wide, large dark green leaves divided into leaflets with sharply toothed edges. A handsome native.

Astilbe chinensis, Chinese astilbe. China, Korea, Japan.

Sun, LS to MS; pinkish flowers on open, slender panicles, late; plant 24 in. (60 cm) high and wide; leaves 2- and 3-ternate, dark green, serrate edges, hairy. An attractive, vigorous garden plant with creeping rootstock. Variety *davidii* has pink flowers on tall, narrow panicles, late; plant 6 ft. (1.8 m) tall and 36 in. (90 cm) wide; leaves 2- and 3-ternate, dark green; larger than the species, needs abundant water and some sun, spectacular. Variety *taquetii* ('Taquetii') is smaller, 4 ft. (1.2 m) tall and 24 in. (60 cm) wide, with bronze-tinged foliage and reddish purple flowers on tall, dense, columnar panicles; var. *pumila* ('Pumila'; dwarf Chinese astilbe) has lilac flowers on short, dense panicles, plant 10 in. (25 cm) tall and 9 in. (23 cm) wide; leaves small, dark green with red tint; small, sun-tolerant, creeping. It is a late-flowerer and good for covering small patches of ground. Available *Astilbe chinensis* cultivars are all hardy to zone 5.

'Finale', bright pink flowers, leaves dark; 20 in. (50 cm) tall and 18 in. (45 cm) wide.

'Intermezzo', salmon-pink flowers; 24 in. (60 cm) tall and 18 in. (45 cm) wide.

'Purpurkerze' ('Purple Candle'), darker, more vivid flowers. An excellent, drought-tolerant cultivar.

'Purpurlanze' ('Purple Lance') also has darker, more vivid flowers than the type. Another excellent, drought-tolerant cultivar.

'Serenade', bright pinkish red flowers, feathery; 20 in. (50 cm) tall and 18 in. (45 cm) wide.

'Spätsommer' ('Late Summer'), pink to pinkish red flowers; 18 in. (45 cm).

'Superba', intense magenta flowers on tall, conical panicles held by strong, brownish stems, late; 4 ft. (1.2 m) tall and 36 in. (90 cm) wide; leaves small, dark green with bronze tint. Outstanding.

'Veronica Klose', dark pink to pinkish red flowers; 18 in. (45 cm).

'Visions' has dark raspberry-pink flowers tightly clustered on flowerstalks to 14 in. (35 cm). Suited for dry regions with periods of drought.

Astilbe ×*crispa*. Garden hybrid.

'Liliput', salmon-pink flowers, reddish green leaves, midseason; very small, 8 in. (20 cm) tall and wide.

'Perkeo', deep pink flowers, reddish green leaves, midseason. At 8 in. (20 cm) tall and 9 in. (23 cm) wide, a great companion plant for miniature hostas.

'Peter Pan', pink flowers; 10 in. (25 cm) tall and 9 in. (23 cm) wide.

Astilbe grandis, giant Chinese astilbe. Southwest China, Sichuan.

Sun, LS to MS; tiny white to creamy white, occasionally light pink flowers carried on massive panicles, midseason; plant to 6 ft. (1.8 m) tall and 5 ft. (1.5 m) wide, large pubescent brownish, later dark green leaves, 3-ternate, divided into ovate leaflets with sharp, doubly serrate edges. A majestic astilbe for the background. Collected by plantsman Dan Hinkley in 1998, this aptly named, truly grand astilbe appears to be the Chinese analogue of our native *Astilbe biternata*, only larger. Needs space.

Astilbe japonica, Japanese astilbe. Japan, southern Honshu, Shikoku, Kyushu.

Sun, LS to MS; white flowers on open, slender panicles, early; plant 30 in. (75 cm) high and 24 in. (60 cm) wide; leaves 2- and 3-ternate, narrow, glossy dark green, margins toothed. Grows in moist, rocky streambeds and ravines, so an excellent companion for *Hosta longipes* (rock hosta). Hybrids involving this species were bred in Germany (note the geographical names); most have medium green foliage.

'Bonn', carmine-red flowers, early; 28 in. (70 cm) tall.

'Bremen', dark pink flowers, early; 24 in. (60 cm) tall and 18 in. (45 cm) wide.

'Deutschland' ('Germany'), white flowers, early; 18 in. (45 cm) tall and 12 in. (30 cm) wide.

'Emden', purplish pink flowers, early; 28 in. (70 cm) tall.

'Europa' ('Europe'), light pink flowers on dense spikes, early; 24 in. (60 cm) tall and 18 in. (45 cm) wide.

'Gladstone', white flowers, early; 24 in. (60 cm) tall and 18 in. (45 cm) wide.

'Koblenz', deep pink to salmon-red flowers, early; 24 in. (60 cm) tall and 18 in. (45 cm) wide.

'Köln' ('Cologne'), deep pink flowers, early; 20 in. (50 cm) tall.

'Mainz', lilac-pink flowers; 28 in. (70 cm) tall.

'Montgomery', deep red flowers, early; 24 in. (60 cm) tall and 18 in. (45 cm) wide. Red-tinted pubescent leaves are nicely serrated.

'Möwe' ('Seagull'), salmon-pink flowers, early; 28 in. (70 cm) tall.

'Peach Blossom' ('Drayton Glory'), peachy pink flowers, early; 24 in. (60 cm) tall and 18 in. (45 cm) wide.

'Red Sentinel', deep crimson flowers, loosely arranged, early; 24 in. (60 cm) tall and 18 in. (45 cm) wide.

'Rheinland', bright pink flowers, early; 20 in. (50 cm) tall and 14 in. (35 cm) wide.

'Washington', white flowers; 28 in. (70 cm) tall.

Astilbe koreana, Korean astilbe. Korea, northern China.

Sun, LS to MS; flowers pink in bud, yellowish white when open, slender, drooping panicles, midseason; plant 14 in. (35 cm) high and wide; leaves 2- and 3-ternate, pubescent, dark brownish green.

Astilbe rivularis, Himalayan astilbe. Himalayas, from Pakistan to Yunnan in southwest China.

Sun, LS to MS; yellowish white flowers on tall, open panicles, late; plant to 5 ft. (1.5 m) high and 36 in. (90 cm) wide; leaves 2- and 3-ternate, large, ovate, pubescent, dark brownish green. Outstanding leaf color for shady gardens.

Astilbe simplicifolia. Japan, Honshu.

Sun, LS to MS; white flowers on slender, nodding panicles, midseason; plant 12 in. (30 cm) high and wide; leaves simple, ovate, glossy bright green, margins coarsely toothed. Rare in the wild and in cultivation, this species nevertheless passed on its

low growth habit to the many hybrids involving it. All cultivars are excellent companions for small hostas, wildflowers, and ferns.

'Aphrodite', red flowers, midseason; 18 in. (45 cm) tall and 24 in. (60 cm) wide, bronze foliage.

'Atrorosea', dark pink flowers, midseason; 18 in. (45 cm) tall and 12 in. (30 cm) wide.

'Bronze Elegance' ('Bronze Eleganz', 'Bronce Elegance'), reddish pink flowers, midseason; 12 in. (30 cm) tall and wide, bronze foliage.

'Carnea', salmon to pink flowers; 12 in. (30 cm) tall and wide, bronze foliage.

'Dunkellachs' ('Dark Salmon'), salmon-pink flowers, midseason; 14 in. (35 cm) tall and 12 in. (30 cm) wide, bronze foliage.

'Gnom' ('Gnome'), light pink flowers, midseason; 8 in. (2 cm) tall and 9 in. (23 cm) wide, reddish green leaves. A fine rock garden subject.

'Hennie Graafland', reddish pink flowers, midseason; 12 in. (30 cm) tall and wide, bronze foliage.

'Inshriach Pink', pale pink, nodding flowers, midseason; 12 in. (30 cm) tall and wide, bronze foliage.

'Peter Barrow', white flowers; 16 in. (40 cm) tall and wide.

'Praecox', pale pink flowers, early; 12 in. (30 cm) tall and wide.

'Praecox Alba', white flowers, early; 12 in. (30 cm) tall and wide.

'Rosea', rose-pink flowers, early; 12 in. (30 cm) tall and wide.

'Snowdrift', white flowers, midseason; 12 in. (30 cm) tall and wide, bronze foliage.

'Sprite', pale pink flowers, early; 20 in. (50 cm) tall and wide.

'William Buchanan', white flowers, midseason; 12 in. (30 cm) tall and 8 in. (20 cm) wide, bronze foliage.

Astilbe thunbergii, Thunberg's astilbe. China, Japan, Honshu, Shikoku.

Sun, LS to MS; white or pink flowers on slender, nodding panicles, midseason; plant 20 in. (50 cm) tall and 14 in. (35 cm) wide; leaves 2- and 3-ternate, on red leafstalks, ovate, leaves and leafstalks hairy, green, margins toothed. Variety *fujisanensis* (Japan, central Honshu) is similar but with double-toothed, small, rigid leaves; var. *sikokumontana* (Japan, Shikoku) is similar but with double-toothed, lance-shaped leaves. The species and its varieties are rare in cultivation but have produced a race of garden hybrids.

'Moerheim' ('Moerheimii'), white flowers, midseason; 36 in. (90 cm) tall and 24 in. (60 cm) wide.

'Professor van der Wielen', white, nodding flowers, midseason; 4 ft. (1.2 m) tall and 36 in. (60 cm) wide.

'Straussenfeder' ('Ostrich Plume'), salmon-pink flowers in open, feathery arrangement, midseason to late; 36 in. (90 cm) tall and 24 in. (60 cm) wide.

Astilboides

Formerly placed in the genus *Rodgersia*, *Astilboides tabularis* (shield-leaf Rodger's flower) is now the only species in the genus *Astilboides*. Native to China and Korea, it grows in moist woodlands and along lakes and streams. In the wild this species grows to immense size: the leaves, which resemble an umbrella blown inside-out by the wind, reach 40 in. (1 m), and the flowerstalks reach 5 ft. (1.5 m) or more. In cultivation it is usually not as grand, getting to about half that size. It gets cold in its natural habitat, so it is not surprising this species dislikes the hot Southeast, even when planted near water. At Hosta Hill, a specimen of long standing is puny when compared to those I have seen in the cool and rain-rich gardens of western North America. Here *Petasites japonicus* is much better for size and stature but not as well behaved—a thug running all over the place. Nevertheless, both are plants of great architectural value in the shady garden. A visitor once asked me why a plant with such large leaves is called *astilboides* (= like an astilbe), and I explained that botanists use the flowers as a point of comparison. In fact, the inflorescence is stately and composed of plumelike panicles of tiny white flowers, much like *Astilbe* only larger. *Astilboides* is classified in the Saxifragaceae.

Propagate by dividing the rhizome before growth starts in very early spring. Sow seed in a cold frame in autumn.

Large slugs and snails can damage young leaf growth, the emerging buds that appear at soil level, and even mature leaves. Army worms and striped caterpillars feed during summer nights, disfiguring the leaves.

Astilboides tabularis, shield-leaf Rodger's flower. Eastern China, North Korea.

Morning sun, LS; tiny creamy white flowers carried on large panicles reaching to 6 ft. (1.8 m); June–August; plant to 36 in. (90 cm) tall and 5 ft. (1.5 m) wide; leaves shieldlike, to 36 in. (90 cm) long, light green, with hairy cover, rounded in outline but with large, toothlike lobes, often deeply incised; leaf stems stout, rounded, upright. A great accent plant near a water feature or as a background grouping in open woodlands, anchoring plantings of hostas and ferns. Absolutely spectacular in flower. Although it requires moist soil, it will not tolerate waterlogged soils: do not place the rhizome below water level when siting on a pond embankment. Maintain soil moisture content with supplemental water during droughts. Suitable for cultivation in zones 4 to 7; further south it languishes. The large leaves, which impart a tropical flavor, are outdone only by the impressive, tall flower spikes with clouds of white flowers. The epithet *tabularis* (= like a table) comes from the resemblance of the leaves to a round table held on stout stems.

Athyrium

Some lucky gardeners inherit native plants, as I did at Hosta Hill. Even the contractor's bulldozers could not wipe out all the lady ferns formerly carpeting the woodland floor, and a short time after we moved in, these persistent denizens of the Georgia woodland resprouted between the roots of pine trees. The genus *Athyrium* consists of many gardenworthy and decorative ferns, including the very popular variegated *Athyrium nipponicum* 'Pictum' (Japanese painted fern), with new fronds reddish pink and soft bluish gray. Here the Japanese painted fern has hybridized with the native lady fern, *A. filix-femina*, resulting in many distinct hybrids—a second gift from nature.

All the lady ferns I grow are rugged and very hardy. They propagate by spores on regular Georgia red clay, on improved soil, and even in the cracks between brick edgings. The taller lady ferns do not like high winds; our gusty spring thunderstorms flatten much of the young growth on taller clumps. I cut the broken stems and shortly new ones rise up, filling the gaps. This fast-growing character is very useful in windy gardens. Over the years, I have grown many clumps of these delightful, herbaceous, long-lived ferns and find them to be of very easy culture. They return every spring without fail, expanding slowly by means of a creeping, branching rootstock to form large clumps of upright stalks bearing delicately divided fronds. Few ferns can beat them for grace and beauty.

The lady ferns are endemic to the temperate and subarctic regions of the northern hemisphere with some southern locations in South America. The genus name comes from the Greek *atharos* (= good breeder), alluding to the reliable viability of the spores. *Athyrium* is classified in the Woodsiaceae.

I have seen lady ferns growing around the Georgia woods in very deep, almost total shade. Here they show up and grow in the darkest corners of the garden, yet they also stand considerable sun. They do best in a light, well-draining woodland soil, rich in organic matter. Lady ferns thrive in our very acid soil, but neutral to slightly alkaline soils also suit them. They require moisture, which seems to pump them up; when drought conditions persist, the stems become brittle and often break. This is not to say that they will not withstand some drought if grown in shade and given supplemental water. Lady ferns make great companion plants for wildflowers, other ferns, and hostas. Their height makes them good subjects to fill in a background, when fronted by lower-growing companions like the gingers *Asarum canadense* or *A. arifolium*. *Athyrium filix-femina* is very winter hardy, native to protected areas of zone 3; in gardens it has proven hardy in zone 4. In the hot, humid southern regions of North America it tolerates adverse conditions such as some drought and considerable heat. Other lady ferns are a little less hardy but robust nevertheless.

Propagate by dividing the creeping rhizome in autumn after the fronds have dropped or in very early spring. Propagation by spores is also relatively easy under the right conditions. The spores must be sown as soon as they are ripe on a coarse commercial mix with a pH of 7 to 8.5 maintained moist at 70°F (21°C). All the lady ferns here have naturalized and propagate without my intervention, so I simply remove young ferns from spots where they are not wanted and transplant them or give them away.

Lady ferns are prone to rusts, but I have not experienced this in my own plantings. Nor do insects seem to bother them.

Species and cultivars listed are herbaceous and lose their top growth in winter.

Athyrium distentifolium, alpine lady fern. North America, Canada, Alaska, also Europe, Iceland, and Asia Minor, in alpine situations.

LS to FS; fronds to 4 ft. (1.2 m), produced in rosettes on slender stalks emerging directly from the rhizome, scaly at the base, stalk either green or reddish brown, grooved, erect, leaning with age; leaves 2- to 3-compound, light green fronds composed of thin leaflets (pinnae), wedge-shaped, narrow, pointed at top, to 10 in. (25 cm) long; subleaflets deeply cut and toothed, mostly blunt-pointed; veins forked; spore cases (sori) roundish, sometimes tightly horseshoe-shaped. Endemic to the alpine regions of North America and Eurasia, hence robust rhizomes and fronds. Variety *americanum* has been separated from the European alpine lady fern; it frond are narrower with leaflets more widely spaced. Hardy to zone 4 but short-lived in hot humid regions. 'Kupferstiel' ('Copperstem') has red stems.

Athyrium filix-femina, lady fern, common lady fern. Cosmopolitan, northern hemisphere, temperate and subarctic zones, also South America.

LS to FS; fronds deciduous, to 36 in. (90 cm) and 12 in. (30 cm) wide, produced in rosettes on slender stalks emerging directly from the rhizome, scaly at the base, either green or reddish brown, grooved, erect, leaning with age; leaves 2- to 3-compound, light green composed of thin leaflets (pinnae), wedge-shaped, usually narrow, pointed at top, to 8 in. (20 cm) long; subleaflets deeply cut and toothed, mostly blunt-pointed; veins forked; spore cases (sori) short, curved, sometimes horseshoe-shaped. This is the ubiquitous, easily cultivated lady fern. The common name, lady fern, is a literal translation of the epithet. Fronds are produced throughout the growing season, so wind- or rain-damaged fronds are quickly replaced by new growth. I recommend removing the broken fronds, to allow delicate new growth to emerge unhindered. Many different forms exist in the wild, including a green-stemmed variant and one with red or brownish stems. **Variety *asplenioides*** (southern lady fern) is found in southern North America, var. *californicum* and var. *cyclosorum* in western North America, and var. *angustum* and var. *michauxii* in northeastern North America. Forma *rubellum*, with pale wine-colored stems, is sometimes available, as is the cultivar 'Rotstiel' ('Red Stem') with a more reddish stem. All are hardy to zone 3, 2 with protection, and are separated by only minor botanical details. By contrast, the differences in the shapes of the fronds are considerable—and quite significant to collectors. Cultivars have been grouped as follows: Cruciatum Group (crested fronds); Cristatum Group (toothed, finely cut, heavily crested fronds); and Plumosum Group (3- to 4-compound fronds with finely divided leaflets and subleaflets). A few of these extreme forms might serve as accents here and there, but most are too outlandish for garden settings. During heavy rains, the crested fronds get waterlogged and so weighted that they break the brittle stems at ground level; only elaborate support structures can prevent this. The following cultivars are not heavily crested and are therefore suitable in the open garden.

'Acroladon', fronds repeatedly branching, resulting in a unusual, ball-shaped clump; to 12 in. (30 cm).

'Fieldii' ('Fieldiae'), tall and strong-growing with paired leaflets forming a cross pattern; to 30 in. (75 cm).

'Frizelliae' (spiral staircase lady fern, Mrs. Frizell's lady fern, tatting fern), very short leaflets shaped into rounded lobes resembling tatting, a handmade lace; to 20 in. (50 cm).

'Frizelliae Cristatum', similar to 'Frizelliae' but with the main frond forked into a 3-tipped top; to 20 in. (50 cm).

'Ghost', a tall form with narrow, paired leaflets of a ghostly gray on reddish brown stems. Makes an elegant and unusual statement in the garden.

'Minutissimum' (dwarf lady fern, small lady fern) makes a dense rosette; to 12 in. (30 cm).

'Setigerum', leaflets reduced to very slender segments; to 20 in. (50 cm).

'Victoriae', narrow, paired leaflets forming a checked pattern; to 40 in. (1 m). Distinctive, strong-growing, and good-looking.

Athyrium nipponicum, Japanese lady fern. China, Taiwan, Korea, Japan.

LS to FS; fronds to 14 in. (35 cm), produced in rosette-shaped clumps on slender stalks emerging directly from the rhizome, scaly at the base, stalk to 18 in. (45 cm), either green or greenish brown, darker near the base, grooved, arching; leaves 2- to 3-compound, green composed of leaflets (pinnae), wedge-shaped, narrow, pointed at top, to 5 in. (13

cm) long; subleaflets deeply cut and toothed, coming to a point; veins forked; spore cases (sori) linear. One of the best ferns for the garden, competing with all comers. Rhizomes and fronds are robust. Spreads vigorously by spores—delicate little Japanese lady ferns come up all over Hosta Hill. The attractive **'Pictum'** (var. *pictum*, 'Metalicum', 'Metallicum Pictum'; Japanese painted fern, Japanese silver painted fern), possibly the most popular lady fern around, is slightly smaller than the type. Its colorful fronds and stalk (stipe) are simply radiant in spring and remain distinct and beautiful well into autumn. The stem is wine-red to purplish red; adjacent leaflets are suffused with reddish to bluish hues, changing to a lighter, metallic gray toward the tips—a distinct bar effect. Coloration in sporlings is variable; some are similar to the mother fern, others may be deep gray, light gray, or reddish gray. Hybrids (**A. nipponicum 'Pictum'** × **A. filix-femina**) volunteer all over Hosta Hill. Some are a blackish gray; some are pink all over when young, turning a soft gray later; another is almost gray in spring and turns almost black in early summer. Many have the erect stature of *A. filix-femina* but show one or more of the attractive colors of *A. nipponicum* 'Pictum'. The Japanese painted fern is a colorful, charming addition to the garden, whether summers are cool or hot. Hardy in zones 4 to 8, 3 with protection.

Athyrium otophorum. China, Korea, Japan.

LS to FS; fronds to 30 in. (75 cm), produced in clumps on slender stalks emerging directly from the rhizome, scaly at the base, stalk either yellowish green or wine-red to purplish brown, grooved, arching; leaves 2-compound, green to greenish gray, composed of leaflets (pinnae), wedge-shaped, narrow, to 3 in. (8 cm) long and 1 in. (2.5 cm) wide, ovate, pointed or blunt at tip, toothed and slightly lobed; veins forked. This Asian lady fern also shows good color, especially in new fronds. Most specimens offered have a beautiful wine-red color on the stalk and petioles with greenish gray leaflets. Not quite as colorful as *Athyrium nipponicum* 'Pictum' but larger and more impressive in the garden. Hardy in zones 5 to 8.

Athyrium pycnocarpon, American glade fern, narrow-leaved spleenwort. North America, Quebec south to Georgia and Louisiana, west to Kansas.

LS to FS; fronds to 36 in. (90 cm) long and 6 in. (15 cm) wide, narrow, lance-shaped with sharp pointed tip, narrowing toward the base; fertile fronds narrower and more erect, sterile fronds longer, more arching; emerging in rosette-shaped clusters from the rhizome, dark and scaly at the base, green above; leaves 3 in. (8 cm) long, very narrow, with sharp tips and rounded base, margins wavy, not toothed, light green; veins 1- to 2-forked; spore cases (sori) long, slightly curved, from mid-vein to margin. A strikingly different fern for the woodland garden or border. The fronds are produced continually during the growing season; any broken fronds are quickly replaced by new growth. Easily cultivated, it is an attractive addition to my woodlands in spring, when the soft, green leaves have a luminous quality, and in autumn, when the fronds turn a seasonal reddish brown. Not as hardy as *A. filix-femina* but useful in more southern regions of zone 6, 5 with protection and depending on microclimate.

Athyrium thelypteroides, silver glade fern, silvery glade fern, silvery spleenwort. North America, southeastern Canada, south to northern Georgia and west to Missouri.

LS to FS; fronds to 36 in. (90 cm) long and 6 in. (15 cm) wide, pointed at tip, tapering toward the base, emerging directly from the rhizome, scaly at the base, stalk green, hairy, stout and erect, but leaning with age; leaves 2-compound, light to yellowish green, leaflets (pinnae) with no stems, wedge-shaped, narrow, pointed at top, to 6 in. (15 cm) long; subleaflets deeply cut with wavy margins, mostly blunt-pointed; veins not forked; spore cases (sori) narrow, straight, silvery at first, later light brown. Resembles the common lady fern, hence its epithet (*thelypteroides* = like a lady [fern]). It has a soft, dull green color. Fine, yellow hairs impart a bright glow, which, together with the many prominent silvery spore cases on the backside, contributes to its gossamer effect when waving in a spring breeze. Easily cultivated and makes an attractive addition to woodlands and the wildflower border. Hardy in zones 5 to 7, 4 with protection.

Begonia

Over the years I have grown various begonias, mostly the rhizomatous tropical and subtropical beauties now gathered in the *Begonia* Rex-Cultorum Group. Obviously, they were in pots on the patio, where their grandiose leaves added bright accents. Now I grow them less and less: they need a lot of care, and arranging watering during our Appalachian jaunts has become bothersome. More than three decades ago, a neighbor gave me *Begonia grandis*, a hardy begonia. That plant's offspring are still with me, a hundredfold and more. Unlike the tropical showpieces, this begonia is truly hardy and perennial, having withstood several nights of −10°F (−23°C) in my garden. Usually classified as a tuberous begonia, it spreads by both seeds and bulblets (tubercles), colonizing wherever it wants. I put up with it because its subtle fragrance perfumes the air and its soft pink flowers grace the garden from August until the first freeze cuts the plants down, usually sometime in December. On taller plants the rose-red underside of the leaves shows here and there, combining with the soft green and distinctive red veins of the upper surface; this show commences long before the plants start flowering, so color is present throughout the growing season.

Begonia grandis is hardy to zone 6, but underground bulblets may survive somewhat colder weather with protection from hard freezes. They are adapted to shady, moist conditions and do not like sun, except during morning hours. Bulblets reach flowering size quickly. Unwanted seedlings and plants are easily removed, but at times I have used a systemic herbicide to keep the population down: I place a large cardboard tube around the begonia so as not to affect adjoining plants and carefully paint its leaves with the herbicide. The tube, covered with plastic, stays in place until the plant dies. Trilliums do not mix well with hardy begonias; hostas and the larger ferns do fine as companions.

The genus was named for Michel Bégon, a patron of botany. It is classified in the begonia family, Begoniaceae.

Propagation is easy: I let the plants do what they want. Why would anyone want to propagate hardy begonias when they do it so confidently and successfully all by themselves?

Slugs and snails can damage new growth emerging in spring; no other pests or diseases are experienced here.

Begonia grandis, hardy begonia, Evan's begonia. Malay Peninsula, southern China, southern Japan.

MS to FS; flowers lightly fragrant, soft pink, 1.2 in. (3 cm) across, male flowers with 4 unequal tepals, female flowers with 2 broad tepals and pink ovaries, hanging down on loose, many-branched stalks with a flower terminating each branch; August to frost; stout succulent stems upright, to 36 in. (90 cm), branched, yellowish green, pink to bright red at the nodes; leaves to 8 in. (20 cm) long and 5 in. (13 cm) wide, broadly ovate, heart-shaped at the base with one lobe much longer and tilted (oblique) toward the other, light olive-green above with veins red-tinted, underneath bright reddish pink with the veins projected and dark red; fruit 3-winged. A variable species, particularly as to leaf coloration and fragrance. In spring, the variant I grow at Hosta Hill has deep red leaf undersides with the veins very dark red underneath and red on the top. The coloration fades a little as flowering time approaches. Elsewhere I have observed plants with little or no fragrance and a much lighter leaf color on the underside. Both the pink- and white-flowered forms are prolific; avoid siting where less vigorous plants might be overwhelmed.

'Alba' (var. *alba*) has flowers that are almost white, with a hint of pink. Leaves are lighter than the type's on the underside, more a light pink; the veins are outlined in a darker color.

'Claret Jug' is virtually identical to the type. Its flowers are pink; leaves are red on the underside.

'Simsii', flowers larger than the type, with the same pink color.

Belamcanda

These short-lived perennials like the hot, dry summers at Hosta Hill. I have grown *Belamcanda flabellata* (blackberry lily) for years, in light to dappled woodland shade; admittedly, it might be more floriferous in full sun, but for me it blooms enough. Throughout its long bloom time, which begins in July, it is a favorite plant in areas that receive a bit of sun in the morning but are in open shade during the heat of the day. I have it poking up between Chinese mayapples, *Podophyllum pleianthum*. The bright orange, red-spotted flowers of *B. chinensis* are a little too much for my taste: orange is a hard color to place in the woodland garden. But when I discovered the yellow-flowered *B. flabellata* 'Hello Yel-low', I just had to accommodate it. Perhaps it is because the flag colors of my birthplace, Munich, are yellow and black—yellow flowers followed by long-lasting, shiny black berries was just the thing. Sometimes yellow blooms are juxtaposed with just-opening black-berried seedpods on the same plant.

Belamcanda flabellata is hardy and lasting if the stout rhizomes are planted shallow and not kept too wet. Hardy to zone 5. Its tall stature allows groups of it to be put here and there in open woodland gardens, and it mixes well with epimediums, hostas, and ferns. Its elegant, irislike leaves add texture to the garden, and the bright yellow flowers of 'Hello Yellow' are like beacons. Although each flower lasts only one day, several bloom at the same time on the branched flowerstalks, in succession, so the overall effect lasts for several weeks. Not quite as conspicuous, the delightful black berries add color to early fall, contrasting with the white fruit of baneberries. The berried pods are great for bringing inside, where their simple beauty lasts all winter in arrangements.

The genus name was adapted in Latinized form from the Asian native vernacular. It is classified in the iris family, Iridaceae. Both species of the genus have been used medicinally by the Chinese to treat ailments of the chest and liver. They are natives of eastern Asia, where they occur in sandy, fast-draining soils; they detest constantly moist or wet soils. Both adapt to lightly shaded conditions and will bloom in open shade, though a place with some morning sun is appreciated. *Belamcanda flabellata* is more shade-tolerant. Here it is planted in soil that is barely improved, somewhat dry, and more important, in an elevated position with good drainage.

Propagate by sowing the large seeds produced in abundance. The seeds are extremely viable; I simply bury seeds where I want another clump and within a few seasons, new plants are in bloom. Division of older clumps also leads quickly to plants of flowering size.

Slugs and snails can damage new growth emerging in spring; no other pests or diseases are experienced here. Crown rot or other fungal rot can be expected where the soil does not drain well or in areas of soggy winter soils. Leaf spot and anthracnose are reported.

Belamcanda chinensis, blackberry lily, leopard flower. Northern India, China, eastern Siberia, Japan.

Sun, LS to WS; flowers bright orange or orange-red, spotted with dark red to maroon, sometimes bright yellow, unspotted or spotted, 1.5 in. (4 cm) across, 6 tepals opening angled upward with the lobe tips pointed, sometimes blunt or notched, filaments deep red to purple; July–September; plant clump-forming, rhizomatous; stems green, stout, upright, to 36 in. (90 cm); leaves basal and placed on the stem, to 12 in. (30 cm) long and 1 in. (2.5 cm) wide, sword-shaped, medium green; fruit 3-parted capsule, shiny black berries grouped to resemble a large blackberry. Variable flower color. Adaptable to some shade; it is up to the gardener to experiment and determine which shady area can still produce flowers. Has naturalized in central and eastern North America from seed carried away from gardens by wildlife; I have seen colonies in northwest and central Georgia growing along the roadside and in open scrub and fields. Most plants offered in commerce are orange with dark red or maroon spots. 'Freckle Face' has yellow flowers spotted with maroon specks. Cultivars come true from seed if isolated.

Belamcanda flabellata, blackberry lily. China, Japan.

Sun, LS to WS; flowers light yellow, usually unspotted or sometimes spotted with dark red to maroon in the center, 2 in. (5 cm) across, 6 tepals opening wide, angled out almost horizontally, with the lobe tips blunt, filaments white; July–September; plant clump-forming, rhizomatous; stems green, stout, upright, to 18 in. (45 cm); leaves basal and placed on the stem, to 8 in. (20 cm) long and 0.8 in. (2 cm) wide, sword-shaped, medium green; fruit 3-parted capsule with many grouped, shiny black berries. Smaller than *Belamcanda chinensis* but with slightly larger flowers, which open wide and have white filaments. **'Hello Yellow'**, a popular selection with pure yellow, unspotted flowers, tolerates shade particularly well.

Blechnum

Most ferns of the genus *Blechnum* are tender and suitable for greenhouses and indoors only. In temperate gardens, the only truly hardy species—and the only one I have cultivated—is *Blechnum spicant* (deer fern), whose long, erect fronds accent my hosta plantings and larger areas of groundcover.

The genus name comes from the Greek *blechnon*, the classic name for a fern; the epithet alludes to the tufted nature of a typical clump. *Blechnum* is classified in the Blechnaceae.

Deer fern is very tolerant of deep shade and requires moist, acidic garden soil. It does best in a light, well-draining woodland soil, rich in organic matter. During hot, dry summers it benefits greatly from supplemental water. If the soil is allowed to dry out, the stems become brittle and collapse. Exposure to sun may scorch the fronds, so site in medium to full shade. Deer fern is a great companion plant for larger wildflowers and other ferns. Hardy to zone 4, 3 with protection.

Propagate by dividing the creeping rhizome in early spring. Keep soil moist to hasten reestablishment. Propagation by spores is also relatively easy; sow spores as soon as they are ripe on a coarse commercial mix with a pH of 5.5 to 6 maintained moist at 70°F (21°C).

Deer fern is prone to rusts and leaf spot, but I have not experienced these. Insects do not seem to bother it, but slugs can injure the emerging young croziers.

Blechnum spicant, deer fern, hard fern. Western North America, Europe, Asia Minor, Japan.

MS to FS; fronds produced in rosettes on slender stalks emerging directly from the rhizome, scaly at the base, stalks dark green, erect; sterile leaves to 20 in. (50 cm), evergreen, dark green composed of closely spaced leaflets (pinnae), tapering from the center to both top and bottom, rising after the fertile fronds, forming a rosette around the fertile fronds, inclined to the horizon; fertile leaves erect, to 28 in. (70 cm), not evergreen but persistent, dark green composed of thin leaflets (pinnae), spaced apart, tapering from the center to both top and bottom; spore cases elongated. This variable fern forms a neat, compact clump and is useful in many places of the garden. Although somewhat evergreen, it is best to remove the fronds in late winter or very early spring to enjoy the beauty of fresh growth. Among its several cultivars are 'Cristatum' (tips of the leaflets branched) and 'Serratum', a form with reflexed and deeply serrated leaflets that are densely arranged. Several more cultivars have been gathered in the *Blechnum* Serratum Group. *Blechnum nipponicum*, a recent importation from Japan, is fully evergreen and hardy to zone 6; its fronds emerge with a bright yellowish red color in spring and eventually rise to 10 in. (25 cm) tall.

Bletilla

The exquisite beauty of tropical orchids is admired by all. Gardeners long for such rare magnificence, but the tender nature of orchids makes them elusive in open, temperate zone gardens. Happily, the splendid lady slippers (*Cypripedium* spp.) and other hardy orchids native to North America can partially satisfy a gardener's dreams of orchid grandeur, but the orchids of North American woods are in the main less showy and have much smaller flowers. There is, however, an exotic orchid hailing from eastern Asia that can easily fulfill a desire for orchid blooms in the garden: *Bletilla striata*. It is readily available from many commercial sources and is of easy culture. The only things it does not like is dry soil and too much sun on its back. I have grown this orchid for years in both improved soil and pure Georgia red clay, which verifies the rugged, undemanding nature of this hardy terrestrial (ground) orchid. Obviously, the plant fares much better when placed in improved soil; a moisture-retentive, friable garden soil that does not dry up in summer is best. The only complaint I have is the bletilla's habit of coming up very early in spring. A late freeze damages the leaves and, if the flowerstalks have already pushed up, destroys the developing blossom. To safeguard against this, I plant bletillas much deeper than recommended, at least 10 in. (25 cm), since early rising soil temperature triggers spring growth here in the South. This usually delays the emergence of leaves and has had no detrimental effect on the plants. If the leaves should surface prematurely, I use a thick layer of pine straw for protection.

The root system is a series of pseudobulbs connected by thick rhizomes. New bulbs are added each season, and the clump slowly expands, eventually forming a large group of plants. I have not found it necessary to dig and divide, unless increase is desired. In more northern climates, bletillas make a great subject for potting and can be overwintered in a cold but frost-free inside area. Bletillas are fragrant, but their sweetly scented blossoms must be close to be appreciated. Hardy to zone 5

with the protection of a deep leaf or pine straw mulch.

Bletillas grow in their native eastern China and Japan at higher elevations, in sheltered spots at woodland margins and clearings, preferring shaded positions. Under cultivation some morning sun is appreciated; however, early emergence may be a problem in sites where the late-winter sun warms up the soil prematurely. The genus name honors Spanish apothecary Louis Blet. *Bletilla* is classified in the Orchidaceae.

Propagate by digging up the pseudobulbs and severing the connecting rhizomes. This is best done in early winter after the leaves have died down. These orchids emerge very early, so division in spring is risky.

Slugs and snails can damage new growth emerging in spring; no other pests or diseases are experienced here. Constantly wet, soggy soils may cause rot of the pseudobulbs. Late freezes can damage early-rising leaves and blooms.

Bletilla ochracea. Eastern China, Japan.

LS to WS; flowers 3–6 per stem, fragrant, light yellow to whitish yellow, pleated lip either dark yellow or flushed with light lavender, to 1 in. (2.5 cm) across; May–June; plant clump-forming, from rhizomatous, flattened pseudobulbs; stems green, stout, upright, to 18 in. (45 cm); leaves basal and placed on the stem, to 12 in. (30 cm) long and 1 in. (2.5 cm) wide, oblong lance-shaped, medium green, heavily pleated, striate. I prefer the form with the dark yellow lip. Still rare but available, sometimes incorrectly as *Bletilla striata* 'Ochracea'. I keep my somewhat finicky specimen in a pot so I can keep my eye on it.

Bletilla striata. Eastern China, Japan.

LS to WS; flowers 3–6 per stem, fragrant, rose-purple, pleated magenta lip, to 1 in. (2.5 cm) across; May–June; plant clump-forming, from rhizomatous, flattened pseudobulbs; stems green, stout, upright, to 24 in. (60 cm); leaves basal and placed on the stem, to 15 in. (38 cm) long and 1 in. (2.5 cm) wide, oblong lance-shaped, medium green, heavily pleated, striate. The epithet *striata* (= ribbed) characterizes the beautifully pleated leaves and lip of the flower. Flower color is variable. Most plants offered have magenta to rose-purple flowers. 'Alba' (f. *alba*) has white flowers with a faint flush of purple on the lip; 'Albostriata' ('Albomarginata') has a thin, white margin on the leaves. 'First Kiss' combines the flowers of 'Alba' with the leaves of 'Albostriata'.

Botrychium

Exploring the wooded, rocky ravine near my home has brought me immense satisfaction. Although I had previously explored wild areas around the world, being able to reach an absolute treasure chest of native plants within a few minutes' walk from my home was a dream come true for me. Sadly, Hurricane Opal felled several tulip poplars and loblolly pines, and poison ivy and kudzu vine invaded the now sunlit areas, obliterating all native undergrowth. But before the invasion, I had admired there several species of grape fern and was hooked on these dainty beauties. The largest was *Botrychium virginianum* (rattlesnake fern), whose broad and finely divided sterile frond could not be missed above the forest litter. I also found *B. dissectum* (cutleaf grape fern) and *B. alabamense*. Needless to say, I rescued all I could find as the area was being overtaken by poison ivy—and paid for this by being assailed by the vicious juices of that scourge. Sometimes it is not easy being enamored of plants. My rashes are long gone, but the grape ferns persist in my garden.

Grape ferns are among the most primitive ferns, the succulent ferns, and all slugs and snails in the neighborhood know about these juicy morsels. Most are not showy and require a place up front to show their unusual and unique features. Natural beauty comes in all shapes and sizes, and I tend to be more grateful for the small wonders in a garden. At Hosta Hill they grow in groups together with diminutive wildflowers and dwarf hostas.

Rarely seen in gardens, grape ferns can be fussy if a complete change of soil takes place during planting. Although not rare in the wild, they should not be dug up unless a rescue situation presents itself. In such a case, remove a large ball of native soil containing the roots. It should be twice as wide as the plant is high and transplanted into garden soil unbroken and at the same depth as found. All the grape ferns I dug up grew in dense Georgia red clay from a rootstock with a few thick, fleshy roots spreading horizontally all around; some roots were over 4 in. (10 cm) deep in the ground. All were transplanted with a ball of native soil.

The terrestrial grape ferns are endemic to eastern and western North America, Eurasia, and Australia. The generic name (*botrychium* = like a grape) alludes to the shape of the gathered spore clusters. *Botrychium* is classified in the adder's tongue family, Ophioglossaceae.

Grape ferns do best in a light, well-draining woodland soil, rich in organic matter and containing some acid, native soil, if possible. All grape ferns are deciduous and form new shoots each year, but some species may be considered semi-evergreen, as their sterile leaves appear in early winter. Hardy to zone 4.

Propagation of grape ferns is problematic: unlike other ferns, they do not seem to naturalize in my garden, and I have tried propagation by spores with dismal results. Gardeners are on their own to face this challenge.

Slugs and snails can be devastating to young growth and the finely divided fronds. I have seen slugs strip the entire frond in a single night. It is essential to eliminate slugs from the area. No other pests or diseases are reported or experienced here.

Botrychium dissectum, dissected grape fern, cutleaf grape fern, lacy grape fern. Eastern North America and eastern Canada, Newfoundland and Nova Scotia south to Georgia and Alabama.

MS to FS; fertile and sterile segments have a common stem at or below ground level, then separate; sterile frond, singular, held on separate erect stem, 3–6 in. (8–15 cm) high, leaf triangular, to 3 in. (8 cm) long, divided into 3 leaflets, semi-leathery, coarse, fleshy, from dark bluish green to light green, bronze in winter, 3–5 in. (8–13 cm) above ground, often held parallel to the ground, lacy cut and intricately lobed, toothed, and scalloped; fertile stem green, erect, 9–15 in. (23–38 cm) tall but often much shorter, spore cluster (sporophyll) at the stem tip, to 2 in. (5 cm) long, spore cases yellowish, bunched like grapes on branched laterals; rootstock erect, fleshy, horizontally branching and spreading. An extremely variable species in terms of leaf shape and divisions. Variety *tenuifolium* is less divided, with narrow, elongated leaflets; f. *elongatum* has much elongated leaflets; and the leaflets of var. *obliquum* arise more obliquely from the stalk. *Botrychium alabamense* is very similar but has shorter leaflets with more rounded lobes. All are much alike, all could serve the same purpose in gardens, and all are hardy to zone 4 with protection. Here the fertile deciduous segment rises in early autumn and matures November–December. The evergreen sterile fronds carry on through the winter, turning bronze after the first frost.

Botrychium virginianum, rattlesnake fern, Virginia grape fern. Eastern North America, Eurasia.

MS to FS; fertile and sterile segments have a common stem; sterile frond deciduous, held on erect stem 12 in. (30 cm) above ground level, leaf triangular, to 10 in. (25 cm) long and 12 in. (30 cm) wide, divided into 3-compound leaflets, light green, of thin substance, not leathery; fertile stem emerging at leaf junction, rising another 12 in. (30 cm), green, erect, topped with a terminal spore cluster (sporophyll) to 2 in. (5 cm) long, spore cases yellowish, bunched like grapes on branched laterals, disappearing soon after the spores ripen; total height to 24 in. (60 cm); rootstock erect, fleshy, horizontally branching and spreading. This species is much larger than the other grape ferns and completely deciduous. It comes up early in spring; a group makes a wonderful, lacy display in the fern glen or among wildflowers. Disappears when exposed to direct sun. **Variety *intermedium***, one of several distinct forms that exist in the wild, has subleaflets that are wider and almost touching. Hardy to zone 3.

Boykinia

The shady garden depends largely on leaf texture to create a diverse portrayal of nature. That is why it is closer to a natural model than sunlit flower borders. *Boykinia aconitifolia* (brook saxifrage), an eastern North American native that is unjustly overlooked by many shade gardeners, is eminently suited to such a natural garden. The flowers are not very showy, true, but they are held in great bunches above the leaves so make themselves known; and their leaves, which resemble those of aconite (hence the epithet), contrast well with ferns, hostas, astilbes, Hakone grass, and all manner of larger wildflowers. It looks great when interplanted with Solomon's seal. Given a fertile, moist, gritty soil, it is of easy culture. As with many other wildflowers, dry soil and too much sun on its back are not appreciated. At Hosta Hill, a nice clump reigns near a shaded water feature. There it has survived severe drought and stifling heat, growing in the pond margins, where water is underneath and not far from the rhizome. It flowers here from July until late September, and its many flowers, though small, contribute in their own dainty way to garden color.

Boykinias are native to North America, western China, and Japan. They grow at higher elevations in sheltered spots at woodland margins and clearings, preferring shaded positions. Though I have diligently searched in Georgia, I have never seen a wild population of *Boykinia aconitifolia* there. North Carolina is another matter: there I saw several fairly large populations in a few isolated mountain valleys, near watercourses. Unfortunately, I do not have the space to emulate such gorgeous wild groups, so a single plant, purchased at a certified wildflower nursery, must do for Hosta Hill.

Most boykinias, with the exception of some of the western species, are hardy to zone 5. The genus was named to honor Samuel Boykin, an eminent field botanist from Georgia, and is classified in the Saxifragaceae. The Japanese and Chinese boykinias are now in the genus *Peltoboykinia*.

Propagate by dividing the rhizome in very early spring before growth starts. Seed sown in a cold frame usually germinates successfully.

Slugs and snails can damage new growth emerging in spring; no other pests or diseases are reported or experienced here.

Boykinia aconitifolia, brook saxifrage. Eastern North America, Appalachians from West Virginia south to Georgia.

LS to WS; flowers small, shallowly bell-shaped, to 0.5 in. (1 cm), on open, branched raceme, 6–21 on each branch, 5 rounded petals, whitish with yellow centers, flowerstalks 10–20 in. (25–50 cm) tall; July–September; plant clump-forming, rhizomatous, slowly spreading; leaf stems green, stout, upright, to 10 in. (25 cm); leaves medium green, with 5–7 lobes, margins coarsely and irregularly toothed, to 6 in. (15 cm) long and 7 in. (18 cm) wide, stem and leaves hairy. *Boykinia jamesii* (Rocky Mountain boykinia), native to the Rocky Mountains from Alberta to Wyoming, has leaves like a heuchera, only more rounded, heart- or kidney-shaped, with 4–10 minor lobes, and purple-violet flowers. It is difficult in open gardens; best for an alpine house or in a shady part of a rock garden.

Boykinia major, mountain boykinia, western boykinia. Western North America, Oregon south to California.

LS to WS; flowers small, shallowly bell-shaped, to 0.5 in. (1 cm), many, on open, branched raceme, 6–21 on each branch, 5 roundish petals, white with whitish yellow centers, flowerstalks 24–36 in. (60–90 cm) tall; July–September; plant clump-forming, rhizomatous, slowly spreading; leaf stems green, stout, upright, to 10 in. (25 cm); leaves dark green, with 5–7 lobes, margins coarsely and irregularly toothed, 8–10 in. (20–25 cm) long and wide. Endemic to the western Cascades. It flowers earlier and is larger than *Boykinia aconitifolia*. A good foliage plant, worth seeking out. *Boykinia occidentalis*, a clump-former, has rounded, heart- or occasionally kidney-shaped leaves with 4–10 minor lobes. It has distribution further north to Vancouver Island in British Columbia and south to southern California. Hardy to zone 8. *Boykinia rotundifolia*, a spreading species from California, has, as its epithet indicates, round, heart-shaped leaves with 4–10 minor lobes. Hardy to zone 7 with protection.

Brunnera

Like most gardeners, I take pride in growing plants to perfection, but I must admit: *Brunnera macrophylla* (Siberian bugloss) is not a plant for gardens in the hot South unless it can be grown in very shady spots along the banks of ponds, streams, or other water features, where moisture in the soil is plentiful and constant. I string mine along, in considerable shade, by giving them plenty of water. They are never vigorous enough to grow into the leaf-meshing groundcovers I have seen in northern gardens. Still, they do look pretty and my wife, Hildegarde, likes their flowers very much, so I put up with their lassitude. Brunneras make wonderful groundcovers in places and climates to their liking, and the variegated forms make great accent plants in the woodland. In spring, their bright purplish blue flowers, held above the leaves, add greatly to the overall palette of the garden.

Brunnera macrophylla is classified in the genus *Brunnera*, but it has been and still is sold in commerce as *Anchusa* and *Myosotis*. The genus was named to honor the Swiss botanist Brunner and is classified in the borage or forget-me-not family,

Boraginaceae. Bugloss is an ancient name applied to several genera of boraginaceous plants.

The large leaves of Siberian bugloss gave rise to the specific name *macrophylla* (= large-leaved). It is reliably winter hardy, thriving in zones 3 to 6. Wherever it is grown, it is essential that the soil stay constantly moist yet well drained. Soils of both high and low fertility are accepted, so long as they are cool. Its heat tolerance is low, so in the South it is best placed in a cool, shady corner. In the North, some morning sun is appreciated; during the heat of the day, some shade is preferred.

Propagate by taking root cuttings of the dormant rhizome in late autumn or very early spring for fastest increase. Sow fresh seed in summer in a warm seed tray; transplant seedlings in late autumn.

Plants are relatively free of pests and diseases.

Brunnera macrophylla, Siberian bugloss. Caucasus to western Siberia.

Morning sun, LS to MS; flowers small, to 0.2 in. (0.5 cm), bright blue to purplish blue or white, on branched panicles to 8 in. (20 cm) long; April–June; plant clump-forming, to 24 in. (60 cm) wide and 18 in. (45 cm) high; stem leaves small, lance-shaped, green; basal leaves large, to 8 in. (20 cm) long, rounded, heart- or kidney-shaped with a pointed tip, sitting on top of tapering, green leafstalks, dark green to grayish green, hairy, felted; rootstock large with thick, dark roots. I bought this plant at a local nursery as *Anchusa myosotidiflora*, and indeed the flowers look much like those of a forget-me-not. Now my label bears the correct name. Cultivars with variegated leaves must not be exposed to direct sun; even a short exposure will brown the lighter leaf areas.

'Betty Bowring' has white flowers.

'Dawson's White' ('Variegata'), leaves have wide, irregular, creamy white margins; flowers blue.

'Hadspen Cream', leaves have narrower, irregular, creamy to yellowish white margins, sometimes also spotted creamy white; flowers blue.

'Langtrees' ('Aluminium Spot'), leaves have a margin irregularly and sparsely spotted with silvery white spots; flowers blue.

'Silver Wings', leaves are large and irregularly spotted with many large silvery white spots, much more pronounced than in 'Langtrees'; flowers blue. A large and vigorous cultivar.

Calanthe

The lovely hardy terrestrial orchids of the genus *Calanthe*, long cultivated in Japanese pot culture, have at last found their way into Western commerce. Gardeners in zone 7 can grow these most cherished and gardenworthy representatives of the orchid family in the open garden. Dainty as they are, they make excellent container subjects, so gardeners further north can also enjoy these beauties and overwinter them in a frost-free place. I grow only one, *Calanthe discolor* 'Eco White', in an elevated container, so I can enjoy the early-spring blossoms up close. This position also keeps it safe from slugs, who have a much more sinister interest in these miracles of nature. The genus has been known to horticulture since Thunberg collected the first species in Japan in the mid-1770s. The species hybridize freely, and most of the commercial offerings are hybrids.

Most calanthes are tender, tropical ground orchids native to eastern Asia, Polynesia, Madagascar, and South America and suitable only for the greenhouse. Of primary interest to gardeners are the species from Korea, China, and Japan, which grow at higher elevations in sheltered spots at woodland margins and clearings, preferring shaded positions. The leaves of these hardy species remain evergreen where temperatures stay above 15°F (−10°C). They do best in a light, well-draining woodland soil, rich in organic matter. During hot, dry summers, calanthes benefit greatly from supplemental water. The soil should never dry out; daily watering is a must for outdoor potted plants. Calanthes tolerate considerable shade, but some early morning sun is appreciated and increases flowering. Site calanthes where their small but splendid flowers can be appreciated. The genus name comes from the Greek *kalos* (= beautiful) and *anthos* (= flower). *Calanthe* is classified in the Orchidaceae.

Propagate by digging up and separating the pseudobulbs after flowering. Seed propagation is for experts only.

Slugs and snails can damage the delicate flowers in spring; no other pests or diseases are experienced here. Fungal leaf spot and mosaic virus are reported.

Calanthe discolor. Japan north to Izu Peninsula, Korea, eastern China.

Some sun, LS to WS; flowers to 20 per stem, to 1.5 in. (4 cm) across but usually smaller, slightly fragrant, tepals chestnut-brown to greenish brown to green, lip broadly 3-lobed, slightly spoon-shaped, light lavender to pink or white; April–June; plant clump-forming, from flattened pseudobulbs; stems green, stout, upright, to 20 in. (50 cm); leaves basal, 3–6 per stem, placed on the stem to 12 in. (30 cm) long and 1–1.5 in. (2.5–4 cm) wide, oblong lance-shaped, medium green, pleated; after flowering the leaves may become horizontal. Variable flower color; the brown-pink combination is seen more than others. Variety *bicolor* looks much like the type but with light yellow tepals; var. *sieboldii* has bright yellow tepals. *Calanthe izu-insularis* comes from the southern Izu Islands and may be a local variant of *C. discolor*; the tepals are rose-pink, and the lip is white with a bright yellow spot at the base. Several hardy cultivars are in commerce.

'Eco Rose', rose-tinged tepals with rosy white lips; a vigorous multiplier.

'Eco White', yellowish white tepals with white lips, mature flowers very white; a floriferous clone, easy to cultivate.

'Kozu' ('Kozu Spice'), a natural hybrid (*Calanthe discolor* × *C. izu-insularis*), has mixed flower colors. More robust than its parents and easy to grow. I have seen it in zone 6 gardens with considerable winter protection.

'Takane', a group of hybrids with or possibly selections of var. *sieboldii* with mixed flower colors. Most have bright yellow tepals with white lips.

Campanula

The beautiful, bell-shaped flowers of campanulas grace many sunny gardens. The genus includes perennial, biennial, and annual species, like *Campanula americana* (American bluebell, tall bellflower), a lanky native annual of eastern North America, which I have seen in bloom along the Blue Ridge Parkway in the Appalachians. The native *C. divaricata* (southern harebell), also frequent in the Smoky Mountain National Park, is well adapted to very light, open shade. The western harebell, *C. scouleri*, is widespread from Alaska to northern California. Some species are suitable for the rock garden, most of them thriving in full sun only; others succeed in partially shaded places but demand a dry soil during summer. To give adequate bloom, most campanulas require at least six hours of full sun—an impossible condition in most shady gardens—and many upright-flowering species resent the hot, southern summer nights, when temperatures do not fall below 75°F (24°C) for weeks on end. Taller varieties require staking when grown under shady conditions, where they reach for the sparse sun and, if not supported, simply flop over. All this makes the selection of *Campanula* species for shady woodland gardens difficult.

Campanula rapunculoides (creeping garden bluebell), a Eurasian perennial, has escaped many gardens and naturalized in parts of North America; it should not be planted, for it may overpower other, less vigorous woodland neighbors. *Campanula alliariifolia* (ivory bellflower) and *C. persicifolia* (peach-leaved bellflower) might be tried. Low-growing **C. poscharskyana** (Serbian bellflower) and *C. portenschlagiana* (Dalmatian bellflower) do a good job of covering ground even in medium shade, although they must have considerable sun for liberal blooming; hardy in zones 4 to 8, very heat-tolerant. Many southern gardeners consider campanulas short-lived and difficult in the shade; their counterparts in zone 6 and colder have better success. Certainly, they are not the carefree, low-maintenance plants most shade gardeners wish for. I consider their inclusion in my garden as temporary experiments: part of the fun of gardening is to see how successful one can be with certain plants under demanding conditions and in particular microclimates.

Campanulas should be grown in well-drained, moist soil of neutral to alkaline reaction; they are damaged by excess moisture. Since most wildflowers and woodland plants are moisture-loving, site selection and choice of companion plants for campanulas should be given considerable thought; it is a real challenge to place them among the many woodland plants that require acid to very acid soil. Many campanulas must be deadheaded or cut back, lest they spread by seed all over the place. Cutting back entirely encourages a second flush of flowers.

The genus is classified in the bluebell or harebell family, Campanulaceae. The common name harebell is a reference to the plants' meadow habitat, which coincides with that of hares. The name bellflower obviously acclaims the shape of the flowers, as does the generic name (*campanula* = little bell). Notwithstanding, the flowers of some species are not at all bell-shaped, but very flat, saucer- or star-shaped.

Propagate by letting the plants do what they want—they seed all over the place. Many species and cultivars come true from seed. Collected seed should be sown in spring; best results are achieved by using a cold frame. Rootstock can be divided in late autumn, after the plants become dormant, or in very early spring.

Many pests and maladies plague campanulas grown out of their primary habitat. They are prone to develop rust, fungal leaf spot, powdery mildew, and crown rot (southern blight), caused by white silk fungus (white mold fungus). Butterfly and moth larvae (caterpillars) and various beetles, particularly weevils, and their grubs can also damage plants. A general-application insecticide may be the only way to solve these problems; systemic insecticides should be used as a last resort and sparingly. Slugs and snails can be damaging to young and old growth alike; they particularly like the flowers.

Campanulas are native to the north temperate zone. Most species suitable for shady gardens are hardy to zone 3. All listed here have been grown in lightly shaded areas with some success.

Campanula alliariifolia, ivory bellflower, spurred bellflower, white bellflower, Caucasian harebell. Caucasus, Asia Minor.

Some sun, LS; flowers many, white, tubular bell-shaped, nodding to one side, 0.8 in. (2 cm) long, with long, spurred petal tips; August to frost; stems upright, leafy, 24–36 in. (60–90 cm), lower stem leaves on long petioles, upper progressively shorter, grayish green, topped with a one-sided flowerstalk; leaves 2–4 in. (5–10 cm) long, basal, heart-shaped, gray-green, densely covered with hair, whitish dense hair beneath, margins toothed; plant clump-forming, somewhat rhizomatous; seeds tiny, abundant. This species is floppy, particularly when grown in some shade, so staking may be necessary. I tried to grow it but failed: it does not tolerate hot, humid weather. It should do better in the higher elevations of southeastern North America but needs more sun further north; a friend gardening in the higher, cooler elevations of northern Georgia has good success with it in light shade, but it does not flower abundantly. Deadhead unless you want it all over the garden. Save some seed to perpetuate this short-lived perennial. 'Ivory Bells' is much like the type but with creamy white flowers; 'Flore Pleno' has double flowers.

Campanula carpatica, Carpathian harebell, Carpathian bellflower, tussock bellflower. Southeastern Europe in the Carpathians and the Transylvanian Alps.

Some sun, LS; flowers many but solitary, bright blue or white, broadly and openly bell-shaped, upturned, to 2 in. (5 cm) across; July–September; stems many, upright, leafy, to 18 in. (45 cm), grayish green; leaves medium to dark green, toothed, to 2 in. (5 cm) long, basal leaves rounded to heart-shaped, upper leaves more triangular; plant clump-forming; seeds tiny, abundant. This species, acclimated to cool elevations, is a good garden plant even in some shade, as long as a cool root run and good drainage is provided. My mother had some lovely blue- and white-flowered cultivars. Here it definitely needs shade during hot afternoons. The flowers are very sensitive to a hot, southern exposure. I mulch it heavily to keep the soil underneath as cool as possible. Admittedly, they never seem to look like Mother's. Somewhat smaller is var. *turbinata* ('Turbinata'). Deadheading is required; spreads prolifically by seed under the right conditions. The many cultivars offered are better in gardens than the species or its variety; some may be intraspecific hybrids.

'Alba', 8 in. (20 cm) tall, white flowers; heart-shaped, hairy leaves.

'Blaue Clips' ('Blue Clips'), 8 in. (20 cm) tall, light sky-blue flowers; comes true from seed.

'Blaumeise' ('Blue Titmouse'), 8 in. (20 cm) tall, violet flowers with white center.

'Blue Moonlight', 8 in. (20 cm) tall, light grayish blue flowers, saucer-shaped.

'Bressingham White', 10 in. (25 cm) tall, white flowers.

'Chewton Joy', 6–8 in. (15–20 cm) tall, very light blue flowers with darker petal margins.

'China Cup', 8 in. (20 cm) tall, dark sky-blue flowers.

'China Doll', 8 in. (20 cm) tall, dark blue flowers.

'Isabel', 8 in. (20 cm) tall, dark blue flowers, saucer-shaped.

'Jewel', 8 in. (20 cm) tall, bright blue flowers.

'Jingle Bells', 8 in. (20 cm) tall, blue and white flowers on the same plant.

'Karl Foerster', 8 in. (20 cm) tall, deep blue flowers.

'Karpatenkrone' ('Crown of Carpathia'), 8 in. (20 cm) tall, light blue flowers.

'Kobaltglocke' ('Cobalt Bell'), 15 in. (38 cm) tall, cobalt-blue flowers.

'Queen of Sheba', 15 in. (38 cm) tall, cobalt-blue flowers.

'Riverslea', 8 in. (20 cm) tall, flowers very large, to 2 in. (5 cm), blue-violet, saucer-shaped.

'Spechtmeise' ('Blue Tit'), 12 in. (30 cm) tall, blue-violet flowers.

'Violetta', 8 in. (20 cm) tall, violet flowers, saucer-shaped.

'Wedgwood Blue', 7 in. (18 cm) tall, grayish violet-blue flowers, compact plant.

'Wedgwood White', 7 in. (18 cm) tall, white flowers, compact plant.

'Weisse Clips' ('White Clips'), 8 in. (20 cm) tall, white, bell-shaped flowers; comes true from seed.

'Wheatley Violet', 8 in. (20 cm) tall, violet-blue flowers.

'White Star', 12 in. (30 cm) tall, large, white, bell-shaped flowers.

'Zwergmöwe' ('Little Gull') 8 in. (20 cm) tall, silvery white flowers.

Campanula takesimana, Korean bellflower. Korea.

Some sun, LS; flowers many, creamy yellow flushed with purple outside and spotted red inside, tubular bell-shaped, 0.8 in. (2 cm) long; August to frost; stems upright, leafy, to 15 in. (38 cm); leaves 3 in. (8 cm) long, basal, heart-shaped, medium green, margins toothed; plant clump-forming, somewhat rhizomatous; seeds tiny, abundant. Its unusually colored, nodding flowers are produced in bunches on several racemes and blend well in a shaded garden. **'Elizabeth'** thrives here with quite a bit of morning sun and heavy shade during hot summer afternoons.

Cardamine and *Pachyphragma*

Years ago, I obtained a plant of *Cardamine diphylla* (two-leaved toothwort) from a wildflower nursery in North Carolina, having seen wild populations of this dainty plant in pinkish white spring bloom. Very soon, I found out that even with a lot of watering it disappeared below ground in late June. Not only in the South but also in northern gardens do most toothworts fade away just when they are counted on to add texture and greenery to the garden. Native North American *C. laciniata* (cutleaf toothwort, crow's toes) evaporates after flowering, as do many of the European species, including one with beautiful, large flowers, *C. waldsteinii*. Thus toothworts rank pretty low on the scale for good, leafy shade garden plants.

Many *Cardamine* species were used to spice up food. The peppery roots were grated and used like horseradish (hence, pepperroot). The commonest common name, toothwort, comes from the plants' use as a popular but ineffective salve for toothaches and also alludes to the rootstock's crinkled shape, which resembles teeth (this gave rise to still another common name, crinkleroot).

I remember one evergreen toothwort from early-spring family excursions in the Bavarian woods. It is the threeleaf toothwort, *Cardamine trifolia*. With snow still on the ground in shaded places, this mat-forming species with snow-white flowers almost passed for another patch of snow. It does not go summer-dormant in zone 7, and its evergreen leaves form a nice groundcover. It did not perform for me initially, letting me know in no uncertain terms that it was just too darned hot or dry, or both. I have moved it to a spot with more shade, and it seems to do much better, even tolerating some dryness.

I am also describing a plant closely related to *Cardamine* that has had the misfortune of being passed among several genera. I include this species, *Pachyphragma macrophylla*, with trepidation, because its tolerance to shade is not yet fully determined. Some gardeners, however, may want to try it.

Toothworts are cosmopolitan in the north temperate zone, growing in moist meadows and woods and other situations. Many native toothworts were once classified under *Dentaria* but have been moved to the genus *Cardamine*, which is classified in the mustard, horseradish, or cabbage family, Cruciferae.

Propagate by dividing the rhizome in very early spring or after flowering, or by taking root cuttings. Seed sown in a cold frame usually germinates successfully.

Slugs and snails can damage new growth emerging in spring. Occasionally, plants develop rust or powdery mildew.

Cardamine raphanifolia. Southeastern Europe, Greece, Turkey.

LS to MS; flowers to 0.8 in. (2 cm) across, white, lilac, or reddish violet, in tight clusters of 6–13; flowerstalks 18–32 in. (45–80 cm) tall; June–July; plant rhizomatous, slowly spreading; leaves compound, 4–6 in. (10–15 cm), glossy, dark green, 3–7 rounded leaflets, margins toothed; evergreen in zone 7. Plants offered in commerce are usually pink-flowered. This is an excellent addition to the moist woodland garden. I have it growing near a water feature, where runoff keeps the ground moist most of the time. In winter, the foliage contributes much to the color and texture of the garden. Hardy to zone 5.

Cardamine trifolia, threeleaf toothwort, threeleaf bittercress, trifoliate bittercress. Central Europe, Germany, northern Italy, Balkans.

LS to MS; flowers to 0.5 in. (1 cm) across, many, bowl-shaped, white or pink with yellow anthers, held in tight, flat bunches facing up; flowerstalks leafless, 8–10 in. (20–25 cm) tall; April–June; plant rhizomatous, slowly spreading; leaves to 3 in. (8 cm), dark green, 3 angularly rounded leaflets, suffused red beneath; evergreen in zone 7. The small flowers are packed tight and on older plants cover the ground almost solidly with white masses. Can stand up to some dryness in the soil, but supplemental water is necessary during very dry summers. Unfortunately, it likes large plots to expand in, so is of limited use in smaller shady gardens. Gardeners with plenty of room should give this evergreen toothwort a try. The mountain people of the Appalachians used *Cardamine trifolia* in salads called creases or cresses (hence, cress). Hardy to zone 5.

Pachyphragma macrophylla. Southeastern Europe, northeastern Turkey into the Caucasus.

Sun, LS; flowers many, pure white, to 0.6 in. (1.5 cm) across in many tight clusters of up to 24 each atop multiple, branching stems to 16 in. (40 cm); May–June; plant rhizomatous, slowly spreading; leaves glossy dark green, roundish, to 5 in. (13 cm) across. Has been cultivated under the name *Cardamine asarifolia* in the British Isles, where it has naturalized in some areas. Rarely seen in North America.

Cardiandra

The great plant hunters of the past are being emulated by modern Siebolds like Dan Hinkley, one of those passionate and generous explorers who share their experiences and their plants. Many of their "discoveries" show up in nursery catalogs first and in A-to-Z works later. In the early 1980s, while doing literary research for my work on the genus *Hosta* at the Holden Arboretum in Cleveland, Ohio, I saw an illustration of *Cardiandra alternifolia* in Siebold and Zuccarini's celebrated *Flora Japonica*, but I had never seen it in gardens. After years of looking for it, I finally found it in Dan's Heronswood Nursery catalog. Now, thanks to Dan, many gardeners have an opportunity to grow this "new" plant.

Siebold found *Cardiandra* in southern Japan on the island of Kyushu; Joseph G. Zuccarini, a Bavarian botanist, helped Siebold with plant identification and first described *Cardiandra alternifolia* in the late 1830s; and Dan rediscovered it for gardeners further north in central Honshu, which describes the approximate the geographic range of this genus. *Cardiandra alternifolia* requires deep, moist, but well-drained woodland soil with an acid reaction. Hardy to zone 5 with protection for the perennating rootstock. *Cardiandra* is classified in the hydrangea family, Hydrangeaceae.

Propagate by taking softwood cuttings very early in the growth cycle. Seed is rarely produced, probably due to the absence of dedicated pollinators. If viable seed is available, it must be sown fresh and as soon as ripe in containers in a cold frame, where seedlings can grow on.

Slugs and snails can damage new growth emerging in spring. I have not seen fungal or viral infections.

Cardiandra alternifolia, Japanese cardiandra. Southern Japan, central Honshu, Shikoku, Kyushu.
LS to WS; floral structure similar to hydrangeas, fertile and sterile flowers in terminal clusters on branched flowerstalks; fertile flowers centrally arranged, many, small, pink; sterile flowers marginal, pinkish white aging to greenish white, composed of 3-sepal lobes, to 0.5 in. (1 cm) across; stems 18–24 in. (45–60 cm) tall, branched; September–October; plant clump-forming, erect; leaves alternate, 3–5 in. (8–13 cm) long, medium to dark green, distinctly veined, broadly lance-shaped to oblong, with a sharply tapering tip, margins finely toothed. This species was first described as having white flowers, but the specimens in commerce are definitely light pink. It was also described as a subshrub; the specimen I grow behaves like an herbaceous perennial, so this technicality did not prevent me from including it in this work. Further south, *Cardiandra formosana* (Formosan cardiandra) brings forth flowers of a deeper color, but it is otherwise similar to *C. alternifolia*; I do not grow *C. formosana*, but its habitat in Taiwan indicates it may not be as hardy as *C. alternifolia*. Another Japanese species, *C. amamioshinensis*, has glossy, toothed, dark green leaves that are opposite, rather than alternate as in the other species; its sterile flowers have somewhat larger, white sepals. All these late-bloomers provide a modest but long-lasting floral display in late summer to early autumn, and the handsomely leaved clumps bring novel texture to the shady garden. 'Flore Pleno' from Japan is the most desirable form; it has sterile double flowers with 6 sepals.

Carex

Carex is a genus with well over 1000 species. Like the grasses, most sedges, as they are commonly called, inhabit sunny habitats, but a few species are indispensable in the shady garden. For many years, I have grown various sedges in the shade—all are troublefree and easy to use. Sedges come in all sizes and shapes and in a wide range of colors, from red to brown, gray to silvery white, orange to coppery, and in every imaginable shade of green. Some species have produced attractively and brightly variegated sports, and these are particularly useful in shady corners, where they add glowing accents. If hostas are the keystones of the shady garden, the sedges provide the trim. Many sedges are evergreen or semi-evergreen in warmer regions of their habitat; others from mild climates, like *Carex siderosticha*, are deciduous. In areas with cold winters, most become deciduous, but the perennating rootstock can be overwintered with good protection where the soil does not freeze hard permanently and deeply.

Sedges are the best filler plants. No matter how small or large a bare spot in the garden, a *Carex* cultivar is ready to fill it. With long, linear, sometimes skinny leaves, sedges provide a rich texture to the garden that is unlike any other. Their grasslike appearance adds diversity and juxtaposes well with the lacy fronds of ferns, the bold leaves of hostas, and the elegant spires of Solomon's seal. The rich, wide blades of the broadleaf sedges, like *Carex plantaginea* and *C. siderosticha*, really appeal to me and make an even better statement in woodland gardens. Some sedges, like *C. grayi* (mace sedge), have attractive fruiting bodies that last for months. At Hosta Hill, some groundcover tasks are left to *C. siderosticha* 'Variegata', a handsome variegated form of the creeping broadleaf sedge; its attractive, creamy white bordered, foot-long leaves liberally cover any given bare spot. Depending on available moisture and soil fertility, it does this either slowly or quickly, but it never becomes invasive; any runners that spread out of bounds are easily removed. Another much-appreciated noncreeping, clumping species, *C. plantaginea* (plantain-leaved sedge), is native to the eastern forests of North America and therefore very much at home in shady gardens; it flourishes here in areas of considerable darkness, from medium to even deeper shade. Some sedges require marshy conditions, but sadly I do not have the space or the wet soil to let them roam. One is the very good-looking *C. pendula*, whose fruiting stems rise well above the dense leaf mound and carry drooping seedheads that look much like the catkins on a birch tree. This sedge is for the boggy ground at the water's edge, and it likes more sun than shade, though I have seen it prosper in gardens that receive considerable shade during the day. Wiry, thin-leaved sedges—like *C. buchanii* (leatherleaf sedge) and *C. comans* (hair sedge), both from New Zealand—are appealing indeed but reportedly short-lived. I have grown *C. comans* 'Frosty Curls' and found it has good lasting qualities.

The genus *Carex* is cosmopolitan; most species are endemic to the temperate and arctic regions. It is classified in the sedge family, Cyperaceae. *Carex* is the classic Latin name for a species of sedge. The several subgenera, including *Eucarex*, *Primocarex*, and *Vignea*, are based on differences in flower morphology. Gardeners interested in natural gardening with native plants will be pleased to learn that several very native North American species are gardenworthy and readily available.

Sedges do best in permanently moist soil. Drainage is of secondary importance, as long as there is no stagnant water in the ground. Soils of both high and low fertility are accepted. To make a creeping sedge grow quickly, as in the case of groundcovers, apply a slow-release fertilizer to give an extra boost to development. Light to medium shade is tolerated; morning sun is appreciated. Broad-leaved sedges prefer some shade during the heat of the day.

Propagate by dividing the dormant clump or creeping rhizome in very early spring before growth starts. Sow seed of cold-region species in a cold frame. Most variegated sedges produce all-green offspring, so division is the best way to obtain variegated increase. Many species creep vigorously, so increase can be achieved every spring by removing unwanted rhizomes from the periphery of the planting.

Large slugs and snails can damage new growth emerging in spring. Rust, smut, and leaf spot are reported, but I have not experienced such maladies here.

The sedges listed here have been grown at Hosta Hill for decades. All are tolerant of considerable shade, and all have survived brief temperature drops to 0°F (−18°C). Many are long-lived and vigorous as long as moisture is in constant supply; nevertheless, they tolerate prolonged periods of dry soils. Flowers are described only if outstanding; inconspicuous flowers are so noted.

Carex comans, hair sedge, New Zealand hair sedge. New Zealand.

Some sun, LS to WS; flowers spikelike, cylindrical, inconspicuous; evergreen leaves almost hairlike, arching, to 18 in. (45 cm) long, 0.1–0.2 in. (3–6 mm) wide, yellowish to whitish green; plant clump-forming, tufted. This sedge can get untidy and needs "combing out" frequently to clean debris from the clump. Hardy to zone 7, 6 with protection. Cultivars include 'Bronze Mound' (bronzy brown leaves) and **'Frosty Curls'** (leaves whitish with white, sometimes curly tips).

Carex conica, miniature sedge, evergreen miniature sedge. Japan, Korea.

Some sun, LS to WS; flowers inconspicuous; evergreen leaves sword-shaped, short 3–5 in. (8–13 cm) long, 0.1 in. (3 mm) wide, dull dark green; plant clump-forming, tufted. This tiny sedge is a slow grower and will not get unruly when planted in small plots or trough gardens. Hardy to zone 5. 'Himekansuge' ('Snowline', 'Variegata', 'Marginata'; variegated miniature sedge) has leaves margined and striped with silvery white.

Carex elata, stiff sedge, tufted sedge. Eastern Europe.

Some sun, LS to WS; flowers overtopping leaf mound, brown; evergreen leaves sword-shaped, 24 in. (60 cm) long, as much as 38 in. (95 cm) in sun, but much shorter in shade, to 0.5 in. (1 cm) wide, green, longitudinally pleated; plant forming dense clumps, tufted. The type is rarely offered, but many yellow-leaved cultivars are in commerce. In spring, these emerge with a bright yellow leaf color, turning yellowish green to light green by midsummer. The greening depends on the amount of shade at a given location; more sun tends to maintain the yellow color. Hardy to zone 5. All forms require constantly moist soil and some direct exposure to sun. 'Aurea' has yellow-margined leaves. The widely available 'Bowles' Golden' ('Bowles's Golden', *Carex flava*, *C. f.* 'Bowles' Golden', *C. stricta* 'Bowles' Golden'; golden tufted sedge) has bright yellow leaves, thinly margined with light green to green. 'Knighthayes' ('Knighthaye's Form') has all-yellow leaves.

Carex fraseri, Fraser's sedge, spring snow sedge. Eastern North America, Appalachians from Pennsylvania to Georgia and Tennessee.

LS to MS; flowers on solitary stalk, to 6 in. (15 cm) tall, showy, creamy white to greenish white, upper male part like an upturned brush, lower female part ball- to egg-shaped, to 0.5 in. (1 cm) across, covered with up to 30 white scales and white threadlike bodies; evergreen leaves broad, to 2 in. (5 cm) wide and 10–24 in. (25–60 cm) long, strap-shaped, leathery, striate lengthwise but lacking a prominent midrib, undulate; plant rhizomatous. The most shade-tolerant sedge available and most attractive during flowering. Its dark green leaves, of heavy substance, drape elegantly along the ground. It is rare and protected in most if not all of its habitat and should never be collected in the wild. A slow grower but well worth the time to see it mature. Makes a great addition to the wild-flower border in company with small ferns, galax, and dwarf Solomon's seal. Some authorities classify it in the genus *Cymophyllus*, from the Greek *kyma* (= wavy) and *phyllon* (= leaf). Thrives in shady, moist corners. Hardy to zone 5.

Carex grayi, mace sedge, morning star sedge. Eastern North America.

Some sun, LS to WS; flowers 1–2 on leaved stalk overtopping leaf mound but surrounded by short, bractlike leaves, 1 in. (2.5 cm) across the spikes, greenish changing to a rich brown when ripe, shaped like a spiked club; deciduous leaves sword-shaped, 12–24 in. (30–60 cm) long, to 0.25 in. (0.6 cm) wide, bright green, longitudinally keeled along center rib; plant forming dense clumps, tufted. Easily one of the most outstanding sedges in the garden. Its ball-shaped fruit, adorned with fierce-looking spikes, recalls a medieval battle flail; it is mean-looking but gentle to the touch and very unusual and attractive. Self-seeds and makes a wonderful give-away plant. Best in some sun; here it grows in woodland shade. Hardy to zone 6b, further north with protection.

Carex morrowii, Japanese sedge. Japan.

Some sun, LS; flowers overtopping leaf mound, brown, inconspicuous; evergreen leaves sword-shaped, 18–24 in. (45–60 cm) long, arching, green, 0.1–0.2 in. (3–6 mm) wide, longitudinally keeled, tapering toward tip; plant forming dense clumps, tufted. One of the best and very long-lived sedges for the shady gardens. The leaves stay fresh and attractive all during the hot summer. Hardy to zone 5, usually evergreen in zone 7. The type is rarely offered, but cultivars with variegated leaves are common. All do best in constantly moist soil. Considerable shade is tolerated; I have several growing in woodland shade, and at Hosta Hill they seem to do best in this situation. Variegation holds best in some shade.

'Aureovariegata' (*Carex hachijoensis* 'Evergold', *C. oshimensis* 'Evergold') has a broad, whitish yellow center in the leaves; center is yellow in shade, creamy white with more sun, the margins are narrow and dark green; clump-forming, elegant.

'Goldband' ('Fisher', 'Fisher's Form', Fisher's Gilt', 'Gilt') has creamy white center banding in the leaves, more white than creamy; clump-forming, elegant.

'Ice Dance', similar to 'Variegata' but rhizomatous; expanding but not invasive.

'Silk Tassel' has very narrow white-variegated leaves forming a silky clump.

'Silver Scepter', white-edged; rhizomatous, expanding.

'Variegata' is the common white-variegated form with thin white margins; slowly expanding.

Carex phyllocephala, Japanese palm sedge. Japan.

Some sun, LS to WS; flowers inconspicuous; leaves sword-shaped, 7–10 in. (18–25 cm) long, first light green, later dark green, 0.5–0.8 in. (1–2 cm) wide, longitudinally keeled along the midrib, midrib projected underneath, striated lengthwise, broadest in the center tapering toward base and tip; leafstalks to 12 in. (30 cm), with leaves emerging along the length, becoming more closely spaced toward top, finally tufted and whorled at the top, palmlike; plant rhizomatous, forming dense clumps with dozens of leafstalks. Very attractive and a good garden sedge. Hardy to zone 6 with protection of the rhizomes; evergreen in zone 7 in mild winters down to 15°F (−10°C) for short periods, otherwise deciduous and herbaceous during prolonged freezing temperatures. The very popular **'Sparkler'** has irregular (some wide, some narrow) white stripes in the leaves, with some leaves more white than green; it is clump-forming, rhizomatous, spreading, but not invasive. It tolerates considerable shade; here it grows with some morning sun but is shaded for the remainder of the day. Site in a protected area in northern gardens. Seeds around, but the seeds produce plain green leaves.

Carex plantaginea, evergreen broadleaf sedge, plantain-leaved sedge. Eastern North America, New Brunswick south to Georgia and Tennessee.

Some sun, LS to WS; flowers blackish brown on spikes, noticeable but not showy; leaves evergreen, lance- or sword-shaped, 7–9 in. (18–23 cm) long, dark green, to 1 in. (2.5 cm) wide, longitudinally keeled along the midrib, midrib projected underneath, striated lengthwise, flattened toward tip, pleated (not flat) along most of their length, with the central vein recessed like a ship's keel and the two adjacent vein pairs elevated, forming a zigzag cross section through the leaf; plant rhizomatous, forming dense, tufted clumps of basal leaves. Native to the moist forests of eastern North America, this species is for northern gardeners who have difficulty growing the Japanese sedges. Makes a wonderful companion plant in the shady woodland garden, grouped with small ferns and small to medium hostas. Planted in tight groups, it makes an excellent groundcover. It has naturalized at Hosta Hill, coming up here and there. The epithet was derived from the resemblance of its leaves to the narrow-leaved plantain, a cosmopolitan weed in North America. No garden should be without this shade-tolerant sedge. Hardy to zone 4; evergreen. Another species native to Eurasia is *Carex sylvatica* with yellowish green leaves to 40 in. (1 m). It is much larger than *C. plantaginea* and more coarse, so not as useful in a garden with smaller plants. In shady gardens, it could be used as a substitute for sun-loving grasses. Hardy to zone 3.

Carex siderosticha, creeping broadleaf sedge. Japan.

Some sun, LS to WS; flowers blackish brown on spikes, noticeable but not ornate; leaves lance- or sword-shaped, 7–10 in. (18–25 cm) long, dark green, to 0.6 in. (1.5 cm) wide, longitudinally keeled along the midrib, midrib projected underneath, striated lengthwise, broadest toward tip and flattened, striated, tapering and narrowing continuously, more keeled toward the base, pleated along most of their length, with the central vein recessed like a ship's keel and the two adjacent vein pairs elevated, forming a zigzag cross section through the leaf; plant rhizomatous, forming dense clumps with dozens of leaves; leaves emerging laterally from the creeping and slowly expanding rhizome. Hardy to zone 6 with protection; evergreen in zone 7 in mild winters down to 15°F (−10°C) for short periods, otherwise deciduous and herbaceous during prolonged hard freezing. The epithet (*siderosticha* = lateral row) is a reference to the plant's growth habit: leaves emerge in a lateral row from the creeping rhizome. Several variegated cultivars are in commerce. These can be used as groundcover in light to woodland shade and have become popular grasslike plants in the shady woodland garden. All require moist conditions and spread fairly rapidly, increasing laterally (to one side) 6–12 in. (15–30 cm) per year. **'Island Brocade'** has yellow edges with occasional irregular, narrow, yellow stripes in the leaves; the leaves are to 8 in. (20 cm) long and 1 in. (2.5 cm) wide. 'Spring Snow' has yellow leaves in spring with a neat dark green border; the leaves, to 8 in. (20 cm) long and 1 in. (2.5 cm) wide, are viridescent and turn all green in summer, providing a striking contrast to the emerging yellow leaves. **'Variegata'** has creamy white, narrow margins with occasional irregular, thin, white stripes in the leaves; the leaves are 8–18 in. (20–45 cm) long and to 1 in. (2.5 cm) wide.

Caulophyllum

American Indians knew many different plants as cohosh; all were used for medicinal purposes. One of them, *Cimicifuga racemosa* (black cohosh), is well known, but others, like *Caulophyllum thalictroides* (blue cohosh), do not turn up as often in shady gardens. American Indians used the underground parts of this species to treat rheumatism, and it was an indispensable aid during childbirth. Its mundane flowers are replaced in early autumn by bright blue berries covered with a waxy, whitish bloom. These attractive fruits are poisonous—children should be warned about them.

Plants are common at high elevations, about 3000 ft. (900 m), in the Great Smoky Mountains. I grow mine in deep shade; they are not as lush and vigorous here but provide a yearly display of berries without fail. Being a "leaf guy," I particularly like the whitish gray dusting that covers the entire plant in early spring. The flowers are tiny, six-pointed stars with a yellowish center and usually greenish brown, sometimes coppery. As with many other North American species, *Caulophyllum thalictroides* has a counterpart in eastern Asia, var. *robustum*.

The cultural conditions of the natural mountain habitat must be approximated as closely as possible if *Caulophyllum thalictroides* is to be successfully cultivated. Do not fertilize; instead, add finely ground compost to the soil before planting and every fall, after the plants become dormant. Site in cool, medium shade in southern gardens, further north in light shade. Keep soil moist at all times; heat resistance is limited if the soil is allowed to dry out. The generic name and epithet in combination allude to the similarity of the stem and leaves to that of meadow rue (*Thalictrum* spp.). The genus is classified in the Berberidaceae.

Propagate by taking rhizome cuttings in very early spring; increase is slow, so patience is advised. Fresh seed can be sown in the ground or in a seed tray.

Fungal leaf spot is reported, but neither pests nor diseases have bothered the blue cohosh here.

Caulophyllum thalictroides, blue cohosh, papoose-root, squawroot, electric light bulb plant. Eastern North America, New Brunswick south to the mountains of South Carolina, Georgia, and Alabama.

MS to FS; flowers small, to 0.5 in. (1 cm), 6 pointed sepals, 6 shorter, hooded petals, clustered together on a branched raceme; April–June; plant herbaceous, clump-forming, rhizomatous; leaves usually 2 on the leafstalk, one near the flowers, another below, green to dark green, covered with whitish dusting in spring; each leaf divided into 9–27 leaflets 1–3 in. (2.5–8 cm) long, 3- to 5-lobed. This eastern wildflower deserves to be planted more frequently. The flowers are ordinary, but its bright blue berries add color to the autumn garden. Hardy to zone 3.

Caulophyllum thalictroides var. *robustum*. Western China, Tibet, eastern Siberia, Sakhalin, northern Japan, Korea.

MS to FS; flowers small, to 0.5 in. (1 cm), 6 pointed sepals, 6 shorter, hooded petals, clustered together on a branched raceme; April–June; plant herbaceous, clump-forming, rhizomatous; leaves usually 2 on the leafstalk, one near the flowers, another below, green; each leaf divided into many leaflets 1–3 in. (2.5–8 cm) long, center leaflets 3-lobed. Very similar to the North American wildflower and as yet scarcely available.

Chamaelirium

Cades Cove is one of the few places where one can take a giant step back into American history. Time has stood still here since the early 1800s, and when I visit this remote hollow in the mountains, I usually leave my car behind and walk for miles to get a real feel for the past. How else can this historic place be truly experienced? I feel sorry for the visitors who rush through this Shangri-la by car; they may stop at a few of the old homesteads, but they miss the little wonders along the many footpaths. One of these is *Chamaelirium luteum* (blazing star), a diminutive wildflower native to the eastern half of North America. In some areas it is rare, but large colonies can still be found, particularly in the Appalachians. Many years ago, while walking with my parents, I discovered a colony of this beauty along Cades Cove Road. The cluster's refined charm made a lasting impression on me, and I finally found a responsible nursery source. The small group of plants now gracing Hosta Hill are mostly male plants, which have a more showy display than the female forms. I interplant them with *Amianthium muscaetoxicum* (fly poison), which blooms a little earlier (a succession of bloom can be had from mid-May until late June by mixing these two species). Later in summer, when the flowers turn greenish yellow, the bent-over flowering spike and raceme remain on the plant and make a modest but interesting early autumn display.

The generic name (*Chamaelirium* = ground [creeping] lily) is a reference to the appearance of immature plants. The epithet comes from the Latin *luteus* (= yellow), for the yellowish flowers. *Chamaelirium* is classified in the Melanthiaceae.

Chamaelirium luteum thrives in open woods, wooded areas, and occasionally thickets. It requires moist, acid soil with a pH of 5 to 5.5. Supplemental water is required during hot, dry periods. It tolerates considerable shade but prefers a more open site with light shade and some morning sun. Hardy to zone 3.

Propagate by division in very early spring. Seed propagation is difficult, requiring the planting of adjacent male and female plants for proper fertilization and seed production.

No pests or diseases affect my plants, though slugs take an occasional bite out of the ground-hugging leaves.

Chamaelirium luteum, blazing star, fairy wand, devil's bit, rattlesnake root, squirrel tail. Eastern North America, southern Ontario, Massachusetts, New York, south to Florida, in mountains from Pennsylvania to Georgia, west to Michigan, Illinois, Ohio, south to Arkansas.

Some sun, LS to WS; flowers tiny, to 0.2 in. (0.5 cm), 3 petals, and 3 sepals, numerous; male and female flowers on separate plants (dioecious), female flowers creamy white with pistils, on long, leafy, upright spike, to 30 in. (75 cm); male flowers more showy, 6 yellow stamens, coming off yellowish white, on elongated raceme to 8 in. (20 cm), on flowerstalk with small bractlike leaves to 24 in. (60 cm) long, first erect, then bending, with raceme tip drooping; May–June; plant herbaceous, clump-forming, with tuberous root; leaves in a basal rosette are elongated, spoon-shaped, green, smooth, 3–8 in. (8–20 cm) long and 0.8–1.5 in. (2–4 cm) wide, blunt-tipped; 3-valved capsule. The Appalachian people thought the male flower spike looked

like a squirrel's tail; other common names were meant as warnings to avoid the extremely bitter taste of the raw root, which, when ingested, induces vomiting and causes severe dizziness. This easily cultivated species should never be planted as a single specimen. It does best as a group of 3 to 5 in company with small ferns, wild gingers, small hostas, and other wildflowers. I started with one plant and now have several. Purchase plants from propagated stock to maintain wild populations.

Chasmanthium

One of the few grasses that can be grown in the shade is *Chasmanthium latifolium* (wild oats), native to the eastern half of North America. Its showy, drooping flowers are shaped much like those of oats grown for food (*Avena sativa*). The one disadvantage to growing these ornamental oats in gardens is their prolific nature. I started with a tiny seedling in a small pot. The grass grew rapidly into a clump and started producing seed the second season. I left the attractive seeds hanging on the grass, and the following spring, little bunches of grass seedlings were coming up all over the place, in both sunny and shady places. The only way to control this bounteous harvest is to cut off the flowering spikes before the ripe seed starts to distribute itself, usually in late autumn after the seedheads turn a nice coppery color. The local flower shop may take the surplus flowerstalks with many thanks, as they are a mainstay in floral arrangements. This grass will grow in deep shade, although it may not flower or become a large clump—which may be a benefit for most gardeners.

Chasmanthium latifolium endures just about any mistreatment and any soil. It even withstands the salty breezes along the coastal regions, and gardeners with salt in their soil and air will find this attractive, versatile grass grass a permanent and easy-to-cultivate addition to shady corners. Here at Hosta Hill, where it seeded itself, its roots penetrate deeply into pure Georgia red clay, rendering it extremely drought-tolerant. I have also seen it grow in the wild in rocky muck along a streambed. In the hot, humid areas of southeastern North America, it definitely appreciates shade; full sun sunburns the grass. In shade, this grass develops a much richer, darker green color; in sun, it bleaches to a yellowish green. The culms are wide-bladed, like small bamboo, with the leaves angling away from the stem at almost right angles. Northern gardeners retain the grass to provide winter interest.

Chasmanthium latifolium is classified in the grass family, Gramineae. Its common names allude to its similarity to food oats.

Propagate by digging up and transplanting the many seedlings this grass produces. Division of older clumps is also a quick way to increase.

This grass seems immune to most known garden pests and diseases; in my experience, nothing affects it.

Chasmanthium latifolium, wild oats, North America wild oats, northern sea oats, northern wild oats, spangle grass, upland sea oats, wild sea oats. North America, southern Canada to New Jersey, west to southern Illinois then south to Florida and west to New Mexico and northern Mexico.

Some sun, LS to WS; flowers overtopping leaf mound, fruit oatlike spikelets to 0.5 in. (1 cm) long, on drooping stems, green turning yellowish green to bronze, breaking up and releasing seed in late autumn to early winter; leaves evergreen, lance-shaped, 5–12 in. (13–30 cm) long, 0.5 in. (1 cm) wide, angled away from the stems at right angles or less, medium green, turning yellowish green in autumn; plant forming dense clumps. This very ornamental grass is clump-forming and does not spread by rhizomes or stolons, like so many other, aggressive grasses. Remove seedheads before they release seeds to prevent its becoming weedy. Hardy to zone 5.

Chelidonium

Consider this entry a warning rather a recommendation. *Chelidonium majus* is one of those pretty pests our grandparents used to grow. It looks like the much-better-behaved *Stylophorum diphyllum* and has an attractive double-flowered form, 'Flore Pleno'. But as my mother found out years ago, this species seeds itself around with unwelcome gusto. Seedlings are easy to remove while they are very small, but an extraordinary effort is required to uproot them once they have anchored themselves in the ground. I know, because I helped Mother rid her garden of this handsome weed. In this case, I am following my mother's advice: unless a large land area is available, where this interloper is welcome to spread itself, it should not be planted. Never should it be allowed to enter smaller gardens, and although it is well adapted to shady gardens and woodland conditions, it is not desirable. This alien has escaped from many gardens and can be found in the wild in many areas of North America. I know of gardeners who, unfortunately, have dug it up in the wild and brought it home, starting the cycle all over again.

Chelidonium majus (greater celandine, celandine poppy, greater celandine poppy, European greater celandine, killwort, sightwort) is a Eurasian species; only minor differences distinguish it from var. *asiatica*, its Asian counterpart. The generic name comes from the Greek *chelodon* (= swallow). Flowering time usually coincides with the arrival of certain species of swallows on European farms; this event was important to my great-grandfather and other farmers in the area as it portended the quick demise of various insect pests, which soon fell prey to the voracious appetite of the birds. In Aristotle's version, swallows bathed the eyes of their young in the plant's juices to strengthen their eyesight, and herbalists used the juice as a cure for sore eyes. Its yellow flowers prompted herbalists to use it as a cure for liver problems.

Chelone

I found turtlehead on a wildflower rescue mission, looking for a plant that would tolerate Georgia red clay. Species of the genus *Chelone* are not frequent in Georgia, but here and there colonies can be found. They particularly like wetland soils with a clay base, and as wetlands disappear, so do the turtleheads. I have observed it frequently along wet stream banks in open, sunny coves of the Appalachian mountains in the Carolinas and Tennessee. Unfortunately, *Chelone glabra* (balmony to early settlers, for its stomach-soothing properties) does not take to shade too well, so I tried the red turtlehead, *C. lyonii*. It is the only turtlehead I am able to grow under mostly shaded conditions. To flower abundantly, all turtleheads need some sun; my plant gets about two hours of morning sun and open shade for the rest of the day. It flowers for about four weeks each September, providing a colorful late summer display. Combine with toad lilies (*Tricyrtis* spp.) for another four weeks of autumn flower color.

The generic name *Chelone* (= tortoise, turtle) comes from the Greek, an allusion to the fancied likeness of the flower to a turtle's head. American Indians used these herbs medicinally for the treatment of liver and gall bladder ailments and as a purgative, laxative, and worm medication. The epithet *lyonii* honors its discoverer, John Lyon; *glabra* refers to the smooth character of the leaves. *Chelone* is classified in the snapdragon or figwort family, Scrophulariaceae.

Turtleheads grow in wetlands, moist open woods, and along stream banks in the mountain valleys. They require moist, acid soil with a pH of 5 to 5.5 and thrive in heavy soils as long as they remain moist or wet. Turtleheads will not endure dry clays; constant moisture is a requirement for best performance Provide supplemental water during hot, dry periods. Turtleheads tolerate considerable shade but prefer a more open site with light shade and some sun. Gardeners should expect some self-seeding, but the spreading is easily controlled. Seedlings usually flower in their second year.

Propagate by division in very early spring. Sow seed in a cold frame in early spring.

Slugs and snails can be a problem. Leaf spot, mildew, and rust are reported but not experienced here.

Chelone glabra, white turtlehead, balmony, shellflower, snakehead, turtlehead. Eastern North America, Newfoundland south to Georgia, west to Minnesota and Missouri.

Some sun, LS; flowers white to pinkish white, tinged lavender near tips, beard white, large, snapdragonlike, 1–1.5 in. (2.5–4 cm) long, tubular, 2-lipped, notched upper lip arches over lower lip, lower lip with beard, carried in terminal clusters on erect flowerstalks to 36 in. (90 cm); July–September; plant herbaceous, clump-forming; stems square; leaves short-stalked and opposite on the stem, medium green, smooth, ovate to lance-shaped with sharply toothed margins, 3–6 in. (8–15 cm) long; fruit in capsule, many winged seeds. Variety *elatior* has a deeper purple coloration in the throat. I have seen the species flower in gardens with considerable shade, and in certain microclimates it may be successful as a perennial for shady gardens. Worth a try. It does best in constantly moist soil and under favorable conditions provides a long bloom period in late summer. Hardy to zone 3.

Chelone lyonii, red turtlehead, pink turtlehead, shellflower, snakehead, turtlehead. Eastern North America, Appalachians, West Virginia, North Carolina, south to Georgia, west to Tennessee.

LS to WS; flowers purple to pinkish red, beard yellow, large, snapdragonlike, 1–1.5 in. (2.5–4 cm) long, tubular, 2-lipped, notched upper lip arches over lower lip, lower lip 3-lobed with beard, carried in terminal clusters on erect flowerstalks to 40 in. (1 m); July–September; plant herbaceous, clump-forming; stems square; leaves on a stalk and opposite on the stem, green, smooth, ovate to lance-shaped with coarsely toothed margins, 2–6 in. (5–15 cm) long; fruit in capsule, many winged seeds. My plant stands up to considerable cold, surviving temperatures to 0°F (−18°C) for short periods. Hardy to zone 4 with protection. 'Hot Lips' has bright pink flowers and purplish bronze new leaves, turning dark green.

Chimaphila and *Pyrola*

The first few times I explored the neighborhood ravine, I completely overlooked *Chimaphila maculata* (pipsissewa), a tiny plant that was growing there in small colonies between the projecting roots of large loblolly pines. The dark green leaves in camouflage dress blended perfectly with dead pine needles and leaf scatter, but during one early-spring excursion into the gulch, I spotted something white and went to investigate. What I saw were the most precious waxy white flowers I had ever seen, hanging in nodding pairs from upright stems. Brushing aside the forest litter and encroaching ivy, escaped from nearby gardens, I uncovered whorls of leathery, dark green leaves marked with a grayish white stripe along the midrib. This time I did not hesitate and dug up a portion of the struggling, partially covered colony, along with a sufficient amount of native soil. Given a better place in my garden with more light and freedom to spread, my pipsissewa group has delighted all comers for over two decades now. I do nothing to maintain pipsissewa, supply no fertilizer, no extra water, and basically just leave it alone. It must like this because it just keeps going on, its evergreen leaves gracing the garden all year and its white flowers brightening up its place in early June.

In the wild I have seen *Chimaphila maculata* all

over southeastern North America, particularly Alabama, Tennessee, and right in my own backyard. I have never spotted *C. umbellata* in Georgia, although it is reported to be frequent in the Southeast. Also not seen in Georgia is what I call the northern pipsissewa, *Pyrola americana*, which I have observed near the Blue Ridge Parkway in Shenandoah National Park.

Both genera thrive in moist to dry coniferous forests in rich woods soil, frequently hiding at the base of large pines. They require very acid soil with a pH of 4.5 to 5, and heavy soils seem no obstacle to the deeply rooted, creeping rhizomes. Supplemental water is not essential but probably appreciated during prolonged droughts, and they are happy in heavy shade. Notwithstanding, they benefit from some dappled light and seem to bloom better that way. Frequently characterized as a cool-summer plant, I have found *Chimaphila* tolerant of dry, hot summers; *Pyrola* is more suited to cool northern areas. Both should be planted in a shady, possibly elevated spot, where the delicate flowers and attractively marked leaves can be closely observed. A group of several of these small plants is much more showy. *Chimaphila* species turn up frequently at local rescue sites and are available in commerce from propagated stock, but *Pyrola* is only occasionally available. Good companion plants for both are the smaller native wild gingers (*Asarum* spp.) and other wildflowers, like galax and autumn ladies' tresses (*Spiranthes cernua*). *Chimaphila* is hardy to zone 4.

The generic name *Chimaphila* (= winter-loving) comes from the Greek, an allusion to its evergreen nature. *Pyrola* is the diminutive of *pyrus* (= pear), for the fancied resemblance of its leaves to those of a pear tree. Pipsissewa is a Creek Indian name based on the belief that the juice of *Chimaphila maculata* reduces kidney stones; American Indians and early settlers throughout the Southeast used its leaves as a component to produce root beer. Its many herbalistic uses include the treatment of colds, urinary ailments, rheumatism, and aches and pains. *Chimaphila* and *Pyrola* are classified in the wintergreen family, Pyrolaceae.

Propagate by dividing the rhizome in winter or very early spring. *Chimaphila* is easy to transplant, but *Pyrola* is difficult—take along considerable native soil to guarantee success. Seed propagation in a very acid growing medium is possible but time-consuming. Stem cuttings may also be rooted in sand over winter.

Slugs and snails can damage new growth emerging in spring; no other pests or diseases are experienced here.

Chimaphila japonica, Japanese wintergreen. Japan.
LS to FS; flowers 1–2, otherwise almost identical to *Chimaphila maculata* but smaller, with stems to 4 in. (10 cm) and leaves broadly lance-shaped to 1.5 in. (4 cm) long. Rarely offered.

Chimaphila maculata, striped pipsissewa, striped wintergreen, pipsissewa, spotted wintergreen, wintergreen, dragon's-tongue, rheumatism root, waxflower. Eastern North America, southern Ontario south to Georgia and Alabama, west to northeastern Illinois and Michigan, south to Kentucky and Tennessee.
LS to FS; flowers 1–5, usually 2, borne on terminal pendent branches atop erect stems 6–10 in. (15–25 cm) tall; flowers wide open, drooping, waxy white, in more open areas sometimes with a pinkish hue, 5-petaled, to 0.6 in. (1.5 cm) across, of thick substance and slightly fragrant; late May–early July; plant rhizomatous, creeping, evergreen; stems woody, partially underground, producing leaves at intervals; leaves 3–4, in tiers of loose whorls, 1–2 in. (2.5–5 cm) long, lance-shaped, sharp-tipped, toothed, leathery dark green with grayish white markings along the midrib (hence *maculata* = spotted, blotched); fruit in brown capsule persisting through winter. This species is more showy than other wintergreens, and with limited space in my garden, I prefer it. Available from many wildflower nurseries.

Chimaphila menziesii, little prince's pine, western prince's pine. Western North America, Cascades.
LS to FS; flowers 1–3; leaf margins finely toothed or smooth. A widespread species in western North America, with most populations concentrated in the Cascades. Rarely offered, it is no improvement over *Chimaphila umbellata*.

Chimaphila umbellata, prince's pine, western prince's pine, common pipsissewa, wintergreen. North America, southern Ontario and Quebec south to Georgia and Alabama, west to the western Cascades, Eurasia, northern and eastern Europe, Japan.

LS to FS; flowers 3–7, borne on terminal pendent branches atop erect stems to 12 in. (30 cm) tall; flowers wide open, drooping, pink, 5-petaled, to 0.6 in. (1.5 cm) across, filaments swollen; June–August; plant rhizomatous, creeping, evergreen; stems woody, partially underground, producing leaves at intervals; leaves in whorls of 3–6 in 2–3 tiers, 1–2 in. (2.5–5 cm) long, lance-shaped, broadest above the middle, toothed, solid dark green; fruit in brown capsule persisting through winter. Variety *cisatlantica* has solid green leaves with conspicuous veins on the leaf underside; var. *occidentalis* lacks these veins. The type is often mixed up with its varieties in commerce.

Pyrola americana, wild lily-of-the-valley, American pyrola, canker lettuce, consumption weed, Indian lettuce, roundleaf wintergreen, roundleaf American wintergreen. North America, British Columbia to Washington and Oregon east to Newfoundland and Nova Scotia and south to Pennsylvania and West Virginia.

LS to FS; flowers 5–20, borne on terminal pendent branches, spirally arranged on erect stems 10–12 in. (25–30 cm) tall; flowers wide open, drooping, to 0.6 in. (1.5 cm) across, petals 5, thick, waxy white, rarely light pink, fragrant, stamens 10 with bright yellow anthers, protruding curved style; July–August; plant rhizomatous, creeping, evergreen; leaves 4–7, basal, 1–2 in. (2.5–5 cm) long, round with long stalk, dark green, leathery, shiny, without markings; fruit in brown capsule persisting through winter. Its Eurasian counterpart, *Pyrola rotundifolia*, is similar but slightly smaller. Both are occasionally offered in commerce. Also smaller but similar is *P. elliptica* (shinleaf, lesser wintergreen, waxflower pyrola) with very waxy flowers of greenish white; it contains aspirinlike substances (salicylates) and was used by American Indians in a shin plaster applied to burns and wounds. *Pyrola secunda* (one-sided wintergreen) is widespread in North America and the most frequently seen species in the wild. Its flowers are arranged to one side on the stem; it is vigorously rhizomatous and makes a good groundcover. The European and western North American *P. picta* (white-veined wintergreen) has the best leaves, to 3 in. (8 cm) long, broadly elliptic, thick and leathery, deep green, with the midrib and side veins distinctly marked with white. Flowers are greenish white to cream on a red stem. The leaves

look very much like those of *Chimaphila maculata*, except they are basal, and are sometimes toothed, as they were in a colony of these dainty plants I observed near the Columbia River Gorge in the western Cascades of Oregon. None of these plants should be removed from the wild unless a rescue situation arises; be sure to dig up sufficient native soil along with the plant in such cases. Most *Pyrola* species are for special garden situations only and are definitely not for novice gardeners.

Chrysogonum

Whenever Latin binomials are difficult to pronounce, and even when they are not, gardeners and suppliers are quick to find new ones. *Chrysogonum virginianum* is fine and fitting for botanists, but gardeners have long called it green and gold (and goldenstar is the new favorite). This species is happy in light shade, and I have seen it growing and blooming in considerable shade. It does best in an open situation where it can receive dappled sun during the day.

Goldenstar is frequent in the Piedmont region of the Carolinas and Georgia, where it grows along the edges of woods and in forest clearings. It tolerates the hot, dry summers of southeastern North America and prefers dry soils, rotting easily if too much moisture is present. I neglect it as much as adjacent plants allow; I do not fertilize it, nor do I water it unless it displays signs of distress during droughts. The pretty yellow, daisylike flowers are produced in great quantity in spring and sporadically in summer. It spreads by stolons and makes a tight cover in relatively little time. I have several expanding clumps growing among a patch of *Silene polypetala* (fringed campion).

The genus name (*Chrysogonum* = golden knee) is a Greek combination alluding to the yellow flowers and jointed stem. *Chrysogonum* is classified in the daisy family, Asteraceae.

Goldenstar requires circumneutral soil with a pH of 6 or slightly higher. It will tolerate somewhat more acid soils; my clumps are growing in improved (one-half of pine bark by volume) clay soil with a pH of 5.5. Supplemental water is necessary only during prolonged droughts.

Propagate by taking runners (stolons) and rooting them in good garden soil. Seed propagation is not necessary and too slow.

Pests and diseases have not damaged my plants. Slugs and snails may take a bite out of newly emerging leaves, but this is only a minor problem with leaf increase so rapid.

Chrysogonum virginianum, goldenstar, golden star, green and gold, golden knee. Eastern North America, central Ohio and Pennsylvania south to Georgia and Florida and west to Mississippi.

Some sun, LS to WS; flowers many but solitary on each branched stem, composed of 5 broad, yellow rays, sometimes notched, 1–1.5 in. (2.5–4 cm) across, with central disk of yellow florets, 5 outer green bracts alternate with the rays (hence, green and gold); April–October; plant stoloniferous, creeping, evergreen south, deciduous north, leaf-stalks reddish; leaves 1–4 in. (2.5–10 cm) long, opposite on stems, heart-shaped, hairy, medium green. An extremely variable species: some forms have long, narrow, and widely separated rays (lobes), others have broad, almost overlapping rays. Leaves are either smooth or have toothed margins. *Chrysogonum australe*, which occurs in the southern part of *C. virginianum*'s range, has a more creeping habit and produces many runners. *Chrysogonum virginianum*, with its more erect, taller habit, is less suitable for groundcover applications but makes a nice companion plant in the open woodland border. During mild winters it is evergreen at Hosta Hill. Hardy to zone 5.

'Allen Bush', a dwarf form with leafy stolons; flowers smaller, yellow.

'Eco Lacquered Spider', a colorful form with very long, purple stolons; the purple color runs into the leaf bases and the leaves are unusually glossy; bloom period somewhat shorter than the type.

'Greystone Gold', a form with overlapping yellow rays and almost round leaves.

'Pierre', softer green leaves and long bloom duration.

Chrysosplenium

As one would expect of members of the vast family of saxifrages, Saxifragaceae, many *Chrysosplenium* species are spreading plants. The few species suitable for shady gardens, most from eastern Asia, are stoloniferous indeed and must be allowed some room to stake out their territory. They adapt well to partial shade; I have small specimens growing and blooming in considerable shade during the day, with a few hours of morning sun. They like an open situation in a woodland setting, bog garden, or wildflower border or near a pond or water feature. I am still not certain how to use these newcomers, but their spreading habit suggests suitability as groundcovers. Here they struggle somewhat during hot, dry summers, but as long as they remain in shade during the heat of the day and supplemental water is supplied, they carry on bravely. I expect them to be much more vigorous in areas of cool summers.

Golden saxifrages, as *Chrysosplenium* species are sometimes called, do not have golden flowers. They are, nevertheless, a bright, sometimes shiny greenish yellow with somewhat darker bracts giving a marvelous two-tone coloration. They are abundant in eastern Asia, where they grow in upland mountain valleys of Yunnan and Sichuan provinces in western China, but they are also found in the moist, deciduous forests of Korea and Japan, and at least one, *Chrysosplenium valdivicum*, is at home in southern Chile, in the cool, moist evergreen woods south of the Bio-Bio River. Golden saxifrages have not been fully tested for cold hardiness, but it can be inferred from other genera endemic to these regions that zone 6 may be the northern limit for all but the Japanese species from central Honshu and those from Korea. A species from northern Scandinavia and arctic Finland, *C. tetrandum*, is much hardier, to zone 1 or 2, depending on microclimate, but it is scarcely available.

Golden saxifrages thrive in moist but well-draining acidic soil with a pH of 5 to 6. Soil fertility does not seem to be very important, and in the wild many populations grow on poor soils. The hot, dry summers of southeastern North America are difficult for the golden saxifrages used to moist and cool forests. I suggest placement in shaded areas where the soil stays cooler, although flowering may diminish. The species are shallow-rooted, so supplemental water is required to keep the top layer of the soil from drying out during prolonged droughts.

Propagate by taking soft cuttings from the plant in early spring and rooting them in good garden soil. Many species are self-layering, and propagation is easily accomplished by transplanting rooted sections of the stems. Alternatively, plants can be divided in very early spring, just as growth commences.

Slugs and snails enjoy the moist, shady environment under these groundcovers and may damage young leaves. No other pest or disease problems are reported.

Chrysosplenium davidianum, golden saxifrage. Western China, Yunnan.

Some sun, LS to WS; flowers many, terminal on branched axillary flowerstalks, greenish yellow with large yellowish green, rounded bracts giving a two-tone appearance, 1.5–2 in. (4–5 cm) across; April–June; plant prostrate, stoloniferously creeping, deciduous; leaves 0.5–1.5 in. (1–4 cm) long, rounded and broadly heart-shaped, medium green, margin scalloped, covered with a coating of fine hair underneath. Hardy to zone 6, may be hardier with protection. Another species from western China in Sichuan province, larger-flowered than *Chrysosplenium davidianum*, is *C. macrophyllum*, which, as the epithet indicates, has large leaves, to 2.5 in. (6 cm) long, green and felty above and purplish underneath. Shade gardeners with some sunny spots may want to try its adaptability to shade.

Chrysosplenium japonicum. Japan, central Honshu, Korea.

Some sun, LS to WS; flowers many, in terminal clusters, greenish yellow with bright yellow, rounded bracts; May–July; plant prostrate, stoloniferously creeping and self-layering, deciduous; leaves opposite, to 1.5 in. (4 cm) long, broadly triangular, but rounded, smooth, medium green, with margin toothed. This species is in commerce but still rarely seen in gardens. Hardy to zone 6, 5 with protection. Another species from south-central Honshu and Korea is *Chrysosplenium macrostemon*, which, as the epithet indicates, has large, showy stamens. Its flowers are small compared to other species and greenish yellow, but the larger bracts are a bright green, and the combination makes a charming display.

Chrysosplenium oppositifolium. Europe.

Some sun, LS to WS; flowers many, inconspicuous; plant prostrate, creeping by means of underground rhizomes, deciduous; leaves small, opposite, forming dense mats of groundcover. Variety *rosulare* is primarily grown as a groundcover and requires watching to be kept in bounds; var. *alpinum* is rarely offered in commerce. *Chrysosplenium alternifolium* is similar but has alternate, rounded leaves; it is native to Eurasia, common in the British Isles and on the Continent with some populations extending to Siberia. A third European species, *C. tetrandum* from the arctic regions of northern Europe, particularly Scandinavia and Finland, is extremely hardy. All require a delicate balance of sun and shade to perform best and are worth a try in shade gardens.

Chrysosplenium valdivicum. South America, southern Chile.

LS to MS; flowers many, clustered in the leaf axils, greenish yellow, 2–2.5 in. (5–6 cm) across; April–June; plant low growing, stoloniferously creeping, self-layering, deciduous; leaves opposite, to 2.5 in. (6 cm) long, rounded and broadly heart-shaped. Hardy to zone 7, may be hardier with protection.

Cimicifuga

One of the first native North American wildflowers I ever planted was black cohosh, *Cimicifuga racemosa*, a stately, architectural plant of great beauty with tall, showy panicles of white flowers. I saw this magnificent wildflower for the first time almost 50 years ago, during a visit to the Appalachians. I espied a white glow in the distance (candles of the woods, the mountain people call it) and fought my way through the underbrush until I stood before a group of towering plants, easily over 7 ft. (2 m) tall. My reverent admiration of the magnificent colony started me on a lifelong love of native plants and gardening with wildflowers. In the past decade, many new species and cultivars of this genus have appeared in commerce—a dream fulfilled—but my first love is still *C. racemosa*.

The generic name *Cimicifuga* is derived from the Latin *cimex* (= bug) and *fugere* (= to drive away). Bugbane (*bane* = to kill) is another common name and one I find equally baffling since flies, attracted to the offensive odor, are the primary pollinators of bugbane. American Indians, who were well acquainted with *Cimicifuga racemosa*, used this native herb to treat snake bites. Early settlers, hoping to drive away bedbugs and other nasty pests, used dried bugbane in their mattress stuffing. Even now, in remote Appalachian areas, a tea made from the leaves treats diarrhea and rheumatism, and its roots are used as a diuretic.

The genus *Cimicifuga* contains many handsome, tall plants for the shady garden. Originating in moist woodlands of almost the entire north temperate zone, they are well adapted to shady, moist conditions. Notwithstanding, the North American species, with their deep-rooting habit, tolerate a considerable lack of moisture. In gardens, an extra supply of water during prolonged droughts is appreciated. Bugbanes do best in a light, well-draining, acid woodland soil, rich in organic matter. Their crowning glory are the tapering panicles of white or pinkish white held high above the loose leaf mounds. Place them against a darker background so the light flowers stand out. The panicles remain upright, turn brown, and provide attractive garden highlights throughout the winter. The leaf mounds are elaborately composed, with each leaf divided into three leaflet segments three times over. Leaflets retain their bright, dark green color into early fall. Some species flower in spring; others raise their panicles in early summer. Most are hardy to zone 5.

Cimicifuga racemosa thrives in considerable shade, but too much shade prevents its flowering. I grow and flower it successfully in medium shade. It likes cool soil, but it succeeds in warmer regions if ample moisture is available. Its best companions are other tall wildflowers and ferns. For best anchorage, the soil should not be too loose; wild plants in Georgia grow in soils containing large amounts of heavy clay, and my plants receive the same treatment. With this good footing, the tall spires withstand considerable winds during heavy spring thunderstorms; I have never had to stake them.

The nomenclature of this genus is in a state of flux; I have maintained the Linnaean order. The species of the genus *Cimicifuga* are herbaceous, clump-forming, erect, long-lived perennials classified in the Ranunculaceae.

Propagate by dividing the rhizome in very early spring. Delay division by at least three years, as young plants do not divide well. Employ a clean, sharp knife for cutting, and apply a dusting of fungicide to keep cuts free of smut or rust. Fresh seed can be sown in small pots in a cold frame, but I find

it much easier to simply strip the seeds from the fruiting panicles and bury them where I want new bugbanes to come up. This method is less productive but with many seeds available, a few seedling always emerge. Most variegated forms are unstable.

Clumps occasionally develop leaf spot, leaf smut, or black rust. These are fungal diseases, and entire plants can be affected unless fungicides are employed. Check plants often for telltale black fungal deposits at the emerging stems. I see occasional weevil damage, but other insect pests do not seem to bother the plants.

Cimicifuga americana, American bugbane, mountain bugbane, summer cohosh. Eastern North America, Pennsylvania south to Georgia and the Carolinas and west to Tennessee.

LS to FS; flowers white, sometimes pink- or red-tinted, small, to 0.5 in. (1 cm) wide, 4–5 sepals, shedding as flower opens, petals minute or absent, stamens numerous, tufted, pistils 3–8 on stalks; flowerstalks 3–6 ft. (0.9–1.8 m), with leaves ascending stalk, erect, with large, bushy, basal leaves, topped with several flowering panicles on branched raceme; July–September; leaves twice divided into 3s, leaflets rounded, heart-shaped, 3- to 5-lobed, toothed, dark green, with pointed tips, 1–3 in. (2.5–8 cm) long; fruit in small capsules. Variability of flower color may be due to differences in microclimate. A good garden plant. Because it does not grow as tall as *Cimicifuga racemosa* and its flowers are more refined, it mixes well with shorter ferns, wildflowers, and medium and large hostas. Further distinguished by its several pistils, on stalks, whereas *C. racemosa* usually has only one sessile (unstalked) pistil.

Cimicifuga biternata, Japanese bugbane, *inushoma* (Jap.). Japan.

LS to FS; flowers white to pinkish white, fragrant, small, to 0.5 in. (1 cm) wide, 4–5 sepals, shedding, petals absent, stamens numerous, tufted; flowerstalks to 40 in. (1 m), erect, smooth, with large, bushy, basal leaves, stem topped with several flowering, densely spike-shaped, bristled racemes; August–September; leaves ternate or twice divided into 3s, leaflets 3–9, rounded, heart-shaped, lobed and sharply, finely toothed and incised, dark green; fruit in small capsules. Similar to *Cimicifuga americana*. The leaf mound is dense and shrublike.

Known to horticulture since its importation from Japan by Siebold the 1830s, this species makes a nice flowering accent in the early autumn garden.

Cimicifuga dahurica. Mongolia to eastern Siberia, northern China, northern Japan.

LS to FS; flowers white to creamy white, sometimes tinged pink, small, 4–5 sepals, shedding, petals resemble inflated stamens, stamens numerous, tufted; flowerstalks 4–6 ft. (1.2–1.8 m), erect, smooth, all leaves basal, stem topped with several lax, compound racemes; August–September; leaves twice or thrice divided into 3s; leaflets rounded to heart-shaped and lobed at base, dark green; fruit in small capsules. A dioecious species and a most unusual bugbane—to me, it looks almost like a goatsbeard, *Aruncus dioicus*, but with flower spikes more defined, if not refined. Male plants are larger in all respects, more floriferous, and better garden specimens; female plants frequently have many simple racemes, which do not give the cloudlike effect of the male plant's compound racemes. If I had room for only one exotic species in my garden, this would be it. Give it plenty of room, as it expands in time.

Cimicifuga elata, western bugbane, Oregon bugbane. Western North America, Washington, Oregon.

LS to FS; flowers white, sometimes pink-tinted, small, to 0.5 in. (1 cm) wide, 4–5 sepals, shedding, petals absent, stamens numerous, tufted; flowerstalks 3–4 ft. (0.9–1.2 m), hairy, leafy, erect, with large, bushy, basal leaves, topped with a single raceme or several panicles on branched raceme; July–September; leaves twice divided into 3s, leaflets small, to 0.6 in. (1.5 cm), rounded, heart-shaped and covered with fine hair, 3-lobed, with lobes lobed again and toothed, dark green; fruit in small capsules. I saw this species on a visit to the Columbia River Gorge and *Cimicifuga laciniata*, another western species, growing in the High Cascades near Mount Hood in Oregon. *Cimicifuga laciniata* has hairy flowerstalks to 6 ft. (1.8 m), with white or creamy white flowers, and is distinguished by its short-clawed, 2-lobed petals and longer pedicels, to 0.5 in. (1 cm); its sepals are oval and shedding. The leaflets are sharply incised, toothed and divided, as the epithet indicates. *Cimicifuga laciniata* is rare in its native habitat but has recently become available, responsibly propagated from seed. A third and equally rare western species is *C. arizonica*

(Arizona bugbane) from the higher elevations of the southern Rocky Mountains in Arizona. It too has flowers with petals but has smooth leaflets, and its flowers are pure white to a creamy or yellowish white. Of the three western species, only *C. elata* is common. The average gardener is better served by the eastern North American species, which are widely propagated, easier to cultivate, and much more showy and satisfying in gardens.

Cimicifuga foetida, fetid bugbane, stinking bugbane, European bugbane. Eurasia, eastern Europe, Mongolia, Siberia, eastern Himalayas.

LS to FS; flowers greenish white with unpleasant odor, small, sepals shedding, petals present, smooth margin, divided, stamens numerous, tufted; flowerstalks 4–7 ft. (1.2–2 m), erect, hairy, simple or divided toward top, all leaves basal, stem remotely topped with dense racemes; August–September; leaves twice or thrice divided into 3s; leaflets oblong, deeply and finely toothed, dark green, terminal leaflet 3-lobed; fruit in small capsules. A good garden plant if one can overlook the fetor during bloom season. Hardy to zone 3.

Cimicifuga heracleifolia, Komarov's bugbane. Northern China, Siberia, Korea.

LS to FS; flowers white, small, 4–5 sepals, shedding, petals absent, stamens numerous, tufted; flowerstalks to 8 ft. (2.5 m), erect, green, all leaves basal, bushy, stem topped with panicles of distinctly separate flowers with short pedicels subtended by bracts on a many-branched raceme; August–September; leaves twice or thrice divided into 3s, leaflets 9–25, broadly ovate, base heart-shaped, 3-lobed, finely toothed, dark green, with pointed tips; fruit in small capsules. A distinctive, robust species that will add much to Western gardens. Its very tall flowering spikes have multiple branches emerging along their length, with each branch clothed in flowers and up to 10 in. (25 cm) long. The individual flowers are larger and more separated on the stems than in other species of *Cimicifuga*, where the individual flowers blend together into a whitish column or spike. The leaflets have good substance. Variety *bifida*, found in central Korea, is ternate only, with 3 leaflets per leaf, and has notched petals in the flowers. It is rarely available.

Cimicifuga japonica, Japanese bugbane, Chinese bugbane. China, Korea, Japan.

LS to FS; flowers white, small, to 0.5 in. (1 cm) wide, 4–5 sepals, shedding as flower opens, petals minute or absent, stamens numerous, tufted, pistils 3–8 on stalks; flowerstalks 24–36 in. (60–90 cm), erect, with no leaves ascending stem, all leaves basal, bushy, stem topped with several flowering, densely arranged panicles on branched raceme; July–September; leaves twice divided into 3s, leaflets rounded, heart-shaped, 3- to 5-lobed, toothed, dark green, with pointed tips, 1–3 in. (2.5–8 cm) long; fruit in small capsules. Very similar to *Cimicifuga americana* and may be its Asian counterpart. Variety *acutiloba* from central Honshu, described in Thunberg's *Flora Japonica* in 1784, has glossy leaflets somewhat larger than the type, with sharply pointed tips. A dwarf form of the type occurs on Cheju Island; these plants have a clump size of 6 in. (15 cm) and flowerstalks to only 8 in. (20 cm).

Cimicifuga mairei. Siberia, Korea, southwestern China, Sichuan, Yunnan.

LS to FS; flowers yellowish white, small, 4–5 sepals, shedding, stamens numerous, tufted; flowerstalks to 8 ft. (2.5 m), erect, green, all leaves basal, bushy, stem topped with flowering panicles on branched raceme; August–September; leaves twice divided into 3s, leaflets broadly ovate, base heart-shaped, 3-lobed, finely toothed, dark green, with a depressed network of veins giving added texture to the leaflets; fruit oblong, seeds with scales. A vigorous species characterized by simultaneously flowering spikes. Its large leaflets make an impressive mound. I have grown it for only a short time, but already it shows great garden potential, enduring long, hot, dry summers with no ill effects, as long as the soil is not allowed to dry out. Other species from China are still rare and seldom seen in gardens. *Cimicifuga brachycarpa* has a multibranched raceme of yellowish flowers; the fruit is short and round (hence the epithet), and the seeds are without scales. *Cimicifuga yunnanensis* has an unbranched raceme of yellowish flowers and a multitude of small leaflets, giving it a shrublike appearance. Purple-flowered *C. purpurea* grows further east in China, in the provinces of Sichuan, Hubei, and Guizhou; I hope this unusual bugbane eventually finds its way into Western gardens.

Cimicifuga racemosa, black cohosh, black snakeroot, fairy candles, snakeroot, rattletop. Eastern North America, Canada, southern Ontario, New England south to Georgia and west to Tennessee and Missouri.

LS to FS; flowers white, with unpleasant odor, small, to 0.5 in. (1 cm) wide, 4–5 sepals, shedding as flower opens, petals absent, stamens numerous, tufted, pistil 1, rarely 2, sessile; flowerstalks 3–8 ft. (0.9–2.5 m), with leaves ascending stalk, erect, with large, bushy, basal leaves, topped with several flowering panicles on branched raceme; June–September; leaves twice divided into 3s, leaflets rounded, heart-shaped, 3- to 5-lobed, sharply toothed, dark green, with pointed tips, 3–4 in. (8–10 cm) long; fruit in small capsules. The best bugbane for the garden. The majestic flowerstalks bloom before all other species, for 4 to 5 weeks; their grandeur encourages one to forget the unpleasant odor they exude. They make a nice display until the first freeze, though I usually cut them down during autumn cleanup. In mild winters they stay up all during the cold season. Widely distributed in commerce, this is a bugbane no garden should be without. Hardy to zone 3 with protection. 'Atropurpurea', which may be part of the *Cimicifuga simplex* Atropurpurea Group, has deep purple leaves in spring; they green up later but keep a dark coloration throughout the season.

Cimicifuga rubifolia, bramble-leaved cohosh. Eastern North America, Georgia, Tennessee.

LS to FS; having observed this plant in Tennessee, I can see why taxonomists elevated the former *Cimicifuga racemosa* var. *cordifolia* to species status. Leaves are 2-ternate but have lateral shoots with 2 leaflets, resulting in a total of up to 9 leaflets per leaf. Leaflets are wider, with heart-shaped bases, 5- to 7-lobed, with the terminal leaflets usually 3-lobed. Lobes are pointed, not rounded, with sharp tips, resembling those of the brambles (*Rubus* spp.) frequent in the area (hence the epithet). Pistils are 1, rarely 2, and sessile (unstalked). Its creamy flowers are not as tall as in *C. racemosa*, and its 2–4 racemes per stalk are more cylindrical, with a rounded rather than a spike-shaped top. It is smaller in all respects except for the size of the leaflets, which are 5–8 in. (13–20 cm) long and have an attractive reddish blush in spring. Rarely offered.

Cimicifuga simplex, autumn snakeroot. Western China, Manchuria, Mongolia, eastern Russia, Kamchatka Peninsula, Sakhalin, Siberia, Japan, Korea.

LS to FS; flowers white, small, sepals small, petals present, smooth margin or slightly 2-lobed, stamens numerous, tufted; flowerstalks to 4 ft. (1.2 m), erect, covered with fine hairs toward top, simple or branched; leaves basal and sometimes on the stem, stem remotely topped with dense racemes to 12 in. (30 cm); August–September; leaves 2- to 3-ternate; leaflets small, 1–3 in. (2.5–8 cm) oblong, sometimes 3-lobed, always deeply and finely toothed, dark green; fruit in small capsules. A popular species characterized by attractive, cylindrical racemes of dense, white flowers. It has a very long bloom period. Variety *matsumurae*, honoring J. Matsumura, who wrote a major work on the Japanese flora, is a later-blooming Japanese form. Hardy to zone 3.

'Armleuchter' ('Candelabra'), white flowers on long stems with multiple racemes, fragrant, pale green leaves.

'Atropurpurea', Atropurpurea Group (a very important group horticulturally; contains variants with purple leaves), white flowers, barely fragrant, reddish purple; coppery leaves fading to brownish green in autumn.

'Braunlaub' ('Brownleaf'), white flowers on long racemes; very dark, brownish green leaves.

'Brunette', lavender-tinted white flowers on compact 8 in. (20 cm) long racemes, fragrant, purple stems; dark reddish purple leaves fading to brownish dark green in autumn.

'Elstead' ('Elstead's Variety'), buds dark pink to purple, opening to white flowers in loose, feathery racemes on purplish stems to 5 ft. (1.5 m); green leaves. A selection of var. *matsumurae*.

'Frau Herms', white flowers on tall racemes, very late bloomer, fragrant; green leaves. A selection of var. *matsumurae*.

'Hillside Black Beauty', Atropurpurea Group, white flowers; blackish purple leaves fading to very dark brownish green in autumn.

'Prichard's Giant', white flowers on very tall racemes, very fragrant; striking green leaves. Heat-tolerant.

'White Pearl', greenish buds opening to pure white flowers on mostly simple, arching racemes, stems to 4 ft. (1.2 m), fragrant; pale green leaves. A selection of var. *matsumurae*.

Claytonia

Spring ephemerals grace the Appalachians. They come early, usually bloom abundantly, and then, as if to signal they have run out of energy, fade away for another year. These fleeting plants are difficult in a shady garden, which relies so heavily on foliage for its paradisian look throughout the season. Nevertheless, I have included the spring beauties (*Claytonia* spp.) because they are harbingers of spring. In the sunny garden, tulips, daffodils, and other bulbous plants announce spring's arrival, but in the shade this task falls to wildflowers. Nothing is more spectacular than a field of spring beauties in bloom. Along the road to Clingmans Dome in the Smoky Mountains, thousands of individual blooms carpet the land like huge pink snowflakes. It's hard to duplicate this effect in a garden, of course, but those who have a small shady corner along a path where small ferns and hostas already grow can tuck a few spring beauties in here and there. Keep your eyes open during the first chilly garden strolls, and spring beauties will be there, announcing the start of a new season.

Spring beauties are short-lived but spread vigorously by self-seeding. Flowers are small but charming, with pink anthers, yellow nectaries, and white or pale pink petals with dark pink veins. I have grown a small colony of them for years and always enjoy their enthusiastic flowering during the early warm days of March. Named for John Clayton, a pioneer botanist in Virginia, spring beauty is found all over North America. Two species represent the genus in gardens, *Claytonia caroliniana* (Carolina spring beauty) and *C. virginica* (Virginia spring beauty). In the wild, particularly in the large Appalachian populations, their habitats frequently overlap, and this conjunction can be emulated in gardens.

Species of the genus *Claytonia* are herbaceous, ephemeral perennials in the purslane family, Portulacaceae. All parts of the plant are edible and nutritious, and the corms especially have a sweet, nutlike flavor; American Indians and early settlers used them in soups, stews, and salads. Originating in moist, open woodlands in the higher elevations, they are well adapted to cool, open woodland shade and moist conditions; yet they can be planted where summers get very hot because they have disappeared underground by the time high temperatures arrive. Obviously, watering during droughts increases a corm's chance of surviving. Hardy to zone 5, 4 with protection.

Plants self-seed. Seed can be sown in the open in autumn.

Mildew can be a problem, but I have not experienced it. Occasionally aphids may be bothersome.

Claytonia caroliniana, Carolina spring beauty, good-morning-spring, mayflower, grassflower, wideleaf spring beauty. Eastern North America, in the mountains from eastern Canada south to Georgia and the Carolinas and west to Tennessee, Missouri, and Minnesota.

LS to FS; flowers white to pink, red-tinted, with dark pink to red veining, small, to 0.8 in. (2 cm) across, 5 petals, 2 sepals, 5 stamens with pink anthers, 3–17 flowers on short, succulent racemes; March–May; plant clump-forming, arising from a corm; leaves usually 2, 2 in. (5 cm) long and 0.8 in. (2 cm) wide, oval to oblong, opposite, smooth dark green, blunt-tipped, on the stem with distinct leafstalks; fruit in small capsule enclosed by 2 sepals. A frequent species in the Smoky Mountains, where I have observed it many times in very early spring in shaded woods, still occasionally snow-covered. It should be planted together with permanent groundcovers, like small ferns and small hostas, that emerge later and cover the areas left open by it.

Claytonia virginica, spring beauty, Virginia spring beauty, common spring beauty, narrowleaf spring beauty, good-morning-spring, mayflower, grassflower, wideleaf spring beauty. Eastern North America, Minnesota east to southern Quebec and New Brunswick south to southwestern Georgia and eastern Texas.

LS to FS; flowers white to pink, red-tinted, with dark pink to red veining, small, to 0.8 in. (2 cm) across, 5 petals, 2 sepals, 5 stamens with pink anthers, 3–17 flowers on short, succulent racemes; March–May; plant clump-forming, arising from a corm; basal leaves usually absent but occasionally many, stems leaves 2–6 in. (5–15 cm) long, to 0.8 in. (2 cm) wide, usually 2 only, narrowly lance-shaped, opposite, smooth dark green, on the stem with no distinguishable leafstalk; fruit in small capsule enclosed by 2 sepals. This species is frequent in the Appalachians. Only its narrow, lance-

shaped leaves distinguish it from *Claytonia caroliniana*, and the same companions are recommended for it. 'Lutea' has orange-red flowers with dark red veining. 'Robusta' is a clone larger than the type, with flowers to 1 in. (2.5 cm) across and flowerstalks to 14 in. (35 cm).

Clintonia

The first time I saw a bead lily was in very early spring, before flowering. I chanced upon what I thought was a patch of lily-of-the-valley, near Rainbow Falls in the Smoky Mountains, but closer examination revealed the colony's true nature. I returned to the same spot in late summer and found the leaf crowns, just as fresh and bright green as the previous spring, topped with glistening dark blue berries. I purchased a few *Clintonia* plants from a Carolina wildflower nursery and planted them in a moist, shady corner of the garden. One was *Clintonia borealis*, and I found out quickly that, even in such a spot, our stifling summers did not appeal to it; it rarely flowers, although the nice, glossy green, barely pleated leaves do carry on. *Clintonia umbellata* flowers, but this mountain dweller needs constant moisture and deep shade to perform on my shady hillock. My bead lilies keep company with highly shade-tolerant wild gingers and uvularias. Even without flowers, the species serve the garden well, providing low-growing leaf cover in deeply shaded areas. Further north and higher up, where summers are cool, bead lilies do exceedingly well. Unfortunately, the balsam fir forests that they and other boreal wildflowers prefer as habitat are rapidly disappearing from the Appalachians, due to beetle infestations. No plants should be taken from the wild.

Some bead lilies have bright, shiny porcelain-blue to blackish blue berries; other species have white berries. The fruit is said to be toxic, but the leaves are edible and taste like cucumber. American Indians and early settlers used the roots, which contain an anti-inflammatory, to treat infections, burns, heart problems, diabetes, and rheumatism.

Clintonia gets its name from DeWitt Clinton, a naturalist and governor of New York. The genus is classified in the Convallariaceae. The epithet *borealis* indicates a bead lily that is at home in northern (boreal) forests; the epithet *umbellatus* refers to the umbrellalike arrangement of the flowers, which are carried in an umbel, on long flowerstalks originating at a common point on the raceme's stem.

Bead lilies thrive in the cool-summer climate of northern forests, but they also do well in the higher elevations of the southern Appalachians. They require constantly damp, acid soil with a pH of 5 and cool soil temperatures. They tolerate considerable shade but prefer a more open site in light shade. Hardy to zone 4, some to zone 3; their ultimate southern heat tolerance and range of cultivation is zone 7a, or, better, 6. My experience in zone 7a shows that bead lilies may not flower when shade is increased to keep them cool, but even without flowers (and, consequently, fruit), the attractive, long-lasting leaves add texture to southern gardens.

Propagate by dividing the rhizome in very early spring. Be sure the division has a growing tip for the new season's growth. Transplants may be slow to establish. Fresh seed can be germinated with the pulp removed and sown in small pots in a cold frame in autumn, but this is a difficult, time-consuming process: patience is advised.

I have seen no disease or insect damage, other than slugs and snails disfiguring new growth.

Clintonia borealis, bluebead, bluebead lily, corn lily, cowtongue, yellow clintonia, yellow woodlily. Eastern North America, Labrador to New England, New York, and New Jersey, in the mountains south to the Carolinas, Georgia, and Tennessee, west to Michigan, Wisconsin, and Minnesota.

LS to MS in the North, FS in the South; flowers small, to 1 in. (2.5 cm) long, greenish yellow to whitish yellow, drooping bell-shaped with 3 recurving petals and 3 petal-like sepals, 6 long stamens arranged umbrellalike, 3–9 per stem, at the top of the slightly hairy flowerstalk, 6–15 in. (15–38 cm) tall, lateral flowerstalks occasionally subtend the main stalk; May–August; plant herbaceous, slowly spreading, rhizomatous; leaves 2–6, basal, shiny medium to dark green, smooth but with minute hairs on the margins, 5–8 in. (13–20 cm) long and 1.5–2.5 in. (4–6 cm) wide, broadly oval to elliptic, slightly keeled along the midrib; fruit, shiny pure blue berry. Ubiquitous in gardens. The leaves, which resemble a cow's tongue in shape, last all season. The striking blue berries are poisonous; watch children around this attractive nuisance.

Clintonia umbellata, speckled wood lily, Clinton's lily, dog plum, speckled clintonia, wild corn. Eastern North America, New York, New Jersey, in the mountains south to the Carolinas, Georgia, and Tennessee.

LS to MS in the North, FS in the South; flowers small, to 0.5 in. (1 cm) long, white, spotted with green and purple, mostly erect but some drooping, star-shaped, with 3 petals and 3 petal-like sepals, 6 long stamens arranged umbrellalike, 5–29 per stem, at the top of the flowerstalk, 16 in. (40 cm) tall, lateral flowerstalks occasionally subtend the main stalk; May–August; plant herbaceous, slowly spreading, rhizomatous; leaves 2–5, basal, shiny medium to dark green, smooth but with minute hairs on the margins, 5–8 in. (13–20 cm) long and 2–2.5 in. (5–6 cm) wide, oblong-elliptic, keeled along the midrib; fruit, black to bluish black berry. The only bead lily I recommend for zone 7. It has done reasonably well here in zone 7a; not sufficiently heat-tolerant to do well in zone 8.

Clintonia uniflora, bride's bonnet, queen's cup, queencup. Western North America, Alaska to California.

LS to MS; flowers small, to 1 in. (2.5 cm) across, pure white, erect, star-shaped, with 3 petals and 3 petal-like sepals, 6 long stamens, arranged singly, rarely 2, at the top of the flowerstalk, to 16 in. (40 cm) tall; May–August; plant herbaceous, slowly spreading, rhizomatous; leaves 2–3, basal, shiny medium to dark green, smooth but with minute hairs on the margins and beneath, 5–8 in. (13–20 cm) long and 2–2.5 in. (5–6 cm) wide, oblong-elliptic, keeled along the midrib; fruit, dark blue to bluish black berry. Widespread in the western mountains and along the coast. May not be any better adapted to southern gardens than its eastern relatives. Another western species, *Clintonia andrewsiana* (western blue bead), is somewhat larger than *C. borealis* and has lovely, bell-shaped flowers of deep rose-purple to purple flowers. It too has blue berries. The western bead lilies have counterparts in eastern Asia; one, *C. udensis* (Asian bead lily), occurs in Siberia, eastern Himalayas, Japan, and probably Korea. It too is similar to *C. borealis*, but its flower color can vary from white, to yellowish green, to dark pink and lilac. The fruit is a blue berry. All Asian bead lilies are rare in the trade and share their North American relatives' love for cool summers.

Convallaria

To me, lilies-of-the-valley will always have a romantic association. They are the first fragrant flowers I remember as a small child. Growing abundantly in my mother's Bavarian garden, they were her favorite "weed," and no matter how many she cut to bring inside to spread their heavy fragrance, there were always more. Here unfortunately, they do not grow as abundantly. This may be a blessing in disguise, because lily-of-the-valley is considered a weed by many northern gardeners, albeit a very charming one. When she moved to the United States, Mother immediately included them in her Detroit garden, where they spread unmercifully.

Pandemic in the north temperate zone, lily-of-the-valley has been known for centuries. Its name turns up in medieval poetry, and in bygone days, it was used as a covering scent for a soapless society. Native North American species *Convallaria montana* —not to be confused with the false lily-of-the-valley, *Maianthemum canadense*—is smaller but otherwise very much like *C. majalis*, the European species. Reported along the Blue Ridge Parkway, at Rocky Knob, it now appears to be very rare in the wild, and several Appalachian states have listed it as a protected plant. On the other hand, it has escaped from gardens and is naturalized in the Shenandoah Valley and elsewhere in North America. I have seen it in small patches in North Georgia forests. Under the right conditions, any species of lily-of-the-valley will spread and propagate in the wild.

The binomial *Convallaria majalis* is from the Latin *convallis* (= valley) and *majalis* (= flowering in May), hence the common names lily-of-the-valley and May lily. The epithet of our native species (*montana* = mountain) refers to its preferred habitat. The genus is placed in the Convallariaceae.

Lily-of-the-valley thrives in the cool-summer climate of Eurasia and is found in many different habitats, including woodlands, mountain meadows, and scrubby mountain slopes. It does exceedingly well in constantly moist, acid soil and cool soil temperatures and can become invasive in such an environment. Further south, it does well in zones 6 and 7, becoming more civilized and turning into a clump-former rather than an aggressive runner. In zone 8 and warmer, it languishes and rarely flowers unless a very shady, cool spot can be provided. Lily-of-the-valley tolerates full shade but prefers a more open site in woodland shade, where it will flower abundantly. It also tolerates full sun if plenty of moisture is supplied during droughts. Hardy to zone 2. When grown in large patches, its small but long-lasting and showy white flowers fill the garden with delicious fragrance. Flowers are followed by attractive red berries; children should be forewarned that these enticing berries are poisonous and will produce a monumental case of stomach upset. The striking, strongly veined leaves carry on from early spring until the first hard freeze cuts them down. Plants make a superb groundcover in shady corners and can be used as edgings or specimens. They must receive occasional attention to be kept in bounds; surplus can be planted elsewhere in the garden or be given away to friends with an appropriate warning as to its wanderlust. Flowering subsides over time as the dense network of rhizomatous roots becomes crowded; if flowering is of primary importance, the planting must be dug up and renewed by separating the young propagating pips and replanting them in fresh or amended soil. Many gardeners use potted plants, particularly the showy variegated forms, for forcing in the home or display on the patio.

Propagate by taking runners with growing tips, called pips, from the underground rhizomatous network. Gardeners with large patches occasionally move entire clumps of the planting elsewhere. Seeding is too slow and not practical in light of the fast production of vegetative propagating pips.

Anthracnose and mold fungi are reported but not experienced here. I have not seen any disease or insect damage, except for an occasional bite taken out of the leaf margins by weevils.

Convallaria majalis, lily-of-the-valley, May lily. Eurasia.

LS to FS; flowers strongly fragrant, small, to 0.6 in. (1.5 cm) across, waxy white, drooping, bell-shaped, 6 segments and recurving tips, hanging from one side, 5–15 per stem, of the arching flowerstalk, 6–12 in. (15–30 cm) tall, arising solitary in the axis of the basal leaves; May–June; plant herbaceous, widely spreading, rhizomatous, with frequent branching nodes; leaves 2–3, basal, shiny medium to dark green, conspicuously veined, smooth, 2–10 in. (4–25 cm) long and 1–3 in. (2.5–8 cm) wide, broadly oval to elliptic, slightly keeled and folded along the midrib; fruit, shiny red to red-orange berry. This is the lily-of-the-valley grown in gardens the world over. Variety *keiskei* from Japan has very short flowerstalks, to 3 in. (8 cm); var. *rosea* has pale pink to rose-pink flowers; var. *transcaucasica*, of uncertain origin, is similar to the type. Forma *picta* has filaments spotted purple at the base.

'Albostriata' ('Albistriata'), leaves striped along the veins with white.

'Aureovariegata' ('Lineata', 'Striata', 'Variegata'), leaves narrowly striped yellow along the veins. Another form has leaves with yellow margins; another, leaves that are spotted with yellowish white. Read catalog descriptions carefully.

'Flore Pleno' ('Plena') has white double flowers.

'Fortin's Giant' ('Fortin's', 'Fortune', 'Fortune's Giant'), a robust selection with wider leaves.

'Hardwick Hall', broad, dark green leaves with pale greenish yellow margins.

'Hikage Nishiki' (= sun shade brocade) is a variegated selection of var. *keiskei* with large white areas in the leaves.

'Prolificans', flowers prolific but small, occasionally grotesque, appearing double-flowered, on a branched inflorescence.

'Rosea Plena' has pink double flowers.

'Vic Pawlowski's Gold', a variegated selection with leaves closely striped with white or clear yellow.

Convallaria montana, lily-of-the-valley, mountain lily. Eastern North America, Pennsylvania south to Carolinas and Georgia and west to Kentucky and Tennessee.

LS to FS; similar to *Convallaria majalis* but smaller and by some considered synonymous. Infrequent in most of its natural range. It is doubtful the plants occasionally offered in commerce are the true species. The widely propagated and available *C. majalis* offers greater horticultural value than this rare mountain lily.

Cornus

Experience is the gardener's greatest teacher. Once gardeners believe they know all there is to know about gardening (and I remain prone to such temerity), failure is certain to follow. *Cornus canadensis* (bunchberry) is a case in point. Many years ago during a visit to my parents' home, I saw great patches of this lovely wildflower in upper Michi-

gan and vowed to duplicate such exhilarating display. Since several references stated this species could be grown from zone 7 north, I presumed it was cool enough in my former zone 6 garden in central Tennessee to maintain a small planting. I did all things right, according to the books, acidifying my alkaline gray clay soil with peat moss and compost, and planted my mail-order bunchberries in autumn. The plants dutifully leafed out in early spring and looked fine for a while, but as the first, almost hot spring days arrived, development came to a halt and no flowers were produced. By the end of the summer, life in the clumps had ceased and I had added another fact to my gardening experience: *C. canadensis* will not grow in the hot summers of the South.

Bunchberry is a northern plant; the southernmost points of its habitat are in the high elevations of the West Virginia mountains and in the Rocky Mountains. It grows in deep, accumulated acid woods soil that is loose and friable and stays constantly moist; it is also seen in bogs across the more northern polar regions. It and its close relative *Cornus suecica* are the only herbs in the genus; some taxonomists have assigned them to the genus *Chamaepericlymenum*, which new unpronounceable generic name gardeners may eventually have to learn to pronounce. The genus *Cornus* is classified in the dogwood family, Cornaceae.

Bunchberry thrives only in very cool-summer climates. Some successes are reported from West Coast, but in general it does well in zone 5 north, possibly zone 6 if all other required growing conditions can be faithfully duplicated. Most important is a very acid, natural, friable humus soil, a goal not easily met in gardens. The total absence of any traces of lime is a must, and clayey soils will contribute to a speedy demise. When given a garden environment to its liking, bunchberry becomes a magnificent, vigorously spreading groundcover for shady areas, with large white flowers (actually bracts) followed by clusters of bright red berries. The striking, whorled leaves carry on from spring until the first hard freeze.

Propagate by taking runners or sods in late autumn or very early spring. Sow seed with the pulp removed immediately after ripening. Germination in a cold frame is difficult and slow unless the right conditions can be met; division is much faster.

Leaf spot and mildew are reported.

Cornus canadensis, bunchberry, crackerberry, creeping dogwood, dwarf cornel, puddingberry. Circumpolar in the north temperate zone, Russia, eastern Siberia, Kamchatka, northern Japan, and the Amur and Yalu river regions of eastern China and North Korea, northern North America from Alaska to Labrador and southern Greenland south to Pennsylvania and West Virginia in the mountains and west to Michigan, Minnesota, and the Rocky Mountains.

LS to WS; flowers composed of 4 large, peripheral white bracts, to 1.5 in. (4 cm) across, flowers centered in a ball-shaped cluster, yellowish green to yellow; May–July; plant 4–8 in. (10–20 cm) high, underground woody but herbaceous, widely spreading, rhizomatous, with frequent branching nodes; leaves 4, green, whorled at the top of the stem, ovate, 1.5–3 in. (4–8 cm) long, broadly ovate, pointed tip, and sunken veins curved into an arc; 1–2 pairs of vestigial on the stem below the main leaves; fruit cluster of red berries. Widespread in northern gardens, and a most attractive groundcover for shady areas. Another herbaceous species from a similar habitat, *Cornus suecica* (northern dwarf cornel), is extremely difficult to establish and cultivate. Do not remove from the wild: chances of a successful transplant are slim to none.

Corydalis

Having seen and admired the enigmatic *Corydalis* in the wild and in both sunny and shady gardens in England and Germany, I thought I'd try this genus in my own garden. I chose **Corydalis lutea** and *C. ochroleuca*, which I had seen luxuriating across the Atlantic, because they were recommended for use in partial shade. I did enjoy the floral display of yellow and whitish flowers and the finely cut foliage, but their sudden demise in midsummer left holes in my garden. That is the first fault I find with the genus: many species are ephemeral and go summer-dormant soon after flowering. And worse was yet to come: ants spread their seed far and wide, and in spring, seedlings came up all over the place, setting up housekeeping in the wildflower garden. My delicate natives had no chance against such weeds, and the only way to get rid of this menace was to rebuild several areas of the garden and use chemicals, which I deplore. Plants that spread so perniciously and then leave holes in the green landscape are not welcome in most small, shady gardens. A friend of mine, aware of my dilemma, told me about *C. scouleri*, native to the Cascades and Olympic Mountains in northwestern North America. He had planted this species in his shady garden in southern Indiana and at first praised its wonderfully dissected, ferny foliage and the captivating rose-pink flowers produced on tall stems; best of all, the bright green sprays of lacy leaves remained fresh all season. But *C. scouleri* soon spread deeply and everywhere in his almost bottomless topsoil, and he is still fighting to control it.

I give these negative comments with apologies to those who like and grow some of the new Asian species of *Corydalis* and more well-behaved cultivars with attractive blue flowers, like 'Blue Panda' and 'Père David'. Many species are small and suitable for sharply drained, somewhat shaded rock gardens, and some of the newer varieties are suitable for the shady garden, but it is difficult to find companions to take over for the corydalis in midsummer.

Not all species and cultivars are perennial, so check catalog descriptions carefully before ordering. Most species listed as suitable for partial shade require considerably more sun than shade. I have talked to many southern gardeners, and we are united in the opinion that one should forget about planting corydalis where summers are hot. For those who garden in cool summers (northwestern and upper midwestern climates), I include a reference that describes some of the older as well as the newer Asian species of *Corydalis*.

The genus takes its name from the Greek *korydalis* (= crested lark), a reference to the look of the spur of the flower. It is classified in the bleeding heart or fumitory family, Fumariaceae. It is native to the northern temperate regions, in North America, Europe, the Himalayas, and eastern China. Some species occur in South Africa. It thrives in the cool woods of Eurasia and is found in many different habitats, including woodlands, mountain meadows, scrubby and rocky mountain slopes, shady rockeries and screes, and in open areas along the shores of lakes and stream banks.

Propagate by taking runners from rhizomatous species or offsets from bulbous species. Sow seed when it is very fresh; it does not survive dry storage for an extended period. Many species self-seed, so seedlings are usually available.

Rust and downy mildew are occasionally bothersome. Slugs and snails can damage young growth and later flowers.

Recommended reading

Hinkley, Daniel J. 1999. "*Corydalis*: Jewels in Many Hues." In *The Explorer's Garden: Rare and Unusual Perennials*. Portland, Oregon: Timber Press.

Cyclamen

The ubiquitous florist's cyclamens are well-known tokens of love, friendship, and admiration. My mother kept several varieties in pots, and they added color to her shady patio. Several *Cyclamen* species are hardy to zone 7 and warmer, possibly zone 5 with dependable snow cover. I have had short-term success siting several hardy cyclamen under protective tree canopies or as underplantings in the shrub border. The first species I tried was *Cyclamen purpurascens*, an evergreen and highly fragrant plant that my grandfather collected for his garden in Austria many years ago. It survived several mild winters under a large loblolly pine but gradually declined in vigor. It probably did not appreciate the acid soil I had sited it in; with azaleas and other acid-loving wildflowers nearby, adding much lime to sweeten the soil here was not feasible. For my second attempt, I chose *C. hederifolium* and a few corms of *C. coum*. Requiring a fairly dry summer dormancy, these cyclamen did well the first season but rotted in short order when adjacent plants needed supplemental water. In short, it is difficult to cultivate cyclamens in small shady gardens, where the requirements for cultivating most other plants are at odds with those demanded by the cyclamens. Gardeners with larger properties—who can provide a separate location for cyclamens, where all their cultural requirements (limey soil, dry summer dormancy, and protection from cold) can be met—should certainly consider including these attractive plants. Potting hardy cyclamens is another way to achieve this isolation and makes the planting portable when inclement weather or other adverse conditions threaten.

Cyclamens, also known as Persian violets, are not violets at all but members of the primrose family, Primulaceae.

Recommended reading

Grey-Wilson, Christopher. 1997. *Cyclamen: A Guide for Gardeners, Horticulturists, and Botanists*. Portland, Oregon: Timber Press.

Cypripedium

Lady slippers are incredibly beautiful, and specialty nurseries now offer these exquisite orchids from time to time. Never purchase bare-root orchids: they may have been dug from wild populations and have no chance of survival in the garden. Seed-raised or tissue-cultured plants fare much better because they are usually shipped potted in a correct soil mix. Even these have exacting cultural requirements, and sadly, many purchased orchids survive but a few seasons and then depart the garden with haste.

Some lady slippers are still common, particularly in eastern North America and Asia. The relative abundance of *Cypripedium acaule* (pink lady slipper) in the dry pinelands of southeastern North America is indicative of its preference for coniferous forest land with soil composed primarily of decayed pine needles. Cultivated specimens are well established in gardens around Atlanta and several places in neighboring western Alabama, all thriving and multiplying in thick accumulations of loblolly pine needles, which make perfect beds for the shallow-rooted orchids. All this points to a relatively thin layer of acid, decomposed pine needle soil over a rock substrate as a base for cultivation. In the wild, the shade provided by tall pines is open and light; such conditions should be replicated in the garden as much as possible.

In cultivation lady slippers do not fare well. Acid-loving orchids require a pH of around 5. I have an abundance of acidic pine needle compost for orchids that require acidic reaction, to which I add a little gritty builders sand and processed pine bark, another ingredient in the soil of natural pine forests. For orchids that require alkaline conditions, I add turkey grit made from crushed seashells. The soil must be loose and friable but should be pressed down after the roots are planted to make good contact. In the absence of suitable pine needle materials, most experts recommend a mix of 2 parts sterilized loam, 2 parts ground oak or beech leaf mold, 1 part ground peat moss, and 1 part coarse grit or sand (turkey grit for varieties requiring alkaline soils).

Lady slippers are regal plants that add a special quality to the garden when successfully established. The easiest lady slipper to grow and maintain—and the only one I can recommend as a "starter" orchid to average gardeners—is *Cypripedium calceolus* (yellow lady slipper); *C. acaule* (pink lady slipper) does reasonably well but does not increase much in my garden; and the most difficult is *C. reginae* (showy lady slipper), which flowers one year and not the next, only to revive itself again or suddenly disappear. I also give Asian native *C. japonicum* a home; it is similar to *C. reginae* and I hope can eventually take its place. None of these orchids are easy garden plants, and I urge beginning gardeners not to buy these beautiful jewels unless they have the knowledge and experience to keep them alive and happy—not an easy task. I hope my admonitions about their care contribute to saving these orchids (many still wild-collected) from death in cultivation.

The lady slippers range throughout North America and Eurasia in a variety of habitats, from dry, open pine forests in the South to cool, moist deciduous woods and bogs further north. Some are extremely hardy plants that can stand up to the rigors of winters as cold as zone 2. The generic name comes from the Greek *kypris* (= Venus) and *pedilon* (= sandal)—a lady slipper indeed. *Cypripedium* is classified in the Orchidaceae.

Lady slippers native to North America are occasionally offered in commerce. Average gardeners will be best served by propagated stock of *Cypripedium calceolus* var. *pubescens*, which is relatively easy to take care of and also much more showy in gardens than some of the minor native species. Among these are *C. californicum* (western lady slipper, California lady slipper), *C. candidum* (small white lady slipper), *C. fasciculatum* from northwestern North America, *C. irapeanum* from Mexico (which is too tender), *C. kentuckiense* (Kentucky lady slipper), *C. montanum* (mountain lady slipper), and *C. passerinum* (sparrow's egg lady slipper). Besides being small and inconspicuous, these species are rare and protected: admire them in their wild habitat or in botanic gardens. Many lady slippers are being imported from Japan and China. Unfortunately, the high monetary value of these orchids has caused wholesale collection from the wild with disastrous effects on wild populations; responsible gardeners will wait until these species can be prop-

agated commercially before they commit to a purchase. Among these Asiatic species are *C. debile*, *C. flavum*, *C. guttatum* and its var. *yatabeanum*, *C. himalaicum*, *C. macranthum*, and *C. yunnanense*.

Propagate by dividing large, established, multi-stemmed clumps in very early spring, when plants are still dormant. The entire clump must be carefully dug and removed with as much soil as possible remaining attached to the fleshy roots. Locate the clump's connecting nodes by feel, minimizing soil disturbance, and divide the clump between stems. Set the bud top of the transplanted division just below the soil surface; lady slippers resent deep planting. Seed propagation is next to impossible: seed is nearly microscopic, a fine dust.

Occasionally, *Botrytis cinerea* (gray mold fungus) threatens these valuable plants. I have not been able to find an environmentally friendly cure that is really effective; only systemic fungicides seem to work. I have not seen any slug or snail damage, but gardeners with larger slugs report flowers being cut off as they open. Rust is sometimes seen, starting as spots on the leaves, then spreading; apply a fungicide immediately. Plants should be checked frequently for gray mold or rust in early spring when new growth emerges.

Cypripedium acaule, pink lady slipper, pink lady's slipper, pink moccasin flower, Noah's ark, squirrel shoes, stemless lady slipper, two-leaved lady slipper, whippoorwill shoe. Eastern North America, Saskatchewan to Newfoundland and Nova Scotia, through New England south to Georgia and South Carolina, west to Minnesota and Illinois, and south to Alabama and Tennessee.

LS to WS; flower on a leafless stalk 6–15 in. (15–38 cm) tall, usually solitary, rarely 2, lip petal inflated, pouchlike to 2.5 in. (6 cm) long, rose- to crimson-pink to rose-purple, veined with red and pleated, with a deep furrow in front, sepals and petals on both sides, greenish brown to maroon, twisted, wavy, lance-shaped, spreading; May–August; plant clump-forming, from a slender rhizome; leaves basal, usually 2, elliptic, pointed, medium green, parallel veins and ribbed, dark green above, finely hairy and silvery beneath; fruit an erect capsule, seed microscopic, in huge numbers. I have seen rare forms in the wild with a white lip petal, but these are not in commerce. Optimum pH is 4 to 5.5. Hardy in zones 3 to 7.

Cypripedium arietinum, ram's head lady slipper, ramshead lady slipper. Eastern North America, Newfoundland west to southwest Quebec and Manitoba, south to New England, New York, Michigan, Minnesota.

LS to WS; flower solitary, on leafy stalk to 12 in. (30 cm) tall, lip petal white veined with crimson and lined with silky white hairs, short, funnel-shaped, with a blunt, conical extension pointing down, resembling a ram's head, top sepal lance-shaped, pointed, green striped brown or maroon, side sepals petals narrowly lance-shaped, twisted, green to greenish purple, all sepals are free; May-July; plant clump-forming, from a slender rhizome; leaves 3–4, on the stem, elliptic, pointed, medium green, parallel veins and ribbed, dark green; fruit an erect capsule, seed microscopic, in huge numbers. This modest and rare lady slipper inhabits damp northern woods and cedar swamps; I saw large populations of it in remote northern Michigan. Of interest only to the collector who must have one of everything. Its flowers are much smaller than those of other species, and it is not at all showy in gardens. I am listing it chiefly to let gardeners know this orchid should not be bought (most commerical stock is wild-collected) or dug in the wild unless a rescue situation presents itself.

Cypripedium calceolus, yellow lady slipper, lady slipper, lady slipper orchid, lady's slipper orchid. North America, central and eastern Europe, east to the Caucasus and Siberia, eastern Asia.

LS to WS; flower fragrant, usually solitary, rarely 2, atop leafy stalk 10–20 in. (25–50 cm) tall; lip petal inflated, pouchlike, 1.5–2 in. (4–5 cm) long, bright yellow to greenish yellow, sometimes spotted or veined red or maroon inside, pleated and with a deep furrow in front; top sepal lance-shaped, twisted; pointed side petals narrowly lance-shaped, spirally twisted, sepal and petals streaked dark maroon, purplish brown or rarely greenish brown; April–August; plant clump-forming, from a slender rhizome; leaves alternately on the stem, 3–4, stem-clasping, elliptic, pointed, medium green above and beneath, deep parallel veins, ribbed; fruit an erect capsule, seed microscopic, in huge numbers. The ubiquitous yellow lady slipper and by far the most easily cultivated lady slipper in gardens. Commercial sources have met the high demand with propagated stock, although some collected

plants are still offered. This is a very long-lived species; the same plants have been cultivated in some botanic gardens for over 70 years. Adaptable to a variety of soils. Optimum pH is 5 to 6.5. *Cypripedium kentuckiense* is very similar, with a large lip and reddish brown sepals and petals; I saw this rare and protected species on Flint Ridge Road in Kentucky's Mammoth Cave National Park. Several varieties occur in the vast range of *C. calceolus*; all are variable; all are hardy to zone 3, with a heat tolerance of zone 8.

Cypripedium calceolus var. *parviflorum*, small yellow lady slipper, small golden-slipper, small yellow moccasin flower, whippoorwill shoe. Northeastern North America, Newfoundland west to British Columbia, south to New England and New Jersey and west to Minnesota, in the mountains south to Georgia.

LS to WS; fragrant flowers smaller than the type, with a lip petal to 1 in. (2.5 cm) long, on shorter stalks to 18 in. (45 cm); leaves less hairy. Closest to the type. Optimum pH is 5 to 6. Occasionally considered the northern version of var. *pubescens* and indeed intermingled with that variety in overlapping areas of habitat. I have seen distinct populations of the two within a few miles of each other.

Cypripedium calceolus var. *planipetalum*, northern yellow lady slipper. Northeastern North America.

Sun, LS; this rare variety inhabits grassy areas of the open limestone tundra north of the habitat of var. *parviflorum*. Its cultivation requirements are impossible to duplicate in gardens. It is considerably smaller than the type, to 8 in. (20 cm) tall, and differs also by the greenish yellow of its sepals and petals. The petals are flat, not twisted, hence the varietal name. *Cypripedium henryi*, an Asian counterpart occasionally offered, is very similar and can be grown from imported Chinese stock.

Cypripedium calceolus var. pubescens, large yellow lady slipper, yellow lady's slipper, American valerian, golden-slipper, large yellow moccasin flower, nerveroot, Noah's ark, umbilroot, Venus-shoe, whippoorwill shoe, yellow Indian-shoe. North America, eastern Canada south to New England and New York, in the mountains south to Georgia, isolated in Alabama and Louisiana, northwest to Minnesota and the Dakotas, and in the west from

Alaska, Yukon region, south to British Columbia, Oregon, and in the mountains to Arizona.

LS to WS; fragrant flowers, larger than the type, with a lip petal 2–2.5 in. (5–6 cm) long, on tall stalks to 28 in. (70 cm); leaves distinctly hairy, hence the varietal name. The most widely grown and showiest variety of yellow lady slipper, by some considered its southern form. Its shoelike inflorescence prompted a host of local names, as did its medicinal uses: American Indians used the dried and powdered roots and sometimes a tea made from dried leaves as a sedative, a remedy for insomnia, and a worming treatment. The hairs of the leaves cause a rash in people who are sensitive to the plant. Natural populations of this variety are intermingled with var. *parviflorum* in many areas of habitat. Available from propagated stock. Optimum pH is 5 to 6.

Cypripedium japonicum, Japanese lady slipper. China, Japan, Taiwan.

LS to WS; flower emerging between and held above the leaves on a leafless stem to 20 in. (50 cm) tall, solitary, lip petal very inflated, pouchlike, large, to 3 in. (8 cm) long, rose- to crimson-pink, spotted with red and pleated, wrinkled, with a deep, fairly wide furrow in front; top sepal lance-shaped, bending down; pointed side petals narrowly lance-shaped, spreading wide, to 4 in. (10 cm) across, sepal and petals pink to rose-pink; June–August; plant clump-forming, from a slender rhizome; leaves 2, opposite, large, 8 in. (20 cm) long and wide, broadly round and fan-shaped, held above and clear of base on hairy stem, dark green, deeply pleated. Easily the most outstanding Asian lady slipper. The leaves are as interesting as the flower, resembling hand fans held horizontally away from the stem. The leaves are deeply pleated, providing striking texture even without flowers. Variety *formosanum*, the southern form from Taiwan, is very similar, but the lip petal is more closed and the furrow more craterlike. Both forms are propagated in Japan and have long been available albeit expensive; also offered from wild stock originating in China, which is unnecessary and unfortunate. This species adapts easily to Western gardens but requires some time to become established. Hardy to zone 4b with protection for the shallow-rooted rhizome; var. *formosanum* is likely less hardy.

Cypripedium reginae, showy lady slipper, showy moccasin flower. Eastern and central North America, Saskatchewan to Newfoundland, through New England in the mountains south to the Carolinas, Tennessee, and Georgia, northwest to Missouri, Minnesota, and North Dakota.

LS to WS; flowers 1–3 on a twisted, leafy stalk 12–36 in. (30–90 cm) tall, usually in the top 1–3 leaf axils; lip petal inflated, pouchlike to 2.5 in. (6 cm) long, mostly white but rose- to crimson-pink in front, veined with deep pink or red and pleated, with a deep furrow in front, sepals and petals on top and both sides white tinged soft pink or pure white, side petals waxy white, lance-shaped, spreading; May–August; plant clump-forming, from a slender rhizome; leaves alternate on hairy stem, 3–7, to 4 in. (10 cm) long, elliptic, pointed, medium to dark green, parallel veins and ribbed; fruit an erect capsule, seed microscopic, in huge numbers. This is the largest and most eye-catching native orchid, common in the states around the Great Lakes and infrequent in the southern Appalachians. Because of its outstanding beauty, it was collected to near extinction in some areas and is now protected. Under no circumstances should it be removed from the wild. Ask questions to determine if plants offered are in fact commercially propagated. This northern orchid does well in northern gardens as long as it is grown in constantly moist, deep muck, duplicating its native habitat, where it inhabits swamps, bogs, and moist to wet forests. It does not fare too well in the South unless given a location in considerable shade and a wet footing. Unfortunately, the shade that keeps it cooler in southern gardens also minimizes flowering, and it may be difficult to grow it as gloriously as it does in the wild. Variety *album*, with creamy white to ivory lip petals (pouches), is uncommon and seldom offered.

Recommended reading

Cribb, Phillip. 1997. *The Genus Cypripedium*. Portland, Oregon: Timber Press.

———, and Christopher Bailes. 1989. *Hardy Orchids*. Portland, Oregon: Timber Press.

Keenan, Philip E. 1998. *Wild Orchids Across North America*. Portland, Oregon: Timber Press.

Cyrtomium

Holly ferns are prolific at Hosta Hill, second only to lady ferns (*Athyrium* spp.). Many years ago, I started with one clump of *Cyrtomium falcatum* 'Rochfordianum', which is evergreen here during all but the coldest winters. In the last three decades, it has been cut down by freezes only four times. I remove the old fronds in spring to let the new, bright green fiddleheads rise up unimpeded. This original clump has spread spores all over my garden and beyond, and each spring brings a new crop of Japanese holly fern to be transplanted or given away. Over the years, I installed a lot of mortared brick curbing, and in moist shade the bricks, some now covered with moss, are a perfect nursery for spores to develop into young ferns. Holly ferns acquired subsequently, like *C. macrophyllum* (large-leaved holly fern) and *C. fortunei* (Fortune's holly fern), have proven just as prolific and are exquisite additions to shady gardens. They make great companion plants for larger hostas and other bold-leaved perennials, and they compete well with smaller azaleas. Their ornamental value is extremely high, and I consider them among the best ferns for the shady garden.

The fiddleheads on these ferns rise early, usually during the middle part of April, so are endangered by late frosts and freezes; a cardboard box or sheet draped over the emerging ferns will usually bring them safely through the cold period. Many southern gardeners simply let the ferns fend for themselves and tolerate some losses among the early fiddleheads. Established clumps usually make up the loss by sending up new growth, and by midspring no trace of the early damage is noticeable. Many northern gardeners consider these ferns too tender for garden use, but with good protection and some snow cover, they can be grown in the open garden. Here in sheltered areas, they have survived temperatures to 0°F (−18°C) for short periods without protection, although I admit that the fronds looked terrible after this onslaught. In northern gardens they become deciduous, of course, but the underground parts have been tested for cold hardiness in zones 6a and 5b with some success, although good protection is a must in these locations. Holly ferns are also great for containers, which can be brought in and overwintered in cool basements after they become dormant. In spring, they can be plunged in the ground in prepared positions and will carry on until the first hard freeze arrives.

Asian holly ferns are native to northern India, China, Korea, and Japan, where they grow in wet or moist locations in forests or along banks of lakes or rivers. The generic name comes from the Greek *kyrtos* (= arched), suggesting the arching habit of the fronds. The American genus *Phanerophlebia* is listed as synonymous in some references. *Cyrtomium* is classified in the Dryopteridaceae.

Place holly ferns in a shaded position, where no direct sun reaches during the heat of the day. Early morning and filtered sun is tolerated. They do best in a light, well-draining, acid woodland soil, rich in organic matter. They do well in the hot, humid southern regions of North America if supplemental water is supplied during droughts.

Propagate by dividing the creeping rhizome in autumn or in very early spring. Propagation by spores is also successful; they should be sown as soon as they are ripe on a coarse commercial mix with a pH of 7 to 8.5 maintained moist at 60–70°F (16–21°C). In many cases, the ferns do their own propagating; I have never had to resort to dividing or sowing spores.

Slugs and snails are no problem here, because the soft fiddleheads come up early when nighttime temperatures are still low and the mollusks inactive. Later the fronds become leathery, and I have not observed any damage. Other pests and maladies do not bother the holly ferns here, but root rot and fungal spots are reported.

Species and cultivars listed form slowly expanding clumps. All are best grown in a sheltered, shady, moist position.

Cyrtomium falcatum, holly fern, Japanese holly fern. Southern Japan and China, Taiwan, Malaysia, India.

LS to FS; fronds produced in rosettes on slender stalks emerging directly from the rhizome, slightly scaly at the base, stalk shiny green, arching; leaves pinnate, to 36 in. (90 cm) long and 10 in. (25 cm) wide; leaflets (pinnae) 6 in. (15 cm) long and to 1.5 in. (4 cm) wide, hollylike on short leafstalks, very shiny dark green above, dull grayish green below, leathery, smooth or slightly toothed, rounded base, wedge-shaped, abruptly narrowed toward tip with upswept tip bending more or less sicklelike to one side, veins imperceptible on top, slightly projected underneath. This fern has a striking habit, and its shiny leaf mound highlight its position in the garden. Overwinter in containers in northern gardens.

'Butterfieldii', leaflets have toothed margins and long, drawn-out tips.

'Compactum', a dwarf form.

'Cristatum' ('Cristata', 'Mayi'), leaflets have crests; fronds are forked and have terminal crests.

'Mandaianum', leaflets are triangular with fringed margins.

'Rochfordianum', leaflets glossy, dark green with coarsely toothed or slightly lobed margins; a vigorous form.

Cyrtomium fortunei, Fortune's holly fern. Southern Japan and China, Korea.

LS to FS; fronds produced in rosettes on slender stalks emerging directly from the rhizome, stalk brownish purple and shiny toward top, densely scaly at the base, less scaly further up, bending down, arching; leaves pinnate, to 24 in. (60 cm) long and 8 in. (20 cm) wide; leaflets (pinnae) 4 in. (10 cm) long and to 1.5 in. (4 cm) wide, sickle-shaped, on short leafstalks, dull dark grayish green above, dull grayish green below, leathery, smooth but irregular, slightly wavy margin, oval, tapering toward tip with upswept tip bending to one side, midrib conspicuously brownish purple above and slightly less underneath. Evergreen here, this fern, with noticeably dark purple stems and midribs on the leaflets, contrasts attractively with yellow hostas. Hardy to zone 6b with protection.

Cyrtomium macrophyllum, large-leaved Japanese holly fern. Southern Japan and China, Korea.

LS to FS; fronds produced in rosettes on slender stalks emerging directly from the rhizome, stalk green, covered densely with large, dark brown scales at the base, less further up, bending down, arching; leaves pinnate, to 18 in. (45 cm) long and 7 in. (18 cm) wide; leaflets (pinnae) opposite on lower stem, alternate toward top, 3.5 in. (9 cm) long and to 2 in. (5 cm) wide, sickle-shaped except terminal leaf cleft, lobed, others on short leafstalks, dull grayish green above, dull greenish gray below, leathery, smooth but irregular, slightly wavy margin, oval, tapering toward tip with upswept tip bending to one side, midrib brownish purple above

and slightly less underneath, veins dark and protruding underneath. Similar to *Cyrtomium fortunei* but with fewer and larger, broader leaflets and a midrib not as distinctly purplish. Unlike many finely divided ferns, outstanding in the garden. Evergreen here during milder winters. Hardy to zone 7a with protection. It can be potted and brought inside further north to make a splendid houseplant or overwintered in a cold basement.

Dactylorhiza

Marsh orchids are rarely seen in North American gardens, perhaps because people think hardy orchids are difficult to cultivate. Thanks to some pioneering work by British gardeners, this supposition is changing, and marsh orchids are finding their way into European, Asian, and North American gardens. Native British species *Dactylorhiza praetermissa* (southern marsh orchid) and *D. purpurella* (northern marsh orchid) are truly gardenworthy, and their earlier introduction has led the way for other marsh orchids. Some of the most outstanding marsh orchids from southwestern Europe and the Atlas Mountains in North Africa have been known since the early 1800s, but older garden books make little mention of them. These striking hardy orchids are now available from specialists; they are not in the standard nursery trade.

Commonly considered sun-loving plants, marsh orchids are also quite adapted to shady gardens. I grow only one species, *Dactylorhiza elata*, but other species have similar cultural requirements. With limited space, I can experience but a small sample of nature's many wonders, and this marsh orchid is a splendid one indeed. I grow it with a few hours of morning sun; it is in shade after 10:00 a.m. Accustomed to a more northern latitude, it seems to appreciate shade in the hot afternoon sun, and high temperatures must be counteracted by plenty of moisture. It definitely does not like dry soil; obviously, a rich, deep, and moisture-retentive soil is a must. It will not grow in clay soil, nor will it endure deep shade, but here it seems to like the light shade provided by loblolly pines. I purchased a single plant of it, just to try it, but to make a real statement in the garden, one ought to have several, at least three, specimens of *D. elata*, whose tall spikes of purple flowers are spectacular in bloom. *Dactylorhiza aristata*, a North American marsh orchid seen only in Alaska, has little chance in the lower 48 states; in any case, the commercially propagated European species are much more showy and better garden plants. Cold hardiness varies; only relatively hardy species are included here. Heat tolerance seems to be good, and my *D. elata* has survived several very hot, dry summers given frequent watering with a trickle system to keep the soil moist. Further north, given marshy conditions, marsh orchids succeed better.

Not all species are truly orchids of the marsh but also inhabit meadows and grasslands with a moist subsoil and headlands. Some species are still sold under the generic name *Orchis*. *Dactylorhiza* is from the Greek *daktylos* (= finger) and *rhiza* (= root), an allusion to the fingerlike tuberous rhizome. The genus is classified in the Orchidaceae.

Marsh orchids are relatively easy of culture if given the right conditions. Mostly, they require a duplication of the wet seepages or mucky marshes they frequent under wild conditions. Those described later will thrive in an open, airy soil of compost, leaf mold, peat moss, and coarse sand. It is crucial to keep this soil moist at all times. Woodland shade with filtered sunlight is tolerated, but some direct morning sun is required for successful flowering. Great strides have been made in the commercial propagation of rare orchids, and obviously only propagated orchids, expensive though they may be, should be purchased. To rip these beauties from their natural habitat is unconscionable.

Propagation by division should be attempted only on larger clumps.

Slugs and snails can be a problem on young plants and just emerging young shoots. Grown under correct conditions, diseases are rare. I have not seen any insect damage on my marsh orchids; even the pesky weevils leave them alone.

Dactylorhiza elata, robust marsh orchid. North Africa, Algeria, southwestern Europe, southern France, Spain, Corsica, Sicily.

Morning sun, LS to WS; flowers small, many, in a tightish raceme, pink, purple, or maroon; side sepals turned down, lance-shaped, lip petal smooth or barely 3-lobed, purple-striped, produced on a leafy flowerstalk, 30–44 in. (75–110 cm) tall; May–August; plant clump-forming, from a slender, branched tuberous rhizome; leaves on the stem, green, 6–14, alternate, narrowly elliptic to lance-shaped, erect, pointed, progressively smaller toward raceme. Among the tallest and showiest orchids in the genus and very popular in Europe. Hardy to zone 6 in sheltered locations; provide some cover during winter in exposed areas. Those with limited space and an equally limited budget should seek this one out. *Dactylorhiza foliosa* (Madeiran orchid) is very similar, with shorter stems to 24 in. (60 cm) and fewer (4–5) leaves; hardy to zone 7.

Dactylorhiza fuchsii, common spotted orchid, spotted marsh orchid. Central Europe east to Mongolia and Siberia, North America, rare in northern Ontario and Newfoundland.

Morning sun, LS to WS; flowers small, many, in a tightish raceme, pale rose-pink, mauve, or white, spotted or streaked with purple or deep red; side sepals turned down, lance-shaped, lip petal deeply 3-lobed with the center lobe elongated and pointed, on a tall leafy, flowerstalks 8–24 in. (20–60 cm) tall; June–August; plant clump-forming, from a slender, branched tuberous rhizome; leaves on the stem, green spotted with purple, 7–12, alternate, lance-shaped elliptic to oblong, erect, pointed, progressively smaller toward raceme. Will not abide acid soils; add dolomitic limestone or ground seashells (turkey grit) to reach the neutral to alkaline conditions this species requires. Tolerates some summer dryness but not the heat of the South. Hardy to zone 6, 5b with protection and in a sheltered spot. *Dactylorhiza maculata* (heath spotted orchid) from the British Isles is very similar but with a 3-lobed lip petal and much shorter midlobe; equally hardy, it requires some sun, light shade, and acidic soil (as its common name might suggest to savvy gardeners).

Danae

In 1994, I received a small plant of *Danae racemosa* as a gift. Not knowing exactly what I had (this sole member of the genus—also written with diaeresis, *Danaë*—did not look like much), I planted it in a large pot, figuring I would move it around until I found a good spot for it. Quickly it grew into a shrublike architectural plant. It remains in the pot and still gets moved around, gracing various spots in the garden—wherever a beautiful, evergreen accent is needed.

Alexandrian laurel, as this species is commonly called, comes from the lands of Alexander the Great (in Greek legend, Danaë was the daughter of King Acrisius of Argos and the mother of Perseus). It is endemic to Turkey and Iran in woodlands and shrubby areas. Widely used during the Italian Renaissance, it is now enjoying its own renaissance in shady gardens. It is not fussy but does prefer a light, moisture-retentive soil. I have it growing in a mix of clay, ground bark, and a little grit. Superficially, it looks like a shrub, but it is actually an evergreen perennial. The stems develop below ground and emerge in spring, much like the shoots of asparagus, rapidly elongating, first erect and later gracefully arching. The bright glossy leaves (actually cladophylls, specialized pseudo-leaves) are exceedingly striking and truly evergreen, almost everlasting (florists love to use them in their arrangements). The dense habit of the plant makes it ideal for the shady woodland garden, to which it contributes winter or summer with equal aplomb. Its flowers are tiny, close to the stem and less conspicuous than the shiny, orange-red berries that add interest later in the season. The genus is related to *Ruscus* (butcher's broom, box holly). It is classified in the Ruscaceae.

Danae racemosa can be used in full shade and in gardens with considerable sun peeking through the branches. It can take full morning sun, but in the South the freshly emerging shoots may be burned if exposed to all-day full sun. At their best, the stems make a shiny green bouquet when brought inside during dreary winter days. Each spring, I cut off stems weathered by falling ice; such pruning in no way hurts the vigor of the plant. Hardy to zone 6 with protection.

Propagate by division in late autumn or very early spring. Seed can be sown in small pots in a cold frame, but it may take several years before the seedlings reach acceptable garden size.

Nothing bothers my Alexandrian laurel. Some caution may be required in early spring, when the soft shoots attract slugs and snails. Once the stems harden, no slug is able to rasp it.

Danae racemosa, Alexandrian laurel. Turkey, Iran.

LS to FS; flowers very small, greenish yellow, inconspicuous, 5–8 on small, terminal racemes on stems to 4 ft. (1.2 m) tall; May–August; plant clump-forming but slowly spreading, rhizoma-tous; true leaves on the stem, early deciduous, persistent leafy cladophylls, bright, glossy green, 1.5 in. (4 cm) long and 1 in. (2.5 cm) wide, alternate, broadly elliptic but asymmetric, pointed, leathery and margins turned down. Together with hellebores and evergreen shrubs and trees, this species is the backbone of the winter garden; in summer it adds architectural interest and later, bright orange-red berries. No garden should be without it.

Darmera

Lately of the genus *Peltiphyllum*, *Darmera peltata* (umbrella plant) has been placed back in the genus under which it was first described. I grow this species and other large, umbrella-leaved plants, like *Astilboides tabularis*, primarily for their bold leaves, which add great texture and tropical character to the shady garden. Native to western North America, *D. peltata* is better suited to southern gardens than the much larger *A. tabularis*, but it does need more shade here than in its native habitat. Its flowers are striking and command attention when they rise up from bare ground before the leaves come to life, but, unfortunately, late frosts and freezes can damage their pristine, early-spring beauty (if they don't cut them down altogether). When I was younger, I installed all kinds of contrivances to protect the blooms from the cold, but now I accept things as they are. I enjoy the starry flowers if nature lets me, and I am thankful for it. If the cold takes them, it makes no sense to get emotional about it. Maybe next year—and so I have another thing to look forward to.

Darmera peltata will grow in partial shade but appreciates some sunny mornings. It requires constantly moist, even boggy soil; site it on the embankment of a pond or by a stream bank to duplicate natural conditions. During periods of drought, provide supplemental water to maintain soil moisture content. Suitable for cultivation in zones 5 to 7; it shows signs of stress during zone 7 summer heat. The epithet (*peltata* = shieldlike) refers to the leaf shape. The older generic name *Peltiphyllum* too means "shieldlike leaf." *Darmera* is classified in the Saxifragaceae.

Propagate by dividing the rhizome before growth starts in very early spring. Seed must be gathered when fresh, usually in midspring; it may germinate as early as autumn.

Large slugs and snails can be very damaging to emerging, soft flowerstalks, leaf growth, and even mature leaves. In summer, army worms, striped caterpillars, and other moth larvae feed during the night, disfiguring the leaves.

Darmera peltata, umbrella plant, Indian rhubarb. Northwestern North America, southwestern Oregon, Siskiyous and northern California, Sierra Nevada.

Morning sun, LS to WS; flowers small, pinkish white or pink, 5-lobed, star-shaped, in dense clusters on red-tinged, thick, hairy, leafless stems, 3–4 ft. (0.9–1.2 m) tall; April–May; in cultivation leafstalks to 36 in. (90 cm) tall, in the wild to 6 ft. (1.8 m); leaves umbrellalike, to 24 in. (60 cm) across, shiny light green, with hairy cover, depressed in the center and rounded in outline but with 10–15 lobes, often deeply incised; leaf stems stout, upright. A great accent plant near a water feature or as a background grouping in open woodlands; also useful as an anchor for plantings of grasses, hostas, and ferns. Spectacular in flower. In autumn, its coppery leaf color adds to the yellows and oranges of the Japanese maples and hostas. **'Nana'**, a dwarf form to 24 in. (60 cm) in height, has much smaller leaves, 9–12 in. (23–30 cm) across, with flowers smaller accordingly. Excellent for adding bold leaf texture to smaller gardens. If not cross-pollinated by the type, its seeds come true.

Deinanthe

Almost unknown to Western gardeners, the species of the genus *Deinanthe*, from the woodlands of Japan and China, are slowly making an appearance and are being appreciated by more than just the collectors. Deinanthes have magnificent large leaves, deeply veined and furrowed all over and toothed or lobed along the margins; such a wonderful spread of handsome foliage adds much textural interest to a shady garden. The flowers are attractive but temporary, so these relatives of hydrangeas earn their keep by providing a striking, long-lasting leaf show. Gardeners in persistently cool, moist climates are lucky: they will be able to successfully cultivate deinanthes, but even then, they may not attain the luxuriant growth seen in the wild. Though I did not, the Atlanta Botanical Garden has had some luck with this genus, so I will try again.

Both species of *Deinanthe* grow in light to medium shade in cool-summer areas and require moist, well-drained, humus-rich soil that will not dry out. They cannot abide heat and drought. The large leaves can be damaged by high winds, so site plants in a sheltered spot. Suitable for cultivation in zones 5 and 6. The genus name, sometimes incorrectly translated as "flower of the gods," is from the Greek *deinos* (= strange) and *anthos* (= flower), noting that the flowers are abnormally large for Hydrangeaceae, in which family the genus is classified.

Propagate by dividing the rhizome before growth starts in very early spring; reestablishment may be slow. Gather seed when fresh and sow in small pots in a cold frame; expect germination to be as slow as the growth rate of the seedlings. Seed may not be produced when grown under garden conditions.

Large slugs and snails can disfigure emerging young growth and even mature leaves.

Deinanthe bifida. Japan, southern and central Honshu.

LS to WS; flowers in terminal clusters, fleshy white with yellow stamens, both fertile and sterile; May–August; leafstalks to 24 in. (60 cm); leaves opposite in pairs, shiny medium to dark green, hairy, to 10 in. (25 cm) long, crinkly and coarse-textured with deeply grooved veins, toothed margins, tip notched, divided into 2 lobes (bifid), hence the epithet. A great foliage plant for cool-summer gardens, adding interesting texture and rich color. Its flowers are modestly showy; it is the leaves that make this a good plant for shady gardens.

Deinanthe caerulea, blue deinanthe. China, Hubei.

LS to WS; flowers in terminal clusters, waxy blue to violet-blue, to 1.5 in. (4 cm) across, rounded lobes with grayish blue to blue stamens; May–August; leafstalks to 18 in. (45 cm); leaves opposite in pairs, shiny medium to dark green, hairy, to 8 in. (20 cm) long, crinkly and coarse-textured with deeply grooved veins, toothed margins, tip pointed, but occasionally notched, 2-lobed. For cool-summer gardens only, this species combines showy, heavenly hued (hence the epithet) flowers with equally showy leaves.

Dennstaedtia

This large genus of attractive subtropical and tropical ferns has only one species hardy enough to be planted in temperate zone gardens: *Dennstaedtia punctilobula* (hayscented fern). Fresh or dry, the fronds exude a pleasant aroma, reminiscent of a freshly mown lawn. The species is epilithic, growing on moisture-retaining sandstone rocks in the boulder-strewn ravines of the Southeast. In 1969, I rescued several clumps before they were wiped out by the urbanization of outer DeKalb County, Georgia, and they have been growing at Hosta Hill ever since. If any fern could be called aggressive in its growth habit, this is it: its creeping rootstock spreads rapidly, sending up solitary fronds all along its length. It forms a solid groundcover in loose, moist soils; here it meanders through heavy Georgia red clay without any problems. I contain its spread by cutting and digging the roots at its perimeter. Best grown in a sheltered, shady, moist position, where adjacent shrub limbs can support the brittle stems during heavy rain and wind (fortunately, new fronds arise quickly to replace any that do break), and better in the woodland than the border, where it could become a nuisance. Other than providing it a little moisture during droughts, I leave it alone, and it does not mind neglect. Hardy to zone 4 and found in zone 8, so quite resistant to heat.

Known since 1803, hayscented fern was variously classified in *Nephrodium* and *Dicksonia*, but the latest placement in *Dennstaedtia* appears to be firm. The generic name honors German botanist August W. Dennstaedt; the epithet *punctilobula* (= small dotted lobes) refers to the shape of the sori on the subleaflets (pinnules). The genus is placed in the Dennstaedtiaceae.

Propagate by dividing the creeping rhizome in autumn or in very early spring. Propagation by spores makes no sense; division is much faster and yields mature divisions.

Slugs like the soft fronds of hayscented fern; take preventive measures to reduce the damage. No other pest or disease bothers them here.

Dennstaedtia punctilobula, hayscented fern. Eastern North America, eastern Canada, south to northern Georgia and west to Arkansas.

LS to FS; fronds to 30 in. (75 cm), produced singly or in small groups at frequent intervals emerging directly from the widely creeping rhizome, scaly and dark brown to black at the base, stalk green, brittle, upright; leaves 2- to 3-compound, shiny yellowish green, later duller, to 16 in. (40 cm) long and 8 in. (20 cm) wide, lance-shaped, tapering at the tip, not stalked; leaflets (pinnae) wedge-shaped, opposite, to 20 pairs, narrow, pointed top; subleaflets (pinnules) numerous, opposite, oblong, deeply cut and toothed, pointed; veins prominent. This fern's fresh color brightens up dark corners in the shady garden.

Dicentra

Bleeding hearts have long been popular flowering plants for the shady garden. Some of the exotic species brought into Western cultivation by Robert Fortune in the 1840s are still fashionable, and native species have come into favor with many North American shade gardeners as part of a campaign to plant native plants. I have seen most of the eastern species in the wild. On a spring outing to the Smoky Mountains, I became enamored with the beautiful, lacy leaves and unusual, delicate flowers of dutchman's breeches, *Dicentra cucullaria*, and I saw it again in patches on the Appalachian Trail near Newfound Gap, where it grows intermixed with *D. canadensis*. These lovely wildflowers are now rare in many areas, victims of habitat loss and unscrupulous poachers. Both species contain alkaloids that have a mildly poisonous effect if ingested; the cattle of early settlers were poisoned by grazing on their emerging leaves. Watch children around these beautiful but baneful plants.

Bleeding hearts are native to the northern temperate regions of North America and Asia. They dislike the very warm temperatures of the south temperate zones but can be found in the cooler habitat of the higher elevations of the southern Appalachians and the Piedmont. A high sugar content in the tuberous rhizomes makes most species reliably winter hardy; they thrive in the temperate climate of zones 3 to 6. Heat tolerance is fairly high as long as water is available in the soil. During warm periods in late winter, particularly here in zone 7, leaves or flowers may emerge very early, and late frosts and freezes may damage the new growth. Take precautions to protect the plants.

Native and exotic bleeding hearts are perennials for shady positions. Many in our woods are ephemerals, taking a long hiatus during summer: their contribution to summer foliage in the shady garden is nonexistent. In general, bleeding hearts prefer a neutral to slightly alkaline soil with a pH of 6.5 to 7.5; I add a handful of turkey grit to my plantings. The soil itself must be well draining, fertile, and light, yet retain moisture; bleeding hearts quickly degenerate in constantly wet or heavy soils. Most bleeding hearts are available in commerce from propagated stock.

The genus takes its name from the Greek *dis* (= two) and *kentron* (= spur), referring to the flowers, which have two enlarged spurs. *Dicentra* is classified in the Fumariaceae.

Downy mildew, leaf spot, rust, and wilt are reported but not seen here. Slugs and snails may damage new growth.

Propagate by dividing the rhizome when dormant in later summer or fall; replant divisions immediately. Seed must be gathered as soon as ripe in spring and sown in small pots in a cold frame or in a flat outside; chilly outside temperatures promote germination.

Dicentra canadensis, squirrel corn, little girl plant, bloomer plant, staggerweed, turkey corn. North America, Quebec, Nova Scotia, south to New England and in the mountains to the Carolinas and northern Georgia, west to Alabama, Tennessee, Missouri, eastern Kansas, and North Dakota.

WS to MS; flowers 4–10 on leafless stalk, fragrant, white to creamy white, with 4 petals, the 2 outer ones forming adjoining, rounded spurs, reminiscent of "an elongated heart or girl's bloomers", and 2 smaller ones white, tipped yellowish white, to 0.8 in. (2 cm) long; April–May; plant to 12 in. (30 cm) tall; root an elongated rhizome with numerous yellow bulblets, reminiscent of corn kernels; leaves basal, triangular, 2-compound, pale bluish green, divided into linear-elliptic, deeply lobed, incised leaflets; fruit an elongated capsule. This summer-dormant species (seen in photo of *Arisaema triphyllum*) makes a wonderful display in the spring garden.

Dicentra chrysantha, golden eardrops. California.

LS to MS; flowers many, up to 75, yellow, with a pungent odor, 4 petals, the 2 outer ones forming adjoining, rounded spurs, heart-shaped, 2 inner ones yellow, tipped purple; April–May; plant large,

to 5 ft. (1.5 m), sparsely leaved. Barely hardy to zone 7a, although it might succeed in protected areas.

Dicentra cucullaria, dutchman's breeches, little boy plant, little blue staggers, staggerweed. North America, Quebec, Nova Scotia, in the mountains in New England south to the Carolinas and northern Georgia, west to Alabama, Tennessee, Missouri, eastern Kansas, Oklahoma and North Dakota, isolated in western North America in eastern Oregon and Washington.

WS to MS; flowers 4–12 on leafless stalk, not fragrant, white to creamy white, with 4 petals, the 2 outer ones forming adjoining, V-shaped, pointed spurs, resembling "inverted dutchman's breeches," and 2 smaller ones, white, tipped yellow, "forming the waistline," to 0.8 in. (2 cm) long; April–May; plant to 16 in. (40 cm) tall; root a cluster of pink oval tubers; leaves basal, triangular, 2-compound, pale bluish green, divided into linear-elliptic, deeply lobed, incised leaflets. Larger than *Dicentra canadensis*, more poisonous and not fragrant, but equally useful in the spring garden, until it becomes summer-dormant.

Dicentra eximia, turkey corn, wild bleeding heart, fringed bleeding heart, staggerweed. Eastern North America, New York south to the Carolinas and northern Georgia, west to Tennessee and West Virginia.

WS to MS; flowers 4–40, not fragrant, hanging from arching, leafless flowerstalks, deep rose-pink to pink, with 4 petals, the 2 outer ones adjoining, with heart-shaped inflated spurs, and 2 smaller, inner ones (the "blood drop"), pink, tipped red, flaring, to 0.8 in. (2 cm) long; April–May; plant usually to 18 in. (45 cm) tall but well-cultivated specimens have reached 36 in. (90 cm); root a stout, scaly rhizome; leaves basal, to 10, triangular, 2-compound, green above, pale bluish green beneath, divided into linear-elliptic, deeply incised leaflets. The very best native species for shady gardens: it does not go summer-dormant like other native species but, provided it receives plenty of moisture, keeps its striking leaves even during the hottest weather, carrying on until late summer and early autumn with occasional sporadic flowering, depending on microclimate. Its pink heart-shaped flowers are similar to those of *Dicentra spectabilis* but a little lighter in color, though it makes up for this by having more of them. It is common in the Appalachians but should be left alone in the wild; the many cultivars in commerce are better garden plants. Many nurseries sell *D. formosa* (western bleeding heart) as *D. eximia*; make inquiries before purchasing. The correct attribution of cultivars to either *D. eximia* or *D. formosa* is uncertain; some of the cultivars listed here are hybrids, involving one or the other of these very similar species. Their long-lasting qualities during summer points to *D. eximia*: most do well in cool summers but suffer in the very hot, dry summers of zones 8 and 9. Here in zone 7a they do well in considerable shade with supplemental water.

'Adrian Bloom', a darker-flowered (almost ruby-red) seedling of 'Bountiful' with a longer bloom period; red-tinted stems, medium green leaves, clump-forming.

'Alba', creamy white flowers with light green leaves.

'Aurora', flowers white, larger than the type; grayish green leaves, spreading, rhizomatous.

'Bacchanal', crimson-red flowers, much larger than the species; grayish green leaves, spreading, rhizomatous.

'Bountiful', purplish pink flowers, much larger than the species, flowering spring and later in summer; red-tinted stems, medium green leaves, clump-forming.

'Coldham', burgundy flowers; fernlike bluish leaves.

'Luxuriant', flowers red, much larger than the species; medium green leaves, spreading, rhizomatous.

'Margery Fish', pure white flowers, much larger than the species; finely divided bluish gray-green leaves.

'Pearl Drops' ('Langtrees'), flowers white tinted pink, much larger than the species; silvery gray-green leaves, vigorously spreading, rhizomatous. A choice cultivar.

'Silversmith', very light creamy white flowers flushed pink; leaves bluish green; clump-forming. An improved 'Alba'.

'Snowflakes', flowers very white.

'Spring Morning', deep pink flowers, late-flowering; leaves medium to dark green; clump-forming.

'Stewart Boothman' ('Boothman's Variety'), deep pink flowers; vigorous, spreading.

'Sweetheart', snow-white flowers.

'Zestful', long-lasting deep rose flowers; grayish green leaves.

Dicentra formosa, western bleeding heart. Western North America, British Columbia south to Oregon, California, Nevada.

WS to MS; very similar to *Dicentra eximia* (indeed, reported in Massachusetts) and by some considered its western form. Flowers in early summer, somewhat later than *D. eximia*. *Dicentra formosa* has diverging regional populations. Subspecies *oregana* occurs in Oregon, subsp. *nevadensis* (Sierran bleeding heart) in Nevada; both differ only in minor details from the type. The leaves of the type are green on top and a dull grayish blue-green beneath, while the other subspecies have bluish green color on both sides. Flowers of some populations have a yellowish cast with pink overtones. Another western species, *D. ochroleuca* from California, has straw-yellow to deep creamy white, purple-tipped flowers. *Dicentra uniflora* (longhorn steer's head) from northern California, Washington, and Idaho is a small, delicate bleeding heart growing in snow beds in well-drained, rocky soils; its flowers have spreading outer petals and paired inner ones (hence the common name). *Dicentra pauciflora* (shorthorn steer's head) also from California and similar to *D. uniflora*, has deeply heart-shaped pink flowers. All these western species and subspecies come from specialized and drier habitats and are not easily transplanted; they should be left alone and admired in the wild. Choose instead from the cultivars listed under *D. eximia* (some hybrids involving *D. formosa*), which are better, longer-lived garden plants with larger, showy flowers.

Dicentra scandens, climbing yellow bleeding heart. Himalayas, western China.

Some sun, LS to WS; flowers 2–14 hanging from fleshy, leafless, arching stalks, yellow or yellowish white, sometimes tipped with pink to purplish pink, with 4 petals, the 2 outer ones adjoining, heart-shaped, elongated, and bending down, 0.8–1 in. (2–2.5 cm) long; April–October; plant veining, climbing; terminal leaves with tendrils. This species and the Nepalese annual *Dicentra torulosa* are the only climbing bleeding hearts. A vigorous species, quite tolerant of hot summers, and most floriferous: the one I grow has climbed up a fence, mingled with Virginia creeper (*Parthenocissus quin-*

quefolia) and blooms from spring until autumn. Hardy to zone 6. 'Athens Yellow' offers hundreds of yellow flowers in equal everblooming succession; it is a climbing plant for the fence row or trellis, and not invasive.

Dicentra spectabilis, bleeding heart, common bleeding heart, old-fashioned bleeding heart, Asian bleeding heart. Siberia, China, Korea, Japan.

WS to MS; flowers 3–15 hanging from fleshy, leafless, arching stalks, deep rose-pink to purplish pink, with 4 petals, the 2 outer ones adjoining, with heart-shaped inflated spurs, and 2 smaller, inner ones (the "blood drop"), pink, tipped red and white, flaring, 0.8–1.2 in. (2–3 cm) long; April–May; plant usually to 4 ft. (1.2 m) tall; root a stout, scaly rhizome; leaves triangular, 5–16 in. (13–40 cm) long, 2-compound, pale green beneath, divided into linear-elliptic, deeply incised leaflets. This species is the common bleeding heart of gardens. The original plant from China first flowered in Europe in 1847, after which it became a fashionable garden plant. For a time it also appeared as a cut flower, but its cut stems have a disagreeable smell so this use was curtailed; in North America it is a favored plant for late-winter forcing in time for Valentine's Day. It has larger flowers than most native species and forms a sizable clump of fernlike grayish green leaves. Although a summer-dormant species, it tolerates considerable sun if given constant moisture, and with that plentiful moisture, its leaves can be preserved until early summer here in the South, and until July or August further north; fill in the blank spaces it leaves with annuals, container plants, or late-emerging perennials. Several other Asian species are occasionally available, but they are more suited for collector's gardens, where they provide a striking spring display of hanging flowers. Among these are *D. macrantha*, a yellow-flowered species from eastern China, and *D. peregrina*, a variable species from eastern Asia with white to purple flowers. Cultivars of *D. spectabilis* include 'Alba' (white flowers), 'Pantaloons' (similar but more vigorous), 'Rosea' (pink flowers), and **'Gold Heart'**, whose unusual yellow leaves and pink flowers make a great color combination in spring.

Diphylleia

On excursions into the Smoky Mountains, I am always on the lookout for handsome plants growing in deep shade. One early spring, I encountered a rarity in a deeply shaded cove near Balsam Mountain, growing on a rocky slope that had water seeping from above. At first sight, it looked almost like the umbrella plant (*Darmera peltata*), but small heads of white flowers rising above the leaves told me otherwise. I had discovered a colony of *Diphylleia cymosa* (umbrella leaf). Gardeners will want to grow this wildflower for its architectural prominence in the garden, its two strikingly tropical-looking leaves, held high on a branched leafstalk, its small but outstanding flowers, and later in autumn, its blue fruit covered with a thin waxy white bloom, much like grapes on the vine.

American Indians used *Diphylleia cymosa* medicinally. An anticancer component has recently been discovered in it, and the search is on for a synthesized equivalent. It is considered rare, but I would correct this to "rarely seen," because one has to get out of the car and hike into remote mountain areas to see it. Umbrella leaf grows in the southern Appalachians, at elevations of 2500 ft. (760 m) above sea level and higher. Where the environment is to its liking, fairly large populations exist. Plants are usually found along rocky mountain streams and seepage areas on rocky slopes, where the ground stays wet most of the time; they like cool, moist conditions and are mostly in medium to full shade. I grow mine in deep shade by the side of a water feature that overflows into an area planted with other moisture-loving plants; even so, umbrella leaf shows considerable heat stress here in zone 7a, and I help it along with frequent, cooling sprays on really hot, dry summer days.

Diphylleia cymosa is an excellent shade garden plant, tough and long-lived. Site it in shade in deep, humus-rich soil that stays moist all year. Hardy in zones 6 and 7, 5 with a heavy winter mulch. It takes some time to mature, so be patient. Assign it a sheltered spot to avoid wind and storm damage to its large leaves, which, in spring, will be overtopped with white flowers held in clusters (cymes, hence the epithet). The generic name comes from the Greek *dis* (= two) and *phyllon* (= leaf), for the two leaves per stem (nonflowering plants usually have only one leaf). *Diphylleia* is classified in the Berberidaceae.

Propagate by dividing the rhizome before growth starts in very early spring. Seed must be gathered when fresh and sown in a cold frame.

Large slugs and snails can be very damaging to exposed portions of the rhizome, emerging growth, and even mature leaves. In summer, army worms, striped caterpillars, and other moth larvae feed during night, disfiguring the leaves.

Diphylleia cymosa, umbrella leaf. Eastern North America, southern Appalachians, Virginia south to northern Georgia and Alabama and west to Tennessee.

MS to FS; flowers small, white, 5 petals and sepals, cup-shaped, with 6 yellow stamens, 6–10, in dense clusters (cymes) above the leaves; May–June; plant clump-forming from a stout rhizome, slowly expanding; leafstalks, reddish, 24–38 in. (60–95 cm) tall; leaves umbrellalike, to 24 in. (60 cm) across, medium green, deeply cleft along the centerline, each half with 5–7 smaller, coarsely toothed lobes; leaf stems stout, upright, usually 2 leaves per stem; fruit a large blue berry coated with a waxy white bloom. A great accent plant near a water feature, as a background grouping in open woodlands, or as a companion to moisture-loving ferns. Variety *grayi*, from the Yunnan Plateau of western China and in the higher elevations of the Japanese Alps of Honshu and further north to Hokkaido, is very similar; it has smaller leaves, which are not as deeply lobed, fewer flowers, and stems suffused with more red. Some botanists rank it as a species, *Diphylleia grayi*. Both var. *grayi* and the type are available in commerce.

Disporopsis

I first became aware of *Disporopsis* several years ago, as an offering in a plant catalog. My lifelong interest in the *Polygonatum/Disporum* complex was piqued, and I ordered all there were to be had. My first acquisition was *Disporopsis pernyi*, which turned out to be a graceful garden plant, easy of culture, and well adapted to southern heat and dryness; it made a nice clump within a few seasons and is now planted among its relatives, Solomon's seals (*Polygonatum* spp.) and fairy bells (*Disporum* spp.). It is evergreen here in zone 7a, but during severe winters, the leaves and stems get burned and bruised by frigid nights and falling ice, so I remove the old stems before new growth appears. Spurred on by

the success of my first *Disporopsis* species, I acquired a clone of *D. fuscopicta*, which has been growing here for several years now. Its almost yellow flowers, which have a brownish purple edge, are marked inside (*fuscopicta* = dark painted). Very heat-tolerant as long as adequate soil moisture is maintained. Thick stems rise from a slowly creeping rhizome that gets larger every season: my plant had two stems at first; it now has two dozen. Stems are densely purple-spotted at the base, becoming lighter green above; along their slightly zigzagging length grows a crop of glossy, wide, dark green leaves that look as if they are made of wax. This plant is also evergreen but seems to be less cold-tolerant than *D. pernyi*. Both disporopsis resemble and can be used like evergreen, succulent Solomon's seals. As such, they bring year-round garden interest. I do not know what their ultimate cold tolerance is, but gardeners in colder areas can easily grow both species in containers, providing plenty of room for growth. Overwinter containers in an area where the temperatures do not fall below freezing, or bring them into the house and admire them in a cool to cold room.

Disporopsis are native to the temperate and subtropical regions of Asia, originating in moist woodlands. They are well adapted to shady, moist conditions; I grow several clumps in the woodland garden, where they thrive in a soil pH of 5.5 to 6.5. They do withstand temporary periods of heat and drought but prefer constantly moist soil. Site where their well-defined, deeply grooved veins can be observed and their leathery leaves touched. (Many gardeners admire their plants with their eyes only, but I love to feel the leaf texture, substance, and resistance: much can be gleaned by touching plants.) Blackish berries in autumn add to the garden merit of disporopsis. The genus is placed in the Convallariaceae.

Propagate by dividing the dormant rhizome in late autumn or very early spring. When completely dormant, the roots can be removed without native soil and divided with a clean, sharp knife. Seed propagation requires a cold frame; division is much more productive.

Large slugs and snails can damage very tender young growth in spring. I have found the plants to be free of pests and diseases.

Disporopsis pernyi is taxonomically well established, but the several other species known in eastern and southern Asia are in a state of nomenclatural flux. As many as 20 species may exist in China alone, so expect additional importations. If future offerings are as exciting as those now in commerce, we gardeners have a lot to look forward to.

Disporopsis arisanensis. Taiwan.

LS to FS; flowers 1–3, white to creamy white, lobe extensions purplish, inside purple-spotted or greenish, 0.5–0.6 in. (1–1.5 cm) long, bell-shaped, tubular, 6-lobed, produced on short pedicels in the leaf axils; May–June; stems thick, finely purple-spotted at the base becoming lighter and greenish above, upright but arching, hairless, to 8 in. (20 cm) tall, unbranched and slightly zigzagging between leaves; leaves alternate, appearing in the upper half of stem, to 4 in. (10 cm) long, 1.5–2.5 in. (4–6 cm) wide, broadly elliptic, with reflexed, pointed tip, veins parallel, 3 principle veins deeply impressed above, projected below; fruit a round, grooved capsule, dark blue to bluish black. Although smaller than some of its relatives in the *Polygonatum/Disporum* complex, this species is evergreen during mild winters in zone 7a and so a valuable plant in the garden. It adapts well to containers large enough for its eventual spread and can be cultivated this way further north with great success. During spring and summer, the pot can be set on the ground or plunged among hardier companions; remove to an overwintering spot before the deep freeze arrives.

Disporopsis fuscopicta. China.

LS to FS; this species reportedly has a stem height of 36 in. (90 cm) based on observations in the wild. The whitish to creamy white spring flowers are like little bells, similar to those of Solomon's seal, but they are smaller. *Disporopsis fuscopicta* is sometimes sold as *D. arisanensis*, and the true identity of commercial plants is still in doubt. The *D. fuscopicta* clone I grow has a stem height of only 24 in. (60 cm) and leaves as wide as *D. arisanensis* but longer, to 6 in. (15 cm). More field work is required to sort this out. In the meantime, several clones are in commerce, and the plants—by whatever name—are striking additions to shady gardens.

Disporopsis pernyi. China, Yunnan, Guangxi, Gizhou.

LS to FS; flowers 1–3, white to creamy white, fragrant, 0.8 in. (2 cm) long, bell-shaped, tubular, 6-lobed with lobes pointed and spreading, recurving, produced on short pedicels in the leaf axils; May–July; stout stems brownish purple at the base becoming lighter and greenish above, upright but arching, hairless, 10–16 in. (25–40 cm) tall, unbranched and slightly zigzagging between leaves; leaves alternate, 4–6 in. (10–15 cm) long, 1–1.5 in. (2.5–4 cm) wide, broadly lance-shaped with reflexed, pointed tip; fruit a round, grooved capsule, dark blue to bluish black. This Chinese species has been known to and appreciated by gardeners north and south for some time as a contributor to a multitextured garden scene. Hardy to zone 5.

Disporum

In most gardens, fairy bells (*Disporum* spp.) have been banished to a dark corner, together with Solomon's seals. There their delicate beauty, which must be observed closely to be appreciated, is wasted. Some larger species may attract attention, but smaller ones get lost in a mass of foliage. What a pity. Luckily, the recent trend toward natural gardens and importations of new species of fairy bells from Asia have renewed interest in both native and exotic members of the genus, and finally, the dainty native North American species are getting the recognition they deserve. I have always admired fairy bells. Many years ago, I found a colony of *Disporum languinosum* (yellow mandarin) in full bloom during a woodland walk in the North Georgia mountains; I bought a plant from a wildflower source, and the spidery beauty of its yellow flowers, drooping on long flowerstalks, has graced Hosta Hill ever since. On another late-summer trip, I collected a few seeds from a second fairy bell; some germinated, and in the end the creamy purple-spotted flowers gave its identity away: it was the archetypal North American species *D. maculatum* (nodding mandarin), which was used medicinally by American Indians and early settlers. Fairy bell, a name generally applied to the species of this genus, originated as a reference to the wispy petals of another native, *D. hookeri*, which resemble the wings of a fairy.

Fairy bells are rhizomatous herbaceous perennials native to the temperate regions of North America and Asia, particularly Korea and Japan. Originating in moist woodlands, they are well adapted to shady, moist conditions. They die down in autumn, but with heavy winter mulching, their hardiness range can be extended. I am excited about the larger Asian species, which add great charm and, in some cases, architectural value to wildflower gardens. If there is room for only one fairy bell, choose *Disporum flavens* from Korea, which grows much larger than native fairy bells; its very strong stems have withstood some nasty spring hailstorms here.

Fairy bells have the same garden uses as Solomon's seal (*Polygonatum* spp.), though they are not quite as large as some. Their culture too is similar. I grow the native species in my woodland garden together with small hostas and ferns. They thrive in soil with a pH of 5.5 to 6.5. Site fairy bells where their well-defined leaf veins can be observed. They do not like very dry conditions and prefer a constantly moist soil; with sufficient moisture, they will last longer into autumn, when red or blackish berries add to their garden merit.

Disporum (= twin seed) is from the Greek, an allusion to the reproductive anatomy of the genus (each chamber of the ovary contains two seeds). The genus is placed in the Colchicaceae.

Propagate by dividing the dormant rhizome in late autumn or very early spring. When completely dormant, the roots can be removed without native soil and divided with a clean, sharp knife. Seed propagation is difficult and slow; root division is much more productive.

Large slugs and snails can damage young growing tips emerging in spring, but fairy bells are otherwise relatively free of pests and diseases. Weevils, a real pest on other plants, have not touched them here.

Species and cultivars listed are herbaceous. Unless otherwise noted, all can be grown in zones 6 to 9. North American species are very hardy; most thrive in zones 4 to 7 and can be grown in zone 3 or colder. Asian species have not been fully tested, but indications are they are hardy to zone 6, 5 with protection. Expect some losses during extreme winters and some divergence from the descriptions: *Disporum* species show considerable variability in the wild.

Disporum bodinieri. Western China.

MS to FS; flowers yellowish, 1 in. (2.5 cm) long, bell-shaped, tubular, 6-lobed, produced on long, branched pedicels in multiples in the leaf axils, an-

thers protruding; May–July; stout stems, upright but leaning, hairless, to 7 ft. (2 m) tall, many-branched, with green leaves to 6 in. (15 cm) long, broadly lance-shaped. But for the sturdy branched stems, this outstanding, large garden plant resembles a Solomon's seal. Stems lean somewhat so the effective height is less—even so, a giant among fairy bells and therefore suitable as an accent or background plant. *Disporum megalanthum* from Sichuan is similarly useful in the garden; its stems reach almost as high, to 6 ft. (1.8 m), and its larger flowers, to 1.2 in. (3 cm), are pure white with attractively contrasting yellow stamens (and anthers not exserted).

Disporum cantoniense, Thai fairy bell. Northern Thailand, Nepal, western and southern China, Japan.

MS to FS; flowers variable, white to pink, deep rose-red, brownish red, or even purple, 0.5–1 in. (1–2.5 cm) long, bell-shaped, tubular, 6-lobed, produced on pedicels in umbels of 3–7, in the leaf axils; May–July; stems upright, hairless, to 5 ft. (1.5 m), occasionally to 7 ft. (2 m) tall, many-branched, with singular, alternate, glossy green leaves to 5 in. (13 cm) long, narrowly to broadly lance-shaped, in some forms grooved veins; ball-shaped fruit is blue to bluish black or red. The nomenclature of this recently collected species is muddled. Possibly several subspecies (or species) are involved, hence the differences in flower color; further expeditions to southeastern Asia should settle the question. Variety *cantoniense* (BSWJ 5290), collected in northern Thailand, has deep rose-red flowers and makes a great addition to gardens. My favorite variant, **Disporum cantoniense (DHHC 724)**, was collected by intrepid plantsman Dan Hinkley in western China. Its stout, smooth, round stems grow to an average of 5 ft. (1.5 m), sometimes higher; they are brownish near the ground and turn progressively to light green at the tips. As many as a dozen branches emerge from the stem. In each of the branch axils, more branches emerge, and this multiplicity of stems, clothed with glossy, green leaves, confers outstanding architectural garden value upon it. Evergreen in zone 7 and warmer, but here in zone 7a it is herbaceous. Another multibranched form, *D. cantoniense* (HWJCM 069), is somewhat smaller, with lovely pink flowers and blue fruit. Even more exciting is **'Aureovariegata'** from Japan; its glossy variegated leaves are carried on sturdy stems to 36 in. (90 cm), and its flowers are white. All these forms give but a meager indication of what is to follow. All become herbaceous in colder regions and are probably evergreen in zone 7. Protect with dry mulch.

Disporum flavens, Korean fairy bell. Korea.

MS to FS; flowers bright yellow, 1 in. (2.5 cm) long, bell-shaped, tubular, 6-lobed, produced on short pedicels in umbels of 1–6, in the leaf axils; May–June; flowerstalks very erect, hairless, dark, brownish near the base, medium green further up, to 36 in. (90 cm) tall, with alternate, multiple branches, the branches also branched; leaves matte dark green above, glossy beneath, to 4 in. (10 cm) long, 2.5 in. (6 cm) wide, broadly ovate to heart-shaped, solitary in the lower part of the main stem, clasping, with the veins deeply sunken on the surface and projected underneath. Makes a slowly expanding clump of upright, multibranched stems clothed with attractive leaves. Tolerates considerable morning sun but requires afternoon shade. Gives a stunning display year after year: 2 weeks of dazzling yellow flowers followed by black, oblong fruit.

Disporum hookeri, drops of gold. North America, British Columbia to Oregon and northern California east to Montana, northern Michigan.

MS to FS; flowers pure white, sometimes creamy to greenish white, 0.5 in. (1 cm) long, bell-shaped, tubular, 6-lobed, produced on long, branched pedicels in umbels of 1–4, in the leaf axils; May–June; stems erect but leaning, upper stems downy, to 32 in. (80 cm) tall, branched, with clasping, green, attractively veined leaves to 6 in. (15 cm) long, ovate to broadly lance-shaped, wavy, in the lower part heart-shaped, clasping, with the leaf tips extended, forming drips. Attractive flowers followed by red-orange, slightly pointed fruit make this native a good garden subject. One must get really close to see the small marvel that is var. *oreganum*, native in Oregon and north and east to Montana, which has, besides hairy style and ovary, the added charm of exserted anthers hanging down below the flower's lobes. Keeping distance in a garden serves the overall impression but ignores all the little wonders.

Disporum languinosum, yellow mandarin, hairy fairy bell, liverberry. Eastern North America, south-

eastern Canada through New England to northern Georgia and Alabama and west to Arkansas.

MS to FS; flowers yellow with long, pointed tepals, to 0.5 in. (1 cm) long, tubular, produced terminally on long pedicels in umbels of 1–3; May–June; flowerstalks erect but leaning, downy, to 24 in. (60 cm), sometimes taller, branched, with downy green leaves to 5 in. (13 cm) long, ovate to narrowly ovate with pointed tips, shiny above and downy beneath. Long in cultivation and a favorite of mine for its attractive flowers (one common name alludes to the yellow silk court color of the mandarins) followed by oblong, red-orange fruit. Very similar to *Uvularia grandiflora*. Plant in groups, just as it occurs in nature, for best effect.

Disporum maculatum, nodding mandarin, spotted fairy bell, spotted disporum, liverberry. Eastern and central North America from southern Michigan and Ohio to northern Georgia and Alabama.

MS to FS; flowers creamy white with purple spots, with separate sepals and petals, to 1 in. (2.5 cm) long, 6-parted, anthers projecting from the perianth, produced terminally on long pedicels in umbels of 1–2; May–June; stems erect but leaning, downy, to 24 in. (60 cm) tall, branched, with downy, stalkless, green leaves to 5 in. (13 cm) long, ovate to narrowly ovate with pointed tips, shiny above and downy beneath, veins conspicuous; fruit red and hairy. A unique native in that the sepals and petals emerge separately from the flower base, like arrowheads with a short extension. The elegant, deeply nodding flowers are ephemeral and all but hidden by the terminal leaf tufts; for best effect, plant in groups and site where the deeply veined leaves can add to garden texture after the spotted (hence the epithet) flowers are gone.

Disporum nantauense, Taiwan fairy bell. Taiwan.

MS to FS; flowers creamy white, 0.5–1 in. (1–2.5 cm) long, bell-shaped, tubular, 6-lobed, produced on long pedicels, usually single, in the leaf axils; May–July; stems low-growing, dark green, hairless, to 12 in. (30 cm), many-branched, with singular, alternate, glossy dark green leaves to 4 in. (10 cm) long, narrowly lance-shaped, with depressed veins; ball-shaped fruit is blue to bluish black. Recently collected but occasionally available. The stems are not as stiffly erect as in other species but just as vigorous, forming little thickets of attractive leaves with showy veins. Hardy to zone 7; good winter protection with a dry mulch extends its range northward, but it becomes herbaceous.

Disporum pullum. Japan.

MS to FS; flowers greenish purple, to 1 in. (2.5 cm) long; May–June; stems erect, sometimes branched, mostly short from 30 in. (75 cm) tall; leaves shiny dark green, small, to 4 in. (10 cm), elliptic, pointed. The species has been known for almost 200 years but is seldom seen. The available cultivar 'Variegatum' has leaves margined with a wide, white edge; it is a spreader, but its charm should make this habit welcome, particularly in the darker corners of the garden.

Disporum sessile, Japanese fairy bell. Japan.

MS to FS; flowers green-tipped white, 1 in. (2.5 cm) long, bell-shaped, tubular, 6-lobed, produced terminally on short, arching pedicels in umbels of 1–3; May–June; stems erect, hairless, forking into 2–5 side branches, to 24 in. (60 cm) tall; leaves smooth, matte dark green, to 4 in. (10 cm) long, 1 in. (2.5 cm) wide, lance-shaped; fruit spherical, black, 2 per flower. The typical all-green species is rarely seen; but subsp. *flavens*, with yellow flowers, and the dwarf var. *inobeanum* are available, and the type's white-variegated sport **'Variegatum'** (variegated fairy bell) has found worldwide acceptance. As with all garden forms, its variegation is changeable and anything but cleanly white-striped. On the same plant, the extremes of variegation can range from leaves mostly white with green stripes to leaves mostly green with white stripes. Its rhizomatous root system branches prolifically and spreads far afield. I consider it downright invasive (digging the roots at Hosta Hill would mean disturbing an adjacent planting of native trilliums), but a little straying is welcome in most gardens. A form with considerably wider leaves covers the ground even better, but I prefer the narrow-leaved 'Variegatum' because it allows a better view of the spring flowers. Occasionally incorrectly offered as a selection of *Disporum pullum*. In Japan, other variously variegated forms of *D. sessile*, primarily used in pot culture, are collected by aficionados with enough money to buy them; mostly white and therefore lacking chlorophyll, these forms are probably too weak for garden purposes.

Disporum smilacinum. Japan, Korea, China.

MS to FS; flowers creamy white, 0.5 in. (1 cm) long, sometimes larger, expanded bell-shaped, starry, usually solitary, rarely 2; May–June; stems erect, sometimes branched, mostly short, 6–20 in. (15–50 cm) tall; leaves shiny dark green, small, to 3 in. (8 cm) long and 2.5 in. (6 cm) wide, broadly elliptic, stalkless; fruit spherical, bluish black. The typical all-green species has wide-ranging rhizomes that expand slowly to make a dense groundcover, and its fairly large flowers contribute to its garden value. Its epithet is the diminutive of the ancient Greek name for the greenbrier vines (*Smilax* spp.), to which this species is broadly related. The many variegated sports of *D. smilacinum* discovered in Japan are gradually making their way into Western nurseries at a reasonable cost; these treasures should be grown where they can be most appreciated.

'Aureovariegata' has glossy leaves with dazzling yellow stripes and a yellow tip in spring; later in the season the variegation becomes creamy white. Long used in Japanese gardens, it makes a lovely groundcover or accent group, although the Japanese prefer to grow such unusual plants in pots.

'Dai Setsurei' (= large snow mountain) has white leaves with green stripes.

'Ginga' (= milky way) has whitish leaves with green flecks and spotting.

'Kinkaku' (= golden pavillion) has yellow leaves with streaky green stripes.

'Ki-no-Tsukasa' (= yellow chief) has a yellow margin and yellow streaks growing from the tip into a green leaf.

'Kinsho' (= golden wing) has bright yellow leaves with delicate green striping.

'Seiki-no-Homare' (= pride of the century) is similar to 'Kinkaku' but with more yellow in the leaf.

Disporum smithii, large-flowered fairy bells. Western North America, British Columbia south to Oregon and northern California.

MS to FS; flowers creamy to greenish white, 1 in. (2.5 cm) long, bell-shaped, tubular, 6-lobed with recurved tips, anthers protruding, produced on long, branched pedicels in umbels of 2–4, mostly terminally; May–June; stems erect but leaning, spotted with red, to 24 in. (60 cm) tall, branched, with wavy-margined green leaves to 5 in. (13 cm) long, ovate to broadly lance-shaped, wavy, in the lower part heart-shaped, clasping; red fruit. Frequently confused with *Disporum hookeri* var. *oreganum*, which is similar but with an unbranched stigma: *D. smithii* has a 3-lobed stigma. This species is threatened by the clear-cutting of its native forest habitats and should be obtained from responsible sources only. A relatively rare white-margined form of it is sometimes seen in gardens. *Disporum trachycarpum*, which also has a 3-lobed stigma, is differentiated by its rough-surfaced fruit (*trachycarpum* = rough fruit), first yellow then bright red; it also differs by not having drooping leaf tips. It ranges from British Columbia south to Oregon and in the higher elevations from North Dakota to Arizona and western New Mexico. Both species should be sited where they can be observed closely.

Disporum uniflorum. Western China, Yunnan.

MS to FS; flowers large, 1.5 in. (4 cm) and longer, creamy white, bell-shaped, tubular, 6-lobed, produced on very long pedicels, to 2.5 in. (6 cm), in multiples of 2–7 in the terminal leaf axils; May–July; stout stems, upright but leaning, hairless, to 40 in. (1 m) tall, branched, with wavy green leaves to 6 in. (15 cm) long, broadly lance-shaped. The acquisition of this outstanding, large garden plant deserves special efforts. It is distinguished by its very large (for the genus) flowers, which (according to photographs taken in Lijiang) hang conspicuously on pedicels that are much longer than the flowers. Sometimes mentioned in connection with *D. flavens*, whose large yellow flowers are borne on short pedicels.

Disporum viridescens. Korea, Japan.

MS to FS; flowers large, greenish white, drooping, star-shaped; May–June; branched stems to 30 in. (75 cm) tall; leaves green, small, to 3 in. (8 cm) long, elliptic; fruit spherical, black. A recent introduction, notable for its flowers. In time the vigorous underground rhizomes expand to make a pretty colony or groundcover. *Disporum lutescens* is a similar yellow-flowered species from southern Honshu and Kyushu in Japan. Both are seldom available.

Dodecatheon

The mountains of northern Georgia are home to many spring ephemerals. They bloom early, store up energy before the trees leaf out or the grasses and subshrubs cover them, and then fade away for another year. One such temporary wonder much admired by me in its native habitat was **Dodecatheon media** (common cowslip, prairie pointer). The few plants I obtained to try in my shady garden did well for the first two seasons, blooming faithfully if briefly in spring and disappearing shortly thereafter, but after a couple of years, they began to decline and finally disappeared altogether. I was disappointed and decided that in future I should visit and admire them in the wild, where large patches make a gorgeous display in early spring. A few in the garden just do not give justice to their great charm. Best adapted to meadows and grassy prairies (and even there they are short-lived plants), they should not be planted where evergreen trees and shrubs shade them out during their early-spring growing cycle. Also, they require a slightly alkaline soil with a pH of 6 to 7.5, something that is difficult to provide in a shady garden, where most plants need high acidity. A few can be tucked in here and there where there is almost full sun before the trees leaf out, but remember: their loveliness is fleeting, and they do not provide the lasting display of attractive foliage so necessary for successful shady gardens.

Dracunculus

Shady gardens are green gardens by nature. Flowers spice up the scene from time to time, but the canvas of the gardener's art is green. For added excitement, I like plants that not only contribute a temporary splash of color but are also weird and wonderfully attractive. *Dracunculus vulgaris* (dragon arum) is certainly one of these: its bizarre flower attracts people even as its stench draws flies. Found all around the Mediterranean region, it may not be very hardy, but it can be potted and grown outdoors in northern gardens. In Detroit, my mother grew one on her patio and overwintered it dry in her basement; it bloomed year after year until an early hard freeze turned it to mush. I grow it for the same reason I grow snake palms (*Amorphophallus* spp.): it combines a beguiling flower with interesting, long-lasting foliage. Hardy to zone 7a; provide some winter mulch in exposed locations. I have it poking up among Solomon's seals, its tuberous root planted at least 6 in. (15 cm) deep; even a short, hard freeze does not penetrate that deep, so

I forgo the mulch. The soil must be well drained and dry in summer; in areas of wet summers, it is better potted. Withhold water after the leaves die down, and add a slow-release fertilizer at the leaf emergence.

Dracunculus (= dragon) belongs in the Araceae. Propagate by separating tuber offsets in autumn or very early spring. Diseases and attacks by insects are uncommon.

Dracunculus vulgaris, dragon arum. Mediterranean region, Asia Minor.

Morning sun, LS to WS; spathe large, 24–36 in. (60–90 cm) long, spathe tube pale green to greenish white outside, spathe blade (hood) broad and flaring, purple inside, dull greenish white or green below, margins wavy and turned down; spadix erect, as long as the spathe limb or slightly longer, shiny dark purple, almost black, foul-smelling; June–July; plant tuberous; leaves fan-shaped, 6–8 in. (15–20 cm) long and 10–14 in. (25–35 cm) wide, with 9–15 segments, middle one largest, all lance-shaped, pointed, dark green, with whitish markings; leaf stems purple-spotted, thick pseudostem, flowerstalk exceeds leafstalks. Not for those with sensitive noses, this species nevertheless fills the craving for weird plants some shade gardeners have.

Dryopteris

Ferns are essential in the shady garden, and the genus *Dryopteris*, which at one time encompassed over 1200 species, contributes prodigiously to the ranks of gardenworthy ferns. Many are classics, outstanding garden ferns of tall stature, and some are even evergreen, providing a conspicuous accent in an otherwise bleak winter landscape. The evergreen *Dryopteris erythrosora* (autumn fern) from Japan, one of my favorites, has naturalized at Hosta Hill. This penchant for naturalizing is shared by *D. affinis* (golden shield fern) from Eurasia, one of the primary ferns in public gardens; its vase-shaped form fits well into the landscape. Very similar is *D. filix-mas* (male fern), a North American native that here turns a wonderful yellow in autumn. Easily the most unusual fern in my garden is *D. sieboldii*, from southern Japan and Taiwan; its fronds have a strange look, and its outline is anything but typical. Some visitors do not even recognize it as a fern.

Dryopteris celsa (log fern) is worth seeking out but seldom offered. It and *D. cristata* (crested wood fern) are both from eastern North America and very hardy. *Dryopteris arguta* (western wood fern, coastal wood fern), which occurs in Oregon and Washington, is limited to zone 7 and warmer.

Ferns in the genus *Dryopteris* are endemic to the north temperate zone. The generic name comes from the Greek *dryas* (= oak) and *pteris* (= fern), an allusion to the common habitat of northern, deciduous oak forests. Fern taxonomy is ever in flux, with genera and species shifted in and out of the various families, but for now *Dryopteris* is in the Dryopteridaceae.

Dryopteris ferns are easy to grow as long as moisture is available to them and they are located in medium shade. Some native species grow in fairly deep shade in the Georgia woods, but occasionally they occupy sites that receive considerable sun. In order to withstand any direct sun during part of the day, they must be grown in moist, fertile soil, and in the South, they must have some shade during midday and afternoon, when the sun is burning hot. They do best in a light, well-draining but constantly moist woodland soil, rich in organic matter. Acid, neutral, or slightly alkaline soils all suit these adaptable ferns. Once established, they tolerate very dry soils for extended periods. *Dryopteris* ferns make great companion plants for wildflowers, other ferns, and hostas. Planted in groups, the taller species make good background plantings.

Propagate by dividing mature rootstocks in autumn or in very early spring. Propagation by spores is also relatively easy under the right conditions. The spores must be sown as soon as they are ripe on a coarse commercial mix with a pH of 7 maintained moist at 70°F (21°C). Most species grown here have naturalized and propagate on regular Georgia red clay, on improved soil, and in the cracks between brick edgings. I simply remove young ferns where they are not wanted and transplant them.

Dryopteris ferns are prone to rusts, but I have not experienced this in my own plantings. Fungal spot and leaf gall have also been reported but have not occurred here. Insects do not bother these fern; neither do slugs or snails.

Species and cultivars listed form slowly expanding clumps. All are rugged, most hardy to zone 4, and they adapt well to the dry, hot conditions of the South.

Dryopteris affinis, golden shield fern, scaly male fern. Europe, Scandinavia south to the Alps and the Mediterranean, southwestern Asia.

LS to FS; fronds 3–4 ft. (0.9–1.2 m) tall and to 12 in. (30 cm) wide, elliptic with tapering or blunt base, produced vase-shaped on slender stalks emerging directly from a knoblike crown, covered with yellow scales, stalk clad in dark orange scales, erect, leaning with age; leaves 2-compound, light pale green fronds composed of thin leaflets (pinnae), wedge-shaped, narrow, pointed at top, 3–6 in. (8–15 cm) long and 0.8–1.5 in. (2–4 cm) wide; subleaflets deeply cut, lobed, and toothed, base blunt, tip pointed; spore cases (sori) roundish, kidney-shaped. A robust, gardenworthy fern that comes true from spores. Here in zone 7a the fronds are evergreen; further north they remain green well into winter. Hardy to zone 6 with protection; will take full sun in northern gardens. Similar but larger-growing is *Dryopteris wallachiana* from India, China, Taiwan, and southern Japan; in the wild its fronds reach to 7 ft. (2 m). Both it and *D. affinis* are beautiful, evergreen ferns for background plantings, but *D. wallachiana* has a wider spread as the tall fronds bend down.

'Congesta Cristata', Cristata Group, a crested dwarf form with congested growth; 8–10 in. (20–25 cm) tall and wide.

'Crispa', Crispa Group, dwarf, congested growth; to 8 in. (20 cm) tall and wide.

'Crispa Barnes', Crispa Group, like 'Crispa' but more open, strongly crisped, and taller, to 30 in. (75 cm).

'Cristata' ('Cristata the King'), Cristata Group, strongly crested, gracefully drooping fronds and strongly crested leaflets; to 40 in. (1 m).

'Cristata Angustata', Cristata Group, a 'Cristata' with narrower fronds, shorter leaflets; to 32 in. (80 cm).

'Cristata Grandiceps Askew', Cristata Group, strong grandiceps form with multibranched crests; to 36 in. (90 cm).

'Cristata Ramosissima Wright' ('Ramosissima'), Cristata Group, very divided branched crests, with leaflets forked repeatedly and ending in a crest; to 32 in. (80 cm).

'Furcans', Cristata Group, strong form, similar to the type but with multibranched crests; to 40 in. (1 m).

'Pinderi', a thin form of the typical species with very narrow, tapering fronds; to 28 in. (70 cm).

'Polydactyla Dadds', Cristata Group, grandiceps form with multibranched crests; to 32 in. (80 cm).

'Polydactyla Mapplebeck', Cristata Group, strong grandiceps form with wide, multibranched crests; to 40 in. (1 m).

'Revolvens', a form with leaflets curved backward and rolled under, creating tubular-shaped fronds to 32 in. (80 cm).

Dryopteris carthusiana, narrow buckler fern, spinulose wood fern, spiny wood fern, evergreen wood fern, fruitful wood fern, fancy fern. North temperate zone, Europe, eastern North America, Newfoundland west to Ontario and Iowa and in the mountains south to Georgia and Alabama.

LS to FS; fronds to 30 in. (75 cm) and 12 in. (30 cm) wide, some reaching 36 in. (90 cm) in length, produced in rosettes on slender stalks emerging directly from the rhizome, scaly and brown at the base, stiffly erect, leaning with age; evergreen but becoming deciduous in severe winter; leaves 2- to 3-compound, light lime-green or pale yellowish green, composed of 10–25 pairs of thin leaflets (pinnae), wedge-shaped, usually narrow, pointed at top, 3–4 in. (8–10 cm) long and 0.8–1.5 in. (2–4 cm) wide; subleaflets deeply cut and toothed, mostly blunt-pointed; veins forked; spore cases (sori) short, curved, sometimes horseshoe-shaped. This extremely variable species is the park fern of Europe, frequently seen planted in large groups. The North American variant known as the evergreen wood fern or fancy fern has 3-compound fronds, with finely divided subleaflets, which explains its frequent use by florists and flower arrangers. Given good soil conditions and plenty of moisture, all variants make good garden subjects, but they can be invasive. I prefer *Dryopteris affinis* or *D. filix-mas*, which are less spreading. Hardy to zone 5.

Dryopteris clintoniana, Clinton's fern, Clinton's shield fern, swamp fern. Eastern North America, Wisconsin to southern Quebec south to northwestern Georgia and northern Alabama, west to Tennessee.

LS to FS; fronds light green, to 38 in. (95 cm) tall and 8 in. (20 cm) wide, oblong, lance-shaped with long tapering tips (which distinguish it from the closely related *Dryopteris cristata*); produced in bundles on slender stalks emerging directly from a thick rhizome covered with large, glossy, blackish scales, stalk chaffish at the ground, clad in dark scales, erect, slightly leaning; leaves 2-compound, evergreen fronds composed of 10–15 pairs of leaflets (pinnae), oblong to lance-shaped, pointed tip, 3–5 in. (8–13 cm) long and 0.8–1.5 in. (2–4 cm) wide; subleaflets deeply cut, lobed, and toothed, base blunt, tip pointed; spore cases (sori) roundish, kidney-shaped, close to midrib. An outstanding, vigorous evergreen fern that requires supplemental moisture during dry periods and is better in cool northern gardens. A good specimen fern, it likes a sheltered spot that protects the tall fronds from being laid flat by high winds. Hardy to zone 4. Some consider it to be a naturally produced, perpetuating interspecific hybrid species, *D. cristata* × *D. goldiana*.

Dryopteris dilatata, broad buckler fern, mountain wood fern. North America, Eurasia, South Africa.

S to FS; fronds 12–38 in. (30–95 cm) and 4–15 in. (10–38 cm) wide, some reaching 6 ft. (1.8 m) in length, triangular with long tapering tips; produced in rosettes on slender stalks emerging directly from a thick rhizome covered with brown scales, stalk clad in brown scales, erect, slightly leaning; leaves 2-compound, evergreen fronds composed of 10–15 pairs of leaflets (pinnae), oblong to lance-shaped, pointed tip, 3–5 in. (8–13 cm) long and 0.8–1.5 in. (2–4 cm) wide; subleaflets deeply cut, lobed, and toothed; spore cases (sori) roundish, kidney-shaped, few, at tip of veins. A large, vigorous garden fern, similar to *Dryopteris carthusiana*. Hardy to zone 5. Cultivars may be better for the smaller garden.

'Crispa Whiteside' ('Crispa'), uniformly crisped fronds; to 16 in. (40 cm).

'Grandiceps', fronds with large, terminal crests; to 20 in. (50 cm).

'Lepidota', leaflets with very thin segments giving an open, lacy appearance.

'Lepidota Cristata', petioles and midrib (frond stalk) grooved and covered with yellowish brown scales, leaflets crested, appearing forked; fronds to 16 in. (40 cm) tall and 6 in. (15 cm) wide.

'Lepidota Grandiceps', similar to 'Grandiceps' with leaflets thin and crested; fronds to 16 in. (40 cm) tall and 6 in. (15 cm) wide.

'Standishii', leaflets very narrow, open appearance; to 16 in. (40 cm).

Dryopteris erythrosora, autumn fern, Japanese shield fern, copper shield fern. Southern China, Taiwan, Philippines, east to Korea and Japan.

LS to FS; fronds evergreen, coppery red when young, turning dark green, to 38 in. (95 cm) tall and 12 in. (30 cm) wide, oblong, lance-shaped with long tapering tips; produced in vase-shaped bundles on slender stalks emerging directly from a thick rhizome covered with reddish brown scales, stalk glossy reddish brown, erect, slightly leaning; leaves 2-compound, evergreen fronds composed of 8–20 pairs of leaflets (pinnae), oblong to lance-shaped, pointed tip, 3–8 in. (8–20 cm) long and 1.5–2.5 in. (4–6 cm) wide; subleaflets deeply cut, lobed, and toothed, tip pointed; spore cases (sori) roundish, kidney-shaped, in pairs. An outstanding, slow-growing, robust fern, indispensable for gardeners with limited space. New fronds emerge during late spring and early summer, providing an eye-catching mix of coppery new and older green fronds. Even the spore cases (sori) are red, hence *erythrosora* (= with red sori), often misspelled *erythrospora* (= with red spores). Established clumps withstand all kinds of weather, including long periods of heat and drought. To keep these ferns showy, provide supplemental water when the soil dries out and site in medium to full shade. The leathery fronds remain upright even during frequent spring storms, but they do appreciate a spot that shelters them from high winds. Slightly more tender than some of the native shield ferns but more hardy than originally thought; I have seen it successfully cultivated to zone 5 in sheltered areas. Variety *cystolepidota* is similar. 'Gracilis' is a highly decorative selection of the species, and 'Purpurascens' (var. *purpurascens*, *Dryopteris purpurella*) offers very red to purple coloration.

Dryopteris filix-mas, male fern. Cosmopolitan in the cool regions of North America, Europe, and Asia.

LS to FS; fronds deciduous, medium to dark green above, light to medium green beneath, 3–5 ft. (0.9–1.5 m) tall and to 20 in. (50 cm) wide, oblong elliptic, with long tapering tips; produced in vase-shaped bundles on slender stalks emerging directly from a thick rhizome covered with brown scales, stalk scaly, erect, slightly leaning; leaves 2-

compound, deciduous fronds composed of 16–30, usually 25 pairs of leaflets (pinnae), oblong to lance-shaped, pointed tip, 3–8 in. (8–20 cm) long and 1.5–2.5 in. (4–6 cm) wide; subleaflets lobed and toothed; spore cases (sori) round, kidney-shaped, very large, near midvein. An extremely variable species with many cultivars. It is easily cultivated under a variety of conditions, but moist soil and medium shade suit it best. Hardy to zone 4. *Dryopteris crassirhizoma* from Asia is similar to but not as hardy as *D. filix-mas*, probably to zone 6.

'Barnesii', a tall form with very narrow fronds, the leaflets are tilted forward with the subleaflets overlapped, giving a crisped appearance; to 40 in. (1 m) long and 6 in. (15 cm) wide.

'Bollandiae', a tall, feathery, often ill-formed but vigorous selection; 16–32 in. (40–80 cm).

'Crispa', Crispa Group, crisped fronds composed of densely overlapping leaflets and subleaflets; to 20 in. (50 cm).

'Crispa Cristata', Cristata Group, fronds crisped and crested; 12–20 in. (30–50 cm).

'Crispa Jackson' ('Cristata Fred Jackson'), Cristata Group, a tall large-crested form; to 32 in. (80 cm).

'Crispa Martindale', Cristata Group, an uncommon, tall, small-crested form with leaflets curving toward tip of frond; to 24 in. (60 cm).

'Cristata' (English crested male fern, king of the male fern), the original crested male fern developed in England, with crests on the tips of the leaflets only. It has been surpassed by cultivars that are more crested and branched.

'Decomposita', a tall, feathery form with much-divided subleaflets, appearing almost 2-compound; 24–32 in. (60–80 cm).

'Depauperata Padley', a small, dark green form with the leaflets merging and combining toward the tip of frond, 8–12 in. (20–30 cm).

'Furcans', like the typical species but with leaflets divided at the tip.

'Grandiceps Willis', large, multibranched form, tasseled terminal crests, with leaflets also tasseled at the tips; 20–28 in. (50–70 cm).

'Incisa', a huge, vigorous selection of the type, to 5 ft. (1.5 m), with fronds to 16 in. (40 cm) wide and narrow leaflets to 1.5 in. (4 cm) wide with long, narrowing tips, incised and cleft.

'Jervisii', a grandiceps form with tasseled frond tips and leaflets; to 4 ft. (1.2 m) tall.

'Linearis', very narrow, crisped, finely divided leaflets; 24–28 in. (60–70 cm).

'Linearis Polydactylon', very narrow, crisped, finely divided leaflets and branching in the frond tips and leaflets; 24–28 in. (60–70 cm).

'Lux-lunea', terminal crests and variegated leaflets; to 20 in. (50 cm).

Dryopteris goldiana, Goldie's fern, giant wood fern, Goldie's shield fern, Goldie's wood fern. Eastern North America, Wisconsin, Great Lakes region, New Brunswick to Ontario, in the mountains south to northeastern Georgia.

LS to FS; fronds shiny dark green, later bronze-tinted, leathery, to 4 ft. (1.2 m) tall and 12 in. (30 cm) wide, broadly lance-shaped with abruptly tapering tips and tapered toward base; produced in bundles on slender stalks emerging directly from a thick rhizome covered with tan scales, stalk, very scaly at base, less so further up, tan to straw-colored, erect, slightly leaning; leaves 2-compound, evergreen fronds composed of 12–16 pairs of leaflets (pinnae), oblong to lance-shaped, tapering at base and tip, pointed tip, short-stalked, backward-tilting, 4–6 in. (10–15 cm) long and 1.5–2.5 in. (4–6 cm) wide; subleaflets deeply cut, incurved margins finely toothed, base and tip blunt; spore cases (sori) roundish, kidney-shaped, widely spaced, nearer to midrib than the margin. This outstanding vigorous species (seen in photo of *Heuchera villosa*) is the giant of the native North American wood ferns. Its backward-tilting leaflets, which give it a somewhat coarse appearance, make it easily recognizable. It is rare in northern Georgia, but large colonies exist in northern states. In the South it requires supplemental moisture during dry periods but once established it is an excellent, long-lasting garden fern for the background and in a shrub border, where it uses the low branches of its neighbors as props during heavy rains. Singly, it makes good specimen fern. Hardy to zone 4, possibly 3, depending on microclimate.

Dryopteris ludoviciana, southern wood fern, sword fern, southern swamp fern, Florida swamp fern. Southeastern North America, western North Carolina south to southwestern Georgia and central Florida and coastal Alabama, Louisiana, and eastern Texas.

LS to FS; fronds shiny medium to dark green above, lighter dull green below, leathery, to 4 ft. (1.2 m) tall and 10 in. (25 cm) wide, oblong, lance-shaped with long tapering tips; produced in a row on slender stalks emerging directly from a thick rhizome covered with beige to bronze scales, stalk chaffish at the ground, clad in beige scales, erect, slightly leaning; leaves 2-compound, evergreen fronds composed of 10–15 pairs of leaflets (pinnae), fertile in the upper half of the frond with the subleaflets longer, narrower, sterile in the lower half with subleaflets shorter, wider; subleaflets oblong to broadly lance-shaped with a blunt tip; spore cases (sori) roundish, kidney-shaped, midway between midrib and margin. In its natural habitat, this vigorous species frequents cypress swamps and wet, swampy woods so requires supplemental moisture during dry periods, especially in the South. Used to heat and humidity, it is a good fern for southern gardens. Same garden uses as *Dryopteris goldiana*. Hardy to zone 7.

Dryopteris marginalis, marginal wood fern, marginal shield fern, leatherleaf wood fern, leather wood fern, evergreen wood fern, fist fern. North America, Nova Scotia west to Ontario and British Columbia, Minnesota, Wisconsin, Great Lakes region, in the mountains south to Georgia and west to Oklahoma.

LS to FS; fronds shiny dark gray to bluish green above and lighter medium green beneath, very leathery, to 36 in. (90 cm) tall and 10 in. (25 cm) wide, broadly lance-shaped with gradually tapering tips and slightly tapered toward base; produced in rosette from a large, swollen part of a thick rhizome covered with very long, to 1 in. (2.5 cm), tan to yellowish brown scales; stalk very scaly at base, less so further up, light green, leaning; leaves 2- to almost 3-compound, evergreen fronds composed of 14–22 pairs of leaflets (pinnae), fertile in the upper half, sterile below, not opposite, lance-shaped and tapering to pointed tip, 2–6 in. (5–15 cm) long and 0.8–1.2 in. (2–3 cm) wide; subleaflets deeply cut, not or barely toothed, base and tip blunt; spore cases (sori) roundish, kidney-shaped, very large and conspicuous, at the margin. An outstanding, vigorous native North American wood fern whose bluish green color and leathery substance make it an ideal accent fern for the garden. Unlike other *Dryopteris* species, which can become invasive, it remains a slowly expanding clump; its large, knobby, aboveground crown of tightly rolled-up fronds looks like a clenched fist. It appreciates supplemental moisture during dry periods, but once established it is an excellent, long-lasting garden fern: in 1970 I rescued a few clumps from a North Georgia wood that was facing development, and they still grow in my garden. Highly adaptable to acid or alkaline, light or even heavy soils, and tolerant of hot, dry summers. Hardy to zone 3.

Dryopteris sieboldii, Siebold's fern. Southern Japan, Taiwan.

LS to FS; fronds dark verdigris-green above, lighter dull grayish green below and covered with felty hair, very leathery, to 30 in. (75 cm) long and 20 in. (50 cm) wide, usually bending down and becoming semierect to subhorizontal; produced in a row on slender stalks emerging directly from a thick rhizome covered with deciduous dark brown scales; evergreen leaves composed of 3–5 pairs of entire leaflets (pinnae), fertile in the upper half of the frond, sterile beneath, usually with a single, terminal leaflet at the tip, which is sometimes forked; leaflets are 6–10 in. (15–25 cm) long and 1–1.5 in. (2.5–4 cm) wide, lance-shaped with an acutely tapering tip, somewhat sickle-shaped in outline, with margins almost smooth to lobed or scalloped or toothed and turned down at the edge, rounded at the base and short-stalked or sometimes sessile, very irregular; spore cases (sori) roundish, kidney-shaped, large and conspicuous, in 2 rows, or partially as a single row along each side of the midrib. The epithet of this most unusual fern honors German physician and plant collector Siebold. Published illustrations frequently show regularly strap-shaped fronds with incised but even margins, but the clones that have naturalized at Hosta Hill are weirdly wonderful. It is reliably evergreen here, having survived brief, nightly dips to 0°F (−18°C) with a deep, dry mulch of pine straw. I have seen it grown in zone 6 gardens, but further north, the leaflets die and new fronds emerge in spring, provided a very thick winter mulch is provided. Where it is simply too cold for too long, it can be overwintered in a pot in a cool basement. Site this peculiar fern along a path where all comers can view and admire it; it is guaranteed to be a conversation plant.

Elephantopus

A weed is sometimes defined as a plant that covers the ground and hinders the growth of superior vegetation. The crucial question for most gardeners is, what constitutes superior vegetation? In my garden, elephant's foot is one answer. I first saw *Elephantopus carolinianus*, one species I grow, during a late summer outing in northern Georgia. A large colony was making a home in a clearing, covering the ground with rosettes of textured, dark green leaves. Smaller leaves came from several nodes further up the stem, and each branch of the raceme was topped with tiny purplish flowers surrounded by three large bracts. The overall impression was that of a lilac haze floating over an emerald sea, and hoping to recreate this pleasant apparition in my own garden, I returned in autumn to collect a few seeds. These I planted in a bare spot, in good soil, but nothing came up the following spring. A few stray seeds had landed on the adjoining walk, however, and there a few small plants emerged: this species abhors fine tilth, preferring to grow on and in heavy clay. Now, years later, it still comes up here and there, sinking its taproots deep into heavy soil and enduring heat, drought, deep shade, being stepped on, and all kinds of other unpleasantries. I even paint mature plants with herbicide from time to time, something I hate to do, but this is the only way to remove them. Digging and leaving a bit of root in the ground is like trying to eliminate dandelions by pulling the top off: the root will make another plant in a hurry. It is, after all, a cultivated weed, so I watch for it during my spring cleanup walks, removing small seedlings quickly where they are not wanted. But I still grow it—I like its attractive leaves at the edge of a garden path, its small but charming flowers, its unusual stature, and its gutsy independence.

Several species are included in the genus *Elephantopus*, which name is from the Greek *elephas* (= elephant) and *podos* or *podion* (= foot). Most are available from specialty wildflower nurseries. Seed can be collected in the wild, but transplanting mature plants with deep taproots is difficult to impossible. Risk this with no wildflower, not even a weed. *Elephantopus* is classified in the Asteraceae.

Propagate by letting plants self-seed. Leave the seed on the ground or collect and sow directly where plants are wanted. Transplanting chance seedlings, which have not yet developed a taproot, is usually successful.

Neither slugs, nor snails, nor any other pest or disease seems to bother these weeds, which we, as gardeners, have the power to elevate to the status of superior vegetation . . .

Elephantopus carolinianus, elephant's foot, leafy-stemmed elephant's foot, Carolina elephant's foot, tobacco weed. Eastern North America, New England in eastern Massachusetts south to Pennsylvania, the Carolinas, Georgia, and Florida, west to eastern Alabama, southeastern Kentucky, and southern Great Lakes region.

LS to WS; flowers very small tubular florets, lilac to purple, sometimes white, with 3 heart-shaped bracts to 1 in. (2.5 cm) long and 0.6 in. (1.5 cm) wide; August–September; stems 10–36 in. (25–90 cm) tall, thin but sturdy, green to dark green and hairy, upright, branching near the top, with basal leaves elliptic to broadly lance-shaped, 4–10 in. (10–25 cm) long and 2–4 in. (5–10 cm) wide, stem leaves smaller and at the branching nodes; leaves shiny above and dull below, dark emerald-green, leathery, veins deeply impressed on top, leaf surface heavily and irregularly wrinkled and crinkled, folded along the midrib. The flowers of this "nice" weed are small but many and long-lasting, and its foliage adds season-long texture to the garden. Hardy to zone 5.

Elephantopus tomentosus, elephant's foot, tobacco weed. Eastern North America, Virginia south to Georgia and Florida, west to Kentucky, Oklahoma, and Texas.

LS to MS; flowers very small tubular florets, rose-pink to light purple fading to white, rarely all white, with 3 heart-shaped bracts to 0.5 in. (1 cm); August–September. This species is almost identical to *Elephantopus carolinianus* but has only a basal rosette of leaves and no conspicuous stem leaves. It is common in the wild but not as abundant as *E. carolinianus*. The widely available *E. nudatus* has most attractive violet flowers and basal leaves only; another southeastern species, *E. elatus*, is rarely, if ever, offered. Both are limited to the Southeast and hardy to zone 6b.

Eomecon

I first saw *Eomecon chionantha* (Chinese snow poppy) on a spring visit to a distant garden. I was bewitched by the umbrellalike, grayish green leaves offset by gracefully nodding or upright, crystalline white flowers. My host offered me a piece of it, unprompted, and proceeded to dig, and I went home the proud owner of a small clump, assured that it would grow even when ripped out of the ground in full flower. Little did I know, I was literally off to the races with this small plant. At first it sat there, losing all its flowers and leaves, but I decided not to give it up for dead. After a hot, dry summer, a few soaking autumn rains brought a new crop of leaves, and I was pleased to see this sign of life. An early hard freeze in November cut down the fresh leaves, and with the autumn cleanup, I forgot all about it. But over winter, in a soil that only rarely freezes to a depth of 3 in. (8 cm)—if at all, in mild years—the stealthy plant spread considerably, faster than I could contain it. I placed soil dug from around its periphery on the compost pile, and in short order it too sprouted snow poppies. I finally dug the entire colony, carefully removing all bits of root from the environs, and painted the still emerging leaves with a systemic herbicide. I did pot up a piece of the plant, for remembrance, and there it remains, straining at its limits, trying to escape.

I am telling this story to warn gardeners about the threat this pretty but crafty species poses in areas of mild winters. Northern gardeners need not worry—deeply freezing soil will kill it. Further south in zone 7 and even 6, however, this poppy can be a serious menace, particularly when planted in good, friable soil, and not a single, tiny piece of it should ever be discarded into the wild. Confine it to a large pot, as I now do.

Eomecon chionantha is native to eastern China, where it covers the banks of lakes and rivers, usually in full sun or light shade. The genus name is from the Greek *heoros* (= eastern) and *mekon* (= poppy); the epithet is from *chion* (= snow) and *anthos* (= flower). The genus is classified in the poppy family, Papaveraceae.

Propagate by dividing the rhizome in very early spring before growth starts. Seed can be sown in a cold frame in spring.

Slugs and snails can damage new growth emerging in spring; no other pests or diseases are reported or experienced here.

Eomecon chionantha, snow poppy, Chinese snow poppy, eastern poppy, poppy of the dawn, Chinese bloodroot. Eastern China.

LS to WS; flowers 1–5, white, shallowly bell-shaped, to 2 in. (5 cm) across, with yellow centers of 70 stamens, terminal on an open, branched flowerstalk to 16 in. (40 cm) tall; May–June; plant rhizomatous, quickly and often invasively spreading; leaf stems light green, stout, upright, in small bundles along the rhizome, 10–12 in. (25–30 cm) tall; leaves dull, leathery, dark grayish green above, light gray-green beneath, veins projected on both sides, very conspicuous below, kidney-shaped with irregularly scalloped margin and a single deep cleft at the base, to 6 in. (15 cm) long and 5 in. (13 cm) wide; sap orange-red, pungent. This charming but potentially invasive poppy makes a solid groundcover with lovely white flowers in spring. It should be planted in the ground only where it has room to expand. I do not recommend this species for small gardens; it may overpower more delicate wildflowers in the woodland border. I admire it safely embraced by a decorative container on the patio. Hardy to zone 6 with protection.

Epimedium

Epimediums, or barrenworts, are easily the most unjustly underused perennial. These modest plants have been around for years, but until recently only astute gardeners seemed to notice and plant them. Once relegated to rock gardens, they are increasingly included in woodland gardens and borders as groundcovers and fill-in plants. The genus name may be traced to *epimedion*, the Greek name for another plant, but a learned friend of mine, who treasures epimediums very much, remarked one day that it should be translated as *epi* (= above) and *medio* (= middle), that is to say "above average." I too like these wonderful plants for the shady garden, so I did not argue much with his interpretation. *Epimedium* is placed in the Berberidaceae.

Epimediums are rhizomatous, long-lived perennials native to the woodlands and shady rockeries of temperate Eurasia and the Far East. Many are evergreen, holding on to their leaves until the new growth in spring appears; in more northern regions, these may turn deciduous. A few species are in fact deciduous, but here all behave like evergreens during mild winters. The leaves arise directly from the rhizome and are compound, usually twice-compound, with one to three leaflets per division, for a total of three to nine leaflets. Each leaflet is finely toothed, emerging green, often with a bronzy tint, and colors up well in autumn. Some are heart-shaped, but lance- and arrow-shaped leaves also occur. Mature leaves are stiff and leathery. In established plants, the leaves form a contiguous canopy that makes an excellent, finely textured ground-cover. Flowers are cup- or saucer-shaped, the petals with or without spurs (distinct, horn-shaped appendages); most are quite small, but some species and cultivars are known for larger flowers, to 3 in. (8 cm). Colors range from whites and yellows, through brownish beiges, to pinks, reds, and purples. Flowering takes place in April and May.

At Hosta Hill, flowers usually emerge and open before the leaves arise in spring, and the thick canopy of old epimedium leaves should be removed beforehand so as not to obscure them. The timing of this leaf removal is crucial: it must be done just before the flowerstalks begin to rise. This happens in late March or early April here, later further north. Late frosts and freezes may cut down the young flowers once the protective old leaf canopy is removed, but waiting too long can also be detrimental, because the young flowering stems might be cut off along with the old foliage. Over the years, I have come to the conclusion that I value epimediums primarily as excellent, attractive, and weed-preventing groundcovers. I enjoy the flowers when I can early in spring, but it is the leaves I really want. My epimedium patches have survived record-low temperatures of −10°F (−23°C) at Hosta Hill; most are reliably hardy to about that. Better still, epimediums also succeed in frost-free southern areas, where little or no winter chilling occurs.

Extensive breeding in Germany and the United Kingdom has yielded hybrid cultivars that deliver outstanding garden value. My very favorite is *Epimedium ×perralchicum* 'Frohnleiten'. This truly spectacular barrenwort has larger leaves than most cultivars, mottled pink in spring and turning mottled shades of deep green later. It and many others sometimes listed as clump-forming actually form patches, covering large areas of ground given the right conditions. I have my *E. ×perralchicum* 'Frohn-leiten' in a well-mulched woodland setting underneath an azalea, where it gets medium shade; its large bright yellow flowers, borne for a few weeks on stems taller than the leaves, always receive accolades from visitors. For the remainder of the year it carpets its area with a foot-high, solid mass of splendid leaves, keeping the soil underneath moist and cool. In another area of the garden, the large, long-spurred flowers of *E. grandiflorum* 'White Queen' light up a dark corner underneath azaleas in early spring.

Epimediums can be grown in varying intensities of shade but are not sun-shy; a few of my patches take considerable southern sun in the afternoon without ill effects. They adapt to a variety of soil conditions, from pH 5.5 to circumneutral. Here they grow in clayey soils, but sandy or even rocky ground poses no obstacle to cultivation. Most epimediums favor moist conditions (some mulch is beneficial), but here even prolonged dry periods do not affect them adversely. Their ability to reliably cover level and sloping ground with dazzling foliage—and do this under all conditions of shade throughout most seasons—makes them top choice for me. Further, their modest yet beguiling floral display is definitely a bonus in spring. It is hard for me to understand why epimediums are not included in more gardens.

The genus *Epimedium* has more than doubled its former count of 20 or so species in recent years. Written records and reports are sufficient to put together brief summaries of most of these new marvels, even if actual garden experience with them is limited. Nomenclature has been a problem for both the classic species and the influx of new discoveries, but lucky for us, the acknowledged expert on the genus, Darrell Probst, is sorting through this taxonomic nightmare, and his efforts have been incorporated here. Thanks to his extensive collections, these new, often larger-flowered epimediums will soon grace Western gardens, turning unconvinced gardeners into epimedium aficionados or even fanatics.

Propagate by dividing the creeping rhizome in late autumn or very early spring. Rhizomes are very shallow in the soil, and their usually pink color is highly noticeable. Dig carefully and divide, making sure each piece has a growing tip.

In spring at Hosta Hill, solitary leafcutter bees take big chunks out of the soft barrenwort leaves;

even more widespread is the damage done by vine weevils, who scallop the leaf margins. I have not experienced any fungal diseases with epimediums, but mosaic virus is occasionally reported.

Species and cultivars listed are hardy to zone 5, unless otherwise noted. Cold hardiness of many of the newer introductions from China is not yet fully determined, but most appear to be hardy to zone 6. Unless otherwise noted, bloom period is early to mid-spring, depending upon location and microclimate; plant height is measured to the tallest point, either flowerstalk or top of leaf mound, whichever is higher. Most species and cultivars listed are rhizomatous, and their horizontal width increases constantly with the age of the plant; horizontal width is therefore not indicated in the descriptions.

Epimedium acuminatum. China, Yunnan, Sichuan.
Sun, LS to MS; flowers to 1.5 in. (4 cm), inner sepals red, petals yellow, sometimes white or light pink, with spurs; leaves divided into 3 lance-shaped leaflets, medium green mottled with pink, red, and even pink shading to yellow, later turning dark green, glaucous beneath; plant to 12 in. (30 cm) tall, slowly spreading, evergreen. This relatively new species from mountainous southwestern China is well known there for its dried roots, which are used as a male aphrodisiac. Leaves are particularly attractive in spring but contribute to the diversity of garden foliage all during the season.

Epimedium alpinum, alpine barrenwort. Southern Europe.
Sun, LS to MS; flowers 0.3–0.5 in. (0.9–1 cm), inner sepals red, petals yellow with spurs; leaves single with 5–9 heart-shaped leaflets; plant to 12 in. (30 cm) tall, spreading, evergreen; excellent for dry shade. The selection 'Shrimp Girl' is smaller, to 8 in. (20 cm), and less spreading.

Epimedium brachyrrhizum. China, Guizhou.
Sun, LS to MS; flowers to 2 in. (5 cm), bicolored, with inner sepals white and petals rose-pink; leaves divided into leaflets, medium green mottled pink; plant to 12 in. (30 cm) tall, slowly spreading, evergreen. Outstanding for its large flowers, which overtop the leaf mound. Often confused with *Epimedium leptorrhizum*: the two are almost alike above ground, but *E. brachyrrhizum* has shorter rhizomes.

Epimedium brevicornu. China, Sichuan.
Sun, LS to MS; flowers small, star-shaped, white, reflexed spurs; leaves divided into many thin leaflets, mostly medium green; plant clump-forming, deciduous, to 18 in. (45 cm) tall. One of the few deciduous species, its many leaflets make it a bushy plant in the garden. Forma *rotundatum* has more rounded leaves.

Epimedium ×*cantabrigiense*. Garden hybrid (*E. alpinum* × *E. pubigerum*).
LS to MS; flowers to 0.5 in. (1 cm), sepals bright red with yellowish petals, short spurs; leaves divided into 2 leaflets, flushed with red in spring, later dark glossy green, spiny margins; plant to 16 in. (40 cm) tall, spreading, evergreen.

Epimedium chlorandrum. China, Sichuan.
Sun, LS to MS; flowers to 1.5 in. (4 cm), soft butter-yellow; leaves divided into 3 lance-shaped leaflets, medium green mottled with red; plant to 12 in. (30 cm) tall, slowly spreading, evergreen. Outstanding for its large-spurred light yellow flowers and long, narrow leaflets, which appear in 3s with small lobes at the base. Foliage is exceptional in spring, an irregular reddish mottling over a pale, almost yellowish green base color.

Epimedium davidii. China, Sichuan.
Sun, LS to MS; flowers to 1 in. (2.5 cm), numerous, petals bright yellow with long spurs, inner sepals dark red; leaves divided into 3–5 ovate leaflets, bronze when young, later bright green; plant to 12 in. (30 cm) tall, spreading, evergreen. The showy flowers are held above the foliage, creating a bright accent in the shady garden. Some plants have insignificant inner sepals; their blooms appear to be all yellow. Several clones, some with creamy white petals, are in commerce.

Epimedium diphyllum. Japan.
Sun, LS to MS; flowers to 0.5 in. (1 cm), white, spurless; leaves divided into 2 leaflets, bright green; plant 8–12 in. (20–30 cm) tall, evergreen to semi-evergreen. Available selections include 'Nanum' (a dwarf form), 'Roseum' (rose-pink flowers), and 'Variegatum' (white-mottled or -speckled leaves in spring, turning all green by early summer).

Acanthus mollis

Acanthus spinosus flower spikes

Acanthus spinosus fruit

Acanthus spinosus 'Spinosissimus'

Achlys triphylla LYNNE HARRISON

Aconitum ×cammarum ALLAN ARMITAGE

Aconitum ×cammarum 'Bicolor' ALLAN ARMITAGE

Aconitum ×cammarum 'Spark's Variety' ALLAN ARMITAGE

Aconitum carmichaelii 'Arendsii' ALLAN ARMITAGE

Aconitum napellus 'Newry Blue' ALLAN ARMITAGE

Acorus gramineus 'Albovariegatus' backed by *A. gramineus* 'Minimus Aureus'

Acorus gramineus 'Ogon'

Actaea alba flower

Actaea alba seed

Adiantum capillus-veneris with *Polygonatum odoratum* 'Variegatum'

Adiantum capillus-veneris frond

Adiantum pedatum with *Polygonatum biflorum*

Aegopodium podagraria 'Variegatum' as a groundcover

Ajuga reptans 'Atropurpurea' in the landscape with *Hosta* 'August Moon'

Ajuga pyramidalis 'Metallica Crispa' as a groundcover

Ajuga reptans 'Jungle Beauty'

Ajuga reptans 'Valfredda' TONY AVENT

Amianthium muscaetoxicum flower spikes
DON JACOBS

Amorphophallus bulbifer inflorescence

Amorphophallus bulbifer fruit

Amorphophallus paeoniifolius inflorescence
TONY AVENT

Amorphophallus rivieri inflorescence

Amorphophallus rivieri stem

Amorphophallus rivieri fruit

Amorphophallus rivieri summer leaves with *Hosta montana* and *Polygonatum odoratum* 'Variegatum'

Anemone ×*hybrida* 'Honorine Jobert'

Anemone ×*hybrida* 'Kriemhilde'

Anemonella thalictroides ALLAN ARMITAGE

Aplectrum hyemale

Aquilegia canadensis ALLAN ARMITAGE

Aquilegia coerulea backed by *Polygonatum odoratum* 'Variegatum' ALLAN ARMITAGE

Aquilegia coerulea 'Candidissima'

Arachniodes simplicior

Arisaema angustatum var. *peninsulae* spathe

Arisaema candidissimum summer leaves with *Adiantum capillus-veneris*

Arisaema candidissimum inflorescence

Arisaema consanguineum inflorescence

Arisaema dracontium inflorescence

Arisaema fargesii inflorescence

Arisaema flavum inflorescence

Arisaema heterophyllum inflorescence

Arisaema limbatum inflorescence

Arisaema ringens inflorescence

Arisaema ringens with hostas

Arisaema saxatile inflorescence

Arisaema serratum 'Silver Pattern'

Arisaema sikokianum inflorescence

Arisaema sikokianum variegated and green leaves

Arisaema speciosum leaves

Arisaema speciosum inflorescence

Arisaema tortuosum fruit

Arisaema tortuosum inflorescence

Arisaema triphyllum, large form, with *Dicentra canadensis*

Arisaema triphyllum with five leaflets

Arisaema triphyllum inflorescence of green form

Arisaema triphyllum var. *atrorubens* with closed spathes

Arisarum proboscideum

Arisarum proboscideum inflorescence

Arum italicum 'Pictum'

Aruncus aethusifolius

Aruncus dioicus

Aruncus dioicus with *Bergenia cordifolia*

Aruncus dioicus var. kamtschaticus

Asarum arifolium

Asarum canadense

Asarum europaeum

Asarum hirsutisepalum

Asarum hirsutisepalum flowers

Asarum kumageanum

Asarum minamitanianum leaf

Asarum minor leaf

Asarum naniflorum

Asarum shuttleworthii

Asarum shuttleworthii 'Gosan Valley'

Asarum speciosum

Asarum splendens with ferns

Asarum speciosum flower

Aspidistra elatior as a mass planting

Aspidistra elatior 'Variegata'

Aspidistra elatior 'Asahi' TONY AVENT

Aspidistra elatior 'Variegata' with hostas and ferns

Aspidistra linearifolia 'Leopard'

Asplenium platyneuron

Asplenium scolopendrium

Asplenium scolopendrium 'Crispum'

Aster divaricatus

Astilbe ×*arendsii* 'Cattleya'

Astilbe ×arendsii 'Irrlicht'

Astilbe ×arendsii 'Weisse Gloria' with hostas

Astilbe chinensis 'Superba' with hostas

Astilbe biternata

Astilbe chinensis 'Visions' TONY AVENT

Astilbe simplicifolia

Astilbe japonica 'Bonn

Athyrium filix-femina var. *asplenioides*

Athyrium filix-femina 'Minutissimum'

Athyrium nipponicum 'Pictum'

Athyrium nipponicum 'Pictum' × *A. filix-femina* hybrid

Athyrium nipponicum 'Pictum' (CENTER LEFT) and *A. filix-femina* (RIGHT) with other ferns

Athyrium otophorum showing colorful young frond with more mature ones

Begonia grandis volunteers surrounding a bench in the garden; in the pot is the tender, cane-stemmed *Begonia* 'Angel Wings'

Begonia grandis flowers

Belamcanda chinensis flowers

Belamcanda chinensis fruit

Bletilla striata flower

Belamcanda flabellata 'Hello Yellow' with
Podophyllum pleianthum

Bletilla ochracea flowers TONY AVENT

Botrychium dissectum spore cluster

Bletilla striata in bloom

Botrychium virginianum var. intermedium (LEFT) and the type
(CENTER RIGHT) with Polygonatum geminiflorum

Brunnera macrophylla 'Dawson's White' HANS HANSEN

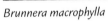

Brunnera macrophylla

Brunnera macrophylla 'Silver Wings' HANS HANSEN

Calanthe discolor 'Eco Rose' (LEFT) and 'Eco White' DON JACOBS

Campanula poscharskyana

Campanula takesimana 'Elizabeth'

Carex comans 'Frosty Curls'

Carex fraseri

Carex grayi

Carex morrowii 'Aureovariegata' with uvularias

Carex phyllocephala with fruit spikes

Carex phyllocephala 'Sparkler'

Carex plantaginea

Carex siderosticha 'Island Brocade'

Carex siderosticha 'Variegata'

Caulophyllum thalictroides

Chamaelirium luteum, emergent leafy scape of female plant (LEFT) and mature racemes of male plant (RIGHT) DON JACOBS

Chelone lyonii

Chasmanthium latifolium

Chimaphila maculata leaf

Chimaphila maculata flower

Chrysogonum virginianum

Chrysogonum virginianum 'Eco Lacquered Spider'

Cimicifuga racemosa raceme showing developing seed capsules (BOTTOM), flowers (CENTER), and buds (TOP)

Cimicifuga racemosa with hostas, lilies, and Solomon's seals

Cimicifuga simplex 'Brunette' autumn color

Claytonia virginica

Clintonia borealis as leaf cover

Clintonia borealis fruit

Clintonia umbellata in bloom

Clintonia umbellata inflorescence

Clintonia umbellata fruit

Convallaria majalis

Convallaria majalis 'Albostriata' with hostas

Cornus canadensis

Corydalis lutea backed by *Stylophorum diphyllum*

Cypripedium acaule flowers

Cypripedium acaule in bloom

Cypripedium calceolus var. *pubescens*

Cyrtomium falcatum 'Rochfordianum'

Cyrtomium falcatum 'Rochfordianum' frond

Cyrtomium fortunei with *Dryopteris sieboldii*

Cyrtomium macrophyllum frond (CENTER) surrounded by *Cyrtomium fortunei*, *Asplenium scolopendrium* (TOP LEFT) and *A. s.* 'Crispum' (BOTTOM LEFT)

Darmera peltata 'Nana'

Danae racemosa

Darmera peltata 'Nana' inflorescence

Deinanthe bifida

Dennstaedtia punctilobula

Dennstaedtia punctilobula in the woodland

Dicentra cucullaria with hostas

Dicentra eximia

Dicentra spectabilis

Dicentra spectabilis 'Gold Heart'

Disporopsis pernyi

Diphylleia cymosa

Disporopsis fuscopicta

Disporopsis fuscopicta flowers

Disporopsis pernyi flowers

Disporum cantoniense (DHHC 724) flowers

Disporum cantoniense (DHHC 724) in bloom

Disporum cantoniense 'Aureovariegata'

Disporum flavens

Disporum languinosum

Disporum sessile 'Variegatum'

Disporum sessile 'Variegatum', another degree of variegation

Disporum smilacinum

Disporum smilacinum 'Aureovariegatum' late in the season

Dodecatheon media

Dodecatheon media inflorescence

Dodecatheon media seed capsules

Dracunculus vulgaris

Dryopteris celsa

Dryopteris dilatata

Dryopteris erythrosora

Dryopteris filix-mas

Dryopteris marginalis with hostas

Dryopteris sieboldii

Elephantopus tomentosus flowers

Elephantopus tomentosus as a groundcover

Eomecon chionantha

Eomecon chionantha flower

Epimedium franchetii

Epimedium ×*perralchicum* 'Frohnleiten'

Epimedium pubigerum

Epimedium ×*versicolor* autumn color

Epimedium ×*versicolor* 'Sulphureum' as a groundcover

Epimedium ×youngianum 'Milky Way'

Erythronium americanum in early bloom

Erythronium americanum showing fully recurved sepals and petals

Farfugium japonicum 'Argentea'

Farfugium japonicum 'Aureomaculata' (LEFT) and typical species (RIGHT)

Farfugium japonicum 'Crispata'

Farfugium japonicum 'Green Dragon'

Farfugium japonicum 'Kagami Jishi' TONY AVENT

Farfugium reniforme TONY AVENT

Galax urceolata as a groundcover

Galax urceolata in bloom

Galium odoratum

Geranium endressii 'Wargrave Pink'

Geranium maculatum as a groundcover

Geranium renardii 'Terra Franche' TONY AVENT

...trifoliata

Goodyera pubescens

Hakonechloa macra 'Aureola'

Helleborus argutifolius

Helleborus argutifolius 'Janet Starnes'

Helleborus cyclophyllus with hosta

Helleborus foetidus naturalized at Hosta Hill

Helleborus foetidus inflorescence

Helleborus lividus with ferns

Helleborus foetidus 'Sopron'

Helleborus odorus leaves

Helleborus odorus in bloom

Helleborus orientalis

Helleborus ×*sternii*

Helonias bullata

Hepatica maxima LYNNE HARRISON

Hepatica acutiloba 'Eco Royal Blue' DON JACOBS

Heuchera americana 'Eco Improved'

Heuchera americana 'Pewter Veil' with Hosta 'Blue Cadet' in bloom

Heuchera villosa in full sun (note slightly wilted leaves) with
Dryopteris goldiana

Heuchera villosa 'Autumn Bride'

Heuchera 'Plum Puddin'

Heuchera 'Snow Angel'

×*Heucherella* 'Kimono' TONY AVENT

Hieracium venosum

Hieracium venosum flowers

Hostas with ferns in the woodland

Hosta fluctuans with grasses in Iwate Prefecture, Japan

Hosta montana f. *macrophylla* HANS HANSEN

Hosta montana 'Aureomarginata' HANS HANSEN

Hosta 'Alex Summers' HANS HANSEN

Hosta 'Cherish' HANS HANSEN

Hosta 'Fair Maiden' with *Helleborus foetidus* HANS HANSEN

Hosta 'Blue Angel' (BACKGROUND) with *H.* 'Midas Touch' (FRONT LEFT) and *H.* 'Tokudama Flavocircinalis' (FRONT RIGHT), edged by *H.* 'Gold Edger'

Hosta 'Blue Cadet' with *Dryopteris erythrosora*

Hosta 'Francee'

Hosta 'Gold Standard'

Hosta 'Great Expectations' with H. 'Birchwood
Parky's Gold' and a blood lily (*Haemanthus coccineus*)

Hosta 'Lakeside Neat Petite'

Hosta 'Liberty' with *Mertensia pulmonarioides* HANS HANSEN

Hosta 'Love Pat' with ferns and blooming *Rodgersia sambucifolia*

Hosta 'On Stage' HANS HANSEN

Hosta 'Ogon Koba' with *Acorus gramineus* 'Minimus Aureus'

Hosta 'Paul's Glory', spilling over brick edging, with other hostas and blooming *Rodgersia henric*

Hosta 'Sagae'

Hosta 'Spritzer' in container underplanted with *H*. 'Undulata Albomarginata' (LOWER LEFT)

Hosta 'Sultana' (TOP LEFT) and *H.* 'Silver Streak' (BOTTOM) with *Adiantum capillus-veneris*

Hosta 'Sum and Substance' (LEFT) and *H.* 'Blue Dimples' (LOWER RIGHT) backed by *H.* 'Gold Standard' and variegated azaleas

Hosta 'Sun Power' shines behind a border of green hostas

Hosta 'Titanic' HANS HANSEN

Hosta 'Tortifrons'

Hosta 'Wide Brim' (LEFT), *H.* 'Halcyon' (CENTER), and *H.* 'Antioch' (RIGHT)

Hydrastis canadensis

Hydrophyllum virginianum in bloom

Iris cristata with *Viola pubescens* var. *eriocarpa* (TOP LEFT), *Helleborus foetidus* (TOP CENTER), and *Carex siderosticha* 'Variegata' (RIGHT)

Hydrophyllum virginianum inflorescence

Iris cristata 'Powder Blue Giant' TONY AVENT

Iris tectorum in bloom

Iris tectorum flowers

Jeffersonia diphylla fruit

Kirengeshoma coreana

effersonia dubia LYNNE HARRISON

Lamium galeobdolon 'Hermann's Pride'

Kirengeshoma palmata with *Hosta* 'Amanuma'

Lamium maculatum 'Beacon Silver' with *Athyrium nipponicum* 'Pictum' as underplantings for a potted *Hosta* 'Hadspen Blue'

Lamium maculatum 'Shell Pink'

Lamium orvala

Lilium michauxii SIGI SCHMID

Lilium 'Enchantment' with hostas

Lilium 'Sun Ray' with hostas

Liriope muscari 'Silver Dragon' showing partial reversion to all green

Liriope muscari 'Variegata' with yellow margins

Liriope muscari 'Variegata' in bloom

Liriope muscari 'Variegata' as a border for a large island bed

Lobelia cardinalis showing purple coloration of new leaves

Lobelia cardinalis inflorescence

Lobelia cardinalis 'Summit Snow'

Lygodium japonicum ascending a dogwood (*Cornus florida*)

Lygodium japonicum showing finely divided fertile fronds against larger sterile fronds

Lysimachia clethroides

Lysimachia japonica 'Minutissima' as a blooming ground-cover with *Saxifraga veitchiana* (RIGHT)

Lysimachia japonica 'Minutissima' flowers

Lysimachia nummularia 'Aurea' as a groundcover fronting hostas

Matteuccia struthiopteris

Maianthemum bifolium

Mazus reptans 'Albus' as a groundcover

Medeola virginiana

Mazus reptans 'Albus' flowers

Mertensia pulmonarioides

Milium effusum 'Aureum'

Mitchella repens as a groundcover

Mitchella repens flowers

Mitella diphylla inflorescence

Mitella nuda 'Variegata'

Omphalodes verna

Mukdenia rossii DON JACOBS

Onoclea sensibilis with Woodwardia areolata (BOTTOM RIGHT), both showing sterile fronds

Onoclea sensibilis ripening spore cases

Ophiopogon japonicus

Ophiopogon japonicus 'Compactus'

Ophiopogon planiscapus 'Nigrescens'

Osmunda cinnamomea

Osmunda regalis woolly-haired fiddleheads in spring

Osmunda regalis as an accent plant

Oxalis triangularis green-leaved form

Pachysandra procumbens in spring

Pachysandra procumbens 'Eco Picture Leaf' DON JACOBS

Pachysandra procumbens gray-green summer leaves with
Disporum sessile 'Variegatum'

Pachysandra terminalis

Panax quinquefolius

Paris polyphylla

Paris polyphylla fruit

Paris verticillata with opening flower bud

Peltoboykinia tellimoides

Peltoboykinia tellimoides flowers

Peltoboykinia watanabei with *Saxifraga stolonifera* (LEFT) and *Aspidistra elatior* 'Variegata' in the background

Petasites japonicus

Phegopteris decursive-pinnata

Petasites japonicus 'Variegatus

Phegopteris hexagonoptera in the woodland

Pinellia cordata

Pinellia tripartita

Pinellia tripartita 'Polly Spout'

Pinellia tripartita 'Polly Spout' inflorescenc

Plantago major 'Variegated'

Platanthera ciliaris with *Hosta longipes* in bloom

Pleioblastus auricomus leaves

Pleioblastus auricomus in container

Podophyllum difforme

Podophyllum difforme showing a different foliar pattern

Podophyllum difforme flowers

Podophyllum hexandrum

Podophyllum hexandrum var. chinense

Podophyllum peltatum in the wild

Podophyllum peltatum underplanted with *Asarum canadense*

Podophyllum pleianthum with *Tiarella cordifolia*

Podophyllum pleianthum flowers

Podophyllum peltatum flower

Podophyllum pleianthum fruit

Pollia japonica with ferns, hostas, and *Heuchera micrantha* 'Palace Purple' (BOTTOM LEFT)

Polygonatum biflorum

Polygonatum biflorum flowers

Polygonatum biflorum fruit

Polygonatum odoratum 'Variegatum'

Polygonatum humile

Polygonatum odoratum 'Variegatum' bordering a walk, underplanted with blooming *Saxifraga veitchiana* and backed by *Lysimachia clethroides*

Polygonatum odoratum 'Striatum'

Polypodium polypodioides

Polypodium polypodioides mature and emerging fronds

Polypodium virginianum covering the face of a huge rock outcrop in a rhododendron forest

Polypodium virginianum

Polystichum acrostichoides

Polystichum polyblepharum

Polystichum ×setigerum

Polystichum tsussimense

Primula prolifera with hostas

Primula veris

Primula vulgaris

Pteridium aquilinium and the author in a forest near Uppsala, Sweden, 1984

Pulmonaria longifolia subsp. *cevennensis*

Pulmonaria officinalis 'Sissinghurst White' with *Polygonatum bi-florum* and underplanted with *Mitchella repens*

Pulmonaria longifolia 'Bertram Anderson' with *Asarum shuttleworthii* 'Callaway'

Pulmonaria longifolia 'Roy Davidson'

Pulmonaria 'Excalibur'

Pulmonaria 'Majeste' HANS HANSEN

Ranunculus repens 'Buttered Popcorn' TONY AVENT

Ranzania japonica LYNNE HARRISON

Rheum palmatum var. *tanguticum*

Rheum palmatum 'Hadspen Crimson'

Rodgersia aesculifolia in autumn ALLAN ARMITAGE

Rodgersia podophylla ALLAN ARMITAGE

Rodgersia sambucifolia with ferns and *Hosta* 'Big Daddy'

Rohdea japonica with *Polygonatum odoratum* 'Variegatum'

Rohdea japonica 'Galle'

Rohdea japonica 'Marginata' backed by *Hakonechloa macra* 'Aureola' (LEFT) and astilbes

Rohdea japonica 'Washitakakuma'
TONY AVENT

Sanguinaria canadensis

Sanguinaria canadensis flowers

Saruma henryi

Saruma henryi in bloom with *Acorus gramineus* 'Minimus Aureus'

Sauromatum venosum

Sasa veitchii

Saxifraga michauxii in bloom (RIGHT FOREGROUND) with *Trillium catesbaei* and *Vancouveria hexandra*

Saxifraga stolonifera leaves and stolons

Saxifraga stolonifera in bloom

Saxifraga umbrosa 'Aureopunctata'

Saxifraga veitchiana in bloom with emerging *Rodgersia sambucifolia*

Selaginella apoda

Selaginella braunii

Selaginella involvens

Selaginella kraussiana 'Aurea'

Selaginella uncinata

Shortia galacifolia DON JACOBS

Silene dioica 'Clifford Moore'

Silene polypetala flowers

Silene virginica

Smilacina purpurea inflorescence of white-flowered form

Silene polypetala in bloom backed by *Adiantum pedatum* with emerging *Veratrum viride* (LEFT CENTER)

Smilacina racemosa in bloom

Smilacina racemosa inflorescence

Smilacina racemosa yellow-leaved form

Smilacina racemosa fruit

Smilacina stellata

Spigelia marilandica in bloom

Spigelia marilandica flowers

Streptopus amplexifolius fruit

Stylophorum diphyllum fruit

Spiranthes cernua

Stylophorum diphyllum flowers DON JACOBS

Stylophorum lasiocarpum

Stylophorum lasiocarpum fruit

Syneilesis palmata

Thalictrum filamentosum var. *tenerum*

Thelypteris noveboracensis

Thelypteris palustris

Tiarella cordifolia 'Eco Running Tapestry'

Tiarella cordifolia 'Eco Slick Rock' leaves

Tiarella cordifolia 'Eco Slick Rock' in bloom

Tiarella cordifolia 'Elizabeth Oliver' leaves

Tiarella cordifolia 'Elizabeth Oliver' in bloom

Tipularia discolor typical leaf (RIGHT) and purple-topped leaf (LEFT)

Tipularia discolor inflorescence

Tiarella wherryi

Tradescantia ohiensis 'Alba' with *Disporopsis pernyi* (BELOW)

Tricyrtis affinis

Tricyrtis flava

Tradescantia virginiana with hostas

Tradescantia 'Sweet Kate' TONY AVENT

Tricyrtis formosana 'Amethystina'

Tricyrtis formosana 'Gates of Heaven'

Tricyrtis hirta in bloom

Tricyrtis hirta with *Hosta* 'Love Pat'

Tricyrtis hirta flowers

Tricyrtis hirta 'Albomarginata'

Tricyrtis macrantha var. *macranthopsis* flowers

Tricyrtis macrantha var. *macranthopsis* in bloom

Tricyrtis macropoda in bloom

Tricyrtis macropoda flowers

Tricyrtis oshumiensis

Tricyrtis oshumiensis flower

Tricyrtis oshumiensis leaf (LEFT) with darker leaf of *T. flava* (RIGHT)

Tricyrtis 'Kohaku'

Tricyrtis 'Togen'

Trillium catesbaei

Trillium catesbaei pink-flowered form DON JACOBS

Trillium cuneatum (BOTTOM) with *T. luteum*

Trillium erectum

rillium erectum var. *album*

Trillium grandiflorum DON JACOBS

rillium grandiflorum, showing new white flowers and older ones fading to pink, with red *T. sulcatum*
ON JACOBS

Trillium lancifolium

Trillium luteum in bloom

Trillium luteum flower SIGI SCHMID

Trillium sessile

Trillium simile in bud

lium simile flower

lium tschonoskii TONY AVENT

lium undulatum DON JACOBS

Trillium vaseyi in bloom

Trillium vaseyi flower

Tupistra chinensis leaves

Tupistra chinensis inflorescence

Tupistra chinensis fruit

Uvularia caroliniana

Uvularia grandiflora

vularia perfoliata flower

Uvularia perfoliata fruit

Uvularia sessilifolia flower

vularia sessilifolia in bloom

Vancouveria hexandra ALLAN ARMITAGE

Veratrum album ALLAN ARMITAGE

Veratrum viride with hardy geraniums and hostas ALLAN ARMITAGE

Veratrum viride inflorescence
ALLAN ARMITAGE

Veronicastrum virginicum flowering among
Lobelia cardinalis

Vinca minor in bloom ALLAN ARMITAGE

Vinca minor as a groundcover ALLAN ARMITAGE

Viola blanda

Viola pubescens var. *eriocarpa* with
Podophyllum pleianthum

Viola pedata ALLAN ARMITAGE

Viola variegata

Waldsteinia lobata

Wasabia japonica LYNNE HARRISON

Woodwardia areolata chainlike spore cases

Woodwardia areolata fertile fronds

Epimedium dolichostemon. China, Sichuan.

Sun, LS to MS; flowers to 2 in. (5 cm), bicolored, petals red, inner sepals white; leaves dark green, in spring mottled with dark greenish gray. As the Greek-based epithet indicates, long stamens are the identifying feature of this species.

Epimedium ecalcaratum. China, Sichuan.

Sun, LS to MS; flowers yellow, bell-shaped, spurless; leaves dark green; plant to 15 in. (38 cm). Still too new to be planted at Hosta Hill; I have seen photographs, and the wonderful, rich yellow flowers form cloudlike masses in early spring. Flowers are unique in that both sepals and petals form a truly bell-shaped perianth, and they are indeed, as the Latin epithet indicates, without spurs.

Epimedium epsteinii. China, Hunan.

Sun, LS to MS; flowers to 1.5 in. (4 cm), petals reddish purple with long spurs, inner sepals broad, white; leaves divided into 3 leaflets, to 3 in. (8 cm) long and 1.5 in. (4 cm) wide, glossy green; plant to 10 in. (25 cm) tall, spreading on long rhizomes, evergreen. Named for Harold Epstein, the famous plantsman. This spreading species with large, attractive flowers makes an excellent groundcover.

Epimedium fangii. China, Sichuan.

Sun, LS to MS; flowers to 1.5 in. (4 cm), petals yellow with narrow spread, inner sepals yellowish white; leaves divided into 3 leaflets, to 3 in. (8 cm) long and 2 in. (5 cm) wide, green; plant 10–12 in. (25–30 cm) tall, spreading on long rhizomes, evergreen. Named for Wen-pei Fang, the noted Chinese author who produced a detailed flora of the environs of Mt. Omei in western Sichuan province. The few flowers this species produces are nonetheless large and exquisite.

Epimedium franchetii. China, Hubei.

Sun, LS to MS; flowers to 1.5 in. (4 cm), inner sepals red to brownish red, sometimes yellowish green, petals yellow with spurs; leaves divided into 3 lance-shaped leaflets, emerging bronze, later turning medium to dark green; plant 12–18 in. (30–45 cm) tall, clump-forming, evergreen. This floriferous species has up to 20 flowers per stem, held above the leaves. Makes a good accent clump in the shady garden.

Epimedium grandiflorum, bishop's hat, longspur barrenwort. China, Korea, Japan.

Sun, LS to MS; flowers 2–3 in. (5–8 cm), with long spurs to 1 in. (2.5 cm) long, rose-colored inner sepals, cup and spurs white; leaves divided into 9 leaflets, reddish coppery when young, later light green, spiny; plant to 12 in. (30 cm) tall, slowly spreading, making large, tight patches, deciduous. Probably the best known of all epimediums and outstanding for its large flowers (hence the epithet) with very long spurs. Recent exploration of the native habitat has revealed various new forms; I am maintaining them as subspecies, but others may list them as varieties. Some subspecies produce flowers among or below the leaf crown; in mild-winter areas, where leaves are evergreen, the old leaves should be removed to expose the emerging flowers.

Subspecies *coelestre*, from mountainous Japan and hardy to zone 3, is a large form with light to greenish yellow flowers produced above the leaves; minute hairs cover both surfaces of the oval leaflets. Subspecies *higoense* from Shikoku Island in Japan is usually small, even diminutive, with much smaller white flowers; it too produces its flowers above the leaves. The leaflets are neatly margined with dark green on a light field in spring, but sadly, this marvelous show is transitory; the upper leaf surface is covered with tiny hairs. Subspecies *koreanum* is among the largest garden epimediums, as its many selections indicate; many of these have yellow or greenish yellow flowers on a mound with bright green leaves: 'Harold Epstein', with very large bright yellow flowers, forms a large clump; and 'La Rocaille', with very large yellow flowers and arrow-shaped leaves, spreads vigorously, tall, to 16 in. (40 cm).

Many of the several cultivars in the *Epimedium grandiflorum* complex produce a second flush of taller leaves after flowering. Consult catalogs for the latest listings.

'Crimson Beauty', dark red flowers with white-tipped spurs, leaves tinted dark bronze in spring.

'Elfenkönigin' ('Queen of Elfs'), large white flowers with long, white spurs, to 2 in. (5 cm); vigorous.

'Koji', dwarf with deep lavender flowers.

'Lilafee' ('Lilac Fairy'), dark lilac flowers, purple-tinted leaves in spring.

'Nanum', dwarf with white flowers.

'Queen Esta', dark lavender flowers, purple-tinted leaves in spring.

'Red Queen', vivid rose-red flowers, large, to 14 in. (35 cm).

'Rose Dwarf', dark rose-pink flowers with spurs, the unusually shaped leaflets are bright green and thinly lance-shaped with a long, tapering tip; small plant.

'Saxton Purple', dark reddish purple flowers with broad white-tipped spurs; leaves tinted dark reddish bronze in spring.

'Silver Queen', silvery white flowers with long spurs, inner sepals flushed rose-pink.

'Sirius', rose-pink flowers above bright, light green leaflets.

'Tama-no-Genpei' (= jewel of Genpei), large dark red-purple inner sepals with white petals fading to lavender on the spurs.

'Violaceum' (f. *violaceum*, var. *violaceum*), dark violet flowers with white-tipped spurs, leaves tinted dark bronze in spring.

'White Queen', very large white flowers with long, white spurs, to 2 in. (5 cm), leaves tinted dark bronze in spring.

'Yubae' ('Rose Queen'), dark rose-pink flowers with white-tipped spurs, leaves tinted dark bronze in spring.

Epimedium leptorrhizum. China, Guizhou.
LS to MS; flowers to 1.5 in. (4 cm), white with broad, whitish pink petal-like spurs that spread widely; leaves divided into 3 leaflets, ovate lance-shaped leaflets, bronze when young, later green, conspicuously veined; plant to 8 in. (20 cm) tall, slowly spreading, evergreen. This vigorous species is being used for hybridizing in England.

Epimedium myrianthum. China.
LS to MS; flowers 0.3–0.5 in. (0.9–1 cm), white inner sepals with dark yellow to brownish yellow petals, very numerous, to 100 per stem; leaves divided, glossy green lightly flecked with pink; plant to 24 in. (60 cm) tall, slowly spreading, evergreen. Although the flowers of this species are tiny, it is remontant (reblooming) and floriferous—very gardenworthy.

Epimedium ogisui. China, Sichuan.
LS to MS; flowers to 1.5 in. (4 cm), 5–12, broad, petal-like inner sepals, white to pinkish white, pet-als white with narrow spurs, produced above the leaves and held in the upper parts of horizontally arranged stems; leaves divided into 3 leaflets, ovate, green, emerging reddish bronze in spring; plant to 10 in. (25 cm) tall, slowly spreading on long rhizomes, evergreen. Named for renowned Japanese botanist Mikinori Ogisu.

Epimedium pauciflorum. China, Sichuan.
LS to MS; flowers to 1.5 in. (4 cm), broad, inner sepals lilac, medium, petals white, streaked with pink, with long spurs, produced above the leaves; leaves divided into 3 leaflets, ovate, green; plant to 8 in. (20 cm) but usually smaller, slowly spreading on long rhizomes, evergreen. Another of the recent accessions from western China, rare but available.

Epimedium ×perralchicum. Garden hybrid (*E. perralderianum* × *E. pinnatum* subsp. *colchicum*).
Sun, LS to MS; flowers to 1 in. (2.5 cm), bright yellow on short stems; leaves divided, green; plant to 16 in. (40 cm) tall, spreading, evergreen.

'Frohnleiten', with flowers to 2.5 in. (6 cm), bright lemon-yellow, held on 16 in. (40 cm) stems, leaves divided bipinnate into 3 leaflets, each with 1–3 large, heart-shaped, lobed leaflets, mottled reddish pink when young, later dark, glossy green, deeply veined, with large spines along wavy margin; plant to 12 in. (30 cm) tall, slowly spreading, making large, open patches. Outstanding garden plant—a few small starts have made sizeable colonies at Hosta Hill. The large, wavy leaflets are particularly attractive in spring, when their strongly mottled appearance approaches variegation.

'Wisley', huge flowers to 3 in. (8 cm) across, sepals and petals bright yellow, spurs tinged reddish or brownish, held on stems to 16 in. (40 cm) tall; luxurious foliage.

Epimedium perralderianum. North Africa, Algeria.
Sun, LS to MS; flowers to 1 in. (2.5 cm), bright yellow, on 12 in. (30 cm) stems; leaves divided bipinnate, each with 3 heart-shaped leaflets, shiny green, with spiny, wavy margin; plant to 12 in. (30 cm) tall, slowly spreading. In cultivation since the 1860s, this species is in the background of many good garden hybrids. Hardy to zone 7, 6 with good protection. The selection 'Weihenstephan' spreads faster and has larger leaves and flowers and deeper green, wavy leaflets.

Epimedium pinnatum. Northern Iran.

Sun, LS to MS; flowers to 0.75 in. (2 cm), inner sepals expanded, broad in the lower half, yellow; petals very small dark reddish to brownish purple with minuscule red spurs, flowers produced above the leaves; leaves divided into 3–9 ovate leaflets, medium to dark green; plant 8–12 in. (20–30 cm) tall, slowly spreading; evergreen, drought-resistant. Subspecies *colchicum* from Turkey and the Caucasus spreads faster and has larger leaves and flowers and deeper green, wavy leaflets; its f. *concolor* has yellow spurs.

Epimedium pubescens. China, Sichuan, Anhui, Shaanxii.

LS to MS; flowers small, inner sepals white, petals yellow, tinged reddish to brownish, with short spurs, produced above the leaves; leaves divided into 3 leaflets, ovate, green; plant clump-forming, large, to 24 in. (60 cm), compact rhizomes, evergreen. Very floriferous and remontant (reblooming).

Epimedium pubigerum. Eastern Balkans, northern Turkey, southern Caucasus.

Sun, LS to MS; flowers to 1.5 in. (4 cm), creamy white to pale yellow, on 20 in. (50 cm) stems, well above the leaves; leaves divided into 9 or more round to ovate, heart-shaped medium green, shiny leaflets with leathery substance; plant to 10 in. (25 cm) tall; evergreen, drought-resistant; floriferous, to 30 flowers per stem.

Epimedium rhizomatosum. Southwest China.

LS to MS; flowers to 0.75 in. (2 cm), petals yellow with short spurs and reddish inner sepals, borne on 18 in. (45 cm) stems; leaves divided, ovate, lance-shaped, glossy green, spiny, glaucous coating below; plant to 15 in. (38 cm) tall, quickly spreading; evergreen; outstanding for its floriferous habit, up to 50 flowers per stem.

Epimedium ×rubrum, red barrenwort. Garden hybrid (*E. alpinum* × *E. grandiflorum*).

LS to MS; flowers to 0.75 in. (2 cm), inner sepals bright red with yellowish petals, short spurs; leaves with 2 leaflets, flushed with red in spring, later dark, glossy green, spiny margins; plant to 16 in. (40 cm) tall, spreading, evergreen. Known since 1854. 'Cobblewood Form' is a vigorous cultivar with a more pinkish cast to the flowers, which are produced well above the more rounded leaves; inner sepals are rose-red with the spurs cream-colored.

Epimedium sagittatum. China, Hubei, Japan.

LS to MS; flowers to 0.5 in. (1 cm), white inner sepals with tiny brownish, cupped petals; leaves divided into 3 spear-shaped leaflets, glossy dark green, to 6 in. (15 cm) long; plant clump-forming, 10–20 in. (25–50 cm) tall, evergreen. Outstanding for its striking foliage.

Epimedium sempervirens. Japan.

Sun, LS to MS; flowers to 0.75 in. (2 cm), with spurs, inner sepals white flushed rose, cup and spurs white, to 10 flowers per stem; leaves divided into 9 leaflets, edged pink when young, green later, spiny; plant to 10 in. (25 cm) tall, slowly spreading, evergreen. A variegated form is known, showing white splashings in the leaflets early, becoming all green later.

'Aurora', dwarf form to 6 in. (15 cm), dark lavender flowers.

'Candy Hearts', inner sepals broad pale pink, petals pink, tinged green; leaflets heart-shaped, flushed pink in spring, dark green later.

'Hanaguruma', large violet flowers; large lance-shaped leaflets. Also offered as *Epimedium sempervirens* (violet form).

'Mars', inner sepals dark rose-pink, petals purple, long, pink spurs with white at the tips; leaflets mottled bronze in spring, dark green later.

'Vega', pure white flowers; leaflets flushed with rose in spring, later green, very glossy in spring, remaining so until late season.

'Violet Queen', large violet flowers; leaflets flushed with rose in spring, later green.

'White Purity', pure white flowers, produced below leaves; large leaves.

Epimedium stellulatum. China, Hubei, Shaanxi.

LS to MS; flowers to 0.5 in. (1 cm), white inner sepals with reddish orange (bronze) petals, spurless, starlike, numerous, up to 40; leaves divided into 2 leaflets, flushed pink in spring turning medium green, glossy, spiny; plant to 12 in. (30 cm) tall, evergreen. 'Wudang Star', with more contrasting brownish petals and lavish flowering habit, is a superb clonal selection.

Epimedium sutchuenense. China, Sichuan.

Sun, LS to MS; flowers to 0.75 in. (2 cm), white flushed with purple inner sepals, petals reddish purple, long spurs, to 20 flowers per stem; leaves divided into 2 leaflets, heart-shaped, glossy, mottled pink when young, later light green, spiny; plant to 12 in. (30 cm) tall, slowly spreading, evergreen.

Epimedium ×versicolor. Garden hybrid (*E. grandiflorum* × *E. pinnatum* subsp. *colchicum*).

LS to MS; flowers to 0.8 in. (2 cm), sepals bright red to orange with spurred yellowish petals on 14 in. (35 cm) stems; leaves divided into 5–13 ovate, heart-shaped leaflets, flushed with bronze in spring, later medium green, spiny margins; plant to 12 in. (30 cm) tall, slowly spreading, evergreen.

'Cupreum', coppery red flowers.

'Neosulphureum', bright yellow flowers.

'Sulphureum' (*E. macranthum* var. *sulphureum*), larger, vigorous, darker yellow flowers, longer spurs, leaflets speckled brown.

'Versicolor', reddish orange flowers fading to a very pale salmon; leaflets green blotched red in spring, green later; vigorous.

Epimedium ×warleyense. Garden hybrid (*E. alpinum* × *E. pinnatum* subsp. *colchicum*).

LS to MS; flowers to 0.5 in. (1 cm), inner sepals bright reddish orange, petals yellow, sometimes tinted brown; leaves divided into 5–9 ovate leaflets, flushed with reddish pink in spring, later medium green, turning orange in autumn; plant to 20 in. (50 cm) tall, slowly spreading, evergreen. If your color preference is toward orange flowers, look for these cultivars. 'Orangekönigin' ('Orange Queen') has deeper orange flowers and is clump-forming rather than spreading; good for situations where a spreading habit would interfere with adjacent plantings.

Epimedium wushanense. China, Sichuan.

LS to MS; flowers to 0.5 in. (1 cm), white to yellowish white, sometimes pinkish small inner sepals, petals condensed into very long, recurving light orange spurs, numerous, 50–100 flowers, on tall stems, usually to 36 in. (90 cm), rarely to 4 ft. (1.2 m); leaves divided into 3 leaflets, elongated, arrow-shaped, to 6 in. (15 cm) long and 1.5 in. (4 cm) wide, mottled with purple in spring turning medium green, spiny-margined; leaf crown to 24 in.

(60 cm) tall, evergreen. Revolutionary. Its truly unusual flowers will surely give rise to new hybrid epimediums for the garden.

Epimedium ×youngianum. Garden hybrid (*E. diphyllum* × *E. grandiflorum*).

LS to MS; flowers to 0.75 in. (2 cm) or smaller, with or without spurs, from white to rose, some to purple; leaves divided into 3–9 narrowly ovate leaflets, flushed with reddish pink in spring, later medium green, toothed, wavy margins; plant to 20 in. (50 cm) tall, slowly spreading.

'Azusa', larger, white flowers with long spurs; leaves lastingly silvery on top.

'Beni Kuyaku', rose-red flowers with inner sepals and petals of similar shapes, resulting in a double-flowered look.

'Fukurasuzume', white inner sepals pink-suffused, petals drooping, spurless; plants are large, to15 in. (38 cm).

'John Gallagher', pale rose flowers.

'Merlin', purple flowers held above foliage.

'Milky Way', pure white flowers with long spurs; leaves silvery on top.

'Niveum' (*Epimedium macranthum* var. *niveum*) has pure white flowers, sometimes spurred; purple-tinted leaves in spring.

'Pink Blush', whitish flowers distinctly flushed rose-pink; a dainty plant, not more than 6 in. (15 cm) in height.

'Roseum' (*Epimedium liliacinum*, *E.* 'Liliacinum'), pale violet to very pale purple flowers.

'Yenomoto' has the largest white flowers; the inner sepals and spurs are very long.

Epipactis

These hardy woodland orchids, native to the Americas and Eurasia, are among the easiest to grow in temperate gardens. The genus has been known for thousands of years; the generic name is in fact the classical Greek name for these terrestrial orchids. Many of the approximately two dozen species are hardy enough for gardens in zone 6 and warmer; in colder areas they can be potted and overwintered inside. The flowers, with spurless lips, are borne on tall, sometimes twisted stalks and appear in colors ranging from yellowish white to greenish brown, orange-red, deep wine-red, and purple. The leaves are lance-shaped and heavily pleated, providing season-long texture for the shady garden. Unlike other unassuming and often overlooked native hardy orchids, *Epipactis gigantea* (giant helleborine) stands tall and is hard to ignore. Other helleborines, as these orchids are commonly called, are equally outstanding and make a prominent display while in flower, usually in late spring or early summer. The best and easiest for moist garden spots are *E. gigantea* and *E. palustris*; I grow these two species and find them to be of relatively easy culture. They require light to medium shade (in the hot South, deep shade) and will spread and colonize in a fertile, humus-rich, deep, and constantly moist soil with a pH of 6.5 to 7 (I sweetened mine up by adding some dolomitic limestone). They dislike being planted too deep. The soil must be kept moist during dry periods. Helleborines mix well with moisture-loving native wildflowers and are great in the moist woodland or even in a bog garden. *Epipactis* is classified in the Orchidaceae.

Propagate by carefully dividing the rhizome after flowering, leaving at least one growing tip on each piece. Seed is microscopic, and seed propagation difficult therefore.

Slugs and snails can be a scourge during latewinter warm-ups, when the foliage begins to emerge. No other pests or diseases bother these native orchids here.

Epipactis atrorubens, broad-leaved helleborine, darkred helleborine. Europe east to the Caucasus, Asia Minor.

LS to MS; flowers 10–25, small, ruby-red to reddish purple, sometimes amber petals and sepals, triangular, to 0.5 in. (1 cm) across; lip with dark green margin, spotted red, short, 2-parted, with a heart-shaped, recurved top, on leafy racemes; June–August; plant rhizomatous, slowly creeping, spreading; stem upright, 10–32 in. (25–80 cm) tall, red-tinged green, often coated with fine hairs, sometimes smooth; leaves 3–10, green, often red-tinged, pleated and broadly lance-shaped, keeled in the center, stem-clasping, spiralling, large and broad toward base, smaller and bractlike toward the top. A high-elevation, lime-loving species, and a challenge even for experienced gardeners in cool, northern gardens; it quickly expired in the hot climate of Hosta Hill. Requires a rocky but well-draining alkaline soil. Suitable for elevated and cooler regions, hardy to zone 6, 5 with protection.

Epipactis purpurata (violet helleborine) from Europe is similar but rarely available.

Epipactis gigantea, giant helleborine, giant orchid, giant stream orchid, chatterbox. Southwestern North America south to northwestern Mexico.

LS to MS; flowers 3–15, larger, greenish yellow or green, sepals flushed purple, tepals veined with brownish purple, triangular, to 1 in. (2.5 cm) across; lip strongly veined and lined with purple or brownish red, short, 2 side lobes yellow, with reflexed, orange top lobe, on leafy, one-sided raceme, each flower subtended by a leafy bract; June–August; plant rhizomatous, slowly creeping, spreading; stem upright, 10–36 in. (25–90 cm) tall, green; leaves alternate, 4–12, green, pleated and keeled along the midrib and broadly lance-shaped, to 8 in. (20 cm) long, stem-clasping, smaller toward the raceme. The easiest helleborine for gardens and also one of the most ornate, with larger flowers than other species. Try this one first. I have seen this stream orchid in naturalized conditions in botanic gardens in Switzerland; gardeners as far north as zone 4b have tried it with some success. It makes itself at home as long as moist conditions are maintained. 'Serpentine Night', a very desirable selection, has dark red stems and leaves. The scarce *Epipactis veratrifolia* (marsh helleborine) from the eastern Mediterranean and Asia is similar but much too tender for most temperate zone gardens, suitable only to zone 8 and warmer.

Epipactis helleborine, helleborine, bastard helleborine. Eurasia.

LS to MS; flowers 10–50, very small, sepals green flushed purple, petals pale green to pink; lip bottom concave, forming a sac with green interior, flushed purple outside, 2 basal projections, top broadly heart-shaped, yellowish, pink or purple; July–August; plant rhizomatous, creeping, sometimes strong-spreading; stem upright, 40 in. (1 m) tall, green; leaves spirally arranged, 3–10, green, pleated and keeled along the midrib and broadly elliptic, 2–6 in. (5–15 cm) long and 1–4 in. (2.5–10 cm) wide, stem-clasping, smaller toward the raceme. This vigorous orchid has naturalized in fertile ground in southeastern Canada, New England, and locally in the District of Columbia, Missouri, and other places. Considered weedy by some. With marshy ground and plenty of moisture during summer, it does spread but never aggressively so, and the offending rhizomes are easily removed. This stream orchid is of easy culture, and its escape into the wilds of North America testifies to its cold hardiness, to zone 6, 5 with protection. The most important ingredient for success is moisture and, for this species, a slightly acid soil. Very small and unexciting flowers, but its leaves add considerable texture to the garden. For showy flowers, I prefer to plant *Epipactis gigantea*.

Epipactis palustris, marsh helleborine. Europe.

LS to MS; flowers 4–18, large, 0.8 in. (2 cm) across, nodding, sepals gray-green to deep reddish brown with red interior, petals creamy yellow, marked or lined with maroon; lip wavy, lined in deep pink inside, with orange spots and the top broad, whitish with yellow at the base, on leafy raceme; July–August; plant rhizomatous, slowly creeping, spreading; stem upright, 10–20 in. (25–50 cm) tall, green; leaves 4–9, spirally arranged, green, hairy, pleated and keeled along the midrib and lance-shaped, 2–6 in. (5–15 cm) long and 1–1.5 in. (2.5–4 cm) wide, stem-clasping, smaller toward the raceme. Floriferous and often considered the prettiest helleborine. Hardy to zone 7a, 6b with protection.

Eranthis

Winter aconites are shade garden plants. I am using the plural because one tuber is never enough: to make any kind of significant planting, it is necessary to buy dozens of them—not out of the question given the very low cost of the tubers. I have tried several species, even those that did not become permanent features in my small garden. It is a lot of fun to see how plants perform and what their idiosyncrasies are in a cultivated environment. Mother had a whole patch of *Eranthis hyemalis* 'Glory' in her garden, and I still remember the outstanding yellow mass of flowers. From her back window, it looked like a gallon of bright yellow paint spilled on the edge of the lawn, still dormant from the winter cold. One autumn she sent me a bunch of tubers, which I planted in the shade under an open-limbed Oregon grape holly (*Mahonia aquifolium*). I was surprised to see the first flowers in the middle of our mild winter, just in time to bloom in concert with the grape holly's gracefully

bunched and drooping yellow candles. But as quickly as the winter aconites appeared, so did they vanish, and by the time the birds were fighting over the grape holly's blue berries there was not a trace of them left. Over several seasons, they showed up, but even self-seeding did not contribute to any kind of persistence. Finally I removed the stragglers and gave the space over to native ferns and wildflowers.

Winter aconites do not like to be disturbed and prefer a neutral or even slightly alkaline soil. My soil was way too acid for them, and our relatively warm winters and dry, hot summers did not agree with them either; my planting in zone 7a was never as lush as Mother's in zone 5, and they do well into zone 4. Also, under shrubs and trees my soil dries up quickly, and winter aconites require a moist soil during their rest period. I remember Mother lifted them from time to time, to separate the tubers, and she replanted them right away so as not to dry them out. This is also a good way to get rapid increase, although under good culture, winter aconites seed freely. They have naturalized in many areas of the world, including parts of North America.

It is not my intention to discourage gardeners from planting winter aconites. For those with plenty of room, they make a wonderful early-spring display. They do not, however, provide the one thing I demand from my shade plants: showy leaves throughout the season, the greens and textures that have transformed Hosta Hill into the shady, restful paradise I wanted it to be. The genus gets its name from the Greek *ar* (= spring) and *anthos* (= flower); it is classified in the Ranunculaceae.

In mild winter regions, early-rising slugs and snails may eat some of the leaves, but leaves are so abundant, no harm is really done. Leaf smut has also been reported. None of these problems would be serious enough to remove them from my want list. In the final analysis, what ousted the winter aconites from my garden was their disappearing act. I hope Mother looks down and forgives me.

Erythronium

Easily one of the daintiest and most charming North American wildflowers, *Erythronium americanum* is abundant in the higher elevations of the Great Smoky Mountains, where I have seen large colonies in April. At Hosta Hill, its nicely mottled, shiny leaves and bright yellow blossoms arrive early, sometimes during the last days of February, and long before the late freezes of spring in April and May. Although frost-resistant to a degree, the flowers usually get cut down. Mother called the plants she grew trout lilies (she preferred that name because my father liked trout fishing). Some say the name came from the Cherokee Indians, who noted the lily's flowering time coincided with the time trout were running in the streams; others claim the name derived from the mottling of the leaves, which brings to mind the speckled brook trout. American Indians used the leaves in a salve to treat ulcers and as a potherb, the cooked tubers as a food starch, and the raw tubers as an emetic.

I liked this and other species of trout lilies in Mother's garden (she always planted shallow-rooted, autumn-flowering annuals to cover the bare spots) but dislike their ephemeral nature here in the South. In the North the leaves last well into summer, providing a nice display, but in warm regions, trout lilies go summer-dormant. A few of my Southern friends grow them nevertheless, treating them as annuals and purchasing new tubers each fall. Further north, the available hybrids' later emergence makes them good garden subjects; they can be interplanted with later-arriving hostas and other perennials, which will cover the spots they leave vacant. The best way and place to plant trout lilies may be as individual groups in the open woodland garden, where the ground does not have to be solidly covered with vegetation and bare spots are natural. But gardens have gotten smaller, leaving few people with the space for large woodland gardens. As one of the early harbingers of spring, trout lilies are definitely worth considering—if a suitable place can be found for them and their ephemeral nature is duly considered.

Trout lilies inhabit deciduous forests at higher elevations in open meadows with considerable early-spring sunshine. They will not tolerate medium to full shade and require fairly cool, constantly damp soil with a pH of 5 to 6. In gardens they prefer an open site with some sun in light or dappled woodland shade. The eastern North American species may be used in more shady situations, but many gardeners complain that they are shy to flower. Hardy to zone 4, some to zone 3. *Erythronium* gets its name from *erythros* (= red), alluding to the reddish brown marbling of the leaves.

The genus is classified in the lily family, Liliaceae.

Propagate by taking offsets or dividing clumps after flowering. Replant divisions or tuber immediately and do not let them dry out. Up to four years are required to produce flowering plants from seed.

I have not seen any disease or insect damage, but rusts, smut, and leaf spot are reported. Slugs and snails can disfigure new growth in spring.

Erythronium americanum, yellow trout lily, yellow adder's tongue, amberbell, yellow fawn lily. Eastern North America, Ontario to New Brunswick and Nova Scotia, south through New England to Georgia and Alabama, west to Tennessee, Arkansas, and Oklahoma, north to Minnesota.

Some sun, LS; flowers 1–1.5 in. (2.5–4 cm) across, solitary, bright sulfur-yellow inside, spotted at base, with 3 recurving petal-like sepals, brownish purple on the outside, and 3 recurving petals with a reddish brown or purple streak, 6 long stamens with yellow or reddish brown anthers, stem 4–10 in. (10–25 cm) tall; late February–early May; plant herbaceous, summer-dormant, slowly spreading, rhizomatous, forming colonies; leaves elliptic, usually 2, basal, erect, shiny dark green mottled with brownish red and grayish green, 3–8 in. (8–20 cm); fruit, egg-shaped capsule with a dimple at its tip. One of the most common early-spring flowers in eastern North America. One local variant has amber flowers. *Erythronium umbilicatum* is in most respects identical except that its fruit has a small beak at its tip, rather than a dimple; reaching into the deciduous woods of South Georgia, it is better adapted to southern gardens but ephemeral nevertheless. *Erythronium albidum* (white trout lily, blonde lilian, white dogtooth violet) has leaves that are narrower and not as prominently mottled and white to pinkish white flowers, purple-tinged on the outside and yellow at the base inside, with yellow anthers; here it flowered better and more reliably than *E. americanum*. The more northern *E. propullans* (Minnesota adder's tongue) has pink flowers.

Erythronium californicum, California fawn lily. Western North America, Coast Ranges of northern California and Oregon.

Some sun, LS; flowers 1–2 in. (2.5–5 cm) across, 2–3 per stem, creamy white with dark orange center markings, with 3 recurving petal-like sepals and 3 petals, 6 long stamens with white anthers, stem 6–14 in. (15–35 cm) tall; April–May; plant herbaceous, bulbous; leaves elliptic, usually 2, basal, erect, lightly mottled brownish green, 1.5–3 in. (4–8 cm) long. This common western species has a relative in central California, *Erythronium tuolumnense* (mother lode trout lily), with up to 7 bright yellow, greenish-lined flowers per flowerstalk; *E. helenae*, *E. citrinum*, and *E. howelii* are also very similar but rarely available. The western species share overlapping habitats and have specialized growing conditions that make them less fitting for eastern gardens. Species from the sunny slopes in western mountain ranges go summer-dormant early and require a fairly long rest period; these include *E. grandiflorum* (glacier lily, avalanche lily, lamb's tongue fawn lily) and *E. hendersonii* from northwestern California and southwestern Oregon, and *E. multiscapoideum* (Sierra fawn lily) from the Sierra Nevada, with multibranched flowerstalks. Other western species are *E. oreganum* from British Columbia south to Oregon, which has wide, flattened filaments but is otherwise similar to *E. californicum*, *E. purpurascens* (purple fawn lily), and *E. revolutum* (western trout lily, mahogany fawn lily) and its pink-flowered var. *johnsonii* from Vancouver Island to northern California. Cultivars of *E. californicum* include 'Pink Beauty' (deep pink flowers that shade to lavender) and the vigorous 'White Beauty' (white flowers with a dark orange throat).

Erythronium dens-canis, dogtooth violet, Asian dogtooth violet, European dogtooth violet, short trout lily. Eurasia.

Some sun, LS; flowers 1.2–1.5 in. (3–4 cm) across, solitary, white, pinkish white, or lilac, with sharply recurved petal-like sepals and 3 petals, and 6 long stamens with purple or deep lilac anthers, 4–6 in. (10–15 cm) tall; late February–early May; plant herbaceous, bulbous; leaves elliptic, usually 2, basal, erect, shiny medium green, 4–6 in. (10–15 cm) long. The first species described in the genus and the one that gave rise to the name dogtooth violet, a translation of its epithet and a reference to the tuber's shape. A very low-growing species with short flowerstalks; site carefully so that its flowers will not be overshadowed by taller neighboring plants. Hardy to zone 2, but unfortunately its heat tolerance is limited: in areas warmer than zone 7, it

is short-lived, lacks vigor, and goes summer-dormant very early.

'Album', pure white flowers.

'Carneum', pink flowers.

'Charmer', white flowers tinged deep red; taller than the type, to 12 in. (30 cm).

'Frans Hals', mottled leaves and larger, light purple flowers.

'Lilac Wonder', small purple flowers with a deep brown spot at the base of the tepals, showing up like a ring of darker color.

'Niveum', white flowers.

'Pink Perfection', larger, true pink flowers to 2 in. (5 cm) across; flowers early.

'Purple King', mauve to bluish purple flowers edged with white and marked with a deep brown in the center; leaves intensely mottled.

'Rose Queen', deep rose-pink flowers; leaves mottled.

'Snowflake', pure white flowers; leaves mottled.

'White Splendor' ('White Splendour'), white flowers with a dark brown or blackish purple center; flowers early.

Erythronium cultivars

All require cool soil and some shade. Hardy to zone 4, best in zones 5 and 6.

'Citronella', bright lemon-yellow flowers with darker yellow anthers, up to 10 flowers per stem, which is 8–14 in. (20–35 cm) tall; leaves shiny, mottled with reddish bronze; similar to 'Pagoda' but flowers later.

'Joanna', creamy yellow flowers flushed pink, up to 8 flowers per stem, which is 10–12 in. (25–30 cm) tall; leaves mottled with dark brown.

'Kondo', sulfur-yellow flowers with darker yellow anthers and reddish brown shading in the center, 3–8 flowers per stem, which is 7–14 in. (18–35 cm) tall; leaves mottled with reddish bronze, but mottling fades after flowering.

'Pagoda', sulfur-yellow flowers with deep yellow anthers and brown centers, 4–10 flowers per stem, which is 6–14 in. (15–35 cm) tall; leaves dark green, glossy, mottled with bronze; a vigorous, popular hybrid cultivar.

Farfugium

Many gardeners are ill at ease trying to vocalize (or even recall) strings of syllables like *Ligularia tussi-*

laginea or *Farfugium tussilagineum*, both binomials applied to a species known as leopard plant. Now it is properly *F. japonicum*, the name originally bestowed by renowned English botanist John Lindley, but I call all forms of this species leopard plant —spots or no spots. Typically it has large, glossy green, umbrellalike leaves with a host of round yellow spots of different sizes, hence the common name; the yellow flowers, held high above the handsome foliage, add a dazzling accent to the late fall garden. In the frigid North, this plant is sold as a houseplant; Mother kept her potted specimen out on the shady patio during the warm season. It did not occur to me to try it in the open garden until I spied the variegated *F. japonicum* 'Argentea' in a North Carolina garden, surrounded by blue hostas and backed by tall, black-stemmed lady ferns; I was told it stayed in the ground during winter, protected by a thick layer of pine straw. I now grow *F. japonicum* and three of its cultivars, including 'Argentea'. All are potted in sterile potting soil. The sterile soil deters smut, black spot, and other fungal diseases to which leopard plants are subject and initially eliminates slugs and snails; potting permits the leaves to overwinter intact, thus giving the plants a headstart in spring. I sink the pots into the ground during the warm season and overwinter them in my cold but frost-free garage, bringing a few in as houseplants. Obviously, gardeners in colder regions where the ground freezes solid can do likewise and enjoy these marvelous, leafy plants all year. Keeping them in pots also allows me to change their positions every spring, and they are great for filling spots left vacant by summer-dormant ephemerals; in such spots, instead of burying them in the ground, I set them on top of it. Wherever they are sited, all elicit questions and expressions of admiration from visitors. To me, they are ideal foliage plants for a shady garden, adding charm, texture, and color.

Leopard plants tolerate deep shade and should not be exposed to the heat of the midday sun, which wilts the leaves considerably. Medium shade is ideal. The soil should be fertile, well-draining, friable, and sterile. A constantly moist soil, to balance the high transpiration rate of the large leaves, is a must; provide water quickly if leaves wilt and place a saucer under potted plants during hot days to retain water. In the ground and protected, the plants survive very cold winter temperatures for short du-

rations, but they perish in frozen soil. Hardy to zone 7a as long as soil does not freeze. Pot and overwinter them further north.

Many gardener still refer to *Farfugium* species and cultivars as ligularias, but the generic name *Ligularia* is now applied only to a related group of hardy perennials. The half-hardy species classified under *Farfugium* have been known since the plant explorer Siebold described them in the mid-1800s; many are still in commerce as *Ligularia* and the even older name *Senecio*. *Farfugium* is classified in the Asteraceae.

Propagate by carefully dividing the rhizome in late winter or very early spring. Care must be taken to obtain pieces with growing tips. Fresh seeds obtained in autumn may be sown in a cold frame. Here occasional self-sown seedlings are found and can be grown on if removed before winter arrives.

Fungal black smut and black spot can be problematic in plants overwintered in the ground. Slugs and snails attack the young growth in early spring.

Farfugium japonicum, leopard plant, green leopard plant, coltsfoot. Eastern China, Korea, Taiwan, Japan.

LS to FS; flowers daisylike with many rayed lobes, light yellow, 1.5–2 in. (4–5 cm) across; 6–14 in clusters on multibranched flowerstalks, green with white woolly coating and conspicuous bracts, 18–28 in. (45–70 cm) tall; September–November; plant clump-forming, to 24 in. (60 cm) wide and 18 in. (45 cm) high; leaves basal, large, 8–12 in. (20–30 cm), rounded, heart- or kidney-shaped, dark green to grayish green, glossy, variably margined, smooth to deeply toothed; atop erect, green leaf stems, coated with a white, woolly covering. The all-green type makes a handsome groundcover or accent plant; it is variable in leaf form: some leaves are almost smooth-margined, others so toothed as to appear lobed. It looks great among ferns and astilbes. The white-splashed var. *lutchuense* (*shiro hakekomi fu* in Japan) is not yet in Western commerce, but other forms selected by Japanese gardeners are now eagerly collected by *Farfugium* aficionados here, including variegated types such as *itofukurin* (= thinly margined), *bota fu* (= blotched), and *chiri fu* (= mottled).

'Argentea' ('Albovariegata', 'Variegata', 'White Wonder') is the white-variegated form. The white can be an almost true white if the plant is sited in some sun; in more shade, the white becomes an ivory with much yellow mixed in. The leaves contain shades of grayish or whitish green. The variegation is difficult to characterize, because each leaf is different, but it is more sectoral (pie-shaped) than mottled or marginal. Known for years but still expensive.

'Aureomaculata' ('Kimon'; leopard ligularia, leopard plant), the classic yellow-spotted leopard plant. The spots are randomly placed and variously sized. Seedlings raised from this cultivar are occasionally variegated, but many revert to the type and are all green.

'Crispata' ('Cristata', 'Chirimen'; parsley ligularia), a particularly interesting green form that has ruffled and crisped margins, reminiscent of fancy parsley. Adds great textural content to the garden. Somewhat smaller than the species but just as vigorous.

'Green Dragon' (dragon ligularia), leaves grotesquely deformed—what the Japanese consider a *ryu* (= dragon) form.

'Kagami Jishi', leaves variegated like 'Aureomaculata' and margined like 'Crispata' but deeply lobed.

'Kimon Chirimen', a hybrid between 'Aureomaculata' and 'Crispata', showing characteristics of both.

'Kinkan' (= corona), leaves with a thin, uniform yellow margin; described as a gold-ring type.

Farfugium reniforme. Southeastern Asia.

LS to FS; flowers daisylike with many rayed lobes, light yellow, 2 in. (5 cm) across; in clusters on multibranched flowerstalks to 36 in. (90 cm); September–October; plant clump-forming with leaves basal, large, thick and glossy green, to 18 in. (45 cm) in diameter, kidney-shaped, smooth-margined; atop erect, green leaf stems. A more "tropical" cultivar suitable for gardens in zones 8 to 10, but with good winter protection, its rhizome is hardy here in zone 7a. Confine to a container in most gardens and overwinter in a frost-free area.

Galax

I first saw *Galax urceolata* (beetleweed) during an autumn hike to Linville Falls in western North Carolina. Unlike everything else, the small, exposed colony was not covered up by dead leaves:

with little or no soil, it clung to the mossy cushion atop a huge exposed rock. In this open position with some sun exposure, the leaves had colored a deep purplish bronze. I have been growing this species for years now, enjoying the display it gives all year long. In late May, the flower spikes are covered with tiny wands of white flowers, and its striking leaves are reliably evergreen, even at high elevations. They look so good, certain populations were decimated by overcollection of the exceptional heart-shaped leaves for floral decorations, and it is now propagated to satisfy this demand. Mountain people still gather the bronze fall leaves for Christmas decorations.

This delightful species has a limited habitat, mostly in the mountains of the southern Appalachians. The genus name comes from the Greek *gala* (= milk) for the milky white flowers. Beetleweed is a single species in the monotypic genus *Galax*, classified in the Diapensiaceae.

For active growth and good flowering, beetleweed requires constantly moist soil of high acidity with a pH of no more than 5.5. In deep shade the leaves remain green and will not color in autumn. Flowering increases in locations with some sun exposure, but the species flowers reliably in medium shade. Moisture is imperative while the flowerstalk elongates in spring; any drying during this time may abort flowering. Once seed is set, the species is remarkably drought-tolerant, surviving long, dry autumn periods. It is available from propagated stock; it should not be collected in the wild.

Propagate by carefully dividing the rhizome in very early spring. Remove all soil so that parts with growing tips can be identified and correctly separated. Replant divisions immediately. I have tried propagating seed obtained from wild populations; a very acid starting mix is a must, as is patience: seedlings take several years to mature. Division is a much faster way to increase.

Fungal and bacterial leaf spot are reported but not seen here in the 30 years I have cultivated these plants. Slugs and snails may disfigure fresh growth, but once the leaf tissue has hardened, they leave the plant alone. Weevils may also take an occasional bite out of the young leaves.

Galax urceolata, beetleweed, coltsfoot, wandflower, wand plant. Southern Appalachians, in the mountains from Virginia south to Georgia, localized in the higher Piedmont, Ohio, New York, and southern New England.

LS to FS; flowers many, tiny, white, 5-petaled, united at base, vase-shaped, in a spikelike cluster on a green, leafless, upright flowerstalk to 32 in. (80 cm); May–June; plant clump-forming, rhizomatous, slowly spreading, to 36 in. (90 cm) wide and 8 in. (20 cm) high; leaves basal, large, 2–4 in. (5–10 cm), rounded, heart- or kidney-shaped, dark green, glossy, toothed margin on thin, wiry leafstalks 5–8 in. (13–20 cm) long. The type is variable in leaf form; some leaves are more toothed than others, and in the wild I have found polyploid forms with much larger leaves, to 6 in. (15 cm) across.

Galium

Bedstraw, the common name for several *Galium* species native to North America, comes from their past use as a mattress fiber. Most are weedy and have no place in the garden. The only one in general use is the Eurasian species *Galium odoratum*, which makes a nice, dense creeping groundcover of star-shaped leaves with many clusters of equally starry white flowers. For good flowering, *Galium odoratum* requires constantly moist soil with a pH of 5.5 to 7. In southern gardens it must have a sunny corner with soil that never dries out; it languishes in the shade. Further north it is much more vigorous and can be planted in medium shade; many gardeners there use it to cover areas in full shade under trees, but, given lots of moisture and fertile soil, it can become invasive. The genus name comes from the Greek *gala* (= milk), either for the milky white flowers or the fact that in the past some species were used to curdle milk. *Galium* is classified in the bedstraw or madder family, Rubiaceae.

Propagate by carefully dividing the runners in very early spring; replant divisions immediately. With the plant's vigorous spreading habit, seed propagation makes little sense.

Fungal and bacterial leaf spot and mildew are reported. Slugs, snails, and other pests rarely bother it.

Galium odoratum, sweet woodruff, woodruff. Eurasia, central Europe to Siberia.

LS to MS; flowers many, tiny, white, fragrant, 5-petaled, star-shaped in clusters; June–July; plant rhizomatous, vigorously spreading, to 18 in. (45 cm) high but usually less; leaves 1.5 in. (4 cm) long, 0.5 in. (1 cm) wide, emerald-green, arranged in whorls of 6–8 leaves on smooth, square leafstalks. An excellent groundcover in moist, shady areas. Naturalized in North America.

Gentiana

The images of two favorite flowers, *Blauer Enzian* (= blue gentian, *Gentiana bavarica*) and *Edelweiss* (*Leontopodium alpinum*), are pervasive in Bavarian folk art. The roots of some alpine gentians, including *G. lutea* (schnapps gentian), are used to make *Enzian Schnapps*, a high-alcohol aperitif whose healing properties and powers as a spring tonic are legendary among Bavarian country folk. The genus has a cosmopolitan distribution and a long history: according to Pliny the Elder, King Gentius of Illyria on the Balkan Peninsula discovered the medicinal value of the genus whose name honors him. On the other side of the Atlantic, American Indians used the plants as a tonic and to treat back pain, and early settlers followed suit and prepared spring bitters, a tonic to purify blood. The genus is classified in the gentian family, Gentianaceae.

Remembering the wonderful gentian displays in the Bavarian Alps, I tried to cultivate alpine gentians raised from seed sent by a friend there, but I found out very quickly that central Tennessee was not the right location to raise a professed state flower of Bavaria. Gentians as a whole are not easy plants to cultivate. Most are suited to full sun situations in the border or rock garden. Only a few are of easy culture and marginally fitting for shady gardens.

The gentians described are tolerant of lightly shaded gardens and accept a variety of soils. They grow best in damp, gritty woodland soil, which should be watered during hot, dry summers; a sandy loam with some peat retains enough moisture and provides the required drainage. Optimum pH is 5 to 6.5, and cool soil is a must. Best suited to cool-summer gardens in zones 4 to 6b; even the species native to the northern Georgia mountains suffer here in zone 7a. Usually I keep difficult plants like gentians potted until I determine the best location for them. This may take a few seasons but keeps the plant roots undisturbed meanwhile.

Propagate by dividing the rhizome in early spring. Seeds can be sown as soon as ripe in pots in a cold frame. Seed germination is tedious.

Slugs and snails can be a problem. Leaf spot has also been reported.

Gentiana andrewsii, closed gentian, bottle gentian, blind gentian. Eastern North America, Saskatchewan to Ontario and Minnesota and through the Great Lakes region east to New England, south in the mountains to Georgia and west to Arkansas.

LS to WS; flowers 2–5, in tight terminal clusters and in the upper leaf axils, sepals 5, petals 5, fused, tubular, bottlelike, closed or nearly so at the lobe tips, dark blue, sometimes white-tipped or all white, 1–1.5 in. (2.5–4 cm) long, on erect stems 12–24 in. (30–60 cm) tall; August–October; plant herbaceous, tufted, clump-forming; leaves form a basal rosette, stem leaves in opposite pairs on the stem below and in a whorl at the top, 2–4 in. (5–10 cm) long, dark green, lance-shaped to oblong, unstalked. This common native gentian is best grown in moist woodland shade in the South and in some sun and light shade in the North. Maintain soil moisture during dry periods. Hardy to zone 4, heat-tolerant to zone 7. The white-flowered 'Alba' (f. *alba*) is sometimes offered.

Gentiana asclepiadea, willow gentian. Eurasia, central Europe to Italy and Greece, extending into Ukraine, the Caucasus, and Asia Minor.

LS to WS; flowers solitary or 2–3, in tight terminal clusters and in the upper leaf axils, sepals 5, petals 5, narrowly bell-shaped with pointed, sometimes reflexed lobe tips, dark blue with purple spots inside, sometimes longitudinally white-striped, or light blue, all white, or red, 1–1.2 in. (2.5–3 cm) long, on erect but leaning stems 20–24 in. (50–60 cm) tall; August–October; plant herbaceous, tufted, clump-forming; leaves in a whorl at the top and many in opposite pairs on the stem below, no basal rosette, 2–3 in. (5–8 cm) long, dark green, lance-shaped to oblong, unstalked. The best gentian for moist shade, trouble-free and of easy culture as long as moisture is maintained. Hardy to zone 6, heat-tolerant to zone 7.

'Alba', flowers white.

'Knightshayes', flowers blue with white throat; smaller than the type.

'Nymans', flowers dark blue with large purple spots inside; plant large with arching stems.

'Phyllis', flowers pale blue; stems tall to 28 in. (70 cm).

Gentiana clausa, closed gentian. Eastern North America, Saskatchewan to Ontario and Minnesota and through the Great Lakes region east to New England, south in the mountains to northern Georgia and west to Arkansas.

LS to WS; features practically identical to *Gentiana andrewsii*. *Gentiana linearis* (narrow-leaved gentian), a more northern species, has narrower leaves and more open flowers. *Gentiana saponaris* (soapwort gentian) has leaves that resemble *Saponaria* and more open flowers; it is well adapted to more southern conditions. Better for northern gardens is *G. decora* (American mountain gentian), with bluish white, closed flowers that are blue-striped. All are available from wildflower nurseries. The very rare native *Gentianopsis crinita* (fringed gentian) and *G. procera* (smaller fringed gentian) are protected species almost everywhere; they should never be removed from the wild.

Geranium

I sometimes call the wild woodland plants of the genus *Geranium* by their common name, cranesbills, to avoid confusion with what most people think of as geraniums, the lovely, tender, window-dressing plants of the genus *Pelargonium*. The generic name is from the Greek *geranos* (= crane), an allusion to the shape of the fruit, which resembles a crane's bill. I first saw cranesbills during a trip to the Smoky Mountains in the early 1950s; there along the trails were large groups of *Geranium maculatum*, which plant American Indians and early settlers used for its astringent and styptic properties and to cure diarrhea. Cultivated cranesbills evolved from such wild woodland species in Europe and North America. Their striking, delicately cut leaves and attractive flowers have earned them a growing following, and new cultivars, including a few with variegated leaves, satisfy the increasing demand for these beauties. That they are low-maintenance plants only adds to the attraction.

Geranium is a wide-ranging genus of about 300 species found throughout the temperate zones, some of which, the hardy cranesbills, are excellent, long-lived foliage perennial plants for the shady garden, including both dry and moist shade. They tolerate a variety of soils but grow best in damp, friable woodland soil, which should be watered during hot, dry summers. Optimum pH is 5 to 7.

Under these conditions they will colonize the bare spots in the woodland garden rapidly, even aggressively, by creeping rhizomes and exploding seed capsules. Gardeners with small plots should think twice before they burden themselves with the task of weeding out unwanted cranesbill seedlings. The problem can be avoided if plants are cut back sharply after flowering; be careful not to cut off too much of the essential, handsome foliage. Deadheading is another solution but requires more time, effort, and dexterity. The nice but temporary flowers can be gaudy; rather than introducing glaring magenta or fierce purple to the tranquil green embrace of a shady garden, choose white or pink cranesbill cultivars when available. The genus is classified in the geranium family, Geraniaceae.

Propagate by dividing the rhizome in early spring. Seed collected from hardy varieties should be sown outdoors as soon as ripe; many species give offspring true to type, but cultivars do not always come true.

Cranesbills are subject to mildews and rusts. Here, vine weevils take chunks out of leaf margins, and aphids, slugs, and snails can be a problem. Plants affected by a virus that distorts the flowers must be destroyed.

Geranium endressii, Endress's cranesbill. Europe, western France, Pyrenees.

LS to WS; flowers many, 1–1.5 in. (2.5–4 cm) long, trumpet-shaped, crowded, terminal, above the leaves, on stems 12–18 in. (30–45 cm) tall, sepals 5, small, petals 5, light pink or salmon-pink, conspicuously notched, veined with darker pink, stamens 10, pistil 1; June–September or later; plant evergreen, clump-forming, spreading by creeping rhizomes; leaves green, 2–6 in. (5–15 cm) long, 5-lobed, each lobe again divided and unevenly toothed; fruit elongated, beaked capsule. This popular and easily cultivated cranesbill has been in gardens since the early 1800s. It spreads by creeping rhizomes and by seed and bears watching. The flowers appear over a long period, and the leaves make a dense groundcover. Hardy in zones 4 to 7, but here in zone 7a it stopped flowering after the nights got too warm in late spring, and it melted out completely during a particularly hot, dry summer, so I no longer grow it. It did very well in my mother's southern Michigan garden, indicating that reasonably cool summers may be the limiting factor. Does best in dry shade in the South, and more sun in northern gardens. A taller selection of the species, **'Wargrave Pink'** ('Wargrave Variety'), has salmon-pink flowers and petals more deeply notched; to 24 in. (60 cm).

Geranium macrorrhizum, bigroot geranium, bigroot cranesbill, scented cranesbill, fetid cranesbill. Southern Europe, southeastern Alps, Balkans, in the Carpathians and Apennines, naturalized in northern Europe and elsewhere.

LS to WS; flowers 2–7, fragrant, mostly paired or in dense clusters, terminal on the branches, above the leaves, shallowly bowl-shaped to flat, sepals 5, dark red, inflated, petals 5, rounded and separate, magenta to reddish purple, petals light to dark pink or white, 0.8–1.5 in. (2–2.5 cm) across, stamens 10, pistil 1; May–August; plant semi-evergreen, mat- to clump-forming, with thick, creeping rhizomes, 6–8 in. (15–20 cm) tall in shade, taller in more sun; leaves basal, 7–8 in. (18–20 cm) wide, green to light green, cut into 5–7 lobes; fruit elongated, beaked capsule. Crush a leaf to release the astringent, mediciney smell that some consider fetid. By far the best cranesbill for southern gardens, happily enduring hot summers in zone 8. Hardy to zone 3. With good drainage and a spot in dry shade, it makes an excellent groundcover, spreading by thick rhizomatous roots.

'Album', flower petals white with a faint blush of pink, sepals pink to light red.

'Bevan's Variety', flower petals deep magenta, sepals bright red.

'Czakor', flowers deep magenta-red; leaves turn purplish in autumn. A Balkan selection.

'Ingwersen's Variety', flowers a muted pink; very light green leaves.

'Lohfelden', flowers soft violet pink, veined with a deeper pink; plant smaller, not as tall.

'Ridsko', flowers magenta pink; leaves glossy green, more deciduous.

'Spessart', flower petals white, sepals pink, similar to 'Album'.

'Variegatum', flowers lilac-pink; leaves grayish green, margined and splashed with creamy to yellowish white. Should receive plenty of fertilizer and no more than light shade.

'Velebit', flower deep magenta-red. A Balkan selection.

Geranium maculatum, spotted wild geranium, wild cranesbill, wild geranium, spotted cranesbill, alumroot. Eastern North America, southern Manitoba and Ontario to New England, south to Georgia and west to Tennessee, Missouri, and Kansas.

LS to WS; flowers 2–5, terminal on the branches, in loose clusters above the leaves, shallowly bowl-shaped, lavender to rose-purple, sometimes white, 1–1.5 in. (2.5–4 cm) across, sepals 5, pointed, petals 5, rounded and separate, stamens 10, pistil 1; April–June; plant rhizomatous, clump-forming, 12–24 in. (30–60 cm) tall; leaves 4–5 in. (10–13 cm) wide, grayish green, sometimes spotted (hence the epithet), cut into 3–7 deeply toothed lobes, short-stalked except basal leaves, which are long-stalked; fruit elongated, beaked capsule. The common wild cranesbill, well suited for moist woodland shade in southern gardens, some sun and light shade in more northern exposures. Self-sows abundantly. Hardy to zone 4, heat-tolerant to zone 8. Does better in hot, southern summers than many European cranesbills as long as moisture is maintained. Its selection 'Album' has white flowers, sometimes with a very pale pinkish cast.

Geranium nodosum. Central and southern Europe, southern France to central Italy, central Balkans.

LS to MS; flowers 2–5, small, to 0.6 in. (1.5 cm) long, trumpet-shaped and erect, terminal, above the leaves, on red-tinted stems 12–18 in. (30–45 cm) tall, sepals 5, small, petals 5, lilac-pink or pink, wedge-shaped, conspicuously notched, lightly veined, stamens 10, pistil 1; June–August; plant herbaceous, clump-forming, rhizomatous; leaves shiny green, basal ones elliptic, 5-lobed, 2–8 in. (5–20 cm) long, stem leaves, lance-shaped, 3-lobed, each lobe unevenly toothed; fruit elongated, beaked capsule. One of the few cranesbills that tolerates deep, dry shade; more damp shade is required in hot-summer areas. It makes large colonies in time, spreading by creeping rhizomes and seed, but it is not as aggressive as *Geranium* ×*oxanianum*. Flowers are sparse but appear over a long period, and the leaves make a dense groundcover of glossy bright green. Hardy in zones 6 and 7.

Geranium ×*oxanianum*. Garden hybrid (*G. endressii* × *G. versicolor*).

LS to WS; dry and moist shade. This hybrid spreads far and wide by seed and is too vigorous for all but very large gardens; it should be used only for covering areas where nothing else will grow, with the proviso that its spread be carefully watched and contained. Once established, its strong, deep root system is virtually impossible to remove. It is usually represented by the century-old 'Claridge Druce', which makes an all-smothering, nearly evergreen groundcover, effectively eliminating both weeds and delicate, valuable woodland plants. Hardy to zone 4.

Geranium phaeum, dusky cranesbill, mourning widow, black widow. Central and southern Europe, Pyrenees to eastern Germany, east to Bulgaria and Ukraine.

LS to MS; flowers 2–9, nodding, in loose, one-sided clusters, terminal on the branches, above the leaves, flat, sepals 5, petals 5, rounded, reflexed, dark maroon to blackish purple with a whitish spot in center, sometimes all white, 0.6 in. (1.5 cm) across, stamens 10, pistil 1; June–August; plant herbaceous, clump-forming, rhizomatous, to 30 in. (75 cm) tall; leaves basal, 4–8 in. (10–20 cm) wide, bright green, sometimes marked purplish green in center, cut into 7–9 lobes, each shallowly lobed and toothed; fruit elongated, beaked capsule. More of an accent plant than a groundcover. It seeds freely, but offspring are variable. Must have good drainage. Takes both dry and moist shade. Hardy to zone 4, heat-tolerant to cool-summer areas of zone 6b or 7a. Variety *lividum* has pale, dull lilac flowers, sometimes bluish lilac.

'Album' (f. *album*), flowers white, sometimes faintly flushed pink, anther bright yellow. Preferable to the dark-flowered type for brightening the shady garden.

'Joan Baker', flowers pale lavender with darker ring in center, to 1 in. (2.5 cm); plant vigorous, to 36 in. (90 cm). A selection of var. *lividum*.

'Langthorne's Blue', flowers violet-blue.

'Lily Lovell', flowers mauve, larger than type; leaves lighter green.

'Majus', flowers larger and plant taller than var. *lividum*.

'Margaret Wilson', flowers similar to the type; robust, yellowish white leaves.

'Samobor', flowers dark like the species; leaves nicely variegated with dark greenish brown.

'Taff's Jester', flowers dark like the species; leaves irregularly mottled with yellow or wholly yellow, splashed with yellowish green and marked with purplish green to maroon in the notches; good variegated foliage but viridescent, turning greener in time.

'Variegatum', flowers dark like the species; leaves irregularly splashed with cream and paler green and occasionally spotted with purplish green to maroon.

Geranium renardii. Eastern Europe to the Caucasus.

Some sun, LS; a widely available species represented in commerce by improved cultivars. Best in dry shade in the South, more sun in the North. **'Terra Franche'**, a heat-tolerant cultivar for southern gardens, bears violet flowers in early summer and has fuzzy, deeply lobed, grayish green leaves; it is suited for the lightly shaded rockery. 'Whiteknights' offers white flowers with a pale lavender background hue and dark lilac veins in early summer; leaves grayish green, deeply lobed.

Geranium versicolor. Southern Europe, Sicily, Balkans.

LS to WS; flowers white with magenta veins. Very similar to *Geranium endressii* and has the same garden uses; its leaves have slightly broader lobes, with margins not as acutely toothed. Needs to be watched: it self-seeds freely and spreads by creeping rhizomes. Makes an excellent groundcover under trees. Best in dry shade in the South, more sun in the North. Takes some summer heat as long as it remains in shade during the hot afternoon hours. Hardy to zone 6.

Recommended reading

Bath, Trevor, and Joy Jones. 1994. *The Gardener's Guide to Growing Hardy Geraniums*. Portland, Oregon: Timber Press.

Gillenia

Gillenia trifoliata (Bowman's root) is a graceful, dainty North American native that deserves to be grown in more gardens. Its white or pinkish flowers have five unruly, uneven, twisted petals, and the twisted stems are many-branched, holding three reddish green leaves at each node. The red sepals remain on the plant after flowering, adding color well into autumn. It adapts easily to different soil conditions, as long as the soil is not allowed to dry out completely. Hardy to zone 4.

Bowman's root was used medicinally by American Indians and early settlers; it is also called false ipecac, short for *ipecacuanha*, a South American species with emetic properties. The genus name honors the German botanist Gillenius. It is classified in the Rosaceae.

Propagate by careful division in late autumn or very early spring. Sow seed in trays in a cold frame in autumn. Given the plant's vigorous spreading habit, seed propagation makes little sense.

Not prone to insect or mollusk damage; rust is an occasional problem.

Gillenia trifoliata, Bowman's root, Indian physic, Indian hippo, false ipecac, fawn's breath. Eastern North America, southern Ontario to New York, west to Michigan, Missouri, and Arkansas, south to Georgia and Alabama.

LS to MS; flowers 2–6, on thin stalks in open clusters above the leaf mound, white or pinkish, to 1.5 in. (4 cm) across, star-shaped, 5 petals, 5 sepals, sepals red, persistent; May–July; plant rhizomatous, clump-forming, 24–36 in. (60–90 cm) high; leaves 2–4 in. (5–10 cm) long and 0.5 in. (1 cm) wide, 3-parted, green, sharply toothed, short-stalked, with tiny bractlike leaf-pair at base. A good, airy addition to the wildflower garden, it looks great planted between shrubs for support and mixes well with hostas and other bold-leaved shade perennials. *Gillenia stipulata* (American ipecac, American ipecacuanha, Indian physic), from southern New York west to Illinois and Ohio and south to Georgia and west to Kansas and Texas, is very similar but with a pair of large bractlike leaves (stipules) at the leaf bases, giving the leaves a 5-parted look. The sepals are not showy red. A more leafy plant and well adapted to southern gardens, it is infrequently offered.

Glaucidium

Known to Western horticulture since Siebold and Zuccarini described it in 1845, *Glaucidium palmatum* was only recently rediscovered and is now offered in commerce. Unfortunately, hot, dry summers are not to its liking, so I must garden without this Japanese beauty. Lucky are the gardeners in more northern regions who can plant and enjoy this excellent and valuable shade garden plant. Large, many-veined, crinkly leaves add great texture to the shady garden; it makes a great companion to hostas, ferns, astilbes, and native wildflowers in the moist woodland border. The genus name suggests its flowers resemble those of the sun-loving horned poppies (*Glaucium* spp.). *Glaucidium* is placed in the peony family, Paeoniaceae.

Native to the mountains of northern Honshu, in Aomori Prefecture, *Glaucidium palmatum* enjoys cool summers. Where summers are hot and dry, water in abundance and site in full shade in a position sheltered from desiccating winds. The woody, rhizomatous rootstock spreads slowly, forming a nice colony in time.

Propagate by carefully dividing the dormant woody rhizomes in very early spring. Seed can be sown in the open in spring, but germination is slow and seedlings take several years to mature.

Slugs and snails are a real problem in spring when the new growth emerges; no other pests or diseases are reported.

Glaucidium palmatum. Japan, northern Honshu.

MS to FS; flowers solitary, terminal, nodding, with 4 wavy, lobed mauve to lilac tepals, formed like petals, to 3 in. (8 cm) across, no sepals, many yellow stamens; May–June; plant clump-forming with woody, rhizomatous rootstock; leaves maple-leaf-shaped, with 6–10 lobes, toothed and incised, crinkled and heavily veined, light green, heart-shaped at the base, 5–10 in. (13–25 cm) long, leaves at bottom are largest and diminish in size toward top. An excellent plant for shady gardens with cool summers. Hardy to zone 4. In zone 7 and warmer, plantings should be considered experimental and probably will not succeed. White-flowered f. *leucanthum* ('Leucanthemum', 'Album') has been known from the wild for many years but is rarely available.

Goodyera

Finding hardy, native woodland orchids practically in ones own backyard is exciting. Discovering *Goodyera pubescens* (rattlesnake plantain) in the rocky ravine near our house was an especially happy happenstance for me, for such a small plant is easily overlooked in the forest litter. Widespread in the temperate zones of Eurasia and North America, except Africa, these are among the easiest orchids to cultivate in gardens. They should be planted close

to walks or in an elevated bed where they can be seen. Their flowers are tiny, but their distinctly and beautifully marked, evergreen leaves present a striking contrast to wild gingers and other low-growing wildflowers. American Indians thought the leaf pattern resembled rattlesnake skin (hence the common name) and therefore used plants to cure snakebites. Gardeners in mild-winter areas can grow species usually sold as terrarium orchids, including *G. foliosa*, *G. hachijoensis*, *G. schlechtendaliana*, and *G. velutina*; in Japan variegated forms of these species, called brocade orchids (*nishiki ran*), have given rise to a new mania in pot culture.

The genus was named to honor the British botanist Goodyer and is classified in the Orchidaceae. Its members make attractive four-season plants in gardens where snow will not cover up the attractive leaves. For best effect, they should be planted in groups. This is facilitated by most species, because they spread rapidly by creeping rhizomes. These orchids grow in the top layer of moist, well-draining soil with a pH of 5 to 6. I grow several species, and here they appreciate occasional watering during hot, dry spells. Their heat tolerance is great, to zones 8 and 9, and they are much more hardy than most references indicate. In the wild, some species occur in zone 4, and I have seen them cultivated in zone 5, but snow cover spoils the winter interest.

Propagate by carefully dividing the rhizomes.

In my garden, nothing in the way of pests or diseases seems to bother these orchids, except that slugs and snails may take an occasional bite out of young leaves. Mealy bugs and aphids are reported but never seen here.

The species of *Goodyera* are variable. Expect considerable differences in the leaf markings and leaf color. All are evergreen in the zones indicated.

Goodyera oblongifolia, giant rattlesnake plantain, Menzies' rattlesnake plantain, green-leaved rattlesnake plantain. North America, northern Maine into southeastern Quebec, British Columbia south through central California and in the Rocky Mountains of Arizona and New Mexico.

MS to FS; flowers 6–30, very small, greenish or yellowish brown, insignificant, one-sided or slightly spiraled on upright flower spikes with scaly bracts, to 20 in. (50 cm); June–August; leaves 3–6, in a tight basal rosette, 3–4 in. (8–10 cm) long, dark green with a conspicuous silvery green stripe on the mid-vein, cross veins not distinctly marked as in other species. Among the larger species in the genus. Hardy to zone 5.

Goodyera pubescens, downy rattlesnake plantain, lattice leaf, rattlesnake orchid, scrofula weed, adder's violet. Eastern North America, southern Ontario, Quebec, Minnesota, and New England, south to central Georgia, Alabama, Tennessee, and west to Missouri and Oklahoma.

MS to FS; flowers numerous, very small, greenish, insignificant, on upright, woolly spikes with scaly bracts and with flowers on all sides, to 16 in. (40 cm); June–August; leaves 3–8, in a tight basal rosette, 2–3 in. (5–8 cm) long, dark grayish to bluish green with conspicuous network of silvery white principal veins and narrower cross veins. Distinctly variegated leaves provide year-round interest. Hardy to zone 5.

Goodyera repens, dwarf rattlesnake plantain, northern rattlesnake plantain, lesser rattlesnake plantain, jewel orchid. Eastern North America, northern Eurasia, British Isles, central Europe, Japan.

MS to FS; flowers many, very small, insignificant, usually one-sided, sometimes slightly spiraled on upright flower spikes with scaly bracts, 4–10 in. (10–25 cm) tall; June–August; leaves 3–4, in a basal rosette, 0.5–1 in. (1–2.5 cm) long, dark bluish green with a network of whitish veins. This widely distributed species is much smaller than *Goodyera pubescens* and not as showy. Hardy to zone 4. Variety *ophioides* (= like a snake) is found from Newfoundland across Canada to Alaska as well as in Minnesota and in the Appalachians south to North Carolina; it too is dwarf, with more distinctly marked silvery white veins in the small leaves. Hardy to zone 3. Very similar and seldom seen is *G. tesselata* (checkered rattlesnake plantain, smooth rattlesnake plantain), a species with smooth, dark green leaves that are checkered with lighter green; it grows in eastern North America on both sides of the Canadian border.

Goodyera schlechtendaliana. China, Taiwan, Korea.
MS to FS; flowers many, white or rose-pink, very small, 4–10 in. (10–25 cm) tall; July–August; leaves in a basal rosette, 0.8–1.5 in. (2–4 cm) long, broadly lance-shaped, dark grayish green with a prominent, silvery white central stripe and a network of whitish veins. A rare species, hardy to zone 6b. Very similar is *Goodyera velutina* from the same habitat; its flowers are larger and white or reddish brown and the leaves are of similar size, maroon underneath, with a velvety texture and a white midrib. Hardy to zone 7b. From Hachijo Island comes *G. hachijoensis* var. *matsumurana*, with whitish flowers flushed pink; its leaves are larger, to 2.5 in. (6 cm) long, medium green, with a central splash of white and a network of white veins. Hardy to zone 7b. All need a sheltered spot and tolerate hot summers as long as moisture is maintained.

Recommended reading
Cribb, Phillip, and Christopher Bailes. 1989. *Hardy Orchids*. Portland, Oregon: Timber Press.

Hakonechloa

My search for the ideal small ornamental grass for shady gardens came to an end when I found *Hakonechloa macra* (Hakone grass). I first saw it in the western Japanese Alps, growing with azaleas and *Hosta longipes* on the rocky banks of a tributary of the Tenryu River in Shizuoka Prefecture. Many years later I saw a variegated form of it in a local nursery, and this graceful, elegant grass has been growing at Hosta Hill ever since.

The generic name is a combination of Hakone (its habitat in the mountainous Hakone region of central Honshu) and the Greek *chloe* (= grass). Plants were previously included in the genus *Phragmites*, where one still finds *Phragmites australis*, the giant sun-loving reed grass native to North America. *Hakonechloa* is classified in the grass family, Gramineae.

Hakone grass requires abundant moisture during its initial spring growth cycle; once the grass has matured in late spring or early summer, it endures incredible heat and drought. Stagnant water in the ground will cause root rot. Soils of low fertility are accepted; slow-release fertilizers give an extra boost to development. The clumps expand slowly by means of creeping rhizomes, but this growth is never invasive. Hardy to zone 6 with protection, heat-tolerant to zone 9.

Propagate by dividing the dormant clumps or creeping rhizomes before growth commences in very early spring.

Other than an occasional bite taken by weevils out of leaf margins, no diseases nor insect assaults have been noted.

Hakonechloa macra, Hakone grass, Japanese reed grass. Japan, central Honshu, Hakone region.

Some sun, LS to MS; flowers and seedpods terminal, in loose, irregular clusters; stems (culms) wiry, smooth, green, arching, 20–26 in. (50–65 cm) long, leaf blades deciduous, 3–8 per stem, 6–12 in. (25–30 cm) long to 0.6 in. (1.5 cm) wide, linear lance-shaped with long, tapering tip, blades smaller near the ground, larger toward the top, then smaller again, light to medium green, shiny on top, dull green beneath; plant clump-forming, slowly expanding by rhizomes, clumps 12–16 in. (30–40 cm) tall. A most graceful and elegant grass for a multitude of uses in gardens. Its dense leaf mounds combine exceedingly well with hostas and other bold-leaved perennials and make a nice accent in fern glades; it is shown to advantage in front of tall-growing wildflowers like Solomon's seals and fairy bells (*Disporum* spp.) and is absolutely stunning in decorative containers. The leaf blades remain on the plant during winter. In moist soils they turn a reddish bronze and provide winter interest; in dry soils they wither and become unsightly, so I remove them. The all-green type is most vigorous and makes a refined addition to the garden where too much variegation might not be desirable. Most available forms are variegated.

'Alboaurea', leaf blades striped with mostly ivory-white, some yellow, and little green; somewhat diminished vigor. 'Albovariegata' is similar but with no yellow.

'Aureola', leaf blades mostly bright yellow, with a few thin, green stripes; excellent, vigorous, and widely available. Well adapted to shady southern gardens; some sun is appreciated in northern latitudes.

Helleborus

Most species of hellebores originate in Eurasia; many grow in the Balkan region of southeastern Europe. What makes them all so outstanding is their excellent winter character. Most hellebores are evergreen and perennial, providing color and interest when deciduous (herbaceous) plants are dormant. I have several growing in my garden, each

an asset, including an imposing *Helleborus argutifolius* (Corsican hellebore) just off the terrace. The hybrids involving *H. orientalis* (Lenten rose) have the most colorful large flowers, though I appreciate their striking foliage much more. Many years ago, my uncle led me to a blooming group of *H. niger* (Christmas rose) in the mountains of my native Bavaria; I am able to grow its fine selection 'Potter's Wheel' by giving copious amounts of water and adding dolomitic limestone to the soil mix.

Ten years ago, I planted a small piece of *Helleborus foetidus* (stinking hellebore) on a northeast-facing slope in the front garden. Spring rains can be heavy in Georgia, and the wet, acid clay soil here was not to the little hellebore's liking. But hellebores are tough, ideal shade plants, and it perked up in early summer, when it became drier and warmer. Nearby hostas overshadowed the small plant, and it stayed hidden (perhaps even forgotten) until the hostas went dormant late that year; it was the only thing in the area that survived the first hard freeze. In its third year, in November, it pushed up a thick, light green stem with fringes on top, which opened into a nodding cluster of greenish flowers. Getting up close to admire it, I detected the faint odor that gives this species its name. It got very cold, to 11°F (−12°C), that first night of bloom, but the flowers survived. The following spring, the flowers turned more green, and finally, a cluster of brownish seedpods developed in the center of each. Before I realized it, the flowering stem had turned black and died, and the seed had scattered all over the place. My one little hellebore is now a thriving, self-sufficient colony of year-round green plants. People complain that *H. foetidus* dies off after seeding. I combat this by cutting most flowering stems before the seeds fully develop, leaving a few stalks to produce seed and to further naturalize my front garden. Plants thus remain vigorous and produce more flowers the following seasons. They are happy even in the dry, hot summers of the southeastern United States. Soils can be anything from clayey to sandy, with a pH of 5.5 to 7. The only conditions *H. foetidus* dislikes are waterlogged soil and wet winters; in these it rots and dies.

Evergreen hellebores are essential perennials for any shady garden. Even deciduous species have wonderfully segmented leaf crowns during summer, so making up for their lack of winter interest.

Hellebores tolerate a wide range of soil conditions as long as they get good drainage. Some like more sun; others tolerate almost full shade. In shadier conditions, plants may be smaller and flowering sparse. With their finely divided leaves hellebores make excellent companions for hostas, woodland flowers, ferns, and other shade plants during the growing season. Flower shape places the genus in the Ranunculaceae.

Propagate by allowing seeds to ripen on the plants; they will scatter in time, yielding many small seedlings. Seeds prefer to germinate in the cracks of brick paving or on minute soil patches in concrete paving: their Mediterranean heritage and liking for dry places is obvious. I once tried moving large seedlings from these seemingly inhospitable places to nice pots filled with superior potting soil; they rewarded me by promptly expiring. Hellebores dislike dividing and transplanting.

Hellebores are susceptible to black fungal rot. Slugs and snails attack the young growth.

Helleborus argutifolius, Corsican hellebore. Mediterranean region, Corsica, Sardinia.

Sun, LS to MS; flowers many, 24–30, light green, bowl- or cup-shaped, facing out or slightly down, sepals 5, large, overlapping, to 2 in. (5 cm) across, stamens many; December–May; plant evergreen, with overwintering flowerstalks, to 4 ft. (1.2 m) tall and 36 in. (90 cm) wide; leaves dark green, on the stem, 3–8 in. (8–20 cm) long, divided into 3 leaflets, center one elliptic, lateral leaflets rounded on the outside edge, leathery, shiny, with very coarsely toothed, spiny margins. An attractive, low-maintenance species whose striking leaves give marvelous winter interest. It produces overwintering, leafy flowering stems and is evergreen in zone 7. Remove the old stems to allow new shoots to develop and flower before summer arrives. Hardy to zone 6 with good protection. It mixes well with the soft green, bold leaves of the Chinese mayapple (*Podophyllum pleianthum*) and assorted hostas and ferns. The selection **'Janet Starnes'** has shorter leaves that are attractively speckled light grayish green.

Helleborus atrorubens, purple hellebore. Northwestern Balkans.

Sun, LS to WS; flowers solitary or 2–3 in loose clusters, deep purple, reddish on the back, sometimes greenish in center or rarely all green, saucer-shaped, facing out, sepals 5, large, 1.5–2 in. (4–5 cm) across, stamens many, on widely branched stems; January–April; plant to 12 in. (30 cm) tall and wide; leaves deciduous, basal, dark green, flushed purple in spring, to 10 in. (25 cm) across, divided into 5 leaflets, the 2 outer leaflets divided again, into 3–5 leaflike lobes, totaling 9–13 elliptic segments, leathery, shiny, with toothed, spiny margins. Rarely seen and small, it requires a place up front where its dark flowers can be appreciated. Hardy to zone 5 and quite heat-tolerant once established. The several named botanical forms are rarely available: f. *cupreus* has reddish brown or gold flowers; f. *hircii* has leaves to 15 segments; f. *incisis* has leaflets more deeply toothed, incised.

Helleborus ×*ballardiae*. Garden hybrid (*H. lividus* × *H. niger*).

Sun, LS to MS; flowers 3–4, white or white flushed with pink inside, turning purplish pink, saucer-shaped, facing out or slightly down, sepals 5, large, overlapping, 2–3 in. (5–8 cm) across, stamens many, overwintering flowerstalks, to 18 in. (45 cm) tall and 12 in. (30 cm) wide; December–April; leaves deep green to deep bluish green with veins outlined in whitish green, on the stem, to 8 in. (20 cm) across, divided into 3–5 leaflets, leathery, shiny, with widely toothed, spiny margins. A great addition with striking, conspicuously variegated leaves. Its leafy overwintering flowering stems are evergreen in zone 7. Hardy to zone 6 with good protection. The popular cultivar 'December Dawn' has white flowers flushed pinkish purple inside, turning dull, grayish purple.

Helleborus cyclophyllus, Grecian hellebore. Southern Balkans, Greece, southern Bulgaria, Macedonia, Albania.

Sun, LS to WS; flowers faintly scented, 4–7 in loose clusters, green to yellowish green, saucer-shaped, facing out or down, sepals 5, large, 2–3 in. (5–8 cm) across, stamens many, on stems 22 in. (55 cm) tall; January–April; plant 16–18 in. (40–45 cm) tall and wide; leaves deciduous, almost basal, light green, conspicuously veined, leathery, finely hairy underneath in spring, to 10 in. (25 cm) across, divided into 7 leaflets, the 2 outer leaflets divided again into leaflike lobes, totaling 9–11 or more elliptic segments, leathery, shiny, with finely toothed margins. An impressive hellebore with great leaf interest and well worth growing. Hardy to zone 6 and very heat-tolerant once established. Another striking species from southeastern Austria ranging across the upper Balkans to the Black Sea is *Helleborus dumetorum*, which has adapted well to hot summers here and is slowly expanding into a striking plant; its flowers are the smallest in the genus, but I like the up to 13 fingerlike, very slender, deciduous leaflets, which add grace to the leaf mound.

Helleborus foetidus, stinking hellebore, bear claw hellebore, bear's foot, dungwort, setterwort, stinkwort. Western and central Europe, Spain and Portugal to Hungary, United Kingdom.

LS to MS; flowers many, 24–48, in loose clusters on light green, erect, overwintering stems with conspicuous, leafy bracts, 0.6–1 in. (1.5–2.5 cm) across, green to pale green, sometimes flushed purple at the sepal tips, bell- or cup-shaped, drooping, sepals 5, stamens many; December–April; plant to 32 in. (80 cm), sometimes taller, and 18 in. (45 cm) wide; leaves evergreen, on the stem, first light then darker or grayish green, leathery, to 9 in. (23 cm) across, divided into leaflets, the 2 outer leaflets divided again into leaflike lobes, totaling 9–11 or more narrowly lance-shaped segments, leathery, shiny, with toothed or entire margins; leaves slightly fetid when crushed. Very hardy and a good garden plant once established, although extremely variable.

'Bowles' Form', leaves more finely divided; plant larger and vigorous.

'Green Giant', plant taller.

'Green Gnome' ('Sierra Nevada Form'), a dwarf form, 8 in. (20 cm) tall.

'Italian Form', like 'Bowles' Form' but more floriferous.

'Miss Jekyll' ('Miss Jekyll's Scented Form'), flowers scented.

'Piccadilly', flowerstalks with red tinting; leaves very dark with grayish overlay.

'Ruth', leaves dark green, deeply cut, turning reddish in autumn.

'Sienna', leaves darker.

'Sopron', leaves metallic, glossy dark green.

'Tros-os-Montes', flowers green and unflushed at sepal tips; leaflets deeply serrated.

'Wester Flisk', flowers yellowish green, edged in reddish brown; leafstalks and stems red-tinted.

Helleborus lividus, Majorcan hellebore. Mediterranean region, Majorca, Cabrera.

LS to MS; flowers 8–10, apple-green inside, flushed pinkish purple outside, 1.2–2 in. (3–5 cm) across, sepals 5, stamens many, in loose clusters on overwintering stems; December–April; plant to 18 in. (45 cm) tall and 12 in. (30 cm) wide; leaves evergreen, dark green or bluish with silvery white veining, divided into 3 leaflets, egg-shaped, with fine and widely spaced teeth. This rare but available species is hardy here in zone 7a in a sheltered spot, where it has endured temperatures of 15°F (−10°C) for short periods. Further north it makes a striking pot subject; remove to a frost-free area during the coldest part of the winter. Its beautiful leaves, veined in silver, are well worth the extra effort.

Helleborus multifidus, lacy hellebore. Italy, Balkans.

LS to MS; flowers green, cup-shaped, drooping, 3–10, 1.5–2 in. (4–5 cm) across, sepals 5, stamens many, in loose clusters on overwintering stems; December–April; plant to 24 in. (60 cm) tall and 16 in. (40 cm) wide; leaves deciduous, medium green, basal, hairy beneath, divided into many leaflets, as many as 40–70 segments. Subspecies *hercegovinus* has more than 100 segments. The lacy appearance of these plants makes them outstanding additions to the garden. Subspecies *bocconei* and subsp. *istriacus* have fewer segments, about 20 and 12, respectively. I grow subsp. *istriacus*; it has overwintering rather than deciduous leaves, the tattered remains of which I remove each spring. All are hardy to zone 7, heat-tolerant to zone 9.

Helleborus niger, Christmas rose, *Christrose* (Ger.), snow rose, winter rose. Swiss, Italian, German, and Austrian Alps to Croatia.

Sun, LS to MS; flowers with pinkish buds, opening to white with a green center, later sometimes turning pinkish; to 3.5 in. (9 cm) across, sepals 5, stamens many, solitary or rarely 2–3 on purplish overwintering stems; plant 8–12 in. (20–30 cm) tall and to 12 in. (30 cm) wide; leaves evergreen, very dark green, leathery, shiny, divided into 7–9 leaflets, untoothed, except toward tip of leaflets. This wonderful hellebore from the Alps is hardy to zone 3 with protection, heat-tolerant to zone 6. Subspecies *macranthus* from the Italian Alps has huge flowers, to 4.5 in. (11 cm) across. Several botanical varieties have been named: var. *angustifolius* with narrower leaflets and smaller white flowers; var. *humilifolius* with smaller leaves on unspotted stems and larger flowers; var. *oblongifolius* with a very long central leaflet that narrows abruptly toward its base; and var. *stenopetalus* with very narrow sepal lobes. Many selections show some of these varietal features.

'Apple Blossom', flowers white flushed rose-pink, more reddish outside.

Blackthorn Group, flowers with pink buds, opening white, turning pink; stems dark.

'De Graff's Variety', flowers whitish turning pale rose.

'Eva', large white flowers to 4.5 in. (11 cm) across.

'Flore Roseo', flowers pink.

'Foliis Variegatis', leaves variegated with cream in spring.

'Louis Cobbett', flowers white suffused with deep pink.

'Madam Fourcade', flowers white, not large; leaves light green; plant smaller.

'Marion', flowers double, with up to 25 sepals.

'Potter's Wheel' ('Ladham's Variety'), flowers white with a green eye, large, 4–5 in. (10–13 cm) across, overlapping sepals; very dark green leaves. I coddle this small plant successfully in full shade with morning sun penetrating its cool corner of the garden.

'Praecox' (All-Saints-Day Christmas rose), flowers late October–early November.

'Riverstone', flowers white, early, slightly fragrant.

'St. Brigid', leaves tall, very dark green, protecting flowers.

'Sunrise', flowers with much pink in the white sepals.

'Sunset', flowers red in bud, white sepals flushed with red, later turning red.

'Trotter's Form', pure white flowers, very long-lasting.

'Wardie Lodge', flowers white tinged pink; leaves narrow, mottled with greenish purple; stem marbled purple.

'White Magic', flowers white; stem tall and darkish.

Helleborus ×*nigercors*. Garden hybrid (*H. argutifolius* × *H. niger*).

Some sun, LS; flowers many, up to 30 or more, white or white flushed with pink inside, sometimes with a bluish cast, saucer-shaped, facing out or slightly down, sepals 5, large, overlapping, 3–4 in. (8–10 cm) across, stamens many, overwintering flowerstalks to 12 in. (30 cm) tall and 24–38 in. (60–95 cm) wide; December–April; leaves medium green, basal and on the stem, 4–12 in. (10–30 cm) long, divided into 3–5 leaflets, leathery, shiny, with widely and coarsely toothed, spiny margins. This group of garden hybrids has showy flowers and leafy flowering stems. Evergreen in zone 7, hardy to zone 6 with protection.

'Alabaster', flowers white with green shading toward center, to 4 in. (10 cm) across.

'Beatrix', flowers smaller, white flushed with green.

Blackthorn Strain, flowers pure white to greenish white with green stripe in the center of sepal.

'Hawkhurst', flowers large, very white but flushed with green; leaves large, very dark green.

Helleborus odorus, fragrant hellebore. Balkans, Greece, Corfu.

Sun, LS to WS; flowers faintly scented, 3–5 in loose clusters, green, sometimes yellowish green, saucer-shaped, facing out, sepals 5, large, 2–3 in. (5–8 cm) across, stamens many, on overwintering stems; January–April; plant 16–18 in. (40–45 cm) tall and wide; leaves evergreen, basal, dark green, leathery, finely hairy underneath in spring, to 16 in. (40 cm) across, divided into 5–7 leaflets, the 2 outer leaflets divided again into leaflike lobes, totaling 9–11 or more elliptic segments, leathery, shiny, with finely toothed margins. An impressive hellebore and well worth growing. Hardy to zone 6, heat-tolerant to zone 8.

Helleborus orientalis, Lenten rose, false rose. Black Sea region, Balkans, Turkey, the Caucasus.

Sun, LS to MS; flowers whitish tinting to green and cream, to 3 in. (8 cm) across, on overwintering, branching stems; plant to 24 in. (60 cm) tall and 20 in. (50 cm) wide; leaves medium to dark green, divided into leaflets, central leaflet undivided, outside leaflets divided into 3–4 leaflets, for a total 7–9 segments, finely toothed. The Balkan subsp. *abchasicus* has flowers tinted with red; subsp. *guttatus* has white flowers with a green center and prominently spotted with red or purple. The type and its subspecies are seldom seen in gardens, but the many orientalis hybrids, sometimes gathered under the names *H.* ×*hybridus* or *H.* ×*orientalis*, are widely available and very popular. Most are variable and represent selected seedling material from crosses of the typical species and its variants with other species, including *H. cyclophyllus, H. odorus, H. purpurascens, H. torquatus,* and *H. viridis.* Most were selected for flower color—white, pink, rose, reddish purple, deep purple, and even blackish. At Hosta Hill, the flowerstalks emerge in late November to early December, and the flowers usually remain closed for the coldest part of the winter; they open fully in late January and remain on the plant until April. New leafstalks develop in early March; as with other hellebores, I remove the flowerstalks before the seeds ripen in April. I have a white-flowered cultivar that comes true from seed, but most hybrids have varying offspring: only vegetatively propagated cultivars are true to name and type, so quiz your supplier carefully. Hybridizers have had only limited success with developing more upright flowers on the orientalis hybrids. Their nodding flower habit makes it difficult to enjoy them, so I have sited some of my plants on a hillside above the walks. Notwithstanding, many hybrids show their intense coloration on the back of the flower, so some landscape effect is derived from this character.

All cultivars listed are similar to the type in stature. All are outstanding and of the easiest culture. Hardy to zone 3 with protection, heat-tolerant to zone 9. At Hosta Hill they have withstood temperatures as low as 0°F (−18°C) and several summers of severe heat and drought.

'Alcyone', flowers metallic pink flushed outside, creamy green inside; plant vigorous, taller.

'Amethyst', flowers bluish mauve with dark edges on the flat sepal lobes; stems reddish purple.

'Andromeda', flowers dark crimson-purple inside and out, slightly glaucous.

'Blowsy', flowers yellow in bud, opening flat to creamy yellow, sepals puckered.

'Blue Spray', flowers blackish purple with a glaucous coating; stems dark purplish green.

'Citron', flowers yellow in bud, opening to yellow outside with a rose-pink haze inside.

'Cosmos', flowers saucer-shaped, greenish white, tinted pink outside and veined dark red, inside pinkish, evenly dotted with dark red spots almost to the edge of the sepals, leaving a narrow band of clear pink at the sepal margins.

'Dawn', flowers to 4 in. (10 cm) across, very pale, shiny pink, later turning coppery red.

'Dusk', flowers purple with blackish veins and speckles toward the sepal tips.

'Early Purple', flowers tinted with red, early.

'Eco Autumn Purple', leaves turn an attractive purplish color in fall.

'Eco Bullseye', flowers white with a red center.

'Eco Golden Eye', flowers purple with darker veins, anthers bright yellow.

'Garnet', flowers deep purplish red, veined darker purple.

'Günter Jürgl', flowers fully double, facing out, green with pink streaks on the back, pinkish speckled with darker pink inside, floriferous.

'John Raithby', flowers uniform lilac with a distinct, even network of purple veins.

Millet Hybrids, flowers white, pink, or red.

'Nocturne', flowers blackish purple, not opening flat, bracts bluish purple.

'Parrot', flowers yellow, hanging down.

'Philip Wilson', flowers nodding, rich pink backs, inside deep pink with deep purple spotting in the center and a clear pink zone near the tips of the sepals.

'Queen of Night', flowers nodding, deep purple, shiny on the back, nectaries yellowish green.

'Snow Queen', flowers fully double, creamy white flushed green at the base.

'Ushba' ('Usba'), flowers yellow in bud, opening to pure white with off-white veins, to 2.5 in. (6 cm) across; stems red-spotted at base.

Helleborus purpurascens. Central Europe into Poland, Czech Republic, Carpathians in Romania to western Ukraine.

Sun, LS; flowers 2–4, grayish purple to greenish dark purple, lighter green shading inside, cup-shaped, pendent and drooping, sepals 5, large, 1.5–2 in. (4–5 cm) across, stamens many, on stems produced in late winter or early spring; January–April; plant herbaceous, to 12 in. (30 cm) tall and wide, but often smaller; leaves deciduous, basal, light green, leathery, finely hairy underneath in spring, to 10 in. (25 cm) across, divided into up to 5 leaflets, each with 2–5 narrow, toothed lobes. This species disappears totally at the onset of winter and pushes up new flowering stems in early spring. Hardy to zone 5 and very heat-tolerant once established.

Helleborus ×*sternii*. Garden hybrid (*H. argutifolius* × *H. lividus*).

Some sun, LS; flowers few, greenish, flushed with pink or maroon, on overwintering stems; December–April; plant clump-forming, of differing proportions; leaves grayish green, veins marked in greenish white, toothed, spiny margins or entire. This group of garden hybrids is extremely variable, a mixture of features resembling either one or the other of the parents. Of easy culture and hardy to zone 7, 6 with protection. *Helleborus niger* crossed with *H.* ×*sternii* yields *H.* ×*ericsmithii*; involving three parents as they do, these plants display an even greater variability. Peruse commercial catalogs for plant descriptions.

'Blackthorn' (Blackthorn Strain), flowers green flushed with pink on purple stems; leaves marbled with silvery gray giving a smoky appearance; plant small.

'Boughton Beauty' (Boughton Beauty Strain), flowers green flushed with pink on purplish pink stems; leaves dark grayish green with conspicuous marbling; plants larger. Beware: many inferior plants are sold under this name.

Helleborus thibetanus, Chinese hellebore. China, Gansu, Hubei, Shaanxi, Sichuan.

Sun, LS to MS; flowers white fading to pink and lastly turning all green, sepals 5, pointed, bell-shaped, 2–2.5 in. (5–6 cm) across, subtending bracts green and very large, 2–5 on purple-tinged stem; plant to 18 in. (45 cm) tall; leaves green, divided into leaflets, central leaflet undivided, outside leaflets divided into subleaflets for a total of 7–9 segments, coarsely saw-toothed. In the wild, this species grows with astilbes and matteuccias, so its culture should be similar; flowers open in March, and leaves die down after the flowerstalks are fully developed in June or July.

Helleborus torquatus. Balkans, Bosnia, Croatia south to Montenegro (Crna Gora).

Sun, LS to MS; flowers small, in shades of green, brown with green stripes, purple inside and out, and deep violet-purple; leaves multidissected, with 12–80 segments. More field work is needed to define this extremely variable species, which is represented in gardens by plants collected in the 1930s. Plants offered under this name may be hybrids. Hardy to zone 6, heat-tolerant to zone 8. Several

seedling strains of the type are offered, and selections include 'Aeneas' (flowers double, green with brown veins outside, green inside), 'Dido' (flowers with green interior, exterior dark purple), and 'Paul Voelcker' (flowers double, lime-green; leaves reddish bronze when young).

Helleborus viridis, green hellebore. Alpine region from Switzerland into Bavaria, northern Italy, and Austria.

Sun, LS to MS; flowers dark green, sometimes yellowish green, 1–2 in. (2.5–5 cm) long, saucer-shaped or flat, nodding, 2–4 on long branching stems; plant 16 in. (40 cm) tall; leaves deciduous, medium to dark green, sometimes purple tinted when young, hairy beneath, leaflets 7, central leaflet undivided, outside leaflets divided into 3 leaflets, for a usual total of 9 segments, irregularly and coarsely toothed. I often observed this species in the foothills of the Alps in Bavaria, where it occurs on limestone. Adding dolomitic limestone to acid soils may speed up its usually slow growth. Subspecies *occidentalis* occurs further west in Germany, France, and Spain and is almost alike but has smooth, not hairy, leaf undersides.

Recommended reading

Ahlburg, Marlene. 1993. *Hellebores*. London: Batsford.

Mathew, Brian. 1967. *Hellebores*. Alpine Garden Society.

Rice, Graham, and Elizabeth Strangman. 1993. *The Gardener's Guide to Growing Hellebores*. Portland, Oregon: Timber Press.

Helonias

Wetlands in North America are under increasing attack; urban expansion is a chief threat. Fortunately, protection has also increased, so that swamp and bog dwellers like *Helonias bullata* (swamp pink) might retain at least some of their habitat. Years ago, wetlands in the way of new residential construction were filled in or drained, and it was on one such occasion that a few friends and I had the opportunity to rescue a colony of swamp pink. It has been growing here ever since and is of easy culture, as long as its specialized habitat is duplicated. My swamp pinks have flourished in an area of dappled shade with some morning sun in a mini-bog, a depression 24 in. (60 cm) deep lined with plastic and filled with rich, acid peat soil with a pH of 4 to 5. The rich green, strappy leaves and fragrant pink flower spikes add much to the garden.

Commercial sources offer propagated stock of swamp pink, which is now rare in the wild and a threatened species in Georgia and the Carolinas; wild plants should never be approached, to protect the habitat. Hardy to zone 5. The generic name comes from the Greek *helo* (= swamp, marshy place), for the plants' preferred habitat. The genus is classified in the Melanthiaceae.

Propagate by taking offsets from the tuberous rhizomes. Fresh seed germinates readily but is rarely produced in cultivation.

No disease or insect damage has been experienced here.

Helonias bullata, swamp pink. Eastern North America, New York to Virginia, in the mountains south to northwestern Georgia.

Some sun, LS to WS; flowers many, 10–30, with 3 petals and 3 sepals, bright pink, with 6 blue-tipped stamens, fragrant, arranged in a dense, terminal, cylindrical raceme, 1–3 in. (2.5–8 cm) long, on hollow, upright flowerstalk with small, leafy bracts, 12–36 in. (30–90 cm) tall; April–May; plant herbaceous, clump-forming, with tuberous rhizome; leaves in basal rosette, evergreen, straplike, bright green, smooth, 3–10 in. (8–25 cm) long and 0.8 in. (2 cm) wide, blunt-tipped; 3-lobed capsule. Here this species flowers frequently; the blue-tipped stamens give an overall purple hue to the flower spike, which elongates further after flowering. As in nature, I have several planted in a solitary group to attract attention to the evergreen leaves.

Heloniopsis

Similar in habit to the native North American swamp pinks of the genus *Helonias*, the species of *Heloniopsis* from Asia have fewer but larger flowers and are suited to more shady locations. They are more at home in moist woodlands than wetlands, but they do require constantly moist soil. In areas of dry summers, installing them in an artificial bog may be a necessity. *Heloniopsis* species are still rare in gardens, but some varieties are commercially imported from Korea and Japan. The broad, lance-shaped green leaves are overtopped with beautiful

nodding flower on bare stems and provide a charming display in spring. They do best when located in cool, shady locations; they dislike heat and dry conditions in southern gardens. Leaves are evergreen and turn purple in winter; in excessive cold, they may become deciduous.

Heloniopsis occurs in sizeable colonies in some areas of its Asian habitat, which includes moist woodlands and forest margins. The generic name, which comes from the Greek, indicates a resemblance to *Helonias*. The genus is classified in the Melanthiaceae.

Propagate by dividing the tuberous rhizomes after flowering in late spring.

Disease or insect damage is rare, but slugs and snail can damage new growth in spring.

Heloniopsis orientalis. Taiwan, Korea, Japan, Sakhalin.

S to WS; flowers 3–12, nodding, tubular with 6 spreading tepals, to 0.6 in. (1.5 cm) across, rose-pink, with 6 stamens and bluish purple anthers, arranged in a loose, upright, reddish, one-sided flowerstalk, to 10 in. (25 cm) tall; May–June; plant herbaceous, clump-forming, with tuberous rhizome; leaves in basal rosette, leathery, broadly lance-shaped, sharp-pointed, dull green, smooth, 3–8 in. (8–20 cm) long and 1–1.5 in. (2.5–4 cm) wide; 3-lobed capsule. The most frequently cultivated species. The variegated forms found in Japan are eagerly collected for pot culture. Hardy to zone 6, 5 with protection. I have seen an irregularly yellow-striped, very small plant that may have been a sport of var. *kawanoi*, a dwarf form of the typical species with a leaf rosette to 4 in. (10 cm) across and stems no more than 5 in. (13 cm) high. Variety *breviscapa* from the southern regions of the habitat has widely funnel-shaped flowers that are either pale pink or white, and the leaf rosette reaches 7–9 in. (18–23 cm) across; still untried in North America, its cold hardiness may be limited to zone 7. Variety *flavida* has greenish white flowers and flowerstalks taller than the type, reaching 16 in. (40 cm).

Hepatica

Hepaticas are also called liverworts. The liver-shaped leaves of *Hepatica acutiloba* were used extensively by American Indians and early settlers to treat liver ailments and other diseases. The generic name is from the Greek *hepas* (= liver), alluding to the leaf shape. Hepaticas are classified in the Ranunculaceae.

In the wild, liverworts occur in North America, Europe, and Asia. In gardens, they are harbingers of spring. Among the earliest-blooming wildflowers, their flowers, which usually open in early March atop the old, overwintering leaf mound, are remarkably frost-resistant; here I have seen occasional flowers from December through February on warm days. Immediately after flowering, new leaves emerge and remain on the plant until the following spring. Hepaticas are very easy to cultivate, and I have never understood why they are so rarely seen in gardens. Even in the heat and drought of southern gardens, these tough, little plants prevail, and it is perhaps because they are little and demure that gardeners often overlook them. I have seen gorgeous wild colonies of both *Hepatica acutiloba* and *H. americana* blooming in northern Georgia and on the Cove Hardwood Nature Trail in the Great Smoky Mountains. In this case nature points the way: as in the wild, large groups of them should be planted along garden paths, where they can be easily observed. Although the flower display is ephemeral, liverworts are great for shady gardens because of their persistent leaf display.

Almost any soil will do as long as it is not water-logged; liverworts in fact grow on heavy clay soils in the wild. Optimum pH is 5 to 7. Hepaticas tolerate considerable dryness, but some watering during droughts is recommended. Fertilizing is not required, but the addition of years-old woods compost is appreciated. Uncover leaf mounds in very early spring so that the flowers can properly develop and show. North American species are hardy to zone 3 and heat-tolerant well into zone 8.

Propagate by division in late autumn. Seed must be fresh and can be germinated by planting in the ground or in a seed tray. Be patient with the seedlings: they are extremely sensitive to transplanting shock and should be kept in seed trays for several seasons.

Large slugs and snails can damage young leaf growth and mature leaves. In summer, army worms and striped caterpillars feed on the leaves during the night.

Hepatica acutiloba, liverleaf, sharp-lobed hepatica, sharp-lobed liverwort, sharp-leaved hepatica. Eastern North America, southern Manitoba and Minnesota to southern Quebec, New England and south to South Carolina, Georgia, Alabama, west to Arkansas and Missouri.

LS to FS; flowers solitary, each on a hairy stem 4–6 in. (10–15 cm) tall, lavender, but also blue, pink, or white, sometimes purple, to 1 in. (2.5 cm) wide, 5–9 (sometimes to 12) petal-like sepals, no petals, 3 green sepal-like, persistent bracts, stamens numerous; March–April; plant herbaceous, clump-forming, with a fibrous roots emanating from a rhizomatous crown; leaves green, to 3 in. (8 cm) across, 3-lobed with pointed tips, sometimes 5- or 7-lobed; fruit seedlike, hairy. Usually seen in limestone regions, here this species grows on acid clay amended with dolomitic limestone; it hybridizes with *Hepatica americana* in the wild. **'Eco Royal Blue'** has blue flowers.

Hepatica americana, round-lobed hepatica, round-lobed liverwort, mayflower, blue anemone, blue liverleaf. Eastern North America, southern Manitoba and Minnesota to Nova Scotia, New England and south to Georgia, Alabama, Florida, west to Arkansas and Missouri.

LS to FS; flowers similar to *Hepatica acutiloba*, except that the leaves are 3-lobed with rounded tips and it has fewer flowers, which are mostly pinkish blue, but also lavender or white. This is the common liverwort widespread in eastern North America. It grows well on acidic soils, where it usually has bluish flowers. Several colors are available in commerce.

Hepatica nobilis, European hepatica. Europe.

LS to FS; flowers solitary, each on a hairy stem 4–5 in. (10–13 cm) tall, lavender, but also pinkish blue or white, to 1 in. (2.5 cm) wide, 6–9 petal-like sepals, no petals, 3 green sepal-like, persistent bracts, stamens numerous; March–April; plant herbaceous, clump-forming; leaves green, sometimes mottled with grayish green, to 3 in. (8 cm) across, 3-lobed with pointed tips, sometimes 5- or 7-lobed. In the wild *Hepatica nobilis* hybridizes with another European species, *H. transsilvanica*, yielding *H. ×media*; among the selections of this naturally occurring hybrid are 'Ballardii' (flowers deep blue with a high number of sepals) and, one of the best, 'Millstream Merlin' (flowers semi-double, dark purplish blue). *Hepatica nobilis* is an extremely variable species; clones with attractively mottled and even ruffled leaves are in commerce, and double-flowered forms are also available, at a cost.

'Ada Scott', flowers double, deep blue.

'Alba', flowers white.

'Alba Plena', flowers double, white.

'Barlowii', flowers full and rounded, bright sky-blue.

'Caerulea' ('Coerulea'), flowers blue.

'Eco Blue Harlequin', flowers blue; leaves marbled in shades of green.

'Little Abington', flowers double, dark blue.

'Marmorata', a selected clone with leaves marbled in silvery gray.

'Plena', flowers double, blue.

'Rosea', flowers pink.

'Rubra', flowers dark rosy red.

'Rubra Plena', flowers double, red to rosy red.

Hepatica nobilis var. *japonica,* Asian hepatica. Korea, Japan.

LS to FS; flowers solitary, each on a hairy stem 4–5 in. (10–13 cm) tall, blue, pink, or white, to 1 in. (2.5 cm) wide, 6–9 narrow, petal-like sepals, giving a star-shaped appearance, stamens numerous; March–April; plant herbaceous, clump-forming; leaves green, sometimes mottled with silvery gray or yellow, to 3 in. (8 cm) across, 3-lobed with pointed tips, sometimes 5- or 7-lobed. Variety *asiatica* from Korea is outstanding in having leaves handsomely mottled with silvery gray. Asian taxonomists prefer to treat these varieties as separate species, but recent rearrangements of the genus have pointed the other way. The Asian hepaticas are variable, and the many forms with variegated leaves are eagerly collected and revered in Japanese pot culture. Confirm details concerning flower color and leaf mottling before ordering.

Other Asian species have been discovered and are slowly reaching Western gardens. *Hepatica yamatutai* from Sichuan province in China is an outstanding hepatica for the garden, with very large flowers and deeply lobed leaves that have a purple cast beneath. *Hepatica henryi,* whose native range is not yet determined, has small flowers of little worth, but its leaves may be attractive enough to bring it into cultivation. Another Asian species is *H. insularis,* which I overlooked searching for the diminutive *Hosta venusta* near Mount Halla on Cheju Island; this lovely dwarf with silver-mottled leaves promises to keep company with small hostas in gardens just as it does in the wild. Hepaticas isolated on Ullung Island speciated into **Hepatica maxima,** which has leaves of a size befitting its epithet; although its flowers are less showy, this species promises to be a great, leafy addition to the shady garden.

Hepatica transsilvanica, Transsylvanian hepatica. Southeastern Europe, Romania, Transsylvania Mountains.

LS to FS; flowers solitary, each on a hairy stem 5 in. (13 cm) tall, mostly blue, but also white and pinkish white, to 1.5 in. (4 cm) across, no petals, 6–9 petal-like sepals, 3 green sepal-like, persistent bracts, stamens numerous; March–April; plant herbaceous, clump-forming; leaves green, sometimes mottled with grayish green, to 4 in. (10 cm) long, 3-lobed or sometimes 5- or 7-lobed with rounded tips, each lobe subdivided into several smaller lobes, giving an almost round appearance. A gardenworthy species, with large flowers and leaves; here it withstands dry conditions better than the other species. The longer, creeping rhizomes of its rootstock give it a welcome spreading habit. Cultivars include 'Buis' (flowers silvery cornflower-blue) and 'Ellison Spence' (flowers double, silvery blue; very floriferous).

Heuchera, ×*Heucherella,* **and** *Tolmiea*

If the Far East is credited with contributing the most popular hostas to the shady garden, then North America must be extolled for being the source of heucheras. In both cases, it was plant breeders who ushered these plants into gardens. Like hostas, heucheras are primarily grown for their attractive, often strikingly variegated leaves. Included here is ×*Heucherella,* a cross between *Heuchera* and *Tiarella* that is used and treated like *Heuchera* in gardens, and *Tolmiea menziesii* (youth-on-age), a western North American species that is similarly useful as a groundcover in shady gardens.

Things were different before the advent of *Heuchera micrantha* 'Palace Purple', a purple-leaved cultivar that inspired many gardeners, including myself, to include heucheras in gardens. Until then, all I grew at Hosta Hill was a native plant, snatched from the bulldozers on a construction site north of Atlanta, with striking leaves but measly flowers that I usually cut off; I think it is *H. parviflora*, but I am not certain, because the nomenclature of the 70-odd species of *Heuchera* is a work in progress. Most species occur in western North America from British Columbia south to Mexico. The eastern species are commonly called alumroot, for the color of the roots' interior; American Indians used them to make a healing poultice applied to burns and other wounds. Many species have insignificant flowers, but some recent selections with more showy flowers or many small flowers do make an impression—*H. sanguinea* 'White Cloud', for example, really looks like a small white cloud from afar. I grow several varieties in my garden and have concluded that the leaf mound, not the flowers, is the glory of these plants.

In the wild, eastern heucheras occupy moist and dry woodlands, sandstone cliffs, and exposed rocky sites; western species are primarily cliff and mountain dwellers. In gardens, they are low-maintenance groundcover and specimen plants and combine well with hostas, ferns, and taller wildflowers like disporums and astilbes. In mild-winter areas, their evergreen leaf mounds provide four-season interest; in northern habitats they are herbaceous unless covered by lasting snow during the coldest periods. Heucheras are very easy to cultivate in light to full shade, and direct sun is tolerated in more northern gardens. Almost all are hardy to zone 4, but heat tolerance is limited; site in deep shade in southern gardens. Moist, but not overly so, soil is ideal. Drainage is key (and for western species, absolutely essential), because saturated soils can cause root rot. I add very coarse sand to the soil mix as well as pine bark pellets. With age, the rootstock lengthens, and the growing tips will eventually be well above ground level. At this point some gardeners cut off the aboveground part, hoping that the roots left in the ground will resprout; I dig up the entire rootstock and replant it deeper. Optimum pH is 5 to 6.

Heuchera honors the German botanist von Heucher. *Tolmiea* honors William Tolmie, an official of the Hudson Bay Company. Heucheras and tolmieas are classified in the Saxifragaceae.

Propagate by division in late autumn. Species seed can be sown, barely covered, in spring after warm weather arrives. Hybrid cultivars must be divided, because seed does not come true.

Large slugs and snails can damage young leaf growth and mature leaves. In summer, army worms and striped caterpillars feed on the leaves and disfigure them. Leaf spot and mildew are reported.

Heuchera americana, rock geranium, common alumroot. Eastern North America, Ontario and Michigan east to New England, south to Georgia and Alabama, west to Oklahoma and Missouri.

Some sun, LS to FS; flowers insignificant, yellowish green to brownish green, in clusters of 3–5 per stalk on multistalked flowering stems 24–36 in. (60–90 cm) tall; April–June; plant evergreen to semi-evergreen, mound-forming, with thick, woody rootstock; leaves in a basal rosette, on long stalks, shiny, leathery, in spring mottled with purplish brown, later all green, hairy beneath, 3–5 in. (8–13 cm) across, heart-shaped with 3–9 lobes, each coarsely toothed. The best species for southern gardens if sited in medium to full shade. For gardening purposes **Heuchera villosa** (hairy alumroot) from the southern part of *H. americana*'s range and *H. richardsonii* from the western and central ranges are essentially the same. **Heuchera villosa 'Autumn Bride'** has velvety leaves of light green with large inflorescences of white flowers. *Heuchera parviflora* is horticulturally the equal of *H. americana*. All adapt well to southern gardens but need to be planted in shade; leaves wilt in too much sun. Several selections of *H. americana* are available; all have flowers from white to whitish or yellowish green and sometimes green tinged with purple.

'Chocolate Veil', leaves to 6 in. (15 cm), deep brown with a purplish cast, veined silvery gray, purple underneath.

'Dale's Silver' ('Dale's Selection', 'Dale's Variety'), leaves mottled silvery gray; tall, to 30 in. (75 cm).

'Eco Improved', leaves to 6 in. (15 cm), grayish foliage edged green with purple veins. An improved 'Eco Magnififolia'.

'Eco Magnififolia', leaves to 6 in. (15 cm), deep brown with a purplish cast, veined silvery gray, purple underneath.

'Eco Running Tapestry', leaves to 6 in. (15 cm), green, heavily veined in dark purplish brown.

'Emerald Veil', emerald-green leaves tinted with silvery gray.

'Garnet', medium green leaves with reddish brown veins.

'Persian Carpet', burgundy-red leaves with dark purplish brown edges and veins, tinted silvery gray in spots.

'Pewter Veil', silvery gray leaves with purplish cast and charcoal-gray veins.

'Purpurea', an old cultivar with purplish brown marbling on the leaves.

'Ruby Veil', ruby-red leaves with a network of silvery gray veins.

'Velvet Night', very dark velvety leaves, greenish black shaded with purple.

Heuchera cylindrica, poker alumroot. Western North America, British Columbia and Alberta, south to Montana, California, and Nevada.

Some sun, LS to FS; flowers insignificant, yellowish green to yellowish white, in clusters of 3–5 per stalk on multistalked flowering stems 24–38 in. (60–95 cm) tall; May–July; plant evergreen to semi-evergreen, mound-forming; leaves in a basal, mounding rosette, coarsely hairy, dark green mottled with lighter green, 1–3 in. (2.5–8 cm) across, heart-shaped with 3–7 rounded lobes, each scalloped. Grown primarily for its striking leaf mound, this species is a good, very hardy foliage plant for more northern gardens, but suffers in the South.

'Alba', creamy white flowers.

'Chartreuse', flowers yellowish green.

'Greenfinch', flowers bright green on tight stalk.

'Green Ivory', whitish flowers with green bases.

'Green Marble', light green marbled leaves and greenish flowers.

'Hyperion', very short scapes with pinkish red flowers with a hint of green.

'Siskiyou Mountains', a cute dwarf with scapes to 4 in. (10 cm) and a small leaf mound.

Heuchera micrantha, crevice alumroot, small-flowered alumroot. Western North America, British Columbia south to Sierra Nevada.

Some sun, LS to FS; flowers small, yellowish white, red anthers, on flowerstalks to 36 in. (90 cm); June–July; plant evergreen to semi-evergreen, mound-forming; leaves in a basal rosette, gray-green, 1–3 in. (2.5–8 cm) across, heart-shaped with 3–7 rounded lobes, each scalloped. Suffers greatly from the summer heat in southern gardens.

'Chocolate Ruffles', large, deep cocoa-brown leaves with heavily ruffled margins that reveal the purple underside; white flowers are small but many and contrast with the dark leaves.

'Lace Ruffles', ruffled leaves with white variegation; shorter flower spikes.

'Montrose Ruby', leaves maroon with silvery markings; flowers creamy white.

'Palace Purple' ('Powis Purple'), a selection (some say of var. *diversifolia*) with deep purplish red leaves, to 6 in. (15 cm) across (seen in photo of *Pollia japonica*). Comes true from seed, but many seed-raised plants lose their deep color and turn dark green by summer. Does well here in spring and fall, but during the summer it's a sad sight.

'Pewter Moon', leaves marbled with pewter, maroon underside; flowers pinkish.

'Ruffles', leaves woolly, bright green, and heavily ruffled; flowers white.

Heuchera sanguinea, coralbells, coral flower. Southwestern North America, New Mexico and Arizona south to Mexico.

Some sun, LS to MS; flowers large, tubular, bell-shaped, to 0.5 in. (1 cm) long, red, rarely pink or white, on flowerstalks 10–20 in. (25–50 cm) tall; May–June; plant evergreen to semi-evergreen, mat- or clump-forming; leaves in a basal rosette, dark green, 0.8–3 in. (2–8 cm) across, kidney- to heart-shaped with 3–7 rounded lobes, each shallowly toothed. In nature, this western species grows on moist shady rocks. It is very hardy in northern gardens, to zone 3, where it needs more sun than shade and flowers persist for up to 7 weeks. Flowering can be extended by cutting spent flowerstalks. It does not grow well in the heavy, acid clay soils of the South. I have experimented with some cultivars, growing them in soil amended with much organic matter and coarse grit for rapid drainage as well as dolomitic limestone and located in full shade. Here the species and its cultivars have a short life span.

'Alba', flowers white.

'Apple Blossom', buds rose-pink opening to pink flowers.

'Brandon Pink', flowers reddish to coral-pink.

'Cherry Splash', flowers rose-red; leaves green with white and yellow splashes.

'Coral Cloud', flowers coral-red; leaves shiny and with crinkled surface.

'Fairy Cups', flowers bright, clear cherry-red; leaves cupped.

'Firesprite', flowers bright rose-red.

'Frosty', flowers bright red; leaves variegated with silvery white.

'Grandiflora', flowers white, very floriferous.

'Jack Frost', flowers rose-red; leaves overlaid in silvery white.

'Maxima', flowers dark crimson-red.

'Mother of Pearl', flowers white tinted with pink.

'Northern Fire', flowers scarlet-red; leaves mottled with silvery white.

'Oxfordii', flowers scarlet-red.

'Pearl Drops', flowers white flushed with pink; arching stems.

'Pluie de Feu' ('Feuerregen', 'Rain of Fire'), flowers bright red, long-lasting.

'Red Spangles', flowers crimson-red, late.

'Schneewittchen' ('Snow White'), flowers pure white.

'Scintillation', flowers deep pink, rimmed in coral-pink.

'Snow Storm', flowers bright clear red; leaves green with silvery white splashings.

'Splendens', flowers scarlet-red, long-lasting.

'Splish Splash', flowers rose-pink; leaves splashed in creamy white.

'Virginalis', flowers pure white.

'White Cloud', flowers white; leaves green mottled with silvery white.

'Winfield Pink', flowers clear pink.

Heuchera cultivars

On the West Coast, Dan Heims and others have come up with many excellent heucheras, and in Europe too breeders continue to generate new cultivars at a fast pace. Many of these cultivars—even those already listed, some would argue—may not be selections of given species but are rather hybrids. These and other hybrids have been loosely gathered under *Heuchera* ×*brizoides*. The original cross was made by Lemoine between *H. americana* and *H. sanguinea*. Later, *H. micrantha* and possibly other species were involved, as well as crosses between hybrids, so correct attribution of this hybrid group is difficult. Most average 24–36 in. (60–90 cm) in height, and, depending on location, flower during early or late summer. Consult the latest catalogs for full listings.

'Bloom's Coral' ('Bloom's Variety'), flowers coral-red.

'Can-Can', flowers red; leaves green overlaid in silvery white with green veins, ruffled margins.

'Carmen', flowers dark red.

'Champaign Bubbles', flowers creamy pink; leaves green with silvery white overlay.

'Chatterbox', flowers rose-pink.

'Freedom', flowers rose-pink, floriferous, late.

'Gloriana', flowers dark pink.

'Gracillima', flowers pink, early.

'Green Ivory', flowers greenish white.

'Huntsman' ('Dennis Davidson'), flowers bright red on short stems.

'Jubilee', flowers light pink, early.

'June Bride', flowers snow-white.

'Lady Romney', flowers light pink.

'Leuchtkäfer' ('Firefly'), flowers fragrant, vermilion-red.

'Mary Rose', flowers deep pink.

'Matin Bells', flowers bright red.

'Mint Frost', flowers pinkish red; leaves silvery green with olive-green veins.

'Mint Julep', flowers red; leaves mint-green with silvery overlay.

'Monet', flowers red; leaves large, green splashed with white.

'Mt. St. Helens', flowers cardinal-red.

'Oakington Jewel', flowers red; leaves greenish bronze.

'Petite Pearl Fairy', flowers pink; leaves dark green splashed with silvery white; dwarf plant.

'Plum Puddin' ('Plum Pudding'), flowers pink; leaves deep burgundy-red with silvery white etching between veins.

'Pretty Polly', flowers light pink.

'Regal Robe', flowers white, leaves silver with lavender.

'Ring of Fire', flowers red; leaves green with silvery white overlay and a thin orange-red margin.

'Rosamundi', flowers coral-pink.

'Ruby Ruffles', flowers red; leaves ruby-red with a silvery white overlay in leaf center, wrinkled and ruffled showing the purple underside.

'Silberregen' ('Silver Rain'), flowers pure white.

'Snow Angel', flowers rose-pink; leaves green with silvery white splotches.

'Taff's Joy', flowers pink; leaves green variegated in yellowish white and shaded pink.

'Torch', flowers dark scarlet-red.

'Velvet Knight', flowers red; leaves dark purple with veins outlined in red.

'Weserlachs' ('Weser Salmon'), flowers salmon-pink.

'Whirlwind', flowers pinkish red; leaves coppery red, wrinkled, and ruffled.

'White Marble', flowers white; leaves green, mottled silvery white.

'Widar', flowers scarlet-red; vigorous.

×*Heucherella*, foamy bells. Hybrid (*Heuchera* × *Tiarella*).

Some sun, LS to FS; the prototype cross, originally made by Lemoine, was probably between *Heuchera* ×*brizoides* and *Tiarella wherryi*. Other crosses have been involved since. Called foamy bells for their more floriferous and dense flowering habit, which is more like *Tiarella*. Because they are sterile, this group of hybrids must be propagated by division. ×*Heucherella alba* has white flowers without stolons. ×*Heucherella tiarelloides* has pink flowers on reddish flowerstalks and is stoloniferous.

'Bridget Bloom', flowers rich pink, floriferous; leaves marbled gray.

'**Kimono**', flowers white with a faint greenish to yellowish undertone, very floriferous in April–May; leaves deeply lobed with a blackish green stripe along the center vein. Huge compared to its parent *Tiarella*, forming clumps to 36 in. (90 cm) across.

'Pink Frost', flowers pink, floriferous; leaves green suffused with silvery white.

'Quicksilver', flowers pink, fading to white; leaves silvery gray with reddish bronze veins.

'Silver Streak', flowers creamy white, floriferous; leaves purple marked with silvery white.

'Snow White', flowers snow-white; leaves green suffused with silvery white.

'Viking Ship', flowers pinkish; leaves silvery white, initially with leafletlike projections, later filling in to a mapleleaf shape.

Tolmiea menziesii, youth-on-age, pickaback plant, piggyback plant, thousand-mothers. Northwestern North America, Oregon and the western Cascades, northern California.

MS to FS; flowers small, barely fragrant, tubular and cup-shaped, to 0.6 in. (1.5 cm) long, red or reddish purple, sepals 5 uneven, petals 4, threadlike, curving, maroon, stamens 3, with orange anthers, 20–50 loosely arranged one-sided on hairy flowerstalks 10–20 in. (25–50 cm) tall; June–August; plant rhizomatous, producing young plants at the intersection of leaf and leafstalk, fast-spreading; leaves mostly basal, hairy, lime-green, to 4 in. (10 cm) across, kidney- to heart-shaped with 3–5 sharp, toothed lobes. Hailing from moist, shady coniferous forests, this species needs deep shade in southern gardens; direct sun may scorch the leaves. In northern gardens it can be grown in lighter shade. Hardy to zone 6. In cold-winter areas, it is grown as an interesting, shade-tolerant houseplant. Its selection 'Taff's Gold' ('Maculata', 'Variegata') has leaves paler green and irregularly speckled, mottled, and spotted with creamy, pale yellow.

Hieracium

As its common name hawkweed indicates, the many species and subspecies of this genus are plainly weeds and mostly sunlovers, but *Hieracium venosum* (rattlesnake weed) grows happily in considerable shade, thriving on neglect. Years ago, I found it among the forest litter in my youngest son Sigi's Bay Creek garden on the outskirts of Atlanta. What attracted me were its many grayish green leaves with conspicuous red to purple veins. Later on, this colony of many individual plants produced tall, leafless stems bearing clusters of bright yellow flowers. The leaves lose some of their striking spring coloration when the weather gets hot.

Rattlesnake weed is native to North America. It grows and flowers in light to medium shade, but for larger plants and more flowers, site it in morning sun. Soil conditions do not matter; here it likes the poor, compacted clay soil under my paths better than the rich soil in adjacent beds. Hardy in zones 3 to 8 and endures hot, dry weather with such aplomb that I just have to love it. The generic name is from the classic Latin name for these weeds. *Hieracium* is classified in the Asteraceae.

Propagation is no problem: this species has not forgotten that it is a weed and spreads itself around the garden. Unwanted seedlings should be removed when young.

My plants seem to be immune to diseases, and insect pests do not bother them.

Hieracium venosum, rattlesnake weed, poor robin's plantain. Eastern North America, southeastern Canada south to Georgia and Alabama.

LS to MS; flowers many, small, yellow, dandelionlike, to 0.5 in. (1 cm) across, in open clusters atop leafless, branching stems to 30 in. (75 cm) tall but usually shorter, around 12 in. (30 cm); May–

August; leaves 4–10, in a basal rosette, elliptic, short leafstalk, blunt tip, 1.5–6 in. (4–15 cm) long, light grayish green with a network of bright red or reddish purple veins that become less noticeable by midsummer; fruit dry with greenish yellow bristles. In time, this species carpets the shady woodland with brightly colored leaves in spring, showy yellow flowers in early summer, and a green groundcover until the first freeze. Plant in groups.

Hosta

Hostas, still offered in some catalogs under the old names funkia or plantain lily, are the aristocrats of the shady garden, remaining handsome from the time they emerge until the first frost turns their leaves a warm buff or golden yellow. My grandfather had several clumps of *Hosta sieboldiana* in a shady corner of his garden, and my sister and I hid under their huge, blue-gray umbrellas of leaves during games of hide-and-go-seek. Occasionally, we broke a leaf stem and provoked his wrath. Opa, as we called him, loved his hostas, and they still grace the garden he so diligently tended. I never forgot their elegant beauty, and when I built my first garden, hostas topped my "must get" perennial list. Unfortunately, no one in Nashville seemed to know what a hosta was in 1957. Luckily, my mother had a few in her Detroit garden and shared them with me. They became the talk of the neighborhood, and I found myself sharing pieces now and then. My interest became so passionate that in the late 1970s, I began a scholarly study of the genus *Hosta*, which culminated in the publication of my monograph, *The Genus* Hosta (Timber Press: Portland, Oregon, 1991).

Having grown many hundreds of hosta cultivars and all the species hostas here at Hosta Hill, I can say without reservation: these plants are simple to use, fit just about anywhere, and require little maintenance other than cleanup—no staking, lifting, dividing, or babying. Most insects do not bother them, although cutworms and large slugs and snails may eat holes through the arising shoots, resulting in perforated leaves. American gardeners meet this challenge by applying toxic poisons, while the more pragmatic Japanese leave things as they are and consider holes in hosta leaves nature's way.

Hostas offer tremendous diversity: plant sizes from tiny crowns fitting into the palm of a hand to huge mounds of shrub-sized proportions; plant habits from erect vase shapes to prostrate starry pinwheels; leaf shapes from grassy straps to near perfectly round circles; leaf textures from flat to dimpled, wrinkled, cupped, or twisted; leaf substances from thin and papery to thick as leather; surface effects from polished and shiny to matte, even powdery white; leaf colors from blue-green to chartreuse, yellow, and almost silvery white; variegation patterns from narrow margins to bright centers on dark surrounds and multicolored streakings and splashings; scapes from tall and erect to oblique, even flat-on-the-ground. Flowers too are diverse, from large, waxy, deliciously fragrant white trumpets to wide-open purple bells, and almost every cool combination in between. By carefully combining early-, average- and late-flowering hostas, a succession of bloom can be established, here from late May through late October or until the first freeze further north. Even the seed capsules show great variety.

Hostas are extremely long-lived as perennials go. Opa's were planted before 1900 and they thrive still. And they are in general affordable, although newly introduced cultivars can be very expensive. Once planted and given reasonable care, hostas multiply faithfully and, in most cases, rapidly. In the final analysis, hostas are makers of gardeners because what makes enthusiastic gardeners out of reluctant ones is the sweet smell of success. Hostas practically guarantee success, and that success inspires gardeners to work harder to achieve more.

Some hosta flowers are worthy of consideration, but it is their foliage—the many shades of green and the multitude of variegation patterns, combined with the different sizes, shapes, textures, and surfaces—that make hostas so useful in shady gardens. Hosta leaf colors are not true colors nor are they permanent. Virtually every hosta lover has, always with some degree of sadness, seen his blue plant turn green in summer's heat, and many a fine golden margin eventually turns a nondescript white. These phenomena deserve explanation.

1. Viridescence. Viridescent hostas turn green. Leaves emerge white, yellow, or very light green and turn green or even dark green.

2. Lutescence. Lutescent hostas turn yellow. Leaves emerge green or chartreuse (yellowish green) and turn yellow or whitish yellow. Much more

subtle than viridescence, lutescence frequently involves only a very slight change from a greenish to a yellowish cast.

3. Albescence. Albescent hostas turn white. Their yellow, yellowish green, or green areas turn to near white. Yellow-margined hostas frequently turn into white-margined ones.

The "blue" of hostas is not a true blue, but a bluish cast caused by a pruinose epidermal wax, called indumentum, which produces a glaucous sheen over a green background color. When the wax is lost—washed off by rain or overhead watering, or diminished by increasing day- and nighttime air temperature differentials—the underlying green color becomes visible. The blue effect lasts much longer under cool and more shady conditions but sooner or later the green will be plain. The attractive "white" of the leaf underside of some species and cultivars is actually a coating of a very fine, opaque white powder. Whatever the true nature of the color, gardeners still admire their blue and white hostas while they appear thus and consider their "turnings" part of the ever-changing look of the garden.

Resist the temptation to cram as many of these colorful plants as possible into a garden—I have seen gardens in which the preponderance of variegated hostas changed the entire scene into a kaleidoscopic monstrosity. Stick with the serenity of a natural garden, in a green palette; the multiplicity of greens offered by different hosta cultivars will assure your garden is both tranquil and diverse, in size and texture as well as in color. Variegated and bright yellow hostas can be utilized in the garden, but sparingly so. Yellow hostas are great for brightening the dark corners of shady gardens, but limit variegated hostas to use as accents, highlighting exceptional vistas in a garden.

By variegated hostas, I mean those with standard, stable variegation, either marginal or center-variegated (a light-colored leaf center with a darker margin). I do not like hostas that have streakings, stripes, blotches, or other irregular variegation on darker (usually green) leaves. In a natural garden setting, these usually very expensive chameleon hostas have no place. Besides their instability (most revert to solid color or margined forms), each leaf on an irregularly variegated plant has a different pattern of streaks and stripes. Streaky

hostas may be fine for collectors and hybridizers, but gardeners should keep away from them, particularly if the goal is a stable, serene landscape. If you absolutely must have one "streaker," site it as an accent plant or pot it up as a patio conversation piece.

Hostas evolved in the land areas bordering the East China Sea and the Sea of Japan. They have been found growing in the wild in eastern China, Korea, the Japanese archipelago (excluding the Ryukyu Islands), and the southern Sikhote-Alin mountains. The Japanese formal (academic) and horticultural name is *giboshi* (the exact transliteration from the Japanese Katakana is *gi-bo-u-shi*). Visiting Japan in the 1690s, the German botanist and medical doctor Kaempfer observed hostas and used a westernized version of the Japanese name, *Gibboosi*, in 1712. Swedish botanist Thunberg assigned the first scientific generic names, *Aletris* in 1780 and *Hemerocallis* (alluding to the ephemeral nature of hosta flowers, each lasting one day only) in 1784. Hostas were introduced to Europe around 1784, when *Hosta plantaginea* was raised in France from seed sent from Macao by French Consul Charles de Guignes. In 1812 the Austrian botanist Trattinnick suggested the genus be classified under the generic name *Hosta*, honoring his contemporary Nicolaus Thomas Host; a few years later in 1817 the German botanist Sprengel published the generic name *Funkia* to honor Heinrich Funk, a Bavarian collector of alpine ferns. In the 1820s, Philipp Franz Balthasar von Siebold, a German eye surgeon and botanist, sent several live hosta specimens to Holland; Siebold had a gardener's eye for plants, including hostas, and he collected and imported many distinct and desirable species and cultivars, many with variegated foliage. Trattinnick's *Hosta* was conserved in 1905 by the International Botanical Congress of Vienna. The genus is now placed in its own family, Hostaceae.

Selecting hosta cultivars for the garden is as vexatious as trying to select daylilies, roses, or daffodils. Here I have listed some of the most popular (as voted annually by the membership of the American Hosta Society—variegated hostas are certainly in vogue!) of the 3000 some registered hosta cultivars and added to that gardenworthy species and cultivars I have grown at Hosta Hill. The bigger hostas—those over 40 in. (1 m) across and over 30 in. (75 cm) high—do take up a lot of room, and to plant several in small city gardens may be a bit too much. Site smaller hostas up front and in groups, either as mass plantings or as edgings along walks, taking care their companions do not overpower them. Site miniature and dwarf hostas—those less than 10 in. (25 cm) across and 6 in. (15 cm) high—in mass plantings of a couple of dozen or more individual plants, ideally in an elevated position, as in a rock garden. For single specimens, the best and safest place is in an elevated ornamental pot, which offers some protection from slugs and allows quick checks for disease or insect damage.

Hostas are herbaceous. Unless otherwise noted, all species and cultivars listed are hardy in zones 4 to 8. No shade requirements are indicated: all are suitable for locations with *some sun and light to medium shade*. In full shade, hostas may not flower. All flowers have six tepals (three sepals and three petals), all similar and of uniform color, and six stamens with yellow or purple anthers; the flowers occur one-sided on the stem, unless otherwise noted.

Hosta capitata, *iya giboshi* (Jap.), *banwool-bibich'u* (Kor.). Korea.

Flowers purple, funnel-shaped, to 2 in. (5 cm) long; June–July; flowerstalk to 20 in. (50 cm), straight, with ridges; plant clump-forming, dome-shaped, 36 in. (90 cm) across, 30 in. (75 cm) high; leaves to 6 in. (15 cm) long and 4 in. (10 cm) wide, green, base heart-shaped, wavy-undulate leaf margin, sunken veins. The flowers are tightly grouped and sit "ball-shaped" (a translation of the Korean name) atop the stem, making this species an interesting garden subject. Highly variable. Both large- and small-leaf forms are found in the wild; usually it is the small-leaf form that is offered.

Hosta clausa, *tsubomi giboshi* (Jap.), *jookug-bibich'u* (Kor.). Korea.

Flowers remain as lavender to light purple buds until they drop off; June–July; flowerstalk to 20 in. (62 cm), smooth, green, leaning; plant clump-forming, 10 in. (25 cm) across, 8 in. (20 cm) high; leaves to 5 in. (13 cm) long and 2 in. (5 cm) wide, green, lance-shaped. Variety *normalis* ('Normalis') has flowers that open; var. *stolonifera* is a nonflowerer that propagates by creeping rhizomes.

Hosta gracillima, small rock hosta, *hime iwa giboshi* (Jap.). Japan.

Flowers purple, funnel-shaped, to 1.5 in. (4 cm) long; June–July; flowerstalk to 10 in. (25 cm), bare, straight; plant clump-forming, 6 in. (15 cm) across, 1.5 in. (4 cm) high; leaves to 2 in. (5 cm) long and 0.5 in. (1 cm) wide, glossy dark green, elliptic lance-shaped, wavy leaf margin. 'Kifukurin Ko Mame', a hybrid with creamy white margins, is similar. Other hybridized forms of the species are 'Rock Princess', 'Sugar Plum Fairy', and the yellow-leaved 'Hydon Sunset'.

Hosta hypoleuca, white-backed hosta, *urajiro giboshi* (Jap.). Japan.

Flowers shiny white, funnel-shaped, to 2 in. (5 cm) long; June–July; flowerstalk to 14 in. (35 cm), leaning; plant clump-forming, 36 in. (90 cm) across, 20 in. (50 cm) high; leaves 12–18 in. (30–45 cm) long and 12 in. (30 cm) wide, glaucous green, base heart-shaped, wavy-undulate leaf margin, with intensely white, powdery coating on the underside. Uncommon in the wild, it clings tenaciously to rock ledges and forms only 1–3, very large leaves. In cultivation it develops into a large clump with 5–7 leaves. 'Maekawa', a selection of the species, is almost identical. Hybrids are 'Azure Snow' (bluish green leaves) and 'Merry Sunshine' (green leaves with yellow margins).

Hosta kikutii, crane-beaked hosta, *hyuga giboshi* (Jap.). Southern Japan.

Flowers white, funnel-shaped, to 2 in. (5 cm) long; July–August; flowerstalk to 20 in. (50 cm), straight but leaning; plant clump-forming, dome-shaped, 18 in. (45 cm) across, 10 in. (25 cm) high; leaves 7–9 in. (18–23 cm) long and 3–4 in. (8–10 cm) wide, green, lance-shaped, flat with closely spaced, sunken veins. Excellent for gardens with hot summers. The selection 'Leuconota' has bluish green leaves with a powdery white coating underneath. Hybrids involving the species include 'Red Neck Heaven' and others with lavender flowers. 'Hyuga Kifukurin' (*Hosta* 'Shelleys') is a natural sport with a narrow yellowish white margin. Variety *polyneuron* has wider leaves with veins very narrowly spaced; variegated hybrids of this variety include 'Wakayama Sudare Shirofukurin' (larger leaves with a narrow white margin) and 'Shikoku Sudare Shirofukurin', also with a crisped, narrow white margin but smaller leaves, to 4 in. (10 cm) long.

Hosta laevigata. Korea.

Flowers light purple, spider-shaped, to 1.5 in. (4 cm) long and across; July–September; flowerstalk to 20 in. (50 cm), straight but leaning, with small stem leaves; plant clump-forming, dome-shaped, 14 in. (35 cm) across, 10 in. (25 cm) high; leaves 7–9 in. (18–23 cm) long and 2–3 in. (5–8 cm) wide, dark green, narrowly lance-shaped, flat with good substance.

Hosta longipes, rock hosta, *iwa giboshi* (Jap.). Japan.

Flowers purple or white suffused with purple, bell-shaped, to 2 in. (5 cm) long; August–October; flowerstalk to 12 in. (30 cm), straight but leaning; plant clump-forming, dome-shaped, 18 in. (45 cm) across, 12 in. (30 cm) high; leaves 5–6 in. (13–15 cm) long and 3–4 in. (8–10 cm) wide, green, heart-shaped, flat with closely spaced, sunken veins; leaf and flowerstalks purple-spotted. This widespread species (seen in photo of *Platanthera ciliaris*) is matchless for hot-summer gardens with long periods of drought. Forma *sparsa* flowers sparsely (hence the epithet) and has purple anthers. The popular f. *hypoglauca* has purple leaf and flowerstalks and a whitish, powdery coating on the leaf underside. 'Urajiro' has near white leaf undersides; other selections include 'Brandywine', 'Setsuko', and 'Tagi'. *Hosta rupifraga* (*hachijo giboshi* in Japan) from Hachijojima is similar to *H. longipes*, but its leaves are thick and bright, shiny green and suited to both hot and cool summers; it flowers sparsely. 'Hydon Twilight' is more floriferous.

Hosta longissima var. *longifolia*, swamp hosta, *hosoba mizu giboshi* (Jap.). Japan.

Flowers purple, funnel-shaped, to 2 in. (5 cm) long; August–September; flowerstalk to 18 in. (45 cm), straight but leaning, with stem leaves; plant clump-forming, dome-shaped, 10 in. (25 cm) across, 5 in. (13 cm) high; leaves 6–7 in. (15–18 cm) long and 0.5–0.6 in. (1–1.5 cm) wide, dark shiny green, flat, narrowly linear lance-shaped. This moisture-loving variety provides an interesting mound of very narrow leaves. 'Asahi Comet' has white margins; 'Asahi Sunray' has yellow margins.

Hosta montana 'Aureomarginata', *kifukurin oba giboshi* (Jap.).

Flowers white, suffused with lavender, funnel-shaped, to 3 in. (8 cm) long; June–July; flowerstalk to 4 ft. (1.2 m), smooth, green; plant clump-forming, 5 ft. (1.5 m) across, 4 ft. (1.2 m) high; leafstalks very long, variegated; leaves to 12 in. (30 cm) long and 7 in. (18 cm) wide, arching, very contracted at base, broadly ovate heart-shaped, deeply ribbed and furrowed at veins, margin with slight waves, sharp twisted tip turned under, surface deep green, dull green below, broad, irregular golden yellow margin. This stately garden plant, which has appeared in the top 10 in the AHS poll, was found as a wild sport in Tokyo Prefecture and first described as a botanical variety in 1928. Young plants have a very elongated leaf; it takes several years for the characteristic heart-shaped leaf to develop. One of the very first hostas to sprout in spring; protect the emerging sprouts from damage by late frosts. During hot, dry summers the leaves have a tendency to burn out; here it goes heat-dormant before any other hosta. A protected site with considerable shade is advised. The comparable 'Yellow River', with a whitish yellow margin, emerges much later, so is not prone to late frost damage; it is the showy centerpiece of many gardens. 'Mountain Snow', a sport of 'Yellow River', is similar but has white margins, and so has 'Frosted Jade', a hybrid of *Hosta montana*. 'Frosted Jade' has a distinctive look and stands out in the garden.

Hosta montana f. *macrophylla*, *oba giboshi* (Jap.). Japan.

Flowers almost white with a hint of lavender, funnel-shaped, to 3 in. (8 cm) long; June–July; flowerstalk to 4 ft. (1.2 m), smooth, green, lasting, fertile bracts, which roll under; plant clump-forming, 6 ft. (1.8 m) across, 4 ft. (1.2 m) high; leafstalks very tall; leaves to 18 in. (45 cm) long, 12 in. (30 cm) wide, arching, very contracted at base, broadly ovate heart-shaped, deeply ribbed and furrowed at veins, margin with slight waves, sharp twisted tip turned under, surface with deep green, dull green below, broad. This large-leaved mountain hosta grows on elevated meadows and at the edge of forests; it grows much faster than *Hosta sieboldiana*, and in warmer regions it is a much better garden hosta. The type is smaller but widespread in Japan and one of the most diverse species found. The hybrids 'Green Acres', 'King Michael', and 'Mikado' are very similar to f. *macrophylla*; the classic hybrid 'Big Sam' is occasionally available and also recommended. Similar green giants, all botanical forms or hybrid progeny of *H. montana*, include 'Amplissima', 'Behemoth', 'Bethel Big Leaf', 'Big Boy', 'Bigfoot', 'Birchwood Elegance', 'Elata', 'Emerald City', 'Godzilla', 'King James', 'Niagara Falls', and 'Tucker Tommy Little'. Yellow-leaved hybrids include 'Alice Gladden', 'Grand Canyon', 'Jackpot', 'Midnight Sun', and 'Stardust'; all grow into very large clumps. **Hosta fluctuans**, a closely related species with undulating, wavy leaves, makes a very large, elegant clump.

Hosta nigrescens, black hosta, *kuro giboshi* (Jap.). Central Japan.

Flowers white, funnel-shaped, to 2 in. (5 cm) long; July–August; flowerstalk to 6 ft. (1.8 m), glaucous green, bare, straight and erect; plant clump-forming, dome-shaped, 30 in. (75 cm) across, 24 in. (60 cm) high; leaves 10–12 in. (25–30 cm) long, 7–9 in. (18–23 cm) wide, very dark green, glaucous, elliptic, keeled (boat-shaped). The black hosta is not actually black, but its sprouts are near dull black initially. The selection 'Elatior' is larger, with bright, shiny green leaves. 'Tall Boy', a hybridized form of the type, has green leaves and very tall flowerstalks, to 7 ft. (2 m).

Hosta plantaginea, August lily, hairpin hosta, *maruba tama-no-kanzashi* (Jap.), *yu-san* (Chin.). China.

Flowers very large, white, very fragrant, funnel-shaped, to 5 in. (13 cm) long with a spread of 3 in. (8 cm); August; flowerstalk to 30 in. (75 cm), light green with stem leaves; plant clump-forming, 30 in. (75 cm) across, 20 in. (50 cm) high; leaves 7 in. (18 cm) long, 5 in. (13 cm) wide, heart-shaped, light glossy green. The best fragrant hosta with the showiest of all hosta flowers, but it requires considerable sun and higher summer temperatures to develop them. Along the Mediterranean coast, for example, it is often seen growing in pots, flowering abundantly. It is the only night-bloomer in the genus; its flowers open late in the afternoon, and their fragrance is most noticeable during evening hours. The light green, shiny leaves provide a beautiful foil. Site near garden seating, walks, or entrances to take full advantage of this species unique look and lovely fragrance. It is a fast grower

when given good, deep soil and can be grown further south than any other hosta, but it does not tolerate droughts well; provide supplemental water beginning in July and continue into September if dry conditions warrant. Difficult to flower in zone 6 and colder. 'Aphrodite' is a selection with double flowers. 'Venus' is also double-flowered, with stamens that have developed into petals. 'Ming Treasure' is a white-margined cultivar. 'Royal Super', a double-flowered sport with creamy white streaks and margins, is smaller than the type. *Hosta plantaginea* has been extensively used as a pod parent to produce fragrant hybrids. One of these, 'Royal Standard', is among the best fragrant hostas for general garden culture; it blooms further north than the species and is easy for beginners. Its flowers are a pure white, about one-half the size of those of *H. plantaginea*.

Hosta pulchella, grandmother mountain hosta, *ubatake giboshi* (Jap.). Japan.

Flowers purple, funnel-shaped, to 1.5 in. (4 cm) long; June–July; flowerstalk to 10 in. (25 cm), bare, green, purple-spotted, straight; plant clump-forming, 6 in. (15 cm) across, 2 in. (5 cm) high; leaves 1–2 in. (2.5–5 cm) long, 0.5 in. (1 cm) wide, glossy dark green, elliptic lance-shaped, wavy leaf margin. 'Kifukurin Ubatake' has leaves with a pale yellow margin. Another hybridized form is the popular 'Stiletto' with longer leaves, to 7 in. (18 cm) long and 1 in. (2.5 cm) wide, with a thin, rippled white margin; it is an excellent edging plant. Several other small plants originated from this species: 'Cody' has shiny green leaves, 'Gaijin' has narrow yellow margins, and the exquisite 'Shiny Penny' is one of the best yellow-leaved miniature hostas for the garden.

Hosta rectifolia, erect hosta, *tachi giboshi* (Jap.). Japan.

Flowers purple, funnel-shaped, to 2 in. (5 cm) long; July–September; flowerstalk to 38 in. (95 cm), smooth, green, with small stem leaves, erect; plant clump-forming, 24 in. (60 cm) across, 20 in. (50 cm) high; leaves 10 in. (25 cm) long and 3–5 in. (8–13 cm) wide, dark green, smooth and shiny, lance-shaped and slightly wavy, erect, with uniform transition to leafstalk. Forma *pruinosa* has bluish green leaves and tall, straight scapes. 'Kifukurin Tachi' has a creamy yellow margin that fades to white; 'Ogon Tachi' is yellow-leaved.

Hosta sieboldiana 'Mira', rhubarb hosta, *daio giboshi* (Jap.). Japan.

Flowers numerous, glossy white, densely packed, elongated bell-shaped, 2 in. (5 cm) long; June–July; flowerstalk to 38 in. (95 cm), upright; plant clump-forming, 65 in. (1.6 m) across, 36 in. (90 cm) high; leaves held horizontally on arching leafstalks, bluish gray, flat when young, slightly rugose at maturity, heart-shaped, with heavy substance, white pruinose back, to 18 in. (45 cm) long and 12 in. (30 cm) wide. First described by Maekawa in 1938 as the rhubarb hosta, for its large size (*daio* translates as "great monarch," which is fitting as well). Just like the species, differing only by its larger leaves, less round and more pointed, and longer flowerstalks; another selection of *Hosta sieboldiana* is the yellow giant 'Semperaurea' from Germany. Cultivars derived from *H. sieboldiana* are usually assigned to the Elegans Group; 'Snowden', a striking hybrid, forms a more upright, stately leaf mound. One of the most unusual variegated sports of *H. sieboldiana* is 'Spilt Milk'. Its variegation consists of stable white streaking and misting throughout the leaf; early in the season, a darker margin appears but changes to grayish green by midsummer. 'Spilt Milk' is a slow grower but well worth the wait, as it is truly outstanding in the garden. Hybrids with *H. sieboldiana* 'Mira' ancestry include 'Gray Cole', a huge specimen with somewhat shorter scapes and much more rugosity. 'Ryan's Big One' and 'Trail's End', with somewhat taller flowerstalks, are choice blue-green giants. 'Big John', considered the largest-leaved hosta in commerce, and all other giant blue hostas serve the same purpose as the species in gardens. All need up to 12 years to fully mature in size; applying a slow-release fertilizer may speed up the process. The large leaf areas transpire profusely, so extra watering is a must during dry summers.

Hosta sieboldii 'Kabitan' (*H.* 'Kabitan').

Flowers deep lavender or violet, funnel-shaped, to 2 in. (5 cm) long; July–August; flowerstalk to 10 in. (25 cm), smooth, green, with small stem leaves, erect; plant clump-forming, 10 in. (25 cm) across, 6 in. (15 cm) high; leaves 5 in. (13 cm) long and 1 in. (2.5 cm) wide, bright yellow with a narrow green margin, smooth, lance-shaped. A very popular small sport of *Hosta sieboldii*. *Hosta sieboldii* f. *spathulata*, the all-green variant found in the wild, is seldom offered, but a hybrid of it, 'Pineapple Poll',

with wavy, narrow leaves and good substance is available. 'Alba' (*H.* 'Weihenstephan') is the white-flowered form. The original green-leaved botanical variant with a white margin, *H. sieboldii* 'Paxton's Original' (*H. sieboldii*, *H. albomarginata*), is now rarely grown. *Hosta sieboldii* 'Mediopicta' is similar and has green streaks in the leaf. *Hosta sieboldii* 'Subcrocea' (*H.* 'Subcrocea') is all yellow and lacks the green margin; it is very similar to an old Japanese hybrid **'Ogon Koba'** ('Wogon', 'Ogon'). The hybrid 'Silver Kabitan' ('Haku-Chu-Han') has white leaves with narrow green margins. A smaller related hybrid is 'Masquerade', with viridescent white leaves that have a thin, green margin; the white turns to greenish white. The hybrid 'Peedee Gold Flash' has been called a 'Kabitan' on steroids; it looks like it but is larger.

Hosta tibae, Nagasaki hosta, *nagasaki giboshi* (Jap.). Japan.

Flowers lavender, light purple-striped, funnel-shaped, to 2 in. (5 cm) long, flowerstalks 20–28 in. (50–70 cm), smooth, green, with small stem leaves, leaning, branched, with 1–4 side branches, each producing a flower cluster; September–October; plant clump-forming, 24 in. (60 cm) across, 18 in. (45 cm) high; leaves 7–9 in. (18–23 cm) long and 4–5 in. (10–13 cm) wide, dark green, smooth and shiny, lance-shaped and slightly wavy. As many as 120 flowers have been counted on one stem and its multiple branches in a late show of color.

Hosta ventricosa, purple hosta, *murasaki giboshi* (Jap.). China, Korea.

Flowers dark purple-striped, bell-shaped, to 2.5 in. (6 cm) long, fragrant; June–July; flowerstalk to 36 in. (90 cm), smooth, green, lasting; plant clump-forming, 36 in. (90 cm) across, 24 in. (60 cm) high; leaves 10 in. (25 cm) long and 8 in. (20 cm) wide, dark glossy green, heart-shaped, waves on the margin and twisted tip. The "dark purple hosta," as the Japanese know it, was among the first hostas to reach England, where it has been grown since 1790. An excellent specimen plant and landscape hosta for mass plantings, borders, and edgings. Always comes true, so seed propagation is easy. Two natural sports of this species have long been known to gardeners. 'Aureomaculata' has viridescent yellow leaves with a wide, irregular dark green margin; the beautiful yellow center turns greenish but never as dark as the margin, so a lighter center is always visible. 'Aureomarginata' ('Variegata') has a dark center and a wide, streaky albescent yellowish white margin that turns ivory-white. 'Little Blue' and 'Peedee Elfinbells' are smaller forms of the species. Yellow cultivars too are known but all seem to be viridescent, turning green as the season progresses; among these are 'Fury of Flame' and 'Gold Flush'.

Hosta venusta, beautiful maiden hosta, *otome giboshi* (Jap.), *hanra-bibich'u* (Kor.). Korea.

Flowers few, lavender, funnel-shaped, to 1.5 in. (4 cm) long; July–August; flowerstalk 8–10 in. (20–25 cm), bare, green, sometimes purple-spotted, straight and with ridges; plant clump-forming, 6 in. (15 cm) across, 3 in. (8 cm) high; leaves 1 in. (2.5 cm) long and wide, satiny dark green, broadly heart-shaped, wavy leaf margin. A variable species. The clone in commerce represents but one of many different forms, some with lance-shaped leaves, others with much larger leaves, all recently found on Cheju Island. It is excellent potted or in the shady rock garden. If planted in the open ground, protect from slugs and snails because its tiny size makes it a midnight snack for a good-sized slug. 'Tiny Tears', 'Thumbnail', and 'Suzuki Thumbnail' are selected smaller forms. The hybrid **'Lakeside Neat Petite'** forms a neat green mound of tight foliage and is very floriferous. 'Gosan Gold Midget' is a yellow hybrid; 'Kinbotan' is small with a creamy yellow margin. *Hosta minor* is the Korean species from which *H. venusta* evolved; it is much larger but has similar features. *Hosta nakaiana* from Korea is used extensively in hybridizing, it is the mother plant of the much larger 'Candy Hearts' and 'Pearl Lake', both welcome in gardens for their tight-clumping habit and floral display. **'Amanuma'** (seen in photo of *Kirengeshoma palmata*) is very similar to *H. nakaiana*.

Hosta yingeri. Korea.

Flowers light purple, spider-shaped, to 1 in. (2.5 cm) long and across, not one-sided, but all around the stem, stamens 6, 3 short and 3 longer ones; August–September; flowerstalk to 24 in. (60 cm), straight but leaning; plant clump-forming, dome-shaped, 18 in. (45 cm) across, 8 in. (20 cm) high; leaves 7 in. (18 cm) long and 3 in. (8 cm) wide, dark glossy green, elliptic, flat with heavy substance. Its spidery flowers make a delightful early autumn display. 'Potomac Pride' has this species in its parentage and has inherited the glossy leaf surface.

Hosta cultivars

'Abba Dabba Do'.

Flowers pale lavender, funnel-shaped, to 2 in. (5 cm) long; June–July; flowerstalk to 40 in. (1 m), with small stem leaves, straight; plant clump-forming, erect, dome-shaped, usually 36 in. (90 cm) across but occasionally much larger, to 5 ft. (1.5 m) wide, 30 in. (75 cm) high; leaves 10 in. (25 cm) long and 7 in. (18 cm) wide, olive-green with a yellow margin that widens with maturity, leaf elongated, tapering to a point, base heart-shaped, wavy-undulate leaf margin, with leafstalks forming a continuous upright arch. 'Abba Dabba Don't' is a reverse sport with a white center and dark green margins; 'Abba Dabba Darling' has a pale yellow center with a two-tone margin of dark green and celadon. Similar cultivars are 'Abba Aloft' and 'Flint Hill' (green leaf and narrow greenish yellow to yellow margin), 'Abba Dew' (lighter yellow-green center with yellow margin), 'Abba at Large' (lutescent yellow center and a darker greenish yellow margin), and 'Sun Banner' (dark green center with yellow margin).

'Allan P. McConnell'.

Flowers purple, bell-shaped, to 1.5 in. (4 cm) long; June–July; flowerstalk to 15 in. (38 cm), straight; plant clump-forming, 18 in. (45 cm) across, 8 in. (20 cm) high; leaves 3 in. (8 cm) long and 2 in. (5 cm) wide, dark green, white margin, oval with heart-shaped base, flat. This sport of *Hosta nakaiana*, with less-pronounced ridges on scape, is an excellent small, white-margined hosta. The reverse form with a white center and a green margin is 'Ivory Pixie'. 'Shades of Mercy' is a sport with white center streaked green and green margin.

'Antioch', Antioch Group.

Flowers lavender, funnel-shaped, to 2 in. (5 cm) long; June–July; flowerstalk to 32 in. (80 cm), smooth, green, with small stem leaves, leaning; plant clump-forming, 36 in. (90 cm) across, 20 in. (50 cm) high; leaves 10 in. (25 cm) long and 8 in. (20 cm) wide, medium green, with white to creamy white margin, heart-shaped. This is a good, variegated garden plant (seen in photo of 'Wide Brim').

Other members of the Antioch Group—'Goldbrook', 'Moerheim', 'Shogun', 'Spinners'—are very similar if not identical. 'Jade Lancer' is alike but slightly larger; 'Fortunei Albomarginata', 'Vivian', and 'Yellow Boy' are comparable but smaller.

'August Moon'.

Flowers whitish, bell-shaped, to 2 in. (5 cm) long; June–July; flowerstalk to 28 in. (70 cm), smooth, green, straight; plant clump-forming, 30 in. (75 cm) across, 20 in. (50 cm) high; leaves 6 in. (15 cm) long and 5 in. (13 cm) wide, yellow, roundish heart-shaped, cupped, crinkled. This yellow hosta (seen in photo of *Ajuga reptans* 'Atropurpurea') is excellent for brightening up dark corners. 'Moon Waves' has more lance-shaped leaves with very wavy margins. 'Abiqua Moonbeam' ('Mayan Moon') is a green-margined sport. 'September Sun', 'Indiana Moonshine', and 'Lunar Magic' have yellow centers and medium to light green margins; 'September Surprise' is similar but with medium to dark green margins. 'Lunar Eclipse' and 'Gosan Moonskirt' have yellow centers and white margins, the former with a drawn-up leaf edge (draw-string margin), the latter with a smooth, flattened white margin. Reverse sports are 'August Beauty', 'Dark Moon', and 'Kiwi Sunlover'; all have the green center and yellow margin. 'Moon Glow' also has a yellow center with white margins. 'Green August Moon' and 'Lunar Night' are all-green forms.

'Birchwood Parky's Gold'.

Flowers lavender, bell-shaped, to 2 in. (5 cm) long; June–July; flowerstalk to 38 in. (95 cm), smooth, green, straight; plant clump-forming, 30 in. (75 cm) across, 18 in. (45 cm) high; leaves 5 in. (13 cm) long and 4 in. (10 cm) wide, yellow, roundish heart-shaped, flat. This classic hosta (seen in photo of 'Great Expectations') is still widely grown; comparable all-yellows are 'Gold Drop' and **'Gold Edger'** (seen in photo of 'Blue Angel'). Related cultivars are 'Birchwood Gold' (yellow but slightly larger), 'Sweet Home Chicago' (yellow center with green margin), and 'Zuzu's Petals' (green center with yellow margin). 'Parky's Prize' is a green-centered sport with greenish yellow margin.

'Black Hills'.

Flowers lavender, funnel-shaped, to 2 in. (5 cm) long; June–July; flowerstalk to 34 in. (85 cm), smooth, green, with small stem leaves; plant clump-forming, 36 in. (90 cm) across, 24 in. (60 cm) high; leaves 8 in. (20 cm) long and 7 in. (18 cm) wide, very dark green, heart-shaped, cupped, rugose. The "black" refers to this classic's leaves, whose darkness may be lessened by increased sun exposure. Other very dark green cultivars include 'Black Beauty', 'Joseph', 'Lakeside Accolade', 'Lakeside Black Satin', 'Lakeside Coal Miner', 'Neat and Tidy', 'Rosedale Spoons', and 'Twisted Sister'.

'Blue Angel'.

Flowers densely packed, numerous, glossy white, elongated bell-shaped, 2 in. (5 cm) long; June–July; flowerstalk to 4 ft. (1.2 m), upright; plant clump-forming, 50 in. (1.3 m) across, 36 in. (90 cm) high; leaves 18 in. (45 cm) long and 12 in. (30 cm) wide, held horizontally on long, upright leafstalks, bluish gray, flat when young, but rugose, corrugated, sometimes twisted at maturity, heart-shaped, with heavy substance, white pruinose back. Similar to *Hosta sieboldiana* (and often confused with 'Elegans'), this imposing hosta has made the top 10 in the AHS poll. Its large size requires careful siting, particularly in smaller gardens. The huge sports 'Angel Eyes' and 'Guardian Angel' make great accents in spring, when their very large wavy leaves have a whitish center variegation; the viridescent center turns bluish green during the summer. 'Grey Ghost' is all creamy white in spring, turning bluish green. 'Green Angel' is an all-green sport.

'Blue Cadet'.

Flowers bell-shaped, lavender, to 2 in. (5 cm) long; June–July; flowerstalk to 26 in. (65 cm), smooth, glaucous blue-green, straight; plant clump-forming, dome-shaped, 28 in. (70 cm) across, 18 in. (45 cm) high; leaves 5 in. (13 cm) long and 4 in. (10 cm) wide, glaucous blue-green, heart-shaped, cupped. Several seedlings are in commerce, all with bluish green leaves, including 'Booka', 'Lynne', and 'Stephen'. 'Banyai's Dancing Girl' is a similar, very floriferous cultivar.

'Blue Moon' ('Halo'), Tardiana Group.

Flowers bell-shaped, whitish mauve, to 1.5 in. (4 cm) long; June–July; flowerstalk to 12 in. (30 cm), smooth, glaucous blue-green, straight; plant clump-forming, dome-shaped, 10 in. (25 cm) across, 6 in. (15 cm) high; leaves 3 in. (8 cm) long and 2 in. (5 cm) wide, glaucous blue-green, heart-shaped, flat. This small blue hosta looks great in a shaded rockery or along a path. 'Cherub' is of similar size but has leaves with a creamy white margin. 'Summer Joy' is a smaller sport with a white center and bluish margins. For gardeners with a lack of space and a desire for a similar but smaller cultivar, 'Baby Bunting' is a good choice, as is its variegated sport 'Hope' (green center, yellowish green margin) and the attractive **'Cherish'** and 'Pandora's Box', with wide green margins that streak into the white center.

'Blue Wedgwood' ('Blue Wave'), Tardiana Group.

Flowers bell-shaped, light lavender, to 2 in. (5 cm) long; June–July; flowerstalk to 16 in. (40 cm), smooth, glaucous blue-green, straight; plant clump-forming, dome-shaped, 24 in. (60 cm) across, 14 in. (35 cm) high; leaves 6 in. (15 cm) long and 5 in. (13 cm) wide, glaucous blue-green, heart-shaped with a wedge-shaped outline, cupped, somewhat puckered. Sometimes confused with **'Blue Dimples'** (Tardiana Group), which has a rounded heart-shaped base with wedge-shaped form (seen in photo of 'Sum and Substance'). Many other, similar plants occur in the Tardiana Group, differing only in size and leaf shape; they serve the same purpose in gardens but should be selected for desired leaf size and shape: 'Blue Arrow', 'Blue Blush', 'Blue Diamond', 'Blue Skies', 'Camelot', 'Devon Blue', 'Dorset Blue', **'Hadspen Blue'** (seen in photo of *Lamium maculatum* 'Beacon Silver'), 'Hadspen Hawk', 'Hadspen Heron', 'Happiness', 'Harmony', 'Irische See', 'Osprey', and 'Sherborne Swift'. 'Punky' is a smaller sport with a yellow center and blue-green margins.

'Bold Ribbons'.

Flowers lavender, funnel-shaped, to 2 in. (5 cm) long; June–July; flowerstalk to 28 in. (70 cm), smooth, green, with small stem leaves, leaning; plant clump-forming, 24 in. (60 cm) across, 16 in. (40 cm) high; leaves 6 in. (15 cm) long and 4 in. (10 cm) wide, medium dark green with white margin, heart-shaped. Its seedling **'Wide Brim'** has yellow margins that change to creamy white and is an excellent hosta for general use. Similar but with less substance in the leaves are 'Neat Splash Rim' and 'Yellow Splash Rim'; 'Ground Master' has creamy white margins.

'Brim Cup'.

Flowers white, bell-shaped, to 2 in. (5 cm) long; June–July; flowerstalk to 18 in. (45 cm), smooth, green, with small stem leaves, leaning; plant clump-forming, 16 in. (40 cm) across, 12 in. (30 cm) high; leaves 6 in. (15 cm) long and 5 in. (13 cm) wide, medium dark green with white margin, heart-shaped. Leaves are attractively cupped, but in some gardens, excessive cupping leads to tears in the margin. 'Java' is an all-green sport.

'Buckshaw Blue'.

Flowers white, bell-shaped, to 2 in. (5 cm) long; June–July; flowerstalk to 14 in. (35 cm), smooth, green, straight; plant clump-forming, 18 in. (45 cm) across, 12 in. (30 cm) high; leaves 6 in. (15 cm) long and 4 in. (10 cm) wide, blue-green, heart-shaped, flat. One of the bluest hostas and holds that color longer than most. Similar to 'Tokudama' but does not have its very cupped leaves. 'Blue Velvet' and 'Moscow Blue' are comparable.

'Candy Hearts'.

Flowers white, bell-shaped, to 2 in. (5 cm) long; June–July; flowerstalk to 26 in. (65 cm), smooth, green, straight; plant clump-forming, 28 in. (70 cm) across, 16 in. (40 cm) high; leaves 6 in. (15 cm) long and 5 in. (13 cm) wide, grayish green with a bluish cast, heart-shaped, flat. Although classified as a blue hosta, this fine landscape hosta is more of a grayish green. The sport **'Fair Maiden'** has a distinct, very wide and streaky white margin and dark green center; 'Heartsong', another sport, has a very narrow, creamy white margin.

'Chinese Sunrise'.

Flowers lavender, bell-shaped, to 2 in. (5 cm) long; June–July; flowerstalk to 28 in. (70 cm), smooth, green, with small stem leaves, leaning; plant clump-forming, 28 in. (70 cm) across, 16 in. (40 cm) high; leaves 6 in. (15 cm) long and 3 in. (8 cm) wide, in spring a beautiful yellow central color with a narrow green margin, lance-shaped. A viridescent sport of *Hosta cathayana*.

'Christmas Tree'.

Flowers white, funnel-shaped, to 2 in. (5 cm) long; June–July; flowerstalk to 32 in. (80 cm), smooth, green, with small stem leaves, leaning; plant clump-forming, 36 in. (90 cm) across, 20 in.

(50 cm) high; leaves 10 in. (25 cm) long and 6 in. (15 cm) wide, medium green, with white to creamy white margin, heart-shaped, wrinkled. A mature 'Christmas Tree' is an awesome display in any garden. 'Pizzazz', similar and slightly smaller, has a crumpled blue-green center and yellowish green margin.

'Crispula', *sazanami giboshi* (Jap.).

Flowers lavender, funnel-shaped, to 2.5 in. (6 cm) long; June–July; flowerstalk to 38 in. (95 cm), smooth, green, lasting; plant clump-forming, 36 in. (90 cm) across, 24 in. (60 cm) high; leaves 10 in. (25 cm) long and 7 in. (18 cm) wide, dark green with a regular white margin, smooth, heart-shaped, with an extended and twisted, sharp tip. A classic and still one of the best white-margined hostas. 'Crispula Viridis' is the all-green form.

'Decorata', *otafuku giboshi* (Jap.).

Flowers deep lavender to purple, bell-shaped, to 2 in. (5 cm) long; June–July; flowerstalk to 20 in. (50 cm), smooth, green, erect; plant clump-forming, 30 in. (75 cm) across, 12 in. (30 cm) high; leaves 6 in. (15 cm) long and 3 in. (8 cm) wide, dark green with a regular white margin, smooth, heart-shaped. Another classic hosta of great garden value. 'Decorata Normalis' is the all-green form. 'Goddess of Athena', a derivative of 'Decorata', has the same striking flowers but wide yellowish margins.

'Dixie Chick'.

Flowers white, funnel-shaped, to 1.5 in. (4 cm) long; June–July; flowerstalk to 12 in. (30 cm), smooth, green, lasting; plant clump-forming, 12 in. (30 cm) across, 4 in. (10 cm) high; leaves 2.5 in. (6 cm) long and 0.6 in. (1.5 cm) wide, dark green, regular creamy white margin with tiny green spots, smooth, glossy, lance-shaped.

'Donahue Piecrust'.

Flowers near white, bell-shaped, to 2 in. (5 cm) long; June–July; flowerstalk to 34 in. (85 cm), smooth, green, with small stem leaves; plant clump-forming, 30 in. (75 cm) across, 24 in. (60 cm) high; leaves 10 in. (25 cm) long and 7 in. (18 cm) wide, dark green, with distinct regular piecrust margins, elongated heart-shaped. Hostas with ruffled piecrust margins always draw a crowd and add to the overall texture of the landscape. The classic 'Ruf-

fles', the very large 'Birchwood Ruffled Queen', and several other landscape hostas have this attractive feature: 'Choo Choo Train', 'Circus Clown', 'Crested Reef', 'Green Piecrust', 'Holly's Honey', 'Lakeside Ripples', 'Mesa Fringe', 'Niagara Falls', 'Permanent Wave', 'Regal Ruffles', 'Ruffles Galore', 'Sea Drift', 'TuTu', and 'Waving Wuffles'. *Hosta pycnophylla* has a neat piecrust margin, and its leaf undersides are coated with a whitish powder; the same can be said for its related hybrids 'Amethyst Joy' and 'Inland Sea'.

'Elegans' (*Hosta sieboldiana* 'Elegans'), Elegans Group. Garden origin.

Flowers numerous, glossy white, densely packed, elongated bell-shaped, 2 in. (5 cm) long; June–July; flowerstalk to 4 ft. (1.2 m), upright; plant clump-forming, 50 in. (1.3 m) across, 36 in. (90 cm) high; leaves 18 in. (45 cm) long and 12 in. (30 cm) wide, held horizontally on long, upright leafstalks, bluish gray, flat when young, but rugose, dimpled, and corrugated at maturity, heart-shaped, with heavy substance, white pruinose back. This most majestic blue-gray hosta has made the top 20 in the AHS poll and is a continual favorite in gardens. Originally described as a botanical variety, it is now known to be Arends' 1905 hybrid 'Robusta' (*Hosta sieboldiana* 'Mira' × *H*. 'Tokudama', which Arends knew as *H. fortunei*), apparently further developed and hybridized. I have seen several distinct plants, all under the name "Elegans." Plants offered in commerce should be considered a group of similar garden plants: all look like the archetypal *H. sieboldiana* but with moderately taller scapes, a slight lavender coloration inside the flower petals, and rounder, more corrugated, and bluer leaves, traits inherited from 'Tokudama'. As with all large hostas, it requires careful siting, and supplemental water is a must to keep this giant happy in warmer regions. Other cultivars in the Elegans Group are derived from and listed under *H. sieboldiana* 'Mira'.

'Fortunei Albomarginata', Fortunei Albomarginata Group.

Flowers lavender, funnel-shaped, to 2.5 in. (6 cm) long; June–July; flowerstalk to 38 in. (95 cm), smooth, green, lasting; plant clump-forming, 36 in. (90 cm) across, 24 in. (60 cm) high; leaves 10 in. (25 cm) long and 7 in. (18 cm) wide, dark green with a regular white margin, smooth, heart-shaped.

Other members of the white-margined Fortunei Albomarginata Group are 'Carol', 'Fisher's Cream Edge', 'North Hills', and 'Zager's White Edge'.

'Fortunei Albopicta', Fortunei Albopicta Group.

Flowers lavender, funnel-shaped, to 2.5 in. (6 cm) long; June–July; flowerstalk to 32 in. (80 cm), smooth, green, lasting; plant clump-forming, 32 in. (80 cm) across, 24 in. (60 cm) high; leaves 8 in. (20 cm) long and 6 in. (15 cm) wide, in spring with a bright yellow center and a dark green margin, smooth, heart-shaped. This is a showy hosta in spring, but its yellow center is viridescent and by early summer it is almost as green as the margin. 'Zager Green Rim' is nearly identical. 'Elizabeth Campbell' is similar, with a wider green margin. 'Chelsea Babe' is similar but smaller. 'Fortunei Aurea' is a smaller, viridescent yellow-leaved form, with no margin; its bright yellow leaves turn green in early summer. 'Granary Gold' is viridescent yellow without the margin and darkens to a yellowish green later. Also viridescent are 'Phyllis Campbell' and 'Sharmon'. 'Fortunei Viridis' is the reverted all-green form of 'Fortunei Albopicta'.

'Fortunei Aureomarginata' ('Ellerbroek', 'Golden Crown', 'Yellow Band'), Fortunei Aureomarginata Group.

Flowers lavender, funnel-shaped, to 2.5 in. (6 cm) long; June–July; flowerstalk to 36 in. (90 cm), smooth, green, lasting; plant clump-forming, 36 in. (90 cm) across, 24 in. (60 cm) high; leaves 10 in. (25 cm) long and 7 in. (18 cm) wide, dark green with a regular yellow margin, smooth, heart-shaped. This is the cultivar that gave the group of yellow-margined hostas its name. 'Kiwi Treasure Trove', 'Twilight', and 'Viette's Yellow Edge' are similar; 'Owen Online' and 'Patience Plus' have reverse variegation with a yellow center and green margins. 'Green Gold' is a distinct sport with a narrow, uniform yellowish margin.

'Fortunei Hyacinthina', Fortunei Group.

Flowers lavender, funnel-shaped, to 2.5 in. (6 cm) long; June–July; flowerstalk to 38 in. (95 cm), smooth, green, lasting; plant clump-forming, 36 in. (90 cm) across, 24 in. (60 cm) high. This quintessential green hosta evolved in Siebold's garden before his death and was listed as early as 1877. Leaves have a slight grayish cast in spring, turning a bright dark green later in the season. It and its many close relatives are hybridized forms of *Hosta montana*. All are about the same size and with few exceptions have lavender to violet flowers that are darker in northern gardens. All are tried and proven garden plants. 'Fortunei Aoki' ('Aoki'), named by Siebold before his death for Aoki Kon'yo (who produced the first Japanese-Dutch dictionary) has a leaf surface that is all over wrinkled and dimpled. 'Fortunei Gigantea' ('Bella') is a bit larger; 'Fortunei Obscura' is somewhat smaller. 'Fortunei Rugosa' has very wrinkled, glaucous leaves that are more green than blue. 'Fortunei Stenantha' is a distinct form, with much lighter and smoother leaf color, short scapes, and flowers with nonspreading lobes, hence the epithet *stenantha* (from *stenos anthos* = narrow flower). 'Freising' has a smaller leaf and pure white flowers. 'Nancy Lindsay' and 'Windsor Gold' have viridescent yellow leaves that turn green later. Several variegated sports are in commerce: 'Alaskan Halo' and 'Arctic Rim' have creamy white margins, as has 'Praying Hands', whose foliage is upright and folded. Stemming from an unstable variegated form of 'Fortunei Hyacinthina' is the very popular 'White Christmas' with a white center and dark green margins; its sport 'Night before Christmas' has wider green margins and is more vigorous. White-centered cultivars tend to burn out, but I have seen some fine specimens in hot southern gardens.

'Fragrant Bouquet'.

Flowers white, fragrant, funnel-shaped, to 2.5 in. (6 cm) long; August; flowerstalk to 30 in. (75 cm), light green with stem leaves; plant clump-forming, 4 ft. (1.2 m) across, 20 in. (50 cm) high; leaves 9 in. (23 cm) long and 8 in. (20 cm) wide, heart-shaped, yellowish to pale light green with creamy white margin. One of the best variegated and fragrant hostas. The soft colors of this hybrid, which has made the top 10 in the AHS poll, blend well with blues and darker greens. A fast grower when given good, deep soil, and an excellent hosta for southern gardens. 'Guacamole' is a similar, very vigorous sport with a yellowish green margin; it has made the top 20 in the AHS poll and is outdone in growth rate only by its all-green sport 'Fried Green Tomatoes'. 'Fried Bananas' is a vigorous all-yellow form. The smaller 'So Sweet' has slightly fragrant flowers and cupped, light green leaves with a creamy white margin; it too is a vigorous, rhizomatous cultivar of great garden value.

'Francee' ('Fortunei Klopping Variegated'), Fortunei Albomarginata Group.

Flowers lavender, funnel-shaped, to 2 in. (5 cm) long; June–July; flowerstalk to 40 in. (1 m), green; plant clump-forming, 36 in. (90 cm) across, 24 in. (60 cm) high; leaves 8 in. (20 cm) long and 5 in. (13 cm) wide, heart-shaped, dark green with narrow white margin. A distinguished, much-tested garden hosta that holds its leaf color, looking marvelous from spring until autumn. This classic hosta has made the top 20 in the AHS poll and is seen in many old gardens; in my garden it is more dignified than its sports 'Patriot', with wide white margins, and 'Minuteman' and 'Trailblazer', which have even wider white margins. Another sport, 'Admiral Halsey', has creamy margins but is otherwise very similar to the latter two. Similar but with narrower leaves and more refined, narrow white margins is 'Gloriosa'. 'Green Gold' has yellow margins that turn white in summer. 'Patriot's Fire' is an interesting cultivar similar to 'Francee'; its green center changes to yellow by summer.

'Frances Williams' ('Golden Circles', 'Yellow Edge').

Flowers white, bell-shaped, to 2 in. (5 cm) long; June–July; flowerstalk to 30 in. (75 cm), green, with variegated leaves; plant clump-forming, 4 ft. (1.2 m) across, 24 in. (60 cm) high; leaves 12 in. (30 cm) long and 11 in. (28 cm) wide, broadly heart-shaped, dimpled and rippled, margins slightly upturned, sharp tip, blue-green, with irregular, wide yellow margin, with streaking toward midrib. Discovered by Frances Williams in 1936, this is easily the most popular sport of *Hosta sieboldiana* ever marketed. Although it has placed in the AHS poll top 20 and is grown the world over, it is a difficult garden plant: most plants sold in North America suffer from marginal necrosis, probably a genetic disorder, which causes the yellow marginal tissue to "burn" and eventually turn brown, develop holes, and disintegrate. Exposure to strong sunlight in early spring and frequent rain seem to exacerbate the malady, and unfortunately, Hosta Hill is no longer embellished by this cultivar. **'Alex Summers'**, derived from 'Gold Regal' and named for the founder of the American Hosta Society, is an excellent, nonburning alternative and looks great

all year long. Many similar variegated forms belong to the Sieboldiana Aureomarginata Group (Frances Williams Group). Among those reported not to burn are 'Aurora Borealis', 'Chicago Frances Williams', 'Dorothy Benedict', 'Eldorado', 'Olive Bailey Langdon', 'Samurai', and 'Squash Edge'. 'Northern Exposure' is similar but has a yellowish white margin that turn white. 'Broadway Frances' is a large sport with bluish green center and wide yellow margin. 'Nifty Fifty' is similar; its more creamy white margin does not burn.

'Geisha' ('Ani Machi').

Flowers lavender, bell-shaped, to 2 in. (5 cm) long; June–July; flowerstalk to 10 in. (25 cm), smooth, green, erect; plant clump-forming, 10 in. (25 cm) across, 4 in. (10 cm) high; leaves 4 in. (10 cm) long and 2 in. (5 cm) wide, yellowish green with an irregular, dark green margin, heart-shaped but twisted and curved along the midrib and the tip curled under. This unusual, colorful cultivar is quite a conversation piece; it is one of the few with curiously twisted leaves, which add incredible textural quality to the garden. Another is 'Mary Marie Ann', with a viridescent yellow leaf that has green margins; its margins are shirred like the edge of a pulled curtain, adding an additional feature to its twisted texture. The best twisted white-centered hosta is **'Silver Streak'** (seen in photo of 'Sultana'), a small cultivar with a pure white center and narrow, irregular green margins; its leaves twist like those of 'Geisha' but they are narrower and smaller.

'Ginko Craig'.

Flowers deep lavender, bell-shaped, to 2 in. (5 cm) long; June–July; flowerstalk to 18 in. (45 cm), smooth, green, erect; plant clump-forming, 10 in. (25 cm) across, 4 in. (10 cm) high; leaves dark green with a white margin, lance-shaped. Two distinct leaf forms exist: slightly corrugated mature leaves 8 in. (20 cm) long and 3 in. (8 cm) wide, with irregular, wavy white margin, and smaller juvenile leaves 6 in. (15 cm) long and 2 in. (5 cm) wide, with a smooth leaf blade and margin. Maturity occurs 4 to 6 years after planting, and the juvenile form can be maintained by frequent dividing. 'Bunchoko' has leaves like the juvenile form but its flowers are white; 'Excalibur', 'Hime', 'Hime Karafuto', and 'Princess of Karafuto' are all similar to the mature plant. 'Gosan Hildegarde' is an all-yellow hybrid involving 'Ginko Craig'.

'Golden Bullion'.

Flowers lavender, bell-shaped, to 2 in. (5 cm) long; June–July; flowerstalk to 20 in. (50 cm), green, straight; plant clump-forming, 28 in. (70 cm) across, 14 in. (35 cm) high; leaves 6 in. (15 cm) long and 4 in. (10 cm) wide, heart-shaped, yellow (lutescent), puckered and slightly cupped. A sturdy, nonburning all-yellow sport of 'Tokudama Flavocircinalis'.

'Golden Medallion'.

Flowers whitish, bell-shaped, to 2 in. (5 cm) long; June–July; flowerstalk to 20 in. (50 cm), green, straight; plant clump-forming, 24 in. (60 cm) across, 14 in. (35 cm) high; leaves 6 in. (15 cm) long and 5 in. (13 cm) wide, rounded, heart-shaped, yellow (lutescent), cupped and puckered. An all-yellow sport of 'Tokudama Aureonebulosa'. 'Abiqua Ariel', 'Aspen Gold', **'Midas Touch'** (seen in photo of 'Blue Angel'), and 'Super Bowl' are similar. Comparable but smaller are 'Golden Prayers' and 'Little Aurora', which itself has sported to 'Tattoo', in which each leaf (yellow center, light green margin) has a dark green "tattoo" in the outline of a maple leaf.

'Golden Sunburst', Golden Sunburst Group.

Flowers white, bell-shaped, to 2 in. (5 cm) long; June–July; flowerstalk to 30 in. (75 cm), green, straight; plant clump-forming, 4 ft. (1.2 m) across, 20 in. (50 cm) high; leaves 13 in. (33 cm) long and 10 in. (25 cm) wide, broadly heart-shaped, dimpled and rippled, margins slightly upturned, sharp tip, yellow (lutescent). A good yellow form but subject to burning. 'Gold Regal', 'Fort Knox', 'Heartache', 'Kasseler Gold', 'Ultraviolet Light', and 'Zounds' serve similar uses in gardens; all take several years to reach their ultimate size.

'Golden Tiara', Tiara Group.

Flowers deep lavender striped with purple, bell-shaped, to 2 in. (5 cm) long; June–July; flowerstalk to 24 in. (60 cm), smooth, green, straight; plant clump-forming, dome-shaped, 24 in. (60 cm) across, 14 in. (35 cm) high; leaves 4 in. (10 cm) long and 3 in. (8 cm) wide, flat, green, heart-shaped, with a neat yellowish green margin that bleaches to near

creamy white in sun. This sport of *Hosta nakaiana* is very popular, widely cultivated, and extremely vigorous, producing multiple flowerstalks even when young. Requires abundant water to stay good-looking. The leaves are thin; in the South plants fade and even go dormant during prolonged droughts unless provided with extra water. 'Grand Tiara', with considerably wider yellow margins, is a superior garden plant. Several other sports in the Tiara Group are of similar stature: 'Diamond Tiara' (medium green with a white margin), 'Emerald Tiara' (viridescent yellow, becoming a deep yellowish green with a dark green margin), 'Emerald Scepter' (very similar but a shade darker), 'Golden Scepter' (yellow), 'Jade Scepter' (all green, similar to the parent species *H. nakaiana*), and 'Platinum Tiara' (yellowish green with a white margin). 'Sweet Tater Pie' is a seedling with yellow leaves that turn green by summer.

'Gold Standard', Fortunei Group.

Flowers lavender, funnel-shaped, to 2 in. (5 cm) long; June–July; flowerstalk to 40 in. (1 m), green, bending, with stem leaves; plant clump-forming, 36 in. (90 cm) across, 20 in. (50 cm) high; leaves 8 in. (20 cm) long and 5 in. (13 cm) wide, heart-shaped, yellow (lutescent) with a dark green margin. This classic hosta, discovered as a sport of 'Fortunei Hyacinthina', retains its parent's vigor and fast increase. An excellent garden plant, it has deservedly made the top 5 in the AHS poll, but needs shade during hot afternoons to keep the bright yellow leaf center from bleaching and burning. 'Janet' is smaller, with a leaf center yellowish white turning to white and a green margin. The sport 'Striptease' has a yellow center and wide green margin with a pure white, irregular line posed at the junction of the main colors; it has placed in the AHS poll top 20. The fine 'Richland Gold' has bright yellow leaves that turn whitish yellow with age. 'Moonlight' has an albescent greenish yellow center and thin, white margins, and 'Richland's Gold Moonlight' has a yellow center with white margins. 'Something Different' has a viridescent yellow center with dark green margins. 'String Bikini' has a dark green leaf with a narrow white center.

'Great Expectations', George Smith Group.

Flowers white, bell-shaped, to 2 in. (5 cm) long; June–July; flowerstalk to 33 in. (84 cm), green, with small stem leaves; plant clump-forming, 40 in. (1 m) across, 24 in. (60 cm) high; leafstalks white, green-margined; leaves 9 in. (23 cm) long and 7 in. (18 cm) wide, broadly heart-shaped, dimpled and rippled, margins slightly upturned, sharp tip, emerging chartreuse turning to creamy white (albescent), with dark bluish green, irregular margin, with streaking toward midrib. One of the best center-variegated sports involving *Hosta sieboldiana*. Can be difficult to establish but its beauty is well worth the effort: it has placed in the top 3 in the AHS poll. As with all other hybrids related to *H. sieboldiana*, it is essential to keep the rhizome actively growing by providing supplemental water during summer droughts, particularly in warmer regions. 'George Smith' is similar but larger. Several other hybrids in the George Smith Group are similar in size and variegation: 'Borwick Beauty', 'Color Glory' and 'Queen of Islip', which here always burn (melt out) in the center, as well as 'Du-Page Delight' and 'Northern Sunray'. Related hybrids are 'Dream Weaver', which is identical to 'Great Expectations' but with very wide margins, and 'Great American Expectations', which is larger, taller, and faster growing.

'Green Fountain'.

Flowers lavender, funnel-shaped, to 2 in. (5 cm) long; June–July; flowerstalk to 38 in. (95 cm), smooth, green, with small stem leaves, erect; plant clump-forming, 36 in. (90 cm) across, 26 in. (65 cm) high; leaves 10 in. (25 cm) long and 3 in. (8 cm) wide, dark green, smooth and shiny, lance-shaped and slightly wavy. This *Hosta kikutii* hybrid forms a distinctive cascading mound in the garden and is excellent for elevated containers. 'Elvis Lives', another *H. kikutii* hybrid, is an excellent grower and has bluish green leaves that turn dark green by midsummer. **'Spritzer'** is similar but has yellow leaves with irregular green streakings in spring; the yellow fades to shades of light green later in the season. 'Golden Fountain' retains its yellow leaf color throughout the season.

'Halcyon', Tardiana Group. Hybrid ('Tardiflora' × 'Elegans').

Flowers bell-shaped, white, to 2 in. (5 cm) long; June–July; flowerstalk to 20 in. (50 cm), smooth, glaucous blue-green, straight; plant clump-forming, dome-shaped, 32 in. (80 cm) across, 18 in. (45 cm) high; leaves 7 in. (18 cm) long and wide, upright on strong leafstalks, glaucous, pronounced blue-green, heart-shaped, flat. The best of the Tardiana Group hybridized by Eric Smith in England, 'Halcyon' (seen in photo of 'Wide Brim') is an excellent garden plant, widely cultivated, and has placed in the AHS poll top 20. 'Chantilly Lace', 'Gay Blade', and 'Sleeping Beauty' are much like but have striking creamy white margins. 'Devon Green' is a green form of 'Halcyon'. 'Tambourine' is a very large striking hybrid with a medium green center and a wide, creamy white margin.

'Honeybells'. Hybrid (*Hosta plantaginea* × *H. sieboldii*).

Flowers almost white with a hint of lavender, funnel-shaped, fragrant, to 2.5 in. (6 cm) long; August; flowerstalk to 5 ft. (1.5 m), smooth, light green, lasting, with small stem leaves; plant clump-forming, 4 ft. (1.2 m) across, 24 in. (60 cm) high; leaves 11 in. (28 cm) long and 8 in. (20 cm) wide, light green, heart-shaped, flat, laxly arching. Sophisticated hosta gardeners may fault me for even mentioning this plant, which they characterize as coarse, primitive, or even artless. But to me, it is a first-love kind of thing—'Honeybells', among the first hostas established at Hosta Hill, is a most vigorous plant, with fragrant flowers, and an excellent, inexpensive hosta for beginners, growing well in both northern and southern gardens. An old hybrid dating back to 1950, it is a fast grower that mounds up quickly and tolerates considerable sun, even in southern regions. Sports of this cultivar are 'Sugar and Cream', with a broad, creamy white margin, and 'Sweet Standard', with splashes of creamy white and yellowish green; 'Sweet Standard' is unstable and reverts to 'Sugar and Cream'. 'Irongate Glamour' is among the best fragrant cultivars with creamy white margins.

'Inniswood'.

Flowers white, bell-shaped, to 2 in. (5 cm) long; June–July; flowerstalk to 30 in. (75 cm), green, erect; plant clump-forming, 4 ft. (1.2 m) across, 24 in. (60 cm) high; leaves 10 in. (25 cm) long and 8 in. (20 cm) wide, broadly heart-shaped, dimpled and rippled, margins slightly upturned, sharp tip, yellow (lutescent) with irregular, wide green margin. A sport of 'Sun Glow', which is similar but with all yellow leaves; 'Innisjade' is the green-leaved sport.

'Invincible'.

Flowers white, slightly fragrant, funnel-shaped, to 2 in. (5 cm) long; June–July; flowerstalk to 20 in. (50 cm), green, with small stem leaves, erect; plant clump-forming, 20 in. (50 cm) across, 10 in. (25 cm) high; leaves 5 in. (13 cm) long and 3 in. (8 cm) wide, broadly heart-shaped, smooth, glossy, rich green, sharp tip. This is one of the best glossy hostas; its shiny leaves beg for attention.

'June', Tardiana Group.

Flowers bell-shaped, lavender, to 2 in. (5 cm) long; June–July; flowerstalk to 18 in. (45 cm), smooth, glaucous blue-green, straight; plant clump-forming, dome-shaped, 30 in. (75 cm) across, 18 in. (45 cm) high; leaves 6 in. (15 cm) long and 4 in. (10 cm) wide, glaucous, with a yellowish center and irregular blue-green margin with streakings toward the midrib, heart-shaped, flat. Has placed in the top 5 in the AHS poll and considered one the best variegated garden sports of the Tardiana Group. Retains its yellow center in some sun. 'Touch of Class' has a wider blue-green margin, and 'May' has greenish yellow leaves.

'Krossa Regal'.

Flowers pale purple, funnel-shaped, to 3 in. (8 cm) long; June–July; flowerstalk to 56 in. (1.4 m), bare, grainy, glaucous blue-green, straight; plant clump-forming, erect leaves vase-shaped, 40 in. (1 m) across, 36 in. (90 cm) high; leaves 9 in. (23 cm) long and 5 in. (13 cm) wide, glaucous blue-green, heart-shaped, wavy-undulate, with long leafstalks erect. This classic hosta, cultivated the world over, is a sterile descendant of *Hosta nigrescens*. Its architectural stature makes it an excellent garden plant; it has made the top 10 in the AHS poll. Tissue culture has produced the sports 'Porcelain Vase' (greenish white center with dark green margins) and 'Regal Providence' (leaves with a yellow center and blue-green margins).

'Lancifolia'.

Flowers lavender, funnel-shaped, to 2 in. (5 cm) long; July–September; flowerstalk to 18 in. (45 cm), smooth, green, with small stem leaves, leaning; plant clump-forming, 30 in. (75 cm) across, 12 in. (30 cm) high; leaves 6 in. (15 cm) long and 2–3 in. (5–8 cm) wide, dark green, smooth and shiny, lance-shaped and slightly wavy. This cultivar has

been grown for many years and is still a good landscape hosta for edgings and mass planting; it blooms late and has attractive, sterile flowers. 'Cathy Late' is a later-blooming variant. Several sports are in commerce: 'Change of Tradition' has green leaves with a thin, white margin and 'New Tradition' has a white leaf with a thin green margin. The viridescent hybrid 'Lancifolia Aurea' has yellow leaves without a margin. 'Inaho' is also broadly related; its yellow leaves with green streaks are quite stable, keeping their yellow well into late summer. *Hosta cathayana* is very similar but has fertile flowers.

'Love Pat'.

Flowers bell-shaped, white, to 2 in. (5 cm) long; June–July; flowerstalk to 20 in. (50 cm), smooth, glaucous blue-green, straight; plant clump-forming, dome-shaped, 32 in. (80 cm) across, 18 in. (45 cm) high; leaves 7 in. (18 cm) long and wide, upright on strong leafstalks, glaucous, pronounced blue-green, heart-shaped, deeply cupped, intensely puckered. This excellent hybridized form of 'Tokudama' has made the top 20 in the AHS poll and is widely cultivated internationally. **'Big Daddy'** (seen in photo of *Rodgersia sambucifolia*) is a somewhat larger version of it, with a clump size to 36 in. (90 cm) across and leaves to 11 in. (28 cm) long. 'Abiqua Drinking Gourd' is similar but has leaves that are cupped to the extreme and very distinct.

'Neat Splash Rim'.

Flowers lavender, funnel-shaped, to 2 in. (5 cm) long; July–September; flowerstalk to 28 in. (70 cm), smooth, green, leaning; plant clump-forming, somewhat vase-shaped, 28 in. (70 cm) across, 12 in. (30 cm) high; leaves 8 in. (20 cm) long and 3 in. (8 cm) wide, dark green with an irregular, creamy white margin, smooth and shiny, lance-shaped and slightly wavy. Derived from the heavily streaked but unstable 'Neat Splash', this is a popular hosta for edgings and accent groups. 'Yellow Splash' is similar to 'Neat Splash' and equally unstable, reverting to the stable 'Yellow Splash Rim'. From 'Neat Splash' comes 'Scooter', a handsome, fast-growing addition at Hosta Hill, and several white-margined forms of similar size: 'Bold Ribbons', 'Coquette', 'Cordelia', 'Crested Surf', 'Ground Master', and 'Little Wonder'. 'Emily Dickinson' is also white-margined and has fragrant flowers.

'On Stage' ('Choko Nishiki').

Flowers pale lavender, funnel-shaped, to 2.5 in. (6 cm) long; June–July; flowerstalk to 32 in. (80 cm); plant clump-forming, 30 in. (75 cm) across, 16 in. (40 cm) high; leafstalks variegated; leaves 9 in. (23 cm) long and 6 in. (15 cm) wide, arching, ovate heart-shaped, deeply ribbed and furrowed at veins, wavy, sharp tip, with viridescent yellow center turning a light green later, with a streaky, irregular dark green margin. This center-variegated beauty, found as a natural sport of *Hosta montana* in Japan, is very popular and has made the top 20 in the AHS poll. It requires careful siting and good, deep soil to develop into an impressive garden plant. Some morning sun helps to bring out the bright yellow color and retain it longer. Some claim to see a difference between 'On Stage' and 'Choko Nishiki', but I consider them synonymous.

'Opipara' ('Bill Brinka').

Flowers lavender, funnel-shaped, to 2 in. (5 cm) long; June–July; flowerstalk to 30 in. (75 cm), smooth, green, with small stem leaves, leaning; plant clump-forming, somewhat vase-shaped, 24 in. (60 cm) across, 15 in. (38 cm) high; leaves 7–9 in. (18–23 cm) long and 4 in. (10 cm) wide, dark green with a wide yellow margin, smooth and shiny, elliptic and slightly wavy. A very popular variegated form from Japan, related to 'Decorata'. Its creeping rhizomes are inherited from its ancestor *Hosta rectifolia*.

'Patriot', Fortunei Albomarginata Group.

Flower lavender, funnel-shaped, to 2 in. (5 cm) long; June–July; flowerstalk to 40 in. (1 m), green; plant clump-forming, 36 in. (90 cm) across, 24 in. (60 cm) high; leaves 8 in. (20 cm) long and 5 in. (13 cm) wide, heart-shaped, dark green with very wide, irregular white margin and some streaking to the leaf midrib. Discovered as a sport of 'Francee', it is one of the best white-margined cultivars available and an excellent garden plant. It has placed in the top 3 in the AHS poll. Similar are 'Admiral Halsey' (margin more creamy white), 'Minuteman' (margin slightly wider), 'Patriots Fire' (margin narrower and center viridescent), and 'Trailblazer'. All useful for brightening up shady garden corners. Sports of 'Patriot' include 'Fire and Ice', 'Loyalist', 'Mademoiselle', and 'Paul Revere', all with reverse variegation (white center with dark green margin).

'Paul's Glory'.

Flowers whitish lavender, bell-shaped, to 2 in. (5 cm) long; June–July; flowerstalk to 28 in. (70 cm), green, with small stem leaves; plant clump-forming, 32 in. (90 cm) across, 24 in. (60 cm) high; leafstalks white, green-margined; leaves 7 in. (18 cm) long and 5 in. (13 cm) wide, ovate heart-shaped, slightly dimpled, emerging chartreuse, turning yellowish white or creamy white (albescent), with dark bluish green, irregular margin. This sport of 'Perry's True Blue' has made the top 5 in the AHS poll. An outstanding garden plant: the color change during spring provides much interest, and it is easily grown and multiplies quickly. Several sports and related cultivars are available. 'Pete's Passion' is similar but with wider green margins. 'Chesterland Gold' and 'Gold Glory' have yellow leaves; 'Peter Ruh' has a green center with yellow margins.

'Pearl Lake'.

Flowers lavender, bell-shaped, to 2 in. (5 cm) long; June–July; flowerstalk to 30 in. (75 cm), smooth, bluish green, straight, with small stem leaves; plant clump-forming, 30 in. (75 cm) across, 18 in. (45 cm) high; leaves 5 in. (13 cm) long and 4 in. (10 cm) wide, grayish green with a bluish cast, heart-shaped, flat. Although classified as a blue hosta, this fine landscape hosta is more of a grayish green. Very floriferous, it gives an outstanding floral display in spring. Similar are the hybrids 'Alston Glenn', 'Rotunda', and 'Tucker Charm', all deep grayish green; 'Granada' and 'Veronica Lake' are yellow-margined sports.

'Piedmont Gold'.

Flowers white suffused with lavender, funnel-shaped, to 2 in. (5 cm) long; June–July; flowerstalk to 36 in. (90 cm), green, erect; plant clump-forming, 4 ft. (1.2 m) across, 24 in. (60 cm) high; leaves 11 in. (28 cm) long and 8 in. (20 cm) wide, broadly heart-shaped, flat, sharp tip, yellow (lutescent). Sensitive to sun exposure; place in considerable shade in southern gardens. It takes time for this cultivar to develop into its large, mature form. Several sports and related seedlings are available. 'Everglades' and 'Moonshine' have a yellow leaf with wide, green margin; so has 'Lakeside Symphony', but it takes time to develop its lighter, lime-green margins and is a bit smaller. 'Satisfaction' is a vigorous cultivar with green leaves and broad yellow margins; 'Evening Magic' has yellow leaves with irregular white margins. 'Hutch' and 'Tucker Tigers' have uniformly light green leaves.

'Regal Splendor'.

Flowers pale lavender, funnel-shaped, to 2.5 in. (6 cm) long; June–July; flowerstalk to 4 ft. (1.2 m), bare, grainy, glaucous blue-green, straight; plant clump-forming, dome-shaped, 40 in. (1 m) across, 36 in. (90 cm) high; leaves 12 in. (30 cm) long and 7 in. (18 cm) wide, glaucous blue-green with creamy yellow margin that turns creamy white, heart-shaped, wavy-undulate, with long leafstalks forming a continuous upright arch. This imposing, stable sport of 'Krossa Regal' has placed in the top 20 in the AHS poll.

'Sagae', *sagae giboshi* (Jap.).

Flowers lavender, funnel-shaped, to 2 in. (5 cm) long; June–July; flowerstalk to 4 ft. (1.2 m), green, with variegated leaves; plant clump-forming, 4 ft. (1.2 m) or more across, 31 in. (79 cm) high; leaves 10–12 in. (25–30 cm) long and 8–9 in. (20–23 cm) wide, broadly heart-shaped, wavy with undulating margin, sharp tip, leaf lobes upturned, glaucous surface and underside, soft olive-green with irregular, wide yellow margin. This hybrid, formerly considered a selection of *Hosta fluctuans*, is among the best variegated landscape hostas. Its bright margins are outstanding, and its tall stature makes it a superb accent plant. Long known and revered in Japan, it has gained the same reputation in Western gardens and has placed in the AHS poll top 3. 'Fat Cat' and 'Ivory Tower' are yellow-leaved sports; **'Liberty'** is an attractive wide-margined sport.

'Shade Fanfare'.

Flowers few, lavender, funnel-shaped, to 2 in. (5 cm) long; June–July; flowerstalk to 24 in. (60 cm), green; plant clump-forming, 24 in. (60 cm) across, 16 in. (40 cm) high; leaves 8 in. (20 cm) long and 7 in. (18 cm) wide, heart-shaped, flat, yellowish green center with a yellowish to creamy white margin. This is the stable form of the streaky sport 'Flamboyant'. Its soft colors make it a dignified garden plant. 'Archangel' and 'Golden Fanfare' are all-yellow sports. 'Verna Jean' has a yellowish center with white margin, while 'Cavalcade' has the same white margin on a medium green leaf.

'Shining Tot'.

Flowers lavender, funnel-shaped, to 1.5 in. (4 cm) long; July–August; flowerstalk to 10 in. (25 cm), bare, green, purple-spotted, straight; plant clump-forming, 6 in. (15 cm) across, 2 in. (5 cm) high; leaves 1–2 in. (2.5–5 cm) long and 0.5 in. (1 cm) wide, glossy dark green, broadly heart-shaped, wavy leaf margin. This popular tiny hosta is similar to *Hosta gracillima* but has rounded leaves. Excellent in the shady rock garden or potted; if planted in the open ground, protect from slugs and snails.

'Sum and Substance'.

Flowers whitish with lavender tint, elongated bell-shaped, 2 in. (5 cm) long; June–July; flowerstalk to 4 ft. (1.2 m), bare, oblique, overtop leaf mound; plant clump-forming, 5 ft. (1.5 m) across, 32 in. (80 cm) high; leaves 20 in. (50 cm) long and 14 in. (35 cm) wide, but usually somewhat smaller, on long leafstalks, yellow (lutescent), flat when young, but rugose, corrugated, and sometimes twisted at maturity, heart-shaped, with heavy substance, white pruinose back. This colossal cultivar needs some sun to go from chartreuse to yellow. Has held the No. 1 spot in the AHS poll. It grows well both in the North and in the hot, humid South. I know of a specimen 10 ft. (3 m) across and 4 ft. (1.2 m) in height; at Hosta Hill a plant has grown from a tiny, tissue-cultured explant into a giant 5 ft. (1.5 m) across and 36 in. (90 cm) high within 4 years. The large leaves have a high transpiration rate, so the plant needs deep soil and much moisture during dry periods to maintain vigorous growth. Several other hostas come close to attaining the size of this colossus; all are more or less yellow or yellowish green, and just one of these yellow giants may be enough for the average garden: 'Blast Off', 'Chartreuse Wedge', 'Choo Choo Train', 'Golden Sculpture', 'Lemon Meringue', 'Sea Monster', 'Solar Flare', 'Straka Gold', and 'Sunlight Sister'. Among the many sports of 'Sum and Substance' are the all-green 'Domaine De Courson' from Belgium and 'Parhelion', a light green with a creamy white edge. Similar but with a yellow margin and a lighter green center are 'Corona' from the Netherlands and 'Tiffney's Godzilla' from the United States. Among the many green-centered, yellow-margined sports of 'Sum and Substance' are 'Bottom Line', 'David A. Haskell', 'Eagle's Nest', 'Lady Isobel Barnett', 'Sum It Up', 'Sum of All', 'Supersonic', and **'Titanic'**. All are majestic. Such very large, variegated hostas should be used only as accents in the quiet, green garden.

'Summer Music'.

Flowers lavender, funnel-shaped, to 2 in. (5 cm) long; June–July; flowerstalk to 20 in. (50 cm) with stem leaves; plant clump-forming, 22 in. (55 cm) across, 10 in. (25 cm) high; leaves 7 in. (18 cm) long and 6 in. (15 cm) wide, heart-shaped, flat, with an albescent white center and a wide irregular green margin streaked with light green. The white center of this newer hybrid, a sport of the all-yellow 'Shade Master', reportedly melts out (burns), so careful siting is recommended; I grow it in a place where it gets a lot of morning sun and afternoon shade. 'Lakeside Meter Maid' (white center, dark green margin) is similar. Sporting also produced the much better-behaved 'Last Dance' (medium green center, wide yellow margin streaking to the center), which does not burn and makes a good garden plant; 'Nickelodeon' is similar, as is 'Summer Breeze' (dark green center, yellow margin).

'Sun Power'.

Flowers pale lavender, funnel-shaped, to 2 in. (5 cm) long; July–August; flowerstalk to 40 in. (1 m), with small stem leaves, straight; plant clump-forming, erect vase-shaped, 36 in. (90 cm) across, 30 in. (75 cm) high; leaves 10 in. (25 cm) long and 7 in. (18 cm) wide, yellowish green to yellow, elongated, tapering to a point, base heart-shaped, wavy-undulate, with leafstalks forming a continuous upright arch. Outstanding for its architectural stature and bright color, it has earned a position in the top 20 of the AHS poll. Similar is 'Sun Banner' with a dark green center and yellow margin. The yellow (lutescent) 'Sea Gold Star' becomes more resplendent as the season advances. 'Abba Dew' has a light green center and bright yellow margins.

'Tardiflora'.

Flowers purple, funnel-shaped, to 2 in. (5 cm) long; September–October; flowerstalk to 12 in. (30 cm), straight but leaning; plant clump-forming, dome-shaped, 18 in. (45 cm) across, 10 in. (25 cm) high; leaves 3–6 in. (8–15 cm) long and 2–3 in. (5–8 cm) wide, glossy dark green, leathery, heart-shaped, erect, with sharp tip; leaf and flowerstalks purple-spotted. This cultivar, which produces yellow an-

thers and many flowers, was crossed by Eric Smith with 'Elegans' (which he knew as *Hosta sieboldiana* 'Elegans') to create the Tardiana Group. The sport **'Tortifrons'** also has yellow anthers and much smaller, skinny leaves, curiously twisted and curled, that flatten out in too much shade; best in almost full sun North, morning sun in the South.

'Tokudama', *tokudama* (Jap.).

Flowers whitish, bell-shaped, to 1.5 in. (4 cm) long; June–July; flowerstalk to 18 in. (45 cm), glaucous green, straight; plant clump-forming, 24 in. (60 cm) across, 14 in. (35 cm) high; leaves 8 in. (20 cm) long and 7 in. (18 cm) wide, rounded heart-shaped, cupped, puckered and dimpled, glaucous, bluish green. This cultivar of unknown origin is a parent of 'Abiqua Drinking Gourd', 'Blue Cadet', 'Blue Umbrellas', 'Elegans', 'Love Pat', and many other blue-green hostas. It is only occasionally seen in gardens, having been largely replaced by its numerous offspring, which is unfortunate, because it makes a striking display with its corrugated blue leaves and white flowers.

'Tokudama Aureonebulosa', *akebono tokudama* (Jap.).

Flowers whitish, bell-shaped, to 1.5 in. (4 cm) long; June–July; flowerstalk to 18 in. (45 cm), glaucous green, straight; plant clump-forming, 24 in. (60 cm) across, 14 in. (35 cm) high; leaves 8 in. (20 cm) long and 7 in. (18 cm) wide, rounded heart-shaped, puckered and dimpled, glaucous, with mottled yellowish green center and an irregular, streaky bluish green margin. In Japan it is known as the "dawn of day" 'Tokudama'. Many similar forms are in commerce: 'Blue Shadows' has more blue streaking in the leaf center; 'Bright Lights' is more vigorous and faster growing; 'Princess Diana' has a narrower but more streaky margin; and 'Tokudama Flavoplanata' has an almost pure yellow center with a very narrow, neat blue-green margin. Most are slow-growing but they are well worth the wait. None like deep shade, and some sun is required for full development. 'Tokudama Ogon Hime', a yellow-leaved dwarf form from Japan, may be the origin of 'Little Aurora', which in turn has given rise to several variegated sports: **'Sultana'** (an exquisite little green hosta with bright yellow margins), 'Delia' and 'Goldbrook Grace' (yellow center, medium green margin), 'Elfin Cup' (yellowish center, creamy white margin), 'Enchantress' (white center, green margin), and 'Just So' (yellow center, narrow dark green margin). 'Shere Khan' (yellow center, thin white margin) is a miniature sport of 'Just So'. 'Vanilla Cream' is an excellent solid pale-yellow hybrid.

'Tokudama Flavocircinalis', *kifukurin tokudama* (Jap.).

Flowers whitish, suffused with lavender, bell-shaped, to 1.5 in. (4 cm) long; June–July; flowerstalk to 20 in. (50 cm), glaucous green, straight but leaning; plant clump-forming, 36 in. (90 cm) across, 18 in. (45 cm) high; leaves 9 in. (23 cm) long and 6 in. (15 cm) wide, broadly elliptic with heart-shaped base, puckered and dimpled, glaucous bluish green with a yellow margin 1.5 in. (4 cm) wide. This cultivar (seen in photo of 'Blue Angel') is larger than 'Tokudama Aureonebulosa' and more showy. Its margins do not burn like those of 'Frances Williams', and it makes a splendid addition to any garden.

'Undulata'.

Flowers lavender, funnel-shaped, to 2 in. (5 cm) long; June–July; flowerstalk to 36 in. (90 cm), green variegated with creamy white or whitish, straight but leaning, with many largish stem leaves; plant clump-forming, 24 in. (60 cm) across, 18 in. (45 cm) high; leaves 6–7 in. (15–18 cm) long and 3–4 in. (8–10 cm) wide, broadly elliptic with heart-shaped base and twisted tip, streaky white in the center and with an irregular margin of dark green with yellowish green and celadon streakings. This "green and white" hosta of old gardens is viridescent; those planted in our grandmothers' gardens have slowly, over decades, turned all green. It is still a good garden cultivar, which can be kept variegated if the green shoots are cut out occasionally. 'Undulata Univittata', an intermediate form, has a narrow white center. The all-green form is 'Undulata Erromena'. All are inexpensive and can be used for mass plantings.

'Undulata Albomarginata'.

Flowers lavender, funnel-shaped, to 2 in. (5 cm) long; June–July; flowerstalk to 36 in. (90 cm), green variegated with creamy white or whitish, straight but leaning, with many largish stem leaves; plant clump-forming, 28 in. (70 cm) across, 18 in. (45

cm) high; leaves 6–7 in. (15–18 cm) long and 3–4 in. (8–10 cm) wide, broadly elliptic with heart-shaped base, dark green with an irregular margin of creamy white to white. Unlike 'Undulata', this cultivar (seen in photo of 'Spritzer') is stable and has long been in cultivation. Among the best inexpensive variegated hostas, it grows in just about any soil; here it has thrived in Georgia red clay for decades. Easy to grow and vigorous.

'Whirlwind', Fortunei Group.

Flowers lavender, funnel-shaped, to 2 in. (5 cm) long; June–July; flowerstalk to 20 in. (50 cm), green, variegated stem leaves; plant clump-forming, 16 in. (40 cm) across, 10 in. (25 cm) high; leaves 6 in. (15 cm) long and 3 in. (8 cm) wide, heart-shaped but contracted and twisted, with a viridescent yellowish green center and an irregular dark green margin. The leaf color shows best in spring and fades to lighter green by early summer. Has made the top 20 in the AHS poll and is a favored conversation hosta, to be planted out as an accent or given prominence in a container on the patio. A garden sport of 'Fortunei Hyacinthina', it has produced other sports, such as 'Second Wind' (a somewhat larger, plain green, glaucous form with cupped leaves) and 'Tradewind' (possibly unstable, with streaked leaves). 'Eternal Flame' has dark green margins on a creamy white center.

Recommended reading

Aden, Paul. 1990. *The Hosta Book*. 2d ed. Portland, Oregon: Timber Press.

Grenfell, Diana. 1996. *The Gardener's Guide to Growing Hostas*. Portland, Oregon: Timber Press.

Schmid, W. George. 1991. *The Genus* Hosta. Portland, Oregon: Timber Press.

Zilis, Mark. 2000. *The Hosta Handbook*. Rochelle, Illinois: Q & Z Nursery.

Hydrastis

American Indians in Virginia used the yellow rootstock of *Hydrastis canadensis* (goldenseal) to produce a dye, and this eastern North American native is still widely used in herbal medicine for its antibacterial, anticonvulsant, sedative, and antihypertensive properties (it contains the alkaloid hydrastine). For its rich medicinal efficacy, it was wild-collected for centuries, with devastating results: the few plants that carry on in nature must never be disturbed, nor should their habitat be threatened. This long-lived, vigorous species is now commercially propagated for medicinal use, and several nurseries offer propagated stock.

I first encountered this plant in an isolated mountain valley in North Georgia. I was taken by the crinkly, rich green leaves, and with permission (I was on private property), I collected a couple of red berries. In a few years, my own plants were blooming and producing seed. The sepals of the flower, which are devoid of petals, fall away very early in the bloom cycle, leaving showy white stamens around several pistils. Easily cultivated, it should be planted in rich, moisture-retentive soil that is never allowed to dry out; watering is essential in hot, dry summers. Optimum pH is 5.5 to 6.5. Hardy to zone 3, but zone 7a in northern Georgia and Alabama seems to be its southern limit. *Hydrastis* is classified in the Ranunculaceae.

Propagate by dividing the rhizome before growth starts in very early spring. Seed can be sown in a cold frame in autumn.

I have never seen slug damage on my plants, nor do diseases and insects bother them.

Hydrastis canadensis, goldenseal, eyeroot, Indian dye, orangeroot, turmeric, yellow puccoon, yellowroot. Eastern North America, along the Canadian border from Minnesota to New England, south to northern Georgia and Alabama, west to Arkansas.

MS to FS; flowers solitary, whitish green, no petals, sepals 3, falling away early, stamens numerous, white; flowerstalk green, hairy, 12–16 in. (30–40 cm); April–May; plant rhizomatous, roots thick, yellow; leaves on the stem, 2, heart-shaped outline but 5- to 7-lobed, irregularly cleft and toothed, very dark green, 6–8 in. (15–20 cm) long, deeply furrowed along the veins and wrinkled all over; fruit red berries. The flowers are ephemeral, but the heavily crinkled leaves add significantly to the texture of shady gardens.

Hydrophyllum

The generic name derives from the Greek *hydor* (= water) and *phyllon* (= leaf), and true to its name, this North American native genus must have abundant moisture to be successfully cultivated. Here *Hydrophyllum virginianum* (Virginia waterleaf) required a trickling soaker hose all summer long; I really like its much-divided leaves, which are attractively mottled with gray in spring, and the whisky appearance of its flowers, whose filaments protrude way beyond the petals. The sour taste of its leaves, which American Indians and early settlers ate as greens, gave rise to many of its common names. Easily cultivated in zones 4 to 6a, it should be planted in perpetually moist but not waterlogged soil with a pH of 6 to 7. The genus is classified in the waterleaf family, Hydrophyllaceae.

Propagate by dividing the creeping rhizome before growth starts in very early spring.

Some slug or snail damage may occur. Lack of water turns the leaves black.

Hydrophyllum virginianum, Virginia waterleaf, Indian salad, John's cabbage, scorpion weed, Shawnee salad. Eastern North America, southern Manitoba to Quebec and western New England, south to North Carolina, west to northern Alabama and Tennessee, northern Arkansas and eastern Kansas.

LS to WS; flowers several, arising from the leaf axils on long stalks, extending above the leaves, drooping, white or dark violet, 5-petaled, bell-shaped, with hairy filaments extending beyond the petals; stem 12–30 in. (30–75 cm); May–August; plant rhizomatous, creeping; leaves compound, on the stem, with 5–7 leaflets, 2–5 in. (5–13 cm) long, green, mottled gray early, lance-shaped, sharply toothed; fruit a capsule. The flower buds curl over like a scorpion's tail. *Hydrophyllum macrophyllum* (large-leaved waterleaf) and *H. canadense* (broadleafed waterleaf) have large, single leaves with a mapleleaf shape. *Hydrophyllum fendleri* (Fendler's waterleaf) and *H. capitatum* (cat's breeches), both from British Columbia and the western Cascades, are equally at home in gardens. All add significantly to the garden's leaf texture and offer interesting flowers.

Iris

All bearded irises and most beardless irises, including the eye-catching Japanese irises, require full sun to be at their showy best. But a few species are surprisingly suitable for shady gardens. One is the native *Iris cristata* (crested iris), which I rescued years ago from a nearby tree-covered hillside threatened with "suburbanization." American Indians used it as a poultice for sores and as a tea, but ingestion can cause severe stomach pains, so early settlers left it alone.

Irises are easily cultivated in any garden soil with a pH of 5 to 7. The rhizome must not be planted too deep or they may rot; close examination of the native North American species in the wild shows the mats of rhizomes growing on top of the ground with the roots reaching into the soil. Hardy to zone 4, and the native North American irises are heat- and drought-tolerant well into zone 8. The genus is named for the Greek goddess of the rainbow and is classified in the Iridaceae; taxonomists have further subdivided the genus into subgenera, sections, and series.

Propagate by dividing the creeping rhizome in late autumn. Seed can be sown as soon as ripe in late summer or early autumn.

Slugs, snails, iris borers, and weevils can be bothersome. Crown rot and rhizome rot occur frequently when the rhizomes are planted too deep or in heavy or waterlogged soils.

Iris cristata, crested iris, crested dwarf iris, dwarf crested iris. Eastern North America, New York west to Illinois, south to Georgia and Alabama and west to Mississippi, Arkansas, and Oklahoma.

Morning sun, LS in the North, WS to MS in the South; flowers violet-blue, sometimes white, usually solitary, rarely 2, atop a short, slender flowerstalk, 2.5 in. (6 cm) long and 3 in. (8 cm) wide, composed of 6 spreading parts, sepals 3, petal-like, crested with white or yellow ridges, streaked with purple, broad, curving down, petals 3, narrower, arching, styles 3, 2-lobed, arching over the sepals, stamens 3, hidden under the styles; April–May; plant rhizomatous, densely mat-forming in more sun, with a more loose habit in more shade, widely spreading, forming colonies; leaves flat, lance-shaped, green, pointed, erect and sheathing the stem, 5–8 in. (13–20 cm) long and 0.6–1 in. (1.5–2.5 cm) wide, short at bloom time but elongating after flowering, with the longer dimension occurring after that time; fruit a 3-sided capsule. This shade-tolerant Evansia iris (subgenus *Limniris*, section *Lophiris*) inhabits the upland forests in its habitat; it is a good garden plant, tolerant of a variety of soils and even some neglect. The blue-flowered *Iris verna* (subgenus *Limniris*, series *Vernae*; dwarf iris) is not as shade-tolerant.

'Alba' (var. *alba*), flowers white.

'Eco Purple Pomp', flowers very dark violet, crests bright yellow brushed with orange.

'McDonald', flowers very pale blue, shading to lavender, crests yellow-orange, center patch (signal) white bordered with darker lavender.

'Navy Blue Gem', flowers dark violet, crests yellow, center patch (signal) white; usually 2 flowers are produced.

'Powder Blue Giant', very large pale blue flowers, to 3.5 in. (9 cm) across, crests yellow, center patch (signal) white bordered with dark blue; leaves larger, to 12 in. (30 cm) tall.

'Shenandoah Sky', flowers medium blue, crests yellow, center patch (signal) white; stems to 6 in. (15 cm) tall; leaves to 7 in. (18 cm) tall.

'Summer Storm', flowers dark violet-blue.

'Vein Mountain', flowers bright pale blue, crests orange, center patch (signal) white bordered by dark purple, usually one-flowered; stems shorter, to 5 in. (13 cm) tall; leaves to 8 in. (20 cm) tall.

Iris foetidissima, gladdon iris, gladwyn, gladwin, gladwine, roast beef plant, scarlet-seeded iris, stinking gladwyn, stinking iris. Western Europe, North Africa, Atlantic Islands.

Morning sun, LS in the North, WS to MS in the South; flowers malodorous when crushed, dull purple, lilac, or topaz tinged with yellow, veins dark purple, 2–3 in. (5–8 cm) across, to 5 per branch on a flowerstalk with 2–3 branches, to 36 in. (90 cm) tall; June–July; plant rhizomatous, vigorous; leaves evergreen, flat, lance-shaped, green, pointed, erect, arranged in fan-shaped tufts, malodorous when crushed, to 30 in. (75 cm) long; fruit a large capsule that splits open in autumn and displays its attractive and showy scarlet seeds. This iris of subgenus *Limniris*, section *Foetidissimae*, is often grown for its ornate seed clusters rather than for its flowers. The leaves are evergreen and provide welcome color during the off-season. Among the most shade-tolerant irises but unfortunately for northern gardeners, it is limited to zone 7a and warmer; it is very heat-tolerant but appreciates supplemental water during dry summers in the South. 'Variegata', with leaves striped creamy white or pale yellow, is eye-catching in the shady garden. Other cultivars include 'Citrina' (var. *citrina*; flowers yellow veined in pale lilac), 'Fructoalba' (seeds white), and 'Lutescens' (var. *lutescens*; flowers pure yellow).

Iris gracilipes, Chinese crested iris, Japanese crested iris. China, Japan.

Morning sun, LS in the North, WS in the South; flowers violet-blue, sometimes white, several, to 3 in. (8 cm) long and 4 in. (10 cm) wide, tube 0.6 in. (1.5 cm) long, falls notched with a violet-veined, white signal, crest yellow to orange with white tips; June–July; plant with slowly creeping rhizome, more or less clump-forming, depending on shade level, with a loose habit in more shade; leaves flat, grasslike, narrowly lance-shaped, green, yellowing after flowering, pointed, erect and partially sheathing the stem, to 12 in. (30 cm) long and 0.6 in. (1.5 cm) wide. This shade-tolerant Evansia iris (subgenus *Limniris*, section *Lophiris*) is well known as a rock garden plant but is also suitable for the woodland garden. It requires well-drained, acid soil. Flowering is curtailed in shade, but the grasslike leaves form an attractive clump. 'Alba' has white flowers.

Iris koreana, Korean iris. Korea.

Morning sun, WS to MS; flowers mostly 2, yellow, to 1.5 in. (4 cm) across with a long tube, sepals 3, falling down with a brown halo on the falls, petals 3, narrower, erect, blooming atop a short, slender flowerstalk to 6 in. (15 cm) long before the leaves expand; April–May; plant clump-forming; leaves flat, lance-shaped, green, pointed, erect and sheathing the stem, 0.6 in. (1.5 cm) wide, short at bloom time but elongating to 15 in. (35 cm) after flowering. This shade-tolerant iris (subgenus *Limniris*, section *Limniris*, series *Chinensis*) tolerates a variety of soils and accepts the hot, dry conditions prevalent in southern gardens, as does *Iris odaesanensis* (subgenus *Limniris*; Odae-san iris), also from Korea, an outstanding clump-former with white flowers to 2 in. (5 cm) across. The falls of *I. odaesanensis* have a yellow signal surrounded by a thin brownish border; it blooms May–June on stems to 8 in. (20 cm). Its green leaves are flat, lance-shaped, pointed, and erect, 0.6 in. (1.5 cm) wide, short at bloom time but elongating to 12 in. (30 cm) after flowering; they sheath the stem.

Iris tectorum, Japanese roof iris, roof iris. Central and southwest China, naturalized in Japan.

Morning sun, LS in the North, WS to MS in the South; flowers blue-lilac, sometimes white, terminal, 2–3 per spathe, to 4 in. (10 cm) across, composed of 6 spreading parts, sepals 3, petal-like, wavy, veined darker, with frilly white crests, spotted purple, curving down, petals 3, wavy, arching, styles 3, 2-lobed, arching over the sepals, stamens 3; May–June; plant rhizomatous, rapidly forming colonies; leaves flat, broadly lance-shaped, shiny green, pointed, erect and sheathing the stem, 12–14 in. (30–35 cm) long and to 1 in. (2.5 cm) wide; fruit a 3-sided capsule. This shade-tolerant Evansia iris (subgenus *Limniris*, section *Lophiris*) has long been grown on the roofs of buildings in Japan, hence the common name. It thrives on neglect and is tolerant of a variety of soils. Hardy to zone 4, very heat-tolerant. Cultivars include 'Alba' (flowers white with yellow streaks on the falls) and 'Variegata' (leaves streaked and striped with creamy white).

Recommended reading

Glasgow, Karen. 1997. *Irises: A Practical Gardening Guide*. Portland, Oregon: Timber Press.

Jeffersonia

Twinleaf is an apt vernacular name for *Jeffersonia diphylla*, whose single leaf is so deeply divided as to look like two separate ones. The genus name honors Thomas Jefferson; the epithet comes the Greek *dis* (= two) and *phyllon* (= leaf), for the two leaves per stem. This once-common native species is now rare, particularly in its southern range. It likes moist conditions and grows in medium to full shade in most of its habitats; in gardens, provide a shady spot and deep, humus-rich soil that stays moist all year. Optimum pH is 7, but native populations in northwestern Georgia flourish on acid soil. *Jeffersonia diphylla* is hardy to zone 4 and heat-tolerant, making it a great wildflower for southern gardens. It takes several years for plants to reach blooming stage, but they are long-lived and excellent candidates for the shady garden. The pretty flowers are ephemeral; but the leaves carry on until autumn, adding to the garden's leaf texture, and the unusual seedpods look like a smoker's pipe with a hinged cover that opens and releases the ripe seed. American Indians used the plant to treat rheumatism, infections, and cramps. Both *J. diphylla* and a very similar Asian species, *J. dubia*, are available in commerce. *Jeffersonia* is classified in the Berberidaceae.

Propagate by dividing the rhizome before growth starts in very early spring. Seed must be gathered when fresh and sown in an open frame.

Large slugs and snails can be very damaging to new growth in early spring. No diseases noted here.

Jeffersonia diphylla, twinleaf, American twinleaf, rheumatism root. North America, except New England, southern Ontario, Iowa, Wisconsin to western New York, south to northwestern Georgia and northern Alabama.

MS to FS; flowers solitary, above the leaves, to 1 in. (2.5 cm) across, white, 8 petals and 4 early falling petal-like sepals, cup-shaped opening to star-shaped, with 8 yellow stamens, on smooth stems, 5–10 in. (13–25 cm) tall, elongating to 18 in. (45 cm) when in fruit; April–May; plant clump-forming; leaves basal, 3–6 in. (8–15 cm) across, grayish green above, glaucous beneath, deeply cleft along the centerline; leaf stems stout, upright; fruit in a capsule with hinged top. A very rare double-flowered form is sometimes offered.

Jeffersonia dubia, Asian twinleaf. South Korea, eastern Russia, China, Manchuria.

MS to FS; smaller and shorter than *Jeffersonia diphylla* with similar flowers, usually blue or lavender-blue, usually not above or equal with the leaves; April–June; plant clump-forming, tufted; leaves basal, 3–5 in. (8–13 cm) across, bluish green above with a purple cast when young, one-sided cleft along the centerline and lobed around margins. Forma *alba* is a naturally occurring white-flowered variant.

Juncus

Two species in the genus *Juncus* are suitable for shady places. Like the sedges (*Carex* spp.), rushes are trouble-free and easy to use. They are grown for their spiky, grasslike, but cylindrical leaves; some are straight, others spiral and twist like a corkscrew, resulting in a bizarre mess of strangely attractive leaves that always elicits comment. These multifarious leaves juxtapose well with the bold foliage of hostas and the tracery of ferns.

In their natural habitat rushes grow in mostly marshy conditions, but any garden soil that holds moisture will suit them, so long as there is no stagnant water in the ground. Many are long-lived and vigorous, and they like sun or shade. Here in zone 7 most turn a yellowish brown after the first few frosts and become dark brown by winter's onset; they grow happily into very hot regions, including zone 9. The rushes listed are good filler and accent plants.

The genus *Juncus* is cosmopolitan in distribution. *Juncus* is the classic Latin name for rush, and the genus is classified in the rush family, Juncaceae.

Propagate by dividing the dormant clumps or creeping rhizomes before growth starts in very early spring. They can be moved at any time provided a good clump of earth is taken with them.

Insects and mollusks leave the rushes alone. Stem rot can be a serious problem in stagnant soils.

Juncus effusus, common rush, soft rush, Japanese mat rush. Cosmopolitan.

Some sun, LS to MS; flowers inconspicuous; leaves green to light yellowish green, erect, cylindrical, with sharp tips, to 5 ft. (1.5 m) long, shorter in shade; plant clump-forming, tufted. Rarely offered but so common, it can be collected; years ago, I dug up a clump from a very shady creek bed on property owned by one of my sons. It multiplied in medium shade, and small tufts now punctuate my woodland. Field-cultivated in Japan to produce tatami mats. Hardy to zone 4.

'Aureus Variegatus' has straight leaves striped with yellowish green.

'Curly Wurly' is a compact selection of 'Spiralis', with spiral leaves pointing everywhere.

'Spiralis' (f. *spiralis*, *Scirpus lacustris* 'Spiralis'; corkscrew rush), spiraling, upright leaves. Makes a great accent plant among hostas and ferns.

'Vittatus', leaves marked with thin, ivory-white bands.

'Zebrinus', leaves broadly banded with greenish white to white.

Juncus inflexus, hard rush, blue rush. Cosmopolitan.

Some sun, LS; flowers inconspicuous; leaves blue-green, erect, straight and cylindrical, with sharp, hard tips, to 4 ft. (1.2 m) long, shorter in shade; plant clump-forming, tufted. This attractive steel-blue rush goes great with yellow hostas. Hardy to zone 4. Cultivars include 'Afro' (blue Medusa rush; same blue as the species but with contorted, corkscrew leaves) and an unusual weeping selection, 'Lovesick Blues' (weeping blue rush).

Kirengeshoma

The first time I saw kirengeshomas in bloom was at a nursery in Vancouver, Washington. From afar, the blooms looked much like those on my *Tricyrtis macrantha* var. *macranthopsis*, a set of gorgeous, nodding, waxy, lemon-yellow bells. I took a piece of this *Kirengeshoma palmata* home with me and have since added another marvelous Asian beauty, *K. coreana*. Both have stood up to the hot, dry summers of zone 7a, but I doubt these exotics will succeed in zones 8 to 10, as some sources indicate. Constant moisture and excellent drainage are essentials, accomplished here by raised-bed planting, as is a cool, shaded location. Kirengeshomas make great companions to hostas, ferns, and astilbes in the moist woodland border. Their large leaves, shaped like maple leaves, carry on until the first freeze. The genus name comes from *ki renge shoma*, the Japanese name for *Anemonopsis*, which resembles this genus. *Kirengeshoma* is classified in the Hydrangeaceae.

Kirengeshomas are hardy to zone 5 with protection. Supplemental water is necessary in warmer zones with hot, dry summers. The rhizomatous rootstock spreads slowly, forming a nice colony in time.

Propagate by carefully dividing the dormant woody rhizomes in very early spring. Seed can be sown in the open in spring, but germination is slow and seedlings take several years to mature.

Slugs and snails are a real problem in spring when the new growth emerges. No other pests or diseases are reported, but lack of drainage leads to root rot and a quick demise.

Kirengeshoma coreana. Korea.

MS to FS; similar to *Kirengeshoma palmata* but yellow flowers not as waxy and with flaring, opening petals, only somewhat nodding, in clusters on stems 5–6 ft. (1.5–1.8 m) tall. Despite its considerably different, more open flowers, some consider this larger plant a variant of *K. palmata*. It is sometimes placed in the genus's Koreana Group.

Kirengeshoma palmata, yellow waxbells. Southern Japan, Kyushu, southern Shikoku.

MS to FS; flowers yellow, 2–4, in terminal clusters on branches from the leaf axils, nodding, tightly bell-shaped with 5 fleshy, overlapping petals, recurved at tips, to 1.5 in. (4 cm) long on flower-stalks 4–5 ft. (1.2–1.5 m); June–July; plant clump-forming with rhizomatous rootstock; leaves opposite, mapleleaf-shaped, with 6–10 lobes, toothed and incised, light green, heart-shaped at the base, 4–8 in. (10–20 cm) long, smaller toward top, those at bottom are larger. An excellent plant for shady garden, with an unforgettable flower show. Takes lighter shade in more northern regions.

Lamium

Most gardenworthy deadnettle cultivars stem from Eurasian species; the several species native to North America, including *Lamium amplexicaule* (henbit), are weedy and rarely used in gardens. The garden forms, primarily used as creeping groundcovers, can be well behaved or invasive, according to cultural conditions. Some have striking variegated leaves that form a dense, multicolored groundcover. In the South they need medium to full shade; further north they tolerate considerable sun. Even and constant moisture and a fertile soil with a pH of 5.5 to 7 are musts everywhere, but such fitting conditions can turn some cultivars into invasive monsters. Site away from delicate wildflowers and small plants; deadnettles will overpower them. Hardy to zone 4. In areas warmer than zone 7b, deadnettles become leggy and must be cut back once or twice a season to 8 in. (20 cm).

Deadnettles lack the stinging hairs of the stinging nettle (*Urtica dioica*), hence the common name. The genus name is the classic Latin for the European deadnettle. They are classified in the Labiatae. New reference works include the genera *Galeobdolon* and *Lamiastrum* in the genus *Lamium*, which arrangement is followed here. These names are still encountered in commerce, in particular *Lamiastrum*.

Propagate by carefully dividing the runners in very early spring; replant divisions immediately. With the plant's vigorous spreading habit, seed propagation makes little sense.

Mildew and leaf spot are reported; larger slugs and snails can be a problem.

Lamium album, archangel, dumb nettle, white deadnettle, snowflake. Eurasia, central Europe to eastern Asia, naturalized in North America.

LS to MS; flowers white, large-lipped above, tubular, to 0.8 in. (2 cm) long, 7–9 in false whorls around the stem; June–July; plant ascending to stoloniferous, spreading, 8–16 in. (20–40 cm) high; leaves oblong, to 3 in. (8 cm) long, toothed and incised, medium green, hairy. Low maintenance; naturalizes easily even in drier soils. Cultivars include 'Friday' (leaves light and darker green with yellow center) and 'Goldflake' (leaves striped yellow).

Lamium galeobdolon, yellow archangel, golden nettle, golden deadnettle. Eurasia, central Europe to western Asia.

LS to FS; flowers yellow to brown-spotted yellow, large-lipped above, tubular, to 0.8 in. (2 cm) long, 3–5 in false whorls around the stem; June–July; plant rhizomatous and stoloniferous, vigorously to invasively spreading, to 24 in. (60 cm) high but usually less; leaves broadly ovate to heart-shaped, to 2.5 in. (6 cm) long, toothed, medium green often mottled with silvery gray, on stolonlike branches. A good, quickly spreading groundcover. Excellent in moist, shady areas; unsightly where soil dries out. Check its spread frequently to keep it from getting out of bounds.

'Florentinum' ('Variegatum', 'Type Ronsdorf', *Galeobdolon argentatum* of gardens), leaves silvery gray in center, green margins; purple in winter; mat-forming.

'Hermann's Pride', leaves smaller, silvery gray-green with conspicuous darker green veins; mat-forming.

'Silber Teppich' ('Silver Carpet'), leaves silvery gray with green veins; clump-forming.

'Silver Angel', leaves silvery gray-green.

'Silver Spangled', leaves coarsely toothed, heavily silver-mottled; mat-forming.

Lamium maculatum, spotted deadnettle. Eurasia, central Europe to western Asia.

LS to FS; flowers reddish purple, sometimes pink or white, large-lipped above, tubular, to 0.8 in. (2 cm) long, 3–5 in false whorls around the stem; June–July; plant ascending, stoloniferous, vigorously spreading, mat-forming, to 8 in. (20 cm) high; leaves broadly ovate to heart-shaped, 1–3 in. (2.5–8 cm) long, heavily toothed, medium green often mottled or centered with silvery white or pink. An excellent, quickly spreading groundcover.

'Album' (f. *album*), flowers white; leaves silvery white mottled.

'Argenteum', flowers reddish; leaves silver-gray mottled.

'Aureum' ('Gold Leaf'), flowers pink; leaves yellow with white center.

'Beacon Silver' ('Beacon's Silver', 'Silbergroschen'), flowers pale pink to lilac; leaves silvery gray with a thin green margin.

'Beedham's White', flowers white; leaves greenish yellow.

'Cannon's Gold', flowers purple; leaves yellow.

'Chequers', flowers deep pink; leaves with silvery gray stripe along midrib.

'Immaculate', flowers purple; leaves green.

'Pink Nancy', flowers pink; leaves silvery gray with thin green margin.

'Pink Pewter', flowers pink; leaves light silvery gray with darker grayish green margin.

'Red Nancy', flowers red; leaves silvery gray.

'Shell Pink', flowers pink, floriferous; leaves green with white blotch.

'Sterling Silver', flowers purple; leaves silvery gray.

'White Nancy', flowers pure white; leaves silvery gray with narrow green margin.

Lamium orvala. Central Europe, Austria to Balkans.

LS to MS; flowers purple to brownish red, large-lipped above, tubular, to 1.5 in. (4 cm) long, in false whorls around the stem; June–July; plant ascending, clump-forming, to 24 in. (60 cm) tall; leaves oblong heart-shaped, 4–6 in. (10–15 cm) long, irregularly toothed and incised, deeply veined, medium gray-green, hairy. A clump-forming species suitable for smaller gardens or pot culture. 'Album' is a white-flowered form.

Lilium

Known and admired throughout recorded history, lilies are symbols of virginity and purity in art and religion and have been a food source for man and animals for centuries. The generic name goes back to the classic name given by the Greeks and Romans to lilies and forms the root for the Liliaceae, in which family the true lilies are classified. Lilies present a predicament to the shade gardener. They like to have their toes in cool, shaded soil but most must have their heads in the sun. My garden's shade is somewhere between dark woodland and medium—not a great environment for most lilies, particularly the new, sun-loving hybrids admired by so many. Luckily, some lilies can stand a fair amount of shade. *Lilium martagon* and its relatives present an opportunity to grow fine lilies in shady realms, and with some care and correct placement, a few native North American lilies too reward the shade gardener.

Using lilies as annuals is a good way to enjoy them in shady places. Asiatic and Oriental *Lilium* hybrids like **'Enchantment'** and **'Sun Ray'** make great companions for hostas in woodland shade. Using bulbous perennials as annuals is a trick I learned from southern landscapers, who use truckloads of tulips as annuals around Atlanta office complexes and parks; the spent bulbs are relegated to the compost heap after flowering because they will not get the winter chilling they need to flower another season. Like tulips, all lily bulbs perform great for the first season, no matter the amount of sun or shade, because of the plentiful food supply stored up in the bulb when it comes from the grower; in woodland shade, they might give a second or possibly a third season of great bloom, but without some full sun, they will surely decline, usually sooner than later. All lilies, even shade-tolerant lilies, must have some sun.

Plant lilies in a fertile, friable, acid soil with plenty of humus. Optimum pH is 4.5 to 6, but the lilies listed are tolerant of a pH up to 6.5. All my lilies are located on sloping ground in berms or raised beds, which is one way to gain the good drainage they require. Constant, even moisture in spring is important for spring growth; in summer lilies prefer a drier soil and withstand droughts quite well; in winter they dislike wet, boggy conditions, which can lead to bulb rot. Some species are hardy to zone 3. The bulbs need winter chilling for several weeks, so lilies do not regenerate well in warm-winter areas of zones 8 and 9. For best effect in woodland gardens, plant in groups of three to five. Lilies combine well with taller-growing perennials and wildflowers; I use them to great effect popping up between hostas and ferns in the shady, woodland border.

Propagate by carefully removing offsets or bulbils from the stems as soon as the plants become dormant. Seed can be sown as soon as ripe in pots in a cold frame.

In some areas, lily beetles and their larvae defoliate the stems, and vine weevils and their larvae attack the leaves and bulbs; basal rot turns the bulbs to mush, and another fungal rot infects the leaves and turns them brown. Such threats can be contained with systemic chemical insecticides or fungicides. Slugs and snails can be a problem in spring when the new growth emerges. Lack of drainage can lead to bulb rot and a quick demise. In open areas, rabbits have developed a craving for lily bulbs; frequently, the only way to prevent them from being eaten is to enclose them in below-ground wire cages. Viral diseases are a problem with many lilies, but those described are relatively resistant.

Lilium martagon, common turk's cap lily, martagon lily, turk's cap, turban lily. Eurasia, Spain across southern Europe to the Caucasus and into Siberia.

Some sun, LS to WS; flowers slightly fragrant or malodorous, pendent or nodding, sepals 3, petal-like, petals 3, glossy pink, mauve, red, or maroon, spotted with purplish or blackish brown, sometimes white with or without spots, tepals very strongly recurved, 2 in. (5 cm) across, stamens exposed, anthers dangling, flowers produced in loose clusters, 6–50, on long, branched flowerstalks, 3–6 ft. (0.9–1.8 m) tall, green shaded with purple or red; July–September; plant bulbous, stem-rooting; leaves in 2–4 whorls of 6–14, to 6 in. (13 cm) long, elliptic to inversely lance-shaped with 7–9 prominent veins, green, sometimes hairy beneath; fruit a capsule. Resistant to most lily diseases and of relatively easy culture: it will need about two hours of full sun and does well in moist, open woodland. Hardy to zone 4, difficult in zone 8 and warmer; I consider zone 7b its southern limit. The long-lasting flowers come earlier than other lilies. Variety *albiflorum* has flowers white with pink spotting; var. *album* has white, unspotted flowers, smaller to 1.5 in. (4 cm) across, and yellow anthers; and var. *cattaniae* has unspotted maroon flowers. The related *Lilium hansonii*, also stem-rooting, is more leafy and has thick-textured tepals of spotted tangerine-orange with more gently recurving tips. 'Early Bird', a selection of *L. ×dalhansonii* (*L. martagon × L. hansonii*), has early, orange-yellow flowers with light spotting carried on stems to 6 ft. (1.8 m) tall. Other Backhouse hybrids (as hybrids between these two species are also known) include 'Dairy Maid' (flowers creamy yellow with dark spotting), 'Marhan' (flowers orange with chestnut-brown spotting on tall stems), 'Shantung' (flowers pinkish mauve with spotting), and 'Sutton Court' (flowers yellowish tangerine with darker spotting).

Lilium philadelphicum, wood lily, red lily, wild orange-red lily, orange cup lily. Eastern and central North America, southern Ontario and Quebec, New England south to the mountains of eastern Kentucky, North Carolina, and northwestern Georgia, west to Texas.

Some sun, LS to WS; flowers opening and facing up, sepals 3, petal-like, petals 3, each forming a separate segment, tapering toward the base, the shanks becoming like a thin stalk with space between the stalks, orange spotted with purplish brown and with a yellowish throat, 2 in. (5 cm) wide, stamens 6, within the flower, flowers 1–5, on long flowerstalks, produced on stems 12–36 in. (30–90 cm) tall; June–August; plant bulbous, producing new bulblets alongside; leaves 4–8, in whorls, 1–4 in. (2.5–10 cm) long, narrowly lance-shaped with pointed tips; fruit a capsule. This is a magnificent lily with separate, seemingly floating tepals supported by very thin, stalklike shanks. It requires a drier location than *Lilium superbum* (it is often considered difficult because it is given too much moisture); its cultural requirements are otherwise similar. Hardy to zone 3, heat-tolerant to zone 7. A related southern species, *L. catesbaei* (southern red lily, pine lily), is found in dry, thin woods and clearings and is suited for more southern gardens in zones 7 and 8; it has a single up-facing flower and alternate leaves along the stem and held upright.

Lilium superbum, American turk's cap lily, lily-royal, swamp lily, turk's cap. Eastern North America, southern New England south to the Carolinas, Georgia, and northern Alabama.

Some sun, LS to WS; flowers nodding sideways or down, sepals 3, petal-like, petals 3, orange with crimson tips and spotted with purplish brown, streaked green at the base, forming a green "star," tepals strongly recurved in turk's cap fashion, 2.5 in. (6 cm) long, stamens exposed, anthers brownish red, dangling, flowers 3–40, on long flowerstalks, produced on stems 3–9 ft. (0.9–2.7 m) tall, green mottled with maroon; July–September; plant bulbous, strongly rhizomatous; leaves in whorls or alternate in the upper part, 4–5 in. (10–13 cm) long, elliptic to lance-shaped with reflexed, pointed tip; fruit a capsule. This is the largest and best of the native lilies for the garden. It needs two hours of sun and does well in the moist woodland. Easily cultivated as long as constant soil moisture is maintained; in the wild it grows in swampy areas and wet woodlands, but it does not tolerate stagnant water conditions. The soil must be acid, a pH of 5 to not over 6. Hardy to zone 3, heat-tolerant to zone 7 as long as moisture is maintained. I grow the much more demure ***Lilium michauxii*** (Carolina lily, Michaux's lily). This native lily (named for the French botanist and explorer of North America, André Michaux) does well in the dark woodland shade, where the sun shines for only a brief period early in the morning; it is much smaller, 12–36 in. (30–90 cm), and rarely has more than 3 flowers on the stem. The leaves are broader toward the tip and whorled. It tolerates somewhat drier conditions and is long-lived once established. Hardy to zone 6, heat-tolerant to zone 8. Both are available from wildflower nurseries and should never be removed from the wild. They mix well with other woodlanders due to their acid soil requirements.

Recommended reading

Jefferson-Brown, Michael, and Harris Howland. 1995. *The Gardener's Guide to Growing Lilies*. Portland, Oregon: Timber Press.

McRae, Edward Austin. 1998. *Lilies: A Guide for Growers and Collectors*. Portland, Oregon: Timber Press.

Liriope

Liriope is an institution in southern gardens. The lilyturf so ubiquitous in the South, *Liriope muscari*, is often characterized as a clumper, but as many gardeners can attest, it spreads vigorously into adjacent lawns when used as an edger. Perhaps all that good fertilizer and water expended on the lawn also benefits the bordering lilyturf, which quickly decides to take over. Lilyturf does not care how hot or dry it gets, or what soil it grows in, or how much or little sun or shade it gets. By now almost every garden has patches of it, so this amiability is no longer appreciated, and one has to haul it off to the garden waste recycling center, where they convert it to good compost.

Mid-twentieth-century references barely mention *Liriope*. Since then, a flood of new cultivars has been developed, many attractively variegated and all—because of their great tolerance to shaded environments—indispensable in the shady garden. I have grown various species of lilyturf in light to deep shade and found all to be troublefree and easy to use. Their abundance of thin, strap-shaped leaves goes great with bold hostas and lacy ferns; they can be used singly as an accent plant, in a row as edgings, or in masses as a maintenance-free groundcover. They are evergreen in the warmer regions of their habitat. In areas with cold winters, most of them become deciduous, but the perennating rootstock can be overwintered with good protection where the soil does not freeze hard permanently and deeply.

The genus *Liriope* is endemic to eastern Asia. It is classified in the Convallariaceae and is closely related to the other genus of lilyturf, *Ophiopogon*.

Liriope thrives anywhere. I have seen it flourish in heavy Georgia red clay without amendments. It does not like stagnant water in the ground. Soils of both high and low fertility are accepted; apply a slow-release fertilizer to give plants intended as groundcovers a quick start. Any kind of shade is tolerated.

Propagate by dividing the dormant clumps in very early spring before growth starts. Sow seed directly in the ground in spring. Many species self-seed.

Leaf spot and root rot are reported but not experienced here. Slugs can be problematic, but they have left my plants alone. The only insect problem has been an occasional bite taken out of a leaf margin by vine weevils.

Liriope exiliflora, lilyturf. China, Taiwan, Japan.

LS to FS; flowers small, many, mauve, loosely arranged in clusters on a purple flowerstalk to 12 in. (30 cm) tall, above the arching leaves; July–September; leaves evergreen, dark green, linear lance-shaped, wider toward the top, tip blunt, leathery, 16 in. (40 cm) long and 0.5 in. (1 cm) wide, midrib keeled, and 6–8 parallel veins grooved; plant clump-forming, tufted, rhizomatous, creeping; fruit clusters of black berries. Spreads faster than other species. Hardy to zone 7a, heat-tolerant to zone 10. The species is rarely available, but its selection 'Silvery Sunproof' ('Ariake Janshige') offers pale violet flowers in loose arrangement and leaves striped white or yellowish white. *Liriope graminifolia* (lilyturf) from China and Japan is similar, but its flowers are a little tighter, and its 4–6 leaves have grasslike parallel veins; often confused with selections of *L. muscari*.

Liriope muscari, big blue lilyturf, blue lilyturf, lilyturf, southern lilyturf. China, Taiwan, Japan.

LS to FS; flowers small, many, bluish violet, sometimes mauve, tightly arranged in a spike-shaped, conical cluster, 0.8 in. (2 cm) wide at bottom and 4–5 in. (10–13 cm) long, on a purplish green flowerstalk to 15 in. (38 cm) tall, above the arching leaves; July–September; leaves evergreen, dark green, linear lance-shaped, wider toward the top, tip blunt, leathery, 10–18 in. (25–45 cm) long, 0.5–0.8 in. (1–2 cm) wide, midrib deeply keeled, and 6–9 parallel veins grooved, forming a zigzag cross section; plant clump-forming, tufted, rhizomatous, expanding slowly or quickly depending on soil conditions; fruit clusters of black berries, stems often bending down with their weight. Hardy to zone 6a, heat-tolerant to zone 10.

'Big Blue', flowers violet-blue; a large selection of the type.

'Christmas Tree' ('Munroe No. 2'), flowers pale lavender or lilac on a conical spike, wide at the bottom; to 15 in. (38 cm) tall.

'Curly Twist', flowers deep lilac shaded to burgundy; leaves dark green, twisted.

'Gigantea' (*Liriope gigantea*), probably a large selection of *L. muscari*.

'Gold Banded' ('Gold Band'), flowers purple; leaves yellow with dark green margins, narrow or wider.

'Grandiflora' (*Liriope grandiflora*), flowers lavender on tall stalk to 24 in. (60 cm).

'Ingwersen', flowers deep violet; leaves dark green.

'John Burch', flowers bluish lavender, often crested like a cockscomb; leaves yellow striped.

'Lilac Beauty', flowers deep lilac, floriferous, on stems to 20 in. (50 cm); leaves dark green.

'Majestic' (*Liriope majestica*), flowers deep lilac, sometimes fused, flattened spike, on tall stems to 20 in. (50 cm), floriferous; leaves dark green.

'Monroe White' ('Munroe No. 1', *Liriope munroei*), flowers larger, pure white, floriferous; leaves wide, dark green; fruit pinkish lavender.

'Royal Purple', flowers bright purple, floriferous; leaves dark green.

'Silver Dragon' ('Gin Ryu'), lilac flowers; leaves irregularly streaked with white, sometimes reverting to all green.

'Silver Midget', flowers lilac-blue on 15 in. (38 cm) stems; wide, dark green leaves. Not a midget plant!

'Tidwell Big Blue', flowers lilac-blue on 12 in. (30 cm) stems; leaves very dark green.

'Variegata' (*Liriope variegata*), flowers violet; leaves green with white to yellow margins and streaks.

'Webster Wideleaf', flowers purple on stems to 18 in. (45 cm); leaves dark green, wider than most cultivars, to 0.8 in. (2 cm) wide.

Liriope spicata, creeping lilyturf, creeping liriope. Southwestern China, Vietnam.

LS to FS; flowers small, many, mauve, loosely arranged in clusters on a brownish violet flowerstalk to 12 in. (30 cm) tall; August–September; leaves evergreen, dark green, linear lance-shaped, tip blunt, leathery, to 12 in. (30 cm) long and narrower than other species; plant rhizomatous, vigorously creeping; fruit clusters of black berries. Spreads faster than all other species and makes an excellent groundcover or turf substitute. Hardy to zone 5, heat-tolerant to zone 10.

'Alba', flowers white.

'Gold Dragon' ('Golden Dragon', 'Kin Ryu'), flowers pale purple, stems to 10 in. (25 cm); leaves narrow, dark green, striped yellow.

'Silver Dragon' ('Gin Ryu'), flowers pale purple, stems to 10 in. (25 cm); leaves narrow, dark green striped silvery white; fruit light green striped darker green. Often confused with *Liriope muscari* 'Silver Dragon', which has stripes more yellowish or ivory.

Lobelia

I must admit, my main reason for growing a bunch of cardinal flowers is to attract hummingbirds, which are easily the most fascinating of all the birds that visit Hosta Hill. I rarely saw them—until my single cardinal flower multiplied into several. Now the territorial hummers put on aerial fights while the large groups of cardinal flowers are in bloom, some in light to medium shade, others where they get some afternoon sun, from late July through the first weeks of September. Cardinal flower, *Lobelia cardinalis*, is a native North American wildflower. Its showy flowers have always attracted people. American Indians brewed a tea from the leaves to treat rheumatism, fevers, colds, and headaches; the roots, which contain alkaloids, are toxic if taken in quantity. It is characterized as short-lived, but this has been no problem here. Given sufficient mois-

ture, the clumps, besides self-seeding prolifically, produce plenty of offsets to carry on. In mild-winter regions new leaf crowns form in late autumn to early winter, and by late spring tall stalks rise clothed with attractive leaves tinged purplish bronze, adding much to the landscape.

Lobelia cardinalis, *L. siphilitica* (great lobelia), and the hybrids of *L.* ×*speciosa* are the only lobelias that will bloom, more or less, in shade. The subtropical *L. splendens*, which was involved in the creation of *L.* ×*speciosa*, requires conditions prevalent in zones 8 and 9.

All lobelias listed have great heat tolerance as long as the soil remains constantly moist and they are grown in shade. A fertile soil with a pH of 4.5 to 6 guarantees success. *Lobelia cardinalis* loves to grow in swampy conditions; *L. siphilitica* prefers somewhat drier, but never dry soil. For best effect in woodland gardens, plant in groups of three to five.

The epithet *cardinalis* alludes to the bright red worn by cardinals in the Catholic church; the epithet *siphilitica* is a reference to the plant's use as a cure for syphilis. The genus name honors the Flemish botanist Lobel. *Lobelia* is classified in the Campanulaceae.

Propagate by removing offsets from clumps in early winter or transplanting self-seeded seedlings.

Mulched crowns are subject to crown rot. Leaf spot, rust, and smut are reported but not experienced here. Larger slugs and snails attack young growth in late winter and early spring. Moth and butterfly larvae, like army worms or cabbage worms, can be troublesome during the flowering season.

Lobelia cardinalis, cardinal flower, Indian pink, scarlet lobelia. Southern Ontario to Quebec and New Brunswick and east in North America, excluding the Dakotas west to Oregon and Washington.

Some sun, LS to WS in the North, LS to MS in the South; flowers brilliant red, to 1.5 in. (4 cm) long, 5-petaled with 2 lips, upper 2-lobed, the lower 3-lobed, reflexed, stamens fused, forming a tube and extending beyond the petals, leaflike bract beneath each flower; flowers many, up to 48, loosely arranged in an elongated cluster to 14 in. (35 cm) long, on erect, green to reddish purple stalks 2–4 ft. (0.6–1.2 m) tall; July–September; leaves alternate, new growth tinged purple, then bright green, often oblong lance-shaped, toothed, to 4 in. (10 cm) long; plant clump-forming, rhizomatous, producing offsets; fruit a capsule with many seeds. Hardy to zone 3, heat-tolerant to zone 9.

'Alba' (f. *alba*), flowers pure white.

'Angel Song', flowers bicolored, salmon and cream.

'Cotton Candy', flowers pinkish white.

'Monet Moment', flowers pink-violet.

'Rosea' (f. *rosea*), flowers rose-pink.

'Rose Beacon', flowers light rosy pink.

'Ruby Slippers', flowers dark ruby-red.

'Summit Snow', flowers pure white.

'Twilight Zone', flowers light rose-pink.

Lobelia siphilitica, great lobelia, great blue lobelia, blue cardinal flower. Eastern North America, western New England, south to Georgia and Alabama, west to Texas, Kansas, and the Dakotas.

Some sun, LS to WS; flowers bright blue, to 1 in. (2.5 cm) long, 5-petaled, with 2 lips, upper 2-lobed, the lower striped with white, and 5 pointed lobes, stamens fused, forming a tube and extending beyond the petals, large leafy bracts surround each flower; flowers many, loosely arranged in an elongated cluster on erect, green to reddish purple stalks 2–5 ft. (0.6–1.5 m) tall; August–September; leaves alternate, bright green, lance-shaped, toothed or sometimes smooth-margined, 3–4 in. (8–10 cm) long; plant clump-forming, rhizomatous, producing offsets; fruit a capsule with many seeds. The flowers of this species are smaller than those of *Lobelia cardinalis* and tend to disappear into the large, leafy bracts, the white-flowered form (the one I use, 'Alba') less so than the blue one ('Nana'). Hardy to zone 5, heat-tolerant to zone 9.

'Alba' (f. *alba*), flowers pure white.

'Nana' (f. *nana*), flowers bright blue; plant to 36 in. (90 cm).

'Nana Alba', flowers pure white; plant smaller than type.

Lobelia ×*speciosa*.

Some sun, WS; these complex hybrids involving *Lobelia cardinalis*, *L. splendens*, and *L. siphilitica* include cultivars of the Compliment series and Fan series, among others. All are hardy to zone 4. Their very bright reds and intense blues should be used cautiously in an introspective shady garden.

'Brightness', flowers cherry-red; leaves green, suffused with bronze.

'Cherry Ripe', flowers cherry-red; leaves green, suffused with maroon.

'Compliment Deep Red', flowers velvety wine-red.

'Compliment Scarlet', flowers scarlet-red.

'Dark Crusader', flowers deep red; leaves greenish brown to maroon.

'Fan Cinnabar Pink', flowers reddish pink.

'Fan Orchid Rose', flowers rose-pink.

'Fan Scarlet', flowers scarlet-red; leaves green with purple cast.

'Gladys Lindley', flowers creamy white, large.

'La Fresco', flowers deep lilac to plum.

'Oakes Ames', flowers scarlet-red; leaves and stems green, suffused with bronze.

'Pink Flamingo', flowers a rich pink.

'Queen Victoria', flowers scarlet-red; leaves and stems greenish purple.

'Robert Landon', flowers cherry-red.

'Rose Beacon', flowers rose-pink.

'Summit White', flowers clear white.

'Will Scarlet', flowers scarlet-red; leaves medium green suffused with dark purple to maroon.

'Wisley', flowers light red; leaves and stems green, suffused with bronze.

Luzula

Woodrushes are grown for their strap-shaped leaves, which form tussocks of glossy green leaves covered with tiny hairs. I consider *Luzula sylvatica* (greater woodrush) one of the best grasslike plants for medium and even full shade. A quick grower, it makes a weed-proof groundcover and competes well with greedy tree and shrub roots, so is very useful in places where no other plants will grow. Small groups combined with ferns and hostas create valuable textural combinations, and its variegated forms are good candidates as accent or container plants. In its natural habitat *L. sylvatica* grows in mostly moist woodlands, but any moisture-retentive yet well-draining garden soil is accepted. It grows remarkably well in dense Georgia red clay and endures periods of drought without much damage.

The genus *Luzula* is widely distributed in the cold and north temperate zones, including North America and Eurasia. Woodlands are a common habitat; some species, like *Luzula nivea* (snowy woodrush), grow minimally in light shade, but *L.*

pilosa and *L. sylvatica* are quite at home in shady gardens. They are evergreen but brown during cold winters and will happily grow into very hot regions, including zone 9, as long as moisture is maintained. Hardy to zone 5; in the coldest areas, plants become herbaceous. The generic name *Luzula* derives from the Italian *lucciola* (= firefly). The genus is classified in the rush family, Juncaceae.

Propagate by dividing clumps in late spring; replant divisions immediately. Woodrush can be moved at any time during the year provided a good clump of earth is taken with it.

Leaf spot and rust are reported. Insects and mollusks leave woodrush alone.

Luzula pilosa, woodrush. Southern, central, and eastern Europe, southwestern Asia.

Some sun, LS to MS; flowers in spikelets, brown, inconspicuous; leaves dark green, distinctly hairy along the margins, parallel-veined, upright, with sharp tips, 4–6 in. (10–55 cm) long and 0.2 in. (5 mm) wide, channeled, midrib slightly keeled; plant tufted, with short rhizomes, slowly creeping. This is a small woodrush for areas with small ferns, hostas, and other dwarf plants, along walks or in elevated spots. Many years ago I collected seeds in Germany, and this modest but faithful woodrush has been growing here ever since. Not invasive but like any creeping plant, it bears watching to keep it in bounds. *Luzula multiflora*, native to North America and Europe, has similar uses in gardens.

Luzula sylvatica, greater woodrush, sylvan woodrush. Southern, central, and eastern Europe, southwestern Asia.

Some sun, LS to MS; flowers in spikelets, chestnut-brown, inconspicuous; leaves dark green, hairy along the margins, parallel-veined, arching or leaning, with sharp tips, 8–10 in. (20–25 cm) long and 0.5–0.8 in. (1–2 cm) wide, channeled, midrib slightly keeled; plant tufted, creeping, forming dense mats of tussocks. Detail-oriented gardeners like the starry, spiky appearance of the bracts on the tiny flowers. The Munich Botanic Garden features many impressive selections.

'Aurea', leaves broader, yellow to straw-yellow in winter, greenish yellow in summer.

'Farnfreunde' (= friend of ferns), leaves tussocks more compact, green; mixes well with smaller ferns.

'Hohe Tatra' (= high Tatra mountains), leaves in upright tufts, green, distinctly hairy.

'Marginata' ('Aureomarginata'), leaves green with a neat yellow margin that turns creamy white to white in summer; spikelets pendent, brown and yellowish.

'Tauernpass' ('Tauern Pass'), leaves wider, bright green, forming low, flat rosettes that turn into large matlike cushions; resists winter browning.

Lygodium

In my shady garden, just about every fern I grow spreads itself around. One of the most fruitful is *Lygodium japonicum* (Japanese climbing fern). Its offspring come up everywhere, even in the middle of paths and cracks in brick paving. Contrary to its delicate appearance, it is robust and withstands heat and drought in the South; it has become weedy in the southeastern states and west into Texas. Its cold tolerance is low, but with winter protection of a thick pinestraw or other mulch, the roots should survive in zone 7 and perhaps 6b; further north I recommend potting and overwintering it in a cool place inside. Its climbing habit is astounding. Here, it clambers up a dogwood, emerging in late April and soon concealing its prop with a multiple layer of finely divided fronds; by July it is usually in the top of the tree, a height of 13 ft. (4 m).

Lygodium japonicum has a North American counterpart in *L. palmatum* (Hartford fern), whose fronds, as the epithet indicates, have ivylike leaflets; it is hardy well into zone 3. Both ferns are deciduous, and new twining croziers rise every spring from slowly spreading underground rootstocks.

Climbing ferns thrive in the deepest shade and require moist, acidic garden soil with a pH of 4.5 to 5.5. They need no maintenance except occasional watering and perhaps a plant tie here and there on smooth surfaces, to help the upward climb. Since they require only a vertical surface, they can be added to gardens with no obvious room for new plants. They make great conversation plants as they climb through shrubs, up tall trees, or over a birdhouse in a shady corner. The Latin generic name (*lygodium* = flexible) is an allusion to the trailing stems. *Lygodium* is classified in the Schizaeaceae.

Propagation is taken care of by the ferns themselves. The fernlets that spring up all over the garden can be dug and transplanted with ease.

Nothing in the way of diseases or insect pests bothers climbing ferns.

Lygodium japonicum, Japanese climbing fern. India, Indochina, China, Malaysia, Japan, Australia.

MS to FS; fronds deciduous, produced in opposite pairs on very long, twining and vining stems; both fertile and sterile fronds are produced on the same stem; sterile leaves 5–9 in. (13–23 cm), dark green composed of alternate leaflets (pinnae), each with 3 subleaflets, the center one much longer; fertile leaves shorter, with margins fringed with narrow, extended lobes that contain the sori; spore cases in double rows, covering lobular leaf margin extensions. An excellent, delicate-looking fern for vertical gardening.

Lygodium palmatum, Hartford fern, Hartford climbing fern. Eastern North America, southern New Hampshire, eastern New York, Kentucky, the Carolinas south to Florida.

LS to FS; fronds deciduous, produced on very long, twining and vining, branched, wiry and brittle stems; both fertile and sterile fronds are produced on the same stem, the fertile leaves are borne at the top of the stem only; sterile leaves light green, evergreen until next year's growth, 2–3 in. (5–8 cm) long and 1.5–2 in. (4–5 cm) wide, shaped like an ivy leaf with 5–7 fingerlike extension, fertile leaves produced in pairs on once-forked leafstalks; sterile leaves similar, but much smaller and more deeply cut, with sori covering the underside; spore cases in double rows, covering underside. Not as robust as *Lygodium japonicum*.

Lysimachia

When gardeners hear the name loosestrife, many think of purple loosestrife, *Lythrum salicaria*, a pretty but vicious invasive that, given sun and wet soil, has taken over acre after acre of our northern wetlands, to the detriment of native plants. But the common name loosestrife is also applied to species in the genus *Lysimachia*. The few *Lysimachia* species that will flower in very light shade, though they are not pests in the wild, are nevertheless a mixed blessing in shady gardens. My first experience was with **Lysimachia clethroides** (gooseneck loosestrife). I had

seen a huge planting of it on a trip to Michigan, and I shall never forget the spectacular sight—hundreds of tapering, goose-necked, nodding white flower spikes all pointing the same way. Upon my return, I tucked three plants into a sunny bed that was not yet shaded by dogwoods, and within a few seasons the interloper had covered the entire plot and was making inroads on my good neighbor's lawn, which I could not allow. To get rid of it was a dreadful job, requiring herbicides. The plant is a little better behaved in shady areas, but nevertheless, I urge all gardeners to think twice before they turn this fiendish beauty loose in a lightly shaded woodland garden: trilliums, fairy wands, beetleweeds, and bloodroots are no match for gooseneck loosestrife. I now admire it in other gardens.

But I dearly love three lysimachias: *Lysimachia congestiflora*, *L. nummularia*, and a dwarf form of *L. japonica*. The three are among the best and fastest-growing groundcovers for small gardens and are planted widely at Hosta Hill. Although they seem to like sun more than shade, I grow them in light to woodland shade, where they are better behaved, growing somewhat more slowly. In too much shade they get loose and straggly.

The genus is named for Lysimachos, the king of Sicily who pacified a mad bull by waving a sheaf of loosestrife. *Lysimachia* is classified in the Primulaceae.

Propagate by taking rooted stem cuttings or by transplanting small sods of established plants. I have never tried seeds; vegetative propagation is much faster in a garden environment.

Rust and leaf spot are reported but not experienced here. Slugs and snails may take an occasional bite, but plants grow so fast, the damage is repaired in no time.

Lysimachia congestiflora, dense-flowered loosestrife, golden globes. China.

Some sun, LS to WS; flowers small, in terminal clusters, upturned, bright yellow, cup-shaped, 0.5–0.8 in. (1–2 cm) across; June–August; plant stoloniferous and mat-forming, noninvasive; leaves opposite or whorled, dark green, slightly hairy, broadly lance-shaped, to 2 in. (5 cm) long. Hardy to zone 6 with protection; it can be used as an annual or container plant further north. 'Eco Dark Satin' (flowers yellow with red throat; leaves dark, satiny green) and 'Outback Sunset' (flowers yellow with red throat; leaves medium green with yellow margin, tinged red in spring) are offered.

Lysimachia japonica. Eurasia.

Some sun, LS to WS; flowers small, 1–3 in the leaf axils, upturned, yellow, cup-shaped to 0.5 in. (1 cm) across; June–August; plant stoloniferous and stem-rooting, prostrate, or sometimes erect, mat-forming, no more than 2 in. (5 cm) high; leaves opposite on long, trailing stems, light green, slightly hairy, roundish oblong, to 1 in. (2.5 cm) long. Hardy to zone 6a, heat-tolerant to zone 9 as long as moisture is maintained. **'Minutissima'** (miniature moneywort) is a dwarf form of the rarely available type, with leaves to 0.5 in. (1 cm) and tiny yellow flowers. A very small plant initially, it spreads quickly, forming pretty mats of tiny leaves that are evergreen here in zone 7; I never have enough of it for myself or to give away. Its stems trail along the ground, sending roots into the soil wherever they touch. Best used as a groundcover for small areas; if used between stepping stones, it should be recessed because it does not take foot traffic too well. I use it in my wildflower border to underplant trilliums, dwarf Solomon's seal, and other delicate woodlanders. It can also be grown in full sun.

Lysimachia nummularia, moneywort, moneyplant, creeping Jenny, creeping Charlie. Eurasia, central Europe to the Caucasus and beyond, naturalized in eastern North America.

Some sun, LS to WS; flowers solitary, upturned, in the leaf axils, yellow, cup-shaped to 0.8 in. (2 cm) across; June–August; plant stoloniferous and stem-rooting, prostrate, or sometimes erect, mat-forming, no more than 3 in. (8 cm) high; leaves opposite on long, trailing stems, light green, slightly hairy, broadly rounded (hence the common and scientific names, from the Latin, *nummus* = coin) to egg-shaped, to 1 in. (2.5 cm) long. Hardy to zone 4, heat-tolerant to zone 8 as long as moisture is maintained. It can become invasive with a combination of full sun and constantly wet soil and will grow into the water along ponds and streams. **'Aurea'** (yellow moneywort, yellow ceeping Jenny) is a very vigorous yellow-leaved selection. In full sun it spreads quickly; in light to woodland shade it is better behaved. Makes a great, tight, yellow groundcover under tall-growing open perennials like

clumps of Solomon's seals, ferns, and small shrubs. It can be grown in full sun. Some gardeners use the all-green type for the same purposes.

Maianthemum

Maianthemum canadense (Canada mayflower) is widespread in the Canadian woodlands but occurs spottily further south. I have always wanted to see these woodland lilies in the wild, not as cultivated specimens planted along public wildflower trails. Finally I did find it just across the state border with North Carolina, on Whiteside Mountain. There among the rock outcrops and large patches of spike moss, among trilliums and wild strawberries, I spotted the small but charming white flowers and then detected their strong fragrance, despite its being a windy day.

Originating in moist woodlands of Eurasia and North America, mayflowers are well adapted to shady, moist conditions. The flowers are ephemeral, but the attractive leaves carry on from spring until autumn and fit well with other perennials with the same life cycle, like small hostas, wild gingers, and the smaller ferns. Optimum pH is 4.5 to 5, and they loathe lack of moisture. Here in the heat of the Piedmont, they grow and spread in very acid, moist soil, but flowering has always been sparse. Further north, they make a wonderful addition to the woodland or wildflower border. Mayflowers are reliably winter hardy; most thrive in the temperate climate of zones 3 to 6, but their heat tolerance is limited. In the hot, dry summers of zone 7, they should be located in deep shade and deep, cool soil with profuse watering during droughts; further south they are out of place. All are rhizomatous herbaceous perennials, so die down in autumn.

Maianthemum species make a carpet of green leaves not unlike that of the true lily-of-the-valley (*Convallaria* spp.); it is hard to tell the two genera apart when plants are not in bloom. Because the flowers are small, plants should be used in front of the border or along paths; they also make a fine groundcover at the base of trees, a difficult spot. Despite the generic name (*maianthemum* = mayflower), plants often do not flower until June in the mountains. The genus is classified in the Convallariaceae.

Propagate by dividing the dormant rhizomes in late autumn or very early spring. Seed may be sown in small pots in a cold frame, but division is much faster and more productive.

Large slugs and snails can damage new growth emerging in spring. Mayflowers are otherwise free of pests and diseases, except for occasional rust and leaf spot.

Maianthemum bifolium, false lily-of-the-valley. Eurasia, western Europe to Japan, western North America, West Coast from Alaska to northern California east to the Cascades.

LS to FS; flowers tiny, very fragrant, white, 4-merous, petals 2 and 2 petal-like sepals, stamens 4, 10–25 on a small, branched flowerstalk on stems to 6 in. (15 cm); May–June; basal leaves 2, to 6 in. (15 cm) long and 3 in. (8 cm) wide, oblong, heart-shaped at base, green, broadly elliptic, dilated with midrib deeply keeled and depressed parallel veins, no stem leaves; fruit a berry, first green, later speckled red, finally red. Rarely available, this species is well worth seeking out and makes a fine groundcover.

Maianthemum canadense, Canada mayflower, mayflower, bead ruby, elf feather, false lily-of-the-valley, May lily, two-leaved Solomon's seal, wild lily-of-the-valley. North America, South Dakota east to Newfoundland, in the mountains south to northern Georgia and eastern Tennessee.

LS to FS; flowers tiny, very fragrant, white, 4-merous, petals 2 and 2 petal-like sepals, stamens 4, 8–22 on a small, branched flowerstalk on stems to 6 in. (15 cm); May–June; leaves 1–3, usually 2, 1–3 in. (2.5–8 cm) long, oblong, heart-shaped at base, almost stalkless or mostly stem-clasping, bright green, elliptic to broadly lance-shaped, with midrib deeply keeled and depressed veins, hairless; fruit a berry, 1- to 2-seeded, first green, later speckled red, finally red. Not a great horticultural subject, but its modest beauty and lovely fragrance fit well into a border with small plants or along paths, where the enticing flowers can be seen.

Maianthemum kamtschaticum, false lily-of-the-valley, western mayflower. Eurasia, western Europe to Japan, western North America, West Coast from Alaska to northern California east to the Cascades.

LS to FS; flowers tiny, very fragrant, white, 4-merous, petals 2 and 2 petal-like sepals, stamens 4, 10–25 on a small, branched flowerstalk on stems to 7 in. (18 cm); May–June; basal leaves 2, to 6 in. (15 cm) long and 3 in. (8 cm) wide, oblong, heart-shaped at base, green, broadly elliptic, dilated with midrib deeply keeled and depressed parallel veins; stem leaves 1–3; fruit a berry, first green, later speckled red, finally red. Highly variable. *Maianthemum dilatatum* (western mayflower) from the Cascades west has stems to 14 in. (35 cm) and larger leaves. Considered by some to be a variety of *M. kamtschaticum*, which is itself sometimes ranked as a somewhat larger subspecies of *M. bifolium*. With classification so confused, it may be difficult to sort out plants in commerce.

Matteuccia

Ostrich ferns are endemic to the temperate regions of North America and Eurasia. The genus is named for the Italian physicist Matteucci and is classified in the Woodsiaceae. The European (slightly smaller) and North American forms of ostrich fern were considered separate species, *Matteuccia struthiopteris* and *M. pennsylvanica*, respectively, but recent authors have combined them as *M. struthiopteris*, a species whose epithet is a combination of the Greek *struthokamelos* (= ostrich) and *pteris* (= fern). *Matteuccia struthiopteris* is an outstanding ornamental fern for the shady garden. It is one of the tallest ferns, very hardy, to zone 2, and equally adapted to hot southern summers, if moisture is maintained during dry spells.

Ostrich ferns are tolerant of even deep shade and yet stand up to considerable sun if grown in perpetually moist, fertile, acid soil with a pH of 5 to 5.5. They make great companion plants for the taller wildflowers, other ferns, and large hostas. Their height makes them good subjects to fill in a background, which is speedily accomplished: the ferns spread quickly by underground runners, producing next year's plants. Highly decorative, they can serve as bold accent plants.

Propagate by removing clusters of new growth from the periphery of the mother plant. Plants also self-sow spores abundantly in moist soil.

I have found these ferns to be trouble-free; no diseases or insect pests are reported.

Matteuccia struthiopteris, ostrich fern, ostrich plume fern, shuttlecock fern. In the cooler regions of eastern North America, Europe east into Russia, eastern Asia.

LS to FS; sterile fronds 4–6 ft. (1.2–1.8 m) long and 12–18 in. (30–45 cm) wide, produced in rosettes on short slender stalks emerging directly from the rhizome, scaly at the base, reddish brown, grooved, erect; sterile leaves rich dark green, deciduous, 3-compound, widest near the top with rapidly pointed tip, gradually tapering down to almost the base, cut into 40 pairs of alternate leaflets; sterile leaflets linear, lance-shaped, narrow, pointed at top, to 7 in. (18 cm) long, composed of up to 30 pairs of subleaflets (lobes), not opposite, wedge-shaped, narrow, rounded, blunt top; fertile leaves to 24 in. (60 cm), lyre-shaped, stiff, hard, leathery, green turning brown, cut into tightly spaced leaflets with rolled-over tips clasping spore cases (sori) like pods; rootstock stout, covered with brown scales, erect, with evenly developed crown, spreading rapidly by rhizomatous runners that grow deeply into the ground. *Matteuccia orientalis* (Asian ostrich fern, Japanese ostrich fern) from northern India, China, Korea, and Japan is not as up-standing and decorative as *Matteuccia struthiopteris* and smaller in all respects; its sterile fronds, to 40 in. (1 m) long, are outward reclined and often prostrate.

Mazus

Gardeners sometimes push the envelope and put plants where they are not supposed to grow. Failure can result, certainly, but plants occasionally turn out to be quite adaptable. I always experiment—it is part of gardening fun for me. *Mazus reptans*, a creeping groundcover, is in the main considered a rock garden plant for sunny areas, and it does make a wonderful, blooming lawn substitute. But I use it in shady areas to underplant cobra lilies (*Arisaema* spp.) and tall, native wildflowers with an open makeup, like Solomon's seals and blue cohosh. Its tight groundcover of leafy rosettes discourages weeds, and here the the green carpet is covered with small, white flowers almost all year. The only months I have not seen flowers are January through March.

Mazus is an Asian genus related to the North American monkeyflowers, including *Mimulus ringens*. *Mazus reptans* is hardy to zone 4, 3 with protection. Heat and drought in southern gardens do not bother it as long as the soil remains wet; the plant helps out in this by making a tight cover that prevents evaporation. It does best with some sun, but here it knits together and flowers in woodland shade. Constant moisture and a fertile soil with a pH of 5.5 to 6 is a must. Supplemental water may be necessary during hot, dry periods. In my son's shady Bay Creek garden, it has escaped the rock-bordered beds and made its way into the walkways, where it competes successfully with grass and moss. Given much sun and a moist environment, it may become invasive; to control this, remove the outer leaf rosettes and transplant them to other locations.

The genus name is from the Greek *mazos* (= teat, nipple), referring to the swellings at the base of the flower. *Mazus* is classified in the Scrophulariaceae.

Propagate by carefully dividing the runners in very early spring; replant divisions immediately. With the plant's vigorous spreading habit, seed propagation makes little sense.

Larger slugs and snails can be a problem, but here plants seem impervious to pests and diseases.

Mazus reptans. Himalayas, northern Pakistan and India, western China.

Some sun, LS to WS; flowers with lobed upper and lower lips, snapdragonlike, purplish blue with lower lip white, orange- to red-spotted, 0.5–0.8 in. (1–2 cm) long, 2–5 in one-sided cluster on prostrate flowerstalks; May to frost; plants prostrate, widely creeping and mat-forming, rooting at the leaf nodes; leaves in rosettes, medium to dark dull green, 0.8–1.2 in. (2–3 cm) long and 0.5 in. (1 cm) wide, egg-shaped with blunt tip, coarsely toothed, crinkled margin. Low maintenance; naturalizes easily even in drier soils. The white-flowered **'Albus'** is very attractive and fits anywhere. *Mazus pumilio* and *M. radicans*, which are native to warmer regions of Indomalaysia and Australasia, are hardy to zones 7 and 6, respectively.

Medeola

Some native North American wildflowers are so modest, one wonders why we should grow them at all. *Medeola virginiana* is unassuming indeed, and I, for one, grow it because I rescued a clump at a road construction project: I would rather it continue to grow in my garden than see it destroyed. American Indians dug up these plants and ate the roots raw for their cucumberlike flavor, but the species is still abundant in more remote areas and is available from some wildflower nurseries. Its nodding flowers are barely seen underneath the whorl of leaves, but in autumn the little plants are outstanding. In mid-September, I observed large populations on Black Rock Mountain in Georgia, and their already yellowing leaves with conspicuous reddish markings and colorful purple berries were the most prominent display on the woodland floor.

Given plenty of moisture and shade as well as friable soil with a pH of 4.5 to 5.5, it also does well in cultivation. Hardy to zone 3; in warm, southern gardens it should be placed in deep shade, where it does well as long as the soil stays moist. A small group of plants makes a nice showing, and in a place to its liking, the plant makes offsets and multiplies rapidly.

The genus is named for the Greek sorceress Medea, alluding to the genus's purported medicinal properties. *Medeola* is classified in the Trilliaceae. Recent chloroplast DNA analysis has shown that it may actually be more closely related to *Polygonatum*, and some taxonomists suggest it belongs in its own family, the Medeolaceae.

Propagate by dividing the rhizome in very early spring before growth starts.

Slugs and snails can damage new growth emerging in spring; no other pests or diseases are experienced here.

Medeola virginiana, Indian cucumber root, cushat lily. Eastern North America, Ontario and Minnesota, Quebec to Nova Scotia south to New England and in the mountains south to Georgia and Florida and west to Arkansas and Minnesota.

LS to WS; flowers 2–9, greenish yellow, nodding, to 0.5 in. (1 cm) long, petals 3, recurved, sepals 3, petal-like, recurved, stigmas 3, long brownish red; May–June; leaves 5–10, arranged in 2 whorls, one midway up stem, 2.5–5 in. (6–13 cm) long, broadly oval to lance-shaped, another at top of stem with 3, sometimes 4 smaller leaves from which spring the flowerstalks, 8–30 in. (20–75 cm) tall; root large, to 3 in. (8 cm) long and 1 in. (2.5 cm) wide; fruit bluish-purple berries. Young, nonflowering plants show only one whorl of leaves. This wildflower is a slow grower when young. Be patient—its colorful autumn display is well worth the wait.

Mertensia

Mother grew rock-hardy Virginia bluebells, and their burst of bloom in early spring was a delight. But when I happened to visit her garden later one summer, I noticed the bluebells were gone—some groundcover had taken over the space. I learned that the lovely bluebells disappear soon after flowering, but I went home with a small plant anyway, and soon found out that in my warmer climate, bluebells went dormant even earlier—another beautiful native plant that leaves a hole in the garden. Bluebells are shallow growers; nothing can be planted on top of them to disguise the empty spot, but if they are sited around an accent hosta, the bluebells come up first and flower just about when the hosta leaves unfurl, making a striking display of blue flowers against yellow and green foliage.

Taxonomists have switched Virginia bluebell's long-established binomial *Mertensia virginica* to *M. pulmonarioides*, meaning it resembles lungwort (*Pulmonaria* spp.). Although the former name is still widely used in commerce, *M. pulmonarioides* will show up more and more. In northern gardens *M. pulmonarioides* is a sun-loving plant; here, it requires some shade. I have replaced it with *M. sibirica*, a better garden plant that does not go dormant after blooming.

The genus name honors the German botanist Mertens. *Mertensia* is classified in the Boraginaceae.

Propagate by dividing the rhizome in very early spring before growth starts, digging carefully to free the thick rootstock completely. Sow seed in small pots in a cold frame; keep constantly moist.

Slugs and snails can damage new growth emerging in spring. Mildew and rust are reported on leaves.

Mertensia pulmonarioides, Virginia bluebells, Virginia cowslip, cowslip, American lungwort, Roanoke bells, tree lungwort. Eastern North America, southern Ontario and Minnesota east to southeastern Maine, New York and south to North Carolina, northwestern Georgia and Alabama and west to Arkansas and eastern Kansas.

Some sun, LS to WS; flowers 5–20, in terminal clusters, pink in bud later bright blue, nodding, trumpet-shaped, to 1 in. (2.5 cm) long, lobes 5, stamens 5, anthers yellow; March–June; leaves deciduous, bluish green, basal and on the stem, basal 2–8 in. (5–20 cm) long, elliptic to egg-shaped, deeply veined; stem leaves smaller, alternate, oval, un-toothed; stems 8–24 in. (20–60 cm) tall. This summer-dormant species (seen in photo of *Hosta* 'Liberty') requires plenty of moisture and a woodland soil with a pH of 6 to 7. Gardeners who grow a lot of acid-loving plants must find or create a circum-neutral spot by adding dolomitic limestone to the soil. Available cultivars are 'Alba' (flowers white) and 'Rubra' (flowers pinkish). *Mertensia sibirica* (Siberian bluebells) from eastern Russia is very similar but grows more dense and taller, with unbranched stems to 30 in. (75 cm). It does not go dormant in summer and is also more tolerant of slightly acid soils; a white-flowered cultivar, 'Alba', is available.

Milium

Nothing brightens a shady garden more than golden yellow foliage. For many years now, *Milium effusum* 'Aureum' has accented Hosta Hill. Not as tidy as *Hakonechloa macra*, this grass is nevertheless extremely useful and trouble-free in the garden. It propagates itself by spreading seed (which comes true), and the small tufts of seedling grass can either be removed and given away or planted elsewhere in the garden. I like it a lot, so let it come up in many places. The yellow tufts juxtapose well with delicate ferns and the bold foliage of blue-green hostas. The blades are evergreen to zone 6, but the plant is deciduous. Hardy to zone 5 with good winter protection, or it can be grown as an annual. Long-lived and vigorous, it will happily grow into very hot regions, including zone 9, as long as moisture is maintained, and yet it tolerates brief periods in dry soil. Use as an accent plant or in groups as a groundcover or combined with other plants. In midsummer and during winter, the foliage is light green, but new growth in late winter or early spring emerges a brilliant yellow.

The genus *Milium* is endemic to North America and Eurasia. *Milium* is the classic Latin name for millet, and the epithet *effusum* (= spreading) too is Latin. The genus is classified in the grass family, Gramineae.

Propagate by division at any time, taking a good clump of soil along and replanting at once.

Insects and mollusks leave it alone, but vine weevils take an occasional bite out of the blades. It is otherwise free of diseases and pests.

Milium effusum, woodrush, millet grass. North America, Eurasia.

Some sun, LS to MS; flowers tiny yellowish spikelets in loose clusters atop green stems; May–June; leaves smooth, strap-shaped, flat, shiny green, erect or arching, with pointed tips, to 18 in. (45 cm) long and 0.2–0.5 in. (0.5–1 cm) wide; plant clump-forming, tufted, spreading. The species is rarely offered. The most widely available form is **'Aureum'** (var. *aureum*, 'Bowles' Golden Grass'), with bright yellow flowers and blades; the blades turn light green with age. Another selection, 'Variegatum', with leaves irregularly striped with white, is not robust and needs more sun than shade.

Mitchella

On one of my excursions into the deeply shaded neighborhood ravine, I found large, flat patches of *Mitchella repens* (partridgeberry). The leaves look much like those of small-leaved boxwood (*Buxus microphylla*), but what attracted me to it were the previous year's large, bright red berries. I brought a few of the rooting branches home and true to another of its names, running box, this trailing evergreen perennial has run all over my garden. I remove it in some places but tolerate it where it covers woodland paths and walks; it gets stepped on a lot, with no ill effect, and is about as rugged a groundcover as any gardener could wish. It looks great in the woodland garden with mosses and low-growing wildflowers. Its flowers occur in pairs, one with a short pistil and long stamens, and the other a long pistil and short stamens, to assure cross-pollination; the two flowers produce one berry, which hangs on for another season, so berries and flowers can be seen at the same time. The berries have a pepperminty flavor and are a favorite food for grouse or wild turkey, but having no such wildlife in my garden, they remain on the plants, adding much color in autumn and through the winter. The species was highly sought after by American Indian women, who used the leaves and berries to brew a tea to aid in childbirth.

With its highly ornamental red berries and shiny, dark green leaves with greenish white veins, it has been overcollected in some areas as a Christmas decoration. Notwithstanding, *Mitchella repens* is still common and almost cosmopolitan in eastern North America. It is hardy to zone 4, 3 with protection. It withstands heat and drought into zone 9, and I have never had to provide supplemental water. It grows in deepest shade and tolerates any exposure except full sun. Fertile soil with a pH of 4.5 to 5.5 is a must for successful flowering. The genus name honors the Virginia botanist Mitchell. *Mitchella* is classified in the Rubiaceae.

Propagate by separating rooted runners in spring and transplanting them immediately. Seed can be sown in pots in a cold frame in autumn, but given the plant's vigorous spreading habit, seed propagation makes little sense.

Here the plant seems impervious to pests and diseases; not even mollusks bother it. Birds and rodents eat the berries.

Mitchella repens, partridgeberry, running box, twinflower, squawberry, squawvine, teaberry, twinberry, two-eyed berry. North America, Ontario and Minnesota east to Nova Scotia, south to Florida, eastern Texas, and eastern Mexico.

LS to FS; flowers terminal, white, rarely shaded pink, in pairs fused at the base, 0.5–0.8 in. (1–2 cm) long, up-facing, petals 4, spreading, funnel-shaped, fringed and bearded inside lobes, either male, staminate with abortive pistil, or female, pistilate with abortive stamens; May–July; plants prostrate, widely creeping and mat-forming, rooting at the leaf nodes; leaves in opposite pairs, shiny dark green, veins greenish white, sometimes white, to 0.8 in. (2 cm) long, broadly egg-shaped with rounded tip; fruit a 2-eyed berry with 8 seeds, brilliant red, sometimes white. An attractive, low-maintenance groundcover that will naturalize even in drier soils. Combines well with tall, open wildflowers and cobra lilies; great under small shrubs. Forma *leucocarpa*, with white berries, is occasionally available. First described by Siebold in the 1850s, *Mitchella undulata* (Japanese partridgeberry) from Korea and Japan has the same tolerance for light to full shade; it has pink flowers with white beards and larger leaves, to 1 in. (2.5 cm), with pointed tip and wavy margin.

Mitella

The name miterwort is often wrongly applied. The false miterworts of the genus *Tiarella* have beautiful, billowing spikes of white flowers; the true miterworts of the genus *Mitella* have inconspicu-

ous flowers whose miraculous shapes—geometric masterpieces of nature—must be seen through a magnifying glass to be appreciated. Miterworts are closely related to heucheras, but their leaves are not as showy. They nevertheless make a well-behaved groundcover for the shady garden, where different shades of green are vital. Most frequently seen in commerce is *Mitella diphylla* (bishop's cap), which I have often observed in northern uplands of Georgia; its stalks with tiny greenish yellow flowers elongate as they mature and flop over, so I usually cut them above the stem leaves and grow the species for the leaves alone. The generic name is the diminutive of the Greek *mitra* (= cap, hat), an allusion to the shape of the fruit, which looks like the official headdress of a bishop. *Mitella* is classified in the Saxifragaceae.

Some species are evergreen, providing four-season interest in mild-winter areas. All are very easy to cultivate in light to full shade, and direct sun is tolerated to a significant degree in more northern gardens. Most are hardy to zone 5. Heat tolerance is also good, particularly for species native to southeastern North America, like *Mitella diphylla* and *M. nuda*, which I have grown successfully for years. The western species are difficult in southern gardens, though. Moist soil is ideal; miterworts respond to it by growing more rapidly into a dense groundcover. Optimum pH is 6 to 7; add some dolomitic limestone to acid soils.

Propagate by division or by taking rooted runners and replanting them immediately in late autumn. The species self-seed freely; seedlings can be removed and relocated in very early spring.

Slugs and snails can damage young leaf growth. Leaf spot and rust are reported but not experienced here.

Mitella breweri, Brewer's miterwort, feathery miterwort. Western North America, British Columbia east to Alberta, Montana, and Idaho, south in the Cascades into California.

LS to FS; flowers greenish yellow, insignificant, petals 5, comblike, feathery, dissected; stems to 10 in. (25 cm) tall; May–July; plant evergreen, slowly spreading; leaves in a basal rosette, medium green, hairy, 2–4 in. (5–10 cm) long, broadly egg-shaped, with 5–11 indistinct, toothed lobes; fruit miter-shaped, splitting open at maturity. This species has the most fanciful flowers of the genus. Hardy to zone 5, best for northern gardens. Several other western species differ only in minor details and flower color. *Mitella caulescens* has 1–3 stem leaves and yellow petals with purple at the base. *Mitella pentandra* (five-stamen miterwort) has greenish petals and conspicuous yellow anthers juxtaposed against a brownish purple flower center; the epithet *pentandra* (= with five stamens) is not very helpful: all miterwort species have 5 stamens. *Mitella trifida* (three-toothed miterwort), endemic to British Columbia south to the southern Cascades, is easily identified by its 3-lobed white petals, which look much like Poseidon's trident, and its more cup-shaped, purplish flowers; very similar is *M. diversifolia*, also from the Cascades.

Mitella diphylla, bishop's cap, miterwort, fairy cap. Eastern North America, Ontario and Michigan east to New England south to Georgia and Alabama, west to Oklahoma and Missouri.

LS to FS; flowers white, insignificant, petals 5, bell-shaped with 7- to 8-fingered divisions, recurved, fringelike, stamens 10, pistil 1; stems to 18 in. (45 cm) tall; April–June; plant slowly spreading; leaves in a basal rosette, medium green, hairy, to 3 in. (8 cm) long, broadly egg-shaped, with 5–11 toothed, shallow lobes; stem leaves 2, opposite, smaller, 2-lobed, toothed; fruit miter-shaped, splitting open at maturity. The pair of stem leaves gave rise to the epithet *diphylla* (= two-leaved). Use as a groundcover or in the wildflower garden with ferns, heucheras, and hostas. ***Mitella nuda*** is very similar but lacks the stem leaves; it has roughly the same North American habitat but is also found in eastern Asia, from Japan to Korea. A handsomely yellow-variegated form of *M. nuda*, from Japan, **'Variegata'** (*M. japonica* 'Variegata'), is now available; stoloniferous, it makes an attractive groundcover in time.

Mukdenia

Many years ago I purchased a specimen of the only species in this monotypic genus, *Mukdenia rossii*, from a West Coast nursery (as *Aceriphyllum rossii*). The former name was very descriptive (*aceriphyllum* = maple leaf): its leaves look very much like that of *Acer saccharum* (sugar maple). Cultivation has been a struggle, and now I understand why: Mukden (the ancestral capital of the Manchu Dynasty and

the old capital of Manchuria), now called Shenyang, is about 400 miles northeast of Beijing, and it gets very cold there. *Mukdenia*, like *Boykinia*, requires cool summers to be really happy. Its soil requirements too are similar: a fertile, clay soil with some grit in it and abundant water at the roots. In southern gardens it needs deep shade to develop its leaves fully, but it may flower only sporadically. My mukdenias do fairly well planted on the margins of a pond, where water is not far from the rhizome. Hardy to zone 4; I consider zone 7 its southern limit. *Mukdenia* is classified in the Saxifragaceae.

Propagate by dividing the rhizome in very early spring before growth starts. Sow seed in pots in a cold frame.

Slugs and snails can damage new growth emerging in spring; no other pests or diseases are reported or experienced here.

Mukdenia rossii. Northeastern China, Korea south to Cheju Island.

LS to WS in the North, MS to FS in the South; flowers small, shallowly bell-shaped, to 0.2 in. (0.5 cm), mostly white, sometimes light pink tepals, with the sepals longer, yellow centers, many in clusters above the leaves, on open, leafless, branched flowerstalks, 10–18 in. (25–45 cm) tall; May–June; plant clump-forming, rhizomatous, slowly spreading; leaf stems green, stout, upright, 6–8 in. (15–20 cm); leaves medium green, bronze-tinged in spring, with 5 lobes, margins coarsely and irregularly toothed, to 7 in. (18 cm) long and 6 in. (15 cm) wide, stem and leaves hairy; fruit ball-shaped capsule with many seeds. This species can be difficult in gardens with hot, dry summers. Although not separated botanically at this time, several forms differ in leaf size, number and shape of leaf lobes, and flower color. The leaves of the more northern variant are said to have a distinct reddish tinge in spring and into early summer; variants originating from tributaries of China's Yalu River and seen in German gardens have pink flowers and more elongated leaves.

Nothoscordum

An obscure wildflower with grasslike leaves, *Nothoscordum bivalve* (false garlic) is usually hidden among forest litter in the wild; about the only time it can be easily spotted is during its bloom period, when the starry white flowers become beacons of sorts. I first saw this plant in the Cedar Sink area of Mammoth Cave National Park, blooming with *Dodecatheon media* in late April to early May. Once planted, it reproduces rapidly by offsets and is easily maintained. I enjoy the modest beauty of this southeastern native every spring and its re-blooming in warm autumns, starting in September. It is sometimes available from wildflower nurseries. Unlike true garlic, its juice is odorless and tasteless. The genus name *Nothoscordum* (= false garlic) is from the Greek. The genus is classified in the Alliaceae.

False garlic thrives in open woods and meadows and is seen in sandy bogs along the coast. It requires damp, well-draining, almost neutral soil with a pH of 6 to 7. It tolerates considerable shade, but prefers a more open site with light shade and some sun.

Propagate by taking bulblets.

Rust and leaf spot are reported but not seen here.

Nothoscordum bivalve, false garlic, grace garlic, scentless garlic, yellow false garlic. Eastern North America, southeastern Nebraska east to Ohio, Indiana, and southeastern Virginia and south to northwestern Georgia and the Georgia Piedmont, coastal plains, Florida into Texas.

Some sun, LS to WS; flowers yellow or yellowish white, 3 petals and 3 petal-like sepals, stamens 6, small, to 0.5 in. (1 cm) long, 3–9 in a terminal cluster, stalk to 18 in. (45 cm) tall, smooth, leafless; April–May and September–October; plant herbaceous, clump-forming, with bulbous root; basal leaves are narrow, straplike, green, smooth, to 12 in. (30 cm) long and 0.2 in. (0.5 cm) wide, blunt-tipped; fruit a capsule. This elegant native should find a place in every wildflower garden. Hardy to zone 5, and it has withstood our very hot, dry summers. *Nothoscordum gracile* (Mexican false garlic) has naturalized in the coastal regions of southeastern North America and on Bermuda; it is semi-tender, hardy to zones 8 and 9, but has been spotted in zone 7. Its flowers are pink or lilac with white.

Omphalodes

I remember *Nabelnuss* (= navelseed) growing in my grandmother's wild garden. What impressed me as a boy were the hundreds of white flowers covering a patch of ground like late spring snow. Our common name too is a reference to the nutletlike seeds, each with a navel-like depression. I never knew what cultivar Grandmother grew, but I assume it was *Omphalodes verna* 'Alba'. *Omphalodes verna* carpets the ground with small, gentian-blue flowers in spring, looking much like forget-me-nots. Of the several annual, biennial, and perennial species in the genus, only *O. cappadocica* and *O. verna* are suited for the shady woodland garden.

Omphalodes species are native to the Mediterranean region, Asia Minor, and Mexico, and are frequently cultivated in European gardens. They deserve to be grown more here in North America. The two species listed will do well; their spring flower display is short but spectacular and is followed by an evergreen or semi-evergreen carpet of medium green leaves. They are primarily grown as groundcover plants.

The generic name also stems from the Greek *omphalos* (= navel), referring to the navel-like depression in the seeds. The genus is classified in the Boraginaceae.

Moist soil is ideal, but it must drain well and remain cool. Optimum pH is 6 to 7; add some dolomitic limestone to acid soils. Given these conditions, navelseed will respond by growing more rapidly into a dense groundcover. In southern gardens a position in cool shade is appreciated; further north, light shade and some sun are tolerated. The species described are hardy to zone 6.

Propagate by seed, sown in pots in a cold frame. The seed capsules are hidden in the foliage, and seed ripens early, so frequent checks are required for successful collection. Propagate cultivars by careful division in early autumn or late winter to early spring, as some do not come true from seed.

Slugs and snails can be very damaging to young growth.

Omphalodes cappadocica, navelseed, navelwort, perennial forget-me-not. Eastern Mediterranean region, Turkey, western Caucasus, Asia Minor.

LS to FS; flowers small, to 0.2 in. (0.5 cm) across, 3–12 on long stalks in loose, terminal clusters, sky-blue with white centers, sepals 5-cleft, petals 5-lobed on short tube, stamens 5; April–June; plant clump-forming, rhizomatous, shortly creeping, erect to ascending, to 10 in. (25 cm) tall; leaves evergreen, basal or alternate, medium green with conspicuous veins, finely hairy, broadly oval to heart-shaped, pointed tip; fruit a capsule with 4 nutlets. The best garden species, being a more bushy plant that does not spread assertively. Cultivars include 'Anthea Bloom' (flowers bright blue, in upright sprays; does not come true from seed), 'Cherry Ingram' (flowers deep blue, larger than the species), 'Lilac Mist' (flowers lilac-pink to mauve, larger than the species), and 'Starry Eyes' (flowers bright sky-blue, narrowly outlined with pinkish white turning white).

Omphalodes verna, blue-eyed Mary, creeping forget-me-not. Southern Europe.

LS to FS; flowers small, to 0.5 in. (1 cm) across, 3–15 in loose, terminal clusters, deep blue with white centers, sepals 5-cleft, petals 5-lobed on short tube, stamens 5; April–June; plant stoloniferous, rhizomatous, widely creeping, to 8 in. (20 cm) tall; leaves semi-evergreen, to 8 in. (20 cm) long and 3 in. (8 cm) wide, medium green with conspicuous veins, finely hairy, broadly oval to heart-shaped, rapidly pointed tip; fruit a capsule with 4 nutlets. It was Marie Antoinette's favorite flower so should really be called blue-eyed Marie. This stoloniferous species spreads rapidly under favorable conditions; it will naturalize and by some reports is invasive. Here it is well behaved, sited out of direct sun, and never overruns companion plants. Unfortunately, its early flowers are sometimes caught by late freezes in April. In southern gardens the leaves are evergreen, but further north they are barely semi-evergreen and may become deciduous. The white-flowered 'Alba' is a natural albino form; 'Grandi-flora' has flowers like the type but larger, to 0.6 in. (1.5 cm) across.

Onoclea

Onoclea sensibilis (sensitive fern) is most unfernlike in appearance—a handsome addition to the shady garden. It just showed up here one day, either from a spore blown in by the winds or as a fernlet brought in with rescued plants. It grows around Stone Mountain and in other nearby habitats in the company of *Woodwardia areolata*, which also prefers marshy land and swamps near rivers or in forest seepages. The undivided leaflets of its light green sterile fronds have attractive wavy margins; its fertile, elongated bead sticks remain on the plant through the winter. Given just about any kind of moist soil, this fern will spread far and wide, making good-looking colonies.

In gardens *Onoclea sensibilis* is tolerant of even deep shade and stands up to considerable sun if grown in perpetually moist, fertile soil. Optimum pH is 5 to 5.5, but it is also tolerant of circumneutral soil with a pH around 7. This fern is very cold-sensitive, collapsing promptly on first appearance of even a mild frost, but its root is hardy to zone 4, so it can be grown in just about any garden in the North. It is equally adapted to hot summers, growing as far south as northern Florida and eastern Texas. Maintain soil moisture during dry periods. It makes a great companion plant for the taller wildflowers, other ferns and large hostas. Allowed to spread, it makes a tall groundcover, weaving itself through all kinds of neighboring plants. It is highly decorative and can serve as a bold accent plant. Do not site where it could overrun small wildflowers or ferns.

The generic name is from the Greek *onos* (= vessel) and *kleio* (= to close), alluding to the beadlike spore clusters that enclose the sori. *Onoclea* is classified in the Athyriaceae.

Propagate by cutting rhizomes from the periphery of the colony. It also self-sows spore abundantly in moist soil.

Rust is reported but not seen here.

Onoclea sensibilis, sensitive fern, bead fern. Eastern North America, Labrador south to Florida and west to Texas and the Dakotas, naturalized in western Europe, northeastern Asia.

LS to FS; sterile fronds oval or broadly triangular, 24–30 in. (60–75 cm) long and 12–15 in. (30–38 cm) wide, produced singly along a creeping rhizome, scaly at the base, brown, erect; sterile leaves light green, deciduous, 6–12 opposite pairs, widest at the bottom with rapidly pointed tip; sterile leaflets widely spaced, light green, wavy, slightly lobed margins, the lowest pair longest, tapering on both ends, veins distinctly netted; upper leaflets progressively smaller, linear, lance-shaped, narrow, pointed top; fertile leaves 12–24 in. (30–60 cm) tall, club-shaped, stiff, hard, leathery, with numerous leaflets, green turning brown, shaped into beadlike divisions that contain the spore cases; rootstock stout, brown, forking and spreading rapidly by rhizomatous runners near surface. No garden should be without this attractive, widely available fern.

Ophiopogon

Lilyturf is widely planted in southern gardens. Most of it is *Liriope*, but the genus *Ophiopogon* too offers attractive species and cultivars of great garden value. A variety of standard, dwarf, and variegated forms are in commerce, all with great tolerance to shade and so indispensable in the shady garden. In Japan the variegated forms, most selections of *Ophiopogon japonicus*, are eagerly collected and used in pot culture.

The common name mondo grass is now applied to all species of *Ophiopogon* by the gardening public. In zone 7 and warmer, they are evergreen. In areas with cold winters, the perennating rootstock can be overwintered with good protection, but where the soils freezes hard permanently and deeply, they cannot be used. Same garden uses as *Liriope*; some dwarf forms knit together to form a dense sod that prevents weeds from growing.

The generic name is from the Greek *ophis* (= snake) and *pogon* (= beard), a fanciful allusion to the shape of the flower cluster. *Ophiopogon* species are endemic to eastern Asia. The genus is classified in the Convallariaceae. It is closely related to the other genus of lilyturf, *Liriope*. The most visible difference is the fruit color: black in *Liriope*, blue in *Ophiopogon*.

Mondo grass flourishes as a lawn substitute in heavy Georgia red clay without amendments. It does not like too much water and will rot if drainage is slow. Soils of both high and low fertility are accepted; apply a slow-release fertilizer to give plants intended as groundcovers a quick start. Any kind of shade is tolerated.

Propagate by dividing the dormant clumps in very early spring before growth commences. Seed propagation can be done in spring by sowing directly into the ground. Many species self-seed.

Leaf spot and root rot are reported but not experienced here. Slugs too are supposedly problematic, but they have left my plantings alone. The only insect problem has been an occasional bite taken out of the leaf margins by vine weevils.

Ophiopogon jaburan, Jaburan lily, Jaburan lilyturf, white lilyturf, white mondo grass, snakebeard. Japan.

Some sun, LS to WS in the North, FS in South; flowers small, many, white, sometimes tinged lilac, 0.5 in. (1 cm) long, arranged in tight clusters on a leafless flowerstalk to 6 in. (15 cm) tall; August–September; leaves evergreen, dark green, linear lance-shaped, tip blunt, leathery, to 24 in. (60 cm) long and 0.2–0.5 in. (0.5–1 cm) wide; plant clump-forming, tufted, widely creeping with subsurface stolons terminating in new plantlets; fruit clusters of blue berries. Spreads fast. Hardy to zone 7, heat-tolerant to zone 10.

'Aureovariegatus', leaves green, striped with yellow.

'Caeruleus', flowers purplish blue, violet.

'Crow's White', leaves variegated with white.

'Nanus' (dwarf mondo grass), leaves short, to 3 in. (8 cm); entire plant dwarf, rarely blooms. Very useful for mass plantings as a groundcover or edger, or between stones along paths.

'Vittatus' ('Argenteovittatus', 'Javanensis', 'Variegatus', *Ophiopogon malayanus*), leaves green, narrowly margined and irregularly striped with yellowish white or white.

Ophiopogon japonicus, mondo grass, Japanese mondo grass. Japan, central and southern Honshu, Shikoku, Kyushu, Korea.

Some sun, LS to WS in the North, FS in the South; flowers small, many, bell-shaped, white, sometimes tinged lilac, 0.2 in. (0.5 cm) long, arranged in tight clusters on a leafless flowerstalk 2–3 in. (5–8 cm) tall; August–September; leaves evergreen, dark green, linear lance-shaped, tip blunt, leathery, 8–12 in. (20–30 cm) long and 0.2 in. (0.5 cm) wide; plant clump-forming, tufted, creeping and expanding; fruit clusters of blue berries. Spreads fast. Hardy to zone 7, heat-tolerant to zone 9.

'Albus', flowers pure white.

'Compactus' ('Minor'), extremely dwarf, leaves short, curling, to 2 in. (5 cm) tall and 4 in. (10 cm) wide.

'Kyoto Dwarf' ('Intermedius'), very dwarf, to 4 in. (10 cm) tall and wide.

'White Dragon' ('Shiro Ryu'), leaves widely striped with white, little green showing in some leaves, to 12 in. (30 cm) long.

Ophiopogon planiscapus, mondo grass, Japanese mondo grass. Japan, Honshu, Shikoku, Kyushu.

Some sun, LS to WS in the North, MS to FS in the South; flowers small, many, bell-shaped, pale purplish white or pinkish white, 0.2 in. (0.5 cm) long, arranged in tight clusters on a leafless flowerstalk to 3 in. (8 cm) tall; August–September; leaves evergreen, dark green, linear lance-shaped, tip blunt, leathery, 6–14 in. (15–35 cm) long and 0.2 in. (0.5 cm) wide; plant clump-forming, tufted, creeping and expanding by means of stolons; fruit clusters of blue to blackish blue berries. Hardy to zone 6, heat-tolerant to zone 9.

'Leucanthus' (*Ophiopogon leucanthus* of gardens), flowers pure white.

'Nigrescens' ('Arabicus', 'Black Dragon', 'Ebony Knight', *Ophiopogon arabicus* of gardens), flowers pinkish; leaves 5–7 in. (13–18 cm) long, almost black; fruit black. This outstanding plant has withstood brief dips to −10°F (−23°C) here with a light cover of pine straw; most seeds come true, although green seedlings show up occasionally.

Osmunda

Before the rolling land that became my neighborhood was subdivided, I surveyed the area, with permission, and was able to rescue several small trees, wildflowers, and ferns. Among the treasures were *Osmunda cinnamomea* (cinnamon fern) and *O. regalis* (royal fern), flowering ferns of *Osmunda*, which genus is cosmopolitan worldwide except for Australasia. The three species described (the two aforementioned and *O. claytoniana*) are deciduous and very hardy, growing well into zone 3; some gardeners report hardiness to zone 2. They do well in even full shade, yet take considerable sun and are extremely tolerant of hot weather—as long as they have wet feet. Moisture at the roots is the secret to having large clumps of flowering ferns; without it, they become squat and stubby—not at all "royal." The genus is named for Osmunder, the Saxon equivalent of the god Thor, who hid his wife and child on an island in a mass of these ferns. *Osmunda* is classified in the flowering fern family, Osmundaceae.

Any moist garden soil with a pH of 4.5 to 7 is acceptable. I have observed *Osmunda cinnamomea* and *O. regalis* growing in the very acid waters of cypress swamps in southern Georgia and in the alkaline seepage area of northwestern Georgia limestone bluffs. Here flowering ferns grow well in regular garden soil that dries out during occasional, pro-longed droughts; with this, they get a little tattered, but I have never lost one to dry conditions. All make great companion plants for taller wildflowers, other ferns, and large hostas.

Propagate by cutting pieces from the periphery of an established clump or colony. They also self-sow spores abundantly in moist soil. Spores are very short-lived and must be sown as soon as ripe in a commercial growing medium at 60°F (16°C).

Rust is reported, but I have found flowering ferns to be insect- and disease-free.

Osmunda cinnamomea, cinnamon fern, fiddleheads, buckhorn. Nearly cosmopolitan in North, Central, and South America, Eurasia.

Sun, LS to FS; sterile fronds 24–36 in. (60–90 cm) tall and 7–9 in. (18–23 cm) wide, in the wild to 5 ft. (1.5 m) tall; produced in clusters from a central rootstock, scaly at the base, brown, erect; sterile leaves light green, lance-shaped, erect or slightly arching, 2-compound with 12–20 nearly opposite pairs of leaflets, pointed tip; sterile leaflets closely spaced but not overlapping, light green, narrowly lance-shaped, pointed at top, wavy, deeply cut, veins distinctly forked; fertile leaves appear and wither first, to 39 in. (90 cm) tall, erect, club-shaped, pointed, with numerous pairs of club-shaped leaflets growing upward, parallel to the stem, forming a clublike mass of leaflets, very bright light green turning to shiny cinnamon-brown; rootstock very stout, brown, expanding with age, partly above ground. No garden should be without this attractive fern. In spring the emerging fiddleheads are covered with tufts of white woolly hair; they were eaten boiled or as a salad by American Indians and early settlers and are still relished by cognoscenti. Both the common and scientific names of this fern allude to the cinnamon color of its fertile leaves; the epithet is from *Cinnamomum zeylandicum*, from the bark of which the spice cinnamon is produced. Cut withered sterile fronds to maintain a tidy appearance.

Osmunda claytoniana, interrupted fern, Clayton's fern. Asia, northern India to Siberia and south to Japan, eastern North America, Manitoba to Newfoundland south to Georgia and west to northern Arkansas.

Sun, LS to FS; sterile fronds 24 in. (60 cm) tall and 7 in. (18 cm) wide, arching outward and arranged vase-shaped, surrounding taller fertile fronds to 36 in. (90 cm), in the center part interrupted by fertile leaflets, lower leaflets more widely spaced; produced in clusters from a central rootstock; sterile leaves light green, lance-shaped, arching outward, 2-compound with 12–20 nearly opposite pairs of leaflets, pointed tip; sterile leaflets almost overlapping, light green, narrowly lance-shaped, pointed at top, deeply cut, veins forked; fertile leaves to 36 in. (90 cm) tall, more erect, closely spaced sterile leaflets in upper half, followed by 3–6 pairs of fertile leaflets, green turning brown, growing upward, parallel to the stem, with sterile leaflets more widely spaced in lower part; rootstock very stout, brown, expanding with age, partly above ground, growing outward, dying in the center, eventually forming a ring of ferns. Like *Osmunda cinnamomea*, its fiddleheads are covered with tufts of white woolly hair in spring. North Georgia seems to be the southern limit of this northern fern; in the wild I have observed it only in Rabun County at the higher elevations. Here in the Georgia Piedmont it languishes a bit, even with supplemental water, but further north it would be an excellent addition to any shady garden.

Osmunda regalis, royal fern, ditch fern, flowering fern, locust fern, snake fern. Nearly cosmopolitan in North, Central, and South America, Eurasia, and Africa.

   Sun, LS to FS; sterile fronds 3–6 ft. (0.9–1.8 m) tall; in spring fiddleheads covered with tufts of brown woolly hair, not as conspicuous as *Osmunda cinnamomea* or *O. claytoniana*; sterile leaves light green, oblong, erect, 2-compound with 4–9 pairs of alternate, widely spaced leaflets looking much like that of locust tree branch; subleaflets widely spaced, translucent light green, narrowly oblong, rounded top, wavy, small, distinct leafstalks, veins forked, distinct main vein; fertile leaflets terminal, light brown, densely clustered and contracted; rootstock very stout, brown, expanding with age, partly above ground. This highly decorative fern can serve as a bold accent, but it must be carefully sited: when grown in good, moist soil, it eventually expands to make a colony to 10 ft. (3 m) in diameter. It does better in gardens with some sun and dappled shade and constantly moist soil. I have seen it grown in South Georgia in full sun at a pond margin, and its stature was absolutely magnificent. In more shady gardens its stems turn brownish or orange-red. Variety *spectabilis* is sometimes recognized as the North American form. Cultivars include 'Crispa' (crisped leaflets and subleaflets), 'Cristata' (distinctly crested leaflets and subleaflets), 'Purpurascens' (fronds flushed reddish bronze to purple in spring), and 'Undulata' (wavy-margined subleaflets).

Oxalis

I first came upon *Oxalis montana* (American wood sorrel) while hiking in the higher elevations of the mountains in northwestern Georgia. The patch I found on a mossy slope in deep shade was huge, and I decided that collecting a tiny bit would do no harm. Transplanted as a sod to Hosta Hill, the dainty mountain plant flourished its first spring, showing pretty white flowers with dark pink veins, but unfortunately did not survive its first hot, dry summer—another lesson complete. It has a somewhat larger relative in western North America, *O. oregana* (redwood sorrel), and is also very similar to *O. acetocella* (European wood sorrel, Irish shamrock). All do well in gardens with damp, cool summers and their cold tolerance leaves nothing to be desired: they grow well into zone 3. In zone 7 they seem to be limited to the high mountain spruce and fir forests.

   Given the right cultural conditions, some species of wood sorrel can become invasive. *Oxalis stricta*, a European species, has naturalized all over North America, becoming the weedy yellow sorrel of American roadsides. The attractive groundcover shamrock *O. violacea* (violet wood sorrel), another North American woodland species, can also be very invasive, spreading stealthily by underground runners; it is very difficult to control in the average garden environment. My experience with it was most unhappy, but gardeners with many acres to cover may want to try it.

   Cultivars of **Oxalis triangularis** (*O. regnellii* 'Triangularis'), on the other hand, have been growing here for years; the clumps have increased in size, but I have not detected any invasive tendencies. All are quite frost-tolerant and have survived several cold winters here in zone 7a. Each petiole carries three triangular leaflets inversely attached at a point of the triangle, with a straight side facing out. The white flowers appear in spurts from late spring until late autumn, and I like the way the leaves, either bright green or reddish purple, fold up in the evening and open again when the sun comes up.

The generic name is from the Greek *oxis* (= acid), alluding to the sour taste of the leaves. The genus is classified in the oxalis family, Oxalidaceae.

Pachysandra

Pachysandra terminalis (Japanese spurge) has been a landscape groundcover since it was brought from Japan and described in 1843 by Siebold and Zuccarini. Among the first groundcovers I planted at Hosta Hill, it has been so prolific that I have not bought another piece of it since. Here it makes a great carpet of attractive evergreen leaves, and its fast-spreading habit has made it a darling of landscapers looking for a uniform, easy-care groundcover for difficult areas. Wet or dry, in shade or in sun, under trees with greedy roots or on steep banks for erosion control--Japanese spurge does it all, with aplomb, and with its low cost and wide availability it is hard to beat. The appealing North American native *P. procumbens* is much more to my liking, with a more open habit that allows its pretty, ground-level flowers to be admired, but unfortunately it is a slow grower, less hardy and a bit more fussy than its Asian counterpart. Both it and *P. stylosum*, a new Asian species, are available from wildflower and specialty nurseries.

All species are evergreen in zone 7 and warmer. In areas with very cold winters the foliage becomes deciduous; the perennating rootstock can be overwintered if given good protection, but plants are of questionable use where soil freezes hard permanently and deeply. All are quite tolerant of very hot, dry summers, carrying on without much watering or other extraordinary care; they should do well into zone 8, perhaps 9.

The generic name is from the Greek *pachys* (= thick) and *andros* (= man, male), for the very thick stamens. The genus is classified in the box family, Buxaceae.

Pachysandra species and cultivars are extremely long-lived and thrive in practically any soil. I have seen them flourish as a lawn substitute in heavy Georgia red clay, and here the genus has provided a weed-excluding groundcover for over 30 years in the same spot. An occasional application of slow-release fertilizers keeps it going. Do not use *Pachysandra terminalis* in flower beds. Its thick rhizomes penetrate all nooks and crannies; I have tried to grow sturdy hostas species in a long-established bed of it and found they could not compete. Much better behaved is *P. procumbens*, which I grow in the company of some delicate trilliums and fairy wands.

Propagate by taking rooted rhizomes from the periphery of the colony. Cuttings can be rooted in early summer. These methods are so successful that seed propagation does not make much sense.

Leaf spot, root rot, and die-back are reported but not experienced here. Nor have I seen slug or snail damage—my plantings carry on year after year, seemingly thriving on neglect.

Pachysandra procumbens, Allegheny pachysandra, Allegheny spurge. Eastern North America, West Virginia and Kentucky to Florida and Louisiana.

WS to FS; flowers small, white, sometimes flushed pink, fragrant, many, on spikes 2–4 in. (5–10 cm) tall, emerging from the leaf axil near ground level, male flowers above, female flowers below; April–May; plant clump-forming, slowly spreading; leaves 3–5 in. (8–13 cm) long on long leafstalks, whorled around the stem, with triangular base and rounded, toothed tip, first light green, later dull gray-green mottled with light brownish gray around the veins with silky, finely hairy surface above, light shiny green below, veins deeply impressed above, projected beneath; stems with the first part trailing along the ground, the terminal part becoming erect, holding leaves to 12 in. (30 cm) high; fruit a 3-beaked capsule. This desirable native is the most gardenworthy pachysandra but does not spread fast enough to be used as a quick groundcover. It is great as an accent colony with ferns and other wildflowers. Evergreen in zone 7, herbaceous and hardy to zone 5 with protection. **'Eco Picture Leaf'** has distinctly variegated spring leaves.

Pachysandra stylosum, Chinese spurge. China.

Sun, LS to FS; flowers small, white, sometimes flushed with pink, on a stubby spike; March–April; leaves shiny light green, leathery; to 12 in. (30 cm) high. This handsome species, relatively new to Western horticulture, brings welcome diversity to garden pachysandras. Like *Pachysandra terminalis*, it spreads by means of widely creeping rhizomelike stems. Hardy to zone 6.

Pachysandra terminalis, pachysandra, Japanese pachysandra, Japanese spurge. China, eastern Sichuan and Hubei east to the Japanese Archipelago.

Sun, LS to FS; flowers small, white, not showy, many, on terminal spikes 0.8–1.5 in. (2–4 cm) long, male flowers above, female flowers below; May–July; plant evergreen, quickly spreading by means of rhizomelike stems; leaves 1–3 in. (2.5–8 cm) long and half as wide, on erect, sometimes branched leafstalks to 12 in. (30 cm), alternate, but grouped in whorls around the main stem or on short side branches, oval to egg-shaped, coarsely toothed near tip, with short leafstalks, dark shiny green, veins not impressed; fruit a white capsule. This almost maintenance-free species grows into a dense groundcover 8–12 in. (20–30 cm) tall and is evergreen into zone 4. Can become invasive in some situations, so check its spread occasionally.

'Green Carpet', leaves darker green than the species; plant more compact, making a 6–8 in. (15–20 cm) tall groundcover.

'Green Sheen', leaves very glossy dark green. An outstanding groundcover for shade.

'Silveredge' ('Silver Edge'), leaves a lighter green with a uniform, thin, silvery white margin. Needs a lot of shade in southern gardens.

'Variegata', leaves have a silvery white margin, more irregular than 'Silveredge'; plant slower growing.

Panax

For centuries ginseng has been used in China as a panacea, and indeed the generic name is from the Greek *pan* (= all) and *akos* (= to cure, to heal). Most ginseng sold in health food stores worldwide comes from roots produced commercially in Korea and the United States. In spite of this, *Panax quinquefolius* (American ginseng) has been since the early 1800s one of the most sought after wild plants in North America. Wild roots are exported to Asia, where collected plants are thought to have greater restorative powers; the choicest cured roots—*jin-chen* (= manlike), for their resemblance to the shape of a man's body—bring exorbitant sums of money there. Thus, despite its being available from commercially propagated stock, the rape of American ginseng continues unabated, and this important species of our native flora is now protected in many areas.

Panax quinquefolius makes a nice accent in the woodland garden, where its brilliant red fruit adds color in the fall; *P. trifolius* (dwarf ginseng), a much smaller and delicate native sometimes seen in the wildflower border or the woodland, is ornamental only and does not yield herbal ginseng. The genus is classified in the Araliaceae.

Propagate by dividing the rhizome in spring. Sow seed in the ground or in containers in autumn.

Root rot and die-back are reported but not experienced here. Nor have I seen slug or snail damage on local plantings.

Panax quinquefolius, American ginseng, ginseng, sang. Eastern North America, Minnesota into Quebec and south in the mountains to the Carolinas and Georgia and west to Nebraska and Oklahoma.

WS to FS; flowers small, greenish, insignificant; April–June; plant clump-forming, deciduous, 10–24 in. (25–60 cm) high; leaves to 12 in. (30 cm) long, 3 on long stalks, each compound with 5 stalked leaflets to 4 in. (10 cm) long, green, slightly and irregularly toothed, coarse; fruit a brilliant red capsule. This native yields herbal ginseng from a fleshy, carrotlike root. Hardy to zone 3, limited heat tolerance: give it a very shady, cool location in hot, southern gardens. The Asian *nin-sin* species (*Panax ginseng, P. pseudoginseng,* and *P. schinseng*) from Korea and northeastern China are also occasionally offered in commerce as ornamentals. A blue-fruited relative of *P. ginseng* (jin-seng) from Sichuan in western China is available under the collection number *Panax* sp. DJHC804. All are useful in the wildflower garden as interesting foliage plants with colorful seed capsules.

Panax trifolius, dwarf ginseng, groundnut, three-leaf ginseng. Eastern North America, Minnesota, Iowa, and Wisconsin into Quebec and east to Nova Scotia, south in the mountains to Georgia and west to Missouri.

WS to FS; flowers small, white, 10–25 arranged in a star shape, emerging from the leaf axil of the main stem; April–June; plant clump-forming, deciduous, to 8 in. (20 cm) high; leaves usually 3 on long stalks, each 3- to 5-parted, with stalkless leaflets to 1.5 in. (4 cm) long, green, slightly and irregularly toothed; fruit a yellowish capsule. This desirable native, which grows from a round tuber (hence, groundnut), is increasingly rare and should never be collected in the wild. Available from propagated stock. Requires a deep, fertile, moist woodland soil with lots of organic matter and a pH of 5 to 7; here it grows in full shade with other delicate wildflowers like trilliums and fairy wands. Hardy to zone 4, limited heat tolerance.

Paris

In the 1970s, on a trip to Germany, I was intrigued by a trilliumlike plant in a private garden. But trilliums have three-part flowers, and these flowers were four-merous. Upon my return, I found this alluring *Paris quadrifolia* (herb paris), a European species known for centuries, had several Asian relatives, and I now grow them along with native trilliums, inviting comparison.

The plant I saw in Germany was labeled *Paris*, but *Daiswa* or *Kinugasa* (formerly *Trillidium*) have been applied by Asian botanists to some species. *Daiswa* stems from *dai swa*, the Nepalese name for these plants, *Kinugasa* from the Japanese, *kinugasaso*. But consensus places most species within the genus *Paris* and that is how they are listed in commerce. That seems a good enough reason for using *Daiswa* and *Kinugasa* as synonyms only, appreciating, of course, that they are the names preferred by many Asian botanists.

Jaded by the grandiose floral displays of sunny gardens, some people who have seen my *Paris* species wonder out loud why I grow these subdued shade plants. My personal answer is that I am as fascinated by them as I am by the cobra lilies. Raising strange plants from exotic places gives me a lot of satisfaction and enjoyment. To me, each plant in my shady garden, whether from our own forests or from far away, adds diversity, and that includes *Paris quadrifolia* and its Asian fellows. From afar the flower of herb paris is unpretentious, but up close it is an absolute marvel. From a knobby purple pistil, eight bright yellow thready petals radiate out in all directions, like the spikes of a compass rose or the spokes of a wheel (wheel lily is a recently coined common name for the genus), set off by four subtending green sepals. Four overlapping leaves form a solid verdant background. The whole composition remains more or less intact until a large cluster of scarlet fruit takes its place. The leaves are as elegant in autumn as they are in spring, and here they

add refinement to a company of trilliums, Solomon's seals, and small ferns.

The name herb paris, known in print since 1578, is the source of the Linnaean generic name *Paris*. It may have been derived from the Latin genitive of *par* (= equal, like), alluding to the analog number of leaf and flower parts in *Paris quadrifolia*. The genus is placed in the Trilliaceae.

The genus is endemic to Europe and eastern Asia. Most species are reliably winter hardy and thrive in the temperate climate of zones 5 to 8. They are rhizomatous herbaceous perennials, so die down in autumn. By mulching the rhizomatous roots heavily for the winter season, their cold hardiness range can be extended. Originating in moist woodlands, they are well adapted to shady, moist conditions. *Paris* species prefer a deep woodland soil with plenty of organic matter, good tilth, and good water-holding capacity, yet reasonably well drained. I grow mine in raised beds. Most do well in considerable shade and tolerate some morning sun. Optimum pH is 5 to 6.5. They go dormant a little early during long, hot, arid summers. Given correct cultural conditions, they are long-lived and form colonies.

Propagate by carefully dividing the dormant rhizome in late autumn or very early spring. I sow seed in place in autumn and let nature take its course.

Large slugs and snails can damage young growth emerging in spring. *Paris* species and cultivars are otherwise free of pests and diseases.

Asian species are extremely variable; expect considerable differences and some misidentification in the various clones offered in commerce.

Paris bashanensis. Western China.

MS to FS; flowers 4-merous, terminal, solitary, petals yellowish, radiating, sepals usually 4, green, broad, persistent; June–July; stems to 40 in. (1 m) tall, but usually much shorter. Very similar to *Paris quadrifolia*. Its leaflets are more lance-shaped and longer; the sepals are conspicuously bent down. Trials in North America are incomplete but success is reported in zone 6.

Paris fargesii. Western China, Yunnan.

MS to FS; flowers 4-merous, terminal, solitary, petals yellowish, radiating, sepals 4, green, broad, persistent; May–July; stems to 6 in. (15 cm) tall; leaves with 4 leaflets, arranged in a whorl on long leafstalks, bright green, net-veined, with pointed tip, to 4 in. (10 cm) long and 3.5 in. (9 cm) wide; fruit a single, nonsplitting vermilion berry. This relatively new species from the mountainous Emei Shan region of western China is short-stemmed and ground-hugging, mixing well with trilliums and small ferns. Variety *brevipedicillata* has knobby anthers and is much taller, to 18 in. (45 cm).

Paris japonica. Japan, central Honshu, Japanese Alps, Shizuoka, Yamanashi.

MS to FS; flowers terminal, solitary, on green flowerstalk 1–3 in. (2.5–8 cm) tall, sepals 8–10, petaloid, white to yellowish white, broadly lance-shaped, large, 1–2 in. (2.5–5 cm) long, 0.5–0.6 in. (1–1.5 cm) wide, persistent, petals yellowish or white, diminutive or sometimes missing; May–July; stems 12–32 in. (30–80 cm) tall; leaves large with 8–12 leaflets, elliptic to oval, arranged in a whorl, bright green, net-veined, with pointed tip, 8–12 in. (20–30 cm) long, 1–3 in. (2.5–8 cm) wide; fruit a single, nonsplitting purple berry, edible. One of the showiest species of the genus but unfortunately tender, requiring special care and soil conditions that duplicate its habitat in volcanic ground. Soil must be rapidly draining, moist during growing season, fairly dry during dormancy, and cool all the time. It is not for the gardening novice. Previously considered an intergeneric hybrid (*Paris verticillata* × *Trillium tschonoskii*), which different chromosome counts and nonconcurrent flowering periods make an impossibility. Hardy to zone 7 with protection. Best as a pot subject in southern gardens with wet winters.

Paris lancifolia. Eastern Himalayas, Nepal, Tibet, China, Taiwan.

MS to FS; flowers terminal, solitary, above the leaves; sepals 5–7, green, narrowly lance-shaped with sharp, drooping tip, 2–3 in. (5–8 cm) long, persistent; petals 4–8, yellowish, to 3 in. (8 cm) long, threadlike; June–July; stems 12–24 in. (30–60 cm) tall; leaves with 6–14, sometimes as many as 22, leaflets high on the stem, to 6 in. (15 cm) long, very narrowly lance-shaped, arranged in a whorl, bright green, net-veined, veins indented, with sharply pointed tip; fruit dull red. A very distinct species with long and narrow leaves growing straight from the stem (sessile). Hardy to zone 7.

Paris polyphylla. Himalayas, northern India, western and southern China, Burma, Thailand, Taiwan.

MS to FS; flowers terminal, solitary, above the leaves on yellowish green flowerstalk, to 6 in. (15 cm) tall; sepals 4–7, green, lance-shaped with drooping tip, 2–4 in. (5–10 cm) long, 0.5–0.8 in. (1–2 cm) wide, persistent; petals 4–6, yellow, to 3 in. (8 cm) long, threadlike, blunt-pointed; June–July; stems 12–36 in. (30–90 cm) tall; leaves with 8–12 leaflets, on purplish leafstalks, sometimes on the stem, broadly lance-shaped, arranged in a whorl, bright green, net-veined, veins indented, with pointed tip, 3–8 in. (8–20 cm) long; fruit a large capsule, splitting, with translucent, scarlet seeds. Widely distributed throughout Asia. Its populations differ in size and by having sessile or nonsessile leaves; the floral features are fairly constant. Variety *nana* is a dwarf form from Sichuan; var. *alba* is from the mountains of western Yunnan, with yellowish white sepals and petals, a white ovary, and bright yellow styles. I have grown a clone of the type from northern India for some time and find it quite adaptable to hot southern summers as long as a cool shady position is provided. If the flowers are not pollinated by a different clone, the flower structure is very long-lasting. Hardy to zone 6, but gardeners should ascertain whether plants offered are from the northern or southern part of the species' habitat.

Paris quadrifolia, herb paris, true-love. Eurasia, Europe to the Caucasus, Siberia, eastern Asia.

MS to FS; flowers terminal, solitary, above the leaves on yellowish green flowerstalk, 2–4 in. (5–10 cm) tall; sepals 4, green, lance-shaped with sharp tip, 1–1.5 in. (2.5–4 cm) long, persistent, petals 4–8, bright yellow, threadlike, flattened, sharply pointed; June–July; stems 6–16 in. (15–40 cm) tall; leaves with 4 leaflets, elliptic, arranged in a whorl on very short leafstalks, bright green, net-veined, with pointed tip, 3–6 in. (8–15 cm) long; fruit large, seeds scarlet to dark brown. Long cultivated in Europe, this species is of easy culture, hardy to zone 5, and quite heat-tolerant in southern gardens if planted in shade to keep the ground cool. The flowers and seeds are poisonous. This is the species named by Linne; the plant described by Thunberg as *Paris quadrifolia* is actually *P. tetraphylla*.

Paris tetraphylla. Japan, northern Honshu, Aomori.

MS to FS; flowers terminal, solitary, above the leaves on green flowerstalk, 2–4 in. (5–10 cm) tall; sepals 4, green, elliptic reflexed with sharp drooping tip, 1–2 in. (2.5–5 cm) long, persistent; petals absent; stamens yellow with purple ovary; June–July; stems 8–10 in. (20–25 cm), sometimes taller; leaves with 4–8 leaflets, tight on the stem, broadly elliptic, arranged in a whorl, bright green, net-veined, veins indented, with pointed tip, 1.5–4 in. (4–10 cm) long; fruit with several purplish black seeds. This stoloniferous species forms colonies of plants and mixes well with other wildflowers. Requires a cool, moist, shady location in gardens with hot, dry summers. Hardy to zone 5.

Paris thibetica. Himalayas, Tibet, northern India, western China, Sichuan.

MS to FS; flowers terminal, solitary, above the leaves on short, green flowerstalk; sepals 5, rarely less or more, green, narrowly lance-shaped with sharp, drooping tip, 2–3 in. (5–8 cm) long, 0.5–0.8 in. (1–2 cm) wide, persistent; petals 4–6, yellowish, to 1.5 in. (4 cm) long, threadlike, stamens yellow; June–July; stems 12–32 in. (30–80 cm) tall; leaves with 6–11 leaflets high on the stem, 5–9 in. (13–23 cm) long, very narrowly lance-shaped, arranged in a whorl, bright green, net-veined, veins indented, with sharply pointed tip; fruit shiny red. From a more northern habitat, this species is similar to *Paris lancifolia* and considered hardy to zone 5.

Paris verticillata. Eurasia, in the Caucasus east to Siberia, China, Korea, Japan.

MS to FS; flowers terminal, solitary, above the leaves on green flowerstalk, 2–6 in. (5–15 cm) tall; sepals 4, green, lance-shaped with sharp tip, 2–4 in. (5–10 cm) long, persistent; petals 4, yellow, 0.6–0.8 in. (1.5–2 cm) long, threadlike; June–July; stems 8–16 in. (20–40 cm) tall; leaves with 4–8 leaflets, tight on the stem or connected with very short leafstalks, broadly lance-shaped, arranged in a whorl, bright green, net-veined, veins conspicuously indented, with pointed tip, 3–5 in. (8–13 cm) long and 1.5–2 in. (4–5 cm) wide; fruit large with several purple seeds. A variable species, due to its wide distribution in dissimilar habitats, but among the easiest to cultivate. Reasonably heat-tolerant if sited in a cool, moist, shady spot. Hardy to zone 5.

Paris violacea. Himalayas, western China.

MS to FS; flowers terminal, solitary, above the leaves on green flowerstalk, 1–2 in. (2.5–5 cm) tall; sepals 4–6, green with grayish white veins, lance-shaped with sharp tip, 2–3 in. (5–8 cm) long, persistent, petals 4–8, greenish yellow, threadlike, sharply pointed; June–July; stems to 8 in. (20 cm) tall; leaves with 4–6 leaflets, lance-shaped, arranged in a whorl on very short leafstalks, green above with netted veins variegated with silvery white, purple beneath, pointed tip; fruit large, seeds scarlet to dark brown. A lovely small species with attractively variegated leaves. Hardy to zone 7.

Paris yunnanensis. Northern India, Tibet, western China, Burma.

MS to FS; flowers terminal, solitary, above the leaves on green flowerstalk, to 7 in. (18 cm); sepals 4–8, green, narrowly lance-shaped, keeled (boat-shaped), with sharp, sometimes drooping tip, 3 in. (8 cm) long, persistent; petals 6–8, green or yellow, to 4 in. (10 cm) long and 0.2–0.5 in. (0.5–1 cm) wide; June–July; stems to 32 in. (80 cm) tall; leaves with 6–8 leaflets, to 6 in. (15 cm) on leafstalks of about the same length or shorter, broadly lance-shaped, arranged in a whorl, bright green, net-veined, veins indented, with pointed tip; fruit large, splitting, with translucent, scarlet seeds. Widely distributed throughout Asia and as a consequence various populations differ greatly. Depending on the origin of a given clone in commerce, a slightly different description may apply. Diagnostic features are the long leafstalks, much longer than in most species, and the narrow, keeled sepals. Hardy to zone 7, 6 with protection.

Peltoboykinia

The *Peltoboykinia* species described are good foliage plants for the natural shady garden, comparable to *Peltiphyllum peltatum*. Their large, lobed, umbrella-like leaves make an excellent groundcover and are particularly useful on the shaded banks of a pond or in wet woodlands. Given deep, fertile, moist, gritty soil, they are of easy culture. At Hosta Hill, nice clumps are maintained through severe droughts and stifling heat with trickle irrigation. They do not appreciate too much sun on their backs.

The genus *Peltoboykinia* is native to southern Japan and possibly China. Its species grow in the mountains in sheltered spots at woodland margins and clearings, preferring shaded positions in moist areas along watercourses. They are hardy to zone 7, 6 with protection of the rhizomatous rootstock. The genus name, with the prefix *pelto* (= peltate, shield-shaped) to differentiate its larger leaves and leaf shape from its close relative *Boykinia*, honors the same Dr. Boykin. It is classified in the Saxifragaceae.

Propagate by dividing the rhizome in very early spring before growth starts. Seed sown in a cold frame usually germinates successfully.

Slugs and snails can damage new growth emerging in spring; no other pests or diseases are reported or experienced here.

Peltoboykinia tellimoides. Southern Japan.

LS to MS; flowers small, shallowly bell-shaped, to 0.5 in. (1 cm), many in terminal clusters, 5 petals, greenish yellow, short-lived, flowerstalks 20–38 in. (50–95 cm) tall, with stem leaves diminishing in size toward top; July–September; plant clump-forming, rhizomatous, spreading; leaf stems green, stout, upright, to 20 in. (50 cm); leaves basal, medium green, round to heart-shaped in outline, with 5–13 deep lobes, lobe tips pointed, margins finely and irregularly toothed, 6–12 in. (15–30 cm) long and 4–10 in. (10–25 cm) wide. Sometimes sold as *Peltoboykinia watanabei*.

Peltoboykinia watanabei, Watanabe's peltoboykinia. Southern Japan.

LS to MS; this species is similar to *Peltoboykinia tellimoides* except that it is larger, to 5 ft. (1.5 m); basal leaves round to heart-shaped in outline, with 5–10 deep lobes, lobe tips pointed, coarsely and sharply toothed, 15–24 in. (38–60 cm) long and 12–20 in. (30–50 cm) wide. A fine spreading groundcover for larger gardens.

Petasites

Among all the hardy plants with large, umbrella-like leaves, *Petasites japonicus* (Japanese butterbur) is king and queen rolled into one. Yet I recommend it with some trepidation. A friend of mine in Delaware planted a clump of this relentless ornamental in his moist woodland; he liked the expanding colony at first, but within a few years he had a stand of butterbur to the exclusion of all other plants in the area, and the colony threatened to take over large patches of the garden. For all I know, he is still doing battle with it at its periphery. Being aware of its propensity for quick invasion, I planted a clump in a large, thick-walled plastic tub, 40 in. (1 m) wide and 18 in. (45 cm) deep, sunk into the ground and filled to the rim with good, friable soil on top of a layer of coarse gravel. To provide some drainage I drilled a few small holes in the bottom. With this arrangement, my clump remains a clump, not an invading army, and I get favorable comments from all comers. The clump, 5 ft. (1.5 m) in diameter, forms a dome of very large, bright green leaves; I grow *P. japonicus* var. *giganteus* and, even confined to its tub, its leaves reach to 30 in. (75 cm) across and stand tall in the landscape. During hot, dry summers I occasionally soak the tub with water to quench the rhizomes' thirst, which is prodigious. Unfortunately, I rarely see the spectacular flowers, which resemble a white bridal bouquet on a large stick, because the thick stems appear in late February, insist on blooming in early March, and so get cut down by our frequent late freezes; all my efforts to somehow protect them have failed. There is only so much room in most gardens, so I recommend the tub method to all who want to plant and enjoy Japanese butterbur without having to do battle with it.

Butterburs require constantly moist, even boggy soil, but they will survive a fortnight without watering. During periods of drought, provide supplemental water to maintain soil moisture content. For larger plants, site butterburs so that they receive some morning sun. Hardy to zone 5; some northern gardeners use butterburs to impart a tropical flavor, as somewhat less imposing substitutes for *Gunnera manicata*, which is too tender in zone 6 and colder. The generic name is from the Greek *petasos* (= hat), a reference to the large hat-like leaves. *Petasites* is classified in the Asteraceae.

Propagate by dividing the rhizome before growth starts in very early spring. All are more or less rampant spreaders and must be confined to a large tub in small gardens. Site with care in open ground.

Large slugs and snails damage emerging, soft flowerstalks and leaf growth. Rust can be troublesome; apply a preventive fungicide.

Petasites albus, white butterbur, white coltsfoot. Eurasia, in the mountains of northern and central Europe east to western Siberia.

Morning sun, LS to MS; flowers small, white to yellowish white, in dense, egg-shaped clusters on thick stems with lance-shaped stem leaves, 6–12 in. (15–30 cm) tall; March–April, arising before the leaves emerge; plants rhizomatous, widely creeping; leaves basal and umbrellalike, rounded, kidney-shaped, 6–16 in. (15–40 cm) across, green, woolly at first, later felty on the underside only, with regular, toothed lobes, on stout, upright stems to 15 in. (38 cm) tall. This gardenworthy species makes a great accent group near water or as a salient feature in open woodlands. Hardy to zone 5. *Petasites fragrans* (winter heliotrope, sweet coltsfoot) from the Mediterranean region is slightly better behaved but too tender for most temperate gardens; it can be tried in zone 7. It is similar to *P. albus*, with pinkish white flowers that permeate the garden with a strong vanilla fragrance. The red-flowered *P. frigidus* from northern Europe is, unfortunately, rarely available. Hardy to zone 5.

Petasites hybridus, bog rhubarb, butterbur. Europe east to northwestern Asia.

Morning sun, LS to MS; flowers small, light pink or sometimes yellow to yellowish white, in dense, egg-shaped clusters on thick stems with stem leaves, to 8 in. (20 cm) tall while in bloom, male plants with withering flowerstalks, female plants with flowerstalks to 30 in. (75 cm); March–April, arising before the leaves emerge; plant rhizomatous, aggressively spreading; leaves umbrellalike, rounded, heart-shaped, to 24 in. (60 cm) across, matte green, covered with fine hairs at first, later smooth, with regular, toothed lobes; leaf stems stout, upright, to 40 in. (1 m) tall. This species has escaped from gardens and naturalized in some parts of North America: gardeners should obtain male (staminate) plants only. Makes an aggressive groundcover or a great accent group in open woodlands. In small gardens it should be contained in a sturdy tub; if planted in the open, check clumps and remove errant rhizomes at regular intervals. Hardy to zone 4 and suitable in southern gardens with hot, dry summers as long as moisture is maintained.

Petasites japonicus, Japanese butterbur, *fuki* (Jap.). Eastern China, Korea, Japan, Sakhalin.

Morning sun, LS to MS; flowers small, yellowish or greenish white, in dense, flatly domed clusters on a subtending rosette of overlapping, light green bracts, held by thick stems to 12 in. (30 cm) tall while in bloom; March–April, arising before the leaves emerge; plant rhizomatous, aggressively spreading; leaves umbrellalike, rounded, heart- or kidney-shaped, to 32 in. (80 cm) across, matte green, covered with fine hairs beneath, with regular lobes, toothed; leaf stems stout, upright, to 40 in. (1 m) tall. Easily the most aggressive of the butterburs, it has naturalized in Europe and North America and should not be allowed to escape into the wild. Can be used as a groundcover or as an anchor for plantings of grasses, hostas, and ferns. In small gardens it should be contained in a sturdy tub; if planted in the open, check clumps and remove errant rhizomes at regular intervals. It is grown commercially in Japan for the edible petioles. Hardy to zone 5 and very heat-tolerant in southern gardens as long as soil remains moist. Variety *giganteus* ('Giganteus') is much larger—too large for smaller gardens. Its leaves are 4–5 ft. (1.2–1.5 m) across, rising on stout stems to 6 ft. (1.8 m). Cultivars include 'Purpureus' (purple fuki), with leaves emerging dark purple to almost purplish black, later fading to purplish green, and flowers flushed with purple; and **'Variegatus'** (variegated butterbur), with leaves irregularly variegated with yellowish or creamy white. 'Variegatus' is a striking plant when contained, but it becomes an almost insufferable blotch on the landscape once it spreads.

Petasites palmatus, sweet coltsfoot, coltsfoot. North America, Newfoundland to Alaska, along the coast south to British Columbia, Oregon, Washington, and California.

Morning sun, LS to MS; flowers small, white to pinkish white, sweetly fragrant, in dense, rounded clusters on a subtending rosette of green bracts, held by stems to 20 in. (50 cm) tall while in bloom; February–April, arising before the leaves emerge; plant rhizomatous, aggressively spreading; leaves umbrellalike, rounded, heart- or kidney-shaped, to 16 in. (40 cm) across, green, with 7–12 toothed lobes, whitish hairy coating beneath; leaf stems stout, upright, to 20 in. (50 cm) tall. The selection 'Golden Palms' has yellow leaves with a metallic sheen (indumentum) and pink flowers rising very early; its spread is not as rampant. Difficult in hot, southern gardens and requires moist and shady conditions. Hardy in zones 6 and 7. *Petasites frigidus* (coltsfoot) grows in higher elevations of the western mountain ranges, particularly the western Cascades, and also in Europe, but it is rarely available in commerce.

Phegopteris

Phegopteris hexagonoptera (southern beech fern) is often rescued from constructions sites in the ever-expanding Atlanta metropolitan area. In the 1800s, botanists confused it with *P. connectilis* (northern beech fern), and indeed their habitat overlaps considerably. The beech ferns provide gardeners with a choice: *P. hexagonoptera* is better adapted to the hot, dry summers of the South, and its cousin *P. connectilis* appreciates the cool, northern woods. Both spread rapidly and can get downright invasive. They should not be planted where smaller ferns or wildflowers could get overtopped by their dense fronds. If exposed to dry conditions for an extended period, they tend to go dormant early; supplemental water extends their growing season.

Both beech ferns are endemic to eastern North America into Canada, but here only *Phegopteris hexagonoptera* is cultivated. It is a rugged, deciduous fern, keeping its bright green well into late summer and early autumn. It is larger and more erect than *P. connectilis* and easily broken by high winds, so site in a sheltered spot. In the wild, it is often bent down by moisture and makes a more or less solid cover in the woodland.

Over the years several scientific names have been applied to this genus, including *Dryopteris*, *Polypodium*, and *Thelypteris*. For now, cryptogamists have settled on *Phegopteris*, from the Greek *phegos* (= acorn) and *pteris* (= fern). The genus is placed in the maidenhair fern family, Thelypteridaceae.

In gardens, beech ferns are tolerant of deep shade but will stand up to considerable sun if grown in a light, well-draining, woodland soil, rich in organic matter. *Phegopteris hexagonoptera* thrives in my acid soil, but neutral to slightly alkaline soils also suit beech ferns. Planted in groups, their height makes them good subjects to fill in a background. They may also be used as a groundcover and fronted by lower-growing companions like hostas or astilbes.

Propagate by dividing the creeping rhizome in autumn after the fronds have dropped or in very early spring. Propagation by spores is possible but

unnecessary, since the spreading habit of the ferns gives plenty of increase.

Diseases, mollusks, and insects do not bother beech ferns.

Species and cultivars listed are widely creeping and form expanding colonies. All are herbaceous and lose their top growth in winter.

Phegopteris connectilis, beech fern, long beech fern, narrow beech fern, northern beech fern. Nearly cosmopolitan in the northern hemisphere, northern United States, and Eurasia.

Some sun, LS to FS; fronds 12–14 in. (30–35 cm) tall, produced tightly in rows along a widely creeping rhizome, stalks scaly at the base, stalk green, darker toward the base, erect, leaning with age; leaves compound, pale green fronds composed of 8–14 double-tapered, opposite leaflets (pinnae), widest in the middle, not winged at the stem, pointed at top, 8–12 in. (20–30 cm) long and to 6 in. (15 cm) wide, widest at the base, the lowest leaflets are widely spaced with lowest pair pointing downward and outward; leaflets deeply cut into 16–24 subleaflets, rounded, lobed, mostly blunt-pointed; veins forked; spore cases (sori) roundish, scattered near the margin. In North America, the southern limit of this species is North Carolina and Tennessee. This fern is narrower than *Phegopteris hexagonoptera*; it also requires more moisture and is unhappy in dry soil. In southern gardens, plant in deep shade in a moist situation. Hardy to zone 3.

Phegopteris hexagonoptera, southern beech fern, American beech fern, broad beech fern. Eastern North America, Quebec to New England, south to northern Florida and Texas.

Some sun, LS to FS; fronds to 24 in. (60 cm) tall, tilting backward from an upright stalk; produced tightly in rows along a vigorously creeping rhizome, stalks scaly at the base, yellowish green, darker toward the base, erect, leaning with age; leaves compound, dull green fronds composed of 8–14 double-tapered, opposite leaflets (pinnae), widest in the middle, winged at the stem, pointed at top, to 16 in. (40 cm) long and widest at the base to 12 in. (30 cm), the lowest leaflets are widely spaced and winged at the stem with the very lowest pointing downward; leaflets deeply cut into 16–24 subleaflets, lobes toothed and mostly blunt-pointed; veins forked and unforked; spore cases (sori) roundish, scattered near the margin. Among the best ferns for southern gardens and holds its own further north. Hardy to zone 4, heat-tolerant to zone 8. ***Phegopteris decursive-pinnata*** from southeastern Asia is larger and more showy—in gardens with enough space for it. Hardy to zone 6, heat-tolerant to zone 8.

Pinellia

Seeing showy cobra lilies and native jacks raising their heads well above hostas and ferns in the garden makes one wonder why we grow smaller things, like pinellias, at all. But many wonders of nature come in small packages, and given a prominent place away from their tall cousins, these tiny beauties add their own charm. Bigger is not always better.

Pinellias must be given a place near garden paths or a perch in a shady rock garden from which to proffer their captivating loveliness. To plant just one will never do—they are best in groups. Just one plant of any of the pinellias described will turn into several or many within a few seasons, and the group will animate its assigned area in the garden. Here they never fail to elicit comments. In southern regions they are ideally suited for shady spots; further north considerable sun is tolerated. During active growth a moist, fertile soil with a pH of 5 to 6 is best, and the tuber likes a relatively dry rest period during winter, so drainage is important. I plant them in a raised bed with a rapidly draining sublayer.

All *Pinellia* species come from eastern Asia, where they grow in deciduous forests and open areas. In southern gardens pinellias do very well, and the several species and cultivars I grow thrive in hot, humid weather. They do not appreciate dry soil; provide supplemental water during droughts. Hardy to zone 6, 5 with protection.

Pinellias are commonly called green dragons and are related to the genus *Arisaema*, except that their flowering stems spring directly from the tuber and apart from separate leaf stems. The genus name honors Giovanni Pinelli, founder of the Naples Botanic Garden. *Pinellia* is classified in the Araceae.

Propagate by taking offsets in autumn; this is the most productive method, since offsets are produced so rapidly. Seed can also be sown as soon as ripe in pots in a cold frame.

I have never experienced any disease or insect problems, and none are reported.

Pinellia cordata, variegated green dragon. China, Korea.

Some sun, LS to WS; inflorescence arising from the tuber, on blackish purple stem to 8 in. (20 cm); spathe to 3 in. (8 cm) long with light green tube with purple veins, with flaring, incurved hood, spadix with long appendage curving upward on a slant or straight up, green; June–July; petiole 6 in. (15 cm) tall, purple to greenish purple; leaves basal, oblong lance-shaped, with heart-shaped base, dark green above with veins outlined in grayish to yellowish green, bright purple beneath, 3–5 in. (8–13 cm) long. With its variegated, dark green leaves and purple stems, this stands out as the best pinellia. Not as rampant as other species, increasing at a moderate pace.

Pinellia petadisecta, green dragon. Western China.

Some sun, LS to WS; inflorescence arising from the tuber, on green stem to 12 in. (30 cm); spathe 4–6 in. (10–15 cm) long with lime-green tube, hood more or less erect, tapering, green, spadix yellowish green; June–July; petiole to 10 in. (25 cm) tall, green; leaves basal, pedate, composed of 7–11 segments, egg- to lance-shaped, green, 4–7 in. (10–18 cm) long. Not as showy as *Pinellia cordata*, this species is larger and holds its own in company with small hostas, ferns, and astilbes. A similar but smaller green dragon from China and Japan, *P. integrifolia*, is rarely offered.

Pinellia tripartita, green dragon. Southern Japan.

Some sun, LS to WS; inflorescence arising from the tuber, on green stem 12–18 in. (30–45 cm); spathe 3–4 in. (8–10 cm) long with light green tube to whitish green, hood erect with tip curved, tapering, light green outside, purplish inside, spadix green with long, green appendage to 10 in. (25 cm) long, first erect, later drooping; June–July; petiole 6–9 in. (15–23 cm) tall, green; leaves basal, with 3 segments, each egg-shaped, pointed, green, 3–8 in. (8–20 cm) long. Another better-behaved pinellia, though it does spread. Forms with spathes purple inside and out are known. It has been used in hybridizing; I hope the several cultivars I saw in Japan with white-variegated leaves eventually appear in commerce. **'Polly Spout'** has flowers that are delicately pink within the spathe and the erect hood; like the species, the spadix extension is up to 10 in. (25 cm) long. It is well behaved and stands out like a pink flag in the wildflower garden, where I've grown it for years.

Plantago

Weeds have the nasty habit of just showing up and making the lives of fastidious gardeners miserable with continuous weeding tasks. Growing them intentionally seems asinine. Many years ago, when I still cultivated a lawn, plantain was a weed only toxic herbicides could eliminate. Seeing our five small children use this poisoned spread as a playground convinced me to do away with it; a portion of it was covered with pine bark and sand, and the rest disappeared under plantings of wildflowers, perennials, and ferns.

But there are a few attractive forms of plantain available to sophisticated gardeners. Purple-leaved and dwarf forms of *Plantago major*, the cosmopolitan common plantain, have been cultivated for some time, but these require full sun; it is the variegated form of *P. major* that has found its way onto the shaded paths of my woodland garden, where it thrives in a thin layer of pine bark on top of Georgia red clay, lighting up the paths with bright spots here and there. This car-track plant, so-called because it prefers to grow on a beaten path or in a rut, is a nice-looking variety with leaves that are beautifully mottled with a lighter green and bright creamy yellow. Like the true weed it is, it does well in the heat and humidity of my southern garden and survives dry periods without additional watering. It seems to prefer to grow on compacted clay with a pH of 5, but any soil, including those with alkaline reaction, seems to suit it. Hardy to zone 4.

Plantago got its name from the classic Latin name for the plant, *plantaginem* (*planta* = sole of the foot), a reference to the prostrate, broadly rounded leaves. It is classified in the plantain family, Plantaginaceae.

The seeds of *Plantago major* 'Variegata' come true. I let it spread by self-seeding, removing juvenile plants where they are not wanted and giving the rest away, since everyone seems to want a piece of it.

I have never experienced any disease problems, but aphids are reported as a sucking pest.

Plantago major **'Variegata'**, common variegated plantain, white man's foot, car-track plant. Cosmopolitan.

Some sun, LS to WS; flowers on a spike, insignificant; leaves basal, to 2 in. (5 cm), in a prostrate rosette, round, heart-shaped at the base, dark green with conspicuous veins, randomly variegated with lighter green and creamy yellow, irregularly toothed margin. This nicely variegated plant is well behaved in shade. In more sunny spots it may seed prolifically, and the seedlings should be removed promptly where not wanted. Similar is f. *contracta* but smaller and dwarf in all respects. 'Marginata', a nice selection of the related *Plantago lanceolata* (English plantain), has leaves with narrow margins of creamy white or pale yellow. For those interested in trying "improved" weeds, several cultivars of *P. major* are offered.

'Atropurpurea', leaves in shades of purple, some with a bronze tinge.

'Contorta', strangely twisted, contorted leaves, monstrous, some with variegation, some not. May be the same as 'Rosularis'.

'Nana', leaves dwarf and prostrate; flowerstalks recumbent.

'Rosularis' (rose plantain), a European selection, leaves contorted, monstrous.

'Rubrifolia', leaves a dark brownish red or maroon.

Platanthera

Most hardy woodland orchids do not survive in gardens, but a few exceptions are offered, like the fringed orchids formerly classified in the genus *Habenaria* and the North American species with fringed lips placed by some taxonomists in *Blepharoglottis*. Both genera have found a secure place for the time being in *Platanthera*, an old Linnaean name from the Greek *platys* (= wide) and *anthera* (= anthers). The genus is classified in the Orchidaceae.

My first encounter with these exquisite orchids was during a midsummer outing in the Great Smoky Mountains, where I came upon a small group of *Platanthera ciliaris*. The bright yellow-orange flowers stood out like beacons among the ferns and subshrubs of the pine forest floor. A few years later I found a commercial source for this species, and it has been growing here ever since. I have seen populations in the mountains of Georgia, the

Carolinas, and southern Michigan, where it grows along roadsides, in bog margins, and more at the edge of forest than deeper into the woods. As native orchids go, it is one of the most charming and still common.

Platanthera species fail in many gardens because incorrect cultural conditions are provided. One of the most important is deep, moist soil that never dries out. Optimum pH is 4 to 5.5. They are best placed in a raised bed mulched with pine needles and plenty of moisture-retaining soil components, such as peat moss. In the South they like woodland shade with some morning sun; in the North they need more sun. Hardy to zone 7, 6 with protection. In the wild I have observed them in sheltered positions in zone 5; they should succeed in similar circumstances in gardens.

Propagate by carefully dividing the tuberous corm.

In my garden, nothing in the way of diseases or insect pests seems to bother these woodland orchids. In southern areas slugs and snails are reported to be a scourge during late-winter warm-ups.

The orchids recommended here are not horticultural subjects for novice gardeners, and many are scarce or rare in the wild. Never remove them from the wild, and do not purchase wild-collected plants.

Platanthera chlorantha, greater butterfly orchid. Europe; British Isles south to northern Mediterranean region and east to the Caucasus.

Some sun, LS to WS; flowers small, fragrant, greenish white, lip petal to 0.5 in. (1 cm), curved downward, strap-shaped, tapering toward end, entire, spur to 1.5 in. (4 cm) long, pointing backward and horizontal, curving slightly downward, upper sepal and 2 lateral petals erect, joined at the tips, 12–30 in a loose cluster on an erect stem to 20 in. (50 cm) high; June–August; leaves 2, basal, glossy green, conspicuously veined, 3–10 in. (8–25 cm) long, oval to elliptic, pointed tip, upper leaves bractlike, much smaller, sheathing stem. A closely related smaller species, *Platanthera bifolia* (lesser butterfly orchid), with whiter flowers suffused with the palest green, is available in Europe. These orchids are not strictly fringed orchids: their lips are strap-shaped, entire organs without fringes.

Platanthera ciliaris, yellow fringed orchid, orange-fringe, orange-plume, rattlesnake master. Southern Wisconsin and east to but rare in New England, also New York south to Georgia and Florida, west to Missouri and Texas.

Some sun, LS to WS; flowers small, bright yellow to yellowish orange, lip to 0.8 in. (2 cm) long, deeply fringed, with spur to 1.5 in. (4 cm), upper sepal and 2 lateral petals erect, spreading, spur long, projecting downward and backward, 24–60 in a cylindrical cluster on an erect stem to 36 in. (90 cm) high; June–August; leaves 2, basal, glossy green, 3–10 in. (8–25 cm) long, lance-shaped, upper leaves much smaller, sheathing stem. This spectacular orchid is great planted where its tall, yellow plumes can overtop companion trilliums, ferns, and medium hostas. *Platanthera cristata* (crested yellow orchid, orange fringed orchid) is a more southern species and very similar with smaller, bright to deep orange flowers with a spur shorter than the fringed lip; *P. blepharoglottis* (white fringed orchid, snow orchid) has slightly larger white flowers and wider leaves but is otherwise similar. Both species are hardy to zone 7. The related *P. integra* (yellow fringeless orchid) has its northern limit in southern New Jersey; it has a rounded, fringeless lip, a short spur, and smaller yellow flowers on stems to 24 in. (60 cm). I have seen it in gardens but have not found it in commerce. Most of these orchids hybridize in the wild, so expect intermediate types.

Platanthera grandiflora, large purple fringed orchid, greater purple fringed orchid, large butterfly orchid, plume royal. Eastern North America, Wisconsin and southern Ontario east to Newfoundland and New England, south to West Virginia and in the mountains to North Carolina, Georgia, and Tennessee.

Some sun, LS to WS; flowers to 1 in. (2.5 cm) long, fragrant, light purple or lavender, lip petal to 1 in. (2.5 cm) with 3 fan-shaped, deeply fringed lobes, spur to 1 in. (2.5 cm) long, backward pointing, upper sepal and 2 lateral petals erect, spreading, 24–58 on an erect spike to 4 ft. (1.2 m) high; June–August; leaves 2, basal, glossy green, 3–10 in. (8–25 cm) long, oval to lance-shaped, upper leaves lance-shaped and much smaller, sheathing stem. *Platanthera psyodes* (small purple fringed orchid, lesser purple fringed orchid, butterfly orchid, fairy fringe, soldier's plume) is very similar but smaller in all respects; it has lavender flowers, stems to 36 in. (90 cm), and several stem as well as basal leaves. More widely available, it can often be found in wet roadside ditches. Cultivating these northern species in hot, dry southern gardens is a challenge.

Recommended reading

Cribb, Phillip, and Christopher Bailes. 1989. *Hardy Orchids*. Portland, Oregon: Timber Press.
Keenan, Philip E. 1998. *Wild Orchids Across North America*. Portland, Oregon: Timber Press.

Podophyllum

One of the first wildflowers I planted was *Podophyllum peltatum* (mayapple). In the 1960s, I saw a huge colony of it along Cades Cove Road, in the Smoky Mountains. I was duly impressed by the canopy of umbrellalike leaves, which gave a glimpse of waxy, white flowers here and there. A single purchased plant, which despite its common name blooms here in April and produces its applelike fruit in early June, has since grown into several large colonies. All parts of the plant are poisonous, except the ripe fruit, which is eaten raw or used in jellies and preserves; it also makes a delicious summer drink when mixed with lemonade. Raccoons and other wildlife love it. American Indians used this species for medicine as well as for food, and early settlers followed suit. Its violent purgative and emetic properties are well known. Sixteen physiologically active compounds have been isolated in it; one, etoposide, is a chemotherapy agent. Unfortunately, this means that the roots of both the American mayapple and *P. hexandrum*, a Himalayan species, are presently collected to the detriment of wild populations.

Podophyllum peltatum is the only North American species; the genus has a much greater representation in Asia. Some taxonomists propose separation of the Himalayan species under *Sinopodophyllum* and the balance of Asian species with malodorous flowers under *Dysosma*; *P. peltatum* would then be the only species retained under *Podophyllum*, but I am retaining the generic name *Podophyllum* for all species, North American and Asian. Plants in commerce, originating from different collections, show considerable clonal differences, and it may take some time to sort out the puzzle. In the meantime, purchase plants from a source guaran-

teeing true-to-name stock. Regardless of what generic name one adopts for these long-lived, elegant plants, all are classified in the Berberidaceae. The genus name is from the Greek *podilon* or *podos* (= foot) and *phyllon* (= leaf).

All *Podophyllum* species are well adapted to shady forests. In the wild their creeping rhizomes form large colonies. *Podophyllum peltatum* does this in a hurry and becomes almost invasive; it crowds out more delicate wildflowers in a loose, woodland soil, a combination that should be avoided in gardens. It mixes well with larger hostas, tall ferns, and taller Solomon's seals, and is useful as a foot-tall deciduous groundcover. The Asian species take time to form a natural-looking group; I used several plants to start a colony so the effect is more immediate. Allow sufficient space for plantings; the leaves of some species become large in time. Underplant mayapples with low-growing, shade-tolerant groundcovers. They prefer a deep woodland soil with plenty of organic matter, good tilth, and good water-holding capacity with a pH of 5.5 to 6.5. All do well in light to medium shade but they also tolerate some sun; I have grown a colony of *P. pleianthum* in considerable morning sun with good results. *Podophyllum peltatum* is hardy to zone 4, but the Asian species are more tender, limited to zone 7, 6 with protection. As long as the rhizomatous rootstock is prevented from freezing, plants can be cultivated as perennials.

Propagate by dividing the rhizome in very early spring before growth starts, making certain that each piece has at least one growth bud. At Hosta Hill *Podophyllum pleianthum* sends new plantlets up from growth buds on the rhizome as well as from adventitious roots, some a considerable distance away from the mother plant. Seed can be sown in a cold frame; germination is usually sporadic. Some Asian species are not self-fertile, so different clones must be grown adjacent to effect fertilization.

Slugs and snails can damage new growth emerging in spring; no other pests or diseases are reported or experienced here.

Podophyllum delavayi. China, northern Yunnan, Sichuan.

LS to MS; flower solitary, sometimes 2–3, petals 6, 0.8 in. (2 cm) long, deep red, flowerstalk green, hairy, emerging from the juncture of the leafstalks; May–June; plant rhizomatous, spreading; stems green, upright, to 8 in. (20 cm) tall; leaves 2, with 4–6 deep lobes, each 3-lobed in turn, but stem side not lobed, coarsely toothed, thick and leathery, to 12 in. (30 cm) long, initially purplish dark green mottled with large blotches of light green to grayish green. Although garden experience with it is still limited, this species promises to be another striking addition to the shady garden.

Podophyllum difforme. China, Hubei.

LS to MS; flowers 3–9, nodding, elongated, bell-shaped, borne just under the leaf node, sepals 6, petals 6–9, 1–1.5 in. (2.5–4 cm), more elongated than those in *Podophyllum versipelle*, deep rosy red to maroon, with ruffled converging tips; April–May; plant rhizomatous, spreading; stems green, at first thickly covered with whitish hair, which later disappears, stout, upright, to 18 in. (45 cm) tall; leaves 2, wider than long, with 2–3 irregular, simple lobes similar to *P. pleianthum*, thick and leathery, 6–9 in. (15–23 cm) long and 9–12 in. (23–30 cm) wide, dark green or grayish green with central blotches and markings along the veins in a mixture of colors from silvery gray to almost cream; fruit small, berry-shaped, yellow when fully ripe. Requirements for growing this exquisite Chinese mayapple in the West are not yet determined, but it is well worth any effort to cultivate it successfully. The fascinating color patterns on the leaves are stunning. Each plant shows a different color pattern: it is impossible to accurately describe it. New growth develops before the arrival of cold weather, so plants may need protection from freezing all winter. It should grow well where winters are mild but may be difficult where they are not.

Podophyllum hexandrum, Himalayan mayapple. Himalayas, Afghanistan east to west-central China.

LS to MS; flower solitary, rarely 2, shallowly bell-shaped, upward pointed or slightly nodding, borne in the leaf axil between the leaves, to 2 in. (5 cm) across, sepals 3, petals 6, waxy white or rose-pink, stamens 6, showy yellow anthers; April–June; plant rhizomatous, spreading; stems green, stout, upright, to 18 in. (45 cm) tall; leaves 2, alternate on flowerstalk, rounded, with 3–5 deep lobes, lobe tips pointed, margins toothed, 6–10 in. (12–25 cm) across, leaf color varies greatly, usually mottled purplish brown to purplish green on green, turning all green; fruit large, bright red, shaped like a

plum, edible, to 1.5 in. (4 cm) long. A species known and cultivated since 1820 and a good foliage plant for the shady garden. Its flowers appear before the leaves fully develop so are not hidden below the foliage like those of *Podophyllum peltatum*. It comes up early so may be damaged by late freezes. The many clones in commerce vary in their patterns of leaf variegation; expect considerable variances in purchased plants. **Variety *chinense*** is a better plant than the type, larger and with pink flowers; its leaves are more divided, with each of the 3–5 lobes further divided into 2–3 sublobes. Variety *majus* ('Majus') looks like the type but is larger in all respects. *Podophyllum aurantiocaule* from China (Yunnan) and Tibet is similar but bears 2–4 creamy yellow flowers and has, as the epithet indicates, yellowish to yellow-orange stems and leafstalks. To confuse matters, pink-flowered forms occasionally occur in cultivation; their leaves are the same size but with 4–7 deep lobes that are finely toothed.

Podophyllum peltatum, mayapple, American mandrake, Indian apple, mandrake, raccoon berry, wild jalap, wild lemon, wild mandrake. Eastern North America, southern Ontario and Minnesota east to Quebec and south to Georgia and Florida, west to Texas.

LS to MS; flower solitary, shallowly bell-shaped, fragrant, nodding, borne in the axil between the leafstalks, to 2 in. (5 cm) across, sepals 3, petals 6–9, waxy white, sometimes pink, stamens 12–18; April–June; plant rhizomatous, vigorously spreading and colonizing; stems green, stout, upright, 12–24 in. (30–60 cm) tall; leaves on nonflowering stems solitary, on flowering stems 2, with leafstalks branching from the same point on the stem, rounded, with 3–9 deep lobes, most lobes deeply cleft, forming 2 lobe tips, margins toothed, 9–12 in. (23–30 cm) across, green, finely hairy beneath; fruit large, usually yellow when ripe, shaped like a plum, edible, 1.5–2 in. (4–5 cm) long. Forma *deamii*, which inhabits the southwestern regions of the habitat, has pink flowers and red fruit. Forma *polycarpum*, a variant with a compound pistil (2–8 carpels), is sometimes available.

Podophyllum pleianthum. Central and southern China, Taiwan.

LS to MS; flowers 2–9, nodding, borne in the leaf axil between the leaves or further up on the leafstalk, very rarely just under the leaf, 2–2.5 in. (5–6 cm) long, bracts 3, enveloping tepals, sepals 6, deep maroon, petals 6–9, dark purplish brown or maroon, malodorous, to attract pollinating flies; May–July; plant rhizomatous, spreading; stems green, stout, upright, to 18 in. (45 cm) tall; leaves 2, alternate on flowering stem, rounded, with 5–9 regular, very shallow lobes, lobe tips pointed, margins with spaced marginal teeth, each ending with a hairlike point, thick and leathery, bright glossy green, 9–15 in. (23–38 cm) across, covered with fine hair underneath; fruit small, berry-shaped, gray to grayish green, sometimes bluish gray but yellow when ripe. The flowers of this species are often hidden beneath the large umbrellalike leaves. I have it planted near the patio so I can look across and see the flowers when I enjoy a brief rest in a low lounge chair. I have had friends get downright horizontal just to see the sensational, dark maroon flowers up close. The spectacular leaves remain fresh and green from the time they unfurl in spring until the first freeze cuts them down. Frequently sold as *Podophyllum versipelle*.

Podophyllum veitchii. China, Sichuan.

LS to MS; flowers 2–6, in a cluster on a hairy flowerstalk, sepal short, petals 6, purple; May–July; plant rhizomatous; leaf stems green, stout, upright, to 12 in. (30 cm) tall; leaves 2, with 6–8 deep, wedge-shaped lobes, each 3-lobed, prominently hairy underneath. A recent offering but I have not seen it.

Podophyllum versipelle. Tibet east to western China, Sichuan, Yunnan.

LS to MS; flowers 5–15, usually 8, open bell-shaped, borne in a drooping cluster at the leaf base on the leafstalk of the upper leaf, sepals 6–9, petals 6, to 1 in. (2.5 cm) long, purplish brown or maroon, stamens 6, malodorous to attract pollinating flies; May–July; plant rhizomatous, spreading little, clump-forming; stems green, stout, upright, to 18 in. (45 cm) tall; leaves 2, alternate on flowering stem, rounded, with 5–8 irregular lobes, deeper than those of *Podophyllum pleianthum*, lobe tips blunt, thick and leathery, bright glossy green, 9–12 in. (23–30 cm) across; fruit small, berry-shaped, gray to grayish green, sometimes bluish gray, yellow when fully ripe. The true *P. versipelle* has been in commerce only since 1999 and is often confused with *P. pleianthum*. There are ways to distinguish the two. For one thing, *P. versipelle* always bears flowers just underneath and at the root of the larger leaf, while *P. pleianthum* has flowers emerging either in the leaf axil or further up on the leafstalk of the larger leaf. Also, *P. pleianthum* has smooth flower-stalks (pedicels), but these are always hairy in *P. versipelle*. Finally, *P. pleianthum* is regularly lobed and had a widely creeping rhizome with budding adventitious roots, while *P. versipelle* has irregularly lobed leaves and a noncreeping rhizome.

Pollia

In the early 1990s I received a gift plant of *Pollia japonica* from a friend of mine, with the warning that this "flowering bamboo" would run. Like all new plants in my garden, it got tender loving care, and I was delighted that first season with its spectacularly tall stems, sweeping leaves, and cute, white flowers followed by bluish black berries. It made a sizeable colony in its second year—and in the third started running away from its designated spot. That autumn I dug up the whole mess and found thick rhizomes spread out in all directions, each with stems rising from nodes at frequent intervals. This was not bamboo, but it certainly behaved like it. Its rhizomes were easily separated, but just to be sure, I screened the soil through a mesh, since any part left behind will make a new plant. I relegated a souvenir rhizome to a large plastic tub with tiny drainage holes, sunk into the ground in the hosta bed. The plant is worth my time because it lends a tropical flavor to the garden and is of very easy culture.

Pollia is a little-known Eurasian genus primarily endemic to the tropics and subtropics, but *Pollia japonica* is hardy enough to be useful in zone 7, 6 with good protection. It can withstand a few degrees of frost, but the first hard freeze will cut it down; further north it makes a bold-looking container subject if overwintered inside. *Kisuji* is an especially attractive yellow-striped form from Japan, but its variegation is reportedly unstable. *Pollia japonica* will grow in any garden soil of good tilth with a pH of 5.5 to 7. Here it spread in heavy clay soil with abandon. The genus name honors Jan van der Poll, who was major of Amsterdam in the 18th century. A relative of *Tradescantia*, *Pollia* is classified in the spiderwort family, Commelinaceae.

Propagate by dividing the rhizome in very early spring before growth starts, making certain that each piece has at least one growth bud. Sow seed in a pot in a warm area.

Slugs and snails can damage new growth emerging in spring; no other pests or diseases are experienced here.

Pollia japonica. Southern Japan, Taiwan, southern China.

Some sun, LS to MS; flowers small, many, white, ball-shaped, in several whorls in a terminal, open cluster, on stalks; May–July; stems straight, to 4 ft. (1.2 m) tall; plant vigorously rhizomatous, spreading; leaves 6–12, singular, glossy green, alternate, to 18 in. (45 cm) long and 2 in. (5 cm) wide, depressed lighter-colored midrib, tapered toward both ends, slightly arching from the stem; fruit small, ball-shaped, very dark blue or bluish black. This species should be contained like bamboo; gardeners with plenty of room can grow it in the open, but its perimeter should be watched closely. An excellent companion to hostas, ferns, and astilbes. The flowers are long-lasting and the berries contrast well with the soft green leaves, making a nice show in autumn. *Pollia condensata* from shady tropical forests in Africa is similar but larger, with stems to 6 ft. (1.8 m); it is too tender to be planted out but makes a nice tropical accent in a container on the patio.

Polygonatum

Several representatives of this genus are native to North America and are frequently seen in gardens. The recent trend toward the natural model in garden design has brought about renewed interest in these native wild plants, and, no longer relegated to a dark corner, they are finally getting the prominence and attention they deserve. To me, Solomon's seals, as they are commonly called, were all along the most elegant of plants, and I always try to find the right place and company to show them off properly. Many years ago, a friend of mine passed along a foot-long rhizome of *Polygonatum odoratum* 'Variegatum'. I planted it in a bare spot among a shady collection of smaller hostas and other low-growing perennials and native wildflowers. The next spring, three graceful, arching 36 in. (90 cm) stalks appeared, lined with alternating, white-mar-

gined leaves and a delightful series of hanging, bell-shaped, creamy white flowers, produced in twos and threes all along the stem. I liked the way my Solomon's seal kept watch over the smaller hostas, looking much like shepherd's crooks. In a few years time, the single rhizome became a truly spectacular mass planting that completely covers the ground. So thick is the growth that few weeds have the energy to survive. Aside from being airy, good-looking, and almost maintenance-free, this small forest of stalks yields an increase year after year. I have another mass planting of variegated Solomon's seal under a pin oak that casts heavy shade; the robust stand fills this darkened space abundantly and carries on from spring until autumn with a display of tiny flowers, delicately variegated leaves, and strings of small, green, ball-shaped seeds that finally turn into silky black pearls.

Polygonatum (= many knees), derived from the Greek, is an allusion to the many joints of the many-branched rhizome; old sources use the generic name *Salomonia*. The origin of the common name Solomon's seal, which first appeared in print in 1534, is uncertain. Some say it refers to the six-pointed star pattern (star of David) visible when the rhizome is cross-sectioned. Others suggest it is a reference to the circular scars left on the rhizomes by previous stalks, which resemble the royal seal of King Solomon. The juice extracted from the rhizomes is used to treat sunburn and earaches. The raw rhizomes are mildly toxic, but American Indians and early settlers ate the starchy roots, either boiled or baked, as potato substitute or in breads. A tea brewed from the leaves is said to be contraceptive. The genus is placed in the Convallariaceae. The taxonomy of the classic as well as recently imported Solomon's seals is somewhat muddled, so expect occasional mislabeling and some changes as new discoveries are classified.

Solomon's seals are rhizomatous herbaceous perennials endemic to the temperate regions of North America, Europe, and eastern Asia. Originating in moist woodlands, Solomon's seals are well adapted to shady, moist conditions, but they can withstand some aridity; in the long, hot summers of southeastern North America, the Eurasian species go dormant a little earlier than the North American natives. Each year every rhizome branch sends up a new stalk, leaving a circular scar on the root when the stem departs in the fall; here in

Georgia I have rescued plants that had scar counts approaching 60, indicating the great age to which these plants can live.

Whether tall or small, Solomon's seals are great additions to any shady garden if properly paired with suitable companion plants. I have grown the Asian *Polygonatum humile* for years; it produces mats of ground-covering stems, barely 4 in. (10 cm) in height, clothed with soft green leaves and has found its way into the woodland and rock gardens, where small hostas and ferns serve as fitting companions. At Hosta Hill it is particularly effective planted in patches of yellow club moss, *Selaginella kraussiana* 'Aurea'. Most native species carry on from spring until autumn, fitting well with other perennials of the same life cycle, like hostas, toad lilies, wild gingers, and epimediums. Obviously, ferns make matchless complementary plants when carefully matched for size.

Solomon's seals prefer a woodland soil with plenty of organic matter, good tilth, and good water-holding capacity, yet well drained. I grow all mine in raised beds. Most tolerate considerable tree root competition. Solomon's seals come close to being maintenance-free plants, thriving and increasing in size year after year without the slightest bit of attention. All I do is remove dead stems after the first freeze and provide a soaking when it has been dry for a few weeks.

Propagate by dividing the dormant rhizome in late autumn or very early spring. I do this after early frosts have turned the leaves pale yellow and finally felled the stems. The rhizomes of the larger species are wide-ranging networks of white roots with pinkish growing tips. Being completely dormant, the roots can be removed without native soil and further cut up with a clean, sharp knife. Each piece should have at least one growing tip. Most species can also be propagated by seed. I simply remove them after they dry up, bury them shallowly in good soil, and let nature take its course. Not all germinate, but the few seedlings that do result grow quickly and can be added to other groups in the garden. If they do not come up, nothing is lost, because division is a lot easier and more productive.

Large slugs and snails can damage new growth emerging in spring, but growth is so fast that usually only the smaller species are harmed. The larvae of saw fly (*Diptera* spp.) and other fly pests are re-

ported to cause damage, but I have not experienced this in my garden.

Unless otherwise noted, all species and cultivars listed can be grown in zones 6 to 9. European and North American species are very hardy and can be grown in zone 4 or colder, as noted. Asian species should be heavily mulched in zone 5 and colder to protect the rhizomes; expect some losses during extreme winters. Note: the descriptions are for cultivated forms in commerce; species show considerable variability in the wild. Expect some divergence as new importations become available.

Polygonatum biflorum, small Solomon's seal, great Solomon's seal. North America, east of the Rocky Mountains and the Sierra Madre in Mexico.

MS to FS; flowers greenish white, 0.5–1 in. (1–2.5 cm) long, hanging, bell-shaped, tubular, 6-lobed, produced 1–4 in the leaf axils; May–July; stems arching, hairless, to 4 ft. (1.2 m) tall; leaves single, alternate, green, to 6 in. (15 cm) long, narrowly to broadly lance-shaped; ball-shaped fruit is black, to 0.5 in. (1 cm) in diameter. This is the popular native Solomon's seal, sold under several synonyms. One, *Polygonatum commutatum* (= changeable), alludes to the changeable nature of this species: some forms grow as tall as 8 ft. (2.5 m), and I have observed small stands of these giants in the Appalachian mountains on private property near Spruce Pine, North Carolina (possibly the variant sold as *P. giganteum*). Some native colonies have individuals in which the flowers always appear in twos, giving rise to the epithet (*biflorum* = two-flowered). A tetraploid form of *P. biflorum* (by some considered a separate species, *P. canaliculatum*) has furrowed leaves. The differing growth patterns may in some instances be due to polyploidy, in others to differing microclimates: the larger forms appear in the higher elevations and in more northern latitudes. The larger forms are useful as overtopping accents in hosta and fern plantings; the smaller forms, allowed to form colonies, make good background screens and groundcover.

Occasionally seen is *Polygonatum racemosum*, which differs from *P. biflorum* by having the flowers borne on axillary branches instead of peduncles; the native habitat of this hardy species from northern Indiana and southern Michigan includes areas of zone 3. *Polygonatum pubescens* (hairy Solomon's seal) grows in eastern North America from eastern

Canada to northern Georgia, where I have observed it in the Appalachian mountains; it is smaller, to 36 in. (90 cm) tall, and differs by having small hairs on the lower veins. Same garden uses as *P. biflorum*.

Polygonatum cathcartii. Eastern Nepal.

MS to FS; flowers creamy yellow, hanging, tubular, 6-lobed, usually 1, sometimes 2, in the leaf axils; May–July; stems to 36 in. (90 cm) tall, purple; leaves broadly lance-shaped, glossy green, to 3 in. (8 cm) long, alternate at the first nodes, subsequently opposite; brown fruit. This Himalayan species, new to cultivation, is similar to *Polygonatum oppositifolium*. In its natural habitat it is found as an epiphyte, hanging from native trees and shrubs. It can also occur growing in the ground, so transfer into a terrestrial garden environment should pose no problems.

Polygonatum cirrhifolium, Sibiricum Group. Nepal, Sikkim.

MS to FS; flowers white, to 1 in. (2.5 cm) long, hanging, bell-shaped, tubular, 6-lobed, produced in clusters in the leaf axils; May–July; stems erect, bending, to 8 ft. (2.5 m) tall; leaves in whorls, green, narrowly lance-shaped, to 6 in. (15 cm) long, coiled-under, tendriled leaf tips, usually 3–5 leaves per node; translucent red fruit. This Himalayan species, new to cultivation, is untested in cold climates. In the wild, its long stems use adjacent trees and shrubs as props, so staking may be required in gardens. Probably hardy to zone 7.

Polygonatum cryptanthum. Korea, Japan.

LS to MS; flowers greenish, to 1 in. (2.5 cm) long, tubular, produced 2 per node; subtended by leaf-like, whitish green bracts, in 1 or more clusters; May–July; stems erect, short, to 15 in. (38 cm) tall; leaves few, ovate, to 4 in. (10 cm) long; bracts remain viable and subtend the bluish fruit. Unusual for its partially hidden flowers, which are subtended by the relatively large bracts, hence *cryptanthum* (= concealed flowers). Related to *Polygonatum involucratum*.

Polygonatum curvistylum, Sibiricum Group. Western China, Sichuan, Yunnan.

MS to FS; flowers white, suffused pink, purple inside, to 1 in. (2.5 cm) long, bell-shaped, narrowest at the throat, tubular, 2 or more, in the leaf axils;

May–July; stems purple, erect but leaning, to 80 in. (2 m) tall; leaves in 5-leaf whorls, green, narrowly lance-shaped, to 6 in. (15 cm) long, leaf tips elongated, sometimes straight, but mostly reflexed, coiled under, tendriled; translucent red ball-shaped fruit. Its whitish pink and purple flowers and dark stems differ from other species and a group planting of it will be outstanding as an accent. This species looks very much like *Polygonatum sibiricum* and may be a subspecific environmental adaption. Populations found in open, rocky ground grow to only 15 in. (38 cm); it is listed as growing to 4 ft. (1.2 m) and has been observed growing much taller, to 10 ft. (3 m). Hardy to zone 5.

Polygonatum falcatum, Japanese Solomon's seal. Japan, Korea.

MS to FS; flowers white, to 1 in. (2.5 cm) long, hanging, greenish white, bell-shaped, tubular, 6-lobed, produced 2–5 in the leaf axils; May–June; stems distinctly arching, hairless, to 6 ft. (1.8 m) tall; leaves single, alternate, green, lance-shaped, to 10 in. (25 cm) long and 2 in. (5 cm) wide; small ball-shaped fruit is bluish dark gray. Very rare in cultivation. A beautiful variegated Solomon's seal often sold and grown as *Polygonatum falcatum* 'Variegatum' is in fact *P. odoratum* 'Variegatum'. The true *P. falcatum*, with leaves much longer and narrower, has been collected in the wild and may soon be in commerce. Hardy to zone 6, 5 with protection.

Polygonatum geminiflorum. Western China.

LS to MS; flowers creamy white, green-tipped, to 1 in. (2.5 cm) long, bell-shaped with flaring lobe tips, tubular, produced 2 per node, hence *geminiflorum* (= twin-flowered), in each individual leaf axil; June–July; stems erect, short, to 15 in. (38 cm) tall; leaves in 3-leaf whorls, shiny green, broadly ovate, short, with tapering tips, to 2 in. (5 cm) long; bluish ball-shaped fruit. This species (seen in photo of *Botrychium virginianum*) is among the smaller Asian Solomon's seals, with attractive white flowers. To highlight its loveliness, keep it in a pot, where it can be observed closely, or in a frontal position in the wildflower or partially shaded rock garden.

Polygonatum graminifolium. Himalayas, western China.

LS to MS; flowers small, ascending, pinkish, produced 1 per node in the leaf axils; June–July;

stems erect, very short, 7–15 in. (18–38 cm) tall; leaves alternate, extremely narrow, grasslike; bluish ball-shaped fruit. One of the smaller Asian Solomon's seals with attractive white flowers. Unusual for its leaves being shaped like blades of grass, hence *graminifolium* (= grasslike leaves). I keep this dainty Solomon's seal in a pot, because large slugs might make a meal of it when it emerges in early spring.

Polygonatum hirtum, wide-leaved Solomon's seal. Central and eastern Europe, east to the Caucasus, China, Japan.

LS to MS; flowers white, green-tipped, to 1 in. (2.5 cm) long, tubular with drawn-in lobe tips, produced 1–5 in the leaf axils; May–July; stems arching, to 36 in. (90 cm) tall; leaves single, alternate, glossy green, to 8 in. (15 cm) long, broadly ovate, to 3 in. (8 cm) wide, hairy underneath (*hirtum* = hairy); ball-shaped fruit is bluish black. Shows some affinity to *Polygonatum odoratum*, but the latter is smaller and not as showy as *P. hirtum*, whose broad, gleaming leaves grab attention even before the large flowers come along and contribute to a marvelous display. Hardy to zone 5. Some authorities connect the European *P. latifolium*, which has black fruit and is reportedly naturalized in Massachusetts, with *P. hirtum*. Specimens of *P. hirtum* collected in China do appear to be more vigorous and larger, and *P. latifolium* var. *robustum* may actually be the Chinese form, for which I maintain the specific name *P. hirtum*.

Polygonatum hookeri. Western China, eastern Himalayas.

LS to MS; flowers light to deep pink, to 1 in. (2.5 cm) long, erect, shortly tubular, with flaring, curving, up-facing lobes, produced singly in the lower leaf axils; May–June; stems erect, short, to 3 in. (8 cm) tall; leaves alternate, deep green, narrowly lance-shaped, with blunt tips, to 2 in. (5 cm) long; small, bluish black ball-shaped fruit. Probably the smallest Asian Solomon's seal and a fine garden plant. Its attractive flowers are unusual in that they face up and for their color. Although initially, the plant's small size requires careful placement in the garden, its vigorous rhizomatous rootstock soon forms expanding colonies. Needs supplemental water during dry periods. Hardy to zone 6.

Polygonatum humile, dwarf Solomon's seal. China, Korea, Japan, Hokkaido to Kyushu.

LS to MS; flowers white, to 0.5 in. (1 cm) long, bell-shaped, tubular, produced in clusters in the leaf axils; May–June; stems erect, hairless, to 8 in. (20 cm) tall, with small singular, alternate, green leaves to 2 in. (5 cm) long, broadly ovate, to 1 in. (2 cm) wide, slightly hairy on the veins beneath; the small ball-shaped fruit is bluish black. Given moist, fertile soil, its rhizomes spread fast and wide, making it an excellent, low-growing groundcover. It becomes ragged and goes dormant early if not supplied with plenty of water during hot, dry summer weather. Hardy to zone 5.

Polygonatum ×*hybridum*, common Solomon's seal, hybrid Solomon's seal, David's harp. Garden hybrid (*P. multiflorum* × *P. odoratum*).

MS to FS; flowers white, 0.5–1 in. (1–2.5 cm) long, hanging, greenish white, bell-shaped, tubular, 6-lobed, produced 2–4 in the leaf axils; May–July; stems erect, barely arching, hairless, to 5 ft. (1.5 m) tall; leaves single, alternate, horizontally held, green, to 8 in. (20 cm) long, broadly lance-shaped; ball-shaped fruit is black, to 0.3 in. (8 mm) in diameter. Mentioned in 18th-century garden books, this gardenworthy, graceful hybrid mixes well with ferns, hostas, and native wildflowers. Although fruiting is scarce, it has naturalized in Europe. Available plants are highly variable and may represent different strains; be careful to select a good plant. The several variegated sports of this hybrid are not as vigorous as the typical plant. Well-known cultivars include 'Flore Pleno' (double-flowered, slightly spreading lobes), 'Striatum' (variegated sport with creamy-striped leaves), 'Variegatum' (very similar if not identical to 'Striatum'), and 'Weihenstephan', an outstanding sterile form of particularly large size and stately architecture.

Polygonatum inflatum. Korea, Japan.

LS to MS; white flowers to 1 in. (2.5 cm) long, tubular, produced 2 per node; subtended by larger whitish green bracts, produced in 1 or more clusters; May–July; stems erect, arching, to 36 in. (90 cm) tall; leaves narrowly lance-shaped, to 4 in. (10 cm) long. A close relative of *Polygonatum involucratum* and similarly appealing.

Polygonatum involucratum. Korea, Japan.

LS to MS; flowers creamy white, to 1 in. (2.5 cm) long, tubular, produced 2 per node; subtended by green, leaflike bracts, to 0.5 in. (1 cm), in 1 or more clusters; May–July; stems erect, short, to 15 in. (38 cm) tall; leaves few, ovate, to 4 in. (10 cm) long; flower bracts remain viable and subtend the bluish fruit. May be of more interest to collectors but the bracted flowers (hence the epithet) and fruits are sure to fascinate gardeners in general.

Polygonatum lasianthum. Korea, Cheju Island, Japan, Hokkaido, Honshu.

LS to MS; flowers green-tipped white, to 1 in. (2.5 cm) long, bell-shaped, tubular, produced alternately in pairs in the leaf axils, held horizontally or slight hanging down; May–June; stems erect, hairless, to 18 in. (45 cm) tall, with small, singular, alternate green leaves to 6 in. (15 cm) long, linear lance-shaped, to 0.8 in. (2 cm) wide; fruit blue. This small Asian Solomon's seal has axillary twin flowers that are semierect, held out nearly horizontally, which allows for better observation of the blooms and makes a lovely display. The rhizomes are widely spreading, resulting in a low-growing groundcover. Available but still scarce in cultivation, it is widespread in South Korea and northern Japan. The flowers of this species are woolly (hairy), hence *lasianthum* (= woolly flower).

Polygonatum multiflorum, Eurasian Solomon's seal, European Solomon's seal. Eurasia, central Europe to western Siberia.

MS to FS; flowers white, 0.5–1 in. (1–2.5 cm) long, hanging on long peduncles, white but green-tipped, bell-shaped, tubular, 6-lobed, produced 2–6 in the leaf axils, usually confined to the lower half of the stem; May–June; stems arching, not angular, hairless, to 36 in. (90 cm) tall, occasionally much shorter; leaves single, alternate, green, broadly lance-shaped, to 6 in. (15 cm) long and 2 in. (5 cm) wide, smooth beneath; small ball-shaped fruit is bluish black. Coming from limestone regions, this species sometimes languishes in areas of high soil acidity; add dolomitic limestone to the soil mix to improve conditions. Some forms have up to 6 flowers per cluster, hence *multiflorum* (= many flowers). Very similar to *Polygonatum odoratum*, which has angled instead of rounded, arching stems. Although *P. multiflorum* is frequently offered in com-

merce, many of these are actually *P. odoratum*; true clones of *P. multiflorum* are seldom seen in gardens. Most variegated and double-flowered forms I have seen labeled *P. multiflorum* are in fact forms of *P. ×hybridum*. Not surprising, *P. multiflorum* of gardens is *P. ×hybridum*.

Polygonatum odoratum, angular Solomon's seal, fragrant Solomon's seal. Widespread in Eurasia, from England and central continental Europe to the Caucasus and Iran, also in western Siberia and Japan.

MS to FS; greenish white flowers with ruffled, skirtlike yellowish green margins, 1 in. (2.5 cm) long, mildly fragrant (lily-scented), hanging, bell-shaped, tubular, 6-lobed, produced 1–4 in the leaf axils; April–June; stems arching but angular, hairless, to 32 in. (80 cm) tall; leaves single, alternate, horizontally held, green, to 6 in. (15 cm) long, broadly elliptic, occurring alternately in two rows along the stem, with wavy, recurving tip; ball-shaped fruit is black. This species is the herbalists' species of old, which accounts for its synonym *officinale* (= used in medicine).

In var. *pluriflorum* ('Pluriflorum'), endemic to Korea and Japan, a majority of the flower clusters on the upper leaf axils have 4–5 individual flowers; it is otherwise similar to the type. Its selection 'Variegatum' is frequently sold as *Polygonatum odoratum* 'Variegatum' or *P. falcatum* 'Variegatum'. When reliable sources offer true specimens of this variety's variegated form, it is worth obtaining, but obviously, confusion reigns supreme and caution is advised when ordering.

Variety *thunbergii* is in all respects similar to the type but grows larger, with stems to 4 ft. (1.2 m), and appears to be more vigorous. Occasionally, plants offered as the typical species are *Polygonatum odoratum* var. *thunbergii*. When the true form is available, it is definitely worth including in the garden.

Polygonatum odoratum is one of the parents of *P. ×hybridum*. The green species is rarely seen in gardens, but many of its cultivars are present in most gardens and make up a majority of Solomon's seals seen.

'Albopictum' has leaves that are white-centered and streaky white. Here it has given rise to another sport with leaves half white and half green along the midrib.

'Flore Pleno' is a double-flowered form with spreading lobes and extensive green markings in the perianth margins.

'Gilt Edge' has a yellow leaf margin. Japanese books illustrate a form that has yellow leaves fading to green at the tips, and other yellow forms are known to aficionados in Japan.

'Grace Barker', similar to 'Striatum'.

'Pumilum' is smaller than the species and often mistaken in commerce for *Polygonatum humile*, which is even smaller.

'Silver Wings', a lesser-known variegated form with broad white margins.

'Striatum', a variegated sport with mostly white-striped leaves and a white margin on most leaves.

'Variegatum', a variegated sport with varying, somewhat streaky, creamy white margins, more articulated toward the tip of the leaf. Probably the best known and most appreciated of all garden-worthy Solomon's seals and widely available. On the same plant, some leaves may have very narrow margins, while others have margins and streaks of considerable width with streaks extending into the leaf toward the midrib. Otherwise this cultivar is as the all-green species. I have included several colonies of this elegant cultivar into the design scheme of Hosta Hill. Some of these groups have 100 or more individual stalks and present a glorious display from spring until the first freeze. No shady garden should be without this extremely vigorous, spreading, drought-tolerant cultivar. Various companion plants are recommended, but I prefer large colonies of this cultivar alone with an underplanting of shade-tolerant, ground-covering *Saxifraga veitchiana*, through which the emerging stems poke up in spring. A larger form with stems to 40 in. (1 m) is offered and may be *Polygonatum odoratum* var. *thunbergii* 'Variegatum'; other than the larger size it is almost impossible to tell the difference. Some forms of *P. odoratum* 'Variegatum' have clusters of 4–5 flowers throughout on the upper leaf axils, and these may in fact be *P. odoratum* var. *pluriflorum* 'Variegatum'.

Polygonatum oppositifolium. Central Nepal, Sikkim.
    MS to FS; flowers white, to 1 in. (2.5 cm) long, hanging, bell-shaped, tubular, 6-lobed, produced in clusters in the leaf axils; June–July; stems erect but nodding, to 4 ft. (1.2 m) tall; leaves leathery dark green, clothing the stem in opposite pairs, to

5 in. (13 cm) long; red fruit. This unusual species, a recent collection from Nepal, makes a fine addition to the woodland garden. Differs from other Himalayan forms by its epiphytic habit; in the wild, it grows in the branches of native stands of rhododendron forest. In-ground cultivation is possible.

Polygonatum prattii. Western China, Yunnan.
    Some sun, LS to WS; flowers pinkish, to 0.5 in. (1 cm) long, bell-shaped, tubular, drooping, produced 2–3 in the leaf axils; May–June; stems erect, to 8 in. (20 cm) tall; the small ball-shaped fruit is a pretty translucent red. I have this dwarf Asian Solomon's seal in a pot, where its dainty structure and colorful flowers and fruits can be appreciated. It is, however, suitable for planting out in the garden if precautions are taken to keep slugs from devouring the young growth in spring. Can take more sun than most Solomon's seals.

Polygonatum punctatum. Eastern Nepal.
    MS to FS; flowers whitish, purple-spotted, to 1 in. (2.5 cm) long, hanging, tubular, 6-lobed; produced 2–3 in the leaf axils; May–July; stems erect, to 18 in. (45 cm) tall; leaves alternately whorled, glossy green, with good substance; fruit dull brownish red. Another recent collection from Nepal, it too is epiphytic, growing in and hanging out of the branches of native stands of rhododendron forest, but in-ground cultivation is easily accomplished. The leaves are evergreen in zone 7; further north they may be disfigured by the cold unless protected. Makes a good subject for potting.

Polygonatum roseum. Central Asia to western Siberia.
    LS to FS; flowers drooping rose-pink (hence the epithet), to 0.5 in. (1 cm) long, tubular, produced singly or in pairs in the leaf axils; May–June; stems arching, channeled, to 36 in. (90 cm) tall; leaves green, to 6 in. (15 cm) long, linear lance-shaped, to 1 in. (2.5 cm) wide, basal leaves alternate, then opposite, sometimes whorled; the small ball-shaped fruit is first red then turns bluish black. Hardy to zone 5.

Polygonatum severtzovii, Sibiricum Group. Western China, northern Afghanistan and eastern Kazakhstan in the Pamir and Tien Shan mountain regions.

MS to FS; very similar to *Polygonatum verticillatum* but differs by having curled leaf tips and red fruit that turns purple when ripe. Its flowers are larger, to 1 in. (2 cm) long, and also bloom May–June; flowerstalks are to 40 in. (1 m) tall. Hardy to zone 5.

Polygonatum sibiricum, Sibiricum Group. Northern China, Mongolia, eastern Siberia, Nepal, Sikkim.

MS to FS; white flowers tinged green, to 1 in. (2.5 cm) long, hanging, bell-shaped, tubular, 6-lobed, produced in clusters in the leaf axils; May–July; stems erect, bending, to 8 ft. (2.5 m) tall; leaves in whorls, grayish green, narrowly lance-shaped, to 6 in. (15 cm) long, margins rolled under, with coiled-under, tendriled leaf tips, usually 3–6 leaves per node, sometimes more; translucent red fruit. This Himalayan species is new to cultivation and untested in cold climates. In the wild, its long stems use adjacent trees and shrubs as props, so staking may be required in gardens. Hardy to zone 7.

Polygonatum Sibiricum Group.

A collective group of Eurasian Solomon's seals with similar morphology, including *Polygonatum cirrhifolium*, *P. curvistylum*, *P. fuscum*, *P. severtzovii*, *P. sibiricum*, *P. stewartianum*, and *P. verticillatum*. Such a gathering allows taxonomists to collect additional data, which refined knowledge may eventually lead to changes in nomenclature. The uniting feature of this group is the scirrhous leaf tip: all leaf tips end in an appendage that is elongated and usually curled under, much like an open tendril. In the wild, these are reported to help prop up the very long stems of the listed species. As with other Solomon's seals, the natural variability of the Sibiricum Group is extensive, and local adaptations are to be expected. Most of the scirrhous *Polygonatum* species are hardy to zone 5. They require a cool, moist summer climate and are short-lived in areas of hot, dry summers.

Polygonatum stewartianum, Sibiricum Group. Temperate regions of Europe and Asia.

MS to FS; flowers pink, purple inside, to 0.5 in. (1 cm) long, bell-shaped with out-facing lobe tips, tubular, produced 2–3 in the leaf axils; May–July; stems erect but slightly leaning, hairless, angular, to 36 in. (90 cm) tall; leaves in 3- to 5-leaf whorls, green, narrowly lance-shaped, with depressed midrib, to 4 in. (10 cm) long, extended leaf tips are pointed, straight to bent down; fruit red, spotted, small. Its bicolored flowers differ from other species, and a group planting of it makes a prominent display. Hardy to zone 5.

Polygonatum verticillatum, Sibiricum Group, whorled Solomon's seal. Temperate regions of Europe and Asia.

MS to FS; white flowers with green fringe, to 0.5 in. (1 cm) long, bell-shaped with out-facing lobe tips, tubular, produced 1–4 in the upper leaf axils; May–June; stems erect, hairless, slightly angular, 4–8 ft. (1.2–2.5 m) tall; leaves stalkless, in 3- to 5-leaf whorls, green, sometimes 2 opposite, narrowly lance-shaped leaves to 6 in. (15 cm) long, with the long leaf tips straight or pointed down; the red ball-shaped fruit is small. This is the primary Eurasian form with whorled leaves, which sets it apart from Solomon's seals with alternate single or opposite leaves. With habitat extending to the Caucasus and Afghanistan, it may be hardy to zone 5. I have been growing it for years, and its performance in the hot summers of southeastern North America is anything but satisfying. Growing in a shaded position and given abundant water still has not convinced the plants to come even close to the typical size found in the wild or in northern gardens. My clumps have slowly multiplied, but the stems barely reach 12 in. (30 cm) and flowering is sparse or absent some years. Variety *rubrum* ('Rubrum') has red-colored stems and leaf petioles.

Polypodium

Many years ago, exploring the wooded, rocky ravine near my home, I stumbled across a rock covered with *Polypodium polypodioides* (resurrection fern). I was always on the lookout for small, moss-covered rocks for the garden, and this particular stone was small enough to be carried home. The small colony of the fern clinging to the rock surface looked miserable—all dry, curled up, and seemingly lifeless. Soon it became a favorite marvel of nature for my small children, who wondered at the magical greening brought on by rainy days after the fern had played dead during dry periods. It was no less amazing for me, and this long-lived fern has been a feature of my garden for decades. The original colony is still growing and expanding, colonizing neighboring rocks in a stone retaining wall.

Resurrection fern is a polypody, a genus of ferns widely cultivated. Many are tropical, but a few are hardy enough to be grown in temperate gardens, planted in the ground or as lithophytes (growing on rocks). Most are small, but they colonize by creeping and branching rhizomes, producing multiple fronds that form eye-catching groups. Cold hardiness varies greatly. They do best in a light, well-draining woodland soil, rich in organic matter, with lots of grit and stones. The rhizomes must be established close to the soil surface, not buried too deeply. All except *Polypodium virginianum* (American wall fern) require an acid soil with a pH of 5.5 to 6.5; wall ferns need an alkaline substrate with a pH of 7 and higher, simulating that found on mortared walls. Once fully established, considerable dryness is tolerated by *P. polypodioides* and *P. virginianum*; they appear dead but revive and green up when moisture is restored. All are trouble-free and require little maintenance. Horticulturally, these ferns stand on their own feet by growing on tree bark and rock faces, which surfaces they soften. Few companions can last under such cultural conditions. All are adapted to medium to full shade but will tolerate some sun.

Hardy polypodies are endemic to eastern and western North America and Europe. The generic name *Polypodium* comes from the Greek *poly* (= many) and *podilon* or *podos* (= foot), alluding to the many footlike scars left on the old rhizome by dead fronds, or alternatively to the many-branched rhizomes. The genus is classified in the polypody family, Polypodiaceae.

Propagate by dividing the rhizome. Propagation from spores is slow but successful; sow spores as soon as they are ripe on a coarse commercial mix with a pH of 7 to 8.5 maintained moist at 70°F (21°C). If a rescue situation presents itself, remove a small, established group completely with its substrate, either a small rock or a piece of bark, and relocate it.

Diseases and insect or mollusk problems rarely occur.

Polypodium polypodioides, resurrection fern, little gray polypody. Eastern North America, southern Illinois and Virginia east to Maryland and Delaware, south to Florida and Texas.

MS to FS; fronds held on separate erect stems, 4–8 in. (10–20 cm) high, leaf oblong to egg-shaped, erect but smaller leaves often prostrate, dark green above and grayish green, scaly beneath, narrow rounded tip; leaflets 6–12 pairs almost cut to the stalk, alternate, sometimes almost opposite, 0.5–1 in. (1–2.5 cm) long, semi-leathery; veins obscure, forked; rootstock woody, slender, horizontally spreading, sometimes matted; spore cases round, prominent, widely spaced at margin. This is a widespread and variable species. The North American form is smaller than some of the subtropical populations. Here, exposed on elevated rock groups, it survives hard freezes down to 0°F (−18°C) for short periods and 10°F (−12°C) for several nights. Hardy to zone 7, 6 with protection. Southward there seems to be no limit to its heat endurance given a habitat to its liking. Its hardiest variety is var. *michauxianum*.

Polypodium virginianum, rockcap fern, rock polypody, American wall fern, Virginia polypody. North America and eastern Asia.

MS to FS; fronds are similar to *Polypodium vulgare* but smaller, 8–10 in. (20–25 cm) long and to 4 in. (10 cm) wide. May be a North American representative of *P. vulgare*; its cultural requirements too are similar. Hardy to zone 5.

Polypodium vulgare, common polypody, wall polypody, adder's fern, golden maidenhair. Almost cosmopolitan in North America, Europe, Africa, and eastern Asia.

MS to FS; fronds held on separate erect stems, to 16 in. (40 cm) high, leaf lance-shaped or triangular, variable, 10–12 in. (25–30 cm) long and to 6 in. (15 cm) wide, erect but younger leaves often prostrate, green above and below, often tinged yellowish green, narrow rounded tip; leaflets 10–20 pairs almost cut to the stalk, alternate, 0.8–2 in. (2–5 cm) long, semi-leathery; veins obscure, forked; rootstock slender, widely spreading horizontally, often matted; spore cases large and round, prominent. This species is widespread and extremely variable, adaptable to many different habitats. Most geographic forms are now considered species: *Polypodium glycyrrhiza* (licorice fern) and *P. hesperium* (western polypody) are both endemic to western North America from Alaska to California. Hardy to zone 5. *Polypodium scouleri* (western leathery polypody) is unusual and attractive but too tender for most gardens, suitable in zones 8 to 10 only. *Polypodium vulgare* cultivars of eastern North American origin are more hardy and can be cultivated well into zone 3; those originating in warmer areas may not be as hardy, but experience shows they can be grown in zone 6 and warmer. The ferns are quite heat-tolerant and have endured high humidity and many hot, dry summers. The best way to establish this fern is to transplant rooted mats of it; cover the mat thinly with soil and weigh it down until the fern settles in its new location. *Polypodium vulgare* has a tendency to sport into all manner of crested, double-crested, branched forms. While these look good isolated in a container or even in a woodland, their presence on rocks in a naturalistic garden is somewhat disturbing. The quiet beauty of the type looks much better in such circumstances than a frizzly crested and branched 'Bifidograndiceps' or a 'Cornubiense Grandiceps'. *Polypodium cambricum* (Welsh polypody, greater polypody) is larger and so fits better in the woodland garden; its cultivars are commonly billed as feathery polypody ferns. For detailed listings of the many forms of these species, all similarly useful in the garden, consult a fern specialist's catalog.

Polystichum

One gift I was glad to receive from nature during the holidays of 1969, a few months after we moved into our new home, was *Polystichum acrostichoides* (Christmas fern). Protected by forking tree roots, a few clumps of this fern had survived the rampage of scarifiers employed to plant a lawn in my backyard woodland. To me the ferns were a blessing and a beginning. Together with a few stalwart lady ferns, Christmas ferns became the modest beginnings of my new garden. Later, after the measly lawn was mercifully snuffed out by me and layers of fallen loblolly pine needles, naturalized Christmas ferns were the first plants to begin the battle of winning back the once rich woodland. This hardy and evergreen fern is a colonizer, one of the most common ferns in northern Georgia. It belongs to the genus *Polystichum*, from the Greek *polys* (= many) and *stichos* (= row), a reference to the sori of some species, which are lined up in neat rows. *Polystichum* is classified in the Dryopteridaceae.

All ferns described are rugged, adapted not only to cold climates but to high heat and humidity. Here they have survived extreme droughts with no injury, and they propagate by spores on regular Georgia red clay, on improved soil, and even in the cracks between brick edgings. The juvenile ferns can be left where they are or relocated and any surplus given away. They are well suited to any shade, from light to dense, and tolerate light sun exposure. They have strong stems and stand up well in high winds during spring storms. Over the years, I have grown many clumps of these long-lived ferns and found they will grow in any soil, including heavy clay, sandy, and stony soils, but a light, fertile woodland soil with plenty of humus is preferred. A soil pH of 5 to 7 is acceptable. Given good cultural conditions, these ferns are low maintenance and of very easy culture. Clumps are easily transplanted year round, so long as a generous ball of earth comes with them.

The *Polystichum* species listed are among the very best garden ferns, most very hardy and evergreen and all gardenworthy and highly decorative. They make great companion plants for taller wildflowers, other ferns, and hostas. They are good subjects for background groundcovers when planted in groups and fronted by lower-growing companions like small hostas, wild gingers, and astilbes. Planted with hellebores, the evergreen species provide a splendid winter display.

Propagate by dividing the rhizome in autumn after the fronds have dropped or in very early spring. Propagation by spores is also fairly easy under the right conditions. The spores must be sown as soon as they are ripe on a coarse commercial mix with a pH of 7 maintained moist at 60–70°F (16–21°C). All the ferns grown here have naturalized and propagate by spores without my intervention.

The only insect problem I have experienced is the larvae of the codling moth, which rolls up the tips of young Christmas fern fronds to make a home. I have never experienced any disease problems, nor are any reported.

Polystichum acrostichoides, Christmas fern, canker brake, dagger fern. Eastern North America, southern Ontario and Minnesota east to Nova Scotia, south to Georgia and Florida, and west to eastern Texas.

LS to FS; fronds to 36 in. (90 cm), produced in rosettes on slender stalks emerging directly from the rhizome, very scaly at the base, stalk green, flattened in front and ridged at the sides, erect at first, but arching with age, fertile fronds taller, more erect; leaves compound, light green, later dark green, lance-shaped, narrow, pointed at top, to 32 in. (80 cm) long and 4 in. (10 cm) wide; leaflets 20–40 pairs, lance-shaped and prominently eared at base, short-stalked, toothed, pointed; veins forked; spore cases (sori) round, in 2 or more rows near midrib. The young fronds of this fern are among the first to rise in spring and provide accents of bright green with silvery white scales. First they are tightly coiled, then they droop backward before becoming erect. I usually remove the old fronds to give the soft croziers an easy path to rise. Christmas fern is used in many areas of North America as a holiday decoration. Hardy to zone 3. In the wild and in my garden, this species spontaneously develops all kinds of unusual leaflet forms: f. *crispum* (wavy or twisted leaflets), f. *cristatum* (fork-tipped leaflets), f. *incisum* (leaflets sharply cut and deeply toothed), and f. *gravesii* (blunt sterile leaflets with a projecting midrib). If many of these ferns are grown, these special forms can be isolated. Some have been named and are occasionally available under a cultivar name. *Polystichum munitum* (western swordfern) from northern and western North America is similar but slightly larger, reaching 4 ft. (1.2 m); its fertile fronds do not narrow toward the tip. Hardy to zone 3. Even more hardy is *P. scopulinum* (western holly fern), which occurs in northwestern North America; it is much smaller, with fronds to 12 in. (30 cm), and is an excellent fern for cold-region gardeners. Hardy to zone 2. A similar western North American fern for horticultural purposes is *P. andersonii*, which occurs in Alaska south to Oregon and east to Montana; its subleaflets are more deeply toothed and the upper side basal subleaflet is larger, giving the leaflet an eared appearance. Hardy to zone 3. While *P. acrostichoides* is excellent for hot, southern gardens, all these western ferns are best in cool northern gardens.

Polystichum aculeatum, hedge fern, hardy shield fern, prickly shield fern. Eurasia, South America.

LS to FS; fronds to 36 in. (90 cm), produced on thick stalks covered with brown scales, arching outward, forming vase-shaped clumps; leaves compound, leathery, glossy green, lance-shaped, tapering toward base, 12–32 in. (30–80 cm) long and 4–8 in. (10–20 cm) wide; leaflets to 50 pairs, mostly alternate but sometimes opposite at base, lance-shaped, pointed and tapering toward base; subleaflets stalked, oblong to oval, angled away from the midrib, spiny-toothed and -tipped; spore cases (sori) round, in 2 rows near midrib. This handsome fern is widely cultivated. Its wide fronds are evergreen and persist into the spring season; they suffer under heavy snow loads, so plant next to supporting shrubs. Expect differences in commercially offered plants of this variable fern.

Polystichum braunii, Braun's holly fern, prickly shield fern. Northeastern North America, Wisconsin east to Newfoundland and south to New York and northeastern Pennsylvania.

LS to FS; fronds to 36 in. (90 cm), produced on thick, scaly stalks, arching outward, forming vase-shaped clumps; leaves compound, leathery, glossy dark green, spiny, elliptic, tapering from the center upward and down to base, 24–36 in. (60–90 cm) long and to 8 in. (20 cm) wide. This fern is similar to the other species but has showy, broad subleaflets that are prickly-toothed and spiny-tipped. Although a most handsome fern for northern gardens, it is not evergreen and usually turns brown after the first few freezes. Hardy to zone 5. Of marginal value for southern gardens; I have tried it here, but it rises early and usually gets cut down by late freezes. **Polystichum ×setigerum** (Alaskan holly fern), its natural hybrid with *P. munitum*, is slightly smaller and a much better subject in the South as long as it is planted in medium to dense shade and soil moisture is maintained. It occurs in Alaska south to British Columbia; hardy to zone 3.

Polystichum polyblepharum, Japanese tassel fern, Japanese holly fern, bear's paw. China, Korea, Japan.

LS to FS; fronds to 36 in. (90 cm), produced closely adjacent on thick stalks covered with glossy, brown scales and arching outward, forming funnel-shaped clumps; leaves compound, leathery, glossy dark green, oblong lance-shaped, abruptly narrowing and pointed top, 18–32 in. (45–80 cm) long and 6–10 in. (15–25 cm) wide; leaflets 24–44 pairs, mostly alternate, oblong lance-shaped, to 5 in. (13 cm) long and 1.5 in. (4 cm) wide, horizontally inclined; subleaflets short-stalked, eared at base, oblong to oval, blunt and spiny-toothed and prickly-tipped, the basal pair bent down and toward the frond tip; veins forked; spore cases (sori) round, in 2 rows near midrib. I was given this fern in 1988 at the trial gardens in Weihenstephan, Bavaria; it has since naturalized and spread all over my garden. One of the finest ferns for the natural green garden. In spring, the tightly spaced young croziers look like a bear's paw, hence one common name. The mature fronds last throughout the winter, retaining their fresh and glossy green. In northern gardens with considerable snow loads, the wide fronds are subject to breaking. Hardy to zone 5. *Polystichum rigens* (stiff bear's paw fern), also from Japan, is similar but smaller, with stiff fronds to 20 in. (50 cm) long; in spring its fronds are a pretty yellow-green, turning dull green later, not as attractive as the glossy green fronds of *P. polyblepharum*. Hardy to zone 7.

Polystichum setiferum, hedge fern, English hedge fern, soft shield fern. Europe.

LS to FS; fronds to 4 ft. (1.2 m), produced on thick stalks covered with brown scales, arching outward, forming vase-shaped clumps; leaves compound, leathery, dark green, oblong lance-shaped, 18–36 in. (45–90 cm) long and 6–10 in. (15–25 cm) wide; leaflets 24–48 pairs, mostly alternate, oblong lance-shaped, to 4 in. (10 cm) long; subleaflets stalked, oblong to oval, angled away from the midrib, spiny-toothed and -tipped; spore cases (sori) round, in 2 rows near midrib. This popular fern is not as hardy as the Japanese species of *Polystichum*. Hardy to zone 7 in sheltered areas, 6 with protection. A multitude of cultivars are available, including some exceptionally attractive variants. For detailed listings, consult a fern specialist's catalog.

Divisilobum Group, fronds finely divided and each subleaflet further divided into sub-subleaflets (3-pinnate), creating a delicate, filigreed pattern of narrowed, leathery segments, much finer than the excellent type.

'Lineare' ('Confluens'), very narrow leaves, leaflets at base missing.

Multilobum Group, fronds finely divided and 3-pinnate, similar to the cultivars in the Divisilobum Group but not narrowed or leathery.

Plumosodivisilobum Group, fronds more finely divided and overlapping at the base; each sub-subleaflet is further divided (4-pinnate) toward the

base, while the segments toward the tip are narrowed, creating an ethereal, feathery appearance of great daintiness.

'Plumosum Bevis' ('Pulcherrimum Bevis', *Polystichum aculeatum* 'Pulcherrimum'), very narrow frond subsegments curving gracefully toward the tip. This very popular English cultivar appears to be sterile and must be propagated vegetatively.

Polystichum tsussimense, dwarf holly fern, Korean rock fern, narrow holly fern, Tsushima fern. Korea, Japan, Tsushima Island.

LS to FS; fronds to 15 in. (38 cm) long and 5 in. (13 cm) wide, arching outward, forming vase-shaped clumps; leaves compound, leathery, dark green, oblong lance-shaped. One of the smallest species but not truly dwarf. Very similar in appearance and detail to *Polystichum acrostichoides* and particularly suited for smaller gardens; in spring its croziers are equally pretty. Hardy to zone 7, 6 with protection.

Primula

I like the color yellow—it fits nicely into a shady garden. One of the most splendid sights I ever saw was the golden yellow primroses in the Asian collection garden of the University of British Columbia. Combined with hostas and other bold Asian foliage plants, the yellow flowers of **Primula prolifera**, adrift in a sea of green foliage, were a beautiful sight in a shaded corner along a watercourse. What attracted me to these showy plants was that there is an almost total absence of such wonders in gardens with hot, dry summers. I have seen *P. japonica* in some southern gardens, usually planted in colonies along the banks of a pond or a stream. This preference for boggy soils makes primulas difficult to mix with perennials that prefer a moist but well-drained site. But I write for gardeners in all types of climates, relying on reports from all over and on the collective wisdom of experts.

Primroses need tender, loving, perpetual care, with the emphasis on perpetual. Many plantings do not succeed in the Southeast (or even in northern and western gardens) because gardeners forget to divide and replant at regular intervals (every two years or even annually) to keep them vigorous. Besides being time-consuming, this keeps the clumps from attaining a large size, and thus the true glory of a drift of primroses escapes many gardeners. Primroses are sometimes considered bedding plants, since one has to dig them up frequently anyhow; in the South, they are planted for late-winter and early-spring bloom and then replaced by summer annuals.

Obviously, there are areas in the world so agreeable that primroses can become weeds in gardens. The western states of North America have such spots. In other northern areas, where the climate is favorable in summer but frigid in winter, the loss of insulating snow cover in late winter means plants are lost to late, hard freezes, as my mother found out in southern Michigan. She liked to fuss with plants, and primroses were among those she fretted over. She watered, divided, and replanted, and her *Primeln*, as she called them, were beautiful. Like her, many gardeners with cool summers and deep, moist soils successfully plant primroses in the shady woodland. Here, *P. sieboldii* frequently gets caught by late freezes—and follows the loss of its flowers by a disappearing act of the foliage when the first hot days arrive.

Consistently moist soil seems to be the main ingredient for successful cultivation of primroses. Even with the best of light, moist soils, the top layer may dry up during droughts, and the shallow-rooted primroses suffer. Even the "easiest" species—including **Primula veris** (cowslip), **P. vulgaris** (common primrose), and *P. sieboldii*—go summer-dormant if water levels are not sufficient. Some species actually prefer heavier soils with clay content; they do not dry out as rapidly. To maintain constantly moist soils, plant primroses along the boggy banks of water features; under these circumstances they do relatively well even in hot, dry summers.

In short, primroses do not provide the lasting foliage so vital in a natural shady garden. Their flowers are dazzling but ephemeral. They require considerable attention from gardeners. I grow all manner of difficult plants—no others are as exasperating and demanding to keep. Still, many experienced gardeners love these plants and would not be without them.

Pteridium

In 1984 I visited Sweden to see the town of Uppsala, where Linnaeus, the father of modern systematic botany, was educated, taught, and later died, in the year 1778. During my stay, on a trip to one of the magnificent forests of northern Sweden, I encountered a huge stand of bracken fern stretching as far as the eye could see. Upon my return home I obtained a piece of *Pteridium aquilinum* and planted it in my fern glen—and so began my love-hate relationship with this regal fern. I loved its branched stems, rising to a stately height, but I hated its invasiveness. Having found my light, fertile woodland soil much to its liking, bracken fern spread into adjacent wildflower beds after just one season. Neither wildflowers nor smaller ferns stood a chance against its aggressiveness. Like submarines, bracken fern rhizomes run fast and deep, ranging as far as 20 ft. (6 m) afield and 10 ft. (3 m) into the ground. Mine had grown 18 in. (45 cm) deep into undisturbed Georgia red clay, and in the end, herbicides were the only solution. The fern glen and a part of a wildflower bed had to be completely rebuilt.

All this raises an obvious question: should such an aggressive fern be included in gardens? *Pteridium aquilinum* is a magnificent fern, and, if carefully placed and watched, it will make a significant contribution to the natural garden. Those with small areas to cultivate can use bracken fern in containers. Planted in the ground in larger woodland areas, it quickly covers a large area with tall, stately fronds and needs constant watching. From time to time, a friend of mine simply removes the fronds around the periphery of the planting and that seems to contain the colony. I still have a bracken fern tucked away in a large container, sunk into the ground. The bottom of the large pot has a small hole with a drain pipe running to an observable position. Every year I repot the fern, removing unwanted rhizomes. The potting soil mix is coarse and fast-draining. With these precautions, a small representation of unruly bracken fern can be enjoyed in a natural garden with informal plantings.

In the hot South, bracken keeps its bright green color into early autumn, and it should do fine in zone 8 as long as moisture is maintained. Further north, it is hardy well into zone 4. Bracken is killed by first frost. Site in a protected area or among shrubs, as strong winds can break the tall stems. A very common fern, bracken occurs in both tropical and temperate zones. This wide distribution has led to the evolution of different local variants. Crested cultivars are offered, but I consider them mere curiosities. The generic name is from the

Greek *pteris* (= fern). The genus is classified in the Dennstaedtiaceae.

Bracken is tolerant of deep shade but stands up to considerable sun if grown in constantly moist soil. It does best in a light, well-draining woodland soil, rich in organic matter. Both acid and alkaline soils are tolerated. Do not plant bracken out in the woodland near small wildflowers and other companions; unless a large, open area away from such small neighbors is available, the fern should be confined to containers.

Propagate by dividing the creeping rhizome in autumn after the fronds have dropped or in very early spring. Propagation by spores is possible, but the spreading habit of the ferns gives plenty of increase, so sowing spores is not necessary for the average gardener.

Diseases, mollusks, and insects do not seem to bother bracken ferns.

Pteridium aquilinium, bracken, bracken fern, brake, pasture brake. Cosmopolitan in the northern hemisphere, North America, and Eurasia, Malaysia, Australasia.

Some sun, LS to FS; fronds to 4 ft. (1.2 m) tall, produced tightly in rows along a widely and deeply creeping rhizome, stalks green, smooth, later turning dark brown, erect, leaning with age; leaves 36 in. (90 cm) wide and long, bright green, compound, usually divided into 3 equal subleaves, triangular in shape and composed of 12–20 tapered, variable, nearly opposite leaflets (pinnae), the lower ones winged at the stem, pointed at top, veins forked; spore cases (sori) in lines near the margin; plant herbaceous, rhizomatous, widely creeping, eventually forming invasive colonies. This strong fern has a majestic prominence and much appeal but has no place in small gardens unless confined to a container.

Pulmonaria

A doctrine of signatures, advanced by a 14th-century German herbalist, held that the outward appearance of plants indicated their predestined use as herbal medicines. Thus, the spotted leaves of *Pulmonaria*, which resembled a diseased lung, were used to treat lung ailments. This gave rise to the ancient German name for this plant, *Lungenkraut*, which in turn became the Old English *lungenwyrt*,

followed later by *lungwort*. *Wyrt* or *wort* in English or *wurz* (= root) or *kraut* in German are very old names used for plants whose parts were used medicinally. Linnaeus gave *Lungenkraut* its scientific name, *Pulmonaria officinalis*.

Pulmonaria officinalis (common lungwort) is endemic to Europe, where it is also called Jerusalem cowslip (Jerusalem is often used in common plant names to signify a variant of a typical and more well-known plant; cowslip relates to its occurrence in meadows, and indeed it is more sun-tolerant than other species). Other *Pulmonaria* species occur in eastern Asia. The generic name is from the Latin *pulmonarius* (= beneficial to the lung), a reference to its alleged efficacy against lung diseases. The genus is classified in the Boraginaceae. The placement of some species is in question. *Pulmonaria montana* is placed in synonymy with *P. rubra* by some authors; others consider it synonymous to *P. mollis*. Based on the color of flowers, which is important to gardeners, I maintain the species status of *P. rubra*. In commerce all three names are used interchangeably, so be wary when ordering.

In gardens pulmonarias are low-maintenance groundcover and specimen plants, combining well with astilbes, hostas, ferns, and taller wildflowers, like Solomon's seals. Many cultivars are available, most with attractively spotted stem leaves that usually appear after flowering. The flowers appear very early, here in late March, later further north. Some flowers emerge red or pink then turn blue later. The bees know when pulmonarias are in bloom because they come out of their hives on warm, late-winter days to visit the nectaries. Where winters are mild, some species described as deciduous are semi-evergreen, but by the time new leaves appear, the old leaves are usually unattractive and are best removed. Many gardeners cut their pulmonarias to the ground right after flowering, which prevents unwanted seeding, reduces mildew, and makes the clumps more attractive by showing new leaves only. In areas where the soil freezes, the roots are reliably hardy to zone 4, but some species are much more hardy, as noted in the descriptions. Heat tolerance is more limiting, however, and in southern gardens they should be located in medium to full shade. Given shade, most will succeed well into zone 8. Moist, but not overly so, soil is ideal. Drainage is more important: saturated soils cause root rot, as does an excessively wet winter. I have all pulmonarias planted in elevated beds, with very coarse sand and pine bark pellets added to the soil mix. Optimum pH is 5 to 7. They are long-lived plants with striking, variegated foliage that lasts into winter as long as supplemental moisture is provided during the hot, dry days of summer.

Propagate by division immediately after flowering or in late autumn. Seed can be sown in the ground, barely covered, or in containers in spring after warm weather arrives.

Large slugs and snails can damage young leaf growth. Powdery mildew is reported but not seen here.

The species attributions of cultivars are conditional and based on recorded information and morphological features; many have been connected with several species. Many lungwort cultivars look similar, and some plants offered may not be true to name. Practically all pulmonaria flowers start out a little red then turn blue, so, as with hostas, it is the leaf sizes, shapes, and patterns that determine which is what. Experts on both sides of the Atlantic have tried to sort things out, but the variability of leaf variegation patterns makes the task difficult.

Pulmonaria angustifolia, blue lungwort, blue cowslip, cowslip lungwort. Northern and central Europe east to the Caucasus.

MS to FS; flowers small, funnel-shaped, red in bud, opening to bright sky-blue, sepals 5, petals 5, in forked clusters on flowerstalks 9–12 in. (23–30 cm) tall; March–May; plant deciduous, mound-forming, slowly creeping rhizome; leaves in a basal rosette, on stalks, bristly, medium to dark green, unspotted, to 16 in. (40 cm) long and 2 in. (5 cm) wide, elongated lance-shaped; stem leaves short-stalked, alternate, smaller. The best species for northern gardens. Hardy to zone 3 with southern limit to the colder parts of zone 7.

'Alba' (f. *alba* of gardens), flowers white; leaves dark green; to 10 in. (25 cm).

'Azurea' (subsp. *azurea*), flowers sky-blue; leaves dark green; to 10 in. (25 cm).

'Beth's Blue', flowers bright blue; leaves medium green, faintly mottled.

'Blaues Meer' ('Blue Sea'), flowers large, gentian-blue.

'Johnson's Blue', flowers deep blue; leaves dark green, small; to 8 in. (20 cm).

'Mawson's Blue' ('Mawson's Variety'), flowers pale blue; leaves dark green, small; to 6 in. (15 cm).

'Munstead Blue', flowers very early, clear blue; leaves dark green, smaller; to 6 in. (15 cm).

'Rubra', flowers early, light red; to 10 in. (25 cm).

'Variegata', flowers blue; leaves variegated with grayish white.

Pulmonaria longifolia, longleaf lungwort, long-leaved lungwort, spotted dog. Western Europe north to the British Isles and east to Sweden.

MS to FS; flowers small, funnel-shaped, violet to purplish, sepals 5, petals 5, in tight clusters on flowerstalks to 12 in. (30 cm); April–May; plant deciduous, mound-forming, slowly creeping rhizome; leaves in a basal rosette, on stalks, bristly and glandular, green spotted with grayish to silvery white, rarely all green, to 18 in. (45 cm) long and 2.5 in. (6 cm) wide, lance-shaped; stem leaves short-stalked, alternate, smaller. Hardy in zones 5 to 8. **Subspecies *cevennensis*** from the Cévennes mountains in France has long, attractively white-spotted leaves with bright blue flowers.

'Bertram Anderson', flowers bright blue; leaves medium green, marked strongly with white.

'Boughton', flowers pale blue, floriferous; leaves green.

'Dordogne', flowers blue; leaves almost completely white, with a thin, white-spotted green margin.

'Lewis Palmer' ('Highdown'), flowers pale blue faintly tinged pink, floriferous; leaves green, vaguely spotted with white; to 14 in. (35 cm).

'Little Star', flowers cobalt-blue, lasting; leaves green spotted with silvery white all over.

'Mary Mottram', flowers bluish; leaves overlaid with silvery white all over, showing a faint green undertone, margin narrowly green.

'Merlin', flowers pale blue, small; leaves white spotted with midrib green.

'Mournful Purple' ('Mournful Widow', 'Mourning Widow'), flowers purple; leaves green, faintly spotted with white.

'Patrick Bates', flowers darkish mauve; leaves distinctly spotted with greenish white.

'Roy Davidson', flowers pale blue to blue, small; leaves densely spotted with white with green midrib and margin.

'Valerie Finnis', flowers pale blue, floriferous; leaves green.

'White Leaf', flowers bluish; leaves overlaid with silvery white all over, showing a faint green undertone, margin narrowly green.

Pulmonaria mollis, soft lungwort. Central Europe, Netherlands, northern France south into the mountains of southern Germany and Switzerland.

MS to FS; flowers small, funnel-shaped, usually pink-tinged at first turning bright blue, sepals 5, petals 5, in clusters on flowerstalks to 15 in. (38 cm); April–May; plant deciduous, mound-forming, creeping rhizome; leaves in a basal rosette, on stalks, softly hairy, medium dull green, unspotted, puckered with darker veins, to 18 in. (45 cm) long and 5 in. (13 cm) wide, elongated elliptic; stem leaves short-stalked, alternate, smaller. I noticed the bright blue, early flowers of this species on a visit to the Bavarian mountains. Some might consider the leaves plain, but I like their velvety appearance and soft green color without the spotting of the common lungwort.

Pulmonaria officinalis, common lungwort, Jerusalem cowslip, soldiers and sailors, spotted dog, virgin's tears. Northern and central Europe, southern Sweden to the Netherlands, Germany south to northern Italy and east into the Balkans.

Some sun, LS to FS; flowers small, funnel-shaped, pink in bud, opening to blue, sepals 5, petals 5, in forked clusters on flowerstalks 9–12 in. (23–30 cm) tall; March–May; plant evergreen, open clump-forming, slowly creeping rhizome; leaves in a basal rosette, on stalks, bristly, medium grayish green, irregularly spotted, streaked, splashed, or mottled with greenish white or dull, leaden white, to 6 in. (15 cm) long and 4 in. (10 cm) wide, oval to elliptic; stem leaves short-stalked, alternate, smaller. This is the ubiquitous, extremely variable lungwort from Europe. Variety *immaculata*, with unspotted leaves, is seldom offered. *Pulmonaria obscura* (obscure lungwort) found in southern England is very similar and may be the British representative of *P. officinalis*. Hardy to zone 5, heat-tolerant to zone 8.

'Alba', flowers white. An older cultivar, still available.

'Bowles' Blue', flowers small, blue to lilac-blue.

'Cambridge Blue' ('Cambridge'), flowers pink opening to light blue, floriferous; leaves mottled white, heart-shaped at base; to 12 in. (30 cm).

'Sissinghurst White' (*P. saccharata* 'Sissinghurst White'), flowers pale pink opening to pure white; leaves large, to 20 in. (25 cm), dark green, densely spotted with white.

'White Wings', flowers white with pink centers; leaves densely speckled with white.

Pulmonaria rubra, red lungwort. Southeastern Europe, Carpathian and Balkan mountains.

MS to FS; flowers small, funnel-shaped, salmon-red to brick-red, sepals 5, petals 5, in open clusters on flowerstalks 12–16 in. (30–40 cm) tall; March–May, some cultivars January–February; plant evergreen, clump-forming, slowly creeping rhizome; leaves in a basal rosette, on stalks, densely hairy with velvety texture, medium to dark green, unspotted, to 12 in. (40 cm) long and 4 in. (10 cm) wide, elliptic; stem leaves short-stalked, alternate, smaller. The only species with red flowers; some forms reach only a pale red, but a few deep red cultivars are available.

'Albocorollata' (var. *alba*, var. *albocorollata*, 'Alba'), flowers white.

'Ann', flowers pale red with lighter streakings; leaves bright medium green.

'Barfield Pink', flowers pink with white veining and margin, early.

'Barfield Ruby', flowers larger, carmine to coral-red; leaves medium green.

'Berries and Cream', flowers raspberry-red; leaves silvery white with a greenish undertone, dark green midrib and margin.

'Beth's Pink', flowers deep coral to deep pink; leaves broader, mottled white.

'Bowles' Red', flowers brick-red, very early; leaves lime-green with few indistinct spots.

'Cleeton Red', flowers a deep red.

'David Ward', flowers coral-red; leaves wide, mint-green with wavy, creamy white margin.

'Diana Chappell', flowers deep pink; leaves broader, mottled white.

'Raspberry Splash', flowers raspberry-red shading to purplish; leaves basal but very upright, densely spotted silvery white.

'Redstart', flowers coral-red, very early; leaves medium lime-green, barely spotted.

Pulmonaria saccharata, Bethlehem sage. Western and southern Europe, southwestern France, Apennines, central Italy.

Some sun, LS to FS; flowers small, funnel-shaped, rose-red opening to bluish, sepals 5, petals 5, in loose clusters on flowerstalks 9–12 in. (23–30 cm) tall; March–May; plant evergreen, clump-forming, slowly creeping rhizome; leaves in a basal rosette, on stalks, bristly and hairy, medium grayish green to green, spotted or mottled with bright, silvery white, to 10 in. (25 cm) long and 4 in. (10 cm) wide, elliptic, narrowing toward the leafstalk, pointed; stem leaves short-stalked or on the stem, alternate, almost the same size as basal leaves. The favored lungwort among gardeners, long cultivated and hardy to zone 4, heat-tolerant to zone 8 if kept moist.

'Alba', flowers large, pure white; leaves variegated silvery white; to 12 in. (30 cm)

'Argentea', Argentea Group, flowers red turning bluish; leaves almost entirely silvery white; to 12 in. (30 cm).

Argentea Group, selected cultivars with much silvery white in the leaves; variegation is variable; flowers red turning bluish.

'Argentifolia', Argentea Group, leaves mostly silvery white.

'Bielefeld', flowers pink; leaves variegated silvery white.

'Dora Bielefeld', flowers clear pink; leaves light lime-green, with some silvery white spots.

'Frühlingshimmel' ('Spring Sky'), flowers large, open, strong light blue; leaves grayish green, vaguely mottled. 'Blauhimmel' ('Blue Sky') and 'Spring Beauty' are virtually identical.

'Leopard', flowers red shading to pink; leaves spotted silvery white.

'Mies Stam', flowers light carmine-red, tinted lilac, floriferous; leaves spotted silvery white.

'Mrs. Kittle', flowers pale blue; leaves with green midrib, more white toward center and a white-spotted green margin.

'Mrs. Moon', flowers lilac, suffused red; leaves profusely spotted with silvery white.

'Pierre's Pure Pink', flowers pure light pink; leaves spotted silvery white all over.

'Pink Dawn', flowers pink turning violet; leaves spotted silvery white.

'Reginald Kaye', flowers rose-pink in bud, opening to violet; leaves with large, silvery white spots over most of the leaves, margin green with white speckles; to 12 in. (30 cm) tall.

'Sissinghurst White'. See *Pulmonaria officinalis* 'Sissinghurst White'

'Tim's Silver', flowers medium blue; leaves mostly silvery white with green picot margin.

Pulmonaria vallarsae. Southern Europe, Italy.

MS to FS; flowers funnel-shaped, violet turning purple, sepals 5, petals 5, in tight clusters on flowerstalks 6–12 in. (15–30 cm) tall; March–May; plant deciduous, clump-forming, slowly creeping rhizome; leaves in a basal rosette, narrowing abruptly to the leafstalk, densely hairy and shiny dark green, spotted with lighter whitish green or white, rarely all green or all silvery white, to 20 in. (50 cm) long and 5 in. (13 cm) wide, elliptic; stem leaves short-stalked, alternate, smaller. Hardy to zone 6 with southern limit to zone 8. The selection 'Margery Fish' has coral-red to reddish violet flowers, turning to intense violet; its leaves, to 6 in. (15 cm) long, are silvery white all over, sometimes faintly and densely spotted a paler greenish at the midrib and margin, with a bright green undertone. Plant to 12 in. (30 cm) tall. Popular but not as hardy as other pulmonarias, to zone 6. Does well in southern gardens.

Pulmonaria cultivars

Pulmonaria species hybridize freely in gardens; these cultivars may be selections of species or hybrids with two or more species involved. All are hardy to zone 5, 4 with protection, and suitable into zone 8 if soil moisture is maintained. Plant in medium to full shade.

'Apple Frost', flowers rose-red in bud, opening to blue; leaves apple-green with silvery white overlay.

'Benediction', flowers blue, floriferous; leaves dark green with some silvery white spots; clumps leafy.

'Beth Chatto', flowers dark blue; leaves heavily spotted with white.

'Blue Ensign', flowers very large, open, deep blue-violet; leaves broad, dark green, unspotted.

'British Sterling', flowers with magenta buds opening to blue; leaves heavily silvery in center with broad green margin.

'Coral Springs', flowers coral-red, floriferous; leaves long, lance-shaped, spotted with grayish white.

'DeVroomen's Pride', flowers bluish; leaves viridescent, silvery white with a thin green margin, turning all green.

'Excalibur' ('Excaliber'), flowers violet-blue, turning pinkish, lasting; leaves elliptic, to 10 in. (25 cm) long, silvery white with a green midrib and thin dark green margin.

'Golden Haze', flowers light blue, early; leaves green with a golden yellow, irregular margin and a yellowish cast all over.

'Majeste' ('Majesty'), flowers reddish in bud, turning blue; leaves shiny silvery white with a very pale greenish undertone.

'Milky Way', flowers red in bud, opening to dark blue, early; leaves heavily spotted with silvery white, vigorous.

'Regal Ruffles', flowers purplish violet, ruffled petals; leaves heavily spotted with silvery white.

'Silver Streamers', flowers light blue with a pink cast; leaves shiny silvery white with a deeply ruffled margin.

'Spilled Milk', flowers rose-pink, turning blue; leaves broad, first with a purplish green cast, turning medium green with a silvery white overlay.

'Trevi Fountain', flowers cobalt-blue with a pinkish cast, long-lasting; leaves speckled with silvery white.

'Victorian Brooch', flowers large, violet with a pinkish cast, long-lasting; leaves speckled with silvery white.

'Weetwood Blue', flowers a clear blue.

Ranunculus

In the early 1950s, my formative years as a gardener, a much older and truly wise friend told me that buttercups are weeds, but being a brash upstart, I did not listen. Besides, my wife, Hildegarde, liked the little beauties with wide-open, bright yellow flowers she had picked in her childhood days. So I dug up a clump from a field of thousands along a country road in Tennessee. The one I planted in my freshly tilled and still sunny, bare border was *Ranunculus acris*, the common European buttercup that has naturalized throughout North America. After a few seasons I had a nice, yellow plot in early spring, and Hildegarde had flowers to brighten the kitchen table. In those days we still had a large patch of grass for our five children to romp on. The weed found this young lawn a wonderful place to spread out in, and I did not have the heart to rein it in. Only the lawn mower kept it from taking over.

The woodland buttercups are the only ones in the genus that grow well under shady conditions. This leaves the shade gardener with nothing but weeds, albeit some exquisitely beautiful ones. In very large gardens with open, lightly shaded areas, buttercups make fine groundcovers, but even there they can get out of hand. Some reference volumes characterize certain species as "not as invasive" or "much less invasive." To me that means invasive, just not as quick at it. Woodland buttercups should not be planted in smaller gardens: they may be "not as invasive," but they are weeds that take over, nevertheless. Among these more or less invasive species are *Ranunculus acris*, the one I wish I had not planted, *R. ficaria* (lesser celandine, figwort), and *R. repens* (creeping buttercup), a fast-moving, beautiful weed.

If suburban gardeners must plant an alien woodland buttercup, they should at least select a cultivar that has attractive leaves: ***Ranunculus repens* 'Buttered Popcorn'** ('Susan's Song'). This yellow variegated buttercup has leaves that are attractive enough for gardeners to tolerate its spreading habit, which is prodigious. The leaves have a yellow center surrounded by a darker green border along the serrated, deeply lobed leaf margin. This stoloniferous cultivar makes a bright groundcover in woodland shade. The solitary yellow flowers appear in spring and from time to time in late autumn and winter. In areas of mild winters, the leaves are evergreen. This selection should not be planted where its vigorous spreading habit will cause problems. Watch closely to see that it does not spread beyond your garden into surrounding natural areas.

Ranzania

Ranzania japonica is slowly entering Western gardens. A close relative of *Podophyllum*, it is the only species in the monotypic genus *Ranzania*, whose name honors the father of Japanese botany, Ono Ranzan. I first saw a specimen at Kew Gardens and later in the Asian collection garden of the University of British Columbia. The leaflets appeared superficially similar to those on my mature clumps of *Saruma henryi*, but the plant grows more like large epimediums, to which it is related; its drooping, cup-shaped mauve flowers are larger than those of epimediums, as are its long-lasting, textured, bright green leaflets. It promises to be an excellent addition, brightening shady gardens with white berries in autumn. *Ranzania* is classified in the Berberidaceae.

This Asian species is well adapted to shady mountain forests, and its creeping rhizomes form small colonies in time. It prefers a woodland soil with plenty of organic matter, good tilth, and good water-holding capacity. Optimum pH is 5.5 to 6. Hardy to zone 7. Site in a sheltered position; it emerges relatively early in spring, and its flowers appear on new growth, before the leaves expand, making it vulnerable to late freezes.

Propagate by dividing the rhizome in very early spring before growth starts, making certain that each piece has a growth bud. Sowing seed is tedious and requires a cold frame, but with patience germination is usually successful. Seedlings take several years to flower.

Slugs and snails can damage young growth emerging in spring.

Ranzania japonica. Southern Japan, Kyushu.

LS to FS; flowers solitary, sometimes in a bundle of 2–5, sepals 6, petal-like, 0.6 in. (1.5 cm) long, rosy lilac, petals tiny, recurving around stamens, stamens 6, on long stems to 4 in. (10 cm) at flowering, elongating to 12 in. (30 cm) in fruit, green; May–June; plant rhizomatous, spreading; leaves expanding after flowering, 2, sometimes 3, each with 3 stalked leaflets, each having 3 lobes, 3–5 in. (8–13 cm) long, rounded, heart-shaped at the base, bright green above, glaucous beneath; fruit a white berry when ripe. Garden experience with this species is limited. At Kew it is grown in the alpine house, and at the University of British Columbia Asian collection garden, it is in a sheltered site. It has been successfully cultivated near the northern coast of Long Island Sound in southern New York (zone 6b), so may be hardy to zone 6 with protection.

Rheum

I will never forget how delicious Mother's rhubarb pie was. Hers had just the right balance of sweet and sour. Back then, I greatly admired *Rhabarber*, as Mother called it, for what it became in a baking dish, but later I appreciated it as an extremely ornamental plant. The difference between the rhubarb grown for food and its ornamental cousins is just that: the former makes great pies and the latter taste terrible but look great in gardens. On a trip to southern England, I saw unbelievable specimens of both ornamental rhubarbs and gunnera; English gardeners, no matter how small their plot might be, always seem to find room for at least one specimen of each. Rhubarb looks much like a smaller gunnera, which is too tender for most northern gardens; in colder climates, rhubarb is frequently seen providing the same tropical look.

Like Mother's *Rhabarber*, most ornamental rhubarbs are sun-loving plants, but some species will grow in light to woodland shade. Very deep soil of at least 24 in. (60 cm) and constant, copious moisture are critical. Even a short period in dry soil leads to early dormancy—and a loss of the gorgeous sight produced by good cultivation. Unfortunately, in southern gardens these ornamental species are a bit difficult. They do not like the heat and cannot stand up to drought, but planted in considerable shade and with a constant supply of water, they will succeed. I have to admit, here they never attain the glorious stature seen in specimens grown in England or in North America further north or on the West Coast. And shade does reduce the beautiful red and purple shading seen in the leaves.

Rheum is the classic Greek name for rhubarb. The genus is classified in the buckwheat family, Polygonaceae.

Propagate by dividing the rhizome in very early spring. Sow seed in pots in a cold frame in early autumn.

Large slugs and snails can damage young growth. Rust occasionally strikes, and southern blight, in which the rhizome rots, is prevalent in warmer regions.

Rheum acuminatum, Sikkim rhubarb. Himalayas, Nepal to southeastern Tibet.

Morning sun, LS to WS; flowers tiny, star-shaped, rose-red to deep pink, sometimes deep red to maroon, in loose clusters on tall, erect, branched flowerstalk to 36 in. (90 cm), often with several stalks per plant; May–July; plant clump-forming; leaves large, to 12 in. (30 cm) long and 10 in. (25 cm) wide, glossy dark green above, purplish green underneath with lighter, prominent veins, heart-shaped to triangular, on long, stout, bright red leafstalks; fruit is a bright red. An ornamental rhubarb of a size suitable for smaller gardens. Its red spring color adds much early in the season, and, given plenty of moisture, it keeps contributing until late autumn. Can be adapted to woodland shade, but some morning sun is helpful to deepen the plant's colors. Hardy to zone 6.

Rheum palmatum, Chinese rhubarb. Northwestern China.

Morning sun, LS to WS; flowers very small, star-shaped, rose-red to deep red, sometimes greenish white, in loose clusters on tall, erect, branched flowerstalk to 6 ft. (1.8 m), with several stalks per plant; May–July; plant clump-forming; leaves very large, to 36 in. (90 cm) long, glossy dark green above, purplish red to red underneath with heavy veining and a cover fine hairs, roundish in outline but deeply lobed, with 4–9 coarsely toothed, incised lobes, borne on long, stout leafstalks; fruit is a bright red. Same garden benefits as *Rheum acuminatum*. Requires deep excavation of the soil to make it feel at home. Not every garden will have the space required to show this giant rhubarb off. Judging by some of the magnificent specimens seen in England, it is well worth its place in the garden if enough area can be made available. I have grown **var. *tanguticum*** for several years near a modest stream. It is puny compared to English specimens but nevertheless adds much interest and color to the streamside. Actually, I like it being smaller, because a full-sized rheum would be overpowering. Hardy to zone 5.

'Atrosanguineum' ('Atropurpureum'), flowers pinkish; leaves crimson-red when young, fading to dark green above, remaining purplish green underneath.

'Bowles' Crimson', flowers red; leaves a bright red beneath; fruit red.

'Hadspen Crimson', flowers red, giant stalks to 15 ft. (5 m); leaves huge, to 40 in. (1 m). I observed this superb cultivar, one of the most outstanding ornamental rhubarbs in cultivation, at Hadspen House in 1988. In shade it will not attain these proportions.

'Irish Bronze', flowers pink; leaves with a reddish bronze tint.

'Red Select', flowers deep red; leaves with a red color.

'Rubrum', flowers red; leaves tinted with maroon-red.

Rodgersia

Superb foliage plants for the shady garden, rodgersias were first discovered on a U.S. expedition to Japan led by Admiral John Rodgers in the mid-1800s (the plant he collected as *Rodgersia japonica* is now *R. podophylla*). An immediate garden success, they have been cultivated ever since, a recognition well deserved. Rodgersias are by far the most majestic of all plants in the Saxifragaceae. Their bold, exquisitely textured leaves are outdone only by their tall flower spikes, which bear clouds of white flowers. Some cultivars have red flowers, but to me the white flowers are much more eye-catching in the myriad greens of a shady garden.

In gardens rodgersias are long-lived specimen plants that require careful placement. They must be given plenty of room to expand, which they do slowly and consistently, eventually making dramatic accent plants or groups. They require little maintenance—a definite advantage. I rarely divide my rodgersias and then only for increase. And rodgersias are suitable at least into zone 5, with some species doing well in zone 4. Other outstanding plants give the much sought after tropical look, but most of these are not very hardy and some are difficult to maintain. Rodgersias tolerate full sun in the North and the hot temperatures of southern gardens if planted in constantly moist, even wet, boggy soil. Given such moisture and a lot of shade, they succeed well into zone 8 if given considerable shade. Mine have succeeded even with some southern sun on their leaves, but they are planted in an artificial bog. Provide a deep soil bed for the ranging, heavy rhizomes, and fertilize in spring, as plants are heavy feeders. Optimum pH is 5 to 6.5.

Site in a sheltered spot: the large leaves of rodgersias act like sails, and the tall leaf stems can break in wind gusts. Mine are in a grouping together with a large (contained) clump of *Petasites japonicus* sheltered by several Kurume azaleas in a small glen. Rodgersias are large plants and can easily overshadow smaller companions. Their leaf canopy is open enough to let its cousin, the shade-tolerant *Saxifraga veitchiana*, be used as a ground-covering underplanting. Rodgersias also make extremely handsome companions to very large chartreuse hostas, like *Hosta* 'Sum and Substance', and the imposing dark green *Dryopteris erythrosora*.

Rodgersias provide intense color during autumn when the leaves turn reddish, orange, and sometimes carmine-red, mixing wonderfully with the autumn color of hostas and Japanese maples.

Rodgersia species are variable, with leaves ranging in tone from reddish purple to deep bronze; these colors develop best in sunny exposures but are seen in shade to some degree. Species planted together in gardens hybridize as merging populations do in the wild (some plants in commerce are in fact interspecific hybrids), and seed-raised plants of garden origin may not be true to name if several species are planted together. True or not, they eventually grow into showy garden hybrids. Cultivars selected on the basis of leaf color vary considerably as well.

Propagate by division immediately after flowering or in late autumn. Seed can be sown in the ground, barely covered, or in containers in spring after warm weather arrives.

Large slugs and snails can damage young leaf growth. Powdery mildew is reported but has not been seen here.

Rodgersia aesculifolia, fingerleaf rodgersia. Western China, Gansu, Hubei, Sichuan.

Sun, LS to FS; flowers white to pale greenish white, small, many, funnel-shaped, sepals 5 becoming larger after fertilization (accrescent), no petals, stamens 10, in dense, forked clusters on flowerstalks 4–6 ft. (1.2–1.8 m) tall; June–July; plant deciduous, mound-forming, slowly creeping rhizomes; leaves palmate, like an outstretched hand, on red-brown stalks below the inflorescence; leaflets 7, sometimes 5 or 9, 4–10 in. (10–25 cm) long, narrowed toward the base but basally overlapping, resembling those of horse chestnut (*Aesculus hippocastanum*), medium to dark green, with deeply impressed, reddish veins, and heavily crinkled, with sharp, occasionally drooping tips irregularly toothed. The dense cover of untidy, reddish brown, woolly hair on the leaf and flowerstalks and both the veins and underside of the toothed leaf margin are identifying features. Some taxonomists consider this species synonymous with *Rodgersia pinnata* while others throw it in with *R. henrici*, which itself is considered *R. pinnata* by some. The plants offered in commerce are also a mixed lot; blame it on nature, who decided to let these magnificent plants hybridize in the wild. If the plant I have

grown for many years under this name turns out to be an imposter, I shall not disown it: its beauty and grandeur have earned it a permanent place in my garden. The selection 'Irish Bronze' (*R. purdomii* 'Irish Bronze') has glossy, bright reddish bronze leaves.

Rodgersia henrici. Southeastern Tibet, northern Burma, western China, Yunnan.

Sun, LS to FS; flowers deep red to reddish purple, small, many, funnel-shaped, sepals 5, not enlarging after fertilization (nonaccrescent), no petals, stamens 10, in dense, forked clusters on flowerstalks 3–5 ft. (0.9–1.5 m) tall; June–July; plant deciduous, mound-forming, slowly creeping rhizomes; leaves on stalks from the stem below the inflorescence, stalks reddish brown; leaflets 5–7, to 12 in. (30 cm) long, not overlapping but emanating from the same point, medium to dark green, with deeply impressed, reddish veins, and heavily crinkled, irregularly toothed. This species (seen in photo of *Hosta* 'Paul's Glory') differs from *Rodgersia aesculifolia* by having red-purple flowers, nonaccrescent sepals, longer and narrower leaves, and a toothed margin that lacks the hairy cover underneath. With such distinguishing features, it is hard to fathom that it has also been linked with and sold as *R. pinnata*. Same garden uses as *R. aesculifolia*.

Rodgersia pinnata, featherleaf rodgersia. Western China, Yunnan, southern Sichuan.

Sun, LS to FS; flowers white, yellowish white, or pink, small, many, funnel-shaped, no petals, sepals 5, stamens 10, in dense, forked clusters on flowerstalks 3–4 ft. (0.9–1.2 m) tall; June–July; plant deciduous, mound-forming, slowly creeping rhizomes; leaves large, to 36 in. (90 cm), on stalks tinged red from the stem below the inflorescence; leaflets 5–9, to 8 in. (20 cm) long, ovate-elliptic, medium to dark green sometimes suffused with reddish bronze, with deeply sunken veins, and crinkled, irregularly toothed. The leaflets are arranged in opposite pairs along the stem (hence the epithet and common name). Frequently the pairs are pseudopinnate (spaced very close together on the stem), like those of *Rodgersia aesculifolia*. The interspecific hybridization of the species in the wild as well as in gardens has distorted the leaf arrangement between pinnate and palmate. Some cultivars may in fact be hybrids with other species.

'Alba', flowers white or yellowish white.

'Elegans', flowers rose-pink to pale pink in dense clusters on a stem to 36 in. (90 cm). A good garden form.

'Purdomii' (*Rodgersia purdomii*; Purdom's rodgersia), white flowers on 36 in. (90 cm) stems; leafstalks and leaflets tinged reddish bronze; leaf arrangement pseudopinnate. Plants I saw in Germany were nearly identical to *R. pinnata*, except with narrower leaflets. Now considered a hybrid.

'Rosea', flowers rose-pink.

'Rubra', flowers deep red.

'Superba', flowers reddish pink to deep pink; leaves and stems suffused with bronze in spring, later dark green. Unfortunately, this widely available form is represented in commerce by uncharacteristic seed-propagated progeny.

Rodgersia podophylla, large fingerleaf rodgersia. Korea, Japan, Hokkaido, northern and central Honshu.

Sun, LS to FS; flowers white, yellowish white, small, many, funnel-shaped, no petals, sepals 5, stamens 10, in dense, forked clusters on flowerstalks 4–7 ft. (1.2–2 m) tall; June–August; plant deciduous, mound-forming, creeping rhizomes, forming large colonies; leaves large, to 16 in. (40 cm), on stalks emerging below the inflorescence; leaflets mostly 5, sometimes to 7, tapering toward base, ovate to triangular with 3–5 deep, jagged lobes at the tip and coarsely toothed at the margin, in spring a glossy reddish bronze, later brownish green and hairy, with deeply sunken veins and intensely crinkled. Easily the best rodgersia for foliage and the first to be introduced in North America. Its truly fingerlike (palmate) leaflets have outstanding texture and color, and the tall spikes of yellowish white flowers are like beacons in the landscape. It has received considerable attention from hybridizers and selectors, yielding the floriferous 'Pagode' (= pagoda; flowers almost pure white, greening later, in pagodalike spikes; leaves bronze, turning bright green), 'Rotlaub' ('Red Leaf'; flowers white; leaves reddish green, turning green), and 'Smaragd' ('Emerald'; white flowers; intense emerald-green leaves).

Rodgersia sambucifolia, featherleaf rodgersia. Western China, Yunnan, southern Sichuan.

Sun, LS to FS; flowers white, usually yellowish white, sometimes pinkish, small, many, funnel-shaped, no petals, sepals 5, stamens 10, in open, forked clusters on flowerstalks 2–4 ft. (0.6–1.2 m) tall, arching at the tip; June–July; plant deciduous, mound-forming, slowly creeping rhizomes; leaves to 30 in. (75 cm), on green stalks, sometimes tinged red below the inflorescence; leaflets 5–11, usually 7, to 8 in. (20 cm) long, ovate-elliptic like those of elderberry (*Sambucus* spp.), medium to dark green, nonglossy, sometimes suffused with reddish bronze, with deeply sunken veins and toothed margin; leaflets pinnate, consistently arranged in wider-spaced opposite pairs along the stem. This smallest of the rodgersias shares habitat with *Rodgersia pinnata*. Highly decorative and an excellent garden plant. The vigorous selection 'Rothaut' ('Red Skin') has whitish flowers and brownish red new leaves, turning dark green.

Rohdea

Some plants are revered with religious fervor in the Far East. One of these is *Rohdea japonica*, the sacred lily. It is particularly held so in Japan, where selected sports have become cherished objects of *koten engei*, the culture of plants in containers. Sacred lily is also grown in gardens, watched over with loving care. Unusually variegated types command huge sums of money, and exhibitions of the greatest rarities are held annually. To possess "the only one in the world" is the goal of many. This has been going on for three centuries, and the culture and admiration of cultivars of this species continues strong.

Rohdea has been known since Thunberg, a pupil of Linnaeus, first described it in his *Flora Japonica* in 1784. The genus was named for German physician and botanist Michael Rohde and is classified in the Convallariaceae. Rohdeas are reliable, evergreen, clump-forming perennials with short, thick rhizomes, usually near soil level. Although rare, during Victorian days, some adventurous people used them as houseplants, and garden books printed in the 1940s characterize them as indoor plants. I have been growing *Rohdea japonica* for over 30 years and find it an excellent subject for the shady garden. In the wild it occurs in southwestern China and in southern Japan, where it is cold enough for it to become deciduous. Hardy to zone 6, 5 with protection. Because of their relatively slow growth rate, rohdeas should be brought indoors in unprotected sites of zone 6, where severe winters may cut down the top growth. Here, I have never given them winter protection, and they have been reliably evergreen with brief dips to 0°F (−18°C). In northern gardens, pot and plunge them during summer and overwinter them as houseplants.

Their tough constitution together with their beautiful, thick leathery leaves make rohdeas ideal for winter gardens, where they make wonderful dark green accents. I have several clumps planted in the company of hellebores and evergreen ferns; the small, greenish white flowers are followed in autumn by big, showy red berries. Rohdeas should not be exposed to full sun but happily endure sun filtered through an open tree canopy. The many variegated forms now available can brighten even the darkest corners of the shady garden; not being agreeable to tissue culture, some still command high prices, but the initial cost is well justified considering the lifetime of pleasure they will give.

Propagate by dividing the rhizome before new growth starts in the spring or in late winter, but remove only new, branching offsets with dormant growth tips. Sow seed in pots in a cold frame.

Plants are relatively disease-free. Slugs and snails do not seem to bother them, but vine weevil larvae will attack the rhizomes.

Rohdea japonica, sacred lily, sacred lily of China, sacred lily of Japan, *omoto* (Jap.). Southeastern China, southern Japan.

LS to FS; flowers small, greenish white, inconspicuous, densely arranged in an elongated cluster near ground level; plant compact, clump-forming, to 18 in. (45 cm) high; leaves in a basal rosette, upright but arching, elongated lance-shaped, dark glossy green arising directly from the rhizome, to 16 in. (40 cm) long and 1–2 in. (2.5–5 cm) wide, midrib deeply keeled, surface pleated with conspicuous parallel veins; fruit large fleshy berries, red, sometimes yellow: The somewhat more tender *Rohdea watanabei* from Taiwan is not be suitable to be planted out in most gardens but could be used in containers everywhere. Over 1000 cultivars of sacred lily, some very rare, have been shown in Japan, mostly at *koten engei* exhibits; many are now offered in commerce under Japanese names. Since the source of the Japanese kanji cannot yet be identified, I have made no attempt to correct them.

'Asian Valley', leaves deeply keeled, dark green with narrow white margin; plant to 10 in. (25 cm) high and 20 in. (50 cm) across.

'Aureostriata', leaves striped with yellow.

'Fuji-no-Yuki' (= snow of Mount Fuji), leaves to 8 in. (20 cm) long and 0.8 in. (2 cm) wide.

'Galle' ('Tyokkwina'; narrow-leaved sacred lily), leaves very narrow, to 18 in. (45 cm) long, 0.8–1 in. (2–1.5 cm) wide; size similar to type (ex U.S. National Arboretum ULNA 39665).

'Ganjaku', leaves deeply keeled, to 6 in. (15 cm) long, striped with thin, creamy white stripes, variable; clump to 6 in. (15 cm) high.

'Godeishu' (= five continents), leaves deeply keeled, to 6 in. (15 cm) long, striped with white stripes that turn whitish yellow, variable; clump more erect than type, to 8 in. (20 cm) high.

'Kin Kirin' (= brocade fiery horse), leaves wavy and not erect but deeply arching, green with broad center and marginal yellow stripes; clump spreading out.

'Marginata', leaves deeply keeled, dark green with narrow white margin; plant to 10 in. (25 cm) high and 20 in. (50 cm) across. An older form of 'Asian Valley'.

'Mure Suzume' (= flock of sparrows), leaves short, with many white stripes, closely spaced toward the margins, variable; plant dwarf, 4–6 in. (10–15 cm) tall and 6 in. (15 cm) wide.

'Striata', leaves dark green striped with white. Similar to but larger than 'Ganjaku'.

'Suncrest', leaves dark green to blackish green, occasional yellowish striping in the leaf blade, variable; clump to 10 in. (25 cm) tall. Distorted leaf tissue forms the highly desired white *ryu* (= dragon) crest in the center of each leaf.

'Washitakakuma', leaves dark green covered with large patches of white, often covering the entire lower portion of the leaf, with a green tip and green streaking into the white part; clump to 18 in. (45 cm) high.

'Yattazu Yan Jaku', leaves dark green blotched with variously sized patches of white; clump to 18 in. (45 cm) high.

Sanguinaria

I do not like plants that evaporate into thin air after a shining moment in spring. Unfortunately, many exquisite native wildflowers belong to this group, but to call *Sanguinaria canadensis* (blood-root) an ephemeral is stretching things a bit. Here it brings great joy in the fleeting days of winter, when its flowers, delicately cradled by the emerging leaves, announce spring. The leaves, after unfolding into a sea of small grayish green umbrellas, carry on for months even in the hot Piedmont of Georgia; a group planted in the full shade of a 30-year-old Japanese fernleaf maple proudly carries its leaves well into the first half of August. For a so-called ephemeral, mid-March to August is not a bad performance. Its individual flowers are short-lived, like most members of the poppy family, but they come one after another for a two-week period in March, an extended period of lovely bloom, during which time they incessantly shed their petals, covering the ground like pristine spring snow. As if shielding themselves from still frosty nights, the flowers close in the evening, opening again in the warming sun of early morning.

Bloodroot was a panacea for American Indians, who used it despite its toxicity to cure just about everything that ails people. Aside from being an insect repellent, a snakebite antidote, a cough medicine, and a rheumatism tonic, the red sap of the roots was used as a dye for making war paint and to stain clothes and baskets. It is a wonder any plants are left. Unlike its Asian cousin *Eomecon chionantha*, *Sanguinaria canadensis* is a well-behaved garden plant, spreading slowly by underground rhizomes; even a small start eventually grows into a sizeable colony. It grows in the wild into the southern reaches of zone 9 and is hardy to zone 3. The genus name comes from the Latin *sanguinarius* (= blood) for its blood-red sap. It is classified in the Papaveraceae.

Bloodroot requires a humus-rich soil with average moisture content and a pH of 5.5 to 7. Even in deep shade it flowers reliably, and the leaves seem to last longer there than in more open areas. Moisture is imperative during spring, but it tolerates considerable dryness later on and during the hot summer when it is dormant. Bloodroot is now protected in some areas and should not be collected in the wild. It can be obtained from propagated stock from several responsible wildflower nurseries or raised from commercial seed.

Propagate by carefully dividing the rhizome after flowering; replant divisions immediately. Sow seed in a cold frame in pots using a commerical seed mix.

Fungal leaf spot is reported, but I have not experienced it.

Sanguinaria canadensis, bloodroot, puccoon root, red puccoon, red Indian paint. Eastern North America, Nebraska and Manitoba east to Nova Scotia, south through New England to Georgia and Florida and west to eastern Texas.

LS to FS; flowers solitary, white, rarely pinkish, open cup-shaped, to 3 in. (8 cm) across, petals 8–12, oval and separate, alternate ones narrower, sepals 2, dropping as the flowers open, stamens many, orange-yellow, on upright flowerstalk to 10 in. (25 cm), leaves curl around the flowerstalk; March–April; plant clump-forming, rhizomatous, slowly spreading, to 8 in. (20 cm) high; leaves basal, heart- to kidney-shaped in outline, 4–10 in. (10–25 cm) long, deeply scalloped with 5–9 rounded lobes, dull bluish green; sap red; fruit a capsule pointed at both ends. The type is variable in leaf form and size. Selections include 'Flore Pleno' ('Multiplex', 'Pleno'), whose longer-lasting, stamenless flowers have petals so numerous as to appear double, and 'Rosea' (unstable flowers, usually pink, sometimes white).

Sasa, Phyllostachys, Pleioblastus, and *Sinarundinaria*

Bamboo plantings usually have full sun shining upon them, and at one time I totally dismissed bamboo for shady gardens. That was before a certain visit to the Asian collection garden of the University of British Columbia, where I saw a huge clump of variegated *Sasa veitchii* growing in considerable shade. Its mass of wide, unbamboolike leaves with whitish margins brightened up a really dark corner near a walkway. This electrifying sight changed my mind about bamboo in shade forever. The genus *Sasa* includes the most shade-tolerant species; *Phyllostachys, Pleioblastus,* and *Sinarundinaria* are other bamboo genera suited for shady conditions.

Shade-tolerance notwithstanding, gardeners should think twice before planting bamboo in the open ground. Years ago I purchased the beautiful golden fishpole bamboo, *Phyllostachys aurea.* At first it clumped up well, but it started running after three seasons, so I constructed an in-ground well of mortared brick, over 40 in. (1 m) in diameter and

24 inches (60 cm) deep, with a thick cement lining on top of a concrete slab. Six years later, the "clump," now 15 ft. (5 m) tall, made a wonderful feature in the garden. Then I noticed new shoots coming up 10 ft. (3 m) from the well. My clump had cracked through the brick and was running as fast as it could. Next followed a two-week travail of searching out all the ranging shoots, breaking up the well, and cutting up the huge root system once confined therein. I then paid a contractor to haul it all off. There may be a landfill somewhere in central Georgia that sports a crown of golden bamboo.

Even the "clumpers" will run, some a lot faster than others. *Sasa pygmea* and **Pleioblastus auricomus**, both dwarf bamboos, are the worst of them all and a most serious menace in gardens. I saw one-half of a very large garden in Ohio overrun by the handsome *P. auricomus*, which has leaves that are beautifully variegated with golden yellow stripes; the root system was so tightly knit, not even a sharpened, narrow spade could cut through it. Mine is safely in a large container, sitting on the bank of a small pond, where it gets some sun during midday. There I can watch it and remove stray runners as they escape through the drain holes. The same goes for *S. veitchii*, a very attractive, shade-tolerant, hardy bamboo for the shady garden; I keep it in an even larger container, atop a stone slab.

Two other widely sold clumping bamboos are *Sinarundinaria murieliae* and *S. nitida*. Both have dense foliage that eventually becomes heavy and imparts a gracefully arching, weeping habit. *Sinarundinaria murieliae* (fountain bamboo, umbrella bamboo) has lighter green stems (culms) and leaves; *S. nitida* has purple stems and darker green leaves. Both eventually grow to a height of 8–12 ft. (2.5–3.6 m), and both bear watching: their rhizomes, although much shorter, nevertheless become rangy in time. In warmer climates I recommend they be confined in large containers, while in areas of cool, short summers they may be committed to the ground. Not as shade-tolerant as *Sasa* species, they do well in the lightly shaded woodland. Hardy to zone 5, 4 with protection. If potted above ground, they require overwintering indoors.

Species of the genus *Sasa*, endemic to eastern Asia, are hardy to zone 6. The generic name is from *zasa*, the Japanese name for this bamboo. The genus is classified in the grass family, Gramineae. *Sasa veitchii* grows in any average garden soil. I have seen it growing in very light as well as very heavy, moist clay soils of average fertility and a pH of 5 to 7. Light to medium shade is tolerated, but some morning sun is appreciated.

Propagate by dividing the creeping rhizome before new growth begins in spring. Include several growing nodes in the cut portion.

Diseases and insect pests are rarely seen.

Sasa veitchii, kuma bamboo grass, *kuma zasa* (Jap.). Japan.

Some sun, LS to FS; flowers inconspicuous; plant rhizomatous, vigorously spreading; stems (culms) slender, to 0.3 in. (0.7 cm) across and 4 ft. (1.2 m) tall, purplish green turning purple later, covered with a glaucous coating of dull white, producing single branches at each node, branches to 40 in. (1 m), each with 4–8 leaves; leaves broadly elliptic with blunt base and tip with short, pointed extension, 7–10 in. (18–25 cm) long, 2–2.5 in. (5–6 cm) wide, conspicuously ribbed and midrib salient, margins hairy, glossy dark green above, dull lighter green beneath, soon developing yellowish white to white margins, some broad, some very narrow, variable from leaf to leaf. In zone 7 this is a rampant grower and requires constant vigilance; further north it may be slightly better behaved but requires watching nevertheless. Best as a subject for a large container; cut back around its perimeter if planted in the ground. The variegation seems to show better in shady gardens.

Sasa tessellata (large-leaved Chinese shade bamboo) is extremely handsome. Its very large leaves—the largest of any hardy bamboo, growing to 24 in. (60 cm) long and 4 in. (10 cm) wide—bestow a vibrant tropical effect to any garden; they are not variegated but beautifully tessellated (they have a prominent mosaiclike veining pattern). Its stems are a pretty yellow with occasional purple blotches, and it grows to a height of 6 ft. (1.8 m). This bamboo is very shade-tolerant but is a rampant grower, particularly in southern gardens with mild winters, where it should be confined in containers. Hardy to zone 6 and, if given much shade, heat-tolerant to zone 9.

Sauromatum

Sauromatum venosum (voodoo lily) was sold as an oddity and coversation plant for many years. The dormant tubers were placed on a shallow container in spring and—one awaited the highly unusual inflorescence. Triggered by warmth, the flower structure rose in just a few days, producing a spathe that quickly peeled back, exposing its pattern of yellow spottily streaked with brownish purple, to reveal a glossy deep purple spadix, showing whitish male flowers at the base. About this time, the flower exuded a nauseating stench. If the plants were grown in an enclosed place, visitors were certain to be driven outdoors, gasping for fresh air. Admiration turned to disgust, and the by then shriveled tubers were quickly thrown out. This was unfortunate, because after the flower dies back, the wonderfully textured, umbrellalike leaf appears, adding a tropical look to the garden. I have grown a group of plants for decades, appreciating the much-divided, large leaves on purple-spotted stalks. Their striking display lasts all summer, until cold temperatures arrive. The leaves of voodoo lilies mix well with ferns, hostas, and astilbes in the shady garden. Avoid siting plants in windswept areas; the large leaves act like sails, and the fleshy leafstalks are easily broken by the twisting action.

Sauromatum is native to tropical Africa and Asia, but in my experience its members are quite hardy. Tubers have been in the ground here for two decades, surviving brief dips to 0°F (−18°C), their only protection being a thick layer of pine straw. In autumn, the leaves endure until night temperatures drop below 45°F (7°C), at which point dormancy is triggered. Where the ground freezes, tubers can be potted and overwintered in a frost-free area. I have grown tubers in potting soil, improved clay, and even mostly clay soil during hot, dry summers and wet winters, and aside from freezing, nothing seems to bother them. For larger plants, site in an acid, well-draining soil with a pH of 5 to 6, containing much organic matter, and apply a small amount of slow-release fertilizer in spring. In shade, the leaves endure southern summers with no visible damage; but when it gets too hot and too dry, they droop a bit, and only watering pumps them back up. I have seen plants growing well into zone 6, and they are extremely well suited further south. Shade is essential in hot, southern gardens, but some sun exposure is tolerated further north. In northern gardens with hard winters, *Sauromatum* makes an excellent foliage subject for containers.

Sauromatum is from the Greek *sauros* (= lizard), alluding to the spotted spathe. The epithet *venosum* (= veined) refers to the heavily veined spathe limb. The genus is placed in the Araceae.

Propagation is easily accomplished by taking offsets from the mature tuber in autumn or by sowing seed in a coarse commercial mix with a pH of 7 maintained moist at 60–70°F (16–21°C).

No diseases reported, nor have I experienced any.

Sauromatum venosum, voodoo lily, monarch of the east, red calla. Tropical East and West Africa, Asia, Himalayas, southern India.

MS to FS; malodorous inflorescence to 18 in. (45 cm) tall; spathe constricted in center, forming an hourglass, tube 2–4 in. (5–10 cm) long and 2.5 in. (6 cm) wide, brownish purple; limb oblong to lance-shaped, 20–28 in. (50–70 cm) long and to 4 in. (10 cm) wide, translucent yellow to greenish yellow with many streaky purple to maroon spots, first erect then folding away, lying on the ground; spadix extension erect, rodlike, deep metallic purple or maroon, to 18 in. (45 cm) long and 0.6 in. (1.5 cm) in diameter at base, slowly tapering toward blunt tip; leaf on fleshy petiole to 30 in. (75 cm) tall, spotted dark olive-green or maroon; leaf solitary, with 7–13, sometimes more leaflets, to 18 in. (45 cm) wide, medium glossy green with prominent veins; fruit at ground level, ball-shaped, to 2.5 in. (6 cm) in diameter, covered with black seed. This aroid is as easy to grow as a daffodil. The inflorescence and its pungent, foul smell last but a day or so. *Sauromatum nubicum* from tropical East and West Africa differs only by its spathe limb being narrower and the leaf segments being wider. Tubers of both species will survive outdoors if the soil does not freeze.

Saxifraga

Every time I look at *Saxifraga stolonifera* (mother-of-thousands), I am reminded of my own mother, who gave me a small piece of it years ago. She had it in a large, flat piece of pottery, encircling a pretty rock she had brought from her beloved Bavarian Alps. This little bit literally turned into the thousands of plants now inhabiting my garden, a testimony to the correctness of the common name. Many places at Hosta Hill—along walks, near rock borders, under shrubs and tall perennials—are brightened by small colonies of this saxifrage, which offers plumes of white flowers in spring and a carpet of colorful, silver-veined leaves for the rest of the year. Here they are evergreen, but Mother brought hers inside during the long, hard Detroit winters.

Saxifraga is a huge genus of, at last count, over 400 species. The generic name comes from the Latin *saxum* (= rock) and *frangere* (= to break). In nature, the tiny seeds of many of the species get caught in the crevices of the rocky landscape in which they grow, and the ensuing plants indeed look as if they had broken the rocks apart. I heard another explanation in Germany concerning the stonelike grains found in the roots of *Saxifraga granulata*, a European species, which indicated to old herbalists believing in the doctrine of signatures that the ingested plant might break up gallstones and kidney stones. The genus is classified in the Saxifragaceae.

Most saxifrages are specialty plants, requiring a sharply drained, alkaline rock garden environment; I tried some of the alpine species in my woodland and was very successful in killing the entire lot of them. But a few woodland saxifrages are indispensable as groundcovers and companions in the shady garden. All species and cultivars described are woodlanders of easy culture and adapted to average, acid woods soil with plenty of humus; here they grow even on the heavy, acid clay soil substrate along my woodland walks, with a pH of 5 or sometimes lower. They tolerate the arid conditions during the long, hot summers in southeastern North America.

A few native North American saxifrages are more difficult but nevertheless interesting additions to the wildflower border if native conditions can be established. I saw *Saxifraga michauxii* on Mount Mitchell in North Carolina at elevations above 6000 ft (over 1800 m), growing on moist rocks; mountain people called it lettuce saxifrage because they ate the leaves in salads and with cooked greens. The same name is applied to *S. micranthidifolia* and *S. pensylvanica*, which were also eaten as food.

Saxifrages are endemic to the subarctic, temperate, and alpine regions of Eurasia, North Africa, and North and South America. The best saxifrages for mild winter woodlands in zone 6 and warmer belong to section *Diptera* (syn. *Irregulares*), marked [DIP] in the species descriptions. Section *Robertso-*

nia (syn. *Gymnoptera*), marked [ROB], includes hardier species suited for gardens in zone 5 and colder. All these are woodland plants suited for all kinds of shade with basal leaf rosettes and clusters of flowers on a leafless, branched stem. The species native to North America are in section *Boraphila*, marked [BOR].

Propagation is easy. Some of the species, like mother-of-thousands, do their own propagating by means of ranging red stolons (as do strawberries), with new plantlets appearing and rooting at the stolon tips; these can be removed and relocated. Division of the dormant rhizome in late autumn or very early spring is also indicated, but each piece should have an ample amount of roots attached. Seed can be sown in place or in an open frame.

Large slugs and snails can damage new growth emerging in spring, but growth is so fast that usually only the smaller species are harmed. The species described are relatively free of pests and diseases.

Saxifraga fortunei [DIP]. China, Japan.

LS to FS; flowers white, sometimes pink, 0.5 in. (1 cm) across, 3 upper petals and 1–2 lower, longer petals, on reddish, branched flowerstalk to 20 in. (50 cm); August–October; plant clump-forming, deciduous or semi-evergreen in mild-winter areas; leaves in a basal rosette, kidney-shaped to roundish, with 7 lobes, heart-shaped base, 2–4 in. (5–10 cm) across, medium green, sometimes purple-rimmed and reddish purple beneath.

Clone 2, flowers pink; leaves burgundy with silvery white streakings.

'Go Nishiki' (= five brocade; 'Five Color'), flowers white; leaves mottled and streaked with 5 colors, mostly greenish and burgundy.

'Rubrifolia', flowers pinkish; leaves and stems red.

'Velvet', flowers light pink; leaves maroon to dark purple with a velvety texture and silvery gray overlay.

'Wada' ('Wada's Mahogany', 'Wada's Variety'), flowers white, very late; leaves and stems dark reddish with reddish brown or mahogany brown accents.

'Windsor', flowers white on tall stems to 24 in. (60 cm); leaves like the species.

Saxifraga stolonifera [DIP], mother-of-thousands, Aaron's beard, beefsteak geranium, beefsteak saxifrage, creeping sailor, strawberry begonia, strawberry geranium. Eastern Asia.

LS to FS; flowers white, spotted yellow or pinkish red, 0.8 in. (2 cm) across, 3–4 upper petals and 1–2 lower, longer petals, on slender green flowerstalk to 24 in. (60 cm); July–October; plant clump-forming, evergreen, spreading by thin, red stolons; leaves long-stalked, in a basal rosette, kidney-shaped to roundish, coarsely toothed, heart-shaped base, 1–4 in. (2.5–10 cm) across, medium to grayish green with silvery gray veins, reddish beneath. In the North this ubiquitous plant is frequently used in dish gardens or hanging baskets; here it spreads all over the place and is removed where not wanted and transplanted or given away as a wonderful pass-along plant. It is easily one of the most easy-care plants in the garden and very well suited to hot southern gardens. Hardy to zone 6 with protection.

'Cuscutiformis' (var. *minor*), flowers white, unspotted, similar to *Saxifraga stolonifera*; leaves round to kidney-shaped, 7- to 9-lobed, to 4 in. (10 cm) across, like the type in color; hardier to zone 5; vigorous enough for a groundcover. The true *S. cuscutiformis* has smaller and white flowers that are spotted yellow and red.

'Eco Butterfly', flowers white; leaves yellow with a butterflylike pattern of contrasting green; prolific multiplier.

'Harvest Moon', flowers white; leaves bright yellow to orange-red, darkening with age; heavy multiplier.

'Maroon Beauty', flowers white; leaves maroon with silvery gray veining and a coating of velvety red hair; good multiplier.

'Tricolor' ('Magic Carpet', *Saxifraga sarmentosa* 'Tricolor'), flowers white; leaves dark green variegated with silvery gray, greenish white, and pink; good multiplier.

Saxifraga ×urbium. Garden hybrid (*S. umbrosa* × *S. hirsuta*, *S. spathularis* × *S. umbrosa*).

LS to FS; flowers tiny, star-shaped, petals white with 2 yellow spots near the base and reddish near the center, many, to 0.5 in. (1 cm) across, in loose clusters on slender, reddish sticky flowerstalk to 14 in. (35 cm) tall; July–September; plant clump-forming, evergreen, spreading vigorously by stolons; leaves in a basal rosette, spoon-shaped, toothed, leathery in texture, 0.8–1.5 in. (2–4 cm) across, medium green. As vigorous as *Saxifraga stolonifera*. Hardy to zone 6.

Selections of *Saxifraga ×urbium* are often sold as *S. umbrosa* [ROB], which species is rarely seen in gardens. **Saxifraga umbrosa** (London pride, porcelain flower, Saint Patrick's cabbage) has larger leaves to 3 in. (8 cm) long, with scalloped edges and crinkled surface. It comes from western Europe and the Pyrenees, and if true is hardy to zone 4. Its var. *hirta* is smaller and has leaves with fringed, hairy edges; var. *primuloides* ('Primuloides') is a miniature *S. umbrosa* reminiscent of a primrose, with rose-pink flowers and tiny leaves; **'Aureopunctata'** ('Variegata') has pink flowers and green leaves with yellow spots. The true *S. umbrosa* and its hybridized forms are vigorous spreaders and make excellent groundcovers even in poor soils. A pH of 5 to 7 is tolerated, but plants resent overly dry soils. Provide supplemental water during droughts in hot southern gardens. This group of plants is better for cool-summer areas. Most cultivars offered are *S. ×urbium*.

'Chambers Pink Pride', flowers pink; leaves like the type.

'Covillei', flowers bicolored, pink and white.

'Elliott's Variety' ('Clarence Elliott', var. *primuloides* 'Elliott's Variety', *Saxifraga primuloides* 'Elliott's Variety'), flowers minute, rose-pink, on 6 in. (15 cm) red stems; leaves small, green above, reddish beneath.

'Ingwersen's Variety', flowers deep red, on 4 in. (10 cm) stems; leaves green suffused with bronze.

Saxifraga veitchiana [DIP]. China.

LS to FS; flowers white, small, spotted yellow or pinkish red, on slender green flowerstalks; July–October; plant clump-forming, evergreen, spreading by red stolons; leaves on bristly stalks, in a basal rosette close to the ground, shallowly scalloped, matte dark green, usually unmarked but sometimes with silvery gray veins, shiny red and bristly beneath. Great for greening the ground underneath taller-growing wildflowers like cobra lilies and Solomon's seals. Here it spreads by stolons and makes a tight, evergreen groundcover within a few seasons. It is not a great bloomer, but its vigor and appealing mat of leaves make up for this. Hardy to zone 5 with protection, evergreen in zone 7. Very tolerant of poor soils, heat, and drought, and easy to care for. At Hosta Hill it has grown from a single plantlet into several large patches of groundcover so tight that weeds are prevented from emerging. Burns in direct sun in southern gardens.

Saxifraga virginiensis [BOR], early saxifrage, eastern saxifrage, Saint Peter's cabbage. Eastern North America, Ontario and Minnesota east to New Brunswick and south through New England to Georgia, west to Oklahoma and Missouri.

LS to FS; flowers white, fragrant, tiny, starlike, sepals 5, petals 5, stamens 10, bright yellow, in clusters on branching green, hairy flowerstalks 6–16 in. (15–40 cm) tall; April–June; plant clump-forming; leaves in a basal rosette, oval to roundish, broadly toothed, 1–3 in. (2.5–8 cm) across, medium green; fruit a 2-beaked brown capsule. This is probably the easiest native to establish in moderately moist woodland gardens. Add coarse sand to the soil to improve drainage and site the plant in a shady spot near moisture-holding, porous rocks.

Saxifraga michauxii [BOR] (Michaux's saxifrage, mountain saxifrage) can also be established, but very cool summers are essential. Its tall, widely branched flowerstalks carry loose clusters of small, star-shaped, white flowers, with petals spotted yellow; the leaves are most attractive, hairy and deeply toothed and purplish brown or maroon beneath. *Saxifraga pensylvanica* [BOR] (swamp saxifrage) has leaves with much finer teeth and a sticky flowerstalk; it inhabits swamps, bogs, and wet areas from New England to North Carolina and west. Another saxifrage for wet areas is *S. micranthidifolia* [BOR] (lettuce saxifrage), a coarser plant with tall, loose flower clusters. Other saxifrages from alpine habitats in western North America include matted saxifrage (*S. bronchialis*), tufted saxifrage (*S. caespitosa*), rusty saxifrage (*S. ferruginea*), northern saxifrage (*S. integrifolia*), wood saxifrage (*S. mertensiana*), western saxifrage (*S. occidentalis*), and Oregon saxifrage (*S. oregana*); most are widespread in the mountains of the Northwest. Native saxifrages are occasionally available from wildflower nurseries and should never be removed from the wild; transplanting and reestablishment are difficult.

Scoliopus

I could not escape the fetor of *Scoliopus bigelowii* (adder's tongue) in bloom, even in an Oregon for-

est. It simply stinks when in flower, and one wonders why anyone would want to include it in the garden. But its odor lasts only a few days in very early spring, after which adder's tongue becomes a fascinating foliage plant with boldly veined, paired leaves that are sometimes spotted with brown blotches. This interesting, modest cousin to the trilliums is placed, along with *Trillium, Daiswa, Kinugasa,* and *Paris,* in the Trilliaceae.

Although suited to zone 7, adder's tongue is not a plant for hot southern gardens and is barely hardy into zone 6b with protection, so its eastern range of cultivation is limited. Since it likes the cool climate of the western Cascades and Siskiyou Mountains, discriminating gardeners in the Northwest and more northern or higher locations with cool, moist summers can enjoy colonies of its attractively mottled leaf mounds. It requires a moist, rich, friable woodland soil with plenty of humus and a pH of 5 to 6.5 in a cool, deeply shaded location. Provide a sheltered spot and mulch with dry pine needles to delay early emergence, preventing damage by late freezes.

Propagate by dividing the dormant rhizome in late autumn or very early spring. Seed should be sown when fresh in pots in a cold frame. Germination is usually delayed and sporadic.

Large slugs and snails can damage new growth emerging in spring. Aphids may be bothersome.

Scoliopus bigelowii, fetid adder's tongue, stink pod, brownies. Western North America, northern California, Oregon.

MS to FS; flowers trilliumlike, to 2 in. (5 cm) across, 1–12 in terminal clusters, sepals 3, broad, to 2 in. (5 cm) across, greenish white striped with deep red to purple along the veins, petals 3, erect, deep brownish purple, on flowerstalks 4–8 in. (10–20 cm); plant rhizomatous, slowly expanding; leaves elliptic to oblong, matte dark green, mottled with maroon to purple spots, conspicuously veined, 4–7 in. (10–18 cm) long and 2–4 in. (5–10 cm) wide. Makes striking colonies under the right cultural conditions.

Scoliopus hallii, Oregon fetid adder's tongue. Western North America, Oregon.

MS to FS; flowers solitary or more, trilliumlike, terminal, sepals 3, broadly lance-shaped, yellowish green mottled with purple, with drooping tips, petals 3, erect, deep brownish purple, on flowerstalks 1–3 in. (2.5–8 cm); plant rhizomatous, slowly expanding; leaves lance-shaped to linear, matte dark green, veined, 3–6 in. (8–15 cm) long and 1–2 in. (2.5–5 cm) wide. This scarce woodlander makes a delightful addition to plantings of trilliums and other wildflowers in gardens where proper cultural conditions can be provided.

Selaginella

Other than ferns and scouring rush, nonflowering plants are rare in gardens. Some of the most unjustly underused belong to the genus *Selaginella* (spike moss, little club moss). The genus was known to Linnaeus in the 18th century but remained virtually unknown to gardeners until recent years, when selected forms of these mosslike plants were propagated and became available. Spike mosses are widespread in northern Georgia woodlands on rock outcrops called flatrocks, whose depressions are frequently covered with mats of them. I have seen spike mosses in more shady conditions in my own neighborhood, growing along rock-strewn streams on moist soil. In gardens they are ideal near watercourses for softening the rock-water transition. I grow several species and cultivars in the deeply shaded, moist areas of my garden, using them primarily as groundcovers in areas where wildflowers do not carpet the ground shoulder-to-shoulder and where the good, bare earth needs a gentle patchwork blanket of yellow, green, gray-green, and brownish green.

The hardiness of spike mosses is often underestimated. For instance, the South African spike moss *Selaginella kraussiana* is billed as being hardy only in zone 10 and warmer, but here it has withstood temperatures to 15°F (−10°C) for several consecutive nights in sheltered areas with a light covering of pine straw. I describe here only spike mosses that are hardy to at least zone 7. These shallow-rooted, lacy plants dry out very quickly; constant moisture is ideal, but many survive brief dry periods and revive when moisture is restored. Most tolerate great heat as long as they are kept moist. Given moisture, many become sturdy and even assertive: the mat-forming species cover considerable areas with cushiony mats, and the stemmed species multiply rapidly, becoming crowded on upright stems. Spike mosses grow in most soils, including sandy and stony soils, as well as moist rock surfaces, but a light, fertile woodland soil with plenty of humus is preferred. A pH of 5 to 7 is acceptable. Given good cultural conditions these ferns are of very easy culture and low maintenance.

Spike mosses have a very fitting scientific name (*selaginella* = little selago; an early name for *Lycopodium selago*, a club moss), alluding to their mosslike nature. *Selaginella* is placed in its own family, the Selaginellaceae.

Propagate by taking rooted stems of the mat-forming species or by transplanting divisions of rhizomes taken from larger clumps. Transplanting is especially easy and may be done year-round; be sure to take along a generous ball of earth. Propagation by spores is also easy; sow spores as soon as they are ripe on a coarse commercial mix with a pH of 7 maintained moist at 70°F (21°C).

Leaf spot is reported. My plants experience occasional stem rot.

Selaginella apoda, meadow spike moss, basket spike moss. Eastern North America, southeastern Canada, New England south to Georgia and Alabama.

LS to FS; stems prostrate, many-branched, branches to 4 in. (10 cm) long; leaves tiny, scalelike, oval, light green, minutely toothed, in 4 rows, 2 lateral rows along the stem widely spaced, 2 inner and upper rows more closely spaced and bunched. This very hardy species should be planted in an up-close rockery along a path, where its fine details can be observed. I received my small colony as a gift from a friend; faithfully kept moist during dry periods, it has graced its garden spot for many years. Hardy to zone 4, possibly 3 with protection. *Selaginella douglasii* (Douglas spike moss), from Idaho west to British Columbia and south to Oregon and northern California, is similar; its multibranched stems 6–16 in. (15–40 cm) form attractive, dark lime-green mats of groundcover. Hardy to zone 6. Another eastern North American native, *S. rupestris* (rock spike moss), is similar to and often seen with *S. apoda*, except that it makes more open, creeping mats. Hardy to zone 6.

Selaginella braunii, arborvitae fern, treelet spike moss. Western China.

LS to FS; stems erect, 12–18 in. (30–45 cm) tall, many-branched in the upper half, with branches forming erect fanlike blades with triangular outline; leaves evergreen, tiny, oval, dark green, 4-ranked along the stems. This hardy, slow-spreading spike moss is similar to *Selaginella involvens* and forms handsome, tightly bunched, upright clumps. Hardy to zone 6.

Selaginella helvetica, Swiss spike moss. Eurasia, in the mountains from the Alps east.

LS to FS; stems prostrate, densely matted, many-branched, forked at the base, to 4 in. (10 cm) long; leaves tiny, flat and pointed, light moss-green, becoming brown when allowed to dry. Quickly forms dense mats that cover the ground, rockery, or stone walls. Hardy to zone 5.

Selaginella involvens, Japanese spike moss. Northeastern India east to Japan.

LS to FS; stems to 12 in. (30 cm) high, many-branched in the upper half, with branches forming erect fanlike blades with triangular outline; leaves tiny, oval, dark green, arranged spirally along the stems. This hardy spike moss forms handsome, tightly bunched, upright clumps. Hardy to zone 6. Its selection 'Aurea' has very light, yellowish green leaves.

Selaginella kraussiana, spreading clubmoss, trailing spike moss, mat spike moss. South Africa, Azores.

LS to FS; stems 6–12 in. (15–30 cm) long, to 1 in. (2.5 cm) high, trailing, matting, and rooting, much-divided and many-branched, with branches forming compound divisions; leaves tiny, oval, bright green. This much-utilized spreading spike moss is universally known and familiar to many in the trade as the "greenhouse weed." Hardy to zone 8; hardy and evergreen in zone 7a if covered with pine straw during winter, and even into 6b if protected from desiccating winter winds. I use its yellow form in several patches as a groundcover among wildflowers and ferns.

'Aurea' (yellow club moss), leaves very bright yellow when young, maturing to a greenish yellow. Makes a good contrast when interplanted with the type.

'Brownii' ('Emerald Isle', *Selaginella brownii*), a compact form with dense growth habit forming cushiony mounds of bright emerald-green to 2 in. (5 cm) high and 8 in. (20 cm) wide.

'Variegata', leaves splashed with creamy white; plant mat-forming.

Selaginella uncinata, peacock moss, rainbow fern, blue spike moss, blue selaginella. China.

LS to FS; stems 12–24 in. (30–60 cm) long, to 1 in. (2.5 cm) high, trailing, matting and rooting, much-divided alternately and many-branched, with branches forming compound divisions; leaves tiny, oval, blue-green with a metallic sheen on new growth. It requires abundant moisture and colors up better in light to woodland shade. A great groundcover that contrasts beautifully with yellow forms of spike moss. Hardy to zone 7a.

Shortia

Most summer tourists who crowd the top of Grandfather Mountain in western North Carolina have never heard of André Michaux, the French botanist explorer who climbed this mountain in 1788, long before there was a paved road to the top. In that year Michaux found a small wildflower in a nearby river valley and included it in his Paris herbarium without ever naming it. The famous American botanist Asa Gray also found it there in 1839; in 1842 he and his colleague John Torrey named it *Shortia galacifolia* to honor their mutual friend, botanist Charles Short of Kentucky. Asa Gray and many others then spent fruitless years scouring the Carolina mountains for another glimpse of this wildflower, only to be outdone by a local teenager, who found a colony of it on the banks of the Catawba River in 1877. Finally, in 1879, the then almost 70-year-old Gray himself found the plant in the wild and declared that with this success he could at last "nunc dimittis" (depart in peace).

One hundred years later, I saw my first colony of Oconee bells, a common name for this native *Shortia*, near the mountain hamlet of Spruce Pine, and I daresay I was just as excited as those erstwhile explorers. A dear friend of mine owns a large tract on a mountainside nearby and permits me to "botanize" there all I want. Within the confines of this large private property, many wildflowers proliferate in an environment that has changed little since American Indians occupied the area. Sadly, this is not the case in most places, where collecting and environmental changes have diminished natural populations to the point of extinction. *Shortia galacifolia* too belongs to this threatened lot, and dam and road construction in the mountain valleys where Oconee bells typically grows have taken a terrible toll. Its interesting history has created an unusual demand for it, and I see it more in gardens nowadays than up in the mountains, which in fact may finally contribute to its survival. This species is protected by locals laws, and some nurseries are now successfully propagating this treasure; it should never be removed from the wild.

Just like the related *Galax*, the charming Oconee bells has a limited habitat, mostly in the southern Appalachians, but I have seen populations in the Piedmont, at lower elevations as far south as northeastern Georgia and northwestern South Carolina. Mountain people call it coltsfoot for the shape of the leaves. The epithet comes from its resemblance to *Galax* (*galacifolia* = with leaves like *Galax*), and *Shortia* is classified in the same family, Diapensiaceae.

For active growth and good flowering, shortias require constantly moist soil with a very acidic pH of 4.5 to 5.5 and plenty of humus and sandy or gritty peat. In the wild it is usually found along stream banks and in wet seepage areas, flowering reliably in medium to full shade, but is also seen in open mountain valleys with light shade. In autumn, the leaves turn a reddish bronze. Moisture is imperative during spring when the flowerstalk elongates.

Propagate by carefully taking rooted runners after flowering; replant immediately and maintain constant moisture to reestablish. Seed propagation is a tedious process, with seedlings taking several years to mature; sow seed in a very acid starting mix in pots in a cold frame. Propagation by division is much faster and more productive.

Slugs and snails occasionally disfigure fresh growth, but once the leaf tissue has hardened, they leave the plant alone. Weevils may also take an occasional bite out of young leaves. No diseases are reported or experienced here.

Shortia galacifolia, Oconee bells, coltsfoot, one-flowered coltsfoot. Southern Appalachians, Virginia, in the mountains from the Carolinas, localized in the upper Piedmont of Georgia and South Carolina.

LS to FS; flowers solitary, large, to 1 in. (2.5 cm) across, nodding, funnel-shaped, white, sometimes pinkish white or bluish toward the margins, petals 5 with 5 irregularly toothed lobes, stamens 10, 5 fertile, yellow, 5 sterile, hidden at the base, on a green, leafless, upright flowerstalk to 8 in. (20 cm); late March–May; plant evergreen, clump-forming, slowly spreading by runners; leaves basal, roundish, leathery, glossy bright green, to 3 in. (8 cm) across, with margins lobed and sharply toothed, on long leafstalks to 5 in. (13 cm) long. Although limited in the wild to a relatively small southeastern habitat in zone 6, it is hardy in zone 5 gardens in New England. Remarkably heat-tolerant as long as moisture is constant. I am cultivating a large-leaved form found in a now flooded mountain valley in North Carolina; it has leaves to 6 in. (15 cm) across.

Shortia soldanelloides, fringed galax, fringe-bells. Japan.

LS to FS; flowers 3–8, nodding and in loose clusters usually pointed to one side of the flowerstalk, to 1 in. (2.5 cm) across, funnel-shaped, deep pink, rarely white with a bluish margin, petals 5 with 5 deeply fringed lobes, stamens 10, 5 fertile, yellowish, alternating with 5 sterile, hidden at the base, upright, reddish flowerstalks 9–12 in. (23–30 cm) tall; May–June; plant evergreen, clump-forming, slowly spreading by runners; leaves basal, oval to roundish and usually heart-shaped at the base, glossy dark green, to 2 in. (5 cm) long, with margins lobed and coarsely toothed. This Asian wildflower was introduced by Siebold to the West. As its epithet suggests, it is similar to *Soldanella alpina* (alpine snowbell). Rarely seen in gardens, it is hardy to zone 6. Several forms have been described, but only one, var. *ilicifolia*, is in commerce; it has smaller leaves to 1.5 in. (4 cm) long with fewer and coarser, almost triangular teeth. Forma *alpina* is smaller and more compact; var. *magna* has larger leaves, to 4 in. (10 cm), that are finely lobed.

Shortia uniflora, Nippon bells. Japan.

LS to FS; flowers solitary, large, to 1 in. (2.5 cm) across, nodding, funnel-shaped but opening wider than *Shortia galacifolia*, first pinkish then fading to white, petals 5 with irregularly toothed lobes, stamens 10, 5 fertile, yellow, 5 sterile, hidden at the base, on a leafless, upright flowerstalk to 8 in. (20 cm); late March–May; plant evergreen, clump-forming, spreading by runners; leaves basal, kidney-shaped to roundish, leathery, glossy bright green, 1–3 in. (2.5–8 cm) long and wide, with margins wavy and toothed, on leafstalks. This Asian counterpart of *S. galacifolia* is similar in all respects but spreads faster and is not as difficult to establish. Hardy to zone 6, 5 with protection. Like Oconee bells, it is quite heat-tolerant provided soil remains moist. 'Grandiflora' has flowers to 1.5 in. (4 cm) across and is more floriferous.

Silene

Silene is a huge genus of plants known commonly as campions (from the Latin for their preferred habitat, open fields) or catchflies (because the sticky sap from their stems and flower bracts tends to do just that). Most species are endemic to the sunny Mediterranean regions of Europe and to mountainous tropical Africa and South America, but a few native North American campions are highly desirable shade-tolerant perennials. One is *Silene polypetala* (fringed campion), now protected in its native habitat but frequently seen in gardens. It has become almost weedy in its decade-long stint at Hosta Hill. Its prostrate runners spread far and wide, rooting along the way. They have even taken over garden paths; visitors gingerly side step the blossoms during spring flowering but later tromp right down on the green, ground-covering leaves without doing much damage. I planted the initial rooted cutting received from a friend in a slightly elevated wildflower bed with very acid soil (pH 4.5); it gets watered frequently because it has many thirsty companions as neighbors. In spring the beautifully fringed petals are produced for a period of three weeks, making an almost solid carpet of pink through which wild gingers and trilliums thrust their foliage. Reports that fringed campion is short-lived have some truth. Some clumps die out for no apparent reason, so I remove every stray runner I see and plant them elsewhere in the garden, where they root readily. That way I always have a supply of this beautiful wildflower and even enough for an occasional give-away.

Silene is classified in the pink family, Caryophyllaceae. For active growth and good flowering, silenes require moist soil with plenty of humus and leaf mold, sandy or gritty content (not limestone) to aid drainage, and a pH of 5 to 5.5.

Propagate by carefully taking rooted runners after flowering or later in autumn and replanting immediately; they are not difficult to establish if moisture is maintained. This is much faster and more productive than sowing seed.

Slugs and snails occasionally disfigure new growth. Rust, smut, and stem rot can occur if the ground is too wet, but I have not experienced these diseases here.

Silene dioica, red campion, morning campion. Europe.

Some sun, LS; flowers grouped on loosely branched stems, roundish, petals 5, notched and open, up-facing, fan-shaped, red to rose-pink, to 1.5 in. (4 cm) across; April–May; plant semi-evergreen, erect, with flowerstalks to 36 in. (90 cm); leaves both basal and on the stem, basal leaves to 8 in. (20 cm) long, stem leaves to 4 in. (10 cm), green. I have seen this species flourishing in light shade from northern Florida to the Georgia Piedmont. The main reasons for trying it in shady gardens are its double-flowered and variegated-leaf forms: **'Clifford Moore'** (leaves dark green with a broad, bright yellow margin), 'Graham's Delight' (leaves striped creamy white), 'Rosea Plena' (flowers double, leaves green), 'Tresevern Gold' (leaves striped yellow), and 'Variegata' (leaves striped white).

Silene polypetala, fringed campion. Southeastern North America, northern Florida to western upland Georgia.

LS to FS; flowers solitary or grouped along flowering tips ascending from the prostrate stems, large, 1.5–2 in. (4–5 cm) across, open and up-facing, fan-shaped, light to rose pink, petals 5, separated with notched and fringed lobes, stamens 10; April–May; plant evergreen, mat-forming, spreading by runners, mostly prostrate, rooting stems, but some stems occasionally erect or ascending, 12–18 in. (30–45 cm) long; leaves opposite, along the stem, spoon-shaped or elliptic, light grayish green, 1–2.5 in. (2.5–6 cm) long, flat to the ground. Rare in the wild, this species should never be removed from its natural habitat; tissue-cultured stock is available from specialist nurseries. Hardy to zone 6. *Silene caroliniana* (wild pink), another native eastern North American species, is similar and also low-growing but requires considerably more sun. It is rarely available and should be left alone in the wild, but its selection 'Millstream Select' seems to tolerate some shade. Ranging from Missouri east to North Carolina is *S. ovata*, with fringed, white petals; erect and very tall, to 5 ft. (1.5

m), its legginess makes it awkward to use. ***Silene virginica*** (fire pink), from New York south to northern Georgia and Alabama and west to Oklahoma, is an attractive wildflower with bright red, deeply notched petals; it requires almost full sun, but its hybrids with *S. polypetala*, smaller and with dark pink, fringed petals, promise to be good, if short-lived, plants for the shady garden.

Smilacina

False Solomon's seal is the traditional common name for this genus, but I prefer Solomon's plume —much more descriptive. Four species are native to the United States but many more are found in Asia, over 30 at last count; some Asiatic species of these woodland lilies are graced with beautiful purple, pink, or yellow flowers, which adds floristic diversity to our already much appreciated white-flowered native species. The showiest by far of these is *Smilacina racemosa*, the several groups of which at Hosta Hill never fail to elicit favorable comments from visitors. Given the right conditions, this species develops into a very large plant with huge feathery flower spikes at the end of the stems. This eye-catching floral display is followed by a striking group of zigzagging lances, clothed with bright green leaves; in late summer the green berries turn pink and red and develop a nice mottled or spotted appearance; finally, before the first freeze cuts down the stems, the leaves turn a spectacular golden color. No shady garden should be without this marvel.

Solomon's plumes are classified in the genus *Smilacina*. This name derives from Greek and is the diminutive of the ancient Greek name for the greenbrier vine, *Smilax*. While the nomenclature of the classic North American species is well established, recently imported species of this genus may take some time to find permanent names. Many underground parts of native species were used for food and medicine, and the smoke from the roots was used as a sedative; Americans Indians and early settlers often mistook plants, with their similar rhizomes, for true Solomon's seals (*Polygonatum* spp.), hence "false." *Smilacina* is placed in the Convallariaceae.

Solomon's plumes are endemic to the temperate regions of North America and temperate Asia. The North American species are reliably winter hardy, most thriving in the temperate climate of zones 4 to 7; both North American and Siberian species are very hardy and can be grown in zone 4 or colder. Species originating in southern Asia are apparently hardy to zone 6 with protection; expect some losses during extreme winters. Unless otherwise noted, all species and cultivars listed can be grown in zones 6 to 9.

Smilacinas are rhizomatous herbaceous perennials, so die down in autumn. Originating in moist woodlands, they are supremely adapted to shady, moist conditions. They dislike lime and prefer a very acid soil with a pH of 4.5; they grow well here in soils with a pH of 5.5. Most native species carry on from spring until autumn, fitting well with other perennials with the same life cycle, like hostas, toad lilies, wild gingers, and epimediums. But they loathe lack of moisture and therefore the long, hot summers of southeastern North America; site in deep shade and water profusely during dry periods to prevent early summer dormancy in hot-summer regions. All Solomon's plumes are great additions to the shady garden, and the large-plumed species like *Smilacina racemosa* are truly outstanding. Ferns make matchless companion plants when carefully matched for size.

Propagate by dividing the dormant rhizome in late autumn or very early spring as described at *Polygonatum*. Seed propagation is also possible, but several years will pass before seedlings reach blooming size. Some *Smilacina* species are dioecious (individual plants are either male or female), so one plant of each sex is required for successful cross-fertilization; do not expect seed set from a single dioecious plant.

Large slugs and snails can damage new growth emerging in spring, but growth is so fast that usually only the smaller species are harmed. Solomon's plumes are otherwise free of pests and diseases.

Smilacina bicolor. Korea.

MS to FS; dioecious; male flowers green, female flowers brownish, on a small, branched flowerstalk; May–June; stems arching, to 18 in. (45 cm) tall; leaves alternate, green, to 4 in. (10 cm) long, elliptic to broadly lance-shaped; orange-red fruit. Still little known in cultivation and rarely available, as is *Smilacina davurica*, which is similar but much smaller, growing to 6 in. (15 cm).

Smilacina forestii. Western China, Yunnan.

MS to FS; flowers pure white, on a small, branched flowerstalk forming the upper 5 in. (13 cm) of the stem; May–June; stems dark purple, arching, to 18 in. (45 cm) tall; leaves alternate, green, to 3 in. (8 cm) long, lance-shaped; orange fruit. Plant rhizomatous, forming large colonies. Rarely available but has proven vigorous and fast-growing in Western garden trials.

Smilacina formosana. Taiwan.

MS to FS; flowers many, diminutive, star-shaped, pure white on a multibranched panicle; April–June; stems to 5 ft. (1.5 m) tall, green; leaves alternately opposed, glossy dark green, to 6 in. (15 cm) long, broadly lance-shaped, with deeply sunken veins. The gleaming leaves are striking and long-lasting; flowers are similar to *Smilacina racemosa* but not as large. Hardy to zone 7 with protection.

Smilacina fusca. Western China, Himalayas, Nepal.

MS to FS; flowers dark purple outside, whitish pink in the throat, arranged in nodding clusters; May–June; stems arching, to 14 in. (35 cm) tall; leaves single, alternate, almost sessile, green, to 5 in. (13 cm) long, elliptic to broadly lance-shaped and distinctly veined and hairy, fringed margins; red fruit. The flowers are sparse but large and beautifully dark, hence *fusca* (= dark-colored, brown). Needs moist but well-drained soil.

Smilacina henryi. Western China, Yunnan.

MS to FS; flowers creamy white to yellow, very fragrant, arranged in large, nodding clusters; May–June; stems arching, to 12 in. (30 cm) tall; leaves single, alternate, green, to 5 in. (13 cm) long, elliptic to lance-shaped; attractive bright orange-red fruit. Requires moist but well-drained soil. Site close to a path or seating to appreciate the lovely floral scent. Hardy to zone 5.

Smilacina japonica. Japan, Korea.

MS to FS; flowers creamy white to white, arranged in nodding clusters; May–June; stems arching, to 24 in. (60 cm) tall; leaves green, covered with fine hairs, singular, closely spaced but alternate, sessile, green, to 4 in. (10 cm) long, broadly elliptic to broadly lance-shaped; red fruit. It will be some time before a shorter, white-margined form (*yuk-izasa shirofukurin*) and other highly prized sports

from Japan enter Western commerce. Variety *luteocarpa* (= yellow fruit) is in all respects similar to the type but has yellow fruit. Variety *robusta* from northern Honshu and Hokkaido is much larger than the type; it differs by its hairy stems, which are also taller, to 5 ft. (1.5 m), and by the fact that the leaves are carried by short leafstalks, not sessile. *Smilacina hondoensis* is a similar, dioecious species with many white flowers on rose-pink stalks, arranged in cloudlike open panicles, and long, hairy stems reaching 8 ft. (2.5 m). Its leaves are differentiated by being fully sessile, like those of *S. japonica*; they are a shiny dark green, large, to 8 in. (20 cm) long, broadly lance-shaped and have the same outstanding, deeply recessed veins. With its prominence, this species will make an attractive accent in the garden even without the flowers. It is, unfortunately, rarely offered. Likewise for *S. yezoensis* (Yezo Solomon's plume), named for its habitat in Yezo, the ancient name for Hokkaido, which has the same striking, deeply veined leaves and green flowers on both male and female plants; the fruit is a brown berry.

Smilacina oleacera. Western China, Yunnan, Himalayas, Nepal.

MS to FS; flowers rose-pink, rarely white, with whitish throat, arranged in nodding clusters and carried on a long, multibranched flowerstalk; May–June; stems smooth green, erect but arching, to 8 ft. (2.5 m) tall; leaves single, alternate, short-stalked, smooth green, to 8 in. (20 cm) long, elliptic to broadly lance-shaped and distinctly veined; red-orange fruit. I grow it in moist but rapid-draining soil in a pot and find it well adapted to our hot summers as long as plenty of water is supplied; I treat this fine specimen like my Himalayan cobra lilies (*Arisaema* spp.) and have not yet mustered the courage to plant it out in the open. Another species from Yunnan is *Smilacina wilsonii* (giant-leaved western Chinese Solomon's plume); its stems reach 4 ft. (1.2 m) and are clothed by ovate leaves, 10 in. (25 cm) long and covered with a dense coat of fine hairs, giving them a felty appearance.

Smilacina purpurea. Western and southwestern China, Himalayas, Nepal, northwestern India.

MS to FS; flowers purple, sometimes white, on a simple flowerstalk, to 10 in. (25 cm), but occasionally branched at the base; April–June; stems to 36 in. (90 cm) tall; leaves 5–11, singular, alternately opposed, green, to 6 in. (15 cm) long, broadly elliptic to very broadly lance-shaped, with deeply sunken veins; red-orange fruit. Frequently occurs with *Smilacina fusca* and like it needs moist but well-drained soil. Should make an interesting accent in the garden, particularly in its purple-flowered form.

Smilacina racemosa, false Solomon's seal, false spikenard, Solomon's feather, Solomon's plume, Solomon's zigzag, treacleberry, wild spikenard. Eastern North America, Canada south to Georgia.

MS to FS; a mass of tiny white flowers arranged in a terminal, branched, pyramidal panicle, up to 7 in. (18 cm) long, individual flowers have a corolla of 6 tepals; May–June; stems arching, zigzagging from leaf node to leaf node, to 36 in. (90 cm) tall; leaves single, alternate in 2 ranks, very short-petioled, green, sometimes yellowish, to 6 in. (15 cm) long, elliptic to broadly lance-shaped and distinctly veined, downy beneath, wavy in the margins; ball-shaped fruit is brownish mottled yellow to red-orange, turning bright red. These elegant plants should be in every shady garden. Best used in masses of 5 or more, which slowly become denser and expand. Individual plants can be spread around the wildflower border. The plant supplies aromatic extracts, and its berries were once used as an antidote for venomous bites. Variety *cylindrica* has cylindrical, not pyramidal, flowering panicles, hence the epithet; it is smaller than the type, with shorter leaves, and makes a fine conversation plant. The western form, var. *amplexicaulis* (fat Solomon), is known from the mountainous regions of southwestern Canada to California and south to New Mexico; it differs by having ovate, closer spaced, stem-clasping leaves. It is sometimes offered but rarely seen in gardens—the type is a better garden subject. The same can be said of another western species ranging from California to British Columbia and east to Montana, *S. sessilifolia* (slim Solomon), which has slim, lance-shaped, sessile leaves on stems reaching 24 in. (60 cm).

Smilacina stellata, starry Solomon's seal, starry Solomon's plume, starflower, star-flowered lily-of-the-valley. Eastern North America, Canada south to Georgia.

MS to FS; small white flowers arranged in a stalklike, terminal cluster, up to 2 in. (5 cm) long,

composed of 4–20 individual flowers, each with a corolla of 6 tepals; May–June; stems arching, zigzagging from leaf node to leaf node, to 6 in. (15 cm) tall, sometimes much shorter; leaves single, alternate, glaucous medium green, to 5 in. (13 cm) long, folded along the midrib, downy beneath; ball-shaped fruit is bright red becoming almost black. Blue berries are reported but I have not seen them. In cultivation since 1633 and, as with its relatives the "true" Solomon's seals, best planted in large groups. Patient gardeners with a paucity of money take heart: a single plant eventually becomes a large group. I plant mine in masses of up to 12 plants, which quickly expand and make a thick but delicate groundcover, becoming more dense as the rhizomes branch and expand. Some gardeners consider starflower invasive, particularly when given conditions to its liking, but I beg to differ. Its pretty, dark green mantle of leaves with early, beautiful flowers and late showy fruit makes up for its prolific hardiness, so I let it run as it wants and simply remove it when it invades areas where it is not desired. Very similar is var. *crassa*, which has evolved in the Atlantic coastal areas apart from the typical upland species; it differs by having attractive, closely spaced, overlapping leaves and, though seldom offered, can be collected during plant rescues.

Smilacina trifolia, three-leafed Solomon's seal, three-leaved starflower. Siberia, eastern North America, northern Canada south to Pennsylvania and west to Minnesota.

MS to FS; flowers white, 6-pointed, arranged in an upright flowerstalk, up to 2 in. (5 cm) long; May–June; flowerstalk sheathed by 3 leaves, sometimes 2 or 4, with tapering bases, to 6 in. (15 cm) tall; fruit deep red. This diminutive species resembles *Maianthemum canadense*, which differs by having 4-pointed flowers. A difficult subject in southern gardens, as its native habitat is cold northern woodlands and bogs. Hardy to zone 3.

Spigelia

One of my favorite flowers is Indian pink, *Spigelia marilandica*. Its fascinating history is similar to that of the well-known *Franklinia alatamaha*: *Spigelia marilandica* was discovered in 1690 in Maryland but —though it is found elsewhere—has not been seen there since; I "discovered" this enchanting species in the wild, in northwestern Georgia, and would not be without it in the garden. Its flower is a marvel of nature, barrel-shaped trumpets of brilliant scarlet outside with five sharply pointed lobes, flaring to reveal a bright yellow inside. The plant, which contains strychnine, was used by American Indians and early settlers to expel intestinal worms; unfortunately, it poisoned more than it cured. *Spigelia*, which name honors Dutch botanist Adrian von der Spigel, is placed in the logania family, Loganiaceae.

Indian pink is seen in rich woodlands and forest margins, primarily in limestone regions. Moist soil with plenty of humus and peat promotes good growth and flowering; the pH should be around 7. One clump of these striking plants is never enough: site a group of five to seven along a path, where the flowers can be closely observed. Prolong the flowering season by removing withered blooms.

Propagate by carefully dividing larger clumps. Sow seed as soon as it is ripe; I put mine in soil right next to the mother plants to increase the group.

Powdery mildew and leaf spot are reported but not seen here.

Spigelia marilandica, Indian pink, Maryland pinkroot, pinkroot, star bloom, worm grass. Eastern North America, Virginia south to northwestern Georgia south to Florida and west to Missouri, southern Indiana, Ohio, Illinois, Oklahoma, and eastern Texas.

LS to WS; flowers 2–10 in terminal, one-sided, curving clusters on a stem 12–24 in. (30–60 cm) tall; flowers large, to 1 in. (2.5 cm) across and 2 in. (5 cm) long, upright, trumpet-shaped, petals 5, fused, scarlet outside with 5 sharply pointed and flaring lobes, yellow inside, stamens 5, yellowish, style protruding; March–June; plant deciduous, clump-forming; leaves stalkless, on the stem, opposite, oval to lance-shaped, green, 2–4 in. (5–10 cm) long, with smooth margins. Available from wildflower nurseries, this dazzling native is still uncommon in gardens and deserves to be more widely grown. Hardy to zone 6 and tolerates the hot summers of higher zones as long as moisture is maintained.

Spiranthes

The genus *Spiranthes* is a bewildering aggregation of some 150 similar species, mostly of tropical origin. Worse, these species hybridize prolifically in nature, creating interspecific hybrids that grow just as profusely as their parents, and even true species have different growth patterns in different habitats. Despite the general confusion, gardeners enjoy these hardy orchids, and several hardy terrestrial species, relatively widespread in the temperate zones of Eurasia and North America, are easily cultivated in open gardens.

In most species the exquisite small flowers are arranged along tall spikes in a spiral, like a plait of tightly braided hair (hence, ladies' tresses). The generic name is from the Greek *spira* or *speira* (= coil, spiral) and *anthos* (= flower), another allusion to the spiraling flowers. The genus is classified in the Orchidaceae. American Indians used *Spiranthes cernua* as an aphrodisiac.

The beautiful, usually white flowers of these striking orchids are so diminutive that a magnifying glass is required to discern their intricate details. Notwithstanding, they make an outstanding floral display in late summer or early autumn, when little else is in bloom in the shady garden. In addition, some species disseminate a lovely fragrance. The leaves are a basal rosette of fleshy, plain green leaves, which present a striking contrast when planted in the company of wild gingers and other low-growing wildflowers. In Japan, colorful variegated-leaf forms are collected for pot culture. Like other plants with small flowers, they should be planted close to walks or in an elevated bed, where the flowers can be better observed.

Ladies' tresses make a better statement in the garden when planted in small groups, but single plants will eventually form small colonies. They like moist, well-draining soil, with a pH of 5 to 6. I grow several species in the top layer of the soil, and here they endure hot, dry weather with occasional watering. Hardiness varies; in the wild in North America some species occur in zone 3. These orchids flower better in woodland shade; they resent and may not flower in deep shade.

Propagate by carefully dividing the dormant tubers. Seed propagation is not recommended.

In my garden, nothing in the way of diseases seems to bother these orchids. Slugs, snails, and vine weevils take an occasional bite out of young leaves.

Spiranthes cernua, autumn ladies' tresses, common ladies' tresses, nodding ladies' tresses, screw-auger. Eastern North America, South Dakota and Ontario east to Nova Scotia and northern New England, and along the coast and in the mountains south to Georgia and Florida and west to Texas.

LS to WS; flowers numerous, very small, creamy white, fragrant and slightly nodding, to 0.5 in. (1 cm) long, side petals and upper sepal united to form a hood, lower lip petal wavy, recurved, with yellow spot in center, flowers arranged in usually 2, rarely more spiraling rows on upright flower spikes, 6–24 in. (15–60 cm) tall; August–October; leaves 3–6, in a tight basal rosette, erect but leaning, to 10 in. (25 cm) long, dark green, narrowly lance-shaped; stem leaves reduced to tight, bract-like scales. Among the largest species and one of the best for gardens. Plants have varying degrees of hardiness, depending on point of origin, but they are usually hardy to zone 5, 4 with protection. Expect considerable variability in commercially available plants. A particularly fragrant variety grows in marshy areas in the southern part of the range; this var. *odorata* (fragrant ladies' tresses, sweet ladies' tresses, swamp ladies' tresses, swamp orchid) is outwardly almost identical to the type but not quite as hardy. *Spiranthes gracilis* (slender ladies' tresses, southern ladies' tresses, green pearl twist) is similar to *S. cernua* but only faintly fragrant, and with a single row of tightly spiraled flowers. Its lip petal has a green stripe in the center. It occurs in southeastern North America, hardy to zone 5. *Spiranthes lacera*, a more northern species, is very much like *S. gracilis* but has leaves that persist during flowering. Both are much smaller than *S. cernua* and not as showy. The rarely offered *S. vernalis* (spring ladies' tresses) has the tallest flowerstalks, to 40 in. (1 m), but this native of southern swamps and marshes is only marginally hardy, to zone 8, perhaps 7b. Also rarely seen in commerce is *S. grayi* (little ladies' tresses, little pearl twist), a dwarf form that would make a nice addition to a moist trough garden. In Europe a yellow-flowered species, *S. ochroleuca*, is occasionally offered; it looks just like *S. cernua* but has greenish yellow to whitish yellow flowers and is in fact of North American derivation.

The same is true for the white-flowered *S. romanzoffiana* (Irish ladies' tresses), which is endemic to northwestern North America, including Alaska, and a few spots on the British Isles; it is sometimes available in England.

Spiranthes sinensis, Asian ladies' tresses. Northern India, China, Taiwan, south to Australia.

LS to WS; flowers white or pink; plant dwarf, similar to *Spiranthes grayi*. Barely hardy in zone 7b, so not suited for northern gardens except as a pot subject. Many sports with variegated leaves have been selected in Japan and are used in pot culture; outstanding cultivars include 'Kikoshi' (= young noble; leaves striped with bright yellow), 'Koyo' (= spiritual uplift; leaves center-variegated with a broad band of yellow), and 'Yuhi' (= great leap; leaves broadly margined with yellow).

Spiranthes spiralis, autumn ladies' tresses, ladies' tresses, European ladies' tresses. Central and southern Europe, Asia Minor.

LS to WS; flowers white, in a spiraling tight row on stems 4–10 in. (10–25 cm) tall. The inflorescence of this very small orchid is densely hairy, and its late-autumn flowering often coincides with the onset of winter—too late to be noticed in northern gardens. Hardy to zone 6.

Streptopus

Plants of this genus are commonly called twisted stalks. As with so many other endemics growing at Hosta Hill, I first spotted *Streptopus roseus* (rose twisted stalk) in bloom in a high mountain valley near the Blue Ridge. So enamored was I with the wonderful, spread-petaled, rose-colored bells that I visited a favorite wildflower nursery along the Blue Ridge Parkway and purchased three plants for the long ride home. They have grown for years now, on the north side of the house, in relatively deep, cool shade and moist, well-drained soil, to which I have added turkey grit made from crushed seashells. Even though my plants are grouped, to maximize impact, their modest springtime flower display is one of those wonders of nature that is best appreciated close up, lying flat on your belly, with the rosy flowers tickling your nose.

The genus name is from the Greek *streptos* (= twisted), an allusion to the flowerstalks; and even the leafy stems below grow in a pronounced zigzag. The genus is placed in the Liliaceae.

Twisted stalks are endemic to the temperate regions of North America, Europe, and temperate Asia, particularly Japan. All species are reliably winter hardy, thriving in the temperate climate of zones 4 to 7; all are rhizomatous herbaceous perennials, so die down in autumn. Originating in moist woodlands, they are well adapted to cool, shady, moist conditions. They prefer slightly acid soil with a pH of 6.5. They will decline in the long, hot summers of southeastern North America unless sited in a moist, cool corner with northern exposure. Other perennials tolerant of deep shade, like wild gingers and epimediums, make good companion plants when carefully matched for size.

Propagate by dividing the dormant rhizome in late autumn or very early spring as described at *Polygonatum*.

Large slugs and snails can damage new growth emerging in spring, but growth is so fast that usually only the smaller species are harmed. Twisted stalks are otherwise free of pests and diseases.

Streptopus amplexifolius, white mandarin. Eurasia, eastern North America, western North America, Alaska south to Oregon and Washington.

MS to FS; flowers greenish white, inconspicuous, to 0.5 in. (1 cm) long, hanging, bell-shaped, tubular, 6-lobed corolla with pointed, upturned lobes, produced 1–4 in the leaf axils; May–July; stems arching, smooth, to 38 in. (95 cm) but mostly shorter, branched below the center; leaves single, alternate, green above and glaucous beneath, minutely toothed in the margin, to 5 in. (13 cm) long and 2 in. (5 cm) wide, narrowly ovate to lance-shaped, heart-shaped at the base and stem-clasping (hence the epithet); oblong fruit is red, to 0.5 in. (1 cm) in diameter. Variety *americanus* (liverberry, scootberry) circumscribes the North American as opposed to the Eurasian variants; var. *denticulatus* has noticeably toothed leaves; var. *oreopolus* has a preference for mountain habitats. All varieties serve the same garden purposes as the type. Twisting leafy stems only adds to the horticultural value, and the gorgeous autumn display of yellowing leaves and bright red fruit on wiry pedicels earn them all a place in the wild garden.

Streptopus roseus, rose mandarin, rose twisted stalk, rosy twisted stalk. North America, Alaska south to British Columbia and northern Oregon, Newfoundland and Labrador west to Michigan and south to New England, Pennsylvania and along the Appalachians south to Georgia and Kentucky.

MS to FS; flowers rose, usually solitary, to 0.5 in. (1 cm) long, hanging, bell-shaped, tubular, 6-lobed corolla with pointed, upturned lobes, produced in the leaf axils of the slightly fringed, upper nodes; April–June; stems arching, finely hairy, to 30 in. (75 cm) but mostly shorter, to 12 in. (30 cm), branched below the center; leaves single, alternate, green above and below, minutely hairy in the margin, to 6 in. (15 cm) long and 2 in. (5 cm) wide, narrowly ovate to lance-shaped and sessile; fruit is red. This North American wildflower, which also offers an autumn display of yellowish leaves and red berries, deserves to be more widely planted. Some distinct geographic forms are offered, usually under the typical species name. Variety *curvipes*, so called for its attractively campanulate flowers with distinctly upturned, pointed lobes, is exceptional; it is distinguished from the eastern populations and mostly segregated in the Northwest, from Alaska to northern Oregon. Variety *perspectus* circumscribes an eastern North American variant with hairy pedicels. Both varieties serve the same garden purposes as the type. From Japan comes *S. streptopoides*, which differs from *S. roseus* by being smaller and having yellowish green-tipped pink flowers; the leaves are to 3 in. (8 cm) long and 1 in. (2.5 cm) wide. As its unhelpful epithet indicates, *S. streptopoides* "looks like a streptopus"; the distinction between it and its var. *japonicus*, which is rarely offered, is minor.

Stylophorum

Stylophorum diphyllum (celandine poppy), like its cousin *Eomecon chionantha* (Chinese snow poppy), can become a self-seeding nuisance given sun and plenty of moisture; but my good-sized clump grows in woodland shade, with dry surrounding soil, and under these conditions, germination is considerably curtailed and the plant spreads little. The few seedlings that do appear can easily be removed and given away, or planted elsewhere. Under more sunny conditions, the attractive seedpods should be removed before seed is scattered all over the place. The species is usually considered endemic to the Midwest, but I have seen populations as far southeast as northwestern Georgia on the Cumberland Plateau. Its occurrence in moist woodlands has given rise to another common name, wood poppy. Hardy to zone 4, and once firmly established, it tolerates the heat in southern gardens as long as moisture to the plant is maintained. Well-cultivated plants have a long flowering period, and here their foliage persists into autumn, unless a drought causes early dormancy. The Asian species require similar conditions for successful cultivation.

The generic name is from the Greek *stylos* (= style) and *phoros* (= to bear), alluding to the long-lasting, distinct style. The genus is classified in the Papaveraceae. The sap of the single North American species, *Stylophorum diphyllum*, is yellow and was used by American Indians as a dye for coloring cloth. Two Chinese species are also available, if rarely, in commerce.

Propagation is easy. Usually the plants self-seed, making plenty of readily transplantable progeny. Division of the rhizomatous roots in very early spring, before growth starts, is also successful; it may take some time for the divisions to become fully established.

Slugs and snails can damage new growth emerging in spring; no other pests or diseases are experienced here.

Stylophorum diphyllum, celandine poppy, wood poppy, flaming poppy, yellow poppy. Central and eastern North America, southern Wisconsin east to Pennsylvania and south to northwestern Georgia, west to Tennessee and Missouri.

LS to WS; flowers 1–5, in terminal clusters on erect, downy, leafy stems to 20 in. (50 cm) tall, brilliant yellow, sepals 2, hairy, petals 4, saucer-shaped and overlapping, 1.5–2 in. (4–5 cm) across, stamens 20–30, yellow, style 1, pillar-shaped; March–May; plant with long, thick, rhizomatous, orange-yellow roots; stem leaves usually 2, rarely 1 or 3, dull, medium green, hairy, oblong to oval, each with 5–7 deeply incised lobes and irregularly, deeply scalloped, 4–10 in. (10–25 cm) long; all other leaves basal, similar; sap yellow; fruit a silvery gray, bristly, egg-shaped capsule that droops before releasing seed. The epithet *diphyllum* (= with two leaves) notes the stem's typical pair of leaves. This gor-

geous wildflower is easy to cultivate and should be planted more. Slowly spreads by self-seeding in time and needs to be watched in lightly shaded areas with good, moist soil.

Stylophorum lasiocarpum, Chinese wood poppy. Central and eastern China.

LS to WS; flowers 2–5, in terminal clusters on erect stems to 16 in. (40 cm) tall, bright orange-yellow, sepals 2, petals 4, saucer-shaped and overlapping, to 2 in. (5 cm) across; March–May; plant with long, thick rhizomatous roots with red sap; leaves basal, medium to dark green, hairy, roundish to oval in outline, each with 4–7 lobes, irregularly scalloped and sharply toothed, to 18 in. (45 cm) long; sap red; fruit a stiffly erect, elongated capsule. Another striking addition to the shady garden. Even when the blooms are gone, the exceptional, frost-resistant leaves of this Asian poppy carry on. The similar *Stylophorum sutchuenense* from western China is smaller, with 3-lobed basal leaves to 12 in. (30 cm) long. Like *S. diphyllum*, both Asian species are reportedly hardy to zone 5 and equally heat-tolerant if supplemental water is provided during droughts.

Symphytum

Symphytum officinale (common comfrey, boneset) has been known for centuries in Europe, where it was planted in royal and monastery gardens primarily to be used in poultices applied to heal broken bones; it is still included in herb gardens and used medicinally the world over. *Symphytum* (from the Greek *symphysis* = the knitting together of bones) has produced several cultivars with true blue flowers and strikingly variegated leaves, which assets would make them desirable garden plants were it not for their aggressive behavior. *Symphytum grandiflorum* with yellow flowers and *S. rubrum* with red flowers make effective but rampant groundcovers 12–18 in. (30–45 cm) tall in the woodland garden. They exclude all weeds, true, but also the more highly desirable denizens of the shade, an aggressiveness that is probably exacerbated by the usually warm, moist spring weather in the Southeast. Many shade gardeners in these parts have regretted planting the groundcover species, and I do not recommend them for small gardens. Taller species like *S. asperum* grow to 5 ft. (1.5

m) and are also pretty but just as pugnacious; many of these require more sun than shade, particularly in northern gardens, and may require staking. I have seen plantings of hybrid comfrey cultivars like the white- and yellow-variegated forms of S. ×uplandicum (S. asperum × S. officinale) in the North, and there complaints about spreading are few. Some gardeners desire the variegated leaves only and therefore cut the plants hard to the ground, so that subsequent growth consists of foliage only—a good way to prevent their seeding around. Still, even small pieces of the fleshy roots sprout new plants, and all things considered, all *Symphytum* species are problematic in the shady garden.

Syneilesis and *Ainsliaea*

I first "discovered" many of my plants at the Asian collection garden of the University of British Columbia. On trips to that woodland wealth of Asian treasures, I made note of plants to get for Hosta Hill, especially those with interesting foliage. One genus that offered striking, boldly textured leaves was at the top of my list for years; *Syneilesis palmata* finally entered commerce, and it has been growing here ever since. The first small potful has slowly expanded into a sizeable colony of outstanding umbrellalike leaves produced on multiple stems and covered with a frosting of tiny white hairs when they emerge in the spring, folded like the leaves of mayapples.

The genus *Syneilesis* is endemic to China, Korea, and Japan in moist, mostly deciduous forests and hillsides. *Syneilesis aconitifolia* and *S. palmata* have proven to be very tolerant of hot, dry summers here and have come through two consecutive severe droughts without showing distress. Here they grow in acid woodland soil high in humus and mixed with old pine needle compost with a pH of 4.5 to 5; the soil in the native habitat is mostly oak humus, so any good garden soil with an acid reaction will do as long it has some capacity to hold moisture. Plants develop nicely in woodland to medium shade, but some sun is required for blooming. For reliable blooming, site in light to woodland shade with some morning sun. Both species are hardy to zone 5, heat-tolerant to zone 8.

Ainsliaea is similar to *Syneilesis*, growing with it in the same habitat, side by side. New explorations by the indefatigable explorer Dan Hinkley have uncovered hardy *Ainsliaea* species that require cultural conditions similar to their relatives in *Syneilesis*. Their flowers are reported to be more showy than those of *Syneilesis*, but it is their striking leaves that add texture and drama to the shady garden.

Both *Syneilesis* and *Ainsliaea* are classified in the Asteraceae. All species listed are deciduous, with perennating rootstock.

Propagate by dividing the rhizome in very early spring before growth starts. I have not seen viable seed produced by these plants. Seed collected in the wild germinates easily if sown in the ground as soon as ripe in autumn, but, for the average gardener, division is much more productive.

Slugs and snails do not seem to like the hairy, young growth and have left my plants alone; no other pests or diseases are reported or experienced here.

Syneilesis aconitifolia, shredded umbrella plant. Northeastern China, Korea, Japan.

LS to WS; flowers many, pink to purplish, in branched clusters on erect, leafy stems to 4 ft. (1.2 m) tall; July–September; plant rhizomatous, slowly expanding but not invasive; leaves on glaucous leafstalks to 24 in. (60 cm) tall, 1 leaf per stalk, folded and mayapplelike when emerging and covered with silky, fine, white hair, expanding umbrellalike, rounded, to 12 in. (30 cm) across, but deeply divided into 7–9 lobes, each lance-shaped, jaggedly toothed and sometimes cleft, grayish green, slightly glaucous. No garden should be without this outstanding foliage plant. The pinkish flowers are on tall stems and not showy; some gardeners cut them so as not to take away from the fantastic fretted texture of the leaves. The common name was bestowed by Tony Avent, another well-known explorer and provider of strange and wonderful plants; I think it is fitting indeed. **Syneilesis palmata**, also from eastern Asia, is very similar but slightly smaller, with leafstalks to 16 in. (40 cm) and leaves expanding to 10 in. (25 cm). The leaves have the same deeply cut and jagged-toothed appearance, but the leaf is somewhat glossy and more of a medium than a gray green. The flowerstalks carry a few fretted stem leaves, diminishing in size toward the top, and rise to 36 in. (90 cm); they are topped with panicles of purplish flowers. In Japan several sports of this species have been discovered, but the usually white variegation is unstable. The rarely seen *Syneilesis intermedia* is smaller; its North American progeny stems from seed collected on Taiwan, so it may not turn out to be as hardy as the northern species.

Ainsliaea acerifolia. North Korea, Japan, northeastern China.

LS to WS; flowers many, white, in branched asterlike clusters on erect stems to 18 in. (45 cm) tall; July–September; plant rhizomatous; leaves medium to dark green, deeply lobed, maplelike, 6–9 in. (15–23 cm) long. The dwarf species *Ainsliaea apiculata* has bundles of much smaller leaves, to 3 in. (8 cm) long, and small flowerstalks, to 6 in. (15 cm), carrying small bunches of white flowers. Still rare in Western gardens, these relatives of *Syneilesis* promise to be great additions to the shady garden. Judging by the climatic conditions in their native habitat, they should be as hardy as the species of *Syneilesis*.

Tellima

North American plant exploration usually proceeded from east to west. Thus, the true miterworts of the genus *Mitella* were found in the eastern regions before a similar plant was discovered in the West. This lone species was first placed in *Mitella*, but, upon closer inspection, a few morphological differences were discovered, and fringecups acquired a scientific name all its own. To indicate the close botanical relationship between the two genera, a nonsense anagram composed of the same letters, *Tellima*, was settled on; *Tellima grandiflora* remains the only species in the genus.

When I first saw fringecups in the foothills of the western Cascades, where it is quite widespread, I too thought it was *Mitella*. Use this western wildflower as a groundcover or in the wildflower garden with ferns, heucheras, and hostas. *Tellima* is classified in the Saxifragaceae.

Fringecups is easily cultivated in light to full shade and tolerates direct sun to a significant degree. Here, sited in medium shade, it accepts hot, dry summers without distress. Moist soil is ideal; fringecups responds to it by growing more rapidly into a dense groundcover. Optimum pH is 6 to 7; add some dolomitic limestone to acid soils. Hardy to zone 6 with protection.

Propagate by division or by taking rooted runners and replanting them immediately in late autumn. The species self-seeds freely; relocate seedlings in very early spring.

Slugs and snails can damage the prostrate leaves.

Tellima grandiflora, fringecups, fringecup, false alumroot. Western North America, western Cascades of Oregon, north to Alaska and south to California.

LS to FS; flowers tiny, 12–34, greenish white, sometimes rose-pink or red, on erect stems to 12 in. (30 cm) tall, insignificant, petals 5, comblike, feathery, dissected, stamens 10, attached to the flower cup rim; May–July; plant evergreen, slowly spreading; leaves in a basal rosette, medium green, hairy, 2–4 in. (5–10 cm) long, triangular to broadly heart- or kidney-shaped, with 5–7 lobes with margins scalloped; fruit a capsule with 2 beaklike projections, which *Mitella* and *Tiarella* do not have. Like *Mitella*, this species has weird flowers that are worth inspecting with a magnifying glass. Its shorter flowerstalks remain more erect than those of its eastern relations.

'Perky', flowers deep red; leaves smaller than the species.

'Purpurteppich' (= purple carpet), flowers greenish white fringed with pink; leaves tinged purplish red on purple stalks.

'Rubra' (var. *rubra*), flowers yellowish or light green; leaves reddish purple; plant more compact than the type.

Thalictrum

Meadow rue comes in two flavors, one delicate and dainty, the other tall and showy. With a genus of over 130 species, a few may qualify as in-betweens. Mother grew a huge cultivar in her sunny border; its purple stems, to 8 ft. (2.5 m) tall, carried clouds of deep lilac flowers, which stood up well to the sometimes fierce Michigan winds (with the help of a stake, I might add). She called it 'Lilac Mist' meadow rue, and its flowers indeed floated like a purplish mist over its striking foliage, which combined the delicacy of the southern maidenhair fern with the color of blue slate. She gave me a piece of it, but it never got a decent start in my hot, shady garden: most tall meadow rues are at home in sunny meadows, so are predestined for the sunny border. Although they can be grown in very light shade, they do best in full sun, and unfortunately, this includes some of the better tall meadow rues, like *Thalictrum actaeifolium*, *T. chelidonii*, *T. dasycarpum*, *T. delavayi*, *T. diffusiflorum*, *T. flavum*, *T. pubescens*, *T. revolutum*, and *T. rochebrunianum*. Most are lanky and require staking, which is fine in an open border but looks terrible in a shady, natural garden. Besides, they are difficult to include with smaller woodland plants.

The graceful woodland species are exceptions, however, and *Thalictrum aquilegiifolium* (common meadow rue) is my favorite among the many I have grown. As its epithet indicates, this Eurasian species has lovely bluish leaves similar to that of columbines (*Aquilegia* spp.) and is easily one of the prettiest smaller meadow rues; it is heat-tolerant and suitable for hot southern gardens. The woodland species native to North America may not have showy flowers, but their finely divided leaves add much to the shady garden; some gardeners use them as they would ferns. Site where their foliage can contrast with other leaf textures. Many of these species were known to American Indians, who used them, among other things, in a brew to unite quarreling couples.

The genus *Thalictrum* is classified in the Ranunculaceae. Some species are dioecious, which means that individual plants are either male or female.

Meadow rue is found in moist, fertile, open woodlands and meadows and along streams, primarily in the north temperate zone. The lower-growing species suited for the shady garden are best planted in small groups in a shady corner. Most like moist, acidic soil with a pH of 5.5 to 6.5. All are hardy to zone 5. Many are listed as heat-tolerant into zone 9, but experience shows that, except for *Thalictrum aquilegiifolium*, this is not true for many of the taller Eurasian species. I have, on the other hand, seen the North American species *T. clavatum*, *T. coriaceum*, and *T. dioicum* growing in the wild in the hot-summer areas of the Georgia Piedmont and in northern Florida and Alabama, so they should adapt well to southern gardens. Watering is necessary in warmer zones with hot, dry summers; with this care, even the superb *T. delavayi* (Yunnan meadow rue) from western China, possibly the best meadow rue for cool-summer gardens, and other meadow rues linger.

Propagate by dividing the rhizome in early spring. Sow seed as soon as ripe in a commercial seed mix, maintained moist at 70°F (21°C). Sterile hybrids must be propagated by division.

Thalictrum aquilegiifolium, common meadow rue. Eurasia.

Sun, LS to MS; dioecious; flowers many, small, appearing lilac, white or deep purple, sepals 4–5, falling away, no petals, stamens many, erect, showy, usually lilac in the male flowers, in showy, loose, branching, flat-topped clusters 3–5 in. (8–13 cm) wide, on flowerstalks 24–36 in. (60–90 cm), sometimes taller; April–June; plant clump-forming, deciduous; leaves compound, divided into many oval to roundish leaflets, bluish green, with 3–5 lobes toward the tip, to 1.5 in. (4 cm) across, usually wider than long, resembling those of the columbine; fruit a swollen, nodding 3-winged, persisting capsule. This handsome species can be planted in medium shade in southern gardens, where it flowers very early, usually around 1 May; in northern gardens, less shade and more sun is best. In all the several available cultivars, it is the showy stamens that provide the flower color.

'Album' (var. *album*) is fairly tall at 30 in. (75 cm), with dainty, pure white flowers that contrast well with its slate-gray foliage. Sadly, the flowers are short-lived but the drooping, winged seed capsules provide prolonged interest. This classic earns its keep in my shady garden primarily as an interesting foliage plant; together with medium-sized blue hostas, its leaves carry on until fall and provide cooling color during the dog days of summer.

'Atropurpureum' (var. *atropurpureum*), flowers dark purple. 'Purpureum' is very similar, except that the color is slightly more subdued.

'Auranticum', flowers reddish orange.

'Dwarf Purple', flowers purple; plant smaller than the species.

'Roseum', flowers pale rose-pink.

'Thundercloud' ('Purple Cloud'), flowers deep purple with larger stamens than the type.

'White Cloud', flowers with yellow-tipped pure white stamens, larger than 'Album'.

Thalictrum dioicum, early meadow rue, spring meadow rue, quicksilver weed. Eastern North America, Ontario, the Dakotas and Minnesota east to Quebec, south to central Georgia and west to Missouri and Arkansas.

Some sun, LS to WS; dioecious; flowers many,

small, greenish white, drooping on male plants, no petals, sepals 4–5, petal-like, stamens many, erect, showy yellow (male plants), purplish pistils (female plants), in showy, loose, branching clusters on smooth, leafy flowerstalks 10–24 in. (25–60 cm) tall; April–May; plant clump-forming, deciduous; leaves compound, divided into many oval to roundish leaflets, matte bluish olive-green above, paler beneath, with 3–4 rounded lobes toward the tip, 0.5–2 in. (1–5 cm) across; fruit egg-shaped, ribbed. An excellent foliage plant for southern gardens, holding up well into autumn, and equally suited to northern gardens well into zone 4, although it will be cut down there by the first hard freeze. Among the earliest blooming meadow rues, but the flowers are mediocre. Similar small woodland species are *Thalictrum debile* and *T. clavatum*, both rarely seen in commerce; I have observed *T. clavatum* (lady rue) in the wild in full shade, so it can be similarly sited in gardens.

Thalictrum filamentosum. Korea.

Some sun, LS to WS; flowers many, small, white, in showy, dense, branching clusters, on smooth, leafy flowerstalks 18 in. (45 cm) tall; April–May; plant clump-forming, deciduous; leaves compound, divided into many oval elliptic leaflets, matte green above, paler beneath. **Variety *tenerum*** is a lower-growing form of this handsome species, of garden origin, with a leaf mound of 12 in. (30 cm). The frothy white flower heads are compact and very long-lasting. An excellent foliage plant for southern gardens, where it holds up well into autumn, and equally adapted to northern gardens well into zone 5, though there it will be cut down by the first hard freeze.

Thalictrum kiusianum. Korea, Japan.

Some sun, LS to WS; dioecious; flowers sparse, small, lilac or mauve, sometimes purple, sepals 4–5, no petals, stamens many, erect, showy, usually purplish, in loose, branching clusters on short flowerstalks to 6 in. (15 cm); June–July; plant mat-forming with prostrate, creeping, rooting stems, deciduous; leaves compound, divided into many roundish leaflets, bluish green with a purplish cast, with 3–5 lobes toward the tip; fruit a ribbed capsule. This very popular species makes a great, albeit deciduous groundcover. Except for its prostrate, stoloniferous habit, it is similar to *Thalictrum aqui-*

legiifolium. T. Nakai named and described *T. kiusianum* (= from Kyushu) and other Korean and Japanese flora in several large works stretching from 1911 into the 1930s; but recent collections in Korea brought to light a species that is practically identical to it, *T. taquetii*, and some now consider the names synonymous. Nomenclatural tangles aside, it is a handsome plant for the shady garden.

Thalictrum minus, lesser meadow rue. Europe, northern and eastern Asia, northwestern, southeastern, and southern Africa.

Some sun, LS to WS; this species is a conglomeration of similar plants, some to 4 ft. (1.2 m), others to less than 18 in. (45 cm), originating over a large habitat, which contributes to their variability. Their flowers are like those of the male *Thalictrum dioicum*, and every bit as insignificant, a drab yellowish staminate color. All can be grown as foliage plants. Among the best is *T. minus* 'Adiantifolium' (*T. adiantifolium*), a superb foliage plant that gets its name from the resemblance of its lacy, ferny leaves to those of *Adiantum pedatum*. The leaf color is a glaucous medium green. It is stoloniferous, spreading out in time but not invasive. My plant, growing in woodland shade, is 24 in. (60 cm) tall, but some variants are a bit taller, all with ferny leaves. Hardy to zone 6, 5 with protection. It tolerates hot southern summers fairly well, demanding an occasional supplemental watering.

Thalictrum orientale. Greece into Asia Minor and east to the Caucasus.

LS to WS; flowers sparse, large, to 1 in. (2.5 cm), sepals petal-like, 4–5, white to lilac, no petals, stamens many, erect but not longer than sepals, purplish, in loose, branching clusters on short flowerstalks to 12 in. (30 cm); May–July; plant clump-forming, deciduous; leaves compound, divided into many roundish leaflets, bluish green with a purplish cast, 3-lobed toward the tip. This smaller, clump-forming species with few but larger flowers is suitable for a moist, shady location.

Thelypteris

No wonder fern lovers are confused. The once large and proud genus *Thelypteris* (an old, pre-Linnaean name for a kind of fern) is a mere shadow of its former self. It has been decimated—of the important hardy species, only New York fern (*Thelypteris nove-boracensis*) and marsh fern (*T. palustris*) are left to hold up the name. The rest are now found in *Dryopteris, Parathelypteris, Phegopteris*, and others; consult the common names in the index to find your favorites. *Thelypteris* is placed in the Thelypteridaceae.

Both species described are widely creeping and form expanding colonies. Both are herbaceous, losing their top growth in winter, and are similar in stature, height, and frond shape. In New York fern, the lower pairs of leaflets diminish rapidly in size, while those on marsh fern remain large and horizontal toward the lower part of the fronds. The only other difference seems to be that marsh fern prefers almost wet soils, while New York fern is more at home in moist open, woodland conditions. Both are hardy to zone 4. Both have a spreading habit, the marsh fern more so. In their natural habitat these ferns occupy sunny sites, but they are suitable for the shady woodland, where they appreciate constantly moist, acid soil with a pH of 5.5 to 6.5. Maintain soil moisture in dry southern gardens to keep these ferns happy and showy. Given plenty of moisture, they will stand up to considerable sun. They are best planted in groups, where the fronds of these ferns can support each other against damage by high winds; a sheltered area in the garden is better than open ground. They provide a good lacy background for lower-growing companions like hostas or astilbes.

Propagate by dividing the creeping rhizome in autumn after the fronds have dropped or in very early spring. Propagation by spores is possible but unnecessary, since the spreading habit of the ferns gives plenty of increase.

Mollusks are sometimes bothersome in the moist garden environment. The high humidity of such sites also leads to mildew, leaf spot and other fungal diseases.

Thelypteris noveboracensis, New York fern. Eastern North America, Newfoundland south to northern Georgia and Alabama and west to Oklahoma.

Some sun, LS to WS; fronds to 18 in. (45 cm) tall and 6 in. (15 cm) wide, produced tightly in tufts along a creeping rhizome, stalks scaly at the base, slightly hairy, smooth and light green above, erect, leaning with age; leaves compound, yellowish green composed of up to 20 stemless leaflets (pinnae), pointed at top, double-tapering, widest in the center, long whitish hair beneath; the lower leaflets are wider spaced and rapidly diminish in size toward the bottom; leaflets cut deeply into 16–24 never-opposite subleaflets with rounded, blunt-pointed lobes; veins rarely forked; spore cases (sori) roundish, scattered near the margin. The delicate, easily broken fronds of this fern brighten a shady corner.

Thelypteris palustris, marsh fern. Eurasia, eastern North America, New England south to Georgia and Florida and west to Texas.

Some sun, LS to WS; fronds to 24 in. (60 cm) tall and 6 in. (15 cm) wide, produced along a creeping rhizome, stalks scaly and blackish at the base, smooth and light to yellowish green above, fertile fronds more erect and taller; leaves compound, yellowish green composed of 10–14 stemless, nearly opposite leaflets (pinnae), the lower pairs shorter than the center leaflets; leaflets cut nearly to the midvein into 10–12 nearly blunt-tipped lobes with the lowest pair perpendicular to the axis, fertile leaflets have constricted margins curving over the spore cases; veins forked; spore cases (sori) roundish, in rows near the veins. This fern develops fronds throughout the summer. Old and new fronds mingle, providing an ethereal display. For best effect, plant several together.

Tiarella

Foamflower is a fitting name for *Tiarella cordifolia*, with its foamy, billowing spikes of white flowers. I have seen colonies of this native North American wildflower in northern Georgia and along Sugarlands Trail in the Great Smoky Mountains, where it is common; the feathery flowers combine into a gleaming, white cloud that beckons from afar through the underbrush. Frankly, I do not understand why this superb wildflower is not grown more in shady gardens: it is a low-maintenance plant that, after flowering for at least four weeks, carries on with striking, variegated leaves, making an attractive groundcover. It has a very high tannin content, which explains its herbalistic use by American Indians and early settlers as a mouthwash, a tonic, and a treatment for many health problems, including indigestion, diarrhea, mouth sores, and diseases of the kidney and bladder.

The species of the genus *Tiarella* have leaves that

are very similar to those of *Mitella diphylla* (miterwort, hence, false miterwort). They are evergreen, providing four-season interest that is heightened by the leaves' turning a purplish bronze at winter's onset. All are very easy to cultivate and must have medium to full shade in the South, but some sun is tolerated in more northern gardens. All are reliably hardy to zone 4, 3 with protection. Heat tolerance is also good, particularly for the species native to southeastern North America, like *Tiarella cordifolia*, and I have grown them successfully for years in medium and deep shade through many hot, dry summers. Moist soil is ideal; the stoloniferous species of false miterworts respond to it by growing more rapidly into a dense groundcover with many flowering spikes in spring. Provide supplemental water during droughts. Optimum pH is 4.5 to 7.

The generic name is the diminutive of the Greek *tiara* (= turban, crown), an allusion either to the shape of the fruit, the shape of the pistil, or the position of the stamens, which rise above the petals to form the points of a crown. *Tiarella* is classified in the Saxifragaceae.

Propagate by dividing the dormant clump or by taking rooted runners and replanting them immediately in late autumn. Under good conditions, plants self-seed freely; remove and relocate seedlings in very early spring. Otherwise sow in pots in a cold frame as soon as ripe.

Slugs and snails can damage plants. Rust is reported, but I have not experienced it here.

Tiarella cordifolia, false miterwort, foamflower, miterwort. Eastern North America, Ontario and Michigan east to Nova Scotia, south through New England and along the Appalachians to northern Georgia and Alabama, west to Tennessee.

MS to FS; flowers many, white, sometimes tinged pink or red, or reddish, small, sepals 5, petals 5, clawed, stamens 10, protruding, brownish anthers, pistils 2, unequal, in a feathery, tight, often conical cluster on leafless stems 6–12 in. (15–30 cm) tall; April–June; plant evergreen, some clones spreading rapidly by stolons, others not as aggressive but stoloniferous; leaves in a basal rosette, on finely hairy stalks, heart-shaped at base, 3- to 5-lobed, similar to those of red maple (*Acer rubrum*), usually finely hairy, medium dull green with the veins outlined in reddish green in spring, veins sunken and surface puckered between, 1.5–3 in. (4–

8 cm) long; fruit 2 capsules, splitting open at one side. This species has the best white flowers in the genus and when planted in groups creates an astoundingly beautiful display. Some of the many available cultivars may be of hybrid origin.

'Albiflora' (f. *albiflora*), flowers white. A selection of the type.

'Cygnet', flowers white, buds rose-colored; leaves deeply lobed and cleft, almost star-shaped, deep green with purple along the midrib.

'Dark Eyes', flowers white; leaves green marked with a large blotch of black; plant clump-forming.

'Eco Eyed Glossy', flowers white, fragrant; leaves medium green, very glossy.

'Eco Rambling Silhouette', flowers white, fragrant; leaves medium green, deeply cleft and lobed; plant stoloniferous.

'Eco Running Tapestry', flowers white; leaves medium green with dark, sometimes red veining; plant stoloniferous.

'Eco Slick Rock' ('Slick Rock'), flowers pinkish, fragrant; leaves deeply cleft, dark green; smaller than the species and spreads vigorously by stolons.

'Eco Splotched Velvet', flowers white; leaves velvety green with a purplish pattern at the leaf base.

'Elizabeth Oliver', flowers white; leaves deeply lobed, green with a blackish purple pattern at the leaf base and along the veins.

'Filigree Lace', hybrid (*Tiarella cordifolia* × *T. trifoliata*), flowers white; leaves lacy, blackish green patch at base.

'George Schenk Pink', flowers light pink; plant clump-forming.

'Heronswood Mist', flowers white; leaves are blotched and marbled with stable, creamy white variegation.

'Ink Blot', flowers pink, floriferous; leaves shiny with large markings of blackish green.

'Iron Butterfly', flowers white; leaves larger than the type and more deeply cleft and broadly marked with purplish black along the midvein.

'Lacquer Leaf', flowers pinkish white, floriferous, tall stems; leaves glossy green.

'Laird of Skye', flowers white, floriferous; leaves dark green, ruffled; plant stoloniferous.

'Lilacina', flowers lilac.

'Major', flowers salmon-rose to wine-red.

'Marmorata', flowers deep purple to maroon; leaves first tinged bronze, later turning dark green with purple spots.

'Mint Chocolate', flowers white tinged pink; leaves deeply lobed, dark green with a large, extended central lobe and marked along the veins with wide, black stripes.

'Ninja', flowers white tinged pink; leaves deeply lobed, dark green and marked in the center with blackish purple, in autumn turning dark purple.

'Pink Bouquet', flowers deep pink.

'Purpurea' (f. *purpurea*), flowers purple.

'Skeleton Key', flowers white; leaves deeply cleft and lobed, dark green with the midrib and minor veins a deep purple, shiny at maturity; plant clumping.

'Spring Symphony', flowers light pink; leaves velvety green with a large central blotch.

'Winterglow', flowers white; leaves with yellow winter color and marked with red blotches.

Tiarella polyphylla, Asian foamflower. Himalayas east to China and Japan.

MS to FS; flowers many, white or pink, small, nodding, sepals 5, petals 5, stamens 10, feathery, in an open cluster on stems to 18 in. (45 cm) tall; April–June; plant evergreen, spreading by stolons; leaves basal, stalked, heart-shaped at base, 3- to 5-lobed, hairy, green, some clones with purple markings, veins sunken, 0.8–2.5 in. (2–6 cm) long; stem leaves 2–3, much smaller. Clones of this species are available, some with attractive, permanent leaf markings in reddish bronze or purple and deep pink, nodding flowers. Very similar to *Tiarella cordifolia*.

Tiarella trifoliata, coolwort, three-leaved foamflower. Western North America, Alaska south to Oregon, western Cascades east to the Rocky Mountains.

MS to FS; flowers many but much less than the eastern species, pinkish white, small, sepals 5, petals 5, threadlike, stamens 10, protruding, yellow anthers, pistils 2, unequal, in a loose, feathery cluster on leafless stems to 16 in. (40 cm) tall; June–September; plant evergreen, without stolons; leaf 3-segmented, basal, 3-lobed center leaflet, 2-lobed lateral leaflets, all toothed, 1–3 in. (2.5–8-cm) long; fruit 2 capsules, splitting open at one side, seeds black. Its selection 'Incarnadine' has pink flowers. The white-flowered *Tiarella laciniata* is very similar, but its leaves are completely divided into 3 deeply cleft and irregularly toothed leaflets; it is rare in its native habitat of southern Alaska south to Oregon

and rarely available. *Tiarella unifoliata* (sugar scoop), which occurs from Alaska into Alberta and western Montana, is widespread but seldom offered. As the species name indicates, it has 1–3 leaves on the stem with secondary flowerstalks emerging from the leaf axils. The primary leafstalk is terminal. The leaves have 3–5 lobes and are toothed, pointed, and unsegmented. Western species are not as hardy, limited to zone 6, 5 with protection. None are as showy as the eastern false miterworts.

Tiarella wherryi, false miterwort, foamflower. Eastern North America, in the Appalachians from Virginia south to Georgia and Alabama, west to Tennessee and Missouri.

MS to FS; flowers many, white, fragrant, small, sepals 5, petals 5, clawed, stamens 10, protruding, reddish yellow anthers, pistils 2, unequal, in a feathery, tight, often conical cluster on leafless stems to 15 in. (38 cm) tall; April–June; plant evergreen, clump-forming, no stolons; leaves in a basal rosette, heart-shaped at base, 3- to 5-lobed, 1.5–3 in. (4–8 cm) long; fruit 2 capsules, splitting open at one side. A nonstoloniferous, more southern form of *Tiarella cordifolia* and very similar to it. It too has showy flower spikes and is good where a spreading plant is not wanted.

'Bronze Beauty', flowers white tinged pink; leaves reddish bronze.

'Dunvegan', flowers white tinged pink, on short stems to 6 in. (15 cm); leaves deeply cleft and lobed, medium green.

'Eco Maple Leaf', flowers white tinged pink, fragrant; leaves mapleleaf-shaped, medium green, marked darker along the veins with red.

'Eco Red Heart', flowers white tinged pink, fragrant; leaves medium green with dark red centers.

'Oakleaf', flowers white tinged pink, floriferous; leaves distinctly lobed like an oak leaf, serrated margins.

Tipularia

In November 1986 the Georgia Botanical Society, founded in 1925, put out the first issue of its new publication, *Tipularia*, the front cover of which featured a line drawing of *Tipularia discolor* (cranefly orchid), a modest but fascinating native orchid endemic to much of eastern North America and found all over Georgia. The dark brownish green leaves appear in early autumn when the deciduous trees lose their leaves, spreading out and carpeting the forest floor, revealing their deep purple underside here and there; they disappear in late spring. In August the flowering stems show up, from bare ground. I grow this orchid primarily as a foliage plant for autumn and winter interest in my shady garden. In the wild it is inconspicuous among the forest litter, but planted in gardens up front and near a walk, the deeply veined leaves provide a show for discriminating gardeners, especially where snow will not cover up the unusual leaves. Site in deep, moist, fertile and acid soil with a pH of 4.5 to 5.5. Hardy to zone 5, very heat- and drought-tolerant in the South.

The species name comes from *discolor* (= with two colors), alluding to the green-above, purple-underneath leaves. The generic name is taken from the insect genus *Tipula*, the craneflies, because the tiny, delicate flowers resemble the spidery legs of these insects. *Tipularia* is classified in the Orchidaceae.

Propagate by carefully dividing the tuberous corm.

In my garden, nothing in the way of diseases or insect pests seems to bother this native orchid. In southern areas slugs are reported to be a scourge during winter warm-ups. Voles and other rodents are fond of the underground corms and occasionally make off with them, so wire mesh protection may be necessary where rodents are active.

Tipularia discolor, cranefly orchid, elfin spur, crippled cranefly, mottled cranefly, resurrection orchid. Eastern North America, Michigan east to New England, where it is localized, becoming common further south in the Carolinas, Georgia, and Florida and west to Tennessee, Arkansas, and southern Indiana.

LS to FS; flowers small, insignificant, reddish purple to yellowish green, or brown, 8–28, on an erect spike 10–24 in. (25–60 cm) tall; August–September; leaf solitary, basal, long-stalked, 3–4 in. (8–10 cm) long and 2–3 in. (5–8 cm) wide, elliptic, from connected underground corms in autumn, dark gray-green to brownish green above, shiny bright purple on the underside, pleated, prominently veined, disappearing before flowering. This species is available from wildflower nurseries, but at Hosta Hill I grow a unique form with purple leaf color both above and beneath, rescued from the wild. *Tipularia japonica* from southern Japan and *T. josephii* from the Himalayas and western China are very similar to *T. discolor*, but I have not yet seen them in commerce.

Tradescantia

Tradescantias are a mixed lot of hardy and tender plants endemic to the Americas, including the hardy North American species, commonly called spiderworts, with which we are concerned. The genus was named to honor John Tradescant and his son, John Tradescant the Younger, both English botanists. Linnaeus named the first plant to reach the European continent *Tradescantia virginiana*, for the colony in which it was collected. This species became the main ingredient in a group of popular hybrids with white, pink, blue, or purple flowers, once known as *T.* ×*andersoniana* and recently placed back in *T. virginiana*. Some authors consider the subspecies and varieties that contributed to these virginiana hybrids mere regional variants of *T. virginiana*; others grant each local variant its own specific status. This complex of similar plants includes four that are distinct enough to be singled out for garden purposes: *T. hirsuticaulis* (hairy spiderwort), a hairy plant with light blue flowers that approximates *T. virginiana*; *T. ohiensis* (Ohio spiderwort), a glaucous, mostly hairless plant; *T. rosea* (rosy spiderwort), which has very narrow, grasslike leaves and rose-pink flowers; and *T. subaspera* (zigzag spiderwort) with stems that obviously zigzag. *Tradescantia* is classified in the Commelinaceae.

A long bloom period is a must if spiderworts are to earn a place in the garden. At Hosta Hill, *Tradescantia virginiana* and *T. ohiensis* have successfully flowered in even woodland shade for years, adding bright white and blue accents to the garden. Each bloom lasts only six to eight hours, even under the best cultural conditions; the flower parts of both species do not drop off but wilt and dissipate by enzymatic action. Remove spent flowers and cut leaves to the ground to encourage reblooming and prevent seed production. The virginiana hybrids, however, must have a lot of sun to bloom abundantly; all that's left when they are finished flowering is bunch of unruly, flopped-over blades to cut back. If one wants to have grassy-looking leaves, several shade-tolerant, ornamental grasses are much better for this purpose.

Spiderworts do well in the wildflower or woodland garden in deep, moist, acid soil with a pH of 5 to 6.5. All spiderworts should be carefully sited because their foliage becomes untidy as the season progresses. From a practical standpoint, any of the hardy spiderworts can be used in gardens in similar fashion. I place them between azaleas, fronted by hostas and other leafy plants that hide the haircuts when the leaves are eventually cut off. In their native habitat all grow in high-light situations like roadsides, meadows, open woods, and clearings, so they should be sited in a partially sunny and lightly shaded spot in the garden to realize abundant flowering. They have a high heat and drought tolerance. Hardy to zone 5.

Propagate by carefully dividing the dormant rootstock in late autumn or very early spring. Self-sown seedlings can be dug and transplanted.

Slugs and snails are troublesome when the fresh shoots start active growth in spring. Spider mites, aphids, and other sucking insects are reported.

Tradescantia ohiensis, spiderwort, trinity. Eastern North America, Minnesota east to Massachusetts, south to Georgia and Florida and west to southern Texas.

Some sun, LS; flowers numerous, in terminal clusters borne over 2 opposite but unequal green bracts, bright blue to rose-pink, rarely white, 1–2 in. (2.5–5 cm) across, sepals 3, narrower, smooth or hairy only at the tips, petals 3, wide open, triangular, stamens 6, showy yellow, on stems to 30 in. (75 cm) tall; April–July; plant clump-forming; leaves stalkless, opposite on the stem, green, hairless and covered with a glaucous bloom, linear to narrowly lance-shaped, keeled, folded lengthwise, to 15 in. (38 cm) long and 1.5 in. (4 cm) wide. This hardy species is similar to *Tradescantia virginiana* and by some considered a subspecies of it. The white-flowered **'Alba'** has blue stamens.

Tradescantia virginiana, common spiderwort, early spiderwort, showy spiderwort, widow's tears. Eastern North America, Minnesota and Wisconsin east to New England, south to Georgia and Alabama and west to Tennessee, Missouri, and Arkansas.

Some sun, LS; flowers numerous, in terminal clusters borne over 2 opposite but unequal green bracts, usually violet-blue, sometimes pink or white, 1–2 in. (2.5–5 cm) across, sepals 3, green and hairy, petals 3, wide open, triangular, stamens 6, showy yellow and hairy, on more or less zigzagging stems to 36 in. (90 cm) tall; April–July; plant clump-forming; leaves stalkless, opposite on the stem, green, stem and leaves very hairy, linear to narrowly lance-shaped, keeled, folded lengthwise, to 15 in. (38 cm) long and 1.5 in. (4 cm) wide. This is the common species, widespread in its habitat. The petals do not drop off but turn into a jellylike liquid (hence, widow's tears). In the past the stems and leaves were used in salads, and even today the edible flowers are used to decorate food and cakes. The hybrid **'Sweet Kate'** ('Blue and Gold') has bright yellow foliage with deep blue flowers; even without flowers, it adds yellow to the garden. Cut to the ground to encourage new leaf growth when the leaf mound becomes unruly.

Tricyrtis

In the late 1950s I wanted to add some autumn-flowering plants to my Nashville garden, so I obtained *Tricyrtis hirta*, a supposedly half-hardy perennial, from a mail-order source; three stems emerged from the rootstock and came through a frosty first winter in zone 6a without problems. The next spring a whole bunch of stems arched forth, clothed with furry, clasping, alternate leaves. The following September, awesome flowers, whitish spotted with bright purple, opened at each leaf axil along the stout stem. My enthusiasm for the genus has not waned since.

Tricyrtis is placed in the Tricyrtidaceae. The generic name is from the Greek *treis* (= three) and *kyrtor* (= swelling), a reference to the three swollen, nectar-bearing cavities at the base of the sepals. The origin of the common name toad lily is unclear; certain species were said to be used to kill toads, and the spotted greenish brown leaves of some species do look a lot like spotted toads. Dan Hinkley, plant explorer extraordinaire, has coined the affectionate nickname toadies, which name I like and use.

Toadies are native to the eastern Himalayas in Nepal and China and range to Japan and further south, to Taiwan (Formosa) and the Philippines. The many variegated sports discovered in Japan have been made subjects for pot culture there. Prized for their colorful foliage, a few of these variegated forms have found their way into gardens. The Japanese name for the genus, *hototogisu*, sometimes turns up as a cultivar name in the West.

Toad lilies are rhizomatous herbaceous perennials. Because they die down in autumn, they can be mulched heavily for the winter season, extending their hardiness range. I have grown *Tricyrtis formosana* (Formosan toad lily) for over a decade now; even though its native island is bisected by the tropic of Cancer, this toad lily has survived brief dips to 0°F (−18°C) here given a cover of dry pine straw 12 in. (30 cm) thick. *Tricyrtis* species get abundant rain in their native habitat. They must have water during prolonged summer droughts; I use soaker hoses, but sometimes even that is not enough. Toad lilies prefer a woodland soil with plenty of organic matter, good tilth, and water-holding capacity, yet well drained; I grow all mine in raised beds in peat moss and pine bark mixed with lots of pine needle compost; pine bark mulch and chips contribute to drainage.

The leafy stems of toad lilies, arching here and there among hostas, astilbes, and ferns, are extraordinary; late in the season, when the garden seems to be worn-out and tired, they display rows of enchanting, orchidlike flowers. Some plants bloom in late autumn, by which time the leaves are unsightly, particularly if the preceding summer has been dry.

Propagation is easy—the plants do it. *Tricyrtis hirta* happily seeds itself all over the place, and I have let it naturalize in some places. Dividing the rhizome is also easily done in the fall. Some of the stoloniferous (actually rhizomatous) species make increase really easy. Simply remove some of the creeping rhizomes from the periphery of the plant in autumn or very early spring.

Slugs and snails bother the young growth in spring. Leaf spot occasionally shows up—roundish spots with brownish purple margins; toad lilies that have suffered through periods of drought are especially vulnerable. Only powerful systemic fungicides prevent anthracnose blight, another malady that strikes toad lilies; I usually just remove affected leaves, but if the disease is widespread on a stem, I remove the entire stem, to prevent infection of other parts of the plant.

Unless otherwise stated, all toad lilies listed can be grown in zones 6 to 9; in zone 5, provide ample mulch to protect the rhizomes and expect some losses during extreme winters. In colder regions with early freezes, the plants may have to be dug and brought inside to prevent the flowers from being spoiled. Keeping plants potted throughout the season facilitates this.

Tricyrtis affinis. Japan, Honshu, Shikoku, Kyushu.
LS to MS; flowers whitish, with brownish purple markings inside, saucer-shaped with petals spreading, up-facing, solitary in several to many of the outer leaf axils, 1 in. (2.5 cm) across; September–October; plant clump-forming, 24 in. (60 cm) tall, stems green changing to brownish at leaf axils, covered with stiff hairs; leaves hairy, to 3 in. (8 cm) long, elliptic, acuminate, dark green with large brownish spots. The brownish "variegated" leaves contrast wonderfully with small yellow hostas.

Tricyrtis flava, *kibanano hototogisu* (Jap.). Japan, Honshu, Kansai, Shikoku, Kyushu.
LS to MS; flowers yellow, with purple markings inside, saucer-shaped with petals spreading, up-facing, solitary or in pairs in the outer leaf axils or terminal, 1 in. (2.5 cm) across; September–October; plant clump-forming, 24 in. (60 cm) tall, stems hairy, dark greenish purple; leaves densely arranged, hairy, to 6 in. (15 cm) long, broadly elliptic, acuminate, medium green, slightly blotched in spring, turning uniform bright green. This species fits nicely into patches of blue-green hostas or darker heucheras, forming expanding clumps of shiny green leaves with good substance. Even when not in flower, its attractive foliage makes a contribution, but its glory season is October, when bunches of bright yellow flowers clothe the stems. I detest staking, but in this case I recommend it: during heavy rains the up-facing flowers fill with water, and the added weight topples the stems. Variety *nana* differs only by its smaller size; its selection 'Chabo' has short stems to 8 in. (20 cm) covered with dark purple leaves, which provide a stunning contrast to the large yellow flowers.

Tricyrtis formosana, Formosan toad lily. Taiwan.
LS to MS; flowers whitish to pinkish, with deep purple markings inside, increasingly darker toward center, petals spreading, up-facing, arranged in cymes at branch terminals, 1 in. (2.5 cm) across; September–October; plant stoloniferous, spreading outward, 30 in. (75 cm) tall, very erect stems,

brownish purple at base changing to light green at tip, covered with tiny hairs; leaves clasping stem, hairy, to 3 in. (8 cm) long, elliptic, acuminate, shiny uniform light green, but some forms have darker green spots, with veins deeply grooved. The flowers of this species, which come off as deep purple, are among the showiest in the autumn garden. My original planting has expanded into a many-stemmed clump 36 in. (90 cm) wide.

'Amethystina' has deep lavender flowers with intense purple spotting and appears much darker.

'Dark Beauty', very dark flowers.

'Gates of Heaven' ('Ogon') is smaller and has bright yellow leaves.

'Samurai' (striped toad lily) has leaves with narrow, white margins and grows to 18 in. (45 cm).

'Seiryu' (= green dragon; 'Hototogisu'), similar to 'Amethystina' but flowers more red.

'Variegata' has distinctly gold-margined leaves.

Tricyrtis hirta, Japanese toad lily. Japan, Honshu, Shikoku, Kyushu.

LS to MS; flowers whitish, spotted with lavender, petals spreading, up-facing, in leaf axils, 1 in. (2.5 cm) across; August–October; plant clump-forming, 24 in. (60 cm) tall, stems arching, green, sometimes brownish at leaf junction, covered with hairs; leaves alternate, clasping stem, hairy, to 5 in. (13 cm) long, oblong-elliptic, acuminate, medium green. The flowers are not as dark as those of *Tricyrtis formosana*, but their arrangement in each leaf axil, with up to 24 flowers per stem, is a marvelous sight on otherwise dreary autumn days. Variety *masamunei* is much like the species but devoid of all hair. *Tricyrtis setochinensis*, broadly related to *T. hirta*, is found and named for its limited habitat along the shores of the Setonaikai, the Japanese Inland Sea; its flowers, carried on the upper part of the 30 in. (75 cm) stem, are densely spotted with purple and somewhat larger. Several cultivars of *T. hirta* are available.

'Alba' (var. *alba* of gardens) has white flowers.

'Albomarginata' has leaves with a narrow white margin.

'Lilac Towers' is similar to the type but has larger lilac flowers.

'Miyazaki' is slightly smaller, to 12 in. (30 cm) tall, but otherwise with arching stems like the type.

'Miyazaki Gold', like 'Miyazaki' but has leaves with narrow, yellow margin.

'White Towers', an albino form with white flowers and pink stamens, is similar to 'Alba'.

Tricyrtis ishiiana. Japan, central Honshu, southern Kanto.

LS to MS; this species closely resembles *Tricyrtis macrantha* (it was once considered a variety of it) but has green stems to 20 in. (50 cm), with smooth green leaves to 4 in. (10 cm), and smaller yellow flowers, arranged in terminal clusters. Once rare in the wild, it is now nursery-propagated. Variety *surugensis* is similar to the species. It has smaller light green leaves on arching stems, which are brownish at the base but light green above; the flowers have dark brown anthers.

Tricyrtis latifolia, broadleaf toad lily. Japan, Honshu, Hokkaido, Shikoku, Kyushu.

LS to MS; flowers light yellow, with deep purple spots inside, petals obliquely spreading, up-facing, arranged in cymes at branch terminals, occasionally in the upper leaf axils, 1 in. (2.5 cm) across; August–October; plant clump-forming, with short rhizomes, 30 in. (75 cm) tall, very erect stems brownish green, darker at leaf axils, covered with tiny hairs; leaves clasping stem, smooth, to 6 in. (15 cm) long and 4 in. (10 cm) wide, rounded heart-shaped, abruptly acuminate, dark green, with veins deeply grooved. This species stands out with its well-rounded leaves and erect habit and can provide a lovely early display in mid-August, blooming along with *Hosta plantaginea* and *H*. 'Royal Standard'. Variety *makinoana* is sometimes mistaken for the type, the only difference being more hairs on the stems and beneath the leaves.

Tricyrtis macrantha. Japan, Shikoku.

LS to MS; flowers deep yellow, bell-shaped, tubular, pendent, richly spotted inside with reddish purple spots, to 1 in. (2.5 cm) long, emerging in clusters (cymes) at ends of branches; September–October; plant clump-forming, 24 in. (60 cm) tall, stems very arching, becoming pendulous, often decumbent, touching the ground, brownish green covered with brown hairs; leaves deeply veined, to 5 in. (13 cm) long, oblong-elliptic, rounded at base, acuminate, dark green. Reported to be hardy to zone 8 only, at Hosta Hill this species has survived brief periods of 5°F (−15°C) without protection, so with protection, gardeners in zone 7 should be able to successfully cultivate it.

***Tricyrtis macrantha* var. *macranthopsis*.** Japan, Honshu, Shikoku, Kyushu.

LS to MS; flowers large, deep yellow, bell-shaped, tubular, pendent, richly spotted inside with bright maroon spots, to 2 in. (5 cm) long, many, emerging in the leaf axils and terminally at ends of branches; September–October; plant clump-forming, 4 ft. (1.2 m) tall, but stems very arching, becoming pendulous, often decumbent, touching the ground, smooth green and without hairs; leaves deeply veined, to 8 in. (20 cm) long, oblong-elliptic, rounded at base and clasping stem, acuminate, dark green. The exquisite drooping flowers of this variety are spectacular, the largest in the genus. In the garden, they can get too close to the ground, where dirt splatters up on them during rainy days, so I elevate the plants in raised beds or in pots on pedestals, to reveal the full details of the floral display. A high position along a rock wall would also suit.

***Tricyrtis macropoda*.** Japan, Honshu, Hokkaido, Shikoku, Kyushu, Korea.

LS to MS; flowers whitish, with purple spots inside, petals obliquely spreading, drooping, downward-facing, arranged on stems terminally in clusters and axillary in the upper leaf axils, 1 in. (2.5 cm) across; August–October; plant clump-forming, to 36 in. (90 cm) tall, stems erect dark green; leaves clasping stem, smooth, to 5 in. (13 cm) long and 2.5 in. (6 cm) wide, nearly heart-shaped, dark green, lacking hairs. Taxonomic splitters recognize f. *hirsuta* (covered with hairs) and f. *glabrescens* (without hairs). Variety *chugokuensis* from Chugoku, the southern district of Honshu, is differentiated by longer pedicels. I have myself seen a very floriferous plant in the Atlanta garden of Ozzie and Jitsuko Johnson: in addition to the terminal flowers, many axillary flowers arise from the leaf axils, reaching down low on the imposing stems; this vigorous new Yungi Temple form of *T. macropoda* measures up to 5 ft. (1.5 m) in height.

***Tricyrtis oshumiensis*.** Japan, southern Kyushu, Kagoshima, Osumi peninsula.

LS to MS; flowers yellow, nearly without spots, petals spreading, up-facing, solitary or in pairs in the outer leaf axils or terminal, 1 in. (2.5 cm) across; August–October; plant clump-forming, 30 in. (75 cm) tall, stems smooth or nearly so, green; leaves smooth, medium green, to 4 in. (10 cm) long and 2 in. (5 cm) wide, narrowly elliptic to oblong, abruptly acute, clasping stem. This species has pretty yellow flowers with a helping of the tiniest pale maroon spots. Its handsome, bright green foliage makes it a great companion plant in the shady garden. Once considered a variety of *Tricyrtis flava*. May need winter protection in zone 6 and colder.

***Tricyrtis perfoliata*.** Japan, Kyushu.

LS to MS; flowers yellow, scarcely purple-spotted inside, petals spreading, up-facing, solitary in the median and outer leaf axils, 1 in. (2.5 cm) across; August–October; plant clump-forming, 30 in. (75 cm) tall, stems smooth, green; leaves smooth, medium green with occasional blotchy shading, to 4 in. (10 cm) long and 2 in. (5 cm) wide, narrowly elliptic, acuminate, distinctly perfoliate. May need winter protection in zone 6 and colder. A potted specimen at Hosta Hill has survived 15°F (−10°C) in the open.

Tricyrtis cultivars

'Amanagawa'. Hybrid (*Tricyrtis perfoliata* × *T. hirta*).

LS to MS; flowers light yellow, with a few speckles, upright, bell-shaped; stems 24 in. (60 cm) tall stems, leaves elliptic, pointed, green with brown speckles.

'Kohaku'. Garden hybrid.

LS to MS; flowers white, widely spotted with dark purple and with yellow throats, produced in the leaf axils, petals spreading, up-facing, 1 in. (2.5 cm) across; September–October; plant clump-forming, to 36 in. (90 cm) tall in good moist soil but usually shorter, stems arching with medium to dark green leaves, clasping stem, hairy, to 3 in. (8 cm) long, oval-elliptic, acuminate and almost heart-shaped at the leaf axil.

'Togen' ('Tojen'). Garden hybrid.

LS to MS; flowers whitish lavender, spotted with light purple and with yellow throat, petals spreading, up-facing, in leaf axils, 1 in. (2.5 cm) across; August–October; stems 36 in. (90 cm) high, erect at first but, weighed down by colossal (for the genus) leaves, they become pendulous, often decumbent, touching the ground, where alternate branches appear at the leaf axils; leaves very large, medium green, clasping stem, hairy, to 12 in. (30 cm) long and 4 in. (10 cm) wide, oblong-elliptic, acuminate at the tip and almost truncate at the leaf axil; plant clump-forming, 4 ft. (1.2 m) tall. This gigantic hybrid of Japanese garden origin, the grandest of all toad lilies at Hosta Hill, can be paired with medium to large hostas and some of the larger ferns. In autumn rains, its leaves and flowers become soaked with moisture and get so heavy that they bend way down, often touching the ground. To keep the wonderful iridescent flowers from becoming soiled, some support here and there is required. I install the stakes early in the spring, before the stems emerge and elongate.

Trillium

Wandering through the Appalachians has been a passion of mine for decades. It has also made me a better gardener, by showing me how trilliums and other wildflowers are meant to grow. Trilliums are also known as wakerobins, toadshades, trinity lilies, and a host of other common names, which attests to their popularity as wildflowers. To see acres of *Trillium grandiflorum* in bloom near my mother's home in southern Michigan was for me a privilege and remains a cherished memory to this day. But my admiration of trilliums goes back to my roots in Europe, where nary a trillium is to be found. They were simply too expensive. As a young student, I could only revere these charmers in botanical gardens. Decades later, when we moved to Georgia, a few jaunts through northern Georgia made it abundantly clear to me that trilliums were everywhere. The Appalachian region of North America is the prehistoric cradle of trilliums.

The recent movement to natural gardening with native plants has put trilliums into the vanguard of flowering plants for the shady garden, and, thankfully, new techniques in trillium propagation have reduced the pressure put on native populations due to collecting (remaining threats include loss of habitat due to development and the appetite of the ever-increasing deer population). In some areas certain species of trillium are abundant; the Virginia Native Plant Society reports that in Shenandoah National Park a contiguous population of 18 million plants exists. Unfortunately, species like *Trillium rugelii* (southern nodding trillium) do not fare as well and are now rare in many areas. All trilliums in the wild should be left alone.

The genus *Trillium* has its widest diversity and distribution in North America. A few species are found in southern Kamchatka, the areas surrounding the Sea of Japan including eastern Russia (Siberia), eastern China (the Amur region), Korea, Japan, and the Himalayas. None are found in Europe or in Asia west and south of the Himalayas; the south temperate zone is devoid of them. Botanists have subdivided the genus into two subgenera, one with stalked trilliums (subgenus *Trillium*), the other with sessile species (subgenus *Phyllantherum*). The stalked ones have flowers on a stalk called a pedicel, and their petals are spreading; the sessile ones have flowers that are stalkless and "sit down" on the topmost whorl of leaves, and their petals are usually erect. Sessile trilliums occur only in eastern North America, and they alone have a feature coveted by gardeners: attractively mottled or patterned leaves. Whether a species is stalked or sessile will be noted in the descriptions.

American Indians used trillium rhizomes as a uterine stimulant during childbirth; other herbalistic uses include treatment of eye problems and all manner of ailments treatable by its astringent properties. The Linnaean name *Trillium*, which dates to 1754, was derived from the Latin *tri* (= three), an allusion to the 3-merous flower and leaf composition. The genus is placed in the Trilliaceae.

Most trilliums are hardy to zone 5. Originating in moist woodlands, they are well adapted to shady, moist conditions. The species from the southern ranges can withstand some lack of moisture; after they are through flowering, they in fact prefer a dry dormant period. The arid summer conditions of southeastern North America cause them to go dormant early; but in the deep shade of a Japanese maple and given supplemental water during dry weather, some of my trilliums provide a leaf show of almost five months, carrying on until late summer. Trilliums prefer a deep woodland soil with plenty of organic matter, good tilth, and good water-holding capacity, yet reasonably well drained. During rescues of native populations, I have found that most wild trilliums are very deeply rooted, so this should be considered when planting them in gardens. Do not site them in soil that is too shallow or which dries out quickly. Given correct cultural conditions, trilliums are extremely long-lived and form extensive colonies in time. Even though they will grow in clay, I grow all mine in raised beds of deep soil mixed with some sandy clay, a little peat moss, pine bark, and lots of pine straw and woods compost. Optimum pH for the southern species is 4 to 5.5; the species common in midwestern habitats, like *Trillium nivale* or *T. recurvatum*, prefer a sweeter soil with a pH of 6 to 7. In my garden, I add dolomitic chips to achieve this pH level.

Propagate by carefully dividing the dormant rhizome in late autumn or very early spring. Seed can be sown in a pot in a protected cold frame placed in shade. It takes five to seven years for seedlings to attain flowering size.

Large slugs and snails can damage young growth emerging in spring. Trilliums are relatively free of pests and diseases here otherwise.

All species are deciduous. Unless otherwise noted, all trilliums are 3-merous, with 3 sepals, 3 petals, 6 stamens, ovary 3- to 6-lobed; leaves 3, whorled. Please note that for stalked trilliums, the flower size is given as measured across the open flower, while in sessile trilliums the flower size is given as the length of the erect petals.

Trillium apetalon, *enreiso* (Jap.). Japan, northern Honshu, Hokkaido, Kurile Islands, southern Sakhalin.

WS to MS; flowers tiny, not showy at all, no petals, only purplish green sepals over plain but unmarked, rich green leaves. This is one for the trillium collector. Hardy to zone 4. Variety *rubricarpum* has red fruit. Another Asian toadshade for collectors, *Trillium smallii* (Kojima Island trillium, *kojima enreiso* in Japan) from western Hokkaido and southern Sakhalin, has petals that are tiny and usually distorted. I find *T. apetalon* relatively easy to cultivate in medium shade in cool, moist, acid soil, but it goes dormant early during the hot season in the Georgia Piedmont.

Trillium catesbaei, Catesby's trillium, rose trillium, rosy wakerobin, bashful wakerobin. Eastern North America, in the mountains and the Piedmont of Virginia, the Carolinas, to Georgia and northern Alabama, west to eastern Tennessee.

WS to MS; flowers stalked, stalk 0.8–1.5 in. (2–4 cm) long, nodding halfway and at the level of the leaves, flowers large, 2–3 in. (5–8 cm) across, sepals green, narrow, recurved, petals opening white, pink, or rose, sometimes deep rose, wavy margins, recurved, anthers yellow; April–June; plant clump-forming, 8–20 in. (20–50 cm) tall; leaves 1.5–3 in. (4–8 cm) long, short-stalked, elliptic, whorled, 5 main veins; fruit a whitish or greenish berry. A good garden form for southern gardens with acid soil. Here it does not multiply well but is attractive and long-lived. Sharing habitat with this species is *Trillium persistens*, which is on the Federal list of endangered plants. I am content with admiring it in the Tallulah Gorge of northeastern Georgia; it is not showy in the open garden. *Trillium catesbaei* is sometimes confused with *T. grandiflorum*, whose flowers turn pink with age. A larger-flowered form from the hollows of the Carolina Appalachians is sometimes listed as *T. catesbaei* var. *macranthum*, but this name is not recognized and is a synonym for *T. cernuum*. Cultivars 'Eco Rose' (flowers large, ruffled, rose-pink) and 'Eco Ivory' (flowers large, ruffled, white turning pink later) are offered.

Trillium cernuum, nodding trillium, northern nodding trillium, ground lily, jew's harp. Eastern North America, Manitoba and the Great Lake States east to Newfoundland and New England, south to New York, Pennsylvania, eastern West Virginia, and southern Virginia.

WS to MS; flowers stalked, stalk 0.6–1.2 in. (1.5–3 cm) long, drooping below the leaves, flowers small, 1.5–2 in. (4–5 cm) across, sepals green, narrowly lance-shaped, recurved, petals white or pink, rarely dark pink, strongly recurved, anthers lavender or pinkish gray; April–June; plant clump-forming, 8–24 in. (20–60 cm) tall; leaves 2.5–4 in. (6–10 cm) long, diamond-shaped, barely stalked, whorled and overlapping, hiding the flower; fruit a dark red berry. This species is not the best garden plant because, true to its name (*cernuum* = drooping), the overlapping leaves hide the small, down-turned flowers. Forma *album* has white flowers; f. *tangerae* is lately considered an interspecific hybrid with *T. erectum*. The type is similar to and frequently confused with *Trillium rugelii* (southern nodding trillium), which occurs much further south, sharing acid soil habitat with *T. catesbaei*; *T. rugelii* is not a showy trillium but a very hardy one, to zone 3.

Trillium chloropetalum, giant trillium, California giant toadshade. Western North America, coastal central California.

WS to MS; flowers sessile, fragrant, sepals green, lance-shaped, blunt-tipped, erect, petals broadly lance-shaped, 2–4 in. (5–10 cm) long and 0.6–1 in. (1.5–2.5 cm) wide, color variable, greenish white, greenish yellow, maroon, dark brown, purplish brown, purplish red, pink, white, or white with red veining, anthers purple; February–April; plant clump-forming, 8–24 in. (20–60 cm) tall; leaves unstalked, greenish mottled strongly or weakly with dark brown, 3–7 in. (8–18 cm) long and wide, rounded diamond-shaped, whorled; fruit a purple berry. Originally considered a form of *Trillium sessile*, this species is still mixed up in commerce with the eastern species, which is much more hardy. Variety *giganteum* is more robust and larger than the type; its flowers are white to deep red, lacking yellow pigment. Both are extremely variable in leaf mottling. Both are good garden plants in mild-winter areas but rise and bloom very early, so are often damaged by late freezes. Not recommended for gardens in zone 5 and colder. Here in zone 7a they need protection from late cold spells. The same goes for two other sessile western species, *T. albidum*, with pure white flowers and slightly more winter hardiness, and *T. angustipetalum*, with narrow, deep red, glossy petals to 0.5 in. (1 cm) wide. Both are sold under the names *T. chloropetalum* and *T. sessile*.

Trillium cuneatum, whippoorwill toadshade, whippoorwill flower, bloody butcher, cuneate trillium, large toadshade, purple toadshade, sweet Betsy, toadshade. Eastern North America, western Carolinas and southern Kentucky south into central Tennessee, the Georgia Piedmont and northern Alabama, Mississippi, and Louisiana.

WS to MS; flowers sessile, faintly fragrant, sepals green to purple-streaked or purple-suffused, lance-shaped, sharp-tipped, erect, petals elliptic to lance-shaped, widest above the middle, 1.2–2.5 in. (3–6 cm) long and 0.5–1 in. (1–2.5 cm) wide, color variable, maroon, purplish brown, purplish green, clear green, yellowish green, yellow, or yellow with purple base, anthers yellow; March–April; plant clump-forming, 6–18 in. (15–45 cm) tall; leaves unstalked, overlapping, darker green mottled strongly or weakly with lighter green or whitish to grayish green, 3–7 in. (8–18 cm) long and 3–5 in. (8–13 cm) wide, oblong-elliptic, whorled; fruit a plain green or purple-streaked berry. This southern trillium

has long been sold as *Trillium sessile* of gardens. It grows over a large area and is extremely variable: its yellow-flowered forms are often mistaken for *T. luteum*, as is its f. *luteum*, which has yellow to greenish yellow flowers. In gardens they serve the same purpose. All forms are hardy to zone 5, but their early appearance in spring may expose them to late freezes. This is an excellent garden trillium with strikingly variegated leaves and a choice of flower colors. It is well adapted to hot, dry summers given supplemental water. From the more western regions of the Southeast come *T. decipiens*, *T. decumbens*, *T. foetidissimum*, *T. gracile*, *T. ludovicianum*, *T. stamineum* (with strange, twisted petals), and *T. underwoodii*. All are attractive and comparable in garden use to *T. cuneatum*, albeit with slight differences in leaves and flowers; but, being from Mississippi and Louisiana and reaching into the coastal plain of the Gulf States, they are programmed by nature to emerge very early, from mid-February to mid-March. Although their rhizomes are very hardy when deeply planted, they repeatedly get cut down by late freezes and disappear. These species have relatively small habitats; they should never be collected in the wild and are better admired in their natural habitat. *Trillium cuneatum* is propagated; it and its cultivars are much better suited to the shady garden.

‘Eco Dappled Lemon’, flowers clear yellow, stamens yellow; leaves heavily marbled; plant to 10 in. (25 cm) tall.

‘Eco Marbled Lime’, flowers light green; leaves marbled light green; plant to 16 in. (40 cm) tall.

‘Eco Midnight’, flowers dark purple; leaves dark purplish green.

‘Eco Mississippi Gold’, flowers yellow; stems purple, leaves marbled lightly with lighter green.

‘Eco Purple Shadows’, flowers dark purple; leaves dark green marbled with lighter shades.

‘Eco Silver Spectacular’, flowers large, deep purple; leaves uniform silver-gray, unmarked.

‘Eco Silver Tiara’, flowers large, deep purple; leaves uniform silver-gray, unmarked.

Trillium erectum, purple trillium, wakerobin, American true love, Bethroot, birthwort, brown Beth, fetid wakerobin, squawroot, stinking Benjamin, stinking Willie. Eastern North America, southeastern Ontario and Michigan east to Nova Scotia, south to New England, New York, and Pennsylvania, and in the Appalachians to northern Georgia and eastern Tennessee.

WS to MS; flowers on straight, erect stalks to 4 in. (10 cm) long, flowers slightly dangling, outward-facing, large, to 3 in. (8 cm) across, slightly malodorous, sepals green, sometimes overlaid with maroon, narrowly lance-shaped, straight, petals straight, prominently veined, purplish brown, maroon, purple, or sometimes white, rarely yellowish green or deep yellow, stamens maroon, anthers yellow; April–June; plant clump-forming, 8–24 in. (20–60 cm) tall; leaves 2–8 in. (5–20 cm) long, diamond-shaped, bright green; fruit a dark red berry. Among the best trilliums for gardens with acid soil. Some individual plants have a more or less fetid odor, but it is mostly less: you must really stick your nose into the flower to perceive it. Here this robust, vigorous species propagates itself in the garden. Its very showy flowers are mainly held erect above the leaves. I have seen entire populations of the white-flowered **var. *album*** in the southern Smoky Mountains. Forma *luteum* has greenish yellow petals. Bicolored sports occur in wild populations. Widely available but extremely variable in commerce. Available cultivars, all with yellow anthers, include 'Eco Gold Star' (flowers yellow), 'Eco Pink Frost' (flowers rose-pink), 'Eco Snow Cap' (flowers pure white), and 'Eco Wine Cap' (flowers wine-red).

Trillium flexipes, bent trillium, Gleason's trillium, white trillium. Eastern North America, Minnesota east to western New York and south to Missouri and Arkansas, in the mountains from eastern Tennessee to northwestern Georgia and northern Alabama.

WS to MS; flowers stalked, stalks straight or angled and rarely declining, not curved, 1.5–5 in. (4–12 cm) long, mostly held above the leaves, flowers large, 2–3 in. (5–8 cm) across, sepals green, lance-shaped, as long as the petals, recurved margins, petals creamy white, rarely maroon or bicolored, with heavy texture, anthers yellow; April–June; plant clump-forming, 8–20 in. (20–50 cm) tall; leaves 3–10 in. (8–25 cm) long, diamond-shaped, unstalked, whorled and almost overlapping; fruit a rosy red to purplish red berry. Often confused with the nodding *Trillium cernuum* and *T. rugelii*, but from a gardener's standpoint, *T. flexipes* is much better: it has a flowerstalk (pedicel) with a kneelike

bend at the point of flower attachment, so facing the flower outward, usually above the leaves. This is a good garden form with long-lasting flowers and leaves, but it must have neutral to slightly alkaline soil. Rarely offered are two off-colored forms, f. *walpolii* (maroon flowers) and f. *billingtonii* (flowers with red in the center and white toward petal tips).

Trillium govanianum, Himalayan triplet lily. Himalayas to western China.

WS to MS; flowers stalked, stalks erect, to 0.5 in. (1 cm) long, flowers held above the leaves, tepals (sepals and petals) alike, purple or maroon, narrowly lance-shaped, to 0.8 in. (2 cm) long, spreading in 6-merous form, stamens 6, purple with yellow anthers, ovary large, purple, with 3 erect, linear purple styles; May–June; plant clump-forming, to 8 in. (20 cm) tall; leaves to 4 in. (10 cm) long and 2 in. (8 cm) wide, with 3 prominent veins, pointed tip, stalked, dark green, whorled. This unusual Asian species looks more like *Paris* and is sure to attract trillium and paris fans alike. It is still rare in cultivation but assumed hardy to zone 5. It requires shade and consistently moist, acid soil. Plant in an elevated container with good potting soil until it is certain to settle in. An elevated position properly displays the small but fascinating flower structure.

Trillium grandiflorum, great white trillium, large-flowered trillium, showy wakerobin, trinity lily, white trillium. Eastern North America, southern Ontario to northeastern Minnesota and Wisconsin east through Michigan, southern Quebec to Maine and New Hampshire south to Ohio and Pennsylvania and in the mountains south to the western Carolinas and northeastern Georgia.

WS to MS; flowers stalked, stalks straight and erect, or slightly angled, 0.8–2 in. (2–5 cm) long, held above the leaves, largest in the genus, 3–4 in. (8–10 cm) across, sepals green, lance-shaped, petals variable, opening white to creamy white and fading to pink or rarely red, with heavy texture, superior forms are conspicuously veined and have undulate margins, anthers yellow; April–June; plant clump-forming, 6–12 in. (15–30 cm) tall; leaves 6–8 in. (15–20 cm) long and 3–6 in. (8–15 cm) wide, diamond-shaped, unstalked, dark green, in spring sometimes marked with purplish brown, prominently veined, whorled, and almost overlapping, persistent until autumn; fruit a 6-angled green berry. This is the trillium my grandfather yearned for and never got. It is the best trillium for gardens, large-flowered and with leaves that carry on until early autumn. It likes slightly acid soil but does well in circumneutral soils. Forma *roseum*, with flowers opening pink to deep pink, is frequently seen in the northern Blue Ridge; f. *polymerum* is a multipetaled form offered in commerce under several cultivar names. Forma *parvum*, a small-flowered form from the northern habitat, has nothing to recommend it to gardens. Due to its wide distribution, considerable variation occurs in the typical species; not all commercial sources provide the largest and best plants.

'Eco Double Gardenia', flowers many-petaled and with petals undulate, turning pinkish.

'Flore Pleno' (f. *flore-pleno*), flowers double, white.

'Green Mutant' (f. *variegatum* sim., f. *viride* sim.), flower petals green with white margin.

'Quicksilver', flowers like the species. A quick-propagating plant that produces side shoots every spring.

'Smith's Double' ('Variety Plena'), flowers double with stamens like small petals.

'Snow Bunting', flowers multipetaled (so-called stacked double) with up to 12 petals, white; plant slow-growing.

'Viride' (f. *viride*), green flowers.

Trillium kamtschaticum, Japanese large-flowered trillium, *obana no enreiso* (Jap.). Japan, northern Honshu, Hokkaido, Kurile Islands, southern Sakhalin, eastern Russia in the Amur and Ussuri regions, northeast China, North Korea.

WS to MS; flowers stalked, stalks straight or angled, 1.5–3 in. (4–8 cm) long, mostly held above the leaves, flowers large, 2–3 in. (5–8 cm) across, sepals green, lance-shaped, as long as the petals, somewhat erect but leaning, petals white or creamy white, with heavy texture, to 2 in. (5 cm) long, anthers yellow; May–June; plant clump-forming, 8–16 in. (20–40 cm) tall; leaves 1.5–7 in. (4–18 cm) long and wide, rounded diamond-shaped, unstalked, whorled and overlapping; fruit a greenish or purple-spotted berry. The Asian counterpart of *Trillium flexipes*, *T. ovatum*, and *T. grandiflorum* and in some cases hard to differentiate from these North American species. Some regional varieties have been named on the basis of fruit color; the

double-flowered f. *plenum* is rarely offered. The forms in commerce have pure white flowers, held horizontally, which last as long as those of the native species. Requires shade and consistently moist, acid soil. It is difficult here during heat and drought. Hardy to zone 4.

Trillium kurabayashii, western whippoorwill toadshade. Western North America, southwestern Oregon, south in northern California, Sierra Nevada.

WS to MS; this is the western equivalent of *Trillium cuneatum*, with slightly larger, conspicuous purplish red or yellow flower and with mottled or solid green leaves. Hardy to zone 6, but its very early appearance in spring exposes it to damage by late freezes. 'Eco Klamath Gold', a selection of the yellow-flowered f. *luteum*, has bright yellow flowers, yellow anthers, and leaves lightly marbled with lighter green.

Trillium lancifolium, lance-leaved trillium, lance-leaf toadshade. Eastern North America, northwestern Georgia and northeastern Alabama, localized in Alabama, Georgia, South Carolina, and southeastern Tennessee.

WS to MS; this is a distinctive species with lance-shaped leaves to 4 in. (10 cm) long and 1 in. (2.5 cm) wide, dark green mottled with lighter green, often slanted down. The linear flowers are relatively small and have sepals that spread out; the sessile, erect petals are maroon, purplish brown, or yellowish brown. Although the rhizome is hardy to zone 5, the leaves, which emerge very early (here in mid-February), are regularly exposed to damage by late freezes. 'Eco Slim' has slim, purple flowers and narrow leaves, lightly marbled with lighter green along the midrib.

Trillium luteum, yellow toadshade, yellow trillium, wax trillium. Eastern North America, western North Carolina in the mountains south to northern Georgia and west to southern Kentucky and eastern Tennessee.

WS to MS; flowers sessile, lemonlike fragrance, sepals green, lance-shaped, sharp-tipped, erect, petals elliptic to lance-shaped, widest near base, 1.2–3 in. (3–8 cm) long and 0.8–1 in. (1–2.5 cm) wide, greenish yellow to lemon-yellow, anthers yellow; April–May; plant clump-forming, 6–16 in. (15–40 cm) tall; leaves unstalked, overlapping, dark green mottled strongly with lighter green or whitish to grayish green with the mottling fading later in the season, 3–7 in. (8–18 cm) long and 2.5–4 in. (6–10 cm) wide, oblong-elliptic, whorled; fruit a plain green or greenish white berry. This excellent and widely available shade garden plant is the only sessile mountain trillium that produces yellow flowers exclusively. Can be recognized by its lemon fragrance. All forms are hardy to zone 5. In hot, southern gardens the yellow-flowered forms of *Trillium cuneatum* are better choices. Rarely available is *T. discolor*, a pale yellow-flowered species from the border of Georgia and South Carolina; it is smaller, with showy, spoon-shaped petals and a more spicy fragrance.

Trillium luteum, the better garden plant, is often confused with two other species: *T. viride* (green trillium, dustleaf toadshade), concentrated in the border region along the Missouri River in eastern Missouri and southern Illinois, and *T. viridescens* (Ozark green trillium, Ozark trillium), concentrated in the Ozark and Quachita Mountains in central and western Arkansas and its borders with Kansas, Oklahoma, and northeastern Texas. These are the plain green trilliums—interesting and quite attractive, but green all over, including the flower, so not showy at all. They are also difficult to cultivate in gardens due to their exacting alluvial and calcareous, sandy soil requirements. Gardeners who want green-flowered trilliums should seek *T. sessile* f. *viridiflorum*.

Trillium nivale, snow trillium, snow wakerobin, dwarf white trillium, dwarf white wood lily. Eastern North America, southern Minnesota east through Iowa, Illinois, Indiana, and Ohio to western Pennsylvania.

WS to MS; flowers stalked, stalks straight, 0.5–0.8 in. (1–2 cm) long, above the leaves, flowers tiny, to 0.8 in. (2 cm) across, sepals bluish green, lance-shaped, shorter than the petals, petals creamy white, anthers yellow; March–May; plant clump-forming, 2–5 in. (5–13 cm) tall; leaves stalked, 1.5–2 in. (4–5 cm) long, green, elliptic, whorled; fruit a greenish white berry. This tiny trillium is popular as a rock garden plant, elevated to display its unassertive beauty. It is too small to be showy in the open garden. Propagates easily from seed. From limestone regions, it requires neutral to alkaline soil. It blooms very early and is often caught by late freezes.

Trillium ovatum, western white trillium, western trillium, white trillium. Western North America, southern British Columbia south to central coastal California and east to eastern Washington and Oregon, isolated further east.

WS to MS; flowers stalked, stalks straight and erect or slightly leaning, 1.2–2 in. (3–5 cm) long, flowers held above the leaves, up-facing, to 3 in. (8 cm) across, sepals green, lance-shaped, petals variable, opening pure white, later fading to pink, anthers yellow; April–July; plant clump-forming, 6–28 in. (15–70 cm) tall; leaves 2–8 in. (5–20 cm) long and 3–6 in. (8–15 cm) wide, diamond-shaped, stalked, medium green, prominently veined, whorled, persistent until autumn; fruit a green or white berry. This western counterpart of *Trillium grandiflorum* is excellent in the garden, where its eye-catching, up-facing flowers provide a prominent display in early spring. Considered the showiest of the western trilliums. Hardy to zone 6, 4 and 5 with protection. Here it blooms very early, sometimes in March, so gets caught by late freezes; for early-warming, southeastern gardens *T. grandiflorum* is better suited. Grounds are sufficient for considering f. *hibbersonii* a separate species, *T. hibbersonii*; it is available under both these names. Being much smaller than *T. ovatum*, it is better used as a rock garden plant. Forma *maculosum* has small flowers and leaves with prominent mottling of maroon to greenish maroon, a unique feature for a stalked trillium. Forma *oettingerii* (Salmon Mountain trillium) is very small, perhaps too small for the open garden. Double-flowered forms include 'Edith' (white) and 'Barbara Walsh' (flowers multipetaled, white with a reddish purple center that turns creamy white and finally deep purple).

Trillium pusillum. Eastern North America, coastal Virginia to South Carolina, west to the Ozark Mountains and eastern Texas.

WS to MS; an extremely variable species of several small disjointed populations of similar plants. Varietal epithets such as var. *alabamicum*, var. *texanum*, var. *ozarkianum*, and var. *virginicum* indicate the locality of a specific pocket of plants. These several varieties have white, up-facing flowers on long flowerstalks. Despite the epithet *pusillum* (= dwarf), not all representatives of the various populations are actually dwarf. Most are protected by local laws. Absolutely none should be dug in the wild. Suppliers of seed-propagated plants should be questioned as to the ultimate size of their offerings. The smaller varieties make excellent rock garden plants, while the larger forms mix well in the woodland or wildflower garden. All are hardy to zone 5. Most require acid and constantly moist, but not soggy, soil.

Trillium recurvatum, prairie trillium, bloody noses, eastern petioled toadshade. Eastern North America, southwestern Michigan and southern Wisconsin south in the Mississippi and Ohio River basin to eastern Texas, northern Louisiana, Mississippi, and Alabama.

WS to MS; flowers sessile, sepals greenish, broadly lance-shaped, sharp-tipped, recurved (hence the epithet), folded back against the stem, returning to horizontal; petals erect, elliptic to lance-shaped with tips bent inward in clawlike fashion, 0.8–2 in. (2–5 cm) long and 0.5–0.8 in. (1–2 cm) wide, dark maroon or dark purple to clear yellow, rarely bicolored, with purple base on yellow, anthers yellow; March–May; plant clump-forming, 6–18 in. (15–45 cm) tall; leaves stalked with leafstalks to 1 in. (2.5 cm), dark green mottled strongly with lighter green or whitish to grayish green, with the mottling fading later in the season, 3–7 in. (8–18 cm) long and 1–3 in. (2.5–8 cm) wide, oblong-elliptic or broadly lance-shaped, whorled; fruit a plain green or green purple-streaked berry. Widespread and variable over its large habitat, it is a good garden plant in eastern North America. Requires a more alkaline soil than the southern trilliums; add dolomitic limestone to acid soils. It does not like the heat and dryness of summers at Hosta Hill, and watering is essential to keep it happy. Forma *luteum* and f. *shayi* ('Shay's Yellow') have yellow flowers; f. *luteum* is better, having clear yellow flowers.

Trillium rivale, brook trillium, brook wakerobin, Siskiyou trillium. Western North America, southern Oregon and northern California in the Siskiyou and Klamath mountains.

WS to MS; flowers stalked, stalks straight, 0.8–4 in. (2–10 cm) long, erect, curving, flowers small, 0.8–1 in. (2–2.5 cm) across, sepals green, lance-shaped, shorter than the petals, petals white or pinkish spotted with purple dots, anthers yellow; March–May; plant clump-forming, 2–6 in. (5–15

cm) tall; leaves 1–3 in. (2.5–8 cm) long, with stalks up to 1.2 in. (3 cm) long, bluish green, showy veins, elliptic to lance-shaped, whorled; fruit a greenish white berry. Unfortunately, this beautiful small trillium requires cool, sandy peat soil or woods soil that should never dry out. In the wild it goes dormant during the first dry period; in gardens supplemental water is a must. Hardy to zone 6. Cultivars include 'Del Norte' (*Trillium rivale* × *Uvularia ovatum*), a natural hybrid similar to the species; 'Eco Pink Cherub' (clear pink flowers); and 'Purple Heart' (flowers with a prominent pattern of purple spots).

Trillium sessile, toadshade, common toadshade, toad trillium, yellow toadshade, nosebleed, bloody butchers. Eastern North America, Ohio, Indiana, northern Kentucky, and Missouri, locally in Virginia, West Virginia, Maryland, and Pennsylvania, and west in central Tennessee, northern Alabama, Arkansas, and eastern Kansas.

WS to MS; flowers sessile with pungent, spicy fragrance, sepals green often suffused or streaked with purple, lance-shaped, rounded tip, flat, petals elliptic to broadly lance-shaped, erect, fleshy, 0.8–1.5 in. (2–4 cm) long and 0.3–0.8 in. (0.7–2 cm) wide, maroon, reddish brown, green or greenish yellow, anthers yellow; March–May; plant clump-forming, 3–10 in. (8–25 cm) tall; leaves unstalked, overlapping, dark green or bluish green, weakly or strongly mottled lighter green or whitish to grayish green with the mottling fading later in the season, 1.5–4 in. (4–10 cm) long and 0.8–3 in. (2–8 cm) wide, elliptic, whorled; fruit a greenish purple berry. With supplemental water, this trillium adapts well to hot, dry summers; unfortunately, it is small and not as prominent as some other species. Hardy to zone 4. Forma *viridiflorum* has yellowish green flowers that are meek in gardens. 'Eco Broad Maroon' has purplish maroon flowers, wide petals, and leaves much broader than the species, slightly marbled in early season, turning all green.

Trillium sulcatum, southern red trillium, Barksdale trillium, rainbow wakerobin, rainbow trillium. Eastern North America, southwestern Virginia and West Virginia to southeastern Kentucky and along the Cumberland Plateau in eastern Tennessee, northwestern Georgia, and northeastern Alabama.

WS to MS; flowers stalked, stalks straight but declined to horizontal, 2–4 in. (5–10 cm) long, flowers held above the leaves, horizontal or slightly drooping, to 2.5 in. (6 cm) across, faintly fragrant, sepals short, green, lance-shaped, margins upturned into channeled tips, petals oblong, from blackish crimson, maroon, red, brownish red, pink, or creamy yellow, anthers yellow; April–May; plant clump-forming, 6–28 in. (15–70 cm) tall; leaves unstalked, 6–8 in. (15–20 cm) long and 4–9 in. (10–23 cm) wide, diamond-shaped, pointed tip, stalked, dark green, whorled; fruit a red berry. This species (seen in photo of *Trillium grandiflorum*) has the widest range of flower colors in the genus; one of the off-color forms, f. *albolutescens*, has yellowish white flowers. The several cultivars are infrequently offered due to slow propagation; these include 'Eco Black Magic' (flowers with near black petals, pistils, and stamen, anthers gray, and sepals purple-tinged), 'Eco Brown Eyes' (flowers creamy yellow with a brown eye), 'Eco Butter Cream' (flowers creamy white with a white eye in each petal), and 'Eco Strawberry Cream' (flowers red with white-eyed petals).

Trillium tschonoskii, mountain woods trillium, white-flowered trillium, *miyama enreiso* or *shirobana enreiso* (Jap.). Japan, northern Honshu, Hokkaido, Kurile Islands, southern Sakhalin, eastern Russia in the Amur and Ussuri regions, northeast China, North Korea into the Himalayas.

FS; very similar to *Trillium kamtschaticum*, but the flowers are a little smaller and nod a little more. The flowers are stalked, with the stalks to 2 in. (5 cm) long. Requires consistently moist, acid soil. My plants have not been here long enough to judge its performance in hot regions, but I expect it will be similar to that of *T. kamtschaticum*. Hardy to zone 4.

Trillium undulatum, painted trillium, painted lady, painted wood lily, striped wakerobin. Eastern North America, Quebec east to Nova Scotia, south through New England, New York to Pennsylvania and in the Appalachians and the Blue Ridge to the Carolinas and northeastern Georgia.

WS to MS; flowers stalked, stalks straight and erect or slightly leaning, 0.8–2 in. (2–5 cm) long, flowers held above the leaves, up-facing, to 2 in. (5 cm) across, sepals short, green, lance-shaped, petals oblong, ruffled, white, marked with dark red in the center with red radiating out along the veins, anthers yellow; April–July; plant clump-forming, 6–24 in. (15–60 cm) tall; leaves 2–7 in. (5–18 cm) long and 3–5 in. (8–13 cm) wide, oblong-elliptic, pointed tip, stalked, dark green with maroon hues early, whorled; fruit a red berry. This cool-weather species is at home in the higher elevations of the mountains and does well in gardens with cool summers as long as it has deep, very acid, and always moist woods soil to grow in. It is intolerant of lime in the soil. Sadly, many specimens of this coveted trillium are installed in lowland gardens, where it barely survives and never is showy. I have tried it here, with unsatisfactory results. An all-white form, f. *enotatum*, completely lacks the wonderful "painted in" red markings of the type and has little to recommend itself to gardeners.

Trillium vaseyi, sweet trillium, sweet Beth, Vasey's trillium. Eastern North America, lower elevations of the Appalachians and the Blue Ridge from the Carolinas to northeastern and central Georgia and eastern Tennessee.

WS to MS; flowers stalked, stalks straight but declined or horizontal, 1.5–3 in. (4–8 cm) long, flowers held at or below the leaves, to 4 in. (10 cm) across, faintly fragrant, sepals short, green, lance-shaped, margins upturned, sulcate, petals oblong, crimson, maroon-red, brownish red, prominently veined, anthers yellow; April–June; plant clump-forming, 6–24 in. (15–60 cm) tall; leaves 4–8 in. (10–20 cm) long and often wider, diamond-shaped, pointed tip, stalked, dark green, whorled; fruit a brown berry. This stately species has the largest flowers in the genus. Unfortunately, they are nodding and so do not show their full beauty from above. I have them on a slope, where the flowers can be observed from the path below. It is well adapted to hot, southern gardens if planted in deep shade and given deep, acid, woods soil and supplemental water. Its foliage lasts well into early autumn—a great garden plant. Hardy to zone 5. I observed another very showy southern trillium, ***Trillium simile*** (sweet white trillium), in the Little River area of the Smoky Mountains; also called the confusing trillium, for its similarity to *T. vaseyi* and *T. erectum*, it has, like *T. erectum*, showy creamy white flowers that contrast well with a black ovary. It is rarely available.

Recommended reading

Case, Frederick W., Jr., and Roberta B. Case. 1997. *Trilliums*. Portland, Oregon: Timber Press.

Jacobs, Don L., and Robert L. Jacobs. 1997. *Trilliums in the Woodland Garden: American Treasures*. Decatur, Georgia: Eco-Gardens.

Tupistra

For a long time now, the hosta crowd has been pining for ruffled leaves and leaf margins. A few hosta cultivars have come close but not as close as the exquisitely wavy, ruffly, pleated *Tupistra chinensis*. Considered a distant cousin of *Rhodea*, the Chinese sacred lily, this species comes from a genus little known and explored. Don Jacobs has brought many plants from China, including this one, and it fulfills the role of a foliage plant for the shady garden as well as hostas do. This curious plant looks either like a small *Rhodea* or a large, lance-shaped, green hosta, with incredibly textured leaves no hosta could match. I have grown it for several years, and it has become a magnet in the garden. Here it has been evergreen through some cold winters, and so it is reported in gardens where minimum temperatures reach 5°F (−15°C). Below that it becomes herbaceous. *Tupistra* is classified in the Liliaceae.

Tupistra chinensis is native to the temperate regions of China and should be hardy to zone 7a, 6 with protection. It originates in moist mountain forests, so it is well adapted to shady, moist conditions. Here it is grown in deep, homemade soil consisting of ground pine bark, peat moss, coarse, gritty sand, and lots of pine needle compost, with some native clay mixed in. The soil tests out with a pH of around 5. This species actually likes hot summers as long as it is placed in medium shade and given profuse watering during dry periods. Luxuriant growth is the result in such conditions; my plant produces multiple offsets on the rhizome that can be removed and planted elsewhere. The plain, nondescript flowers cluster around a short stem that is partially hidden in the center of the leaves—which are the plant's true glory. In mild-winter gardens, this plant is a standout summer or winter, providing year-round garden interest. Further north, in snow country, it loses its leaves, but the rhizome is fairly hardy if protected. I suggest installation in a pot, which can be plunged in spring and removed to a frost-free area during winter.

Tupistra is a marvelous foliage plant when mixed with ferns, astilbes, hellebores, and wildflowers in the shady woodland garden. It does not like exposure to too much sun but will tolerate some morning sun.

Propagate by dividing the rhizome or removing offsets in late autumn or very early spring. Each piece should have a growing tip.

Large slugs and snails can be damaging in spring. I have not experienced any diseases on my plants.

Tupistra chinensis, China ruffled lily. Southern China.

LS to FS; flowers small, light brownish yellow, inconspicuous, densely arranged in an elongated cluster near ground level; plant compact, evergreen in mild-winter areas, clump-forming, to 24 in. (60 cm) high and wide; leaves in a basal rosette, upright but deeply arching, elongated and narrowly lance-shaped, medium matte green, arising directly from the rhizome, to 24 in. (60 cm) long and 2.5–3 in. (6–8 cm) wide, midrib deeply keeled, forming a V-shape in cross section, deeply ruffled, dimpled, and wrinkled, particularly near the margin, with parallel veins conspicuous. A highly desirable addition to the shady garden, providing incredible foliage texture wherever it is planted. 'Eco China Ruffles', a selected form of the type, is offered.

Uvularia

Guided by the doctrine of signatures, early botanists decided that the lovely, bell-shaped flowers of this genus (hence, bellwort) look much like the uvula hanging from the soft palate in the human throat. Consequently, bellwort was used for the treatment of throat ailments. It was also used by American Indians as a sedative and tonic. Long ago, the young shoots of several species were boiled and eaten like asparagus.

All bellworts are herbaceous. They are endemic to the temperate regions of eastern North America and thrive in zones 4 to 8. Originating in cool, moist woodlands, they are well adapted to shady, moist conditions, but their distribution favors limestone regions, thus they prefer a somewhat alkaline soil with a pH of 6.5 to 7. Bellworts prefer a constantly moist soil; given that, the clumps are long-lasting. I plant *Uvularia grandiflora* (large-flowered bellwort), which is given such importance in European gardens, in company with smaller ferns and hostas, where it makes an outstanding addition. The smaller species require careful placement to show their delicate beauty. I mix them with groups of native wildflowers, planted close and up front, where these indigenous marvels can be appreciated. Although the flowers are ephemeral, the elegant stems of rich green leaves contribute to the overall effect in the garden most of the year.

The genus is placed in the Uvulariaceae. Bellworts are closely related to Solomon's seals and disporums but are differentiated by having a three-lobed, dry seed capsule rather than fleshy berries. As with many other genera, the nomenclature of this relatively small genus is, nevertheless, still confused; some species are separated on the basis of minor botanical details. For example, *Uvularia caroliniana* has a style parted down the middle, while the style of *U. sessilifolia* is parted only one-third of its length. Such minuscule detail is of no consequence to gardeners, but plant size certainly is, so the larger Carolina bellwort might be more attractive to those seeking a larger specimen. I have grown these native species for years in the woodland garden. They are of easy culture; the only conditions they loathe are hot, dry summers and overly wet, soggy winter soils.

Propagate by dividing the dormant rhizome in late autumn or very early spring. Each piece should have a growing tip.

Large slugs and snails can damage new growth emerging in spring, and rust and leaf spot are occasionally reported, but these lovely natives are otherwise free of pests and diseases in my experience.

Uvularia caroliniana, mountain bellwort, Carolina bellwort. Eastern North America, New Jersey to West Virginia and south to Georgia and Alabama.

MS to FS; flowers greenish yellow, mostly solitary, rarely 2, terminal, 1 in. (2.5 cm) long, hanging, narrowly bell-shaped, tubular; April–June; stems forked into 1, rarely 2 branches, hairless, to 20 in. (50 cm) tall; plant rhizomatous, slowly creeping; stems straight; leaves single, alternate, sessile (not pierced by the stem, but clasping it), elliptic, glossy green, with minuscule serrations in the leaf margins, to 3 in. (8 cm) long; fruit 3-winged. The

lustrous leaves distinguish this species from other bellworts, which have fleecy veneers. A conversation plant, it makes a nice garden display.

Uvularia floridana, Florida bellwort. Eastern North America, southern Georgia and Alabama, northern Florida.

MS to FS; flowers greenish yellow, mostly solitary, rarely 2, terminal, 1 in. (2.5 cm) long, hanging, narrowly bell-shaped, tubular; April–June; stems forked into 1, rarely 2 branches, hairless, to 12 in. (30 cm) tall; leaves single, alternate, sessile (clasping the stem), elliptic, glossy green, to 2 in. (5 cm) long; fruit 3-winged.

Uvularia grandiflora, large-flowered bellwort, large bellwort, big merrybells, cornflower, large merrybells, merrybells, strawflower, wood daffodil. Eastern North America, Quebec west to Minnesota and south to Tennessee and Oklahoma.

MS to FS; flowers bright greenish yellow, mostly solitary, rarely 2–3, terminal, 2 in. (5 cm) long, hanging, bell-shaped, tubular, 6-lobed with free tepals having twisted tips; April–May; plant rhizomatous, slowly creeping; stems forked into 1, rarely 2 branches, hairless, to 32 in. (80 cm) tall; leaves single, alternate, perfoliate (pierced by the stem), green, downy beneath when young, to 5 in. (13 cm) long, elliptic to ovate, with lance-shaped tips; the stems emerge straight but have arching tops, which causes the terminal leaves to point down; fruit 3-winged, to 0.5 in. (1 cm) in diameter. The most important species in the genus. Its rhizomes are slowly spreading, so steadily increasing the clump size, and its large flowers are an important benefit. Makes a splendid accent plant in the shady border when planted among small ferns, hostas, and the shorter epimediums or other low-growing groundcovers. Even after the flowers have passed, the slowly expanding, leafy clumps add to the composition of the garden. Given plenty of water, the clumps last until late summer or early fall. 'Pallida' (*U. pallida* of gardens, *U. grandiflora* var. *pallida*) has flowers of an anemic yellow; I have seen this cultivar in English gardens and being accustomed to the deep lemon-yellow blossoms of this species at Hosta Hill, I consider this a lesser form.

Uvularia perfoliata, bellwort, perfoliate bellwort, mealy bellwort, strawbells. Eastern North America,

Quebec to Ohio and south to northern Florida and northern Louisiana.

MS to FS; flowers pale yellow, mostly solitary, rarely 2, terminal, 1 in. (2.5 cm) long, hanging, bell-shaped, tubular, 6-lobed with free tepals having twisted tips; April–June; plant clump-forming; stems forked, hairless, to 24 in. (60 cm) tall, straight, in the upper part arching and bending down, with singular, alternate, perfoliate (pierced by the stem) leaves; leaves medium green, hairless, to 4 in. (10 cm) long, elliptic to ovate, with lance-shaped tips pointing down. A smaller version of *Uvularia grandiflora*, also with leaves pierced by the stem but totally so, as its common and specific names indicate. *Uvularia perfoliata* is further distinguished by its overall smaller stature, much smaller flowers, and hairless leaves that are smooth on both sides. Not frequent in gardens. It is a clump-former, so cannot be counted on as a groundcover. The attractive hybrid 'Sunbonnet' (*U. perfoliata* × *U. grandiflora*) is larger than *U. perfoliata*, with larger, bright yellow flowers.

Uvularia sessilifolia, sessile bellwort, strawbells, strawlilies, wild oats. Eastern North America, New Brunswick, Nova Scotia, to New England, south to Georgia and Alabama, west to North Dakota and Missouri.

MS to FS; flowers pale greenish yellow, mostly solitary, rarely 2, terminal, 1 in. (2.5 cm) long, hanging, narrowly bell-shaped, tubular, the tepals not separate and twisting, but the tips flaring, bell-shaped; April–June; plant rhizomatous, widely creeping; stems forked into 1, rarely 2 branches, hairless, to 16 in. (40 cm) tall; leaves single, alternate, sessile (not pierced by the stem, but clasping it), yellowish green above, pale green to gray-green beneath, to 3 in. (8 cm) long, elliptic to ovate to oblong lance-shaped; fruit 3-winged capsule. Smaller and more delicate than other bellworts. Its mostly solitary flowers are pretty and deserve a place where they can be noticed and observed. I keep a small colony in a raised stone bed adjacent to a path. If given good soil and plenty of moisture, its rhizomes spread briskly and far afield; a small start quickly forms a delightful carpet of yellowish green leaves. *Uvularia puberula* is similarly useful in the garden but spreads at a slower rate. Cultivars of *U. sessilifolia* include 'Cobblewood Gold' (yellow leaves, much brighter than the species) and 'Cobblewood

Variegated' ('Variegata'; leaves showing a clear white, narrow margin).

Vancouveria

The modest members of *Vancouveria* are at last being recognized as refined plants for the shady garden. Although some experts told me that it would not grow in my hot Piedmont garden, I had to try anyway and got several plants of *Vancouveria hexandra* (inside-out flower). As delicate as this plant looks, it is a tough one. It has survived two consecutive severe droughts, an ice storm of epic proportions, and all other manner of insults. Admittedly, it is not as exuberant as I have seen it in its western habitat, but it keeps coming back, season after season. Characterized as deciduous, it is almost evergreen here, but falling pinecones, ice particles, and other natural abuses usually tear up the plants so much that the leaves might as well be cut in early spring. I usually do it when I give my epimediums a haircut, before the flowers emerge. The way to grow it here seems to be profuse watering and planting in deep shade.

Vancouveria occurs only in western North America from Washington and Oregon to northern California. The generic name honors British explorer George Vancouver, who circumnavigated Vancouver Island in the 1790s. The genus is classified in the Berberidaceae.

Vancouverias can be grown in varying intensities of shade. Here the species are placed in medium shade, but they will tolerate some morning sun, and in northern or western gardens increasing sun exposure is accepted. They are hardy to zone 5; heat tolerance limit is somewhere in zone 7, depending on microclimate. Originating in moist woodlands, they are well adapted to shady, moist conditions and prefer a deep woodland soil with plenty of organic matter, good tilth, and good water-holding capacity, yet reasonably well drained. Given good cultural conditions, some species may become invasive and form a tight groundcover. Consider this when siting plants next to more fragile natives. I use them just like epimediums. Vancouverias are not spectacular plants, but they have a refined appearance and serve well when interplanted with hostas and stalked wildflowers like Solomon's seals and disporums, which rise up through their carpet of foliage. Their modest yet captivating floral display is definitely a bonus in spring.

Propagate by dividing the rhizome in early spring, making sure that each piece has a growing tip. This is much faster than using seed, which must be sown as soon as it is ripe in pots in a cold frame. Rhizomes are easy to locate because last season's leaves are still present.

Vine weevils occasionally scallop the leaf margins here at Hosta Hill.

Vancouveria hexandra, inside-out flower. Western North America, Washington to southern Oregon and northern California.

WS to FS; flowers small, 8–42, nodding, to 0.5 in. (1 cm), white, sepals 12–15, in 2 sets, outer set of 9 small, falling away early, inner set of 6 petal-like, white, spotted red, bent down, petals white, bent down, stamens 6, yellow; May–June, on leafless stems 10–18 in. (25–45 cm); plant rhizomatous, spreading, sometimes vigorously; leaves deciduous, compound, to 16 in. (40 cm) long, divided into 9–27 leaflets, light green, broadly heart-shaped, many 3-lobed, 1 in. (2.5 cm) long and 0.6 in. (1.5 cm) wide. When grown well, this species has the grace of maidenhair fern. Its flower literally turns inside-out (hence, the common name), first shedding the outer sepals, then curling the inner sepals and petals, exposing the stamens. Sometimes called American barrenwort for its similarity to epimedium. *Vancouveria chrysantha* (golden vancouveria) grows a little further south and has fewer and yellow flowers but is otherwise very similar; its basal leaves have evergreen leaflets, shiny dark green above and glaucous, hairy beneath, leathery and diamond-shaped with wavy margins. A little less hardy but should do fine into zone 7. *Vancouveria planipetala* (redwood ivy) from southern Oregon to central California, has leaflets that look much like those of ivy and are just as leathery and shiny; its flowers, small bells of white shaded with lavender hues, open May–June on leafless stems to 18 in. (45 cm). This species also spreads but at a much slower pace. Patience is required before it will knit together, but this best of the vancouverias is worth the wait: it makes an attractive, blooming groundcover, lower-growing than *V. hexandra*. Hardy to zone 6.

Veratrum

Some foliage plants are so attractive in spring that gardeners must forgive them for disappearing when the heat of the summer arrives. False hellebores are among these beauties. Their large, gracefully arching and strongly veined and pleated leaves, clasping and climbing up on tall stems, provide an early-spring display that is not soon forgotten. False hellebores are common in temperate North America and Eurasia, but they have been overlooked by many gardeners. The notion that gardens must have many colorful, showy flowers, in a Victorian sense, has kept many great foliage plants from being planted until recently. Thankfully the green garden movement, which depends mostly on foliage to paint a natural garden scene, has changed things. False hellebores fit this scheme perfectly. They have no bright colors to attract—only tall, branched spikes of green flowers, some whitish green, other blackish green, all green in some shade or another. The leaves are also a rich, bright green, but their deep, parallel folds, like tight pleats on a girl's skirt, are their real glory. The overall textural vision, as they emerge in early spring, unfurling just like hosta leaves, is like no other.

Veratrum is from the Latin *vere atrum* (= truly black), alluding to the black color of the roots. Long ago, the name was used for the true hellebores, hence the generic common name, false hellebore. *Veratrum viride* is known as Indian poke (from *pocan*, an American Indian term for herbs dried and smoked like tobacco), itchweed (contact with the leaves may cause skin irritation), and corn lily (from afar, it looks like a cornstalk); I remember my grandfather calling it *Giftgermer* (= the German poison), as it was responsible for poisoning cows on the lush, alpine meadows of Bavaria. The genus is placed in the Melanthiaceae. All parts of the plant are poisonous, containing several medicinal compounds, including veratrin. American Indians used minute quantities to reduce blood pressure and larger amounts to determine new chiefs: the one who tolerated (or survived) the poisonous concoction was determined fit to rule.

False hellebores, originating as they do in moist woodlands and meadows, are well adapted to shady, moist conditions. Here they grow in deep woods soil mixed with a little gritty sand and lots of pine needle compost. The soil must be acid with a pH of 4.5 to 5.5. Southern species do better in hot summer gardens, naturally; the more northern species have a heat-tolerance limit to zone 7, unless they are grown in swampy conditions. Many consider these wetland plants, and although common they should not be removed from wetlands. Plants usually go dormant in midsummer, after displaying their tall, plumelike flowers; the later-blooming European and Asian species remain green longer. False hellebores are marvelous foliage plants when mixed with ferns, astilbes, true hellebores, hostas, and other stout wildflowers in the shady woodland garden. As long as the soil stays moist, they tolerate considerable sun in northern gardens. Most species are hardy to zone 6.

Propagate by dividing the rhizome in very early spring. Seed propagation is tedious and not as productive.

Large slugs and snails seem to like these poisonous plants, especially in spring. Caterpillars never touch them. Rust and fungal leaf spot are reported but not seen here.

Veratrum album, European white hellebore. Northern Eurasia, North Africa.

Some sun, LS to FS; flower structure similar to *Veratrum viride*, but the flowers are larger, star-shaped, to 0.6 in. (1.5 cm) across, green outside and whitish inside, densely arranged on a branched flowerstalk to 4 ft. (1.2 m); leaves typical; July–August; plant compact, 24 in. (60 cm) tall, clump-forming. In better forms, the branched flowering spike has an almost white appearance, hence the epithet (*album* = white). It flowers later than the eastern species and is occasionally offered in commerce. Hardy to zone 5.

Veratrum californicum, California false hellebore, corn lily, skunk cabbage. Western North America, Washington to southern California and east to Montana, Colorado, and New Mexico.

Some sun, LS to WS; flower structure similar to *Veratrum viride*, but the flowers are among the largest in the genus, star-shaped, to 0.8 in. (2 cm) across, green outside and yellowish inside, veined inside, densely arranged on a branched flowerstalk to 6 ft. (1.8 m); July–August; plant compact, clump-forming; leaves basal, 16 in. (40 cm) long and 8 in. (20 cm) wide, outstandingly pleated and ribbed

along parallel veins. This species has the widest leaves. It flowers later than the eastern species and is rarely offered in commerce. Hardy to zone 5 but requires more sun than other species.

Veratrum nigrum, black hellebore, European black hellebore. Central and southern Europe east to Siberia, northern China, Korea.

Some sun, LS to FS; flowers small, star-shaped, to 0.6 in. (1.5 cm) across, sepals 3, petal-like, petals 3, stamens 6, curved, malodorous, dark maroon to blackish purple, green striped, densely arranged on a branched flowerstalk 2–4 ft. (0.6–1.2 m) tall; June–August; plant compact, clump-forming; leaves mostly basal, arching, broadly elliptic or lance-shaped, light green, hairless, to 14 in. (35 cm) long and 8 in. (20 cm) wide, outstandingly pleated and ribbed along parallel veins. Also found in Alaska, according to some reports. A smaller species, coveted by connoisseurs. Its blackish flowers make a vivid contrast with the light green leaves. Unfortunately, it is hard to find in commerce.

Veratrum viride, white hellebore, American white hellebore, American false hellebore, false hellebore, corn lily, Indian poke, itchweed. North America, Washington, Oregon, and California, and Minnesota east to New Brunswick, Quebec, and New England, south to the mountains Georgia and Tennessee.

Some sun, LS to FS; flowers small, star-shaped, to 0.5 in. (1 cm) across, sepals 3, petal-like, petals 3, stamens 6, curved, inconspicuous green or yellowish green, densely arranged on a branched flowerstalk 3–7 ft. (0.9–2 m) tall; May–July; plant compact, clump-forming; leaves mostly basal, a few on the stem, clasping, arching, elongated and lance-shaped, light green, arising directly from the rhizome, 6–12 in. (15–30 cm) long and 3–6 in. (8–15 cm) wide, outstandingly pleated and ribbed along parallel veins. Hardy to zone 3. Highly conspicuous and striking in early spring to early summer, it is available from wildflower nurseries. Very similar is *Veratrum parviflorum* (small-flowered false hellebore), seen in the woods from Virginia south to Georgia and Tennessee; it seems to survive our heat better than other species. Wood's false hellebore, *V. woodsii*, has greenish purple to blackish purple flowers and is endemic further west in Iowa and Ohio south to Missouri and Kansas; it tolerates drier conditions. Unfortunately, both these smaller species are rarely offered.

Veratrum wilsonii, Chinese false hellebore. Central and southern Europe east to Siberia, Korea, northern, western, and southern China, Yunnan, Sichuan.

Some sun, LS to WS; flowers small, star-shaped, to 1 in. (2.5 cm) across, sepals 3, petal-like, petals 3, stamens 6, curved, white, green-striped, densely arranged on a branched flowerstalk to 36 in. (90 cm) tall, occasionally to 5 ft. (1.5 m); June–July; plant compact, clump-forming; leaves mostly basal, arching, strap-shaped, light green, hairless, to 20 in. (50 cm) long and 1–1.5 in. (2.5–4 cm) wide, with parallel veins conspicuous. The straplike leaves are not as showy as those of European and North American species. *Veratrum taliense*, also from Yunnan, has similar, narrow leaves and large flowers on long stalks. Both these Chinese species need more sun than shade. I have seen them in European gardens but not in North America.

Veronicastrum

Several years ago, on a visit to Mammoth Cave National Park, I was duly impressed by the stately, showy wildflower *Veronicastrum virginicum* (Culver's root). Books and friends told me that it needs a lot more sun than shade so, for a while, I lived with the memory of this visit; but when Hurricane Opal took out some tall trees nearby, opening up a window to the west, I just had to try. My plants may not be as luxurious as those grown in full sun, but they are gorgeous nevertheless, mixed with a bunch of *Lobelia cardinalis* (cardinal flower). The white spikes of Culver's root contrast well with the late-blooming flowers of the brilliant red cardinal flower, whose stout stems lend support to the weaker-stemmed Culver's root.

Linnaeus placed the plant in *Veronica*, but later botanists considered it a lesser veronica; the generic name therefore honors Saint Veronica, with the addition of the Latin *aster*, as *astrum* (= false, the lesser of). Early settlers learned from American Indians, who used *Veronicastrum virginicum* in purification rites, that the root also contains a powerful emetic and cathartic, leptandrine, which was ingested as a tea brewed from the dried roots. This medicinal use was published by a Doctor Culver,

hence the common name. The genus is classified in the Scrophulariaceae.

Both *Veronicastrum virginicum*, a North American species, and the Eurasian *V. sibiricum* are hardy to zone 3 and tolerate hot summers as long as plenty of water is provided to maintain soil moisture. Originating in moist, open woodlands, thickets, prairies, and meadows, they abide lightly shaded and moist conditions but grow best in more sun than shade.

Propagate by dividing larger rootstocks in very early spring into several segments, each with a growing bud. Sow seed when ripe in pots in a cold frame in autumn.

Fungal leaf spot and mildew are reported.

Veronicastrum virginicum, Culver's root, Culver's physic, blackroot, Bowman's root. Eastern North America, Manitoba east to New England and south to northwestern Florida, west to eastern Texas and the Dakotas.

Some sun, LS to WS; flowers many, terminal in spikelike, narrowly cylindrical clusters, small, white or pale bluish lavender, petals 4, united into a tube with the upper lobe tips separate, spreading, stamens 2, projecting beyond the petal tips; plant clump-forming, with fibrous, yellow rootstock, erect, unbranched, 3–6 ft. (0.9–1.8 m) tall; leaves 2–6 in. (5–15 cm) long, lance-shaped, sharply toothed and tipped, whorled along the stem in groups of 3–9, diminishing in size toward the top; fruit an egg-shaped capsule with many seeds. Here it is in the shade from morning until early afternoon and then gets several hours of hot afternoon sun, which seems enough to keep it happy. I grow it in deep, acid woods soil mixed with lots of pine needle compost; optimum pH is 5 to 6.5. This species is generally white-flowered, but the lavender form is also seen in commerce, so gardeners should ascertain the color when ordering. Two cultivars are offered as well, 'Album' (flowers white) and 'Roseum' (flowers pinkish). It is hoped that the attractive, blue-flowered Eurasian *Veronicastrum sibiricum*, rarely seen in gardens, will become more widely available.

Vinca

This southern European alien has escaped from gardens, naturalizing in northern Europe and setting up housekeeping in the woods and roadsides of the New World. Thankfully, periwinkle is much better behaved than some other alien plants. Its glossy leaves and attractive flowers are welcome, and it is often used as a lawn substitute under trees or in the shady shrub border, where it knits together to make a dense, evergreen groundcover with a long flowering period. It can become invasive, however; it should not be planted where it can overrun delicate wildflowers or other small plants.

Vinca, which is actually considered a subshrub, is native to shady woodlands in central and southern Europe east to the Caucasus. It was well known in ancient times: the name *Vinca*, from the classical Latin *vincio* (= to bind), was used by the Roman polymath Pliny the Elder; *pervinca* was the basis for the name periwinkle. *Vinca* is classified in the dogbane family, Apocynaceae. Only one species of periwinkle is useful in all temperate regions, *Vinca minor*, which is hardy to zone 4 and heat-tolerant well into zone 9. Watering is required to keep it neat during hot, dry summers. I have seen flourishing plantings along the Georgia coast in zone 8b. Periwinkle tolerates considerable shade, becoming more docile in shady areas. Unfortunately, shade also reduces flowering, but periwinkle's function as a groundcover is not curtailed. It prefers a moist soil, rich in organic matter with a pH of 5 to 7, but I have known it to grow in unimproved clay.

Propagate by separating rooted sections of the stems in late summer.

Diseases and insect pests do not seem to bother the plants too much, although I have seen aphids sucking on the new shoots. Dieback can occur.

Vinca major, greater periwinkle, blue button, band plant. Southwestern Europe to northeastern Asia Minor and southern Caucasus.

Some sun, LS to MS; similar to *Vinca minor* but more shrubby, with prostrate as well as more erect stems, to 18 in. (45 cm). Hardy to zone 7, but I have seen it used by some daring gardeners in zone 6. It requires warm, well-drained dry sites; it does not do well in cool, moist, or damp situations. It makes a taller groundcover but is difficult to protect; even here in the Georgia Piedmont it has been killed to the ground during severe winters, so I no longer plant it. *Vinca minor* makes a denser, much lower-growing, very hardy groundcover. *Vinca major* subsp. *hirsuta* has hairy sepals and lance-shaped

leaves. *Vinca difformis* from southwestern Europe, Morocco, and Algeria has striking flowers with 5 separate, diamond-shaped, sharply pointed lobes; gardeners are often attracted to it, but they should resist the impulse to acquire: this species is suitable to almost subtropical climates in zone 9 and warmer only. *Vinca herbacea* from eastern Europe and western Asia is hardy to zone 5 but unfortunately herbaceous and therefore not evergreen-groundcover material.

Vinca minor, lesser periwinkle, common periwinkle, creeping myrtle, running myrtle. Southern Europe, east to the Black Sea region and the Caucasus.

Some sun, LS to MS; flowers solitary in the leaf axils, purplish blue with a white center, sometimes light blue, reddish purple, or white, sepals 5, small, petals united into a corolla, tubular, with 5 wide-spreading, overlapping lobe tips, 1–1.2 in. (2.5–3 cm) across, stamens 5, inserted in tube; April–May; plant evergreen, trailing, prostrate, mat-forming with nonflowering stems rooting at all nodes, 4–8 in. (10–20 cm) high; leaves elliptic or lance-shaped, glossy dark green, smooth margins, produced opposite at intervals along the stems.

'Alba' (f. *alba*), flowers white.

'Alba Variegata' ('Alba Aureovariegata'), flowers white; leaves with light yellow margin.

'Alboplena', flowers white, double.

'Argenteovariegata' ('Variegata'), flowers violet to lilac-blue; leaves with white to creamy white margin.

'Atropurpurea' ('Burgundy', 'Purpurea', 'Rubra', 'Punicea'), flowers reddish purple.

'Azurea Flore Pleno' ('Azureaplena', 'Caerulea Plena', 'Caeruleoplena'), flowers blue, double.

'Cuprea', flowers coppery red.

'Gertrude Jekyll', flowers creamy white, floriferous.

'Grüner Teppich' ('Green Carpet'), flowers sparse, pale lavender-blue; leaves large; plant with dense growth.

'La Grave' ('Bowles' Blue', 'Bowles' Variety', 'Bowlesii', *Vinca bowlesii* of gardens), flowers lavender-blue, large.

'Multiplex' ('Alpina', 'Double Burgundy'), flowers reddish plum-purple, double.

'Oland Blue', flowers light lavender-blue.

'Plena', flowers blue, double.

Viola

Many gardeners have a love-hate relationship with violets. Years ago, I gave in to Hildegarde and planted a few Johnny-jump-ups (*Viola pedunculata*) in my garden; those pretty little violets quickly spread all over the place. Even worse are the many native violets that in no time take over sections of the landscape; in my opinion and with few exceptions, they are obnoxious weeds. Here in the Georgia Piedmont *V. sororia* and *V. obliqua* have invaded lawns, and together with wild onions (*Allium cernuum*) make the lawn keepers' lives miserable. Worse yet, tons of potent herbicides are released into the environment to kill off the interlopers. The root of the problem is the cleistogamous nature of these plants. This fancy word means that two sets of flowers are produced. The first set blooms normally, on stems, but the second set lies close to the ground, where it usually develops no petals and self-pollinates. When ripe, the hidden seed capsules burst and spew out a barrage of seeds. Many germinate in short order, creating new plantlets at the periphery of the mother plant, which only appears to spread by stolons or creeping rhizomes. Another debit is the fact that many violets like more sun than shade, particularly in northern gardens. While they tolerate some shade in the sun-drenched South, further north they become plants for full sun.

No matter, some people still love them, and obviously, there must be some good in a genus composed of over 500 species. In late autumn around Atlanta, patches of pansies (*Viola* ×*wittrockiana*) are planted by mailboxes, at apartment entrances, and in small beds at streetside. They are short-lived perennials used as annuals; by the time hot weather arrives, they usually have been replaced by heat-resistant summer-flowering bedding plants. Many violets are small to tiny plants, and rock gardeners love them. They cultivate such treasures as *V. beckwithii* (Great Basin violet), a difficult species from California, or the world's smallest violet, *V. verecunda* var. *yakusimana*, a dwarf with 0.3 in. (7 mm) round leaves that spreads just like the big ones but, because it is so small, never becomes a real nuisance.

The genus *Viola* (the classical name used by the Romans for these plants and adopted by Linnaeus) is distributed throughout the temperate regions of the world. Violas were favorite Victorian flowers and associated with romance. I remember bringing little posies of *Veilchen* to the girl of my dreams; it must have helped because Hildegarde accepted my proposal of marriage, and we still love each other after 50 years. People still present them as gifts, candy them, and use them in flavorings, perfumes, and potpourris. Violet leaves are high in vitamins A and C, so herbalists now suggest that they be used in salads or cooked as greens to add valuable antioxidants to the diet. *Viola odorata* (sweet violet) is the species primarily used for these purposes; it is more suited to sunny areas, barely hardy in zone 7b, and not tolerant of hot, dry weather, so is rarely seen in North American gardens. Violets are classified in the violet family, Violaceae.

Most gardeners have no trouble identifying violets, and yet the taxonomy of native violets is an unmitigated nightmare. There are 50 or so violets endemic to the southern Appalachians alone, and all hybridize freely. No surprise, then, that native species offered in commerce are often misidentified interspecific hybrids. Many are similar and have equal garden value, except for the flower color, perhaps, which is variable. Notwithstanding, I do hazard descriptions for a few of the more outstanding species. For the shady, natural garden, selections from the wild species are better suited, most of them being perennial evergreen or semi-evergreen plants. Be warned: they still can spread far and wide in the garden. Peruse catalogs for the latest cultivar offerings.

Many native violets are hardy to zone 3. The Eurasian species are generally more tender, to zone 6 or 7. Heat tolerance is greater in the widespread species. Many are tolerant of varying soil conditions; optimum pH is 5 to 7. Obviously a deep woodland soil with plenty of organic matter, good tilth, and good water-holding capacity is to their advantage. They will even grow in acid clay soils, which does not seem to alter their proclivity for territorial takeover.

Propagate by transplanting seedlings, which are usually produced in great numbers. Some species are relatively short-lived, so propagation is necessary to rejuvenate the population.

Large slugs, snails, and sucking insects are frequent troubles. Crown rot, root rot, leaf spot, mildew, and a host of other diseases are reported.

For all species described, flowers are usually solitary or few, mostly nodding or facing out, stalked;

5-merous, with 5 sepals, 5 unequal, free petals, 2 upper ones more or less erect, 2 lateral ones spreading, 1 lower petal liplike with straight or hooked spurs or pouched; 5 stamens. Bloom time is April–June, unless otherwise noted. All (with the exception of *Viola pedata*) are more or less vigorously spreading: unless conscientiously controlled, most will become pernicious weeds in the garden.

Viola adunca, hooked spur violet, western dog violet. Northwestern to northeastern North America.

Some sun, LS to WS; flowers fragrant, violet to lavender with white eyes and white, hooked spur; leaves green, oval, finely hairy, to 1.5 in. (4 cm); plant semi-evergreen, self-seeds freely. Hardy in zones 4 to 8. 'Alba' has white flowers.

Viola biflora, twin-flowered violet. Eurasia, northwestern North America.

Some sun, LS to WS; flowers yellow with dark purple veins on lower petals, spurs; leaves pale green, kidney-shaped, finely hairy, to 1.5 in. (4 cm); plant herbaceous, creeping. Hardy in zones 4 to 8.

Viola blanda, sweet white violet, Willdenow violet, woodland white violet. North America, Minnesota east to Quebec and New England and south to Georgia and Tennessee.

Some sun, LS to WS; flowers white, upper petals bent back and twisted, lower petal purple-veined, spurs; leaves green, heart-shaped, deeply lobed and pointed, to 2.5 in. (6 cm); plant evergreen, self-seeds freely. Hardy in zones 2 to 7.

Viola canadensis, Canada violet, tall white violet. North America, across Canada and the northern United States, south to South Carolina and Alabama and further west.

Some sun, LS to WS; flowers fragrant, inside white, outside purple-tinged, yellow center, lower petal bearded; leaves green, heart-shaped, pointed, to 2.5 in. (6 cm); plant evergreen, self-seeds freely. Hardy in zones 2 to 7.

Viola canina, dog violet, heath violet. Europe, western Asia.

Some sun, LS to WS; flowers blue, violet, or white, spurs white or yellow; leaves green, heart- or kidney-shaped, to 0.8 in. (2 cm); plant semi-evergreen. 'Alba' has white flowers.

Viola conspersa, American dog violet. Eastern North America, Minnesota east to Nova Scotia south to western Carolinas, northern Alabama, and west to Oklahoma.

Some sun, LS to WS; flowers bluish violet, sometimes white, lateral petals bearded, lower petal purple-veined, spur purple-tinged; leaves green, heart-shaped, scalloped, to 2 in. (5 cm); plant evergreen. Hardy in zones 4 to 7.

Viola dissecta, dog violet, heath violet. Japan.

Some sun, LS to WS; flowers fragrant, rose-pink, spur; leaves dark green, divided into 3 segments that are further divided; plant evergreen. Hardy in zones 6 to 9.

Viola glabella, stream violet. Eurasia, northwestern North America.

Some sun, LS to WS; flowers yellow with dark purple veins on lower petals, spur; leaves pale green, kidney-shaped, toothed, to 3 in. (8 cm); plant herbaceous, rhizomatous, vigorously creeping. Hardy in zones 5 to 7.

Viola labradorica, Labrador violet. Northeastern North America, Labrador, Greenland.

Some sun, LS to WS; flowers solitary, violet to pale purple, spurred; leaves green, flushed purple in spring, kidney-shaped, finely hairy, toothed, to 1.5 in. (4 cm); plant semi-evergreen, self-seeds freely. Abides hot southern summers if given plenty of moisture, remaining attractive but inactive, coming to life in autumn and carrying on all during winter (in snow-free areas) until late spring. Hardy in zones 2 to 8.

Viola lutea, mountain pansy, mountain violet. Western and central Europe in the mountains.

Some sun, LS to WS; flowers usually yellow, but also blue-violet or red-violet, or all colors mixed, similar to *Viola tricolor*, short spurs; leaves green, broadly lance-shaped, lobed or entire, to 0.8 in. (2 cm); plant evergreen, spreading. Hardy in zones 5 to 8.

Viola obliqua, marsh blue violet. Eastern North America, Newfoundland to northern Georgia and west to Arkansas, sporadically throughout.

Some sun, LS to WS; flowers bluish violet, sometimes white with blue veins, short spurs; leaves green, heart-shaped, scalloped, to 3.5 in. (9 cm); plant herbaceous, spreading. Hardy in zones 4 to

7. Flower colors include 'Alba' (white), 'Alice Witter' (white with red eye), 'Bicolor' (white with violet eye), 'Gloriole' (white with blue eye), 'Red Giant' (red, large), 'Rosea' (rose-pink), and 'Snow Princess' (pure white).

Viola pedata, birdfoot violet, bird's foot violet, crowfoot violet, pansy violet. Eastern North America.

Some sun, LS to WS; flowers large, to 1.4 in. (4 cm) across, petals beardless, upper petals deep blue-violet, lower 3 petals pale violet or whitish, with violet veins, grooved and spurred, anthers bright orange; March–June; leaves fan-shaped, 3-lobed, the lateral lobes divided into 3–5 linear to spoon-shaped lobes, slightly toothed; plant semi-evergreen, clump-forming, not invasive. Without doubt, the best violet for the shady wildflower garden—well behaved and not as invasive as other violets. It is not cleistogamous, however, and unfortunately produces seed sparsely. Quite variable. White-flowered forms occur. Needs well-draining soil; I grow it in a raised bed in an acid soil mixture of peat, coarse sand, and ground pine bark over a layer of pea gravel. Moisture is essential during hot, dry weather, and frequent watering is required if the soil is as fast-draining as it should be. The modest beauty of this wildflower is well worth the effort. Does not transplant well and should never be removed from the wild. Hardy in zones 4 to 8. Other violets have similar, deeply segmented leaves, but they are aggressive and seed freely. They include *Viola brittoniana* (coast violet) from Maine south and in the mountains to Georgia; *V. pedatifida* (prairie violet) in central North America from the prairies of Canada south to Oklahoma; and *V. palmata* (early blue violet, wood violet), which occurs from Illinois east to Pennsylvania south. These are rarely offered and often difficult garden subjects. Cultivars of *V. pedata* include 'Artist's Palette' (flowers with whitish violet lower petals with a dark center stripe) and 'Bicolor' (flowers bicolored, dark and light violet).

Viola pubescens, downy yellow violet. Eastern North America, Nebraska, Minnesota, and Ontario east to Quebec and New England and south to upland Virginia and west to Tennessee and Missouri.

Some sun, LS to WS; flowers yellow with purple veins; leaves on the stem, green, finely hairy and downy, heart-shaped, margins scalloped, to 5 in.

(13 cm) long; plant clump-forming, self-seeds freely. Hardy in zones 4 to 7. **Variety *eriocarpa*** (smooth yellow violet) is common in the same region and has a few basal leaves and a hairless stem. Also with yellow flowers is *V. nuttallii* (prairie violet), with lance-shaped leaves; it extends west to the Rocky Mountains. *Viola tripartita* (three-part-leaved violet) has deeply 3-lobed leaves and yellow flowers; it is endemic to Ohio and West Virginia and south, in the mountains, sharing habitat with *V. hastata* (halberd-leaved violet), which also has yellow flowers and triangular leaves. All these natives self-seed freely.

Viola riviniana, dog violet, wood violet. Europe into the Mediterranean region, Asia Minor east to the Caucasus and Iran.

Some sun, LS to FS; flowers large, to 1 in. (2.5 cm) across, pale violet to pale purple, spur long, notched, white, yellowish white or pale purple; leaves green, basal, rounded to kidney-shaped, toothed, to 1.5 in. (4 cm); plant semi-evergreen, self-seeds freely. Hardy in zones 5 to 8. A very attractive selection with leaves that are blackish to purplish green, more or less permanently, is 'Purpurea' (*V. riviniana* Purpurea Group, *V. labradorica* var. *purpurea*). Under whatever name, with its dark leaves, this is one of the most attractive violets for the garden—and just as invasive as the rest of them.

Viola sororia, sister violet, common blue violet. North America.

Some sun, LS to WS; flowers to 0.8 in. (2 cm), blue, white, or white with purple veins, 2 lateral petals bearded, lower petal longer and spurred; leaves green, hairy, heart-shaped, margins scalloped, to 5 in. (13 cm) long; plant clump-forming, self-seeds freely. Hardy in zones 5 to 8. *Viola papilionacea*, considered by some a synonym of *V. sororia*, has smooth leaves without hairs and other minor differences; its var. *priceana* (*V. priceana*; Confederate violet), which covers the former Confederate States like the proverbial dew, also has smooth leaves and larger, gray-blue flowers. It has become a pernicious weed in many southern gardens and lawns and is attractive but very aggressive. Cultivars of *V. sororia* include 'Albiflora' ('Immaculata'; flowers pure white), 'Freckles' (flowers white with purple spots), and 'Partly Cloudy' (flowers violet; leaves heart-shaped, green mottled with white).

Viola variegata, variegated violet. Siberia and China, Manchuria, south to Korea and Japan.

Some sun, LS to WS; flowers violet; leaves kidney-shaped, silvery gray with dark green patches between veins, reddish purple beneath, to 0.8 in. (2 cm); plant herbaceous, clump-forming, spreading, self-seeds freely. Hardy in zones 6 to 8. Variety *nipponica* (frequently mislabeled *Viola koreana*) is the form most seen in commerce; it has beautifully variegated, cyclamenlike leaves of silvery green with dark grayish green fields between the veins. Some authors include *V. variegata* with *V. tricolor* (Johnny-jump-up), a very short-lived perennial grown mostly as an annual that self-seeds prolifically. *Viola variegata* is also considered a short-lived perennial and behaves in culture just like *V. tricolor*. It too seeds prolifically. Unfortunately, this violet is intolerant of hot, dry summers. Here, even supplied with plenty of water, it goes heat-dormant. It is not hardy in areas of cold winters without snow cover, so needs plenty of protection in zones 6 and 7. Several species with variegated leaves have recently been imported from eastern Asia. Their specific origin may or may not be *V. variegata*. Cultivars include 'Dancing Geisha' (flowers light violet or white; leaves silvery gray variegated, toothed) and 'Syletta' (flowers pale violet; leaves variegated).

Waldsteinia

The species of *Waldsteinia* make an attractive groundcover with strawberrylike foliage and bright, yellow flowers in spring. Being a relative of the true strawberry, these plants also spread by means of creeping and rooting stems, but they are not as aggressive and can be controlled. The southern species do better in zones 6 and 7, while those native further north do not like the hot, dry summers at Hosta Hill and require cooler summers. All prefer placement in shady woodland gardens in moist, humus-rich soil with a pH of 5 to 6. During dry summers, extra watering is required.

The generic name honors the Austrian botanist Count von Waldstein-Wartemberg. The genus is classified in the Rosaceae.

Propagate by removing and replanting rooted runners in very early spring.

Large slugs and snails can damage young growth emerging in spring. Plants are otherwise relatively free of pests and diseases.

Waldsteinia fragarioides, barren strawberry, dry strawberry. Eastern North America, Minnesota and southern Ontario east to Quebec and New Brunswick, south through New England and in the uplands to Georgia, Alabama, and Tennessee, localized in Missouri and Indiana.

Some sun, LS to MS; flowers bright yellow, 3–8 in pairs on branched stem, to 0.8 in. (2 cm) across, sepals 5 united into a cup, petals 5, stamens many, showy yellow, pistils 3–6; April–June; plant strawberrylike, mat-forming, spreading by creeping rhizomes near the surface; leaves on long stalks, divided into 3 leaflets, green, softly hairy, lower part wedge-shaped, rounded, deeply scalloped and toothed tip, 1–2 in. (2.5–5 cm) long and wide. Subspecies *doniana* differs by having narrower leaves, longer than wide; it occurs in the southern part of the habitat from Virginia to northeastern Alabama and approaches *Waldsteinia lobata* in leaf form. Both it and the type knit into a solid, matlike groundcover 8 in. (20 cm) tall. Unfortunately, the flowers do not often penetrate the leaf cover. Despite the name (*fragarioides* = like a wild strawberry), the fruit is an inedible, dry berry. Hardy to zone 3 but not happy in the heat of zones 7 and 8, so best used in cool-summer areas of zone 6 and colder. Two southern species are better suited for southern gardens in zones 7 and 8. One, *W. parviflora*, occurs from Virginia south to northern Georgia, and is similar to *W. fragarioides* except that it has smaller, narrow-petaled, more star-shaped flowers to 0.5 in. (1 cm). **Waldsteinia lobata** (lobed barren strawberry) from the Georgia and Alabama uplands is the other; this rare species, whose leaflets have 3–5 deep lobes, is on Georgia's Protected Plants list and should never be removed from the wild.

Waldsteinia ternata. Eurasia, central and southeastern Europe east to Siberia, Sakhalin, and northern Japan.

Some sun, LS to FS; flowers bright yellow, 3–7 on branched stem, to 0.8 in. (2 cm) across, sepals 5, united into a cup, petals 5, stamens many, yellow; April–June; plant semi-evergreen, mat-forming, spreading by creeping rhizomes; leaves on short stalks, divided into 3 leaflets, green, softly hairy, diamond-shaped, rounded, deeply toothed tip, 1–2 in. (2.5–5 cm) long and wide, terminal leaflet larger, longer and more oval. This species forms a semi-evergreen ground-covering mat. Readily available in commerce, hardy to zone 3. Here in zone 7a it does not like hot, dry summers but with plenty of water and in deep shade it does reasonably well, and the leaves turn an attractive purplish green after the first frosts. It is best in zone 6 and colder. *Waldsteinia geoides* (erect barren strawberry) has stems that are more upright but is otherwise very similar; it occurs in the European Balkans region into Asia Minor and is hardy to zone 5.

Wasabia

Gardeners the world over experiment with all kinds of plants to see if they can add to the overall beauty and texture of the landscape. When I see purple cabbage planted as a decorative, late-autumn ornamental in our mild-winter areas, I often wonder if Japanese gardeners are amused by this use of a vegetable. Westerners might be just as intrigued about *Wasabia japonica* (Japanese horseradish) being used as a foliage plant. There is really no reason why this plant (used in Japan to prepare *wasabi*, a biting sushi sauce) should not also be used to add leafy texture to our shady gardens.

The leaves of Japanese horseradish—which is in the same family as our ornamental cabbage, Cruciferae—are much more suited to shade. They are highly ornamental—large, dark green, and textured with a network of deeply furrowed veins. The white, star-shaped flowers on a branched stem are a bonus in late spring. Japanese horseradish grows well in shady woodland gardens in moist, deep, humus-rich soil with a pH of 5 to 6. During dry summers, extra watering is required. The generic name is derived from the Japanese vernacular for this plant, *wasabi*.

Propagate by dividing the rhizome in very early spring.

Large slugs and snails can damage young growth emerging in spring. Plants are otherwise relatively free of pests and diseases.

Wasabia japonica, Japanese horseradish, *wasabi* (Jap.). Japan, southern Honshu, Shikoku, Kyushu.

LS to FS; flowers 4-merous, sepals 4, petals 4, white, on a shortly branched stalk to 12 in. (30 cm); May–June; leaves basal, on 6 in. (15 cm) stalks, dark shiny green, rounded, kidney-shaped, with deeply cleft, heart-shaped base and irregularly and coarsely toothed and cleft margin, veins deeply im-

pressed above and projected below, 5–7 in. (13–18 cm) long and to 6 in. (15 cm) wide; plant herbaceous, clump-forming, rhizomatous. Cultivated as a food crop all over Japan but rarely seen in gardens, this species adds a new dimension to the shady foliage garden. Another species, *Wasabia tenuis*, is not yet seen in Western gardens.

Woodsia

One native fern growing on my property in Georgia is *Woodsia obtusa* (common woodsia). I found a few clumps between protruding roots of my loblolly pines. I transplanted the clumps, and they are still with me, adding much to the leafy texture of the garden and adding winter interest with evergreen sterile fronds. Common woodsia is found all over the northern Georgia upland. Although common in limestone regions, it also occurs on acid soil. First discovered in Pennsylvania in 1804 and described as *Polypodium obtusum*, it was later classified in *Woodsia*, which name honors English architect and botanist Joseph Woods. The genus is classified in the Woodsiaceae.

Woodsias are good garden ferns, adapted not only to cold climates but to high heat. Here they have survived extreme droughts. They are well suited to any shade, from light to full, and will tolerate light sun exposure. They are somewhat delicate and do best in sheltered areas, but their constitution allows them to grow in just about any soil type, particularly well-drained rocky and gritty soils. Here they grow in gritty, acid clay soil sweetened with dolomitic limestone; the pH is 5 to 7.5. Although evergreen here in zone 7a, the fronds become deciduous in zone 6 and colder. They are excellent among rocks in the shady garden and make good companion for wildflowers, other ferns, and the smaller hostas.

Propagate by dividing the rhizome in autumn or in very early spring. Propagation by spores is also fairly easy under the right conditions. The spores must be sown as soon as they are ripe on a coarse commercial mix with a pH of 7 maintained moist at 60–70°F (16–21°C).

No insect damage or diseases experienced or reported.

Woodsia ilvensis, rusty cliff fern, rusty woodsia, fragrant woodsia. Northern Eurasia, northern North

America, northern United States and Canada in Greenland and the subarctic.

LS to FS; fronds to 10 in. (25 cm) tall and 1.5 in. (4 cm) wide, produced in tight tufts, often forming dense mats, grayish white underside, turning rust-brown during dry summers but greening again when moisture arrives in autumn; leaves compound, green covered with dense white woolly hair, later turning rusty brown, lance-shaped, narrow, pointed at top, to 6 in. (15 cm) long and 1 in. (2.5 cm) wide; cut into leaflets, to 12 pairs, nearly opposite, stalkless, but lower leaflets sometimes stalked, oval, pointed, cut into 6–8 variable and rounded lobes, or stalkless subleaflets; veins forked; spore cases (sori) round, near margin. Too small to planted in the woodland, this fern is perfect for an elevated rockery, where its silvery white fiddleheads can be observed up close. It turns rusty brown during the dry period but greens up during fall rains. Two other tiny evergreen ferns from northern North America and Eurasia are *Woodsia alpina* (northern woodsia, alpine woodsia), with erect fronds up to 7 in. (18 cm), and the even smaller *W. glabella* (smooth woodsia), with fronds to 5 in. (13 cm). All hardy to zone 2.

Woodsia obtusa, blunt-lobed woodsia, blunt-lobed cliff fern, cliff fern, common woodsia. Eastern North America, common from Canada south to northern Georgia and Florida.

LS to FS; fronds 15–20 in. (38–50 cm) tall, produced in tight clusters on stalks emerging directly from the fibrous-rooted rhizome, very scaly at the base, stalk orange at base, yellowish above, downy when young, flattened in front, erect, fertile fronds taller, more erect, annual, sterile fronds shorter, semi-evergreen; leaves compound, dull green, lance-shaped, narrow, pointed at top, to 14 in. (35 cm) long and 3 in. (8 cm) wide; cut into leaflets, to 15 pairs, nearly opposite, short-stalked, upper leaflets pointed, lower leaflets blunt or rounded, lance-shaped, toothed, hairy when young; subleaflets stalkless, nearly opposite, oblong, cut into lobelike pairs rather than distinct subleaflets, irregularly and finely toothed; veins forked; spore cases (sori) round, in 2 interrupted rows near margin, indusium starlike. The tallest of the woodsias. Its fronds are covered with white hairs when young, giving the fern a pale, almost glaucous appearance.

Woodsia polystichoides, Japanese woodsia. Japan, Korea, China, Manchuria.

LS to FS; fronds to 14 in. (35 cm) tall and 2 in. (5 cm) wide, produced in tight clusters, linear to lance-shaped, semi-evergreen; cut into leathery leaflets, 12–36 pairs, lance-shaped, nearly opposite, short-stalked or stalkless, eared at the base, pointed tip; veins forked. This fern, having leathery fronds with eared leaflets, looks like a *Polystichum* species, as the epithet indicates. Among the larger woodsias and a good fern for northern gardens, hardy to zone 4. It is not happy where summers are hot and dry, so I gave up on it and replaced it with a holly fern, which gives a much better display year-round. *Woodsia manchuriensis* (Manchurian woodsia) is larger and may be used similarly.

Woodsia scopulina, Rocky Mountain woodsia. Western North America, Alaska to northern California.

LS to FS; fronds to 14 in. (35 cm) tall and 3 in. (8 cm) wide, produced in tight clusters, lance-shaped, semi-evergreen; cut into leaflets, 12–25 pairs, lance-shaped, nearly opposite, short-stalked; subleaflets strap-shaped, notched; veins forked. This western woodsia has two counterparts in eastern North America: *Woodsia appalachiana* (Appalachian woodsia), considered synonymous by some, and *W. cathcartiana*, endemic along the Canadian border in Minnesota and Michigan east to western New York. Distinct regional populations of western species, such as *W. oregana* (Oregon woodsia), have been separated as well. All are smaller ferns with upright, ruffled fronds that fit well into a small rockery in the woodland garden. All are hardy to zone 4. I have tried only *W. appalachiana* and find that it's better to admire in its native habitat: it does not like the heat of the Georgia Piedmont. Species growing in the mountains further north and west are obviously more suited to cool-summer areas of northern and western North America and Europe.

Woodwardia

Woodwardia areolata (netted chain fern) is a fern native to Georgia that I have never seen in the wild; it looks much like a smaller sensitive fern, *Onoclea sensibilis*, so is often overlooked. It is also the most prevalent fern at Hosta Hill. A small start of it received from a friend has grown into expansive, upright colonies. I was warned that it would spread, but this did not truly characterize its sprawling habit. I like it, and it is not invasive in the sense of bamboo. It simply sprawls on top of the ground and is easily pulled up when it gets too rambunctious. I let it knit through hosta plantings, where it fills the empty spaces with attractive green fronds, first sterile and later fertile. It likes to grow on pure, acid clay, which absorbs large amounts of water. This fern loves wet places and will grow in swampy areas. Since the hostas get watered during dry periods, the ferns benefit from this and grow luxuriantly. Smaller and even medium hostas may get overwhelmed by this vigorous fern, so it should be teamed up with very large hostas only. It has no place in the wildflower garden, where it will smother the more delicate denizens of the woods. Sun or shade, it makes a tall groundcover in wet, otherwise unproductive areas. The sterile fronds are deciduous, but the fertile ones remain upright all during the winter, providing interest. The common name makes reference to the chainlike arrangement of the spore cases, which occur in double lines along the midrib. Linnaeus called it *Acrostichum areolatum*, but a few decades later the species was placed in *Woodwardia*, which honors English botanist Thomas Woodward. The genus is classified in the Blechnaceae.

Chain ferns are excellent garden ferns and are of the easiest culture as long as some moisture is maintained. They are hardy to zone 5 and tolerant of the high heat here in the Georgia Piedmont, where they survive extreme droughts year after year. These rugged ferns require no coddling; they are well suited to any shade from light to full and will grow in full sun. They grow in just about any soil type, from light to heavy, as long as it is moist and acid with a pH of 4 to 6. They are excellent for filling in bare spots in difficult areas and for closing up voids in the shady perennial garden. They make a nice background for shaded, small ponds and water features.

Propagate by dividing the creeping rhizome in early spring. Propagation by spores is complicated and unnecessary.

No insect damage or diseases experienced or reported.

Woodwardia areolata, netted chain fern, dimorphic chain fern, marsh fern, swamp fern. Eastern North America, New England south to Georgia and Florida and west to Louisiana.

Some sun, LS to FS; sterile and fertile fronds separate; sterile fronds deciduous, taller, oval, green, to 24 in. (60 cm) tall and 6 in. (15 cm) wide, produced along a widely creeping rhizome, cut into 7–12 pairs of nearly opposite leaflets, lance-shaped, narrow, pointed at top, to 3 in. (8 cm) long and 0.5 in. (1 cm) wide, margins wavy, finely toothed, stalkless and winged at stem, except the lower pairs, which are very short-stalked; veins prominently raised, netted (hence the epithet); fertile fronds remaining through winter, shorter, also cut into leaflets but much more narrow and contracted, with margins rolled over the chainlike rows of spore cases. Hardy to zone 5 and tolerant of heat and drought.

Woodwardia virginica, Virginia chain fern. Eastern North America, Nova Scotia south through Virginia to southern Georgia and Florida and west to southeastern Texas.

Some sun, LS to FS; fronds deciduous, to 5 ft. (1.5 m) but usually shorter, produced in tight clusters on stalks emerging directly from a widely creeping rhizome, brown scales at the base, stalk very long, stout, erect, shiny purplish brown, lower part swollen, thickened; leaves yellowish green in spring, dark green later, lance-shaped, broadest in the middle, pointed at top, to 4 ft. (1.2 m) long and 10 in. (25 cm) wide; cut into 13–18 leaflets, closely spaced, nearly opposite, sterile and fertile leaflets the same; subleaflets rounded at tip; inner veins netted, chainlike, outer veins free, forked; spore cases chainlike along the midrib. Much larger than *Woodwardia areolata* and suitable for background plantings in the woodland garden. Hardy to zone 5 and quite heat-tolerant, as indicated by its happy survival here through 3 consecutive blistering droughts. The evergreen *W. radicans* (European chain fern) from southwestern Europe is even larger but more tender, hardy in zones 8 and 9 only. The giant of all chain ferns is *W. fimbricata* (giant chain fern), endemic along the Pacific Coast from British Columbia to southern California; its deciduous fronds can reach 10 ft. (3 m) but it too is not hardy. Gardeners from zone 7 and colder should not plant these half-tender ferns in open gardens; notwithstanding, they make imposing container plants if overwintered in a frost-free location.

Plant Sources

In years past, many rare plants were available in the United Kingdom or in Europe or Asian countries only; but this situation has changed drastically, and most, if not all, of the more unusual plants described in this book can now be obtained from domestic sources. A list of U.S. mail-order sources follows; most supply live plants. Obviously, plants can also be raised from seed by patient gardeners, but the results are often uncertain, and the effect in the garden is not as immediate. For a complete list of plant nurseries in the United Kingdom, acquire the latest edition of the *RHS Plant Finder*, edited by Tony Lord, which contains sources for over 70,000 plants. Finally, gardeners with access to e-commerce can use their favorite search engines to investigate the countless web sites offering seed or live plants. Many of the following mail-order sources, as well as those overseas, now likely have e-mail addresses and conduct business via the Internet.

André Viette Farm and Nursery
Route 1, Box 16
Fishersville, VA 22939

Arrowhead Alpines
Box 857
Fowlerville, MI 48836

Asiatica
Box 270
Lewisberry, PA 17339

Boehlke's Woodland Gardens
5890 Wausaukee Road
West Bend, WI 53095

Busse Gardens
17160 245th Avenue
Big Lake, MN 55309

Camellia Forest Nursery
125 Carolina Forest Road
Chapel Hill, NC 27516

Collector's Nursery
16804 NE 102nd Avenue
Battle Ground, WA 98604

Flower Place Plant Farm
Box 4865
Meridian, MS 39304

Forestfarm Nursery
990 Tetherow Road
Williams, OR 97544-9599

Garden in the Woods
Hemenway Road
Framington, MA 01701

Garden Visions
63 Williamsville Road
Hubbardston, MA 01452-1315

Gardens of the Blue Ridge
Box 10
Pineola, NC 28662

Great Lakes Wild Flowers
Box 1923
Milwaukee, WI 53201

Heronswood Nursery, Ltd.
7530 NE 288th Street
Kingston, WA 98346

Klehm Nursery
4210 North Duncan Road
Champaign, IL 61821

Lee Gardens
25986 Sauder Road
Tremont, IL 61568

Mid-Atlantic Wildflowers
Star Route, Box 226
Gloucester Point, VA 23062

Native Gardens
5737 Fisher Lane
Greenback, TN 37742

Natural Gardens
4804 Shell Lane
Knoxville, TN 37918

Nature's Garden
Route 1, Box 488
Beaverton, OR 97007

Naylor Creek Nursery
2610 West Valley Road
Chimacum, WA 98325

Niche Gardens
1111 Dawson Road
Chapel Hill, NC 27516

Oregon Trail Gardens
1810 SE Troge Road
Boring, OR 97009-9646

Piccadilly Farm
1971 Whippoorwill Road
Bishop, GA 30621

Plant Delights Nursery
9241 Sauls Road
Raleigh, NC 27603

Prairie Moon Nursery
Route 3, Box 163
Winona, MN 55371

Putney Nursery, Inc.
Route 5
Putney, VT 05346

Robyn's Nest Nursery
7802 NE 63rd Street
Vancouver, WA 98662

Roslyn Nursery
211 Burrs Lane
Dix Hills, NY 11746

Siskiyou Rare Plant Nursery
2825 Cummings Road
Medford, OR 97501

Sperka's Woodland Acres Nursery
Route 2
Civitz, WI 54114

Wayside Gardens
Box 1
Hodges, SC 29695-0001

We-Du Nurseries
Route 5, Box 724
Marion, NC 28752

Weston Nurseries, Inc.
Box 186, Route 135
Hopkinton, MA 01748

White Flower Farm
Box 50, Route 63
Litchfield, CT 06759-0050

Woodlanders Inc.
1128 Colleton Avenue
Aiken, SC 29801

Yucca Do Nursery
Box 907
Hempstead, TX 77445

U.S. Department of Agriculture Hardiness Zone Map

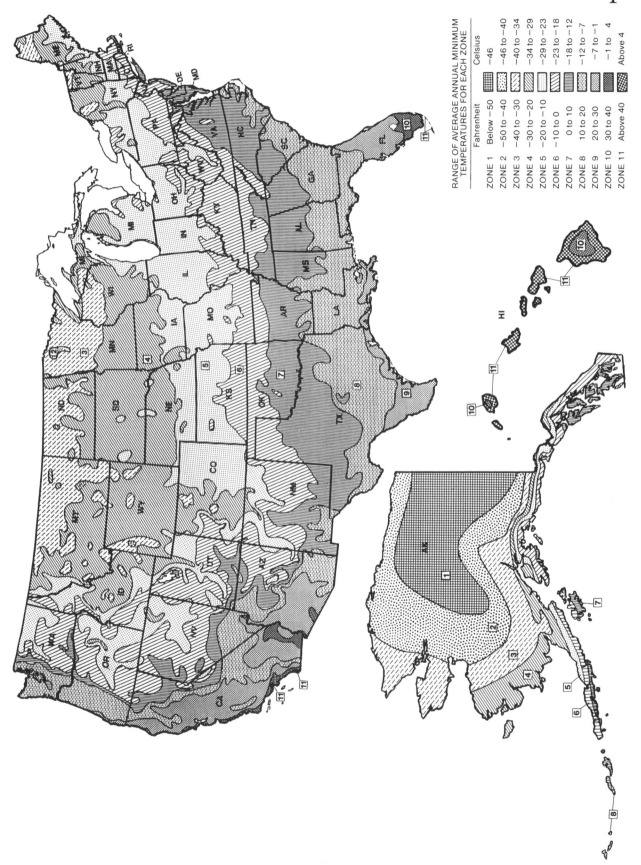

RANGE OF AVERAGE ANNUAL MINIMUM
TEMPERATURES FOR EACH ZONE

	Fahrenheit	Celsius
ZONE 1	Below −50	−46
ZONE 2	−50 to −40	−46 to −40
ZONE 3	−40 to −30	−40 to −34
ZONE 4	−30 to −20	−34 to −29
ZONE 5	−20 to −10	−29 to −23
ZONE 6	−10 to 0	−23 to −18
ZONE 7	0 to 10	−18 to −12
ZONE 8	10 to 20	−12 to −7
ZONE 9	20 to 30	−7 to −1
ZONE 10	30 to 40	−1 to 4
ZONE 11	Above 40	Above 4

Index of Plant Names

Aaron's beard. See *Saxifraga stolonifera*
Acanthaceae, 57
Acanthus, 57–58
Acanthus balcanicus. See *Acanthus hungaricus*
Acanthus boissieri. See *Acanthus dioscoridis*
Acanthus dioscoridis, 57
Acanthus hirsutus, 57
Acanthus hungaricus, 57
Acanthus longifolius. See *Acanthus hungaricus*
Acanthus lusitanicus. See *Acanthus mollis*
Acanthus mollis, 57–58
Acanthus montanus, 57
Acanthus perringii. See *Acanthus dioscoridis*
Acanthus schottii. See *Acanthus hungaricus*
Acanthus spinosus, 58
Acanthus syriacus, 57
Aceriphyllum rossii. See *Mukdenia rossii*
Achlys, 58
Achlys japonica, 58
Achlys triphylla, 58
Achlys triphylla var. *japonica*. See *Achlys japonica*
Aconitum, 59–61
Aconitum ×*acutum*. See *Aconitum* ×*cammarum*
Aconitum alboviolaceum, 59
Aconitum anthora, 60
Aconitum ×*arendsii*. See *Aconitum carmichaelii*
Aconitum bartlettii, 60
Aconitum ×*bicolor*. See *Aconitum* ×*cammarum*
Aconitum ×*cammarum*, 60

Aconitum carmichaelii, 60
Aconitum carmichaelii var. *wilsonii*, 60
Aconitum henryi, 60
Aconitum ×*intermedium*. See *Aconitum* ×*cammarum*
Aconitum lycoctonum, 60
Aconitum lycoctonum var. *pyrenaicum*, 60
Aconitum lycoctonum subsp. *vulparia*, 60
Aconitum napellus, 61
Aconitum napellus subsp. *compactum*, 61
Aconitum napellus subsp. *tauricum*, 61
Aconitum ottonianum. See *Aconitum* ×*cammarum*
Aconitum septentrionale. See *Aconitum lycoctonum*
Aconitum stoerkianum. See *Aconitum* ×*cammarum*
Aconitum wilsonii. See *Aconitum carmichaelii* var. *wilsonii*
Acoraceae, 61
Acorus, 61–62
Acorus calamus, 61
Acorus gramineus, 61, 62
Acrostichum alpinum. See *Woodsia alpina*
Acrostichum areolatum. See *Woodwardia areolata*
Acrostichum ilvense. See *Woodsia ilvensis*
Acrostichum polypodioides. See *Polypodium polypodioides*
Acrostichum thelypteris. See *Thelypteris palustris*
Actaea, 62–64
Actaea acuminata. See *Actaea spicata* var. *acuminata*

Actaea alba, 63
Actaea alba f. *pachycarpa*, 63
Actaea arguta. See *Actaea rubra* subsp. *arguta*
Actaea asiatica, 63
Actaea cimicifuga. See *Cimicifuga foetida*
Actaea erythrocarpa, 63
Actaea erythrocarpa of gardens. See *Actaea rubra*
Actaea japonica. See *Cimicifuga japonica*
Actaea nigra. See *Actaea spicata*
Actaea pachypoda. See *Actaea alba*
Actaea pachypoda f. *rubricarpa*. See *Actaea alba* f. *pachycarpa*
Actaea rubra, 63
Actaea rubra subsp. *arguta*, 63
Actaea rubra f. *neglecta*, 63
Actaea spicata, 63
Actaea spicata var. *acuminata*, 64
Actaea spicata var. *rubra*. See *Actaea erythrocarpa*
Adam and Eve orchid. See *Aplectrum hyemale*
adder's fern. See *Polypodium vulgare*
adder's violet. See *Goodyera pubescens*
Adiantaceae, 64
Adiantum, 64–66
Adiantum aleuticum. See *Adiantum pedatum* subsp. *aleuticum*
Adiantum aleuticum subsp. *subpumilum*. See *Adiantum pedatum* subsp. *subpumilum*
Adiantum altadena of gardens. See *Adiantum capillus-veneris*
Adiantum capillus-veneris, 64
Adiantum obrienii of gardens. See *Adiantum capillus-veneris*
Adiantum pedatum, 65

Adiantum pedatum subsp. *aleuticum*, 65

Adiantum pedatum subsp. *calderi*, 65

Adiantum pedatum subsp. *subpumilum*, 65

Adiantum venustum, 66

Aegopodium, 66–67

Aegopodium podagraria 'Variegatum', 66

Ainsliaea, 304–305

Ainsliaea acerifolia, 305

Ainsliaea apiculata, 305

Ajuga, 67–69

Ajuga alpina. See *Ajuga genevensis*

Ajuga genevensis, 67

Ajuga incisa, 67

Ajuga lobata, 67

Ajuga metallica of gardens. See *Ajuga pyramidalis*

Ajuga pyramidalis, 68

Ajuga repens. See *Ajuga reptans*

Ajuga reptans, 68

Ajuga rugosa. See *Ajuga genevensis*

Ajuga tottenhamii of gardens. See *Ajuga reptans*

akebono tokudama, 224

Alaskan holly fern. See *Polystichum* ×*setigerum*

Aletris, 208

Aleutian maidenhair fern. See *Adiantum pedatum* subsp. *aleuticum*

Alexandrian laurel. See *Danae racemosa*

Allegheny pachysandra. See *Pachysandra procumbens*

Allegheny spurge. See *Pachysandra procumbens*

Alliaceae, 246

Allium bivalve. See *Nothoscordum bivalve*

Allium cernuum, 331

Allium inodorum. See *Nothoscordum gracile*

All-Saints-Day Christmas rose, 197

alpine barrenwort. See *Epimedium alpinum*

alpine lady fern. See *Athyrium distentifolium*

alpine snowbell. See *Soldanella alpina*

alpine woodsia. See *Woodsia alpina*

alumroot. See *Geranium maculatum*

amagi kanaoi. See *Asarum muramatsui*

amberbell. See *Erythronium americanum*

Amenopsis, 75

American beech fern. See *Phegopteris hexagonoptera*

American bluebell. See *Campanula americana*

American bugbane. See *Cimicifuga americana*

American dog violet. See *Viola conspersa*

American false hellebore. See *Veratrum viride*

American ginseng. See *Panax quinquefolius*

American glade fern. See *Athyrium pycnocarpon*

American ipecac. See *Gillenia stipulata*

American ipecacuanha. See *Gillenia stipulata*

American lungwort. See *Mertensia pulmonarioides*

American maidenhair fern. See *Adiantum pedatum*

American maidenhair. See *Adiantum pedatum*

American mandrake. See *Podophyllum peltatum*

American mountain gentian. See *Gentiana decora*

American pyrola. See *Pyrola americana*

American spikenard. See *Aralia racemosa*

American true love. See *Trillium erectum*

American turk's cap lily. See *Lilium superbum*

American twinleaf. See *Jeffersonia diphylla*

American valerian. See *Cypripedium calceolus* var. *pubescens*

American wall fern. See *Polypodium virginianum*

American white hellebore. See *Veratrum viride*

American wood sorrel. See *Oxalis montana*

Amianthium, 69

Amianthium muscaetoxicum, 69

Amianthium muscitoxicum. See *Amianthium muscaetoxicum*

Amorphophallus, 70–72

Amorphophallus bulbifer, 71

Amorphophallus campanulatus. See *Amorphophallus paeoniifolius*

Amorphophallus konjac. See *Amorphophallus rivieri* var. *konjac*

Amorphophallus paeoniifolius, 71

Amorphophallus rivieri, 71

Amorphophallus rivieri var. *konjac*, 71

Amorphophallus titanum, 71

Amur cobra lily. See *Arisaema amurense*

Anchistea virginica. See *Woodwardia virginica*

Anchusa, 123

Anchusa myosotidiflora. See *Brunnera macrophylla*

Anemone, 72–74

Anemone acutiloba. See *Hepatica acutiloba*

Anemone blanda, 72

Anemone ×*elegans*. See *Anemone* ×*hybrida*

Anemone hepatica. See *Hepatica nobilis*

Anemone hupehensis, 73

Anemone hupehensis var. *japonica*, 73

Anemone ×*hybrida*, 73

Anemone japonica. See *Anemone hupehensis*

Anemone japonica of gardens. See *Anemone* ×*hybrida*

Anemone sylvestris, 72

Anemone thalictroides. See *Anemonella thalictroides*

Anemone tomentosa, 74

Anemone transsilvanica. See *Hepatica transsilvanica*

Anemone vitifolia, 74

Anemone vitifolia of gardens. See *Anemone tomentosa*

Anemone vitifolia var. *tomentosa*. See *Anemone tomentosa*

Anemonella, 74–75

Anemonella thalictroides, 74, 75

Anemonopsis, 75–76

Anemonopsis macrophylla, 76

angular Solomon's seal. See *Polygonatum odoratum*

Aplectrum, 76

Aplectrum hyemale, 76

Aplectrum unguiculatum, 76

Apocynaceae, 330

Appalachian woodsia. See *Woodsia appalachiana*

appendixless cobra lily. See *Arisaema exappendiculatum*

Aquilegia, 76–79

Aquilegia canadensis, 77

Aquilegia coerulea, 78

Aquilegia vulgaris, 78

Aquilegia vulgaris var. *clematiflora*. See *Aquilegia vulgaris* var. *stellata*

Aquilegia vulgaris var. *stellata*, 78

Araceae, 70, 82, 93, 94, 168, 259, 289. See also Acoraceae

Arachniodes, 79

Arachniodes aristata, 79

Arachniodes simplicior, 79

Arachniodes standishii, 79

Aralia, 79–81

Aralia cachemirica, 80

Aralia californica, 80, 81
Aralia continentalis. See *Aralia cordata*
Aralia cordata, 80
Aralia elata, 79
Aralia nudicaulis, 80
Aralia racemosa, 81
Aralia spinosa, 80
Araliaceae, 80
arborvitae fern. See *Selaginella braunii*
archangel. See *Lamium album*
Arisaema, 81–93
Arisaema abbreviatum. See *Arisaema flavum*
Arisaema affine. See *Arisaema concinnum*
Arisaema aleinatum. See *Arisaema concinnum*
Arisaema amurense, 83
Arisaema amurense var. *denticulatum*, 83
Arisaema amurense var. *robustum*, 83
Arisaema angustatum, 83
Arisaema angustatum var. *peninsulae*, 83
Arisaema angustatum var. *peninsulae* f. *variegata*, 83
Arisaema atrorubens. See *Arisaema triphyllum* var. *atrorubens*
Arisaema candidissimum, 83
Arisaema concinnum, 83
Arisaema consanguineum, 84
Arisaema cornutum. See *Arisaema jaquemontii*
Arisaema costatum, 84
Arisaema costatum var. *sikkimense*. See *Arisaema propinquum*
Arisaema curvatum. See *Arisaema tortuosum*
Arisaema dolosum. See *Arisaema intermedium*
Arisaema dracontium, 81, 84
Arisaema elephas, 84
Arisaema erubescens, 85
Arisaema erubescens var. *consanguineum*. See *Arisaema consanguineum*
Arisaema exappendiculatum, 85
Arisaema exile. See *Arisaema jaquemontii*
Arisaema fargesii, 85
Arisaema flavum, 85
Arisaema franchetianum, 83
Arisaema griffithii, 85
Arisaema griffithii var. *pradhanii*, 86
Arisaema griffithii var. *verrucosum*, 86
Arisaema helleborifolium. See *Arisaema tortuosum*
Arisaema heterophyllum, 86
Arisaema hookeri. See *Arisaema griffithii*

Arisaema hookerianum. See *Arisaema griffithii*
Arisaema intermedium, 86
Arisaema intermedium var. *biflagellatum*, 86
Arisaema intermedium var. *propinquum*. See *Arisaema propinquum*
Arisaema iyoanum, 86
Arisaema iyoanum subsp. *nakaianum*, 86
Arisaema japonicum. See *Arisaema serratum*
Arisaema jaquemontii, 86
Arisaema kishidae. See *Arisaema serratum*
Arisaema kiushianum, 87
Arisaema limbatum, 87
Arisaema maximowiczii, 87
Arisaema minamitanii, 87
Arisaema negishii, 87
Arisaema nepenthoides, 88
Arisaema ochraceum. See *Arisaema nepenthoides*
Arisaema pradhanii. See *Arisaema griffithii* var. *pradhanii*
Arisaema praecox. See *Arisaema ringens*
Arisaema propinquum, 88
Arisaema ringens, 83. 88
Arisaema ringens f. *glaucescens*, 88
Arisaema ringens of gardens. See *Arisaema robustum*
Arisaema robustum, 89
Arisaema saxatile, 89
Arisaema sazensoo, 89
Arisaema serratum, 89
Arisaema sikkimense. See *Arisaema propinquum*
Arisaema sikokianum, 90
Arisaema speciosum, 82, 90
Arisaema speciosum var. *mirabile*, 90
Arisaema stewardsonii. See *Arisaema triphyllum* subsp. *stewardsonii*
Arisaema stracheyanum. See *Arisaema intermedium*
Arisaema taiwanense, 82, 90
Arisaema tashiroi, 91
Arisaema ternatipartitum, 91
Arisaema thunbergii, 91
Arisaema thunbergii subsp. *urashima*, 91
Arisaema tortuosum, 91
Arisaema triphyllum, 81, 92
Arisaema triphyllum var. *atrorubens*, 92
Arisaema triphyllum subsp. *stewardsonii*, 92
Arisaema urashima. See *Arisaema thunbergii* subsp. *urashima*

Arisaema utile, 86
Arisaema verrucosum var. *utile*. See *Arisaema utile*
Arisaema vituperatum. See *Arisaema consanguineum*
Arisaema wallichianum. See *Arisaema propinquum*
Arisaema wallichianum var. *sikkimense*. See *Arisaema propinquum*
Arisaema yamatense, 92
Arisaema yamatense var. *sugimotoi*, 93
Arisaema yunnanense, 93
Arisarum, 93
Arisarum proboscideum, 93
Arisarum vulgare, 93
Aristolochia macrophylla, 98
Aristolochiaceae, 96
Arizona bugbane. See *Cimicifuga arizonica*
arrowhead ginger. See *Asarum arifolium*
arrowhead hart's tongue fern, 109
Arum, 93–94
Arum cornutum. See *Sauromatum venosum*
Arum dracunculus. See *Dracunculus vulgaris*
Arum erubescens. See *Arisaema erubescens*
Arum flavum. See *Arisaema flavum*
Arum italicum, 93, 94
Arum italicum subsp. *albispathum*, 94
Arum italicum var. *marmoratum*, 94
Arum italicum subsp. *neglectum*, 94
Arum maculatum, 93
Arum nepenthoides. See *Arisaema nepenthoides*
Arum speciosum. See *Arisaema speciosum*
Arum tortuosum. See *Arisaema tortuosum*
Aruncus, 94–96
Aruncus aethusifolius, 94, 95
Aruncus astilboides, 95
Aruncus dioicus, 94, 95
Aruncus dioicus var. *astilboides*. See *Aruncus astilboides*
Aruncus dioicus var. *kamtschaticus*, 95, 96
Aruncus parvulus, 96
Aruncus plumosus of gardens. See *Aruncus dioicus*
Aruncus sinensis, 96
Aruncus.sylvester. See *Aruncus dioicus*
Aruncus vulgaris. See *Aruncus dioicus*
Aruncus vulgaris var. *astilboides*. See *Aruncus astilboides*
Arundinaria murieliae. See *Sinarundinaria murieliae*

Arundinaria nitida. See *Sinarundinaria nitida*

Arundinaria ragamowskii. See *Sasa tessellata*

Arundinaria veitchii. See *Sasa veitchii*

Asarabacca, 96

Asarabacca europaeum. See *Asarum europaeum*

Asarum, 96–104

Asarum albivenium. See *Asarum blumei*

Asarum arifolium, 97, 98

Asarum arifolium var. *ruthii*. See *Asarum ruthii*

Asarum asaroides, 98

Asarum asperum, 98

Asarum blumei, 98

Asarum campaniforme, 98

Asarum canadense, 97, 99

Asarum canadense var. *acuminatum*, 99

Asarum canadense var. *reflexum*, 99

Asarum cardiophyllum. See *Asarum caudigerum* var. *cardiophyllum*

Asarum caudatum, 99

Asarum caudatum f. *alba* of gardens, 99

Asarum caudigerum, 99

Asarum caudigerum var. *cardiophyllum*, 99

Asarum caulescens, 97, 99

Asarum celsum, 99

Asarum chinense. See *Asarum sinense*

Asarum controversum, 98

Asarum costatum, 100

Asarum dimitiatum, 100

Asarum dissitum, 100

Asarum europaeum, 100

Asarum europaeum var. *caucasicum*, 100

Asarum fauriei, 101

Asarum fudsinoi, 100

Asarum gelasinum, 100

Asarum grandiflorum. See *Asarum arifolium*

Asarum gusk, 100

Asarum hartwegii, 100

Asarum heterophyllum, 104

Asarum hexalobum, 100

Asarum himalayicum, 103

Asarum hirsutisepalum, 97, 100

Asarum ikegamii, 101

Asarum infrapurpureum, 100

Asarum kiusianum, 101

Asarum kiusianum var. *tubulosum*, 101

Asarum kooyanum, 102

Asarum kumageanum, 97, 101

Asarum kumageanum var. *satakeanum*, 101

Asarum leucosepalum, 100

Asarum lewisii, 102

Asarum macranthum, 101

Asarum magnificum, 101

Asarum marmoratum. See *Asarum hartwegii*

Asarum maximum, 101

Asarum megacalyx, 101

Asarum minamitanianum, 97, 101

Asarum minor, 102

Asarum minus. See *Asarum minor*

Asarum monodoriflorum, 100

Asarum muramatsui, 98

Asarum naniflorum, 102

Asarum niponicum, 102

Asarum nipponicum. See *Asarum niponicum*

Asarum rigescens, 102

Asarum ruthii, 97, 98

Asarum sakawanum, 102

Asarum satsumense, 98

Asarum savatieri, 97, 102

Asarum shuttleworthii, 96, 102

Asarum shuttleworthii var. *harperi*, 102

Asarum sieboldii, 103

Asarum sinense, 103

Asarum speciosum, 103

Asarum splendens, 103

Asarum stellatum, 103

Asarum subglobosum, 103

Asarum takaoi, 104

Asarum tamaense, 102

Asarum thunbergii. See *Asarum asaroides*

Asarum trigynum, 103

Asarum unzen, 98

Asarum virginicum, 97, 104

Asarum yakusimense. See *Asarum hirsutisepalum*

Asarum yoshikawae, 104

ashweed. See *Aegopodium podagraria* 'Variegatum'

Asian bead lily. See *Clintonia udensis*

Asian bleeding heart. See *Dicentra spectabilis*

Asian dogtooth violet. See *Erythronium dens-canis*

Asian foamflower. See *Tiarella polyphylla*

Asian hepatica. See *Hepatica nobilis* var. *japonica*

Asian ladies' tresses. See *Spiranthes sinensis*

Asian ostrich fern. See *Matteuccia orientalis*

Asian twinleaf. See *Jeffersonia dubia*

Asiasarum, 96

Asperula odorata. See *Galium odoratum*

Aspidistra, 104–106

Aspidistra caespitosa, 105

Aspidistra elatior, 104, 106

Aspidistra linearifolia, 106

Aspidistra lurida, 106

Aspidistra lurida of gardens. See *Aspidistra elatior*

Aspidistra typica, 106

Aspidium angulare. See *Polystichum setiferum*

Aspidium falcatum. See *Cyrtomium falcatum*

Aspidium goldianum. See *Dryopteris goldiana*

Aspidium marginale. See *Dryopteris marginalis*

Aspidium noveboracense. See *Thelypteris noveboracensis*

Aspidium obtusum. See *Woodsia obtusa*

Aspidium spinulosum. See *Dryopteris carthusiana*

Aspidium thelypteris. See *Thelypteris palustris*

Aspidium tsussimense. See *Polystichum tsussimense*

Aspleniaceae, 107

Asplenium, 106–109

Asplenium acrostichoides. See *Polystichum acrostichoides*

Asplenium angustifolium. See *Athyrium pycnocarpon*

Asplenium ceterach, 107

Asplenium ebeneum. See *Asplenium platyneuron*

Asplenium filix-femina. See *Athyrium filix-femina*

Asplenium montanum, 109

Asplenium pinnatifidum, 109

Asplenium platyneuron, 106, 107

Asplenium resiliens, 108

Asplenium rhizophyllum, 108

Asplenium ruta-muraria, 107

Asplenium scolopendrium, 108

Asplenium scolopendrium var. *americanum*, 108

Asplenium trichomanes, 109

Asplenium trichomanes subsp. *pachyrachis*, 109

Asplenium trichomanoides. See *Asplenium trichomanes*

Aster, 109–110

Aster divaricatus, 109

Aster lateriflorus, 110

Aster tataricus, 109

Aster umbellatus, 110

Asteraceae, 137, 173, 304

Astilbe, 110–114

Astilbe ×*arendsii*, 110, 111

Astilbe astilboides, 110

Astilbe biternata, 112

Astilbe chinensis, 112

Astilbe chinensis var. *davidii*, 110, 112

Astilbe chinensis var. *pumila*, 112
Astilbe chinensis var. *taquetii*, 112
Astilbe ×*crispa*, 112
Astilbe decandra. See *Astilbe biternata*
Astilbe grandis, 112
Astilbe japonica, 112
Astilbe koreana, 113
Astilbe pinnata. See *Rodgersia pinnata*
Astilbe rivularis, 113
Astilbe simplicifolia, 113
Astilbe thunbergii, 110, 113
Astilbe thunbergii var. *fujisanensis*, 113
Astilbe thunbergii var. *sikokumontana*, 113
Astilboides, 114
Astilboides tabularis, 114
Athyriaceae, 247
Athyrium, 114–117
Athyrium alpestre. See *Athyrium distentifolium*
Athyrium bourgaei. See *Athyrium filix-femina*
Athyrium distentifolium, 115
Athyrium distentifolium var. *americanum*, 115
Athyrium filix-femina, 114, 115
Athyrium filix-femina var. *angustum*, 115
Athyrium filix-femina var. *asplenioides*, 115
Athyrium filix-femina var. *californicum*, 115
Athyrium filix-femina var. *cyclosorum*, 115
Athyrium filix-femina var. *michauxii*, 115
Athyrium filix-femina f. *rubellum*, 115
Athyrium goeringianum. See *Athyrium nipponicum*
Athyrium matsamurae. See *Athyrium nipponicum*
Athyrium niponicum. See *Athyrium nipponicum*
Athyrium nipponicum, 114, 116
Athyrium nipponicum var. *pictum*, 116
Athyrium otophorum, 116
Athyrium paucifrons. See *Athyrium filix-femina*
Athyrium pycnocarpon, 116
Athyrium thelypteroides, 117
Athyrium uropteron. See *Athyrium nipponicum*
atsumi kanaoi. See *Asarum rigescens*
August lily. See *Hosta plantaginea*
Austrian arum. See *Arum maculatum*
autumn fern. See *Dryopteris erythrosora*
autumn ladies' tresses. See *Spiranthes cernua*; *S. spiralis*

autumn snakeroot. See *Cimicifuga simplex*
avalanche lily. See *Erythronium grandiflorum*
Avena sativa, 133
azure monkshood. See *Aconitum carmichaelii*

badger's bane. See *Aconitum lycoctonum*
balmony. See *Chelone glabra*
Bambusa ragamowskii. See *Sasa tessellata*
Bambusa veitchii. See *Sasa veitchii*
band plant. See *Vinca major*
banwool-bibich'u. See *Hosta capitata*
Barksdale trillium. See *Trillium sulcatum*
barren strawberry. See *Waldsteinia fragarioides*
barroom plant. See *Aspidistra elatior*
bashful wakerobin. See *Trillium catesbaei*
basket spike moss. See *Selaginella apoda*
bastard helleborine. See *Epipactis helleborine*
bead fern. See *Onoclea sensibilis*
bead ruby. See *Maianthemum canadense*
bear claw hellebore. See *Helleborus foetidus*
bear's breeches. See *Acanthus mollis*
bear's foot. See *Aconitum napellus*; *Helleborus foetidus*
bear's paw. See *Polystichum polyblepharum*
beautiful maiden hosta. See *Hosta venusta*
beech fern. See *Phegopteris connectilis*
beefsteak geranium. See *Saxifraga stolonifera*
beefsteak saxifrage. See *Saxifraga stolonifera*
beetleweed. See *Galax urceolata*
Begonia, 117–118
Begonia discolor. See *Begonia grandis*
Begonia evansiana. See *Begonia grandis*
Begonia grandis, 117, 118
Begonia grandis var. *alba*, 118
Begonia grandis subsp. *evansiana*. See *Begonia grandis*
Begoniaceae, 117
Belamcanda, 118–119
Belamcanda chinensis, 118, 119
Belamcanda flabellata, 118, 119
bellwort. See *Uvularia*
bent trillium. See *Trillium flexipes*

Berberidaceae, 132, 161, 174, 228, 262, 282, 326
Bethlehem sage. See *Pulmonaria saccharata*
Bethroot. See *Trillium erectum*
big blue lilyturf. See *Liriope muscari*
big merrybells. See *Uvularia grandiflora*
bigroot cranesbill. See *Geranium macrorrhizum*
bigroot geranium. See *Geranium macrorrhizum*
birdfoot violet. See *Viola pedata*
bird's foot violet. See *Viola pedata*
birthwort. See *Trillium erectum*
bishop's cap. See *Mitella diphylla*
bishop's hat. See *Epimedium grandiflorum*
bishop's weed. See *Aegopodium podagraria* 'Variegatum'
black baneberry. See *Actaea spicata*
blackberry lily. See *Belamcanda chinensis*; *B. flabellata*
black cohosh. See *Cimicifuga racemosa*
black dwarf Japanese wild ginger. See *Asarum yoshikawae*
black hellebore. See *Veratrum nigrum*
black hosta. See *Hosta nigrescens*
black maidenhair. See *Adiantum capillus-veneris*
blackroot. See *Veronicastrum virginicum*
black snakeroot. See *Cimicifuga racemosa*
blackstem spleenwort. See *Asplenium platyneuron*; *A. resiliens*
black widow. See *Geranium phaeum*
blazing star. See *Chamaelirium luteum*
Blechnaceae, 119, 337
Blechnum, 119–120
Blechnum nipponicum, 120
Blechnum spicant, 120
Blechnum virginicum. See *Woodwardia virginica*
bleeding heart. See *Dicentra spectabilis*
Blepharoglottis, 260
Blepharoglottis ciliaris. See *Platanthera ciliaris*
Blepharoglottis cristata. See *Platanthera cristata*
Blepharoglottis grandiflora. See *Platanthera grandiflora*
Blepharoglottis integra. See *Platanthera integra*
Blepharoglottis psyodes. See *Platanthera psyodes*
Bletia hyacinthina. See *Bletilla striata*
Bletia striata. See *Bletilla striata*
Bletilla, 120–121

Bletilla hyacinthina. See *Bletilla striata*
Bletilla ochracea, 120
Bletilla striata, 120
Bletilla striata f. *alba*, 120
blind gentian. See *Gentiana andrewsii*
blonde lilian. See *Erythronium albidum*
bloodroot. See *Sanguinaria canadensis*
bloody butcher. See *Trillium cuneatum*
bloody butchers. See *Trillium sessile*
bloody noses. See *Trillium recurvatum*
bloomer plant. See *Dicentra canadensis*
blue anemone. See *Hepatica americana*
bluebead. See *Clintonia borealis*
bluebead lily. See *Clintonia borealis*
blue bugle. See *Ajuga genevensis*
blue bugleweed. See *Ajuga genevensis*
blue button. See *Vinca major*
blue cardinal flower. See *Lobelia siphilitica*
blue cohosh. See *Caulophyllum thalictroides*
blue cowslip. See *Pulmonaria angustifolia*
blue deinanthe. See *Deinanthe caerulea*
blue-eyed Mary. See *Omphalodes verna*
blue lilyturf. See *Liriope muscari*
blue liverleaf. See *Hepatica americana*
blue lungwort. See *Pulmonaria angustifolia*
blue Medusa rush. See *Juncus inflexus*
blue rush. See *Juncus inflexus*
blue selaginella. See *Selaginella uncinata*
blue spike moss. See *Selaginella uncinata*
Blume's cobra lily. See *Arisaema intermedium*
blunt-lobed cliff fern. See *Woodsia obtusa*
blunt-lobed woodsia. See *Woodsia obtusa*
blushing cobra lily. See *Arisaema erubescens*
bog rhubarb. See *Petasites hybridus*
boneset. See *Symphytum officinale*
Boraginaceae, 123, 242, 246, 277
Boraphila, 290
Botrychium, 121–122
Botrychium alabamense, 121
Botrychium dissectum, 121
Botrychium dissectum f. *elongatum*, 121
Botrychium dissectum var. *obliquum*, 121

Botrychium dissectum var. *tenuifolium*, 121
Botrychium virginianum, 122
Botrychium virginianum var. *intermedium*, 122
bottle gentian. See *Gentiana andrewsii*
Bowman's root. See *Gillenia trifoliata*; *Veronicastrum virginicum*
box holly. See *Ruscus*
Boykinia, 122–123
Boykinia aconitifolia, 122
Boykinia heucheriformis. See *Boykinia jamesii*
Boykinia jamesii, 122
Boykinia major, 123
Boykinia occidentalis, 123
Boykinia rotundifolia, 123
Boykinia tellimoides. See *Peltoboykinia tellimoides*
Boykinia watanabei. See *Peltoboykinia watanabei*
Brachycyrtis macrantha. See *Tricyrtis macrantha*
bracken. See *Pteridium aquilinium*
bracken fern. See *Pteridium aquilinium*
brake. See *Pteridium aquilinium*
bramble-leaved cohosh. See · *Cimicifuga rubifolia*
Braun's holly fern. See *Polystichum braunii*
Brewer's miterwort. See *Mitella breweri*
bride's bonnet. See *Clintonia uniflora*
bride's feathers. See *Aruncus dioicus*
broad beech fern. See *Phegopteris hexagonoptera*
broad buckler fern. See *Dryopteris dilatata*
broad-leafed waterleaf. See *Hydrophyllum canadense*
broadleaf toad lily. See *Tricyrtis latifolia*
broad-leaved helleborine. See *Epipactis atrorubens*
brocade orchid. See *Goodyera*
brook saxifrage. See *Boykinia aconitifolia*
brook trillium. See *Trillium rivale*
brook wakerobin. See *Trillium rivale*
brown Beth. See *Trillium erectum*
brownies. See *Scoliopus bigelowii*
brownstem spleenwort. See *Asplenium platyneuron*
Brunnera, 123
Brunnera macrophylla, 123
buckhorn. See *Osmunda cinnamomea*
bulb-bearing snake palm. See *Amorphophallus bulbifer*

bunchberry. See *Cornus canadensis*
butcher's broom. See *Ruscus*
butterbur. See *Petasites hybridus*
butterfly orchid. See *Platanthera psyodes*
Buxaceae, 251
Buxus microphylla, 243

calamus. See *Acorus calamus*
calamusroot. See *Acorus calamus*
Calanthe, 124
Calanthe discolor, 124
Calanthe discolor var. *bicolor*, 124
Calanthe discolor var. *sieboldii*, 124
Calanthe izu-insularis, 124
Calanthe sieboldii. See *Calanthe discolor* var. *sieboldii*
Calanthe sieboldii var. *flava*. See *Calanthe discolor* var. *sieboldii*
Calanthe striata. See *Calanthe discolor* var. *bicolor*
Calanthe striata var. *bicolor*. See *Calanthe discolor* var. *bicolor*
calico aster. See *Aster lateriflorus*
California false hellebore. See *Veratrum californicum*
California fawn lily. See *Erythronium californicum*
California giant toadshade. See *Trillium chloropetalum*
California lady slipper. See *Cypripedium californicum*
California spikenard. See *Aralia californica*
Campanula, 124–126
Campanula alliariifolia, 125
Campanula americana, 124
Campanula carpatica, 126
Campanula carpatica var. *turbinata*, 126
Campanula divaricata, 124
Campanula persicifolia, 125
Campanula portenschlagiana, 125
Campanula poscharskyana, 125
Campanula rapunculoides, 125
Campanula scouleri, 124
Campanula takesimana, 126
Campanula turbinata. See *Campanula carpatica* var. *turbinata*
Campanulaceae, 125, 235
Camptosorus rhizophyllus. See *Asplenium rhizophyllum*
Campylandra chinensis. See *Tupistra chinensis*
Canada columbine. See *Aquilegia canadensis*
Canada mayflower. See *Maianthemum canadense*
Canada violet. See *Viola canadensis*

Canadian columbine. See *Aquilegia canadensis*
Canadian ginger. See *Asarum canadense*
Canadian snakeroot. See *Asarum canadense*
canker brake. See *Polystichum acrostichoides*
canker lettuce. See *Pyrola americana*
Cardamine, 126–127
Cardamine asarifolia. See *Pachyphragma macrophylla*
Cardamine diphylla, 127
Cardamine laciniata, 127
Cardamine latifolia. See *Cardamine raphanifolia*
Cardamine raphanifolia, 127
Cardamine trifolia, 127
Cardamine waldsteinii, 127
Cardiandra, 128
Cardiandra alternifolia, 128
Cardiandra amamioshinensis, 128
Cardiandra formosana, 128
cardinal flower. See *Lobelia cardinalis*
Carex, 128–132
Carex acuta. See *Carex elata*
Carex buchanii, 129
Carex comans, 129
Carex conica, 129
Carex elata, 130
Carex flava, 130
Carex fraseri, 130
Carex grayi, 130
Carex hachijoensis, 130
Carex japonica of gardens. See *Carex morrowii*
Carex oshimensis, 130
Carex pendula, 129
Carex phyllocephala, 131
Carex plantaginea, 129, 131
Carex pulchella. See *Carex comans*
Carex reticulosa. See *Carex elata*
Carex siderosticha, 129, 131
Carex stricta. See *Carex elata*
Carex sylvatica, 131
Carolina bellwort. See *Uvularia caroliniana*
Carolina elephant's foot. See *Elephantopus carolinianus*
Carolina lily. See *Lilium michauxii*
Carolina spring beauty. See *Claytonia caroliniana*
Carpathian bellflower. See *Campanula carpatica*
Carpathian harebell. See *Campanula carpatica*
carpet bugle. See *Ajuga reptans*
carpet bugleweed. See *Ajuga reptans*

car-track plant. See *Plantago major* 'Variegata'
Caryophyllaceae, 296
cast-iron plant. See *Aspidistra elatior*; *A. typica*
cat's breeches. See *Hydrophyllum capitatum*
Catesby's trillium. See *Trillium catesbaei*
Caucasian harebell. See *Campanula alliariifolia*
Caulophyllum, 132
Caulophyllum thalictroides, 132
Caulophyllum thalictroides var. *robustum*, 132
celandine poppy. See *Chelidonium majus*; *Stylophorum diphyllum*
Ceterach, 106
Ceterach officinarum. See *Asplenium ceterach*
Chamaelirium, 132–133
Chamaelirium luteum, 132, 133
Chamaepericlymenum, 147
Chamaepericlymenum canadense. See *Cornus canadensis*
Chamaepericlymenum suecicum. See *Cornus suecica*
Chasmanthium, 133–134
Chasmanthium latifolium, 133, 134
chatterbox. See *Epipactis gigantea*
checkered rattlesnake plantain. See *Goodyera tesselata*
Chelidonium, 134
Chelidonium majus, 134
Chelidonium majus var. *asiatica*, 134
Chelone, 134–135
Chelone glabra, 134, 135
Chelone glabra var. *elatior*, 135
Chelone glabra var. *montana* of gardens. See *Chelone glabra* var. *elatior*
Chelone lyonii, 135
Chelone montana. See *Chelone glabra* var. *elatior*
Chimaphila, 135–137
Chimaphila astyla. See *Chimaphila japonica*
Chimaphila japonica, 136
Chimaphila maculata, 135, 136
Chimaphila menziesii, 136
Chimaphila occidentalis. See *Chimaphila umbellata* var. *occidentalis*
Chimaphila umbellata, 136
Chimaphila umbellata var. *cisatlantica*, 136
Chimaphila umbellata var. *occidentalis*, 136
China ruffled lily. See *Tupistra chinensis*

Chinese anemone. See *Anemone hupehensis*
Chinese astilbe. See *Astilbe chinensis*
Chinese bloodroot. See *Eomecon chionantha*
Chinese bugbane. See *Cimicifuga japonica*
Chinese crested iris. See *Iris gracilipes*
Chinese false hellebore. See *Veratrum wilsonii*
Chinese ginger. See *Asarum sinense*
Chinese goatsbeard. See *Aruncus sinensis*
Chinese hellebore. See *Helleborus thibetanus*
Chinese rhubarb. See *Rheum palmatum*
Chinese snow poppy. See *Eomecon chionantha*
Chinese spurge. See *Pachysandra stylosum*
Chinese wild ginger. See *Asarum splendens*
Chinese wood poppy. See *Stylophorum lasiocarpum*
Christmas fern. See *Polystichum acrostichoides*
Christmas rose. See *Helleborus niger*
Christrose. See *Helleborus niger*
Chrosperma muscitoxicum. See *Amianthium muscaetoxicum*
Chrysogonum, 137–138
Chrysogonum australe, 137
Chrysogonum virginianum, 137, 138
Chrysosplenium, 138–139
Chrysosplenium alpinum. See *Chrysosplenium oppositifolium* var. *alpinum*
Chrysosplenium alternifolium, 139
Chrysosplenium auriculatum. See *Chrysosplenium oppositifolium*
Chrysosplenium davidianum, 139
Chrysosplenium geoides. See *Chrysosplenium alternifolium*
Chrysosplenium japonicum, 139
Chrysosplenium macrophyllum, 139
Chrysosplenium macrostemon, 139
Chrysosplenium nivale. See *Chrysosplenium alternifolium*
Chrysosplenium octandrum. See *Chrysosplenium oppositifolium*
Chrysosplenium oppositifolium, 139
Chrysosplenium oppositifolium var. *alpinum*, 139
Chrysosplenium oppositifolium var. *rosulare*, 139
Chrysosplenium repens. See *Chrysosplenium oppositifolium*

Chrysosplenium rotundifolium. See
    Chrysosplenium alternifolium
Chrysosplenium tetrandum, 138, 139
Chrysosplenium valdivicum, 138, 139
Cimicifuga, 139–143
Cimicifuga acerina. See *Cimicifuga
    japonica*
Cimicifuga acerina of gardens. See
    Cimicifuga biternata
Cimicifuga americana, 140
Cimicifuga arizonica, 141
Cimicifuga biternata, 140
Cimicifuga brachycarpa, 142
Cimicifuga dahurica, 141
Cimicifuga elata, 141
Cimicifuga europaea. See *Cimicifuga
    foetida*
Cimicifuga foetida, 141
Cimicifuga heracleifolia, 141
Cimicifuga heracleifolia var. *bifida*, 141
Cimicifuga japonica, 142
Cimicifuga japonica var. *acerina*. See
    Cimicifuga japonica
Cimicifuga japonica var. *acerina* of
    gardens. See *Cimicifuga biternata*
Cimicifuga japonica var. *acutiloba*, 142
Cimicifuga laciniata, 141
Cimicifuga mairei, 142
Cimicifuga purpurea, 142
Cimicifuga racemosa, 142
Cimicifuga racemosa var. *cordifolia*. See
    Cimicifuga rubifolia
Cimicifuga ramosa of gardens. See
    Cimicifuga simplex
Cimicifuga rubifolia, 142
Cimicifuga simplex, 143
Cimicifuga simplex var. *matsumurae*,
    143
Cimicifuga yunnanensis, 142
cinnamon fern. See *Osmunda
    cinnamomea*
Clayton's fern. See *Osmunda
    claytoniana*
Claytonia, 143–144
Claytonia caroliniana, 143, 144
Claytonia virginica, 143, 144
cliff fern. See *Woodsia obtusa*
climbing yellow bleeding heart. See
    Dicentra scandens
Clintonia, 144–145
Clintonia alpina. See *Clintonia udensis*
Clintonia andrewsiana, 145
Clintonia borealis, 144, 145
Clintonia udensis, 145
Clintonia umbellata, 144, 145
Clintonia uniflora, 145
Clinton's fern. See *Dryopteris
    clintoniana*
Clinton's lily. See *Clintonia umbellata*

Clinton's shield fern. See *Dryopteris
    clintoniana*
closed gentian. See *Gentiana
    andrewsii*; *G. clausa*
clumping anemone. See *Anemone
    vitifolia*
cockscomb hart's tongue fern. See
    Asplenium scolopendrium 'Cristata'
Colchicaceae, 164
coltsfoot. See *Farfugium japonicum*;
    Galax urceolata; *Petasites palmatus*;
    P. frigidus; *Shortia galacifolia*
Commelinaceae, 264, 311
common alumroot. See *Heuchera
    americana*
common bear's breeches. See
    Acanthus mollis
common bleeding heart. See *Dicentra
    spectabilis*
common blue violet. See *Viola sororia*
common bugleweed. See *Ajuga
    reptans*
common columbine. See *Aquilegia
    vulgaris*
common ladies' tresses. See
    Spiranthes cernua
common lady fern. See *Athyrium filix-
    femina*
common lungwort. See *Pulmonaria
    officinalis*
common meadow rue. See
    Thalictrum aquilegiifolium
common monkshood. See *Aconitum
    napellus*
common periwinkle. See *Vinca minor*
common pipsissewa. See *Chimaphila
    umbellata*
common polypody. See *Polypodium
    vulgare*
common primrose. See *Primula
    vulgaris*
common rush. See *Juncus effusus*
common Solomon's seal. See
    Polygonatum ×*hybridum*
common spiderwort. See
    Tradescantia virginiana
common spotted orchid. See
    Dactylorhiza fuchsii
common spring beauty. See
    Claytonia virginica
common toadshade. See *Trillium
    sessile*
common turk's cap lily. See *Lilium
    martagon*
common variegated plantain. See
    Plantago major 'Variegata'
common woodsia. See *Woodsia obtusa*
common comfrey. See *Symphytum
    officinale*

Compositae. See Asteraceae
Confederate violet. See *Viola
    papilionacea* var. *priceana*
confusing trillium. See *Trillium simile*
consanguineous cobra lily. See
    Arisaema consanguineum
consumption weed. See *Pyrola
    americana*
Convallaria, 146–186147, 239
Convallaria bifolia. See *Maianthemum
    bifolium*
Convallaria keiskei. See *Convallaria
    majalis* var. *keiskei*
Convallaria keiski. See *Convallaria
    majalis* var. *keiskei*
Convallaria majalis, 146
Convallaria majalis var. *keiskei*, 147
Convallaria majalis var. *keiski*. See
    Convallaria majalis var. *keiskei*
Convallaria majalis f. *picta*, 147
Convallaria majalis f. *rosea*. See
    Convallaria majalis var. *rosea*
Convallaria majalis var. *rosea*, 147
Convallaria majalis var. *transcaucasica*,
    147
Convallaria majuscula. See *Convallaria
    montana*
Convallaria montana, 146, 147
Convallaria transcaucasica. See
    Convallaria majalis var.
    transcaucasica
Convallariaceae, 105, 144, 146, 162,
    234, 239, 248, 265, 285, 297
coolwort. See *Tiarella trifoliata*
copper shield fern. See *Dryopteris
    erythrosora*
coralbells. See *Heuchera sanguinea*
coralberry. See *Actaea rubra*
coral flower. See *Heuchera sanguinea*
Cornaceae, 147
cornflower. See *Uvularia grandiflora*
corn lily. See *Clintonia borealis*;
    Veratrum californicum; *V. viride*
Cornus, 147–148
Cornus canadensis, 147, 148
Cornus suecica, 147, 148
corpse flower. See *Amorphophallus
    titanum*
Corsican hellebore. See *Helleborus
    argutifolius*
Corydalis, 148–149
Corydalis lutea, 148
Corydalis ochroleuca, 148
Corydalis scouleri, 148
cowslip. See *Mertensia pulmonarioides*;
    Primula veris
cowslip lungwort. See *Pulmonaria
    angustifolia*
cowtongue. See *Clintonia borealis*

crackerberry. See *Cornus canadensis*
crane-beaked hosta. See *Hosta kikutii*
cranefly orchid. See *Tipularia discolor*
creeping broadleaf sedge. See *Carex siderosticha*
creeping buttercup. See *Ranunculus repens*
creeping Charlie. See *Lysimachia nummularia*
creeping dogwood. See *Cornus canadensis*
creeping forget-me-not. See *Omphalodes verna*
creeping garden bluebell. See *Campanula rapunculoides*
creeping Jenny. See *Lysimachia nummularia*
creeping lilyturf. See *Liriope spicata*
creeping liriope. See *Liriope spicata*
creeping myrtle. See *Vinca minor*
creeping sailor. See *Saxifraga stolonifera*
crested dwarf iris. See *Iris cristata*
crested iris. See *Iris cristata*
crested yellow orchid. See *Platanthera cristata*
crevice alumroot. See *Heuchera micrantha*
crippled cranefly. See *Tipularia discolor*
crowfoot violet. See *Viola pedata*
crow poison. See *Amianthium muscaetoxicum*
crow's toes. See *Cardamine laciniata*
Cruciferae, 127, 335
Culver's physic. See *Veronicastrum virginicum*
Culver's root. See *Veronicastrum virginicum*
cuneate trillium. See *Trillium cuneatum*
cushat lily. See *Medeola virginiana*
cutleaf grape fern. See *Botrychium dissectum*
cutleaf toothwort. See *Cardamine laciniata*
Cyclamen, 149
Cyclamen coum, 149
Cyclamen europaeum. See *Cyclamen purpurascens*
Cyclamen hederifolium, 149
Cyclamen purpurascens, 149
Cymophyllus, 130
Cymophyllus fraseri. See *Carex fraseri*
Cymophyllus fraserianus. See *Carex fraseri*
Cyperaceae, 129
Cypripedium, 149–152
Cypripedium acaule, 149, 150

Cypripedium arietinum, 151
Cypripedium calceolus, 151
Cypripedium calceolus var. *parviflorum*, 151
Cypripedium calceolus var. *planipetalum*, 151
Cypripedium calceolus var. *pubescens*, 151
Cypripedium californicum, 150
Cypripedium candidum, 150
Cypripedium debile, 150
Cypripedium fasciculatum, 150
Cypripedium flavum, 150
Cypripedium guttatum, 150
Cypripedium guttatum var. *yatabeanum*, 150
Cypripedium henryi, 151
Cypripedium himalaicum, 150
Cypripedium humile. See *Cypripedium acaule*
Cypripedium irapeanum, 150
Cypripedium japonicum, 152
Cypripedium japonicum var. *formosanum*, 152
Cypripedium kentuckiense, 150
Cypripedium macranthum, 150
Cypripedium montanum, 150
Cypripedium parviflorum. See *Cypripedium calceolus* var. *parviflorum*
Cypripedium parviflorum var. *pubescens*. See *Cypripedium calceolus* var. *pubescens*
Cypripedium passerinum, 150
Cypripedium pubescens. See *Cypripedium calceolus* var. *pubescens*
Cypripedium reginae, 152
Cypripedium reginae var. *album*, 152
Cypripedium spectabile. See *Cypripedium reginae*
Cypripedium yunnanense, 150
Cyrtomium, 153–154
Cyrtomium falcatum, 153
Cyrtomium fortunei, 153, 154
Cyrtomium macrophyllum, 153, 154

Dactylorchis foliosa. See *Dactylorhiza foliosa*
Dactylorchis maculata. See *Dactylorhiza maculata*
Dactylorhiza, 154–155
Dactylorhiza aristata, 154
Dactylorhiza elata, 154
Dactylorhiza foliosa, 155
Dactylorhiza fuchsii, 155
Dactylorhiza maculata, 155
Dactylorhiza maculata subsp. *fuchsii*. See *Dactylorhiza fuchsii*
Dactylorhiza praetermissa, 154

Dactylorhiza purpurella, 154
dagger fern. See *Polystichum acrostichoides*
daio giboshi. See *Hosta sieboldiana* 'Mira'
Daiswa, 253
Daiswa fargesii. See *Paris fargesii*
Daiswa hainanensis. See *Paris hainanensis*
Daiswa japonica. See *Paris japonica*
Daiswa lancifolia. See *Paris lancifolia*
Daiswa polyphylla. See *Paris polyphylla*
Daiswa polyphylla var. *alba*. See *Paris polyphylla* var. *alba*
Daiswa thibetica. See *Paris thibetica*
Daiswa violacea. See *Paris violacea*
Daiswa yunnanensis. See *Paris yunnanensis*
Dalmatian bellflower. See *Campanula portenschlagiana*
Danae, 155–156
Danae laurus. See *Danae racemosa*
Danae racemosa, 155, 156
dark-red helleborine. See *Epipactis atrorubens*
Darmera, 156–157
Darmera peltata, 156, 157
David's harp. See *Polygonatum* ×*hybridum*
deer fern. See *Blechnum spicant*
deerfoot. See *Achlys triphylla*
Deinanthe, 157
Deinanthe bifida, 157
Deinanthe caerulea, 157
Dennstaedtia, 158
Dennstaedtiaceae, 158, 277
Dennstaedtia punctilobula, 158
dense-flowered loosestrife. See *Lysimachia congestiflora*
Dentaria, 127
Dentaria diphylla. See *Cardamine diphylla*
Dentaria laciniata. See *Cardamine laciniata*
Deparia acrostichoides. See *Athyrium thelypteroides*
devil's bit. See *Chamaelirium luteum*
devil's tongue. See *Amorphophallus rivieri*
devil's walking stick. See *Aralia spinosa*
Diapensiaceae, 186, 295
Dicentra, 158–161
Dicentra canadensis, 158, 159
Dicentra chrysantha, 159
Dicentra eximia, 159
Dicentra eximia of gardens. See *Dicentra formosa*
Dicentra formosa, 160

Dicentra formosa subsp. *nevadensis*, 160

Dicentra formosa subsp. *oregana*, 160

Dicentra glauca of gardens. See *Dicentra formosa*

Dicentra macrantha, 161

Dicentra nevadensis. See *Dicentra formosa* subsp. *nevadensis*

Dicentra occidentalis. See *Dicentra cucullaria*

Dicentra ochroleuca, 160

Dicentra oregana. See *Dicentra formosa* subsp. *oregana*

Dicentra pauciflora, 160

Dicentra peregrina, 161

Dicentra plumosa of gardens. See *Dicentra formosa*

Dicentra pusilla. See *Dicentra peregrina*

Dicentra scandens, 160

Dicentra spectabilis, 161

Dicentra thalictrifolia. See *Dicentra scandens*

Dicentra torulosa, 160

Dicentra uniflora, 160

Dicksonia, 158

dimorphic chain fern. See *Woodwardia areolata*

Diphylleia, 161–162

Diphylleia cymosa, 161, 162

Diphylleia cymosa var. *grayi*, 162

Diphylleia grayi. See *Diphylleia cymosa* var. *grayi*

Diplazium acrostichoides. See *Athyrium thelypteroides*

Diplazium pycnocarpon. See *Athyrium pycnocarpon*

Diptera, 266

Disporopsis, 162–163

Disporopsis arisanensis, 163

Disporopsis fuscopicta, 162, 163

Disporopsis pernyi, 162, 163

Disporum, 163–167

Disporum bodinieri, 164

Disporum cantoniense, 164

Disporum flavens, 165

Disporum hookeri, 163, 165

Disporum hookeri var. *oreganum*, 165

Disporum languinosum, 163, 165

Disporum lutescens, 167

Disporum maculatum, 163, 165

Disporum megalanthum, 164

Disporum nantauense, 165

Disporum pullum, 166

Disporum sessile, 166

Disporum sessile subsp. *flavens*, 166

Disporum sessile var. *inobeanum*, 166

Disporum smilacinum, 166

Disporum smithii, 166

Disporum trachycarpum, 167

Disporum uniflorum, 167

Disporum viridescens, 167

dissected grape fern. See *Botrychium dissectum*

ditch fern. See *Osmunda regalis*

Dochafa flava. See *Arisaema flavum*

Dodecatheon, 167

Dodecatheon media, 167

dog plum. See *Clintonia umbellata*

dogtooth violet. See *Erythronium dens-canis*

dog violet. See *Viola canina*; *V. dissecta*; *V. riviniana*

doll's eyes. See *Actaea alba*

Douglas spike moss. See *Selaginella douglasii*

downy rattlesnake plantain. See *Goodyera pubescens*

downy yellow violet. See *Viola pubescens*

Dracunculus, 167–168

Dracunculus vulgaris, 167, 168

dragon arum. See *Arisaema dracontium*; *Dracunculus vulgaris*

dragon ligularia, 186

dragonroot. See *Arisaema triphyllum*

dragon's-tongue. See *Chimaphila maculata*

drops of gold. See *Disporum hookeri*

Dryopteridaceae, 79, 168

Dryopteris, 168–172

Dryopteris acrostichoides. See *Polystichum acrostichoides*

Dryopteris affinis, 168, 169

Dryopteris arguta, 168

Dryopteris austriaca. See *Dryopteris dilatata*

Dryopteris borreri. See *Dryopteris affinis*

Dryopteris carthusiana, 168, 169

Dryopteris celsa, 168

Dryopteris clintoniana, 169

Dryopteris crassirhizoma, 171

Dryopteris cristata, 168

Dryopteris cristata var. *clintoniana*. See *Dryopteris clintoniana*

Dryopteris cystolepidota. See *Dryopteris erythrosora* var. *cystolepidota*

Dryopteris dilatata, 170

Dryopteris erythrosora, 168, 170

Dryopteris erythrosora var. *cystolepidota*, 170

Dryopteris erythrosora var. *purpurascens*, 170

Dryopteris filix-mas, 170

Dryopteris filix-mas var. *crassirhizoma*. See *Dryopteris crassirhizoma*

Dryopteris floridana. See *Dryopteris ludoviciana*

Dryopteris goldiana, 171

Dryopteris hexagonoptera. See *Phegopteris hexagonoptera*

Dryopteris intermedia. See *Dryopteris carthusiana*

Dryopteris ludoviciana, 171

Dryopteris marginalis, 171

Dryopteris noveboracensis. See *Thelypteris noveboracensis*

Dryopteris paleacea. See *Dryopteris affinis*

Dryopteris phegopteris. See *Phegopteris connectilis*

Dryopteris pseudomas. See *Dryopteris affinis*

Dryopteris purpurella, 170

Dryopteris setosa. See *Dryopteris crassirhizoma*

Dryopteris sieboldii, 168, 172

Dryopteris spinulosa. See *Dryopteris carthusiana*

Dryopteris spinulosa var. *americana*. See *Dryopteris dilatata*

Dryopteris spinulosa var. *intermedia*. See *Dryopteris carthusiana*

Dryopteris thelypteris. See *Thelypteris palustris*

Dryopteris wallachiana, 169

dry strawberry. See *Waldsteinia fragarioides*

duddergrass. See *Adiantum capillus-veneris*

dumb nettle. See *Lamium album*

dungwort. See *Helleborus foetidus*

dusky cranesbill. See *Geranium phaeum*

dustleaf toadshade. See *Trillium viride*

dutchman's breeches. See *Dicentra cucullaria*

dwarf Chinese astilbe, 112

dwarf cornel. See *Cornus canadensis*

dwarf crested iris. See *Iris cristata*

dwarf ginseng. See *Panax trifolius*

dwarf goatsbeard. See *Aruncus aethusifolius*; *A. parvulus*

dwarf golden sweet flag, 62

dwarf holly fern. See *Polystichum tsussimense*

dwarf iris. See *Iris verna*

dwarf maidenhair fern. See *Adiantum pedatum* subsp. *subpumilum*

dwarf mondo grass, 248

dwarf rattlesnake plantain. See *Goodyera repens*

dwarf Solomon's seal. See *Polygonatum humile*

dwarf white trillium. See *Trillium nivale*

dwarf white wood lily. See *Trillium nivale*
Dysosma, 262
Dysosma delavayi. See *Podophyllum delavayi*
Dysosma difforme. See *Podophyllum difforme*
Dysosma pleiantha. See *Podophyllum pleianthum*
Dysosma tsaytuense. See *Podophyllum aurantiocaule*
Dysosma veitchii. See *Podophyllum veitchii*
Dysosma versipelle. See *Podophyllum versipelle*

early meadow rue. See *Thalictrum dioicum*
early red maidenhair fern, 65
early saxifrage. See *Saxifraga virginiensis*
early spiderwort. See *Tradescantia virginiana*
eastern petioled toadshade. See *Trillium recurvatum*
eastern poppy. See *Eomecon chionantha*
eastern saxifrage. See *Saxifraga virginiensis*
ebony spleenwort. See *Asplenium platyneuron*
Ehrendorferia chrysantha. See *Dicentra chrysantha*
Ehrendorferia ochroleuca. See *Dicentra ochroleuca*
electric light bulb plant. See *Caulophyllum thalictroides*
elegant cobra lily. See *Arisaema concinnum*
Elephantopus, 173
Elephantopus carolinianus, 173
Elephantopus elatus, 173
Elephantopus nudatus, 173
Elephantopus tomentosus, 173
elephant's foot. See *Elephantopus carolinianus*; *E. tomentosus*
elephant yam. See *Amorphophallus paeoniifolius*
elf feather. See *Maianthemum canadense*
elfin spur. See *Tipularia discolor*
elk clover. See *Aralia californica*
Endress's cranesbill. See *Geranium endressii*
English crested male fern, 171
English hedge fern. See *Polystichum setiferum*
English plantain. See *Plantago lanceolata*
Eomecon, 174

Eomecon chionantha, 174
Epimedium, 174–180
Epimedium acuminatum, 176
Epimedium alpinum, 176
Epimedium alpinum var. *rubrum*. See *Epimedium* ×*rubrum*
Epimedium brachyrrhizum, 176
Epimedium brevicornu, 176
Epimedium brevicornu f. *rotundatum*, 176
Epimedium ×*cantabrigiense*, 176
Epimedium chlorandrum, 176
Epimedium ×*coccineum*. See *Epimedium* ×*rubrum*
Epimedium davidii, 176
Epimedium diphyllum, 176
Epimedium dolichostemon, 177
Epimedium ecalcaratum, 177
Epimedium epsteinii, 177
Epimedium fangii, 177
Epimedium franchetii, 177
Epimedium grandiflorum, 175, 177
Epimedium grandiflorum subsp. *coelestre*, 177
Epimedium grandiflorum var. *coelestre*. See *Epimedium grandiflorum* subsp. *coelestre*
Epimedium grandiflorum f. *flavescens*. See *Epimedium grandiflorum* subsp. *koreanum*
Epimedium grandiflorum subsp. *higoense*, 177
Epimedium grandiflorum var. *higoense*. See *Epimedium grandiflorum* subsp. *higoense*
Epimedium grandiflorum subsp. *koreanum*, 177
Epimedium grandiflorum f. *normale*. See *Epimedium grandiflorum*
Epimedium grandiflorum subsp. *sempervirens*. See *Epimedium sempervirens*
Epimedium grandiflorum f. *violaceum*, 178
Epimedium grandiflorum var. *violaceum*, 178
Epimedium koreanum. See *Epimedium grandiflorum* subsp. *koreanum*
Epimedium leptorrhizum, 178
Epimedium liliacinum, 180
Epimedium macranthum. See *Epimedium grandiflorum*
Epimedium macranthum var. *niveum*, 180
Epimedium macranthum var. *sulphureum*, 180
Epimedium macranthum var. *versicolor*. See *Epimedium* ×*versicolor*
Epimedium myrianthum, 178

Epimedium ogisui, 178
Epimedium pauciflorum, 178
Epimedium ×*perralchicum*, 178
Epimedium perralderianum, 178
Epimedium pinnatum, 179
Epimedium pinnatum subsp. *colchicum*, 179
Epimedium pinnatum subsp. *colchicum* f. *concolor*, 179
Epimedium pinnatum subsp. *elegans*. See *Epimedium pinnatum* subsp. *colchicum*
Epimedium pubescens, 179
Epimedium pubigerum, 179
Epimedium purpureum. See *Epimedium* ×*rubrum*
Epimedium ×*rubrum*, 179
Epimedium sagittatum, 179
Epimedium sempervirens, 179
Epimedium stellulatum, 179
Epimedium sutchuenense, 180
Epimedium ×*versicolor*, 180
Epimedium ×*warleyense*, 180
Epimedium wushanense, 180
Epimedium ×*youngianum*, 180
Epipactis, 180–182
Epipactis atrorubens, 181
Epipactis gigantea, 182
Epipactis helleborine, 181
Epipactis palustris, 182
Epipactis pubescens. See *Goodyera pubescens*
Epipactis purpurata, 181
Epipactis repens. See *Goodyera repens*
Epipactis rubiginosa. See *Epipactis atrorubens*
Epipactis tesselata. See *Goodyera tesselata*
Epipactis veratrifolia, 181
Eranthis, 182
Eranthis hyemalis, 182
erect barren strawberry. See *Waldsteinia geoides*
erect hosta. See *Hosta rectifolia*
Erythronium, 182–184
Erythronium albidum, 183
Erythronium americanum, 182, 183
Erythronium californicum, 183
Erythronium citrinum, 184
Erythronium dens-canis, 184
Erythronium giganteum. See *Erythronium grandiflorum*
Erythronium grandiflorum, 184
Erythronium hartwegii. See *Erythronium multiscapoideum*
Erythronium helenae, 184
Erythronium hendersonii, 184
Erythronium howelii, 184
Erythronium multiscapoideum, 184

Erythronium obtusatum. See
    Erythronium grandiflorum
Erythronium oreganum, 184
Erythronium propullans, 184
Erythronium purdyi. See *Erythronium
    multiscapoideum*
Erythronium purpurascens, 184
Erythronium revolutum, 184
Erythronium revolutum var. *johnsonii*,
    184
Erythronium smithii. See *Erythronium
    revolutum*
Erythronium tuolumnense, 184
Erythronium umbilicatum, 183
Erythronium cultivars, 184
Eucarex, 129
Eurasian Solomon's seal. See
    Polygonatum multiflorum
European asarabacca. See *Asarum
    europaeum*
European black hellebore. See
    Veratrum nigrum
European bugbane. See *Cimicifuga
    foetida*
European chain fern. See
    Woodwardia radicans
European columbine. See *Aquilegia
    vulgaris*
European crowfoot. See *Aquilegia
    vulgaris*
European dogtooth violet. See
    Erythronium dens-canis
European ginger. See *Asarum
    europaeum*
European greater celandine. See
    Chelidonium majus
European hepatica. See *Hepatica
    nobilis*
European ladies' tresses. See
    Spiranthes spiralis
European red baneberry. See *Actaea
    erythrocarpa*
European Solomon's seal. See
    Polygonatum multiflorum
European white hellebore. See
    Veratrum album
European wood sorrel. See *Oxalis
    acetocella*
Evan's begonia. See *Begonia grandis*
evergreen broadleaf sedge. See *Carex
    plantaginea*
evergreen miniature sedge. See *Carex
    conica*
evergreen wood fern. See *Dryopteris
    carthusiana; D. marginalis*
eyeroot. See *Hydrastis canadensis*

fairy candles. See *Cimicifuga racemosa*
fairy cap. See *Mitella diphylla*

fairy fringe. See *Platanthera psyodes*
fairy wand. See *Chamaelirium luteum*
false alumroot. See *Tellima
    grandiflora*
false anemone. See *Anemonopsis
    macrophylla*
false garlic. See *Nothoscordum bivalve*
false goatsbeard. See *Astilbe biternata*
false hellebore. See *Veratrum viride*
false ipecac. See *Gillenia trifoliata*
false lily-of-the-valley. See
    *Maianthemum bifolium;
    M. canadense; M. kamtschaticum*
false miterwort. See *Tiarella cordifolia;
    T. wherryi*
false rose. See *Helleborus orientalis*
false rue anemone. See *Isopyrum
    biternata; I. thalictroides*
false Solomon's seal. See *Smilacina
    racemosa*
false spikenard. See *Smilacina
    racemosa*
fancy fern. See *Dryopteris carthusiana*
Farfugium, 184–186
Farfugium grande. See *Farfugium
    japonicum*
Farfugium japonicum, 185
Farfugium japonicum var. *lutchuense*,
    185
Farfugium kaempferi. See *Farfugium
    japonicum*
Farfugium reniforme, 186
Farfugium tussilagineum. See *Farfugium
    japonicum*
Fargesia murieliae. See *Sinarundinaria
    murieliae*
Fargesia nitida. See *Sinarundinaria
    nitida*
Fargesia spathacea of gardens. See
    Sinarundinaria murieliae
fat Solomon. See *Smilacina racemosa*
    var. *amplexicaulis*
fawn's breath. See *Gillenia trifoliata*
featherleaf rodgersia. See *Rodgersia
    pinnata; R. sambucifolia*
feathery miterwort. See *Mitella
    breweri*
Fendler's waterleaf. See
    Hydrophyllum fendleri
fetid adder's tongue. See *Scoliopus
    bigelowii*
fetid bugbane. See *Cimicifuga foetida*
fetid cranesbill. See *Geranium
    macrorrhizum*
fetid wakerobin. See *Trillium erectum*
fiddleheads. See *Osmunda
    cinnamomea*
figwort. See *Ranunculus ficaria*
Filipendula, 94

fingerleaf rodgersia. See *Rodgersia
    aesculifolia*
fire pink. See *Silene virginica*
Fissipes acaulis. See *Cypripedium
    acaule*
fist fern. See *Dryopteris marginalis*
five-finger fern. See *Adiantum
    pedatum*
five-stamen miterwort. See *Mitella
    pentandra*
flagroot. See *Acorus calamus*
flaming poppy. See *Stylophorum
    diphyllum*
flattop aster. See *Aster umbellatus*
Florida bellwort. See *Uvularia
    floridana*
Florida swamp fern. See *Dryopteris
    ludoviciana*
flowering fern. See *Osmunda regalis*
fly poison. See *Amianthium
    muscaetoxicum*
foamflower. See *Tiarella cordifolia;
    T. wherryi*
foamy bells. See ×*Heucherella*
Formosan cardiandra. See
    Cardiandra formosana
Formosan toad lily. See *Tricyrtis
    formosana*
Fortune's holly fern. See *Cyrtomium
    fortunei*
fountain bamboo. See *Sinarundinaria
    murieliae*
fragrant hellebore. See *Helleborus
    odorus*
fragrant ladies' tresses. See *Spiranthes
    cernua* var. *odorata*
fragrant Solomon's seal. See
    Polygonatum odoratum
fragrant woodsia. See *Woodsia ilvensis*
Fraser's sedge. See *Carex fraseri*
friar's cap. See *Aconitum napellus*
fringe-bells. See *Shortia soldanelloides*
fringecup. See *Tellima grandiflora*
fringecups. See *Tellima grandiflora*
fringed bleeding heart. See *Dicentra
    eximia*
fringed campion. See *Silene polypetala*
fringed galax. See *Shortia
    soldanelloides*
fringed gentian. See *Gentianopsis
    crinita*
fruitful wood fern. See *Dryopteris
    carthusiana*
fuki. See *Petasites japonicus*
Fumariaceae, 148, 159
Funkia. See *Hosta*
futaba aoi. See *Asarum caulescens*

Galax, 186–187

Galax aphylla. See *Galax urceolata*
Galax urceolata, 186
Galeobdolon, 230
Galeobdolon argentatum of gardens, 231
Galeobdolon luteum. See *Lamium galeobdolon*
Galeopsis galeobdolon. See *Lamium galeobdolon*
Galium, 187
Galium apparine, 187
Galium odoratum, 187
gaping mouth cobra lily. See *Arisaema ringens*
garden columbine. See *Aquilegia vulgaris*
garden monkshood. See *Aconitum napellus*
garden wolfsbane. See *Aconitum napellus*
Geneva bugle. See *Ajuga genevensis*
Gentiana, 187–188
Gentiana andrewsii, 188
Gentiana andrewsii f. *alba*, 188
Gentiana asclepiadea, 188
Gentiana bavarica, 187
Gentiana crinita. See *Gentianopsis crinita*
Gentiana decora, 188
Gentiana linearis, 188
Gentiana lutea, 188
Gentiana procera. See *Gentianopsis procera*
Gentiana puberula. See *Gentiana saponaris*
Gentiana saponaris, 188
Gentianaceae, 187
Gentianopsis crinita, 188
Gentianopsis procera, 188
Geraniaceae, 189
Geranium, 188–191
Geranium endressii, 189
Geranium macrorrhizum, 189
Geranium maculatum, 190
Geranium nodosum, 190
Geranium ×*oxanianum*, 190
Geranium phaeum, 190
Geranium phaeum f. *album*, 190
Geranium phaeum var. *lividum*, 190
Geranium renardii, 191
Geranium striatum. See *Geranium versicolor*
Geranium versicolor, 191
giant chain fern. See *Woodwardia fimbricata*
giant Chinese astilbe. See *Astilbe grandis*
giant helleborine. See *Epipactis gigantea*

giant-leaved western Chinese Solomon's plume. See *Smilacina wilsonii*
giant orchid. See *Epipactis gigantea*
giant rattlesnake plantain. See *Goodyera oblongifolia*
giant stream orchid. See *Epipactis gigantea*
giant trillium. See *Trillium chloropetalum*
giant wood fern. See *Dryopteris goldiana*
giboshi. See *Hosta*
Giftgermer. See *Veratrum viride*
Gillenia, 191
Gillenia stipulata, 191
Gillenia trifoliata, 191
ginger root. See *Asarum canadense*
ginseng. See *Panax quinquefolius*
glacier lily. See *Erythronium grandiflorum*
gladdon iris. See *Iris foetidissima*
gladwin. See *Iris foetidissima*
gladwine. See *Iris foetidissima*
gladwyn. See *Iris foetidissima*
Glaucidium, 191–192
Glaucidium palmatum, 191, 192
Glaucidium palmatum f. *leucanthum*, 192
Glaucium, 192
Gleason's trillium. See *Trillium flexipes*
goat's beard. See *Aruncus dioicus*
goatsbeard. See *Aruncus dioicus*
golden deadnettle. See *Lamium galeobdolon*
golden eardrops. See *Dicentra chrysantha*
golden fishpole bamboo. See *Phyllostachys aurea*
golden globes. See *Lysimachia congestiflora*
golden hart's tongue fern, 108
golden knee. See *Chrysogonum virginianum*
golden maidenhair. See *Polypodium vulgare*
golden nettle. See *Lamium galeobdolon*
golden saxifrage. See *Chrysosplenium davidianum*
goldenseal. See *Hydrastis canadensis*
golden shield fern. See *Dryopteris affinis*
golden-slipper. See *Cypripedium calceolus* var. *pubescens*
golden star. See *Chrysogonum virginianum*
goldenstar. See *Chrysogonum virginianum*

golden tufted sedge, 130
golden vancouveria. See *Vancouveria chrysantha*
Goldie's fern. See *Dryopteris goldiana*
Goldie's shield fern. See *Dryopteris goldiana*
Goldie's wood fern. See *Dryopteris goldiana*
good-morning-spring. See *Claytonia caroliniana; C. virginica*
Goodyera, 192–193
Goodyera decipiens. See *Goodyera oblongifolia*
Goodyera foliosa, 192
Goodyera hachijoensis, 192
Goodyera hachijoensis var. *matsumurana*, 193
Goodyera menziesii. See *Goodyera oblongifolia*
Goodyera oblongifolia, 192
Goodyera pubescens, 193
Goodyera repens, 193
Goodyera repens var. *ophioides*, 193
Goodyera schlechtendaliana, 192, 193
Goodyera tesselata, 193
Goodyera velutina, 193
gooseneck loosestrife. See *Lysimachia clethroides*
goutweed. See *Aegopodium podagraria* 'Variegatum'
grace garlic. See *Nothoscordum bivalve*
Gramineae, 134, 193, 143, 288
grandmother mountain hosta. See *Hosta pulchella*
granny's bonnet. See *Aquilegia vulgaris*
grape leaf anemone. See *Anemone vitifolia*
grassflower. See *Claytonia caroliniana; C. virginica*
grassy sweet flag. See *Acorus gramineus*
Great Basin violet. See *Viola beckwithii*
great blue lobelia. See *Lobelia siphilitica*
greater butterfly orchid. See *Platanthera chlorantha*
greater celandine. See *Chelidonium majus*
greater celandine poppy. See *Chelidonium majus*
greater periwinkle. See *Vinca major*
greater polypody. See *Polypodium cambricum*
greater purple fringed orchid. See *Platanthera grandiflora*
greater woodrush. See *Luzula sylvatica*

great lobelia. See *Lobelia siphilitica*
great Solomon's seal. See
    Polygonatum biflorum
great white trillium. See *Trillium
    grandiflorum*
Grecian hellebore. See *Helleborus
    cyclophyllus*
green and gold. See *Chrysogonum
    virginianum*
green dragon. See *Arisaema
    dracontium; Pinellia petadisecta;
    P. tripartita*
green hellebore. See *Helleborus viridis*
green-leaved rattlesnake plantain.
    See *Goodyera oblongifolia*
green leopard plant. See *Farfugium
    japonicum*
green pearl twist. See *Spiranthes
    gracilis*
green trillium. See *Trillium viride*
Griffith's cobra lily. See *Arisaema
    griffithii*
ground ash. See *Aegopodium
    podagraria* 'Variegatum'
ground elder. See *Aegopodium
    podagraria* 'Variegatum'
ground lily. See *Trillium cernuum*
groundnut. See *Panax trifolius*
Gymnocarpium phegopteris. See
    Phegopteris connectilis
Gymnoptera, 290

Habenaria, 260
Habenaria blepharoglottis. See
    Platanthera blepharoglottis
Habenaria ciliaris. See *Platanthera
    ciliaris*
Habenaria cristata. See *Platanthera
    cristata*
Habenaria fimbricata. See *Platanthera
    grandiflora*
Habenaria integra. See *Platanthera
    integra*
Habenaria psyodes var. *grandiflora*. See
    Platanthera grandiflora
hachijo giboshi. See *Hosta rupifraga*
hairpin hosta. See *Hosta plantaginea*
hair sedge. See *Carex comans*
hairy alumroot. See *Heuchera villosa*
hairy fairy bell. See *Disporum
    languinosum*
hairy Solomon's seal. See
    Polygonatum pubescens
hairy spiderwort. See *Tradescantia
    hirsuticaulis*
Hakonechloa, 193–194
Hakonechloa macra, 193, 194
Hakone grass. See *Hakonechloa
    macra*

halberd-leaved violet. See *Viola
    hastata*
hanra-bibich'u. See *Hosta venusta*
hard fern. See *Blechnum spicant*
hard rush. See *Juncus inflexus*
hardy begonia. See *Begonia grandis*
hardy shield fern. See *Polystichum
    aculeatum*
Hartford climbing fern. See
    Lygodium palmatum
Hartford fern. See *Lygodium
    palmatum*
hart's tongue fern. See *Asplenium
    scolopendrium*
Hartweg's ginger. See *Asarum
    hartwegii*
hayscented fern. See *Dennstaedtia
    punctilobula*
heartleaf. See *Asarum arifolium*
heartleaf ginger. See *Asarum arifolium*
heath spotted orchid. See
    Dactylorhiza maculata
heath violet. See *Viola canina;
    V. dissecta*
hedge fern. See *Polystichum aculeatum;
    P. setiferum*
Hedyscepe canterburyana, 70
helleborine. See *Epipactis helleborine*
Helleborus, 194–199
Helleborus abchasicus. See *Helleborus
    orientalis* subsp. *abchasicus*
Helleborus angustifolius. See *Helleborus
    multifidus*
Helleborus antiquorum. See *Helleborus
    orientalis*
Helleborus argutifolius, 194, 195
Helleborus atropurpureus. See
    Helleborus atrorubens
Helleborus atrorubens, 195
Helleborus atrorubens f. *cupreus*, 195
Helleborus atrorubens of gardens. See
    Helleborus orientalis subsp.
    abchasicus
Helleborus atrorubens f. *hircii*, 195
Helleborus atrorubens f. *incisis*, 195
Helleborus ×ballardiae, 195
Helleborus bocconei. See *Helleborus
    multifidus* subsp. *bocconei*
Helleborus caucasicus. See *Helleborus
    orientalis*
Helleborus colchicus. See *Helleborus
    orientalis* subsp. *abchasicus*
Helleborus corsicus. See *Helleborus
    argutifolius*
Helleborus corsicus subsp. *lividus*. See
    Helleborus lividus
Helleborus cupreus. See *Helleborus
    atrorubens* f. *cupreus*
Helleborus cyclophyllus, 195

Helleborus dumetorum, 196
Helleborus dumetorum subsp.
    atrorubens. See *Helleborus
    atrorubens*
Helleborus ×ericsmithii, 199
Helleborus foetidus, 196
Helleborus guttatus. See *Helleborus
    orientalis* subsp. *guttatus*
Helleborus ×hybridus, 198
Helleborus intermedius. See *Helleborus
    atrorubens* f. *incisis*
Helleborus istriacus. See *Helleborus
    multifidus* subsp. *istriacus*
Helleborus kochii. See *Helleborus
    orientalis*
Helleborus kotchyi. See *Helleborus
    orientalis*
Helleborus lividus. See *Helleborus
    argutifolius*
Helleborus lividus subsp. *corsicus*. See
    Helleborus argutifolius
Helleborus macranthus. See *Helleborus
    niger* subsp. *macranthus*
Helleborus multifidus, 196
Helleborus multifidus subsp. *bocconei*,
    196
Helleborus multifidus subsp.
    hercegovinus, 196
Helleborus multifidus subsp. *istriacus*,
    196
Helleborus multifidus subsp. *serbicus*.
    See *Helleborus torquatus*
Helleborus niger, 196
Helleborus niger var. *angustifolius*, 196
Helleborus niger var. *humilifolius*, 197
Helleborus niger subsp. *macranthus*,
    196
Helleborus niger var. *oblongifolius*, 197
Helleborus niger var. *stenopetalus*, 197
Helleborus ×nigercors, 197
Helleborus ×nigriliv of gardens. See
    Helleborus ×ballardiae
Helleborus odorus, 197
Helleborus odorus subsp. *laxus*. See
    Helleborus multifidus subsp.
    istriacus
Helleborus olympicus. See *Helleborus
    orientalis*
Helleborus orientalis, 197, 198
Helleborus ×orientalis, 198
Helleborus orientalis subsp. *abchasicus*,
    197
Helleborus orientalis subsp. *guttatus*,
    197
Helleborus pallidus. See *Helleborus
    dumetorum*
Helleborus polychromus. See *Helleborus
    orientalis*
Helleborus purpurascens, 198

Helleborus siculus. See *Helleborus multifidus* subsp. *bocconei*
Helleborus ×*sternii*, 199
Helleborus thibetanus, 199
Helleborus torquatus, 199
Helleborus viridis, 199
Helleborus viridis var. *cyclophyllus.* See *Helleborus cyclophyllus*
Helleborus viridis var. *dumetorum.* See *Helleborus dumetorum*
Helleborus viridis subsp. *occidentalis*, 199
helmet flower. See *Aconitum napellus*
Helonias, 199–200
Helonias bullata, 200
Heloniopsis, 200
Heloniopsis breviscapa. See *Heloniopsis orientalis* var. *breviscapa*
Heloniopsis grandiflora. See *Heloniopsis orientalis* var. *breviscapa*
Heloniopsis japonica. See *Heloniopsis orientalis*
Heloniopsis orientalis, 200
Heloniopsis orientalis var. *breviscapa*, 200
Heloniopsis orientalis var. *flavid*, 200
Heloniopsis orientalis var. *kawanoi*, 200
Hemerocallis, 105, 208
Hepatica, 200–202
Hepatica acutiloba, 201
Hepatica americana, 201
Hepatica angulosa. See *Hepatica transsilvanica*
Hepatica asiatica. See *Hepatica nobilis* var. *asiatica*
Hepatica henryi, 202
Hepatica insularis, 202
Hepatica japonica. See *Hepatica nobilis* var. *japonica*
Hepatica maxima, 202
Hepatica ×*media*, 201
Hepatica nobilis, 201
Hepatica nobilis var. *acuta.* See *Hepatica acutiloba*; *H. nobilis*
Hepatica nobilis subsp. *americana.* See *Hepatica americana*
Hepatica nobilis var. *asiatica*, 202
Hepatica nobilis var. *japonica*, 202
Hepatica nobilis var. *obtusa.* See *Hepatica americana*
Hepatica transsilvanica, 201
Hepatica triloba. See *Hepatica nobilis*
Hepatica yamatutai, 202
herb Gerard. See *Aegopodium podagraria* 'Variegatum'
herb paris. See *Paris quadrifolia*
Heterotropa, 96
Heuchera, 202–206

Heuchera acerifolia. See *Heuchera villosa*
Heuchera americana, 203
Heuchera barbarossa. See *Heuchera micrantha*
Heuchera ×*brizoides.* See *Heuchera* cultivars
Heuchera caulescens. See *Heuchera villosa*
Heuchera ciliata. See *Heuchera richardsonii*
Heuchera crinita. See *Heuchera villosa*
Heuchera cylindrica, 204
Heuchera diversifolia. See *Heuchera micrantha*
Heuchera glaberrima. See *Heuchera micrantha*
Heuchera lloydii. See *Heuchera micrantha*
Heuchera longipetala. See *Heuchera micrantha*
Heuchera lucida. See *Heuchera americana*
Heuchera macrorhiza. See *Heuchera villosa*
Heuchera micrantha, 204
Heuchera missouriensis. See *Heuchera parviflora*
Heuchera nuttallii. See *Heuchera micrantha*
Heuchera parviflora, 203
Heuchera richardsonii, 203
Heuchera rugelii. See *Heuchera parviflora*
Heuchera sanguinea, 204
Heuchera squamosa. See *Heuchera villosa*
Heuchera villosa, 203
Heuchera cultivars, 205
×*Heucherella*, 206
Hexastylis, 96
Hexastylis arifolia. See *Asarum arifolium*
Hexastylis arifolia var. *ruthii.* See *Asarum ruthii*
Hexastylis heterophylla. See *Asarum virginicum*
Hexastylis lewisii. See *Asarum lewisii*
Hexastylis memmingeri. See *Asarum virginicum*
Hexastylis minor. See *Asarum minor*
Hexastylis naniflora. See *Asarum naniflorum*
Hexastylis shuttleworthii. See *Asarum shuttleworthii*
Hexastylis speciosa. See *Asarum speciosum*
Hexastylis virginica. See *Asarum virginicum*

Hieracium, 206–207
Hieracium venosum, 206
Himalayan astilbe. See *Astilbe rivularis*
Himalayan maidenhair fern. See *Adiantum venustum*
Himalayan mayapple. See *Podophyllum hexandrum*
Himalayan triplet lily. See *Trillium govanianum*
Himalayan wild ginger. See *Asarum himalayicum*
hime iwa giboshi. See *Hosta gracillima*
hime takaoi. See *Asarum takaoi*
holly fern. See *Cyrtomium falcatum*
hooked spur violet. See *Viola adunca*
horseshoe fern. See *Adiantum pedatum*
hosoba mizu giboshi. See *Hosta longissima* var. *longifolia*
Hosta, 207–225
Hosta albomarginata, 212
Hosta capitata, 209
Hosta cathayana, 221
Hosta clausa, 209
Hosta clausa var. *normalis*, 209
Hosta clausa var. *stolonifera*, 209
Hosta fluctuans, 211
Hosta gracillima, 209
Hosta hypoleuca, 209
Hosta kikutii, 209
Hosta kikutii var. *polyneuron*, 209
Hosta laevigata, 210
Hosta longipes, 210
Hosta longipes f. *hypoglauca*, 210
Hosta longipes f. *sparsa*, 210
Hosta longissima, 210
Hosta longissima var. *longifolia*, 210
Hosta minor, 213
Hosta montana, 210
Hosta montana f. *macrophylla*, 210
Hosta montana 'Aureomarginata', 210
Hosta nakaiana, 213
Hosta nigrescens, 211
Hosta plantaginea, 211
Hosta pulchella, 211
Hosta pycnophylla, 216
Hosta rectifolia, 211
Hosta rectifolia f. *pruinosa*, 211
Hosta rupifraga, 210
Hosta sieboldiana, 212
Hosta sieboldiana 'Mira', 212
Hosta sieboldii, 212
Hosta sieboldii f. *spathulata*, 212
Hosta sieboldii 'Kabitan', 212
Hosta tibae, 212
Hosta ventricosa, 212
Hosta venusta, 213
Hosta yingeri, 213

Hosta cultivars, 213–225
Hostaceae, 208
hototogisu. See *Tricyrtis*
Hungarian bear's breeches. See
    Acanthus hungaricus
hybrid Solomon's seal. See
    Polygonatum ×*hybridum*
Hydrangeaceae, 128, 157, 230
Hydrastis, 225–226
Hydrastis canadensis, 225, 226
Hydrophyllaceae, 226
Hydrophyllum, 226
Hydrophyllum canadense, 226
Hydrophyllum capitatum, 226
Hydrophyllum fendleri, 226
Hydrophyllum macrophyllum, 226
Hydrophyllum virginianum, 226
Hydrosme, 70
Hydrosme rivieri. See *Amorphophallus
    rivieri*
hyuga giboshi. See *Hosta kikutii*

Ibidium. See *Spiranthes*
Indian apple. See *Podophyllum
    peltatum*
Indian cucumber root. See *Medeola
    virginiana*
Indian dye. See *Hydrastis canadensis*
Indian ginger snakeroot. See *Asarum
    canadense*
Indian hippo. See *Gillenia trifoliata*
Indian lettuce. See *Pyrola americana*
Indian physic. See *Gillenia stipulata*;
    G. trifoliata
Indian pink. See *Lobelia cardinalis*;
    Spigelia marilandica
Indian poke. See *Veratrum viride*
Indian rhubarb. See *Darmera peltata*
Indian salad. See *Hydrophyllum
    virginianum*
Indian snake palm. See
    Amorphophallus bulbifer
Indian turnip. See *Arisaema
    dracontium*; *A. triphyllum*
Indocalamus tessellatus. See *Sasa
    tessellata*
inside-out flower. See *Vancouveria
    hexandra*
interrupted fern. See *Osmunda
    claytoniana*
inushoma. See *Cimicifuga biternata*
Iridaceae, 118, 227
Iris, 226–228
Iris cristata, 226, 227
Iris cristata var. *alba*, 227
Iris foetidissima, 227
Iris foetidissima var. *citrina*, 227
Iris foetidissima var. *lutescens*, 227
Iris gracilipes, 228

Iris koreana, 228
Iris odaesanensis, 228
Iris tectorum, 228
Iris verna, 227
Irish ladies' tresses. See *Spiranthes
    romanzoffiana*
Irish shamrock. See *Oxalis acetocella*
iron plant. See *Aspidistra elatior*
Irregulares, 290
Isopyrum biternata, 75
Isopyrum thalictroides, 75
Italian arum. See *Arum italicum*
itchweed. See *Veratrum viride*
ivory bellflower. See *Campanula
    alliariifolia*
iwa giboshi. See *Hosta longipes*
iya giboshi. See *Hosta capitata*

Jaburan lily. See *Ophiopogon jaburan*
Jaburan lilyturf. See *Ophiopogon
    jaburan*
jack-in-the-pulpit. See *Arisaema
    triphyllum*
jade ribbon plant. See *Aspidistra
    caespitosa*
Japanese anemone. See *Anemone
    hupehensis* var. *japonica*
Japanese anemone of gardens. See
    Anemone ×*hybrida*
Japanese astilbe. See *Astilbe japonica*
Japanese baneberry. See *Actaea
    asiatica*
Japanese bugbane. See *Cimicifuga
    biternata*; *C. japonica*
Japanese butterbur. See *Petasites
    japonicus*
Japanese cardiandra. See *Cardiandra
    alternifolia*
Japanese climbing fern. See *Lygodium
    japonicum*
Japanese cobra lily. See *Arisaema
    iyoanum*; *A. serratum*
Japanese crested iris. See *Iris gracilipes*
Japanese deerfoot. See *Achlys japonica*
Japanese fairy bell. See *Disporum
    sessile*
Japanese goatsbeard. See *Aruncus
    astilboides*
Japanese holly fern. See *Cyrtomium
    falcatum*; *Polystichum
    polyblepharum*
Japanese horseradish. See *Wasabia
    japonica*
Japanese lady fern. See *Athyrium
    nipponicum*
Japanese lady slipper. See
    Cypripedium japonicum
Japanese large-flowered trillium. See
    Trillium kamtschaticum

Japanese mat rush. See *Juncus
    effusus*
Japanese mondo grass. See
    Ophiopogon japonicus; *O. planiscapus*
Japanese ostrich fern. See *Matteuccia
    orientalis*
Japanese pachysandra. See
    Pachysandra terminalis
Japanese painted fern, 116
Japanese palm sedge. See *Carex
    phyllocephala*
Japanese partridgeberry. See
    Mitchella undulata
Japanese reed grass. See *Hakonechloa
    macra*
Japanese roof iris. See *Iris tectorum*
Japanese sedge. See *Carex morrowii*
Japanese shield fern. See *Dryopteris
    erythrosora*
Japanese silver painted fern, 116
Japanese Solomon's seal. See
    Polygonatum falcatum
Japanese spike moss. See *Selaginella
    involvens*
Japanese spikenard. See *Aralia
    cordata*
Japanese spurge. See *Pachysandra
    terminalis*
Japanese tassel fern. See *Polystichum
    polyblepharum*
Japanese toad lily. See *Tricyrtis hirta*
Japanese wild ginger. See *Asarum
    caulescens*; *A. niponicum*
Japanese wintergreen. See *Chimaphila
    japonica*
Japanese woodsia. See *Woodsia
    polystichoides*
Japonasarum, 96
Jaquemont's cobra lily. See *Arisaema
    jaquemontii*
Jeffersonia, 228–229
Jeffersonia diphylla, 228, 229
Jeffersonia dubia, 228, 229
Jeffersonia dubia f. *alba*, 229
Jerusalem cowslip. See *Pulmonaria
    officinalis*
jew's harp. See *Trillium cernuum*
jewel orchid. See *Goodyera repens*
jin-seng. See *Panax ginseng*
Johnny-jump-up. See *Viola
    pedunculata*; *V. tricolor*
John's cabbage. See *Hydrophyllum
    virginianum*
jookug-bibich'u. See *Hosta clausa*
Juncaceae, 229, 237
Juncus, 229
Juncus communis of gardens. See
    Juncus effusus
Juncus effusus, 229

Juncus effusus f. *spiralis*, 229
Juncus inflexus, 229

kamo aoi. See *Asarum caulescens*
kanto kanaoi. See *Asarum niponicum*
Kaye's hart's tongue fern, 108
Kentucky lady slipper. See
  Cypripedium kentuckiense
kibanano hototogisu. See *Tricyrtis flava*
kifukurin oba giboshi. See *Hosta
  montana* 'Aureomarginata'
kifukurin tokudama, 225
killwort. See *Chelidonium majus*
king of the male fern, 171
Kinugasa, 253
Kinugasa japonica. See *Paris japonica*
kinugasaso, 253
ki renge shoma, 230
Kirengeshoma, 230
Kirengeshoma coreana, 230
Kirengeshoma palmata, 230
kiwi asarum. See *Asarum
  campaniforme*
kiwi ginger. See *Asarum campaniforme*
kiwi kanaoi. See *Asarum campaniforme*
kojima enreiso. See *Trillium smallii*
Komarov's bugbane. See *Cimicifuga
  heracleifolia*
konjac snake palm. See
  Amorphophallus rivieri
Korean astilbe. See *Astilbe koreana*
Korean fairy bell. See *Disporum
  flavens*
Korean goatsbeard. See *Aruncus
  aethusifolius*
Korean iris. See *Iris koreana*
Korean rock fern. See *Polystichum
  tsussimense*
koshino kanaoi. See *Asarum megacalyx*
kuma bamboo grass. See *Sasa veitchii*
kuma zasa. See *Sasa veitchii*
kuro giboshi. See *Hosta nigrescens*
kurohime takaoi. See *Asarum
  yoshikawae*
kuwaiba kanaoi. See *Asarum
  kumageanum*
Kyushu cobra lily. See *Arisaema
  kiushianum*

Labiatae, 67
Labrador violet. See *Viola labradorica*
lacy grape fern. See *Botrychium
  dissectum*
lacy hellebore. See *Helleborus
  multifidus*
ladies' tresses. See *Spiranthes spiralis*
lady fern. See *Athyrium filix-femina*
lady rue. See *Thalictrum clavatum*
lady slipper. See *Cypripedium calceolus*

lady slipper orchid. See *Cypripedium
  calceolus*
lady's slipper orchid. See
  Cypripedium calceolus
lamb's tongue fawn lily. See
  Erythronium grandiflorum
Lamiastrum, 230
Lamiastrum galeobdolon. See *Lamium
  galeobdolon*
Lamium, 230–231
Lamium album, 230
Lamium amplexicaule, 230
Lamium galeobdolon, 231
Lamium luteum. See *Lamium
  galeobdolon*
Lamium maculatum, 231
Lamium maculatum f. *album*, 231
Lamium orvala, 231
Lamium vulgatum var. *album.* See
  Lamium album
Lamprocapnos spectabilis. See *Dicentra
  spectabilis*
lance-leaf toadshade. See *Trillium
  lancifolium*
lance-leaved trillium. See *Trillium
  lancifolium*
large bellwort. See *Uvularia
  grandiflora*
large butterfly orchid. See *Platanthera
  grandiflora*
large fingerleaf rodgersia. See
  Rodgersia podophylla
large-flowered bellwort. See *Uvularia
  grandiflora*
large-flowered fairy bells. See
  Disporum smithii
large-flowered trillium. See *Trillium
  grandiflorum*
large-leaved Chinese shade bamboo.
  See *Sasa tessellata*
large-leaved Japanese holly fern. See
  Cyrtomium macrophyllum
large-leaved waterleaf. See
  Hydrophyllum macrophyllum
large merrybells. See *Uvularia
  grandiflora*
large purple fringed orchid. See
  Platanthera grandiflora
large toadshade. See *Trillium
  cuneatum*
large yellow lady slipper. See
  Cypripedium calceolus var. *pubescens*
large yellow moccasin flower. See
  Cypripedium calceolus var. *pubescens*
Lastrea thelypteris. See *Thelypteris
  palustris*
lattice leaf. See *Goodyera pubescens*
leafy-stemmed elephant's foot. See
  Elephantopus carolinianus

leatherleaf sedge. See *Carex buchanii*
leatherleaf wood fern. See *Dryopteris
  marginalis*
leather wood fern. See *Dryopteris
  marginalis*
Lemmon's wild ginger. See *Asarum
  lemmonii*
Lenten rose. See *Helleborus orientalis*
Leonurus galeobdolon. See *Lamium
  galeobdolon*
leopard flower. See *Belamcanda
  chinensis*
leopard ligularia, 186
leopard palm. See *Amorphophallus
  rivieri*
leopard plant. See *Farfugium
  japonicum*
Leptandra virginica. See *Veronicastrum
  virginicum*
lesser butterfly orchid. See
  Platanthera bifolia
lesser celandine. See *Ranunculus
  ficaria*
lesser meadow rue. See *Thalictrum
  minus*
lesser periwinkle. See *Vinca minor*
lesser purple fringed orchid. See
  Platanthera psyodes
lesser rattlesnake plantain. See
  Goodyera repens
lesser wintergreen. See *Pyrola
  elliptica*
lettuce saxifrage. See *Saxifraga
  michauxii*; *S. micranthidifolia*;
  S. pensylvanica
licorice fern. See *Polypodium
  glycyrrhiza*
life-of-man. See *Aralia racemosa*
Ligularia kaempferi. See *Farfugium
  japonicum*
Ligularia tussilaginea. See *Farfugium
  japonicum*
Liliaceae, 183, 231, 324. See also
  Alliaceae; Colchicaceae;
  Convallariaceae; Hostaceae;
  Medeolaceae; Melanthiaceae;
  Ruscaceae; Tricyrtidaceae;
  Trilliaceae; Uvulariaceae
Lilium, 231–233
Lilium canadense var. *superbum* of
  gardens. See *Lilium superbum*
Lilium catesbaei, 233
Lilium ×*dalhansonii*, 232
Lilium hansonii, 232
Lilium martagon, 232
Lilium martagon var. *albiflorum*, 232
Lilium martagon var. *album*, 232
Lilium martagon var. *cattaniae*, 232
Lilium michauxii, 233

Lilium montanum. See *Lilium philadelphicum*
Lilium philadelphicum, 233
Lilium superbum, 233
lily-royal. See *Lilium superbum*
lilyturf. See *Liriope exiliflora*; *L. graminifolia*; *L. muscari*
lily-of-the-valley. See *Convallaria majalis*; *C. montana*
Limniris, 227, 228
Liriope, 233–235
Liriope exiliflora, 234
Liriope gigantea, 234
Liriope graminifolia, 234
Liriope graminifolia var. *densiflora.* See *Liriope muscari*
Liriope graminifolia of gardens. See *Liriope muscari*
Liriope grandiflora, 234
Liriope japonica. See *Ophiopogon japonicus*
Liriope majestica, 234
Liriope munroei, 234
Liriope muscari, 233, 234
Liriope muscari var. *densiflora* of gardens. See *Liriope muscari*
Liriope muscari var. *exiliflora.* See *Liriope exiliflora*
Liriope platyphylla. See *Liriope muscari*
Liriope spicata, 235
Liriope variegata, 235
little blue staggers. See *Dicentra cucullaria*
little boy plant. See *Dicentra cucullaria*
little brown jugs. See *Asarum arifolium*; *A. ruthii*; *A. shuttleworthii*; *A. virginicum*
little girl plant. See *Dicentra canadensis*
little gray polypody. See *Polypodium polypodioides*
little ladies' tresses. See *Spiranthes grayi*
little pearl twist. See *Spiranthes grayi*
little prince's pine. See *Chimaphila menziesii*
liverberry. See *Disporum languinosum*; *D. maculatum*; *Streptopus amplexifolius* var. *americanus*
liverleaf. See *Hepatica acutiloba*
lobed barren strawberry. See *Waldsteinia lobata*
lobed spleenwort. See *Asplenium pinnatifidum*
Lobelia, 235–236
Lobelia cardinalis, 235
Lobelia cardinalis f. *alba*, 236
Lobelia cardinalis f. *rosea*, 236

Lobelia siphilitica, 236
Lobelia siphilitica f. *alba*, 236
Lobelia siphilitica f. *nana*, 236
Lobelia splendens, 236
locust fern. See *Osmunda regalis*
Loganiaceae, 300
London pride. See *Saxifraga umbrosa*
long beech fern. See *Phegopteris connectilis*
longhorn steer's head. See *Dicentra uniflora*
longleaf lungwort. See *Pulmonaria longifolia*
long-leaved lungwort. See *Pulmonaria longifolia*
longspur barrenwort. See *Epimedium grandiflorum*
Lophiris, 227, 228
Lorinseria areolata. See *Woodwardia areolata*
Lunathyrium thelypteroides. See *Athyrium thelypteroides*
Luzula, 236–237
Luzula maxima. See *Luzula sylvatica*
Luzula multiflora, 237
Luzula nivea, 236
Luzula pilosa, 237
Luzula sylvatica, 236, 237
Lychnis dioicus. See *Silene dioica*
Lychnis sylvestris. See *Silene dioica*
Lycopodium apodum. See *Selaginella apoda*
Lycopodium selago, 293
Lycopus, 67
Lygodium, 237–238
Lygodium japonicum, 237, 238
Lygodium palmatum, 237, 238
Lysimachia, 238–239
Lysimachia clethroides, 238
Lysimachia congestiflora, 238
Lysimachia japonica, 239
Lysimachia nummularia, 239
Lythrum, 238
Lythrum salicaria, 238

mace sedge. See *Carex grayi*
Madeiran orchid. See *Dactylorhiza foliosa*
mahogany fawn lily. See *Erythronium revolutum*
Mahonia aquifolium, 182
Maianthemum, 239–240
Maianthemum bifolium, 240
Maianthemum bifolium subsp. *kamtschaticum.* See *Maianthemum kamtschaticum*
Maianthemum canadense, 239, 240
Maianthemum dilatatum, 240
Maianthemum kamtschaticum, 240

Maianthemum kamtschaticum var. *dilatatum.* See *Maianthemum dilatatum*
Maianthemum racemosum. See *Smilacina racemosa*
maidenhair spleenwort. See *Asplenium trichomanes*
Majorcan hellebore. See *Helleborus lividus*
male fern. See *Dryopteris filix-mas*
Manchurian woodsia. See *Woodsia manchuriensis*
mandrake. See *Podophyllum peltatum*
marginal shield fern. See *Dryopteris marginalis*
marginal wood fern. See *Dryopteris marginalis*
marsh blue violet. See *Viola obliqua*
marsh fern. See *Thelypteris palustris*; *Woodwardia areolata*
marsh helleborine. See *Epipactis palustris*; *E. veratrifolia*
martagon lily. See *Lilium martagon*
maruba kanaoi. See *Asarum tamaense*
maruba tama-no-kanzashi. See *Hosta plantaginea*
marumi kanaoi. See *Asarum subglobosum*
Maryland pinkroot. See *Spigelia marilandica*
mat spike moss. See *Selaginella kraussiana*
matted saxifrage. See *Saxifraga bronchialis*
Matteuccia, 240–241
Matteuccia nodulosa. See *Matteuccia struthiopteris*
Matteuccia orientalis, 241
Matteuccia pennsylvanica. See *Matteuccia struthiopteris*
Matteuccia struthiopteris, 240, 241
mayapple. See *Podophyllum peltatum*
mayflower. See *Claytonia caroliniana*; *C. virginica*; *Hepatica americana*; *Maianthemum canadense*
May lily. See *Convallaria majalis*; *Maianthemum canadense*
Mazus, 241
Mazus pumilio, 241
Mazus radicans, 241
Mazus reptans, 241
meadow spike moss. See *Selaginella apoda*
mealy bellwort. See *Uvularia perfoliata*
Medeola, 241–242
Medeola virginiana, 241, 242
Medeolaceae, 242
Melandrium diurnum. See *Silene dioica*

Melandrium rubrum. See *Silene dioica*
Melanthiaceae, 69
Menzies' rattlesnake plantain. See *Goodyera oblongifolia*
merrybells. See *Uvularia grandiflora*
Mertensia, 242–243
Mertensia asiatica. See *Mertensia simplicissima*
Mertensia pterocarpa. See *Mertensia sibirica*
Mertensia pulmonarioides, 242
Mertensia sibirica, 243
Mertensia virginica. See *Mertensia pulmonarioides*
Mexican false garlic. See *Nothoscordum gracile*
Michaux's lily. See *Lilium michauxii*
Michaux's saxifrage. See *Saxifraga michauxii*
Micranthes virginiensis. See *Saxifraga virginiensis*
Milium, 243
Milium effusum, 243
Milium effusum var. *aureum*, 243
millet grass. See *Milium effusum*
Mimulus ringens, 241
miniature moneywort, 239
miniature sedge. See *Carex conica*
Minnesota adder's tongue. See *Erythronium propullans*
Mitchella, 243–244
Mitchella repens, 243, 244
Mitchella repens f. *leucocarpa*, 244
Mitchella repens var. *undulata*. See *Mitchella undulata*
Mitchella undulata, 244
Mitella, 244–245
Mitella breweri, 244
Mitella caulescens, 245
Mitella diphylla, 244, 245
Mitella diversifolia, 245
Mitella grandiflora. See *Tellima grandiflora*
Mitella micrantha. See *Mitella trifida*
Mitella nuda, 245
Mitella pentandra, 245
Mitella trifida, 245
Mitella violacea. See *Mitella trifida*
miterwort. See *Mitella diphylla*; *Tiarella cordifolia*
miyabi kanaoi. See *Asarum celsum*
miyako aoi. See *Asarum asperum*
miyama enreiso. See *Trillium tschonoskii*
Moldavian monkshood. See *Aconitum lycoctonum* subsp. *vulparia*
monarch of the east. See *Sauromatum venosum*

mondo grass. See *Ophiopogon japonicus*; *O. planiscapus*
Mondo jaburan. See *Ophiopogon jaburan*
Mondo japonicum. See *Ophiopogon japonicus*
moneyplant. See *Lysimachia nummularia*
moneywort. See *Lysimachia nummularia*
monkey cup. See *Nepenthes refflesiana*
morning campion. See *Silene dioica*
morning star sedge. See *Carex grayi*
mother lode trout lily. See *Erythronium tuolumnense*
mother-of-thousands. See *Saxifraga stolonifera*
mottled cranefly. See *Tipularia discolor*
mottled wild ginger. See *Asarum shuttleworthii*
mountain bellwort. See *Uvularia caroliniana*
mountain boykinia. See *Boykinia major*
mountain bugbane. See *Cimicifuga americana*
mountain lady slipper. See *Cypripedium montanum*
mountain lily. See *Convallaria montana*
mountain maidenhair fern. See *Adiantum venustum*
mountain pansy. See *Viola lutea*
mountain saxifrage. See *Saxifraga michauxii*
mountain spleenwort. See *Asplenium montanum*
mountain thistle. See *Acanthus montanus*
mountain violet. See *Viola lutea*
mountain wood fern. See *Dryopteris dilatata*
mountain woods trillium. See *Trillium tschonoskii*
mourning widow. See *Geranium phaeum*
mouse plant. See *Arisarum proboscideum*
mouse tail ginger. See *Asarum minamitanianum*
mousetail plant. See *Arisarum proboscideum*
Mukdenia, 245
Mukdenia rossii, 245
murasaki giboshi. See *Hosta ventricosa*
Muricauda dracontium. See *Arisaema dracontium*

Myosotis macrophylla. See *Brunnera macrophylla*
Myosotis, 123
myrtle flag. See *Acorus calamus*

nagasaki giboshi. See *Hosta tibae*
Nagasaki hosta. See *Hosta tibae*
Napellus firmum. See *Aconitum napellus*
narrow beech fern. See *Phegopteris connectilis*
narrow buckler fern. See *Dryopteris carthusiana*
narrow holly fern. See *Polystichum tsussimense*
narrowleaf spring beauty. See *Claytonia virginica*
narrow-leaved cast-iron plant. See *Aspidistra linearifolia*
narrow-leaved gentian. See *Gentiana linearis*
narrow-leaved hart's tongue fern, 108
narrow-leaved spleenwort. See *Athyrium pycnocarpon*
navelseed. See *Omphalodes cappadocica*
navelwort. See *Omphalodes cappadocica*
necklaceweed. See *Actaea alba*
nepenthes-like cobra lily. See *Arisaema nepenthoides*
Nepenthes refflesiana, 88
Nephrodium, 158
Nephrodium acrostichoides. See *Polystichum acrostichoides*
nerveroot. See *Cypripedium calceolus* var. *pubescens*
netted chain fern. See *Woodwardia areolata*
New York fern. See *Thelypteris noveboracensis*
New Zealand hair sedge. See *Carex comans*
nin-sin, 252
Nippon bells. See *Shortia uniflora*
nishiki ran, 192
Noah's ark. See *Cypripedium acaule*; *C. calceolus* var. *pubescens*
nodding ladies' tresses. See *Spiranthes cernua*
nodding mandarin. See *Disporum maculatum*
nodding trillium. See *Trillium cernuum*
North America wild oats. See *Chasmanthium latifolium*
northern beech fern. See *Phegopteris connectilis*
northern bugle. See *Ajuga pyramidalis*

northern dwarf cornel. See *Cornus suecica*

northern maidenhair fern. See *Adiantum pedatum*

northern maidenhair. See *Adiantum pedatum*

northern monkshood. See *Aconitum lycoctonum*

northern nodding trillium. See *Trillium cernuum*

northern rattlesnake plantain. See *Goodyera repens*

northern saxifrage. See *Saxifraga integrifolia*

northern sea oats. See *Chasmanthium latifolium*

northern wild oats. See *Chasmanthium latifolium*

northern woodsia. See *Woodsia alpina*

northern yellow lady slipper. See *Cypripedium calceolus* var. *planipetalum*

nosebleed. See *Trillium sessile*

Nothoscordum, 245–246

Nothoscordum bivalve, 245, 246

Nothoscordum fragrans. See *Nothoscordum gracile*

Nothoscordum gracile, 246

Nothoscordum inodorum of gardens. See *Nothoscordum gracile*

Nothoscordum striatum. See *Nothoscordum bivalve*

Oakesia puberula. See *Uvularia caroliniana*

Oakesia sessilifolia. See *Uvularia sessilifolia*

Oakesiella sessilifolia. See *Uvularia sessilifolia*

oba giboshi. See *Hosta montana* f. *macrophylla*

obana no enreiso. See *Trillium kamtschaticum*

obscure lungwort. See *Pulmonaria obscura*

Oconee bells. See *Shortia galacifolia*

Odae-san iris. See *Iris odaesanensis*

Ohio spiderwort. See *Tradescantia ohiensis*

old-fashioned bleeding heart. See *Dicentra spectabilis*

omoto. See *Rohdea japonica*

Omphalodes, 246–247

Omphalodes cappadocica, 246

Omphalodes cornifolia of gardens. See *Omphalodes cappadocica*

Omphalodes loykae. See *Omphalodes cappadocica*

Omphalodes verna, 246, 247

onaga kanaoi. See *Asarum minamitanianum*

one-flowered coltsfoot. See *Shortia galacifolia*

one-sided wintergreen. See *Pyrola secunda*

oni kanaoi. See *Asarum hirsutisepalum*

Onoclea, 247–248

Onoclea nodulosa. See *Matteuccia struthiopteris*

Onoclea sensibilis, 247

Onoclea struthiopteris. See *Matteuccia struthiopteris*

Ophioglossaceae, 121

Ophiopogon, 248–249

Ophiopogon arabicus of gardens, 249

Ophiopogon jaburan, 248

Ophiopogon japonicus, 248

Ophiopogon leucanthus of gardens, 249

Ophiopogon malayanus, 248

Ophiopogon muscari. See *Liriope muscari*

Ophiopogon planiscapus, 248

Ophiopogon spicatus. See *Liriope spicata*

orange cup lily. See *Lilium philadelphicum*

orange-fringe. See *Platanthera ciliaris*

orange fringed orchid. See *Platanthera cristata*

orange-plume. See *Platanthera ciliaris*

orangeroot. See *Hydrastis canadensis*

Orchidaceae, 76, 120, 124, 150, 155, 181, 192, 260, 300, 311

Orchis, 155, 311

Orchis discolor. See *Tipularia discolor*

Orchis elata. See *Dactylorhiza elata*

Orchis foliosa. See *Dactylorhiza foliosa*

Orchis fuchsii. See *Dactylorhiza fuchsii*

Orchis maculata. See *Dactylorhiza maculata*

Orchis maderensis of gardens. See *Dactylorhiza foliosa*

Oregon bugbane. See *Cimicifuga elata*

Oregon fetid adder's tongue. See *Scoliopus hallii*

Oregon saxifrage. See *Saxifraga oregana*

Oregon woodsia. See *Woodsia oregana*

Osmunda, 249–250

Osmunda cinnamonea. See *Osmunda cinnamomea*

Osmunda cinnamomea, 249

Osmunda claytoniana, 249

Osmunda regalis, 249, 250

Osmunda regalis var. *spectabilis*, 250

Osmundaceae, 249

ostrich fern. See *Matteuccia struthiopteris*

ostrich plume fern. See *Matteuccia struthiopteris*

otafuku giboshi, 216

otome giboshi. See *Hosta venusta*

otome kanaoi. See *Asarum savatieri*

owlface cobra lily. See *Arisaema flavum*

Oxalidaceae, 251

Oxalis, 250–251

Oxalis acetocella, 250

Oxalis montana, 250

Oxalis oregana, 250

Oxalis regnellii, 250

Oxalis stricta, 250

Oxalis triangularis, 250

Oxalis violacea, 250

Ozark green trillium. See *Trillium viridescens*

Ozark trillium. See *Trillium viridescens*

Pachyphragma, 126–127

Pachyphragma macrophylla, 127

Pachysandra, 251–252

Pachysandra procumbens, 251

Pachysandra stylosa. See *Pachysandra stylosum*

Pachysandra stylosum, 251

Pachysandra terminalis, 251, 252

Paeoniaceae, 192

painted lady. See *Trillium undulatum*

painted trillium. See *Trillium undulatum*

painted wood lily. See *Trillium undulatum*

Panax, 152–153

Panax ginseng, 152

Panax pseudoginseng, 252

Panax quinquefolius, 252

Panax schinseng, 252

Panax trifolius, 252

panda face ginger. See *Asarum maximum*

panda kanaoi. See *Asarum maximum*

pansy violet. See *Viola pedata*

Papaveraceae, 148, 174, 287, 303

papooseroot. See *Caulophyllum thalictroides*

Parathelypteris, 308

Parathelypteris noveboracensis. See *Thelypteris noveboracensis*

Pardanthus chinensis. See *Belamcanda chinensis*

Paris, 253–255

Paris bashanensis, 253

Paris dahurica. See *Paris verticillata*

Paris fargesii, 253

Paris fargesii var. *brevipedicillata*, 253

Paris hexaphylla. See *Paris verticillata*

Paris hexaphylla f. *purpurea*. See *Paris verticillata*
Paris japonica, 254
Paris lancifolia, 255
Paris obovata. See *Paris verticillata*
Paris polyphylla, 254
Paris polyphylla var. *alba*, 254
Paris polyphylla var. *nana*, 254
Paris polyphylla var. *thibetica*. See *Paris thibetica*
Paris quadrifolia, 253, 254
Paris tetraphylla, 255
Paris thibetica, 255
Paris verticillata, 255
Paris violacea, 255
Paris yakusimensis. See *Paris tetraphylla*
Paris yunnanensis, 255
partridgeberry. See *Mitchella repens*
pasture brake. See *Pteridium aquilinium*
peach-leaved bellflower. See *Campanula persicifolia*
peacock moss. See *Selaginella uncinata*
Pelargonium, 188
Peltiphyllum, 156
Peltiphyllum peltatum. See *Darmera peltata*
Peltoboykinia, 255–256
Peltoboykinia tellimoides, 256
Peltoboykinia watanabei, 256
peony-leaved snake palm. See *Amorphophallus paeoniifolius*
Peramium pubescens. See *Goodyera pubescens*
perennial forget-me-not. See *Omphalodes cappadocica*
perfoliate bellwort. See *Uvularia perfoliata*
Persian violet. See *Cyclamen*
Petasites, 256–258
Petasites albus, 257
Petasites fragrans, 257
Petasites frigidus, 257
Petasites hybridus, 257
Petasites japonicus, 256, 257
Petasites japonicus var. *giganteus*, 256, 257
Petasites palmatus, 257
petty morel. See *Aralia racemosa*
Phanerophlebia, 153
Phanerophlebia fortunei. See *Cyrtomium fortunei*
Phanerophlebia macrophyllum. See *Cyrtomium macrophyllum*
Phegopteris, 258–259
Phegopteris connectilis, 258
Phegopteris decursive-pinnata, 259

Phegopteris hexagonoptera, 258
Phegopteris vulgaris. See *Phegopteris connectilis*
Phragmites, 193
Phragmites australis, 193
Phragmites macra. See *Hakonechloa macra*
Phyllantherum, 316
Phyllantherum recurvatum. See *Trillium recurvatum*
Phyllitis, 106
Phyllitis scolopendrium. See *Asplenium scolopendrium*
Phyllostachys aurea, 287
pickaback plant. See *Tolmiea menziesii*
pig arisaema. See *Arisaema speciosum*
pig flower. See *Asarum arifolium*; *A. virginicum*
pig ginger. See *Asarum arifolium*
piggyback plant. See *Tolmiea menziesii*
pine lily. See *Lilium catesbaei*
Pinellia, 259–260
Pinellia cordata, 259
Pinellia integrifolia, 259
Pinellia petadisecta, 259
Pinellia tripartita, 259
pink lady slipper. See *Cypripedium acaule*
pink lady's slipper. See *Cypripedium acaule*
pink moccasin flower. See *Cypripedium acaule*
pinkroot. See *Spigelia marilandica*
pink turtlehead. See *Chelone lyonii*
pipsissewa. See *Chimaphila maculata*
Plagiorhegma dubia. See *Jeffersonia dubia*
Plagiorhegma dubium. See *Jeffersonia dubia*
Plantaginaceae, 260
Plantago, 260
Plantago asiatica f. *contracta*, 260
Plantago asiatica 'Variegata' of gardens. See *Plantago major* 'Variegata'
Plantago lanceolata, 260
Plantago major, 260
Plantago major 'Variegata', 260
plantain-leaved sedge. See *Carex plantaginea*
plantain lily. See *Hosta*
Platanthera, 260–262
Platanthera bifolia, 261
Platanthera blepharoglottis, 261
Platanthera chlorantha, 261
Platanthera ciliaris, 260, 261
Platanthera cristata, 261

Platanthera fimbricata. See *Platanthera grandiflora*
Platanthera grandiflora, 261
Platanthera integra, 261
Platanthera montana. See *Platanthera chlorantha*
Platanthera psyodes, 261
Pleioblastus auricomus, 287, 288
Pleopeltis polypodioides. See *Polypodium polypodioides*
plume royal. See *Platanthera grandiflora*
pocan, 327
Podophyllum, 262–264
Podophyllum aurantiocaule, 263
Podophyllum delavayi, 262
Podophyllum difforme, 263
Podophyllum emodi. See *Podophyllum hexandrum*
Podophyllum hexandrum, 263
Podophyllum hexandrum var. *chinense*, 263
Podophyllum hexandrum var. *majus*, 263
Podophyllum japonicum. See *Ranzania japonica*
Podophyllum onzoi. See *Podophyllum pleianthum*
Podophyllum peltatum, 263
Podophyllum peltatum f. *deamii*, 263
Podophyllum peltatum f. *polycarpum*, 263
Podophyllum pleianthum, 263
Podophyllum sikkimense. See *Podophyllum aurantiocaule*
Podophyllum veitchii, 264
Podophyllum versipelle, 264
poker alumroot. See *Heuchera cylindrica*
Pollia, 264–265
Pollia condensata, 265
Pollia japonica, 264, 265
Polygonaceae, 282
Polygonatum, 265–271
Polygonatum biflorum, 266
Polygonatum canaliculatum. See *Polygonatum biflorum*
Polygonatum cathcartii, 267
Polygonatum cirrhifolium, 267
Polygonatum commutatum f. *racemosum*. See *Polygonatum racemosum*
Polygonatum commutatum. See *Polygonatum biflorum*
Polygonatum cryptanthum, 267
Polygonatum curvistylum, 267
Polygonatum cyrtonema of gardens. See *Disporopsis pernyi*
Polygonatum falcatum, 267

Polygonatum fuscum, 271
Polygonatum geminiflorum, 267
Polygonatum giganteum. See
    Polygonatum biflorum
Polygonatum graminifolium, 267
Polygonatum hirtum, 268
Polygonatum hookeri, 268
Polygonatum humile, 266, 268
Polygonatum ×*hybridum*, 268
Polygonatum inflatum, 268
Polygonatum involucratum, 269
Polygonatum japonicum of gardens.
    See *Polygonatum odoratum*
Polygonatum japonicum var. *thunbergii*.
    See *Polygonatum odoratum* var.
    thunbergii
Polygonatum lasianthum, 269
Polygonatum latifolium, 268
Polygonatum latifolium var. *robustum*,
    268
Polygonatum multiflorum, 269
Polygonatum multiflorum of gardens.
    See *Polygonatum* ×*hybridum*
Polygonatum odoratum, 265, 269
Polygonatum odoratum var.
    pluriflorum, 269
Polygonatum odoratum var. *thunbergii*,
    269
Polygonatum officinale. See
    Polygonatum odoratum
Polygonatum oppositifolium, 270
Polygonatum prattii, 270
Polygonatum pubescens, 266
Polygonatum punctatum, 270
Polygonatum racemosum, 266
Polygonatum roseum, 270
Polygonatum severtzovii, 270, 271
Polygonatum sibiricum, 271
Polygonatum stewartianum, 271
Polygonatum thunbergii. See
    Polygonatum odoratum var.
    thunbergii
Polygonatum verticillatum, 271
Polygonatum verticillatum var. *rubrum*,
    271
Polygonatum vulgare. See *Polygonatum*
    odoratum
Polypodiaceae, 272
Polypodium, 271–273
Polypodium cambricum, 273
Polypodium glycyrrhiza, 272
Polypodium hesperium, 272
Polypodium hexagonopterum. See
    Phegopteris hexagonoptera
Polypodium incanum. See *Polypodium*
    polypodioides
Polypodium interjectum var.
    cambricum. See *Polypodium*
    cambricum

Polypodium marginale. See *Dryopteris*
    marginalis
Polypodium obtusum. See *Woodsia*
    obtusa
Polypodium phegopteris. See *Phegopteris*
    connectilis
Polypodium polypodioides, 271, 272
Polypodium polypodioides var.
    michauxianum, 272
Polypodium scouleri, 272
Polypodium virginianum, 272
Polypodium vulgare, 272
Polypodium vulgare var. *columbianum*.
    See *Polypodium hesperium*
Polypodium vulgare var. *occidentale*. See
    Polypodium glycyrrhiza
Polypodium vulgare subsp. *prionodes*.
    See *Polypodium cambricum*
Polystichum, 273–275
Polystichum acrostichoides, 273
Polystichum acrostichoides f. *crispum*,
    274
Polystichum acrostichoides f. *cristatum*,
    274
Polystichum acrostichoides f. *gravesii*, 274
Polystichum acrostichoides f. *incisum*,
    274
Polystichum aculeatum, 274
Polystichum aculeatum var. *japonicum*.
    See *Polystichum polyblepharum*
Polystichum andersonii, 274
Polystichum angulare. See *Polystichum*
    setiferum
Polystichum aristatum var. *simplicium*.
    See *Arachniodes simplicior*
Polystichum braunii, 274
Polystichum falcatum. See *Cyrtomium*
    falcatum
Polystichum falcatum var. *fortunei*. See
    Cyrtomium fortunei
Polystichum japonicum. See *Polystichum*
    polyblepharum
Polystichum lobatum. See *Polystichum*
    aculeatum
Polystichum munitum, 274
Polystichum polyblepharum, 274
Polystichum rigens, 275
Polystichum scopulinum, 274
Polystichum setiferum, 275
Polystichum ×*setigerum*, 274
Polystichum simplicius. See *Arachniodes*
    simplicior
Polystichum standishii. See *Arachniodes*
    standishii
Polystichum tsussimense, 275
poor robin's plantain. See *Hieracium*
    venosum
poppy of the dawn. See *Eomecon*
    chionantha

porcelain flower. See *Saxifraga*
    umbrosa
Porteranthus stipulatus. See *Gillenia*
    stipulata
Porteranthus trifoliatus. See *Gillenia*
    trifoliata
Portulacaceae, 143
prairie trillium. See *Trillium*
    recurvatum
prairie violet. See *Viola nuttallii*
prickly shield fern. See *Polystichum*
    aculeatum; *P. braunii*
Primocarex, 129
Primula, 275–276
Primula helodoxa. See *Primula*
    prolifera
Primula japonica, 275
Primula prolifera, 275
Primula sieboldii, 276
Primula veris, 276
Primula vulgaris, 276
Primulaceae, 238
prince's pine. See *Chimaphila*
    umbellata
Prosartes. See *Disporum*
Prosartes hookeri. See *Disporum hookeri*
Prosartes oregana. See *Disporum*
    hookeri var. *oreganum*
Pteridium, 276–277
Pteridium aquilinum, 276, 277
Pteris nodulosa. See *Matteuccia*
    struthiopteris
Pteris pennsylvanica. See *Matteuccia*
    struthiopteris
Pterolobium biebersteinii. See
    Pachyphragma macrophylla
puccoon root. See *Sanguinaria*
    canadensis
puddingberry. See *Cornus canadensis*
Pulmonaria, 277–281
Pulmonaria angustifolia, 278
Pulmonaria angustifolia f. *alba* of
    gardens, 278
Pulmonaria angustifolia subsp. *azurea*,
    278
Pulmonaria azurea. See *Pulmonaria*
    angustifolia; *P. officinalis*
Pulmonaria longifolia, 278
Pulmonaria longifolia subsp.
    cevennensis, 278
Pulmonaria mollis, 279
Pulmonaria montana. See *Pulmonaria*
    mollis
Pulmonaria obscura, 279
Pulmonaria officinalis, 279
Pulmonaria officinalis var. *immaculata*,
    279
Pulmonaria picta. See *Pulmonaria*
    saccharata

Pulmonaria rubra, 279
Pulmonaria rubra var. *alba*, 279
Pulmonaria rubra var. *albocorollata*, 279
Pulmonaria saccharata, 279, 280
Pulmonaria vallarsae, 280
Pulmonaria cultivars, 280, 281
punga pung. See *Amorphophallus paeoniifolius*
Purdom's rodgersia, 285
purple fawn lily. See *Erythronium purpurascens*
purple fuki, 257
purple hellebore. See *Helleborus atrorubens*
purple hosta. See *Hosta ventricosa*
purple jack. See *Arisaema triphyllum* var. *atrorubens*
purple loosestrife. See *Lythrum salicaria*
purple toadshade. See *Trillium cuneatum*
purple trillium. See *Trillium erectum*
puttyroot. See *Aplectrum hyemale*
pyramidal bugle. See *Ajuga pyramidalis*
pyramidal Chinese ginger. See *Saruma henryi*
Pyrola, 135–137
Pyrola americana, 136, 137
Pyrola elliptica, 137
Pyrola picta, 137
Pyrola rotundifolia, 137
Pyrola rotundifolia var. *americana*. See *Pyrola americana*
Pyrola secunda, 137
Pyrola umbellata. See *Chimaphila umbellata*
Pyrolaceae, 136

queencup. See *Clintonia uniflora*
queen's cup. See *Clintonia uniflora*
quicksilver weed. See *Thalictrum dioicum*

raccoon berry. See *Podophyllum peltatum*
rainbow fern. See *Selaginella uncinata*
rainbow trillium. See *Trillium sulcatum*
rainbow wakerobin. See *Trillium sulcatum*
ram's head lady slipper. See *Cypripedium arietinum*
ramshead lady slipper. See *Cypripedium arietinum*
Ranunculaceae, 59, 62, 72, 75, 77, 140, 182, 195, 201, 226, 306
Ranunculus, 281

Ranunculus acris, 281
Ranunculus ficaria, 281
Ranunculus repens, 281
ranyo aoi. See *Asarum blumei*
Ranzania, 281–282
Ranzania japonica, 282
rattlesnake fern. See *Botrychium virginianum*
rattlesnake master. See *Platanthera ciliaris*
rattlesnake orchid. See *Goodyera pubescens*
rattlesnake root. See *Chamaelirium luteum*
rattlesnake weed. See *Hieracium venosum*
rattletop. See *Cimicifuga racemosa*
red baneberry. See *Actaea rubra*
red barrenwort. See *Epimedium* ×*rubrum*
red calla. See *Sauromatum venosum*
red campion. See *Silene dioica*
red Indian paint. See *Sanguinaria canadensis*
red lily. See *Lilium philadelphicum*
red lungwort. See *Pulmonaria rubra*
red puccoon. See *Sanguinaria canadensis*
red turtlehead. See *Chelone lyonii*
redwood ivy. See *Vancouveria planipetala*
redwood sorrel. See *Oxalis oregana*
resurrection fern. See *Polypodium polypodioides*
resurrection orchid. See *Aplectrum hyemale*; *Tipularia discolor*
Rheum, 282–283
Rheum acuminatum, 282
Rheum palmatum, 283
Rheum palmatum var. *dissectum*. See *Rheum palmatum* var. *tanguticum*
Rheum palmatum var. *tanguticum*, 283
rheumatism root. See *Chimaphila maculata*; *Jeffersonia diphylla*
rhubarb hosta. See *Hosta sieboldiana* 'Mira'
ribbed cobra lily. See *Arisaema costatum*
ringent cobra lily. See *Arisaema ringens*
Roanoke bells. See *Mertensia pulmonarioides*
roast beef plant. See *Iris foetidissima*
Robertsonia, 290
robust cobra lily. See *Arisaema robustum*
robust marsh orchid. See *Dactylorhiza elata*
rock bells. See *Aquilegia canadensis*

rockcap fern. See *Polypodium virginianum*
rock-dwelling cobra lily. See *Arisaema saxatile*
rock geranium. See *Heuchera americana*
rock hosta. See *Hosta longipes*
rock polypody. See *Polypodium virginianum*
rock spike moss. See *Selaginella rupestris*
Rocky Mountain boykinia. See *Boykinia jamesii*
Rocky Mountain columbine. See *Aquilegia coerulea*
Rocky Mountain woodsia. See *Woodsia scopulina*
Rodgersia, 283–285
Rodgersia aesculifolia, 284
Rodgersia henrici, 284
Rodgersia japonica. See *Rodgersia podophylla*
Rodgersia pinnata, 284
Rodgersia podophylla, 283, 285
Rodgersia purdomii, 285
Rodgersia sambucifolia, 285
Rodgersia tabularis. See *Astilboides tabularis*
Rohdea, 285–286
Rohdea japonica, 285, 286
Rohdea watanabei, 286
roof iris. See *Iris tectorum*
Rosaceae, 94
rose mandarin. See *Streptopus roseus*
rose plantain, 260
rose trillium. See *Trillium catesbaei*
rose twisted stalk. See *Streptopus roseus*
rosy spiderwort. See *Tradescantia rosea*
rosy twisted stalk. See *Streptopus roseus*
rosy wakerobin. See *Trillium catesbaei*
roundleaf American wintergreen. See *Pyrola americana*
roundleaf wintergreen. See *Pyrola americana*
round-leaved Japanese ginger. See *Asarum tamaense*
round-lobed hepatica. See *Hepatica americana*
round-lobed liverwort. See *Hepatica americana*
royal fern. See *Osmunda regalis*
Rubiaceae, 187, 244
ruby jack. See *Arisaema triphyllum* var. *atrorubens*
rue anemone. See *Anemonella thalictroides*

running box. See *Mitchella repens*
running myrtle. See *Vinca minor*
Ruscaceae, 156
Ruscus, 156
rusty-back fern. See *Asplenium ceterach*
rusty cliff fern. See *Woodsia ilvensis*
rusty saxifrage. See *Saxifraga ferruginea*
rusty woodsia. See *Woodsia ilvensis*

sacred lily. See *Rohdea japonica*
sacred lily of China. See *Rohdea japonica*
sacred lily of Japan. See *Rohdea japonica*
sagae giboshi, 223
Saint Patrick's cabbage. See *Saxifraga umbrosa*
Saint Peter's cabbage. See *Saxifraga virginiensis*
sakawa saishin. See *Asarum sakawanum*
Salmon Mountain trillium. See *Trillium ovatum* f. *oettingerii*
Salomonia, 265
sang. See *Panax quinquefolius*
Sanguinaria, 286–287
Sanguinaria canadensis, 287
sanko kanaoi. See *Asarum trigynum*
sanyo aoi. See *Asarum hexalobum*
Saponaria, 188
Saruma, 96, 104
Saruma henryi, 104
Sasa, 287–288
Sasa albomarginata. See *Sasa veitchii*
Sasa auricoma. See *Pleioblastus auricomus*
Sasa pygmea, 288
Sasa tessellata, 288
Sasa veitchii, 288
Sasamorpha tessellata. See *Sasa tessellata*
satsuma aoi. See *Asarum satsumense*
Sauromatum, 288–289
Sauromatum guttatum. See *Sauromatum venosum*
Sauromatum nubicum, 289
Sauromatum venosum, 289
Saxifraga, 289–292
Saxifraga aconitifolia. See *Boykinia aconitifolia*
Saxifraga bronchialis, 292
Saxifraga caespitosa, 292
Saxifraga cortusifolia var. *fortunei*. See *Saxifraga fortunei*
Saxifraga cuscutiformis, 291
Saxifraga ferruginea, 292
Saxifraga fortunei, 290

Saxifraga granulata, 290
Saxifraga integrifolia, 292
Saxifraga mertensiana, 292
Saxifraga michauxii, 290, 292
Saxifraga micranthidifolia, 290, 292
Saxifraga occidentalis, 292
Saxifraga oregana, 292
Saxifraga peltata. See *Darmera peltata*
Saxifraga pensylvanica, 290, 292
Saxifraga primuloides, 291
Saxifraga sarmentosa. See *Saxifraga stolonifera*
Saxifraga serratifolia. See *Saxifraga umbrosa*
Saxifraga stolonifera, 291
Saxifraga stolonifera var. *minor*, 291
Saxifraga tellimoides. See *Peltoboykinia tellimoides*
Saxifraga umbrosa, 291
Saxifraga umbrosa var. *hirta*, 291
Saxifraga umbrosa var. *primuloides*, 291
Saxifraga ×*urbium*, 291
Saxifraga veitchiana, 291
Saxifraga virginiensis, 292
Saxifraga watanabei. See *Peltoboykinia watanabei*
Saxifragaceae, 110, 114, 122, 138, 156, 203, 244, 245, 256, 283, 290, 305, 309
sazanami giboshi, 216
scale fern. See *Asplenium ceterach*
scaly male fern. See *Dryopteris affinis*
scarlet lobelia. See *Lobelia cardinalis*
scarlet-seeded iris. See *Iris foetidissima*
scented cranesbill. See *Geranium macrorrhizum*
scentless garlic. See *Nothoscordum bivalve*
Schizaeaceae, 237
Schizocodon ilicifolium. See *Shortia soldanelloides* var. *ilicifolia*
Schizocodon soldanelloides. See *Shortia soldanelloides*
Schizocodon soldanelloides f. *alpinum*. See *Shortia soldanelloides* f. *alpina*
Schizocodon soldanelloides var. *macrophyllum* of gardens. See *Shortia soldanelloides* var. *magna*
Scirpus lacustris. See *Juncus effusus*
Scoliopus, 292–293
Scoliopus bigelovii. See *Scoliopus bigelowii*
Scoliopus bigelowii, 292
Scoliopus hallii, 292
Scolopendrium officinale. See *Asplenium scolopendrium*
Scolopendrium vulgare. See *Asplenium scolopendrium*

scootberry. See *Streptopus amplexicaulis* var. *americanus*
scorpion weed. See *Hydrophyllum virginianum*
screw-auger. See *Spiranthes cernua*
scrofula weed. See *Goodyera pubescens*
Scrophulariaceae, 135, 241, 329
Selaginella, 293, 294
Selaginella apoda, 293
Selaginella apus. See *Selaginella apoda*
Selaginella azorica. See *Selaginella kraussiana*
Selaginella braunii, 293
Selaginella brownii, 294
Selaginella caulescens. See *Selaginella involvens*
Selaginella densa of gardens. See *Selaginella apoda*
Selaginella douglasii, 293
Selaginella helvetica, 294
Selaginella involvens, 294
Selaginella japonica. See *Selaginella involvens*
Selaginella kraussiana, 294
Selaginella rupestris, 293
Selaginella uncinata, 294
Selaginellaceae, 293
Senecio, 185
Senecio kaempferi. See *Farfugium japonicum*
sensitive fern. See *Onoclea sensibilis*
Serapias gigantea. See *Epipactis gigantea*
Serbian bellflower. See *Campanula poscharskyana*
sessile bellwort. See *Uvularia sessilifolia*
setterwort. See *Helleborus foetidus*
sharp-leaved hepatica. See *Hepatica acutiloba*
sharp-lobed hepatica. See *Hepatica acutiloba*
sharp-lobed liverwort. See *Hepatica acutiloba*
Shawnee salad. See *Hydrophyllum virginianum*
shellflower. See *Chelone glabra*; *C. lyonii*
shield-leaf Rodger's flower. See *Astilboides tabularis*
Shikoku cobra lily. See *Arisaema sikokianum*
shinleaf. See *Pyrola elliptica*
shirobana enreiso. See *Trillium tschonoskii*
shiro hakekomi fu. See *Farfugium japonicum* var. *lutchuense*
shorthorn steer's head. See *Dicentra pauciflora*
Shortia, 294–296

Shortia galacifolia, 294, 295
Shortia macrophylla of gardens. See *Shortia soldanelloides* var. *magna*
Shortia soldanelloides, 295
Shortia soldanelloides f. *alpina*, 295
Shortia soldanelloides var. *ilicifolia*, 295
Shortia soldanelloides var. *magna*, 295
Shortia uniflora, 295
short trout lily. See *Erythronium denscanis*
showy cobra lily. See *Arisaema speciosum*
showy lady slipper. See *Cypripedium reginae*
showy moccasin flower. See *Cypripedium reginae*
showy spiderwort. See *Tradescantia virginiana*
showy wakerobin. See *Trillium grandiflorum*
shredded umbrella plant. See *Syneilesis aconitifolium*
shuttlecock fern. See *Matteuccia struthiopteris*
Shuttleworth's ginger. See *Asarum shuttleworthii*
Siberian bluebells. See *Mertensia sibirica*
Siberian bugloss. See *Brunnera macrophylla*
Siebold's fern. See *Dryopteris sieboldii*
Sierra fawn lily. See *Erythronium multiscapoideum*
Sierran bleeding heart. See *Dicentra formosa* subsp. *nevadensis*
Sierra wild ginger. See *Asarum hartwegii*
sightwort. See *Chelidonium majus*
Sikkim rhubarb. See *Rheum acuminatum*
Silene, 296, 297
Silene baldwynii. See *Silene polypetala*
Silene caroliniana, 296
Silene dioica, 296
Silene ovata, 296
Silene polypetala, 296
Silene virginica, 297
silver glade fern. See *Athyrium thelypteroides*
silvery glade fern. See *Athyrium thelypteroides*
silvery spleenwort. See *Athyrium thelypteroides*
Sinarundinaria murieliae, 288
Sinarundinaria nitida, 288
Sinopodophyllum, 262
Sinopodophyllum hexandrum. See *Podophyllum hexandrum*
Siskiyou trillium. See *Trillium rivale*

sister violet. See *Viola sororia*
skunk cabbage. See *Veratrum californicum*
slender ladies' tresses. See *Spiranthes gracilis*
slim Solomon. See *Smilacina sessilifolia*
small cast-iron plant. See *Aspidistra lurida*
smaller fringed gentian. See *Gentianopsis procera*
small-flowered alumroot. See *Heuchera micrantha*
small-flowered false hellebore. See *Veratrum parviflorum*
small-flowered ginger. See *Asarum naniflorum*
small golden-slipper. See *Cypripedium calceolus* var. *parviflorum*
small Japanese wild ginger. See *Asarum takaoi*
small purple fringed orchid. See *Platanthera psyodes*
small rock hosta. See *Hosta gracillima*
small Solomon's seal. See *Polygonatum biflorum*
small white lady slipper. See *Cypripedium candidum*
small yellow lady slipper. See *Cypripedium calceolus* var. *parviflorum*
small yellow moccasin flower. See *Cypripedium calceolus* var. *parviflorum*
Smilacina, 297–299
Smilacina amplexicaulis. See *Smilacina racemosa* var. *amplexicaulis*
Smilacina bicolor, 297
Smilacina bifolia. See *Maianthemum bifolium*
Smilacina davurica, 297
Smilacina forestii, 298
Smilacina formosana, 298
Smilacina fusca, 298
Smilacina henryi, 298
Smilacina hondoensis, 298
Smilacina japonica, 298
Smilacina japonica var. *luteocarpa*, 298
Smilacina japonica var. *robusta*, 298
Smilacina oleacera, 298
Smilacina purpurea, 298
Smilacina racemosa, 297, 299
Smilacina racemosa var. *amplexicaulis*, 299
Smilacina racemosa var. *cylindrica*, 299
Smilacina sessilifolia, 299
Smilacina stellata, 299
Smilacina stellata var. *crassa*, 299

Smilacina trifolia, 299
Smilacina wilsonii, 298
Smilacina yezoensis, 298
Smilax, 297
smooth rattlesnake plantain. See *Goodyera tesselata*
smooth woodsia. See *Woodsia glabella*
smooth yellow violet. See *Viola pubescens* var. *eriocarpa*
snakebeard. See *Ophiopogon jaburan*
snakeberry. See *Actaea rubra*
snake fern. See *Osmunda regalis*
snakehead. See *Chelone glabra*; *C. lyonii*
snake palm. See *Amorphophallus rivieri*
snakeroot. See *Cimicifuga racemosa*
snowflake. See *Lamium album*
snow orchid. See *Platanthera blepharoglottis*
snow poppy. See *Eomecon chionantha*
snow rose. See *Helleborus niger*
snow trillium. See *Trillium nivale*
snow wakerobin. See *Trillium nivale*
snowy woodrush. See *Luzula nivea*
soapwort gentian. See *Gentiana saponaris*
soft lungwort. See *Pulmonaria mollis*
soft rush. See *Juncus effusus*
soft shield fern. See *Polystichum setiferum*
Soldanella alpina, 295
soldier's cap. See *Aconitum napellus*
soldier's plume. See *Platanthera psyodes*
soldiers and sailors. See *Pulmonaria officinalis*
Solomon's feather. See *Smilacina racemosa*
Solomon's plume. See *Smilacina racemosa*
Solomon's seal. See *Polygonatum*
Solomon's zigzag. See *Smilacina racemosa*
soshinka, 99
southern beech fern. See *Phegopteris hexagonoptera*
southern harebell. See *Campanula divaricata*
southern ladies' tresses. See *Spiranthes gracilis*
southern lilyturf. See *Liriope muscari*
southern maidenhair. See *Adiantum capillus-veneris*
southern maidenhair fern. See *Adiantum capillus-veneris*
southern nodding trillium. See *Trillium rugelii*
southern red lily. See *Lilium catesbaei*

southern red trillium. See *Trillium sulcatum*

southern swamp fern. See *Dryopteris ludoviciana*

southern wood fern. See *Dryopteris ludoviciana*

spangle grass. See *Chasmanthium latifolium*

sparrow's egg lady slipper. See *Cypripedium passerinum*

speckled clintonia. See *Clintonia umbellata*

speckled wood lily. See *Clintonia umbellata*

Spigelia, 299–300

Spigelia marilandica, 299, 300

spikenard. See *Aralia racemosa*

spinulose wood fern. See *Dryopteris carthusiana*

spiny bear's breeches. See *Acanthus spinosus*

spiny wood fern. See *Dryopteris carthusiana*

Spiraea, 94

Spiraea aruncus. See *Aruncus dioicus*

Spiraea stipulata. See *Gillenia stipulata*

Spiraea trifoliata. See *Gillenia trifoliata*

Spiranthes, 300–301

Spiranthes cernua, 301

Spiranthes cernua var. *odorata*, 301

Spiranthes gracilis, 301

Spiranthes grayi, 301

Spiranthes lacera, 301

Spiranthes lacera var. *gracilis*. See *Spiranthes gracilis*

Spiranthes ochroleuca, 301

Spiranthes odorata. See *Spiranthes cernua* var. *odorata*

Spiranthes romanzoffiana, 301

Spiranthes sinensis, 301

Spiranthes spiralis, 301

Spiranthes vernalis, 301

spotted cranesbill. See *Geranium maculatum*

spotted deadnettle. See *Lamium maculatum*

spotted disporum. See *Disporum maculatum*

spotted dog. See *Pulmonaria longifolia*; *P. officinalis*

spotted fairy bell. See *Disporum maculatum*

spotted marsh orchid. See *Dactylorhiza fuchsii*

spotted wild geranium. See *Geranium maculatum*

spotted wintergreen. See *Chimaphila maculata*

spreading clubmoss. See *Selaginella kraussiana*

spring beauty. See *Claytonia virginica*

spring ladies' tresses. See *Spiranthes vernalis*

spring meadow rue. See *Thalictrum dioicum*

spring snow sedge. See *Carex fraseri*

spurred bellflower. See *Campanula alliariifolia*

squawberry. See *Mitchella repens*

squawroot. See *Caulophyllum thalictroides*; *Trillium erectum*

squawvine. See *Mitchella repens*

squirrel corn. See *Dicentra canadensis*

squirrel shoes. See *Cypripedium acaule*

squirrel tail. See *Chamaelirium luteum*

staggerweed. See *Dicentra canadensis*; *D. cucullaria*; *D. eximia*

star bloom. See *Spigelia marilandica*

starflower. See *Smilacina stellata*

star-flowered lily-of-the-valley. See *Smilacina stellata*

starry ginger. See *Asarum stellatum*

starry Solomon's plume. See *Smilacina stellata*

starry Solomon's seal. See *Smilacina stellata*

stemless lady slipper. See *Cypripedium acaule*

stiff bear's paw fern. See *Polystichum rigens*

stiff sedge. See *Carex elata*

stinking Benjamin. See *Trillium erectum*

stinking bugbane. See *Cimicifuga foetida*

stinking gladwyn. See *Iris foetidissima*

stinking hellebore. See *Helleborus foetidus*

stinking iris. See *Iris foetidissima*

stinking Willie. See *Trillium erectum*

stink pod. See *Scoliopus bigelowii*

stinkwort. See *Helleborus foetidus*

strawbells. See *Uvularia perfoliata*; *U. sessilifolia*

strawberry begonia. See *Saxifraga stolonifera*

strawberry geranium. See *Saxifraga stolonifera*

strawflower. See *Uvularia grandiflora*

strawlilies. See *Uvularia sessilifolia*

stream violet. See *Viola glabella*

Streptopus, 301–302

Streptopus amplexifolius, 302

Streptopus amplexifolius var. *americanus*, 302

Streptopus amplexifolius var. *denticulatus*, 302

Streptopus amplexifolius var. *oreopolus*, 302

Streptopus curvipes. See *Streptopus roseus* var. *curvipes*

Streptopus languinosus. See *Disporum languinosum*

Streptopus roseus, 301, 302

Streptopus roseus var. *curvipes*, 302

Streptopus roseus var. *perspectus*, 302

Streptopus streptopoides, 302

Streptopus streptopoides var. *japonicus*, 302

striped pipsissewa. See *Chimaphila maculata*

striped wakerobin. See *Trillium undulatum*

striped wintergreen. See *Chimaphila maculata*

Struthiopteris germanica. See *Matteuccia struthiopteris*

Struthiopteris orientalis. See *Matteuccia orientalis*

Struthiopteris spicant. See *Blechnum spicant*

Stylophorum, 302–303

Stylophorum diphyllum, 302, 303

Stylophorum lasiocarpum, 303

Stylophorum sutchuenense, 303

sugar scoop. See *Tiarella unifoliata*

summer cohosh. See *Cimicifuga americana*

sungure-to. See *Arisaema speciosum*

swamp fern. See *Dryopteris clintoniana*; *Woodwardia areolata*

swamp hosta. See *Hosta longissima* var. *longifolia*

swamp ladies' tresses. See *Spiranthes cernua* var. *odorata*

swamp lily. See *Lilium superbum*

swamp orchid. See *Spiranthes cernua* var. *odorata*

swamp pink. See *Helonias bullata*

swamp saxifrage. See *Saxifraga pensylvanica*

sweet-after-death. See *Achlys triphylla*

sweet Beth. See *Trillium vaseyi*

sweet Betsy. See *Trillium cuneatum*

sweet calamus. See *Acorus calamus*

sweet coltsfoot. See *Petasites fragrans*; *P. palmatus*

sweet flag. See *Acorus calamus*

sweet ladies' tresses. See *Spiranthes cernua* var. *odorata*

sweetleaf. See *Achlys triphylla*

sweet trillium. See *Trillium vaseyi*

sweet white trillium. See *Trillium simile*

sweet white violet. See *Viola blanda*

sweet woodruff. See *Galium odoratum*

Swiss spike moss. See *Selaginella helvetica*
sword fern. See *Dryopteris ludoviciana*
sylvan woodrush. See *Luzula sylvatica*
Symphytum, 303
Symphytum asperum, 303
Symphytum grandiflorum, 303
Symphytum officinale, 303
Symphytum peregrinum. See *Symphytum* ×*uplandicum*
Symphytum rubrum, 303
Symphytum ×*uplandicum*, 304
Syndesmon thalictroides. See *Anemonella thalictroides*
Syneilesis, 304–305
Syneilesis aconitifolia, 304
Syneilesis intermedia, 305
Syneilesis palmata, 304

tachi giboshi. See *Hosta rectifolia*
tairin aoi. See *Asarum asaroides*
Taiwanese cobra lily. See *Arisaema taiwanense*
Taiwan fairy bell. See *Disporum nantauense*
tall bellflower. See *Campanula americana*
tall cobra lily. See *Arisaema tortuosum*
tall white violet. See *Viola canadensis*
tamano kanaoi. See *Asarum tamaense*
tasseled hart's tongue fern, 108
Tatarian aster. See *Aster tataricus*
teaberry. See *Mitchella repens*
Telesonix jamesii. See *Boykinia jamesii*
Telingo potato. See *Amorphophallus paeoniifolius*
Tellima, 305
Tellima breviflora. See *Tellima grandiflora*
Tellima grandiflora, 305
Tellima grandiflora var. *rubra*, 305
Tellima odorata. See *Tellima grandiflora*
Thai fairy bell. See *Disporum cantoniense*
Thalictrum, 305–307
Thalictrum actaeifolium, 306
Thalictrum adiantifolium, 307
Thalictrum anemonoides. See *Anemonella thalictroides*
Thalictrum aquilegiifolium, 306
Thalictrum aquilegiifolium var. *album*, 306
Thalictrum aquilegiifolium var. *atropurpureum*, 306
Thalictrum babingtonii. See *Thalictrum minus*
Thalictrum chelidonii, 306
Thalictrum clavatum, 306, 307

Thalictrum coriaceum, 306
Thalictrum dasycarpum, 306
Thalictrum debile, 307
Thalictrum delavayi, 306
Thalictrum diffusiflorum, 306
Thalictrum dioicum, 306
Thalictrum filamentosum, 305
Thalictrum filamentosum var. *tenerum*, 307
Thalictrum flavum, 306
Thalictrum foetidus. See *Thalictrum minus*
Thalictrum kiusianum, 307
Thalictrum kochii. See *Thalictrum minus*
Thalictrum majus. See *Thalictrum minus*
Thalictrum minus, 307
Thalictrum orientale, 307
Thalictrum polygamum. See *Thalictrum pubescens*
Thalictrum pubescens, 306
Thalictrum revolutum, 306
Thalictrum rochebrunianum, 306
Thalictrum taquetii, 307
Thalictrum thalictroides. See *Anemonella thalictroides*
Thamnocalamus spathaceus of gardens. See *Sinarundinaria murieliae*
Thelypteridaceae, 258, 308
Thelypteris, 307–308
Thelypteris decursive-pinnata. See *Phegopteris decursive-pinnata*
Thelypteris hexagonoptera. See *Phegopteris hexagonoptera*
Thelypteris noveboracensis, 308
Thelypteris palustris, 308
Thelypteris phegopteris. See *Phegopteris connectilis*
Therofon major. See *Boykinia major*
Therofon rotundifolia. See *Boykinia rotundifolia*
Thlaspi macrophyllum. See *Pachyphragma macrophylla*
thousand-mothers. See *Tolmiea menziesii*
threeleaf bittercress. See *Cardamine trifolia*
three-leafed Solomon's seal. See *Smilacina trifolia*
three-leaf ginseng. See *Panax trifolius*
threeleaf toothwort. See *Cardamine trifolia*
three-leaved foamflower. See *Tiarella trifoliata*
three-leaved starflower. See *Smilacina trifolia*
three-part-leaved violet. See *Viola tripartita*

Thunberg's astilbe. See *Astilbe thunbergii*
Thunberg's cobra lily. See *Arisaema thunbergii*
Tiarella, 308–310
Tiarella alterniflora. See *Tellima grandiflora*
Tiarella cordifolia, 308, 309
Tiarella cordifolia f. *albiflora*, 309
Tiarella cordifolia var. *collina.* See *Tiarella wherryi*
Tiarella cordifolia f. *purpurea*, 309
Tiarella laciniata, 310
Tiarella polyphylla, 310
Tiarella rhombifolia. See *Tiarella trifoliata*
Tiarella stenopetala. See *Tiarella trifoliata*
Tiarella trifoliata, 310
Tiarella unifoliata, 310
Tiarella wherryi, 210
Tipularia, 310–311
Tipularia discolor, 310, 311
Tipularia japonica, 311
Tipularia josephii, 311
Tipularia unifolia. See *Tipularia discolor*
titan arum. See *Amorphophallus titanum*
toadshade. See *Trillium cuneatum*; *T. sessile*
toad trillium. See *Trillium sessile*
tobacco weed. See *Elephantopus carolinianus*; *E. tomentosus*
tokudama, 224
Tolmiea, 202, 206
Tolmiea menziesii, 206
tortuous cobra lily. See *Arisaema tortuosum*
Tosa wild ginger. See *Asarum costatum*
tosano aoi. See *Asarum costatum*
Tradescantia, 311–312
Tradescantia ×*andersoniana.* See *Tradescantia virginiana*
Tradescantia canaliculata. See *Tradescantia ohiensis*
Tradescantia caricifolia. See *Tradescantia ohiensis*
Tradescantia hirsuticaulis, 311
Tradescantia ohiensis, 311
Tradescantia paludosa. See *Tradescantia ohiensis*
Tradescantia reflexa. See *Tradescantia ohiensis*
Tradescantia rosea, 311
Tradescantia subaspera, 311
Tradescantia virginiana, 311, 312
Tradescantia virginica. See *Tradescantia virginiana*

trailing spike moss. See *Selaginella kraussiana*

Transsylvanian hepatica. See *Hepatica transsilvanica*

treacleberry. See *Smilacina racemosa*

treelet spike moss. See *Selaginella braunii*

tree lungwort. See *Mertensia pulmonarioides*

Tricyrtidaceae, 312

Tricyrtis, 312–316

Tricyrtis affinis, 313

Tricyrtis bakeri. See *Tricyrtis latifolia*

Tricyrtis flava, 313

Tricyrtis flava var. *nana*, 313

Tricyrtis formosana, 313

Tricyrtis hirta, 312, 314

Tricyrtis hirta var. *alba* of gardens, 314

Tricyrtis hirta var. *masamunei*, 314

Tricyrtis ishiiana, 314

Tricyrtis ishiiana var. *surugensis*, 314

Tricyrtis japonica. See *Tricyrtis hirta*

Tricyrtis kyusyensis. See *Tricyrtis flava*

Tricyrtis kyusyensis var. *pseudoflava*. See *Tricyrtis flava* var. *nana*

Tricyrtis latifolia, 314

Tricyrtis latifolia var. *makinoana*, 314

Tricyrtis macrantha, 314

Tricyrtis macrantha var. *ishiiana*. See *Tricyrtis ishiiana*

Tricyrtis macrantha var. *macranthopsis*, 315

Tricyrtis macranthopsis. See *Tricyrtis macrantha* var. *macranthopsis*

Tricyrtis macropoda, 315

Tricyrtis macropoda f. *glabrescens*, 315

Tricyrtis macropoda f. *hirsuta*, 315

Tricyrtis macropoda var. *chugokuensis*, 315

Tricyrtis nana. See *Tricyrtis flava* var. *nana*

Tricyrtis oshumiensis, 315

Tricyrtis perfoliata, 315

Tricyrtis puberula. See *Tricyrtis latifolia*

Tricyrtis setochinensis, 314

Tricyrtis stolonifera. See *Tricyrtis formosana*

Tricyrtis yatabeana. See *Tricyrtis flava*

Tricyrtis cultivars, 315–316

trifoliate bittercress. See *Cardamine trifolia*

Trilliaceae, 242, 253, 292, 316

Trillidium, 253

Trillidium govanianum. See *Trillium govanianum*

Trillidium japonicum. See *Paris japonica*

Trillium, 316–324

Trillium affine. See *Trillium catesbaei*

Trillium albidum, 318

Trillium album. See *Trillium flexipes*

Trillium amabile. See *Trillium smallii*

Trillium angustipetalum, 318

Trillium apetalon, 317

Trillium apetalon var. *rubricarpum*, 317

Trillium atropurpureum. See *Trillium erectum*

Trillium californicum. See *Trillium ovatum*

Trillium camschatcense. See *Trillium kamtschaticum*

Trillium catesbaei, 317

Trillium catesbaei var. *macranthum*. See *Trillium cernuum*

Trillium catesbyi. See *Trillium catesbaei*

Trillium cernuum, 317, 319

Trillium cernuum f. *album*, 317

Trillium cernuum var. *macranthum*. See *Trillium cernuum*

Trillium cernuum f. *tangerae*, 317

Trillium chloropetalum, 317

Trillium chloropetalum var. *giganteum*, 318

Trillium crassifolium. See *Trillium ovatum*

Trillium cuneatum, 318

Trillium cuneatum f. *luteum*, 318

Trillium decipiens, 318

Trillium declinatum. See *Trillium flexipes*

Trillium decumbens, 318

Trillium discolor, 320

Trillium erectum, 318

Trillium erectum f. *albiflorum*. See *Trillium erectum* var. *album*

Trillium erectum var. *album*, 319

Trillium erectum var. *atropurpureum*. See *Trillium erectum*

Trillium erectum var. *declinatum*. See *Trillium flexipes*

Trillium erectum var. *japonicum*. See *Trillium kamtschaticum*

Trillium erectum f. *luteum*, 319

Trillium erectum var. *rubrum*. See *Trillium erectum*

Trillium erectum var. *vaseyi*. See *Trillium vaseyi*

Trillium erythrocarpum. See *Trillium grandiflorum*; *T. undulatum*

Trillium flexipes, 319

Trillium flexipes f. *billingtonii*, 319

Trillium flexipes f. *walpolii*, 319

Trillium foetidissimum, 318

Trillium foetidum. See *Trillium erectum*

Trillium giganteum var. *chloropetalum*. See *Trillium chloropetalum*

Trillium gleasonii. See *Trillium flexipes*

Trillium govanianum, 319

Trillium gracile, 318

Trillium grandiflorum, 316, 319

Trillium grandiflorum f. *flore-pleno*, 320

Trillium grandiflorum f. *parvum*, 320

Trillium grandiflorum f. *polymerum*, 320

Trillium grandiflorum f. *roseum*, 320

Trillium grandiflorum f. *variegatum*, 320

Trillium grandiflorum f. *viride*, 320

Trillium hibbersonii. See *Trillium ovatum* f. *hibbersonii*

Trillium hugeri. See *Trillium cuneatum*

Trillium hugeri f. *flavum*. See *Trillium luteum*

Trillium isanthum. See *Trillium sessile*

Trillium kamtschaticum, 320

Trillium kamtschaticum f. *plenum*, 320

Trillium kurabayashii, 320

Trillium kurabayashii f. *luteum*, 320

Trillium lanceolatum. See *Trillium lancifolium*

Trillium lancifolium, 320

Trillium longiflorum. See *Trillium sessile*

Trillium ludovicianum, 318

Trillium luteum, 320

Trillium membranaceum. See *Trillium sessile*

Trillium nervosum. See *Trillium catesbaei*

Trillium nivale, 321

Trillium nutans. See *Trillium erectum*

Trillium obovatum. See *Trillium kamtschaticum*

Trillium ovatum, 321

Trillium ovatum f. *hibbersonii*, 321

Trillium ovatum f. *maculosum*, 321

Trillium ovatum f. *oettingerii*, 321

Trillium ovatum var. *stenosepalum*. See *Trillium ovatum*

Trillium pallasii. See *Trillium kamtschaticum*

Trillium persistens, 317

Trillium pictum. See *Trillium undulatum*

Trillium purpureum. See *Trillium erectum*

Trillium pusillum, 321

Trillium pusillum var. *alabamicum*, 321

Trillium pusillum var. *ozarkianum*, 321

Trillium pusillum var. *texanum*, 321

Trillium pusillum var. *virginicum*, 321

Trillium recurvatum, 322

Trillium recurvatum f. *lanceolatum*. See *Trillium lancifolium*

Trillium recurvatum f. *luteum*, 322

Trillium recurvatum f. *shayi*, 322

Trillium reflexum. See *Trillium recurvatum*

Trillium rhomboideum var. *grandiflorum.* See *Trillium grandiflorum*

Trillium rhomboideum. See *Trillium erectum*

Trillium rivale, 322

Trillium rotundifolium. See *Trillium sessile*

Trillium rugelii, 316, 317, 319

Trillium scouleri. See *Trillium ovatum*

Trillium sessile, 322

Trillium sessile var. *boreale.* See *Trillium sessile*

Trillium sessile var. *californicum.* See *Trillium chloropetalum* var. *giganteum*

Trillium sessile var. *chloropetalum.* See *Trillium chloropetalum* var. *giganteum*

Trillium sessile of gardens. See *Trillium cuneatum*

Trillium sessile f. *luteum.* See *Trillium luteum*

Trillium sessile var. *nuttallii.* See *Trillium viridescens*

Trillium sessile var. *praecox.* See *Trillium cuneatum*

Trillium sessile var. *viridescens.* See *Trillium viridescens*

Trillium sessile f. *viridiflorum,* 322

Trillium simile, 323

Trillium smallii, 317

Trillium smallii var. *maximowiczii.* See *Trillium smallii*

Trillium stamineum, 318

Trillium stenanthes. See *Trillium viridescens*

Trillium stylosum. See *Trillium catesbaei*

Trillium sulcatum, 322

Trillium sulcatum f. *albolutescens,* 322

Trillium tinctorum. See *Trillium sessile*

Trillium tschonoskii, 323

Trillium tschonoskii f. *violacea.* See *Trillium tschonoskii*

Trillium underwoodii, 318

Trillium underwoodii var. *luteum.* See *Trillium luteum*

Trillium undulatum, 323

Trillium undulatum f. *enotatum,* 323

Trillium unguiculatum. See *Trillium recurvatum*

Trillium vaseyi, 323

Trillium venosum. See *Trillium ovatum*

Trillium viride, 321

Trillium viride var. *luteum.* See *Trillium luteum*

Trillium viridescens, 321

trinity. See *Tradescantia ohiensis*

trinity lily. See *Trillium grandiflorum*

true columbine. See *Aquilegia vulgaris*

true northern maidenhair fern. See *Adiantum pedatum* subsp. *aleuticum*

true-love. See *Paris quadrifolia*

tsubomi giboshi. See *Hosta clausa*

tsukushi aoi. See *Asarum kiusianum*

Tsushima fern. See *Polystichum tsussimense*

tufted saxifrage. See *Saxifraga caespitosa*

tufted sedge. See *Carex elata*

Tupistra, 324

Tupistra chinensis, 324

turban lily. See *Lilium martagon*

turk's cap. See *Aconitum napellus; Lilium martagon; L. superbum*

turkey corn. See *Dicentra canadensis; D. eximia*

turmeric. See *Hydrastis canadensis*

turtlehead. See *Chelone glabra; C. lyonii*

Tussilago alba. See *Petasites albus*

Tussilago hybrida. See *Petasites hybridus*

Tussilago japonicum. See *Farfugium japonicum*

tussock bellflower. See *Campanula carpatica*

twinberry. See *Mitchella repens*

twinflower. See *Mitchella repens*

twin-flowered violet. See *Viola biflora*

twin hart's tongue fern, 109

twinleaf. See *Jeffersonia diphylla*

two-eyed berry. See *Mitchella repens*

two-leaved lady slipper. See *Cypripedium acaule*

two-leaved Solomon's seal. See *Maianthemum canadense*

two-leaved toothwort. See *Cardamine diphylla*

ubatake giboshi. See *Hosta pulchella*

udo. See *Aralia cordata*

Umbelliferae, 66

umbilroot. See *Cypripedium calceolus* var. *pubescens*

umbrella arum. See *Amorphophallus rivieri*

umbrella bamboo. See *Sinarundinaria murieliae*

umbrella leaf. See *Diphylleia cymosa*

umbrella plant. See *Darmera peltata*

undulate hart's tongue fern, 109

Unifolium canadense. See *Maianthemum canadense*

Uniola latifolia. See *Chasmanthium latifolium*

unzen kanaoi. See *Asarum unzen*

upland sea oats. See *Chasmanthium latifolium*

upright bugle. See *Ajuga genevensis*

upright bugleweed. See *Ajuga genevensis*

upright Chinese ginger. See *Saruma henryi*

upside-down fern. See *Arachniodes standishii*

urajiro giboshi. See *Hosta hypoleuca*

Urtica dioica, 230

usuba saishin. See *Asarum sieboldii*

Uvularia, 324–326

Uvularia caroliniana, 325

Uvularia floridana, 325

Uvularia grandiflora, 325

Uvularia grandiflora var. *pallida,* 325

Uvularia pallida of gardens, 325

Uvularia perfoliata, 325

Uvularia puberula, 326

Uvularia pudica. See *Uvularia caroliniana*

Uvularia sessifolia. See *Uvularia sessilifolia*

Uvularia sessilifolia, 326

Uvulariaceae, 325

Vagnera amplexicaulis. See *Smilacina racemosa* var. *amplexicaulis*

Vagnera racemosa. See *Smilacina racemosa*

Vagnera sessilifolia. See *Smilacina sessilifolia*

Vagnera stellata. See *Smilacina stellata*

Vancouveria, 326–327

Vancouveria chrysantha, 327

Vancouveria hexandra, 327

Vancouveria planipetala, 327

vanilla leaf. See *Achlys triphylla*

variegated butterbur, 257

variegated green dragon. See *Pinellia cordata*

variegated Japanese angelica tree. See *Aralia elata*

variegated miniature sedge, 130

variegated shield fern. See *Arachniodes simplicior*

variegated sweet flag, 61

variegated violet. See *Viola variegata*

Vasey's trillium. See *Trillium vaseyi*

Venus' hair fern. See *Adiantum venustum*

Venushair fern. See *Adiantum capillus-veneris*

Venus maidenhair. See *Adiantum capillus-veneris*

Venus-shoe. See *Cypripedium calceolus* var. *pubescens*

Veratrum, 327–329
Veratrum album, 328
Veratrum californicum, 328
Veratrum eschscholtzii. See *Veratrum viride*
Veratrum mengtzeanum. See *Veratrum wilsonii*
Veratrum nigrum, 328
Veratrum parviflorum, 328
Veratrum taliense, 329
Veratrum ussuriense. See *Veratrum nigrum*
Veratrum viride, 328
Veratrum wilsonii, 329
Veratrum woodsii, 328
Veronica virginica. See *Veronicastrum virginicum*
Veronicastrum, 329
Veronicastrum sibiricum, 329
Veronicastrum virginicum, 329
Vignea, 129
Vinca, 329–330
Vinca acutiflora. See *Vinca difformis*
Vinca bowlesii of gardens, 330
Vinca difformis, 330
Vinca herbacea, 330
Vinca libanotica. See *Vinca herbacea*
Vinca major, 330
Vinca major subsp. *hirsuta*, 330
Vinca media. See *Vinca difformis*
Vinca minor, 330
Vinca minor f. *alba*, 330
Vinca pubescens. See *Vinca major* subsp. *hirsuta*
Viola, 331–334
Viola adunca, 332
Viola adunca var. *labradorica.* See *Viola labradorica*
Viola beckwithii, 331
Viola biflora, 332
Viola blanda, 332
Viola brittoniana, 333
Viola canadensis, 332
Viola canina, 332
Viola conspersa, 332
Viola cucullata. See *Viola obliqua*
Viola dissecta, 332
Viola dissecta var. *chaerophylloides.* See *Viola dissecta*
Viola dissecta var. *eizanensis.* See *Viola dissecta*
Viola eriocarpa. See *Viola pubescens* var. *eriocarpa*
Viola glabella, 332
Viola hastata, 333
Viola koreana. See *Viola variegata* var. *nipponica*
Viola koreana of gardens. See *Viola variegata*

Viola labradorica, 332
Viola labradorica var. *purpurea*, 332
Viola lutea, 332
Viola lutea subsp. *splendens.* See *Viola lutea*
Viola nuttallii, 333
Viola obliqua, 332
Viola odorata, 331
Viola palmata, 333
Viola papilionacea, 333
Viola papilionacea var. *priceana*, 333
Viola pedata, 333
Viola pedata var. *concolor.* See *Viola pedata*
Viola pedata var. *lineariloba.* See *Viola pedata*
Viola pedatifida, 333
Viola pedunculata, 331
Viola pennsylvanica. See *Viola pubescens* var. *eriocarpa*
Viola priceana. See *Viola papilionacea* var. *priceana*
Viola pubescens, 333
Viola pubescens var. *eriocarpa*, 333
Viola riviniana, 331
Viola sororia, 333
Viola tricolor, 332
Viola tripartita, 333
Viola variegata, 334
Viola variegata var. *nipponica*, 334
Viola verecunda var. *yakusimana*, 334
Viola ×*wittrockiana*, 331
Violaceae, 331
violet helleborine. See *Epipactis purpurata*
violet wood sorrel. See *Oxalis violacea*
Virginia bluebells. See *Mertensia pulmonarioides*
Virginia chain fern. See *Woodwardia virginica*
Virginia cowslip. See *Mertensia pulmonarioides*
Virginia grape fern. See *Botrychium virginianum*
Virginia heartleaf. See *Asarum virginicum*
Virginia polypody. See *Polypodium virginianum*
Virginia spring beauty. See *Claytonia virginica*
Virginia waterleaf. See *Hydrophyllum virginianum*
virgin's tears. See *Pulmonaria officinalis*
voodoo lily. See *Sauromatum venosum*

wakerobin. See *Trillium erectum*
Waldsteinia, 334–335
Waldsteinia fragarioides, 334

Waldsteinia fragarioides subsp. *doniana*, 334
Waldsteinia geoides, 335
Waldsteinia lobata, 334
Waldsteinia parviflora, 334
Waldsteinia sibirica. See *Waldsteinia ternata*
Waldsteinia ternata, 334
Waldsteinia trifolia. See *Waldsteinia ternata*
walking fern. See *Asplenium rhizophyllum*
walking spleenwort. See *Asplenium rhizophyllum*
wall polypody. See *Polypodium vulgare*
Wallich's cobra lily. See *Arisaema propinquum*
wandflower. See *Galax urceolata*
wand plant. See *Galax urceolata*
wasabi. See *Wasabia japonica*
Wasabia, 335
Wasabia japonica, 335
Wasabia tenuis, 335
Watanabe's peltoboykinia. See *Peltoboykinia watanabei*
wavy-frond hart's tongue fern, 108
waxflower. See *Chimaphila maculata*
waxflower pyrola. See *Pyrola elliptica*
wax trillium. See *Trillium luteum*
weeping blue rush, 229
Welsh polypody. See *Polypodium cambricum*
western bleeding heart. See *Dicentra formosa*
western blue bead. See *Clintonia andrewsiana*
western boykinia. See *Boykinia major*
western bugbane. See *Cimicifuga elata*
western dog violet. See *Viola adunca*
western harebell. See *Campanula scouleri*
western holly fern. See *Polystichum scopulinum*
western leathery polypody. See *Polypodium scouleri*
western mayflower. See *Maianthemum dilatatum*; *M. kamtschaticum*
western polypody. See *Polypodium hesperium*
western prince's pine. See *Chimaphila menziesii*; *C. umbellata*
western swordfern. See *Polystichum munitum*
western trillium. See *Trillium ovatum*
western trout lily. See *Erythronium revolutum*

western whippoorwill toadshade. See *Trillium kurabayashii*

western white trillium. See *Trillium ovatum*

western wild ginger. See *Asarum caudatum*

wheel lily. See *Paris*

whippoorwill flower. See *Trillium cuneatum*

whippoorwill shoe. See *Cypripedium acaule; C. calceolus* var. *parviflorum; C. c.* var. *pubescens*

whippoorwill toadshade. See *Trillium cuneatum*

white-backed hosta. See *Hosta hypoleuca*

white baneberry. See *Actaea alba*

whitebeads. See *Actaea alba*

white bellflower. See *Campanula alliariifolia*

white butterbur. See *Petasites albus*

white cobra lily. See *Arisaema candidissimum*

white cohosh. See *Actaea alba*

white coltsfoot. See *Petasites albus*

white deadnettle. See *Lamium album*

white dogtooth violet. See *Erythronium albidum*

white-flowered trillium. See *Trillium tschonoskii*

white fringed orchid. See *Platanthera blepharoglottis*

white hellebore. See *Veratrum viride*

white lilyturf. See *Ophiopogon jaburan*

white man's foot. See *Plantago major* 'Variegata'

white mandarin. See *Streptopus amplexifolius*

white mondo grass. See *Ophiopogon jaburan*

white trillium. See *Trillium flexipes; T. grandiflorum; T. ovatum*

white trout lily. See *Erythronium albidum*

white turtlehead. See *Chelone glabra*

white-veined wintergreen. See *Pyrola picta*

white wood aster. See *Aster divaricatus*

whorled Solomon's seal. See *Polygonatum verticillatum*

wideleaf spring beauty. See *Claytonia caroliniana; C. virginica*

wide-leaved Solomon's seal. See *Polygonatum hirtum*

widow's tears. See *Tradescantia virginiana*

wild bleeding heart. See *Dicentra eximia*

wild columbine. See *Aquilegia canadensis*

wild corn. See *Clintonia umbellata*

wild cranesbill. See *Geranium maculatum*

wild garlic. See *Allium canadense*

wild geranium. See *Geranium maculatum*

wild ginger. See *Asarum arifolium; A. canadense; A. shuttleworthii*

wild jalap. See *Podophyllum peltatum*

wild lemon. See *Podophyllum peltatum*

wild lily-of-the-valley. See *Maianthemum canadense; Pyrola americana*

wild mandrake. See *Podophyllum peltatum*

wild oats. See *Chasmanthium latifolium; Uvularia sessilifolia*

wild orange-red lily. See *Lilium philadelphicum*

wild pink. See *Silene caroliniana*

wild sarsaparilla. See *Aralia nudicaulis*

wild sea oats. See *Chasmanthium latifolium*

wild spikenard. See *Smilacina racemosa*

Willdenow violet. See *Viola blanda*

willow gentian. See *Gentiana asclepiadea*

windflower. See *Anemone; Anemonella thalictroides*

wintergreen. See *Chimaphila maculata; C. umbellata*

winter heliotrope. See *Petasites fragrans*

winter rose. See *Helleborus niger*

wolf's bane. See *Aconitum lycoctonum*

wolfsbane. See *Aconitum lycoctonum*

wood daffodil. See *Uvularia grandiflora*

woodland white violet. See *Viola blanda*

wood lily. See *Lilium philadelphicum*

wood poppy. See *Stylophorum diphyllum*

woodruff. See *Galium odoratum*

woodrush. See *Luzula pilosa; Milium effusum*

wood saxifrage. See *Saxifraga mertensiana*

Wood's false hellebore. See *Veratrum woodsii*

Woodsia, 335–336

Woodsia alpina, 336

Woodsia appalachiana, 336

Woodsia cathcartiana, 336

Woodsia frigida. See *Woodsia ilvensis*

Woodsia glabella, 336

Woodsia hyperborea var. *rifidula*. See *Woodsia ilvensis*

Woodsia ilvensis, 335

Woodsia manchuriensis, 336

Woodsia obtusa, 336

Woodsia oregana, 336

Woodsia perriniana. See *Woodsia obtusa*

Woodsia polystichoides, 336

Woodsia scopulina, 336

Woodsiaceae, 240, 335

wood violet. See *Viola palmata; V. riviniana*

Woodwardia, 336–337

Woodwardia angustifolia. See *Woodwardia areolata*

Woodwardia areolata, 337

Woodwardia fimbricata, 337

Woodwardia radicans, 337

Woodwardia virginica, 337

worm grass. See *Spigelia marilandica*

Yatabea japonica. See *Ranzania japonica*

yellow adder's tongue. See *Erythronium americanum*

yellow archangel. See *Lamium galeobdolon*

yellow clintonia. See *Clintonia borealis*

yellow club moss, 294

yellow cobra plant. See *Arisaema nepenthoides*

yellow ceeping Jenny, 239

yellow false garlic. See *Nothoscordum bivalve*

yellow fawn lily. See *Erythronium americanum*

yellow-flowered cobra lily. See *Arisaema flavum*

yellow fringed orchid. See *Platanthera ciliaris*

yellow fringeless orchid. See *Platanthera integra*

yellow Indian-shoe. See *Cypripedium calceolus* var. *pubescens*

yellow lady slipper. See *Cypripedium calceolus*

yellow lady's slipper. See *Cypripedium calceolus* var. *pubescens*

yellow mandarin. See *Disporum languinosum*

yellow moneywort, 239

yellow poppy. See *Stylophorum diphyllum*

yellow puccoon. See *Hydrastis canadensis*

yellowroot. See *Hydrastis canadensis*

yellow toadshade. See *Trillium luteum; T. sessile*

yellow trillium. See *Trillium luteum*

yellow trout lily. See *Erythronium americanum*

yellow waxbells. See *Kirengeshoma palmata*

yellow woodlily. See *Clintonia borealis*

Yezo Solomon's plume. See *Smilacina yezoensis*

youth-on-age. See *Tolmiea menziesii*

yu-san. See *Hosta plantaginea*

yukiguni kanaoi. See *Asarum ikegamii*

yukizasa shirofukurin, 298

Yunnan meadow rue. See *Thalictrum delavayi*

zasa, 288

Zigadenus muscitoxicum. See *Amianthium muscaetoxicum*

zigzag spiderwort. See *Tradescantia subaspera*